ISTORY IN DISPUTE

ADVISORY BOARD

HISTORY IN DISPUTE

Volume **17**

**Twentieth-Century
European Social and
Political Movements:
Second Series**

Edited by **Paul du Quenoy**

A MANLY, INC. BOOK

**ST. JAMES
PRESS®**

THOMSON

—★—™

GALE

Detroit • New York • San Diego • San Francisco • Cleveland • New Haven, Conn. • Waterville, Maine • London • Munich

History in Dispute
Volume 17: Twentieth-Century European Social and Political Movements, Second Series
Paul du Quenoy

Editorial Directors
Matthew J. Bruccoli and Richard Layman

Series Editor
Anthony J. Scotti Jr.

LIBRARY OF CONGRESS CONTROL NUMBER: 00-266495
1-55862-480-5

Printed in the United States of America
10 9 8 7 6 5 4 3 2 1

CONTENTS

CONTENTS

CONTENTS

CONTENTS

CONTENTS

ABOUT THE SERIES

History in Dispute is an ongoing series designed to present, in an informative and lively pro-con format, different perspectives on major historical events drawn from all time periods and from all parts of the globe. The series was developed in response to requests from librarians and educators for a history-reference source that will help students hone essential critical-thinking skills while serving as a valuable research tool for class assignments.

Individual volumes in the series concentrate on specific themes, eras, or subjects intended to correspond to the way history is studied at the academic level. For example, early volumes cover such topics as the Cold War, American Social and Political Movements, and World War II. Volume subtitles make it easy for users to identify contents at a glance and facilitate searching for specific subjects in library catalogues.

Each volume of *History in Dispute* includes up to fifty entries, centered on the overall theme of that volume and chosen by an advisory board of historians for their relevance to the curriculum. Entries are arranged alphabetically by the name of the event or issue in its most common form. (Thus,

in Volume 1, the issue "Was detente a success?" is presented under the chapter heading "Detente.")

Each entry begins with a brief statement of the opposing points of view on the topic, followed by a short essay summarizing the issue and outlining the controversy. At the heart of the entry, designed to engage students' interest while providing essential information, are the two or more lengthy essays, written specifically for this publication by experts in the field, each presenting one side of the dispute.

In addition to this substantial prose explication, entries also include excerpts from primary-source documents, other useful information typeset in easy-to-locate shaded boxes, detailed entry bibliographies, and photographs or illustrations appropriate to the issue.

Other features of *History in Dispute* volumes include: individual volume introductions by academic experts, tables of contents that identify both the issues and the controversies, chronologies of events, names and credentials of advisers, brief biographies of contributors, thorough volume bibliographies for more information on the topic, and a comprehensive subject index.

ACKNOWLEDGMENTS

Philip B. Dematteis, *Production manager.*

Kathy Lawler Merlette, *Office manager.*

Ann M. Cheschi and Carol A. Cheschi, *Administrative support.*

Ann-Marie Holland, *Accounting.*

Sally R. Evans, *Copyediting supervisor.* Phyllis A. Avant, Caryl Brown, Melissa D. Hinton, Philip I. Jones, Rebecca Mayo, Nadirah Rahimah Shabazz, and Nancy E. Smith, *Copyediting staff.*

Zoe R. Cook, *Series team leader, layout and graphics.* Janet E. Hill, *Layout and graphics supervisor.* Sydney E. Hammock, *Graphics and prepress.*

William Mathes Straney and Walter W. Ross, *Photography editors.*

Amber L. Coker, *Permissions editor.*

James F. Tidd Jr., *Database manager.*

Joseph M. Bruccoli, *Digital photographic copy work.*

Donald K. Starling, *Systems manager.*

Kathleen M. Flanagan, *Typesetting supervisor.* Patricia Marie Flanagan, Mark J. McEwan, and Pamela D. Norton, *Typesetting staff.*

Walter W. Ross, *Library researcher.*

The staff of the Thomas Cooper Library, University of South Carolina are unfailingly helpful: Tucker Taylor, *Circulation department head, Thomas Cooper Library, University of South Carolina.* John Brunswick, *Interlibrary-loan department head.* Virginia W. Weathers, *Reference department head.* Brette Barclay, Marilee Birchfield, Paul Cammarata, Gary Geer, Michael Macan, Tom Marcil, and Sharon Verba, *Reference librarians.*

PERMISSIONS

PICTURES

Pp. 3, 19, 78, 122, 136, 194, 256: Bettmann/CORBIS.

P. 16: AP Photo/Jacques Brinon, APA5324647.

P. 27: Paul Seheult; Eye Ubiquitous/CORBIS.

P. 34: Board of Trustees of the University of South Carolina.

P. 45: Bauhaus archiv/museum fur gestaltung, Berlin.

Pp. 55, 117, 264: Hulton-Deutsch/CORBIS.

P. 60: ©MARCOU/SIPA, Image # 386108_000001.

P. 71: Richard Melloul/CORBIS SYGMA.

P. 85: Courtesy of *Izvestia*, ©1993.

P. 92: ©Hulton Archive/Getty, Image # HP7287.

P. 97: David Turnley/CORBIS.

P. 106: U.S. Army.

P. 133: Yann Arthus-Bertrand/CORBIS.

P. 148: AP Photo/Hidajet Delic, APA7094545.

P. 155: T.C.W. Blanning, ed., *The Oxford Illustrated History of Modern Europe* (Oxford & New York: Oxford University Press, 1996).

Pp. 160, 170: Peter Turnley/CORBIS.

P. 174: Getty/FPJ Historical Selects.

P. 186: By permission of Roger-Viollet.

P. 199: Harlingue Viollet.

P. 207: Ruben Sprich/Reuters/CORBIS.

P. 215: Reuters/Peter Kujundzik/archive photos.

P. 223: Jos Fuste Raga/CORBIS.

P. 232: Alain Nogues/CORBIS SYGMA.

P. 236: Salmer, Barcelona.

P. 245: Yevgeny Khaldei/CORBIS.

P. 273: Jean Bernard Vernier/CORBIS SYGMA.

P. 277: Reuters/CORBIS.

P. 289: "Full map of Europe AD 1900," map ©2003, Christos Nüssli, Milieu 30, CH-1400 Yverdon <http://www.euratlas.com/big/big1900.htm>.

Pp. 290, 292: Maps from *An Encyclopedia of World History*, 6/e edited by Peter N. Stearns. Copyright ©2001 by Houghton Mifflin Company. Reprinted by permission of Houghton Mifflin Company. All rights reserved.

P. 291: From *The Encyclopedia of World History*, edited by William L. Langer (New York: Harry N. Abrams, 1968), map of "Europe in 1939," courtesy of Rand McNally & Co., p. 1041. Map © by RMC, R.L. 04-S-34. www.randmcnally.com.

TEXT

P. 53: Ramsay MacDonald, *Ramsay MacDonald's Political Writings*, edited by Bernard Barker (London: Penguin, 1972), pp. 161–163.

Pp. 100–101: Rezak Hukanovic, *The Tenth Circle of Hell: A Memoir of Life in the Death Camps of Bosnia*, translated by Colleen London and Midhat Ridjanovic, edited by Ammiel Alcalay (Oslo: Sypress Forlag, 1993; New York: Basic Books, 1996), pp. 55–56, 60–64.

P. 109: August Kubizek, *Young Hitler: The Story of Our Friendship*, translated by E. V. Anderson (London: Wingate, 1954), pp. 64–66.

P. 139: "The Bund Meeting," *New York Times,* 22 February 1939, p. 20; copyright © 1939 by The New York Times Co. Reprinted with permission.

P. 153: Janusz Bardach and Kathleen Gleeson, *Man Is Wolf to Man: Surviving the Gulag* (Berkeley: University of California Press, 1998), pp. 160–162.

P. 177: Adolf Hitler, *Mein Kampf* (New York: Stackpole Sons, 1939), pp. 364–366, 369–370.

Pp. 184–185: Michael Oakeshott, *The Social and Political Doctrines of Contemporary Europe,* third revised edition (Cambridge: Cambridge University Press, 1942; New York: Macmillan, 1942), pp. 164–168.

P. 239: Cary Nelson and Jefferson Hendricks, eds., *Madrid 1937: Letters of the Abraham Lincoln Brigade from the Spanish Civil War* (London & New York: Routledge, 1996), pp. 187–188.

Pp. 278–279: Simone de Beauvoir, "Introduction," *The Second Sex,* translated by H. M. Parshley (New York: Knopf, 1953); by permission of Alfred A. Knopf, Inc. Courtesy of Rosica Colin Ltd., the literary agent for Simone de Beauvoir's Estate.

PERMISSIONS

PREFACE

History in Dispute, Volume 17: Twentieth-Century European Social and Political Movements, Second Series explores new contours in the historiography of modern Europe. While *History in Dispute, Volume 16: Twentieth-Century European Social and Political Movements, First Series* examined political, diplomatic, and military themes, *Volume 17* delves broadly into disputed questions of culture, society, ideas, and economics, topics that now enjoy a notable vogue in the historical profession. This new vein of inquiry is an attempt to assess previously overlooked roots and causes of events and investigate the engines of long-term continuities.

Contributions to *Volume 17* are therefore much more thematic than those in the previous volume. When individuals and events are studied, they are presented as part of larger contexts and longer continuities. Conflict, for example, is examined in broader terms than raw battlefield contests. The volume's chapter on World War I is concerned with its effects, or lack thereof, on movements in European cultural life. The Spanish Civil War chapter focuses on its ideological bases and ramifications. The essays on European integration look to the traumas of World War II and the decolonization era to find the process's origins and rationale.

The roles of individual nations are also viewed over a longer duration. The volume seeks to discuss two important powers on Europe's extremities—Britain and Russia—in terms of their evolving national and international identities. A third important nation in Europe's twentieth-century history, the United States, is appreciated in terms of its cultural influence and the relative dangers it may pose for native national cultures.

Chapters dealing with philosophy and political ideology add further perspectives. They highlight debates on the nature of fascism, the importance of nationalism, the evolution of socialism, and the larger political and social meanings of existentialism. More case-specific questions, including the comparability of Nazism and communism and continuities between the regimes of Vladimir Lenin and Josef Stalin, offer rival interpretations of their relevance and developments.

Evolving institutions and conceptions of society are also brought to the forefront in this volume. The twentieth century saw the rise of the welfare state, the beginnings of an international system of justice, the emancipation of women, and the emergence of a culture that deeply reflected irrationality and the psychological effects of modernity.

Economic change complemented the social and intellectual transitions, and several chapters investigate pertinent topics. These include the causes of the Great Depression, German economic crises, and the evolution of social class identities.

It is, of course, the contributors who should receive most of the credit for this work. Without their efforts it would not be. They vary greatly in age, background, outlook, and profession. Many are accomplished professors of considerable reputation and experience. An effort has been made to include scholarship by experts who have pursued careers outside of academia, in the belief that their professional insights will enhance the overall quality of the work and add perspectives that are often not found in the ivory tower. The reader should be aware that some contributors either elected to argue sides of issues that do not reflect their personal or professional opinions, or responded affirmatively to my request that they do so. It is my belief that the ability, willingness, and courage to express an argument that contradicts one's own view represents an exercise in skill as well as in wisdom. Indeed, my mentor Professor David Goldfrank and I have indulged in this idea by writing both sides of some chapters, in effect arguing against ourselves. The staffs at Manly, Inc., and St. James Press also deserve meritorious recognition. Coordinating the work of more than forty contributors and an editor who was in Russia during much of the time this book was being produced required logistical accommodations that would not have been possible a decade ago.

—PAUL DU QUENOY,
GEORGETOWN UNIVERSITY

CHRONOLOGY

1900

Twenty-five percent of the world's population resides in Europe; six of the eight major world powers are located in this region. (*See* **Age of Progress** *and* **Short Twentieth Century**)

29 JULY: Italian king Umberto I is assassinated by an anarchist; he is replaced on the throne by his son Victor Emmanuel III.

1901

22 JANUARY: Victoria, the queen of England, dies, and her eldest son takes the throne as Edward VII. (*See* **Britain as Part of Europe**)

1902

30 JANUARY: Great Britain and Japan form an alliance in order to block Russian expansion in the Far East. (*See* **Russia as Part of the West**)

31 MAY: Great Britain and the Boer Republics sign a peace treaty ending the Boer War, which began in 1899.

1904

8 FEBRUARY: Japan breaks diplomatic relations with Russia, with whom it had been contesting control of Korea and Manchuria, and attacks the Russian fleet at Port Arthur, sparking the Russo-Japanese War.

8 APRIL: Largely in response to the growing power of Germany, Great Britain and France agree to settle outstanding disagreements, especially concerning their colonies, and establish the Entente Cordial.

1905

22 JANUARY: Russian soldiers in St. Petersburg fire upon demonstrators who are calling for shorter working hours and better labor conditions; more than 130 people are killed and hundreds injured in this incident, known as "Bloody Sunday."

5 SEPTEMBER: The Treaty of Portsmouth ends the Russo-Japanese War; Russia loses control of Port Arthur and Sakhalin Island.

1906

16 JANUARY–7 APRIL: The international Algeciras Conference is held to settle a dispute between Germany and France over French claims to a protectorate in Morocco. France succeeds in getting its claims recognized.

FEBRUARY: The battleship HMS *Dreadnought* is launched, resulting in the start of a naval arms race.

10 MAY–21 JULY: The Duma, the national representative body of Russia, meets for the first time; the assembly is the result of Tsar Nicholas II's October Manifesto (1905), in which he changed Russia to a constitutional monarchy.

22 NOVEMBER: Land-privatization reforms, giving peasants control of their land, are decreed by Russian prime minister Petr Stolypin.

1907

Great Britain and Russia sign the Agreement Concerning Persia, Afghanistan, and Tibet (establishing the Anglo-Russian Entente).

1908

7 OCTOBER: Bosnia-Herzegovina is annexed by the Austro-Hungarian Empire. (*See* **Nationalism**)

1911

10 AUGUST: The British Parliament limits the power of veto of the House of Lords. (*See* **Class Identities**)

18 SEPTEMBER: Stolypin is assassinated.

1912

8 OCTOBER: Bulgaria, Greece, Montenegro, and Serbia unite to fight against Turkey when the Turks refuse to grant Macedonian autonomy. By 1913 the Turks are defeated, but internal squabbling soon leads to a second Balkan conflict.

1914

28 JUNE: Archduke Franz Ferdinand, heir to the Habsburg throne, and his wife, Sofia, are assassinated by Serbian anarchist Gavrilo Princip in Sarajevo. (*See* **Age of Progress, Cultural Watershed,** *and* **Short Twentieth Century**)

28 JULY: Austria declares war on Serbia.

1 AUGUST: Russia and France mobilize for war; Germany declares war on Russia; World War I begins.

3 AUGUST: Germany declares war on France.

4 AUGUST: Britain enters World War I against Germany.

26–30 AUGUST: The Germans defeat Russian troops in northeastern Poland at the Battle of Tannenberg.

5 SEPTEMBER: Russia, Great Britain, and France sign the Treaty of London, stating that there will be no separate peace with Germany. (*See* **Russia as Part of the West**)

6–15 SEPTEMBER: The Russians suffer another defeat at the Battle of the Masurian Lakes.

1915

JANUARY: Austro-Hungarian forces launch an offensive in the Carpathian Mountains.

22 MARCH: Russian forces capture the Galician fortress of Przemysl.

7 MAY: The British passenger liner *Lusitania* is sunk by a German U-boat in the Irish Sea, killing 1,198 people and enraging American sentiment against the Germans.

1916

JANUARY–FEBRUARY: U.S. president Woodrow Wilson sends adviser Colonel Edward M. House to Europe to seek mediation between the conflicting sides, but they are unreceptive to the overture.

21 FEBRUARY–JULY: A battle is fought for control of the area around the fortress at Verdun, with casualties to both sides reaching eight hundred thousand men.

24–29 APRIL: Irish republicans revolt against British rule in the Easter Rebellion; the rebels are defeated and put on trial.

4 JUNE: A massive Russian attack against Austro-Hungarian forces, known as the Brusilov Offensive, commences on the Eastern Front. The Germans are forced to remove troops from the Western Front to counter the threat.

1 JULY–19 NOVEMBER: More than one million men are killed during the Battle of the Somme in France.

21 NOVEMBER: Austro-Hungarian emperor Franz Joseph dies.

5 DECEMBER: Germany institutes the "Auxiliary Service Law," which declares that all able-bodied men between the ages of fifteen and sixty not already in the army are liable for civilian service.

12 DECEMBER: German chancellor Theobald von Bethmann-Hollweg proposes peace negotiations; his proposal is turned down by the Allies.

18 DECEMBER: Wilson renews an offer to mediate a compromise between the belligerents, as Germany agrees that it will evacuate occupied territories in Western Europe but not lands held in Eastern Europe; the offer is rejected by the Allies.

1917

King George V of England changes the royal name from Saxe-Coburg-Gotha to Windsor. (*See* **Britain as a Part of Europe**)

22 JANUARY: President Wilson, during a speech to the U.S. Senate, appeals to the World War I combatants to seek "peace without victory."

31 JANUARY: Germany announces its decision to renew unrestricted submarine warfare against all shipping in British waters.

15 MARCH: Tsar Nicholas II abdicates the throne; he and his family are arrested on 21 March; members from the Russian Duma form a Provisional Government. (*See* **French and Russian Revolutions**)

6 APRIL: The United States enters World War I on the side of the Allies.

1 AUGUST: Pope Benedict XV proposes a compromise peace, including Germany's withdrawal from Belgium and France; Allied withdrawal from German colonies; withdrawal of Central Powers troops from Serbia, Montenegro, and Romania; and the creation of an independent Poland. The proposal is rejected by both sides.

3 SEPTEMBER: The United States recognizes the Czecho-Slovak National Council as the ruling government in Austria-Hungary.

7–8 NOVEMBER: Bolsheviks seize the Russian capital, Petrograd, overthrow the Provisional Government led by Aleksandr Kerensky, and touch off a brutal civil war that lasts until 1920. Vladimir Lenin becomes the leader of the Soviet state. (*See* **French and Russian Revolutions**)

20 DECEMBER: The Extraordinary Commission to Combat Counterrevolution, Speculation, and Sabotage (Cheka, or Soviet secret police) is established.

1918

8 JANUARY: Wilson issues the "Fourteen Points," his vision for postwar peace, to include such elements as open covenants, freedom of navigation, free trade, reduced national armaments, and a cooperative international league.

19 JANUARY: Russia's democratically elected Constituent Assembly meets and is dispersed by the Bolshevik government.

3 MARCH: Soviet Russia and the Central Powers sign the Treaty of Brest-Litovsk, ending the war on the Eastern Front.

SPRING: Fifteen Allied nations—including Britain, France, the United States, and Japan— send troops into Soviet Russia in an attempt to intervene in the Revolution.

16/17 JULY: Nicholas II and his wife and children are executed.

29 OCTOBER: The National Council of Croats, Serbs, and Slovenes declares the formation of Yugoslavia. (*See* **Nationalism and Public Opinion**)

9 NOVEMBER: The German Republic is proclaimed.

11 NOVEMBER: An armistice ending World War I goes into effect.

1919

JANUARY: A radical uprising of the German Spartacists, a communist group, is suppressed by the republican government.

5 JANUARY: The *Nationalsozialistische Deutsche Arbeiterpartei* (National Socialist German Workers' Party, or Nazi Party) is formed in Germany. (*See* **Origins of Fascism**)

18 JANUARY: The Paris Peace Conference begins.

6 FEBRUARY–11 AUGUST: An assembly meets in Weimar, adopting a constitution that forms the government that rules Germany until 1933.

4 MARCH: Czechoslovak forces shoot fifty-four Sudeten Germans protesting the Czech annexation of their land.

28 JUNE: The Versailles Treaty is signed, to take effect in January 1920. Germany

accepts all responsibility for World War I, limitations on the size and power of its armed forces, territorial losses, and the responsibility to pay reparations eventually fixed in the amount of $33 billion. (*See* **Economic and Political Changes** *and* **Origins of Fascism**)

1920

16 JANUARY: The League of Nations is formally inaugurated, and the Paris Peace Conference officially ends.

1921

The *Sturmabteilung* (SA, known as Storm Troopers or Brownshirts) is formed by the Nazi Party.

13 DECEMBER: The United States, Great Britain, Japan, and France sign the Four-Powers Pact, establishing procedures for settling disputes in the Pacific dependencies.

1922

6 FEBRUARY: The United States, Great Britain, Japan, France, and Italy sign the Five-Power Naval Limitation Treaty, establishing limitations on the size of naval fleets and vessels.

2 APRIL: Josef Stalin becomes general secretary of the Communist Party of Soviet Russia. (*See* **Leninism vs. Stalinism**)

31 OCTOBER: Benito Mussolini, leader of the Fascist Party, becomes prime minister of Italy. (*See* **International Fascism** *and* **Origins of Fascism**)

DECEMBER: The Irish Free State is established.

30 DECEMBER: Soviet Russia formally becomes the Union of Soviet Socialist Republics (U.S.S.R.).

1923

French and Belgian troops occupy the industrial Ruhr region after Germany defaults on its World War I reparations debt.

8–9 NOVEMBER: Adolf Hitler and the Nazi Party attempt to start an insurrection against the Weimar Republic in what becomes known as the Beer Hall Putsch. Police halt a march, and Hitler later serves eight months in prison, where he starts work on *Mein Kampf* (My Struggle). (*See* **Nazism and Communism**)

1924

21 JANUARY: Lenin dies, and Stalin, who has been accumulating power during Lenin's last

years of life, gradually emerges as the new dictator. (*See* **Leninism vs. Stalinism**)

16 AUGUST: The Dawes Plan reduces Germany's reparations owed to around $9 billion and provides loans to help pay them. (*See* **German Economic Crises**)

1925
APRIL: Paul von Hindenburg is elected president of Germany.

1 DECEMBER: Germany, France, Belgium, Great Britain, and Italy agree to guarantee peace in Western Europe by signing the Locarno Treaty. (*See* **Pacifism**)

1926
Germany joins the League of Nations.

1928
The Right-wing *Croix de feu* (Cross of Fire) is founded in France. (*See* **International Fascism**)

Stalin launches the first Five Year Plan for economic development.

20 JUNE: Croatian Peasant Party leader Stjepan Radic is mortally wounded by a rival member of Parliament (he dies on 8 August), prompting King Alexander to declare a royal dictatorship the following January and to eliminate all ethnic-based political parties. Alexander establishes Yugoslavia and divides the country into administrative districts. (*See* **Nationalism**)

27 AUGUST: The Kellogg-Briand Pact, an attempt to outlaw war as a weapon of national policy, is signed in Paris. (*See* **Pacifism**)

1929
7 JUNE: The Young Plan reduces Germany's reparations again and extends payments for fifty-nine years. (*See* **German Economic Crises**)

29 OCTOBER: The Stock Market in New York crashes, signaling the start of the worldwide Great Depression. (*See* **Great Depression**)

1931
14 APRIL: Spain becomes a Republic after Alfonso XIII is sent into exile. (*See* **Spanish Civil War**)

1 JULY: U.S. president Herbert Hoover proposes a moratorium on German reparations.

11 DECEMBER: Great Britain establishes the policy of granting self-government to its colonies, in the Statute of Westminster, leading to the "British Commonwealth." The dominions affected are Australia, Canada, Ireland, New Zealand, and Newfoundland. (*See* **Britain as Part of Europe**)

1932
2 FEBRUARY: Sixty-one nations send delegations to the League of Nations Disarmament Conference in Geneva, which continues into 1934.

JULY: Elections in Germany give the Nazi Party the largest representation in Parliament; Hindenburg is reelected as president, but Hitler comes in second in the vote.

1933
30 JANUARY: Adolf Hitler is appointed chancellor of Germany by Hindenburg.

27 FEBRUARY: A fire at the Reichstag building, allegedly set by Dutch communist Marinus van der Lubbe, allows Hitler to overthrow constitutional guarantees and aggressively attack his opponents. Elections on 5 March give the Nazi Party nearly 44 percent of the popular vote.

23 MARCH: The Reichstag passes the Enabling Bill, which gives complete power to Hitler. His government begins establishing concentration camps for opponents of the regime.

JUNE: The World Economic Conference is held in London. (*See* **Economic and Political Changes**)

16 NOVEMBER: The Soviet Union and the United States establish diplomatic relations.

1934
6 FEBRUARY: A Right-wing mob tries to storm the French Chamber of Deputies. (*See* **International Fascism**)

29–30 JUNE: Hitler orders a bloody purge of the SA, in what becomes known as the Night of the Long Knives.

2 AUGUST: Hitler declares himself *Führer* (leader) of the Third Reich.

1935
3 MAY: The Soviet Union and France sign a Treaty of Mutual Assistance.

16 MAY: Czechoslovakia and the U.S.S.R. conclude a mutual assistance pact.

JULY: Great Britain institutes the Government of India Act, extending representative government and suffrage in India.

15 SEPTEMBER: The Nazis pass the Nuremberg Laws, which deprive German Jews of citizenship and protect the purity of "German" blood. (*See* **Genocide**)

3 OCTOBER: Italy invades Abyssinia (Ethiopia).

1936
7 MARCH: Hitler sends troops into the Rhineland.

APRIL–MAY: The Left-leaning antifascist Popular Front, led by Léon Blum, comes to power in France. (*See* **European Socialism**)

17 JULY: Following several days of political murders, conservative generals begin an uprising to overthrow the Spanish government, leading to the Spanish Civil War. The rebels (rightists) are initially blocked by a coalition of leftist groups that support the Republic. General Francisco Franco appeals to Germany and Italy for aid to overthrow the government. The Soviet Union and France support the loyalists. (*See* **Spanish Civil War**)

AUGUST: At the Lyon Conference, France, Germany, Great Britain, and Italy agree to halt supplies from reaching both sides in the Spanish Civil War.

29 SEPTEMBER: A provisional ruling military junta chooses Franco as commander in chief of the Nationalists, and he is then appointed the leader of Spain.

25 OCTOBER: Germany and Italy sign a treaty forming the Axis.

25 NOVEMBER: Germany and Japan sign the Anti-Comintern Pact, aimed at stopping the spread of communist (and hence Soviet) power; Italy joins the pact on 6 November 1937. (*See* **Nazism and Communism**)

11 DECEMBER: George VI becomes king of England after the abdication of Edward VIII.

1937
26 APRIL: German aircraft under Franco's command bomb the Basque town of Guernica.

1 JUNE: Stalin begins to purge military officers in the Red Army.

1938
11–12 MARCH: Nazi troops are sent into Austria, and the country is annexed by Germany.

SEPTEMBER: Hitler invades the Sudetenland (in Czechoslovakia) and annexes it to Germany.

30 SEPTEMBER: British prime minister Neville Chamberlain and French premier Edouard Daladier meet with Hitler and Italian dictator Mussolini in Munich; the Munich Agreement allows Czech territory to remain in German hands. (*See* **Pacifism**)

1939
28 MARCH: The Nationalists win their fight to overthrow the Republicans, and the Spanish Civil War ends.

23 AUGUST: The Soviet Union and Nazi Germany sign the Molotov-Ribbentrop agreement, a nonaggression pact.

1 SEPTEMBER: Nazi Germany attacks Poland, initiating World War II. (*See* **Age of Progress**)

3 SEPTEMBER: France and Great Britain declare war on Germany.

18 SEPTEMBER: In accordance with a secret provision of the Molotov-Ribbentrop Agreement, the Soviets invade Poland from the east and annex territory.

30 NOVEMBER: Soviet troops invade Finland; the Winter War lasts until Finland yields in March 1940.

1940
SPRING: More than fifteen thousand Polish officers are murdered by the Soviets (they had been prisoners since September 1939). (*See* **International Justice**)

10 MAY: The Germans launch an offensive westward, overrunning Luxembourg, the Netherlands, and Belgium. Chamberlain resigns, and Winston Churchill becomes the prime minister of England.

10 JUNE: Italy declares war on France.

17 JUNE: The Red Army invades Latvia and Estonia, and the Soviet Union later officially annexes these countries, as well as Lithuania.

22 JUNE: France signs an armistice with Germany.

27 JUNE: The Soviet Union annexes Bukovina and Bessarabia from Romania.

10 JULY: Henri-Philippe Pétain forms the Vichy government in France.

7 SEPTEMBER: The German Blitz against England begins.

27 SEPTEMBER: The Tripartite Pact (Axis) is signed by Germany, Italy, and Japan.

28 OCTOBER: Italy invades Greece.

1941
11 MARCH: Through the Lend-Lease Act the United States provides material support to Great Britain. The act also provides help to other Allies, including the Soviet Union, which receives $11.3 billion. (*See* **Economic and Political Changes**)

27 MARCH: General Dusan Simovic leads a coup that topples Dragisa Cvetkovic's government after it had signed the Anti-Comintern Pact (25 March). Hitler responds by invading Yugoslavia.

22 JUNE: Hitler launches Operation Barbarossa against the Soviet Union. At this time Germany also begins mass executions of Jews in extermination camps and in occupied territories. (*See* **Genocide**)

14 AUGUST: The United States and Great Britain pledge to assist each other in resisting aggression, respecting sovereign rights and territories, collaborating in economic progress, and seeking world peace in the Atlantic Charter; twenty-four additional nations affirm the charter in January 1942. (*See* **Economic and Political Changes**)

7 DECEMBER: Japanese planes attack the American naval base at Pearl Harbor, Hawaii, which results in the United States declaring war on Japan the following day.

11 DECEMBER: Germany and Italy declare war on the United States; the United States declares war against them.

1942

1 JANUARY: The Big Three (United States, Great Britain, and Soviet Union) and twenty-three other nations conclude a pact in Washington, D.C., not to make separate armistices with the Axis.

MAY: Regular deportations of Jews to Nazi death camps begin.

MAY: Soviet foreign minister Vyacheslav Molotov visits London and Washington and requests that the Allies open a second front against Germany.

AUGUST: At the Moscow Conference, Stalin, Churchill, and U.S. envoy W. Averell Harriman discuss the opening of a second front in Europe.

1943

12–23 JANUARY: At the Casablanca Conference, Roosevelt and Churchill insist on the unconditional surrender of Germany.

2 FEBRUARY: German troops at Stalingrad surrender to Soviet forces, marking a turning point in the war.

28 NOVEMBER–1 DECEMBER: Roosevelt, Stalin, and Churchill meet in Tehran, Iran, to discuss the opening of a second front in Europe and other issues.

1944

6 JUNE: The Allies invade Normandy to open a second front in Western Europe.

JULY: The Polish Committee of National Liberation (PKWN) is established to administer territories liberated by the Soviet Red Army.

21 AUGUST–7 OCTOBER: The foundations of the United Nations (UN) are established at the Dumbarton Oaks Conference.

26 AUGUST: Free French leader Charles de Gaulle enters Paris.

1945

4–11 FEBRUARY: Roosevelt, Stalin, and Churchill meet in Yalta to discuss postwar plans, and the Soviet Union is given much latitude in how to deal with occupied countries in Eastern Europe. The text of the agreements made at the conference is published as the Declaration on Liberated Europe.

13–14 FEBRUARY: The German city of Dresden is firebombed by Allied bombers; the city is destroyed; and between 35,000 and 135,000 people are killed.

6 MARCH: Romania forms a communist government led by Petru Groza.

12 APRIL: While vacationing in Warm Springs, Georgia, Roosevelt suffers a cerebral hemorrhage and dies; the vice president, Harry S Truman, is sworn in as president.

28 APRIL: Mussolini and his mistress are captured while trying to flee Italy and are executed.

30 APRIL: Hitler, along with his mistress and several associates, commits suicide in Berlin.

7–8 MAY: Germany surrenders to the Allies.

26 JUNE: The UN Charter is signed in San Francisco. (*See* **Age of Progress**)

17 JULY–2 AUGUST: Stalin, Churchill, and Truman meet at the Potsdam Conference, agreeing to divide Germany (and Berlin) into four occupied zones, to hold war crimes trials, and to seek the unconditional surrender of Japan. (*See* **International Justice**)

6 AUGUST: The United States drops an atomic bomb on Hiroshima, Japan; three days later it drops another nuclear device on Nagasaki. Japan surrenders on 2 September.

29 NOVEMBER: The Federal People's Republic of Yugoslavia is established, and Josip Broz Tito becomes prime minister.

1946

1 FEBRUARY: Hungary becomes a republic.

9 FEBRUARY: Stalin declares that the world is broken into "two camps" and that the Soviets cannot coexist with their former allies.

5 MARCH: Winston Churchill makes a speech in Fulton, Missouri, warning the West of a Communist "Iron Curtain" descending in Eastern Europe.

CHRONOLOGY

9 MAY: Victor Emmanuel III of Italy officially abdicates in favor of his son Umberto, but a plebiscite establishes a republic, and both men go into exile. (*See* **Public Opinion**)

8 SEPTEMBER: Bulgaria declares itself a republic and abolishes its monarchy.

2 DECEMBER: The British and American occupied zones of Germany unite, to be later joined by the French (1948); the Soviets continue to control the fourth region.

1947

19 JANUARY: The Polish Communist Party wins power in state elections.

12 MARCH: The Truman Doctrine, which establishes the U.S. policy of blocking the spread of communism and provides assistance to Greece and Turkey, is announced by President Truman.

5 JUNE: In an address at Harvard University, U.S. secretary of state George C. Marshall advances the concept of American help to rebuild Europe, largely to counter potential expansion of communism. Over the next four years more than $13 billion is provided to sixteen European nations. (*See* **Economic and Political Changes**)

14–15 AUGUST: Great Britain grants independence to India and Pakistan.

31 AUGUST: The communists gain power in Hungary.

4 DECEMBER: Bulgaria becomes the People's Republic of Bulgaria.

1948

25 FEBRUARY: A coup d'état in Czechoslovakia replaces a coalition government with a communist regime.

17 MARCH: Britain, France, Belgium, the Netherlands, and Luxembourg sign the Brussels Pact for common defense.

6 APRIL: Finland signs a nonaggression pact with the Soviet Union.

24 JUNE: Stalin orders all ground traffic into and out of Berlin to be halted. The Americans respond with an airlift of supplies into the city that lasts until the end of September 1949 (the blockade is lifted 12 May 1949).

28 JUNE: Yugoslavia is expelled from the Cominform, the agency of international communism founded by the Soviets in 1947.

1949

25 JANUARY: The Soviet Union founds the Council for Mutual Economic Assistance (COMECON).

4 APRIL: The North Atlantic Treaty Organization (NATO) is formed. Members include Belgium, Canada, Denmark, France, Iceland, Italy, Luxembourg, the Netherlands, Norway, Portugal, Spain, the United Kingdom, and the United States. (*See* **Economic and Political Changes** *and* **European Integration**)

23 MAY: The Federal Republic of Germany (West Germany) is established; in response the Soviets form the German Democratic Republic (East Germany) in October.

29 AUGUST: The U.S.S.R. explodes its first atomic bomb.

1950

Approximately 15.3 percent of the world's population resides in Europe.

25 JUNE: The Korean War begins as North Korean troops attack the South. The United States and United Nations respond by sending troops. Belgium, France, Great Britain, Greece, Italy, Luxembourg, the Netherlands, Norway, and Sweden will supply troops during the conflict. The war rages until 1953.

1951

18 APRIL: Belgium, France, the Federal Republic of Germany, Italy, Luxembourg, and the Netherlands sign the Treaty of Paris, establishing the European Coal and Steel Community (ECSC). (*See* **European Integration**)

1952

30 APRIL: Tito refuses to accept an offer to join NATO.

27 MAY: A European Defense Community is proposed.

2 OCTOBER: Great Britain becomes a nuclear power with the test of its first such weapon.

1953

5 MARCH: Stalin dies.

2 JUNE: Elizabeth II is crowned queen of the United Kingdom at Westminster Abbey.

18 JUNE: Rioting erupts in East Germany, and the protesters are suppressed by Soviet troops.

1954

7 MAY: French troops are defeated at Dien Bien Phu, initiating a withdrawal of France from its colonial empire in Indochina.

1955

5 MAY: The Allied occupation of West Germany officially ends.

14 MAY: The Warsaw Treaty of Friendship, Cooperation, and Mutual Assistance (commonly known as the Warsaw Pact) establishes a mutual-defense organization including the Soviet Union, Albania, Bulgaria, Czechoslovakia, East Germany, Hungary, Poland, and Romania.

1956

14 FEBRUARY: Soviet leader Nikita Khrushchev makes a "secret speech" at the Twentieth Congress of the Communist Party of the Soviet Union, denouncing Stalin's cult of personality. (*See* **Stalin's Economic Policies**)

26 JULY: Egyptian leader Gamal Abdel Nasser nationalizes the Suez Canal.

21 OCTOBER: Rioting occurs in Poland.

23 OCTOBER: Hungarian students in Budapest stage a protest, gaining public support and eliciting police response. (*See* **Public Opinion**)

29 OCTOBER: Israel attacks Egypt.

1 NOVEMBER: Hungary withdraws from the Warsaw Pact.

4 NOVEMBER: Soviet tanks enter Budapest and depose Nagy, who is later abducted and executed in 1958.

5–6 NOVEMBER: Anglo-French forces land in the Suez Canal zone in response to Nasser's nationalization of the canal.

22 DECEMBER: Responding to Soviet and American opposition, British and French troops withdraw from Egypt.

1957

25 MARCH: Belgium, France, West Germany, Italy, Luxembourg, and the Netherlands sign two treaties in Rome, one of which establishes the European Economic Community (EEC) while the other sets plans for the peaceful pursuit of atomic energy development. The EEC goes into effect on 1 January 1958. (*See* **Economic and Political Changes** *and* **European Integration**)

4 OCTOBER: The Soviet Union launches the Sputnik satellite into orbit.

1958

3 FEBRUARY: Belgium, the Netherlands, and Luxembourg form the Benelux Economic Union (to come into force in 1960).

31 MAY: The Fourth Republic ends in France as de Gaulle is named prime minister; the Fifth Republic is inaugurated 5 October.

10 NOVEMBER: Khrushchev demands that unless talks are held concerning the reunification of Germany, he will deny Western access to Berlin. (*See* **Russia as Part of the West**)

21 DECEMBER: Charles de Gaulle is elected president of France. (*See* **Public Opinion**)

1959

3 NOVEMBER: De Gaulle announces his intention to withdraw France from NATO.

1960

13 FEBRUARY: France explodes its first nuclear weapon.

1961

12–13 AUGUST: East Germany begins sealing off East Berlin from West Berlin, constructing the Berlin Wall, in an attempt to stop the exodus of East Germans to the West.

1962

1 JULY: France, after a referendum, grants Algeria independence.

1963

22 JANUARY: France and Germany sign the Treaty of Elysée, a declaration of cooperation. (*See* **European Integration**)

1964

13–14 OCTOBER: Khrushchev is removed from power and replaced by Leonid Brezhnev.

1966

7 MARCH: France pulls out of the military component of NATO.

1967

Greek leader Stephanos Stephanopoulos is overthrown in a military coup.

1968

20 AUGUST: Warsaw Pact forces invade Czechoslovakia to counter the rise of a liberal communist government.

12 SEPTEMBER: Albania withdraws from the Warsaw Pact.

1969

27 APRIL: De Gaulle resigns, and Georges Pompidou becomes president in June.

1970

West German leader Willy Brandt, seeking improved relations with East Germany and the Soviet Union, formulates his *Ostpolitik* (eastern policy). (*See* **Russia as Part of the West**)

1972

22–30 MAY: The United States and Soviet Union sign the first Strategic Arms Limitations Talks (SALT) Treaty.

5 SEPTEMBER: Eleven Israeli athletes and coaches are killed during a terrorist attack at the Munich Olympic games. Five Black September (Palestinian) terrorists and a German policeman also die.

1973

1 JANUARY: Great Britain, Ireland, and Denmark join the EEC. (*See* **European Integration**)

1974

14 AUGUST: Greece withdraws from NATO in a dispute over the handling of the Turkish invasion of Cyprus.

1975

20 NOVEMBER: Spanish dictator Franco dies; two days later Juan Carlos becomes the king of Spain.

1976

10 NOVEMBER: The Convention on the Suppression of Terrorism is adopted by the Committee of Foreign Ministers of the Council of Europe. (*See* **International Justice**)

1978

16 MARCH: Italian former prime minister Aldo Moro is kidnapped and later murdered by members of the Red Brigades.

1979

27 AUGUST: British Lord Mountbatten, a relative of the queen, is assassinated by the Irish Republican Army (IRA), which blows up his sailboat.

24–25 DECEMBER: Soviet troops invade Afghanistan.

1980

Approximately 10.8 percent of the world's population resides in Europe.

4 MAY: Yugoslavian leader Tito dies.

14 AUGUST: Lech Walesa leads massive shipyard strikes in Poland.

1981

23 FEBRUARY: Juan Carlos blocks a coup attempt by the Spanish military.

1982

Spain joins NATO.

9 MAY–14 JUNE: Great Britain fights against and defeats Argentine forces in the Falkland Islands.

10 NOVEMBER: Brezhnev dies.

1983

1 SEPTEMBER: The Soviet Union shoots down a Korean airliner over the Sea of Japan.

30 DECEMBER: U.S. Pershing missiles are deployed in West Germany.

1985

11 MARCH: Mikhail Gorbachev is selected general secretary of the Communist Party of the Soviet Union.

7 OCTOBER: Terrorist Abu Abbas hijacks the Italian ocean liner *Achille Lauro* and murders an American Jewish passenger.

19 NOVEMBER: U.S. president Ronald Reagan meets with Gorbachev in Geneva; the two leaders talk amicably for about an hour, although they disagree about Reagan's "Star Wars" policy.

27 DECEMBER: Palestinians led by Abu Nidal simultaneously attack airports in Rome and Vienna, killing twenty travelers.

1986

Spain, Portugal, and Greece join the EEC.

11–12 OCTOBER: Reagan and Gorbachev meet in Reykjavik and propose a reduction in long-range missiles.

1987

8 DECEMBER: The United States and Soviet Union sign the Intermediate Range Nuclear Forces (INF) Treaty, which provides for the removal of their nuclear missiles from Europe.

1988

14 APRIL: The Soviet Union agrees to withdraw its troops from Afghanistan.

6 DECEMBER: Gorbachev announces Soviet troop reductions for Eastern Europe.

21 DECEMBER: Libyan terrorists destroy Pan American flight 103 over Lockerbie, Scotland, killing 270 people.

1989

9 FEBRUARY: The Soviet Union withdraws its last troops from Afghanistan.

20–21 FEBRUARY: Hungary establishes a new constitution that omits the leading role of the Communist Party. (*See* **European Socialism** *and* **Public Opinion**)

4 JUNE: Representatives of the labor party Solidarity win a majority of parliamentary seats in the first free elections in Poland since before World War II.

9 NOVEMBER: East Germany opens its borders.

22 DECEMBER: Romanian leader Nicolae Ceauşescu is overthrown; he is executed on 25 December.

1990

11 MARCH: Lithuania declares its independence from the Soviet Union. (*See* **Public Opinion**)

3 OCTOBER: East and West Germany reunite.

19 NOVEMBER: The Treaty on Conventional Armed Forces in Europe (CFE Treaty), limiting the number of weapons possessed by the Soviet and Western sides on the Continent, is signed.

22 DECEMBER: Walesa is sworn in as president of Poland.

26 DECEMBER: Serbian leader Slobodan Miloševic becomes president of Yugoslavia. (*See* **Punishing Former Communists**)

1991

APRIL–SEPTEMBER: As the constituent republics declare their independence, the Soviet Union begins to dissolve. (*See* **Short Twentieth Century**)

12 JUNE: Yeltsin is elected president of the Russian Federation.

19 JUNE: Russian troops complete their withdrawal from Hungary.

25 JUNE: Slovenia and Croatia secede from Yugoslavia. Bosnia-Herzegovina and Macedonia soon follow. (*See* **Nationalism**)

19–21 AUGUST: Gorbachev is held under house arrest during a coup attempt by hard-liners.

25 DECEMBER: Gorbachev resigns as leader of the Soviet Union. Yeltsin and the presidents of Ukraine and Belarus (Belorussia) establish the Commonwealth of Independent States (CIS).

1992

Serbia invades Bosnia, instituting a program of "ethnic cleansing" and initiating the Bosnian Civil War. (*See* **Genocide**)

7 FEBRUARY: The European Union (EU) is formally established, based on the Treaty of European Union signed in Maastricht, Netherlands. By 1995 the union will include Austria, Belgium, Denmark, Finland, France, Germany, Greece, Ireland, Italy, Luxembourg, the Netherlands, Portugal, Spain, Sweden, and the United Kingdom. (*See* **Economic and Political Changes** *and* **European Integration**)

1993

1 JANUARY: Czechoslovakia peacefully divides into the Czech Republic and Slovakia. (*See* **Nationalism**)

23 JULY: The British Parliament ratifies the Maastricht Treaty.

1994

DECEMBER: Yeltsin sends Russian troops into the breakaway republic of Chechnya.

1995

Austria, Sweden, and Finland join the EU.

14 DECEMBER: The Dayton Accords, an attempt to broker peace in Bosnia-Herzegovina, are signed. U.S. troops will police the peace under UN auspices.

1998

Miloševic begins moving military and paramilitary units into Kosovo.

17 JULY: The bodies of Nicholas II and his family are interred in the Cathedral of Saints Peter and Paul in St. Petersburg; he is granted canonization on 20 August 2000 by the Russian Orthodox Church.

1999

1 JANUARY: The euro, the monetary unit and currency of the EU, is introduced. It will replace the national currencies of all EU member states except Britain, Denmark, and Sweden in 2002.

MARCH: Poland, Hungary, and the Czech Republic join NATO.

MARCH–APRIL: A U.S.-led NATO bombing campaign commences in Yugoslavia to stop "ethnic cleansing" of ethnic Albanians in Kosovo. An international peacekeeping force subsequently occupies Kosovo.

31 DECEMBER: Yeltsin resigns, and Prime Minister Vladimir Putin becomes acting president of Russia. Putin is elected president in March 2000. (*See* **Age of Progress**)

CHRONOLOGY

AGE OF PROGRESS

Was the twentieth century an era of progress?

Viewpoint: Yes. The twentieth century was a period of immense social and technological strides that enriched humanity.

Viewpoint: No. The twentieth century was an era of immense destruction and dysfunction that harmed humanity far more than helped it.

The twentieth century was characterized by many ambiguities. Does its final balance sheet represent progress for humanity or decline? Many clear signs point to the progress that the first essay highlights. Advances in medicine, technology, agriculture, transportation, and communication all made the world a better and safer place to live than in any previous century. The political, military, and diplomatic efforts that led to the destruction of Nazi Germany and the Soviet Union, the two most virulent threats to peace and liberty, established liberal democracy and free-market economics as the bases of modern society. Regardless of the challenges, humanity accomplished much between 1900 and 2000. The second essay looks at the century in terms of its unprecedented destruction, great threats to peace and liberty, and humanity's development of the capacity to destroy itself. These factors can hardly recommend the twentieth century as an era of progress.

Viewpoint:
Yes. The twentieth century was a period of immense social and technological strides that enriched humanity.

From the vantage point of the early twenty-first century, one may see the twentieth century as a particularly troubling time in human history. The twentieth century produced two devastating world wars, nuclear weapons, ballistic missiles, long-range jets, other weapons that promised greater destruction in any future conflicts and the apparent democratization of destructive capacity as even terrorist groups threatened to obtain chemical, biological, or nuclear weapons. While some of the developments of the twentieth

century appear ominous, on balance the century was one of remarkable progress: two particularly noxious and virulent forms of totalitarianism were eliminated; democracy made the transition from being the exception to the norm in Europe and spread elsewhere in the world; and technological advances led to significant improvements in medicine and the general quality of life.

Perhaps the most distinctive developments in international politics concerned the rise and fall of Nazi Germany and the Soviet Union. While these nations and their ideologies were both products of the twentieth century, they were both defeated in that century. The crimes of the Nazis obviously figure prominently in any cataloguing of human depravity. The killing of six million Jews in the Holocaust was just the start of Adolf Hitler's villainy. Slavs,

Gypsies, and others were also killed in large numbers. Through the combined efforts of democratic nations like the United States and Great Britain in combination with the Soviet Union, Nazi villainy was brought to an end. The fate of the Nazi leaders and their former subjects also was revealing. Rather than being subjected to whatever punishment the victorious powers decided to impose, the Nazi leaders were tried at Nuremberg in proceedings based on rule of law rather than the whim of the victors. The people of East Germany were subjected to further totalitarianism under Soviet direction before the collapse of East European communism in 1989, but the American, British, and French zones developed democratic habits and practices in the form of the German Federal Republic. Breaking from traditions of autocracy and totalitarianism in the German past, Konrad Adenauer served as chancellor of West Germany in its formative years and led his nation into an era of democracy and renewed contribution to civilization.

Germans in the eastern portion of that country were forced to wait until 1990 for reunification into one Germany, but their triumph was part of another major step forward: Germany was reunified as part of the triumph of the Western democracies over Soviet-style communism in the Cold War. It was not, as is sometimes posited, a victory for the United States over Russia; rather the Cold War was a victory for the democratic nations of Western Europe, Canada, and the United States over the Soviet leadership and Soviet-supported dictators elsewhere in Eastern Europe. The importance of this victory cannot be overstated: while the Nazis' popularity was limited by their own ideology as champions of Aryan racial superiority, Soviet communism was an ideology that had considerable appeal to peoples looking to emerge from European colonial domination. The Russians had a long history of expansion and subjugating different peoples under their imperial domination, but this expansion had occurred in contiguous territory. The communist leaders of the Soviet Union plausibly could argue that they had triumphed both over Russian imperialism and Nazi totalitarianism and that their ideology promoted economic development in a framework of justice and equality. Given concerns about capitalism in the wake of the Great Depression and worries among Western political leaders that the depression would return once the Western economies no longer benefited from the stimulus of wartime demand, the apparent success of Soviet efforts at industrialization further contributed to their appeal.

Despite the ability of the Soviets to posture as champions of economic progress in a framework of peace, justice, and equality, the capitalist

democracies ultimately prevailed. The leaders of the United States or other Western nations were not always wise and beneficent in their policies, nor were the costs of victory as low as they might have been. However, in defeating Soviet-style communism, the Western leaders triumphed over a seductive ideology whose proponents as late as the mid 1980s appeared likely to remain in power in Russia and many other places far into the foreseeable future. When Ronald Reagan visited the British Parliament in the early 1980s and proclaimed that the last pages of Marxist history were being written as he spoke, many took this statement as evidence of the American president's simplemindedness. Less than a decade later, however, the Russian and East European component of Marxism-Leninism was in fact on the scrap heap.

Despite the expectations of many that the Soviets would endure into the foreseeable future, that their problems were no more profound than those gripping capitalism in the 1970s, and that the Cold War looked much like a stalemate that was draining to both sides, the capitalist democracies emerged victorious when Mikhail Gorbachev's attempts at greater openness lay bare the magnitude of the system's failures. Gorbachev's unwillingness to deal with rebellion in his East European neighbors the way his predecessors had dealt with prior outbreaks in Hungary in 1956 and Czechoslovakia in 1968—and the way he had started to deal with rebellions in Latvia, Lithuania, and other parts of the Union of Soviet Socialist Republics (U.S.S.R.) in 1989–1991—permitted the final collapse of the system Gorbachev himself continued to believe in.

The development of nuclear weaponry continues to threaten the safety of humanity, but the caution this induced among the Americans and Soviets did restrain the superpowers during potentially dangerous crises after 1945. At the close of World War II, the likelihood of another general European war could not be discounted. Josef Stalin himself expected another Russo-German conflict in another twenty-five years, and many in Western Europe were fearful both of the Soviets and of a possibly revanchist Germany. The threat posed by nuclear weapons, combined with the development of a sustainable approach to dealing with Germany and maintaining a status quo in Europe, prevented another general European war. That another general war did not break out in Europe may be of little consolation to the inhabitants of Latin American, African, and Asian areas that were visited by "limited" or "low-intensity" warfare during the Cold War, but such conflicts in earlier times might have escalated into general wars involving many powers. In an era of nuclear weapons and

AGE OF PROGRESS

2   HISTORY IN DISPUTE, VOLUME 17: TWENTIETH-CENTURY EUROPEAN SOCIAL AND POLITICAL MOVEMENTS, SECOND SERIES

superpower rivalry, however, these conflicts did not become apocalyptic.

Not only did the United States and the Soviet Union avoid the miscalculations or escalations that could have rendered much of the earth uninhabitable, but they also gradually found ways to impose greater control over the nuclear arms race. The Strategic Arms Limitations Treaties (SALT) set ceilings for weapons development in 1972 and 1979. More importantly, the Intermediate-Ranged Nuclear Forces (INF) Treaty of 1987 eliminated an entire class of nuclear weapons, exceeding even the aims of the Nuclear Freeze Movement popular in the Western democracies in the early 1980s, which sought to prevent further deployment of nuclear weapons.

Containment of the superpower rivalry and the defeat of Nazi and Soviet totalitarianism were not the only noteworthy features of European politics during the twentieth century. By the year 2000, democracy was far more prevalent in European politics than it had been in 1900. The great European empires—Russian, German, Austro-Hungarian, and Ottoman—all collapsed during the twentieth century. This development facilitated the emergence of democratic nation-states in central and eastern Europe. Just as the one-time imperial subjects of Europe were permitted to establish their own nations in the twentieth century, the great overseas empires controlled from Europe almost completely dis-

appeared between 1945 and 1962. Peoples once subject to European imperial rule won their independence in these years. Admittedly, few of these nations became storybook examples of peaceful transition to enlightened leadership ratified by regular and free elections. Yet, as the Chinese proverb says, "the journey of a thousand miles begins with a single step," and the twentieth century saw first steps taken that were essential prerequisites for further improvement.

The loss of imperial holdings simultaneously weakened and strengthened European powers. While nations like Belgium and the Netherlands saw their power diminished with the loss of their overseas empires, they nonetheless became more-credible advocates for political democracy and more capable of playing a humanitarian role in international affairs. In fact, the use of troops by the United Nations (UN) to try to keep peace in volatile regions was another praiseworthy development of the twentieth century. Learning from the failures of the League of Nations, planners of the UN took steps to ensure that even at the height of Cold War hostility, UN peacekeepers were playing roles in various contested areas around the globe.

In keeping with the benefits of political developments in the twentieth century were the rejections during the century of long-standing bias on the basis of race or ethnicity. The American system of racial segregation as a matter of law began to unravel during the 1950s. The indige-

The Bradenburg Gate, at the dividing line between East and West Berlin, behind barbed wire, November 1961

(Bettmann/CORBIS)

AGE OF PROGRESS

OPTIMISM IS IN ORDER

On 8 June 1982 U.S. president Ronald Reagan spoke before the British House of Commons:

We're approaching the end of a bloody century plagued by a terrible political invention—totalitarianism. Optimism comes less easily today, not because democracy is less vigorous, but because democracy's enemies have refined their instruments of repression. Yet optimism is in order because day by day democracy is proving itself to be a not at all fragile flower. From Stettin on the Baltic to Varna on the Black Sea, the regimes planted by totalitarianism have had more than thirty years to establish their legitimacy. But none—not one regime—has yet been able to risk free elections. Regimes planted by bayonets do not take root.

The strength of the Solidarity movement in Poland demonstrates the truth told in an underground joke in the Soviet Union. It is that the Soviet Union would remain a one-party nation even if an opposition party were permitted because everyone would join the opposition party. . . .

Historians looking back at our time will note the consistent restraint and peaceful intentions of the West. They will note that it was the democracies who refused to use the threat of their nuclear monopoly in the forties and early fifties for territorial or imperial gain. Had that nuclear monopoly been in the hands of the Communist world, the map of Europe—indeed, the world—would look very different today. And certainly they will note it was not the democracies that invaded Afghanistan or suppressed Polish Solidarity or used chemical and toxin warfare in Afghanistan and Southeast Asia.

If history teaches anything, it teaches self-delusion in the face of unpleasant facts is folly. We see around us today the marks of our terrible dilemma—predictions of doomsday, antinuclear demonstrations, an arms race in which the West must, for its own protection, be an unwilling participant. At the same time we see totalitarian forces in the world who seek subversion and conflict around the globe to further their barbarous assault on the human spirit. What, then, is our course? Must civilization perish in a hail of fiery atoms? Must freedom wither in a quiet, deadening accommodation with totalitarian evil?

Sir Winston Churchill refused to accept the inevitability of war or even that it was imminent. He said, "I do not believe that Soviet Russia desires war. What they desire is the fruits of war and the indefinite expansion of their power and doctrines. But what we have to consider here today while time remains is the permanent prevention of war and the establishment of conditions of freedom and democracy as rapidly as possible in all countries."

Well, this is precisely our mission today: to preserve freedom as well as peace. It may not be easy to see; but I believe we live now at a turning point.

In an ironic sense Karl Marx was right. We are witnessing today a great revolutionary crisis, a crisis where the demands of the economic order are conflicting directly with those of the political order. But the crisis is happening not in the free, non-Marxist West but in the home of Marxism-Leninism, the Soviet Union. It is the Soviet Union that runs against the tide of history by denying human freedom and human dignity to its citizens. It also is in deep economic difficulty. The rate of growth in the national product has been steadily declining since the fifties and is less than half of what it was then.

The dimensions of this failure are astounding: a country which employs one-fifth of its population in agriculture is unable to feed its own people. Were it not for the private sector, the tiny private sector tolerated in Soviet agriculture, the country might be on the brink of famine. These private plots occupy a bare 3 percent of the arable land but account for nearly one-quarter of Soviet farm output and nearly one-third of meat products and vegetables. Overcentralized, with little or no incentives, year after year the Soviet system pours its best resources into the making of instruments of destruction. The constant shrinkage of economic growth combined with the growth of military production is putting a heavy strain on the Soviet people. What we see here is a political structure that no longer corresponds to its economic base, a society where productive forces are hampered by political ones.

The decay of the Soviet experiment should come as no surprise to us. Wherever the comparisons have been made between free and closed societies—West Germany and East Germany, Austria and Czechoslovakia, Malaysia and Vietnam—it is the democratic countries that are prosperous and responsive to the needs of their people. And one of the simple but overwhelming facts of our time is this: of all the millions of refugees we've seen in the modern world, their flight is always away from, not toward the Communist world. Today on the NATO line, our military forces face east to prevent a possible invasion. On the other side of the line, the Soviet forces also face east to prevent their people from leaving.

The hard evidence of totalitarian rule has caused in mankind an uprising of the intellect and will. Whether it is the growth of the new schools of economics in America or England or the appearance of the so-called new philosophers in France, there is one unifying thread running through the intellectual work of these groups—rejection of the arbitrary power of the state, the refusal to subordinate the rights of the individual to the superstate, the realization that collectivism stifles all the best human impulses. . . .

The objective I propose is quite simple to state: to foster the infrastructure of democracy, the system of a free press, unions, political parties, universities, which allows a people to choose their own way to develop their own culture, to reconcile their own differences through peaceful means. . . .

What I am describing now is a plan and a hope for the long term—the march of freedom and democracy which will leave Marxism-Leninism on the ash heap of history as it has left other tyrannies which stifle the freedom and muzzle the self-expression of the people. And that's why we must continue our efforts to strengthen NATO even as we move forward with our zero-option initiative

in the negotiations on intermediate-range forces and our proposal for a one-third reduction in strategic ballistic missile warheads.

Our military strength is a prerequisite to peace, but let it be clear we maintain this strength in the hope it will never be used, for the ultimate determinant in the struggle that's now going on in the world will not be bombs and rockets but a test of wills and ideas, a trial of spiritual resolve, the values we hold, the beliefs we cherish, the ideals to which we are dedicated.

The British people know that, given strong leadership, time, and a little bit of hope, the forces of good ultimately rally and triumph over evil. Here among you is the cradle of self-government, the Mother of Parliaments. Here is the enduring greatness of the British contribution to mankind, the great civilized ideas: individual liberty, representative government, and the rule of law under God.

I've often wondered about the shyness of some of us in the West about standing for these ideals that have done so much to ease the plight of man and the hardships of our imperfect world. This reluctance to use those vast resources at our command reminds me of the elderly lady whose home was bombed in the blitz. As the rescuers moved about, they found a bottle of brandy she'd stored behind the staircase, which was all that was left standing. And since she was barely conscious, one of the workers pulled the cork to give her a taste of it. She came around immediately and said, "Here now—there now, put it back. That's for emergencies."

Well, the emergency is upon us. Let us be shy no longer. Let us go to our strength. Let us offer hope. Let us tell the world that a new age is not only possible but probable.

Source: *Ronald Reagan, "Speech to the House of Commons," 8 June 1982, From Revolution to Reconstruction website <http://odur.let.rug.nl/~usa/P/rr40/speeches/empire.htm>.*

AGE OF PROGRESS

nous peoples of former European colonies gained rights that had been denied them in the days of colonial rule. With the emergence of independent nations in Africa and Asia, and in particular with Cold War concerns motivating leaders on both sides of the Iron Curtain, fashionable racism and ethnic discrimination fell out of fashion. Not all racial and ethnic hostility disappeared, obviously, but among citizens of the most powerful nations such was no longer viewed as acceptable. Also, the leading democracies would act sometimes to attack racist policies, as occurred peacefully when Britain used its influence in Rhodesia (present-day Zimbabwe), its former colony, to oversee the end of that state's minority white rule in 1980, and when international pressure led to the end of white rule in South Africa in 1994. It could also occur forcefully when, for example, the Serbs of the former Yugoslavia attempted to impose "ethnic cleansing" on Bosnia and Kosovo. In those cases the UN and the North Atlantic Treaty Organization (NATO) intervened to prevent further atrocities. Particularly in the case of Kosovo in 1999, NATO members participated in an international effort that was not easily defended under traditional conceptions of national interest or security. These efforts by a coalition of Europeans and their American allies attempted to prevent perpetuation of a moral outrage. While the use of force to fight ethnic cleansing did not become standard international practice, any such use of force marked a major step forward from the practices of the early twentieth century.

Politics, however, may not have been the field in which the greatest advances were made. Technological developments have improved medicine, communications, and the general quality of life. In addition, advancements in technology promised to offer still greater gains in the future. The development of penicillin during World War II was a major advance for medicine presaging the development of a range of antibiotic medications that have helped improve life expectancy and the quality of life during those years. Doctors developed vaccines against some of the most problematic diseases, especially polio. Medical procedures were developed to provide noninvasive treatments for patients who previously would have required invasive surgeries. Treatments have been developed to reduce the death rates from various forms of cancer. The treatment of human immunodeficiency virus (HIV), which causes AIDS, has developed to the point where infection with the virus no longer involves the short-term death sentence that such infection brought when the disease first came to the attention of public-health officials in the 1980s.

Medicine alone is not the sole beneficiary of technological progress. Great strides were made during the twentieth century in telecommunications. At the start of the twentieth century, telegraph cables were particularly important and the telephone was an invention that would grow in popularity. By the end of the century, cellular telephones, personal computers, the Internet, and fax machines had revolutionized the way people in advanced nations communicated for work or leisure. Leisure pursuits were developed further as radio gave way to television, which was improved through the spread of cable television, videocassette recorders, DVD players, and the introduction of high definition television (HDTV). Improvement in communications and media that can serve entertainment or educational functions gives hope for future improvements, not just in advanced nations already able to enjoy such technologies but elsewhere around the globe. As communication becomes easier and people are able to learn more about distant parts of the world, they will have the opportunity to respond to issues that arise with the same reformist impulses that helped spread democracy, end European empires, and alter relationships between different racial and ethnic groups.

Anyone looking at the world in the early twenty-first century can see plenty of problems and challenges threatening the peace and security of most of the human population. Despite these problems and challenges, however, the political and technological developments of the twentieth century have left the human race better equipped to address those unresolved issues remaining before it.

–JOHN A. SOARES JR.,
CINCINNATI

Viewpoint:
No. The twentieth century was an era of immense destruction and dysfunction that harmed humanity far more than helped it.

While odd to consider at the beginning of the twenty-first century, the concept of progress, the inevitable and highly desirable progress of mankind, is a relatively new phenomenon. Its origins are rooted in the European Enlightenment of the seventeenth and eighteenth centuries. Starting with the philosophy of John Locke, the notion that man was shaped by his environment began to take root. Associated with this concept was the conclusion that if the environment were altered, that is, if society were reformed, the result would be an enlightened

AGE OF PROGRESS

and advanced man. True progress was the creation of this better world and a better man. In *Progress of the Human Mind* (1793), philosopher Antoine Condorcet concisely defines progress as "the continuous reduction of inequalities between people and nations; the destruction of prejudice and ignorance; the growth of reason, tolerance, humanity, freedom and happiness." Over time, progress became the philosophical ideal of the Enlightenment and an accepted fact for our modern world.

The twentieth century began on a note of optimism that nearly defies description. The rapid industrialization of the last quarter of the nineteenth century, the incredible increase in scientific knowledge already translated into technology that affected people's lives, the improvements in legal rights, sanitation, medicine, and education, and finally, the relative peace of the period all led people to believe that they were on an unstoppable tide of prosperity. Tyranny, barbarism, hunger, ignorance, disease were on their way out. Even war would become obsolete. That was what the twentieth century was supposed to look like.

In retrospect we know that it fell far short of the mark. The idealism of the fin de siècle, having survived a myriad collection of wars, insurrections, and rebellions in the early years of the century, died a horrible death by the winter of 1914. When the war in Europe began, it was expected to last three months; the troops would be home by Christmas.

World War I dramatically demonstrated man's newly found technological prowess. More people were killed in World War I than in the previous thousand years of European warfare. The poison gases used along the Western Front, rail guns capable of shooting many miles, aerial bombardment, machine guns, submarines, tanks, barbed wire, and the endless days and nights of artillery fire trapping men in trenches sometimes mired in freezing mud, created a hell on earth heretofore unimaginable. Added to the battlefield casualties were millions of civilians who were also victims of the new total war; a conflict that lasted four years, not three months, and consumed the complete resources of the nations involved. In 1919 the weakened world was then struck by one of the worst epidemics since the plague: more people died of influenza than had been killed by the war.

As the war ended and peace was being fought for, new promises of progress were made. World War I was called the "war to end all wars." In 1918 Woodrow Wilson made famous his Fourteen Points, which were the popularly accepted basis for the peace. Democracy, self-determination, and a "general association of nations" were to be the foundation of the new world. As one

British delegate explained, "We were preparing not Peace only, but Eternal Peace." Unfortunately, even as the peace was hammered out, the next war was being prepared. Fighting continued along the borders of Italy and rapidly led to the rise of a new type of leader, a new type of government, and a new ideology. Fascism and Mussolini had arrived in Italy by 1922.

In *Destin du siècle* (1931) the French historian Jean-Richard Bloch described the modern age. He said that "it was defined by its unlimitedness, its concept of power without religious or moral counterweight." The decades of the 1920s and 1930s saw increasing constitutional crises and the failure of democracy and capitalism. The concept of self-determination barely survived the peace process, let alone the interwar period. The League of Nations, this new "general association," was not even joined by its original sponsor, the United States, and proved repeatedly to be a weak and ineffective tool for resolving conflict. By 1939 the world had entered its second total war of the century. Mechanized armies devastated whole countries; populations were herded and slaughtered with factory-like efficiency; and the whole struggle ended with an atomic blast. It is impossible to determine how many died, and at some level it becomes irrelevant. Whether the Nazi camps killed eighteen million or twenty million, whether the Japanese murdered ten million or twelve million in China, or whether the Russians lost 18 percent or 20 percent of their population, it is all equally incomprehensible. The human mind simply cannot grasp, nor really accept, losses this great. Even harder to understand than the numbers were the ways in which people were coldly exterminated, and human life ceased to have any value or meaning.

Unlike the end of the "war to end all wars" the peace process that concluded World War II did not even suggest the possibility of eternal peace; instead it set the stage for the next war. Europe was rapidly divided in two, and the rest of the world increasingly felt the pressure to choose a side. Slowly, some tried to evolve a third alternative, but it required an Olympic talent to walk that beam without falling.

With the Soviet detonation of the atomic bomb in 1949, we became a world hiding under our desks, awaiting a war that many believed really would be the last, leaving no one standing to fight another day. Perhaps one of the first limits the twentieth century encountered was the limit to fear itself; after a time life went on. People could not live perpetually terrified of nuclear holocaust so they simply lived. Governments got past their fear of total annihilation by using alternatives to total war. This approach gave rise to the Korean War (officially a "police action") of the early 1950s; a variety of insurrections in the Third World where the two superpowers coached from the sidelines; and endless nonviolent competitions over chessboards, on hockey rinks, and in space.

In 1989 the Berlin Wall was torn down, and by 1991 the Cold War, such as we knew it, was finally over. Suddenly we were a world with only one superpower, as the Soviet Union, the "evil empire," collapsed. In a fury of self-righteous vindication the United States with or without its allies devoted itself to creating a "New World Order" in its own image. Not everyone was as firmly convinced that the collapse of the Soviet Union meant that the American way of life was the only viable path. One-fifth of the world's population, in China, still lived under a functioning communist system, but that seemed to escape the notice of most Americans. What was brought home in a couple of fiery explosions in September 2001 was that there was a new fear—terrorism. Not even the superpower was immune to this threat.

As for the world at large, the First Persian Gulf War, begun in 1990, continued with sanctions and regular bombing raids against Iraq that lasted into the next century. Yugoslavia disintegrated into a tangled mess that no one could unravel, and fewer cared to try. In 1999, as the century ended, the North Atlantic Treaty Organization (NATO, the organization created to defend Europe against the now defunct Eastern bloc), spearheaded by the United States, bypassed the United Nations (UN) and launched a "humanitarian bombing" campaign against Yugoslavia to stop a "holocaust" of a few thousand people in Kosovo. This one move potentially destroyed one of the most concrete examples of our progress. The UN and the concurrent system of international law that had been so carefully constructed after World War II were undermined by those strong enough to act unilaterally. World War I ended the Concert of Europe as a stable international order. The bombing of Yugoslavia by NATO demonstrated clearly that the twentieth century was ending with no international order other than that endowed by power of might. Meanwhile, in Africa a true holocaust was under way in Rwanda, where hundreds of thousands perished in a matter of weeks in a civil war between Hutu and Tutsi, while the world was concerned by unsettling economic conditions and bleak forecasts. Sadly the century ended much as it began with conflicts too numerous to count.

Nineteenth-century hopes of an end to war and the early-twentieth-century hope for an institution of peace seemed more ephemeral in 2000 than they had in 1900. As for the twentieth-century record on barbarism and tyranny: even photo-graphs fail to convey the true horror. Millions died in the name of progress, of creating a new man or a new and improved society. Under the Ottoman Turks in 1915 the "first modern attempt to eliminate an entire population was made," resulting in the deaths of 1.5 million Armenians. In the 1920s the Bolsheviks established the dictatorship of the proletariat to usher in a communist society, and millions perished. In the 1930s a new Japan was being created; Chinese and Koreans proved to be inconvenient and died in the millions. The Nazi policies of the 1940s removed a variety of "undesirables" from the face of the earth: Poles, Russians, Serbs, Jews, Gypsies, homosexuals, and communists, none of whom had a place in the new world order. In taking the "Great Leap Forward" the Chinese found that it was necessary to sacrifice millions of their own people during the 1950s. In the 1970s Pol Pot and the Khmer Rouge achieved distinction by eliminating 2 million Cambodians, almost one-third of the country's population. Perhaps one of the most bizarre examples of barbarism came out during the 1986 trial of Jean-Bedel Bokassa, president/emperor of the Central African Republic/Empire, convicted of the mass murder and cannibalism of schoolchildren. This twentieth-century man who had been educated by missionaries and served with distinction in the French army during World War II, overthrew the elected president of the Central African Republic in 1964, promised the abolition of the bourgeoisie in 1965, and crowned himself emperor in 1977. Not wanting to miss any of the trends of his day, he briefly converted to Islam following a meeting with Muamar Quaddafi. Released after serving six years in prison, he died in his villa in 1996, leaving behind his 17 wives and 55 children. In the 1990s, forty years after Josef Stalin's death, official confirmation finally became available for the suffering and deaths of tens of millions under his totalitarian dictatorship. Even in the twentieth century he stands alone.

Among the victims of this century were those who survived, though their homes did not—to many the twentieth century was aptly named the century of the refugee. By the 1990s we had long since grown accustomed to seeing the fleeing columns of people with their earthly possessions overloaded upon trucks, cars, tractors, cattle, or their own backs. Some found new homes; many gave birth to the next generation in refugee camps. Some camps, like those in Palestine or across the border from Tibet, have existed for half a century. A certain portion of the world's population became marginalized.

This observation can also be made for a surprisingly large geographic segment of the globe, encompassing more than one-half the world's

y

AGE OF PROGRESS

population. While there is no denying that in certain countries material well-being improved, it was mostly in the nations that were among the wealthy in the 1800s. The gap between the First World and the Third World continued in every respect, for with poverty came disease, malnutrition, famine, war, and ignorance. The horrific epidemic of AIDS in Africa and the world's inability to stem the tide is a case in point.

Even for the wealthy elite of the West the end of the century has brought a host of problems. The gap between rich and poor appears to be increasing yet again, and many nations are reevaluating social programs that have extended beyond their ability to maintain. The common measure of economic health, "gross domestic product," has itself come into question as a useful barometer of prosperity. Does the speed of growth truly matter if it is accompanied by pollution, the destruction of natural resources, congestion, the breakup of the community, longer working hours, less family time, and the abandonment of the old, ill, and infirm? The collapse of the Soviet Union seemed to support the conclusion that its communist system was bankrupt. Yet, the last decade has shown that capitalism in its myriad incarnations does not hold all the solutions to the world's economic woes. In the end both systems support an elitist world with few haves and many have-nots.

For that part of the world that has reached a point beyond subsistence, the most immediate measure of progress is technological innovation and the speed of that innovation. The computer purchased two years ago is obsolete, and by next year the VCR will have to go—we must be moving forward. On the Internet we read that a new treatment plan was developed to help AIDS patients with lymphatic cancer—we do not ask how many have access to this care. On television a new game is advertised, and it must be progress that our children have one more reason to sit in front of a small screen, alone, blowing up fictitious folk. From an early age their toys come with loud and fast sounds and flashing lights— we are told this too is progress; it helps their development. It doesn't matter that they do not have the attention span necessary to read a magazine, let alone a book. Our industries are booming; our population is expanding; this is progress—the destruction of our environment seems to matter to too few.

There is no question that discoveries in medicine have saved countless lives, that new techniques in agriculture have made it possible to feed millions more, that we have established a global information network, that we have made the world a smaller place with our trains, planes, and automobiles, and that we have walked on the moon. Yet, we are still just as ready to use our technology for ill as for good. With the expansion of our understanding of infectious disease came cures and biological weapons. We still suffer from prejudice and ignorance. It is hard to believe that we have entered the twenty-first century with the looming specter of war between Islam and the lands of Christendom, as if we have returned to the Middle Ages. And, like that largely preliterate society, we know little about them and they, little about us. While the information superhighway hums with millions of messages daily, the urban myth thrives—the replacement of the old stories of witches, the fountain of youth, and alchemists' gold. Our new technological world defends us from the environment but cannot save the environment from us. We are slowly becoming aware of this dilemma but are not yet sure how much we care. Our modern gadgets give us the illusion of ease and self-sufficiency; we need no longer depend on anyone—consequently we find ourselves increasingly alone. We have become a society obsessed with mental health, where drugs such as Prozac and Ritalin are dispensed with abandon, and everyone should have a therapist, for we, in the non-war-torn, economically prosperous, politically stable, technologically advanced world suffer from "stress." In terms of scope, humanity's most monumental twentieth-century discovery is that it has the ability to destroy itself. We may even possess a variety of options on how: nuclear Armageddon, environmental catastrophe, or biological and chemical warfare. Perhaps that is why we are so "stressed."

–JULIJANA BUDJEVAC,
WASHINGTON, D.C.

References

Jean-Richard Bloch, *Destin du siècle* (Paris: Rieder, 1931).

Martin Gilbert, *A History of the Twentieth Century* (New York: Perennial, 2000).

Eric J. Hobsbawm, *The Age of Extremes: A History of the World, 1914–1991* (New York: Vintage, 1996).

Michael Howard and William Roger Louis, *The Oxford History of the Twentieth Century* (Oxford: Oxford University Press, 1998).

Hans Koning, "Notes on the Twentieth Century," *Atlantic Monthly,* 280 (September 1997): 90–100.

J. M. Roberts, *Twentieth Century: The History of the World, 1901 to 2000* (New York: Penguin, 1999).

AGE OF PROGRESS

AMERICANIZATION

Has Americanization been a significant threat to European cultural life?

Viewpoint: Yes. Europeans, mesmerized by American military prowess and economic prosperity, willingly adapted trappings of American culture, compromising their traditional cultural identity.

Viewpoint: No. The flow of cultural influences is multidirectional, and American culture legitimately enjoys mass popularity in Europe.

A major fact or, some would say, consequence of America's rising power in the twentieth century was the expansion of its culture throughout the world, particularly in Europe. To the alarm and disgust of some critics, American music and movies were already gaining popularity after World War I. After the major U.S. contribution to winning World War II, American culture grew more and more influential, impacting not just arts and entertainment but also dress, cuisine, and even language. European cultural critics deplored the proliferation of McDonald's, Hollywood, and American popular music. France has adopted, or attempted to adopt, legislation restricting the importation of American cultural products and limiting public and commercial use of the English language.

Is "Americanization" as serious a phenomenon as its critics have alleged? One argument suggests that the business practices of the producers of American culture led to market saturation and cultural penetration, damaging traditional European identities and replacing them with the crass values of consumerism and materialism. In contrast, the counterargument suggests that American culture has been pervasive because it enjoys legitimate popularity in market economies where consumers are free to choose from among many national cultures and traditions. If the choice of Europeans favors America, then so be it. A corollary to this argument also posits that the movement of cultural influences is and has always been multidirectional, and that many cultures, including European and American, have been both the source and object of far-reaching influence. The contours of this debate offer reflection on accelerating processes of globalization, growing international interdependence, and blossoming intercultural exchange.

Viewpoint:
Yes. Europeans, mesmerized by American military prowess and economic prosperity, willingly adapted trappings of American culture, compromising their traditional cultural identity.

The debate on the meaning, nature, and effects of "Americanization" on the world—and on Europe in particular—has its origins in the rise of the United States to a dominant position in the international system during the first decades of the twentieth century. No single definition can encapsulate the qualitative and quantitative expansion of American hegemony over almost all spheres of political, military, economic, social, and cultural life. This trend has been contextualized in different ways, depending not only on specific national viewpoints but also on the wider political milieu and on the sort of ethical values that European societies have attached to it at different stages during the twentieth century. For example, while U.S. intervention in European affairs in the aftermath of World War I was overwhelmingly endorsed and applauded by public opinion in many European countries as a force of renewal and a potent alternative to the discredited "old" values of the Continent, in recent years it has been regarded with increasing skepticism or sometimes outright hostility as a force that dilutes cultural identities and exercises undue political and economic control over the world.

At the peace negotiations that followed World War I, U.S. president Woodrow Wilson's "Fourteen Points" represented a form of idealist (and perhaps, with hindsight, naive) reorientation of political decision making in the direction of open diplomacy, moral consistency, and respect for popular feeling. U.S. involvement was regarded as the attempt of a "new" international force to remedy old habits and onerous legacies in an ailing Continent that had shown itself incapable of erecting a stable framework for the collective welfare of its peoples. European fascination with the United States continued well into the 1920s, aided by the increasing U.S. financial involvement in the reconstruction of the war-ravaged countries (especially Germany) and a series of peace-oriented initiatives, such as the League of Nations and the Kellogg-Briand Pact (1928), that renounced violence as a legitimate weapon for solving international disputes. Even if the United States seemed to revert to a position of political isolationism in the aftermath of the Versailles Treaty

(1919)—a trend that resulted in the rejection of Wilson's own contribution to the creation of the League of Nations—American involvement continued and was widely associated with conditions of sociopolitical and economic stability. The same impression was reinforced after 1929, when the world economic crash caused the withdrawal of American capital and plunged Europe into an unprecedented and demoralizing crisis.

The European fascination with American novelty extended into the cultural sphere even during the 1930s, when other forms of U.S. economic and political involvement seemed to wane in the shadow of severe domestic problems. At a time of rapid expansion in mass culture, American experiments with new forms of cultural expression (for example, popular cinema) and the incorporation of modern technology into cultural artifacts added a further layer of veneer to Americanization. Hollywood movies gradually became focal points of a culture that seemed to bind diverse European audiences together much more than any other force originating in the Continent itself. The introduction of jazz in Europe provided the opportunity for the conceptualization of a dissident youth culture that was even informed by a rebellious political spirit (for example, against authoritarianism and fascism). European culture appeared incapable of generating innovation any longer and was increasingly losing the initiative to a much more dynamic reservoir of modernity coming from the other side of the Atlantic. At the same time, native culture seemed unable to resist erosion in response to mass-produced American influences nor to incorporate effectively the spirit of novelty.

During World War II and, in particular, after its devastating conclusion, U.S. involvement in Europe became not only more manifold and intense but was also associated with a claim to bipolar loyalty. During the Cold War, the endorsement of Americanization became—consciously or unconsciously—coterminous with a statement of ideological and political loyalty, a choice between diametrically opposed worldviews and ethical visions. This sort of rigid dualism left little space for the reconceptualization of a distinct "European" identity in the aftermath of World War II. What started perhaps as an ideological statement and a form of defense against a formidable "enemy" became an often uncritical or uncontrollable process that saturated European political, economic, and cultural space. The Americanization of European politics flourished in the Cold War, as economic assistance was often identified with political-ideological hegemony and often with a military presence.

AMERICANIZATION

A TOTAL FASCINATION

In a 30 November 2000 address at the French Institute Alliance in New York, French ambassador François Bujon de l'Estang touched on the French view of the United States:

To be sure, and as I said earlier, the United States exerts on the French a total fascination. The global picture of a land of opportunities, exceptional entrepreneurship, incredible business success stories and rapid and enormous money rewards is universally accepted. Hollywood and Broadway have conveyed an image of glamour that the French love. They love the United States under the features of John Wayne, Humphrey Bogart, Marilyn Monroe or Frank Sinatra, and with the colors of *Gone with the Wind.*

It's not unusual to hear a Frenchman returning from his first visit to the United States say that he felt as if he knew the country before he arrived because he'd "been there" in American movies.

Yet negative stereotypes linger on. The most complete caricature is perhaps seen in the famous French TV program, "Les Guignols de l'Info," a daily puppet show which lampoons various prominent individuals. The American is depicted as a coarse, unscrupulous person with a Sylvester Stallone appearance and voice, representing an imaginary enterprise called "World Company," and forever brandishing a wad of dollars to buy everything that can be bought.

Many people in France, as you can tell from the polls, think of America as a violent society, gun-toting and trigger-happy, riven by growing social inequalities and by a deep-seated, all-pervasive racism. The ghettos and the gaps in social coverage project the image of a harsh society without pity for the frail, where the dollar is king and little else matters.

In the same article I mentioned a few minutes ago, Stanley Hoffman refers to "the fairly large black spots in America: 2 million people in jail, housing segregation, almost 50% of the voting-age population not voting, enormous inequalities in income and fortunes, the frequently dilapidated state of public services in a country that systematically distrusts the state, and so on". Lots of French people find this unbelievable and are amazed at these dark spots in American society; they're shocked that the death penalty is still in force and by the fact that, in the year 2000, 42 million Americans have no health coverage.

Politicians and media commentators also frequently denounce the U.S. lack of knowledge of the rest of the world, its hegemonic pretensions, insularity and heavy-handedness. Although the same criticism is also frequently heard in many other countries around the world, there again French propensity to being very vocal and for theorizing is very much in evidence.

Again, there's a negative backdrop to these stereotypes.

French intellectuals especially are quick to criticize what they perceive to be the all-consuming nature of the American market. They see it essentially as a danger in terms of both their voluntarist conception of policy and their conviction that the protection of the weakest requires a significant degree of regulation. Viviane Forrester's work, *L'Horreur économique,* a major hit in French bookshops, expresses some French liberal intellectuals' rejection of an American model, deliberately caricatured with expressions like "unfettered capitalism" and "cowboy capitalism." But even outside their circle, you'll find echoes of their way of thinking in the political world. Some of you will remember De Gaulle's famous retort that: "French policy is not made on the floor of the Stock Exchange." Prime Minister Lionel Jospin summed it up nicely when he said, during his visit to the U.S. in 1998, "Yes to a market economy, but no to a market society."

Many French intellectuals frequently speak of the American way of life as all ephemera, glitz and gadgets. It's also fashionable among these same people to criticize what they perceive to be the absence of historical perspective, cultural depth and long-term vision among Americans.

In short, the image of the United States in France continues to be dogged by real prejudices although, mirroring what happens in the U.S. for anti-French feelings, they do tend to weaken the further you get from Parisian intellectual circles and the closer you go to the heartland of France, where American visitors, of their own admission, are very warmly received.

Source: *François Bujon de l'Estang, "France and the United States: Seen Through Each Other's Eyes," 30 November 2000, Embassy of France website <http://www.info-france-usa.org/news/statmnts/2000/be3011.asp>.*

AMERICANIZATION

How did European countries react to this seemingly uncontrolled infiltration by the symbols of U.S. power and cultural domination? In the 1950s the momentum for European integration seemed to generate conditions that would facilitate in the near future the recasting of a distinct European identity. Until the 1980s, however, the European Economic Community (EEC) remained exactly what its temporary title suggested—an economic agreement among a small number of countries that possessed limited momentum and even less political muscle to detach the need for political affinity with the United States from the ongoing process of U.S.-derived saturation of the European socio-economic and cultural space. Only France embarked on a systematic policy aimed at limiting Americanizing trends. French president Charles de Gaulle twice blocked the integration of the United Kingdom into the European Union (EU), fearing that Britain would become the portal for a stronger representation of U.S. interests in the institution. At the same time, a combination of positive incentives geared toward reviving domestic cultural creation and resisting infiltration proved ineffective in reversing the long-term trend toward an increasingly Americanized culture. American symbols continued to exercise an almost unassailable magnetism, as they were associated with images of innovation and modernity. Some commentators have even described the phenomenon as a superbly successful "cultural imperialism" that saturated Europe's consumer sphere.

In this respect, the greatest danger that Americanization poses for an autonomous European identity consists in the paralyzing effect that the former has on the latter. The way that American political supremacy, economic might, and cultural expansion have permeated distinct regional and national cultures has stifled the autochthonous force of innovation and generated a complacency that no formal political initiative can overcome. During General Agreement on Tariffs and Trade (GATT, 1993) negotiations for the liberalization of international trade, European cinema demanded recognition that it constituted a special cultural product in need of some form of protection. However commendable such an initiative was, it did little to reverse the trend toward a further disruptive Americanization of European culture.

At the same time that European states are trying to enforce a regulation in the flow of American cultural artifacts and popular consumer symbols in one particular area, U.S. symbols continue to colonize public spaces and collective imageries. The opening of a McDonald's on Piazza di Spagna in Rome (a place not simply of superbly harmonious architectural beauty but also of supremely *Roman* flavor) was received with almost unanimous anger by the city's population. Similar sentiments targeted the creation of the first European Disneyland park in the outskirts of Paris. Isolating, however, the effect from its fundamental cause—the overpowering and paralyzing effect of Americanization—conceals a crucial truth. The strength of Americanization does not lie in the sum of its particular components. It is, rather, symptomatic of both a wider process of succumbing to a cultural and social idiom that has already assumed the character of a norm, and of the absence of a powerful antidote that can mobilize the currents of a distinct European-ness.

In the last decade of the twentieth century, the collapse of the Soviet bloc and the recognition that the United States constituted the only real superpower in the international system resulted in a further expansion of Americanization into the Continent—this time in Eastern Europe. The traditional identification of an anti-Soviet agenda with the West, and of "Western" with "American," have effected a dizzying penetration of public and private spheres with symbols and trends emblematic of this spectacular transition to a postcommunist reality. Globalization has become the new catchphrase, provoking a similar sort of ideological bipolarity separating those who enthusiastically celebrate its opportunities for openness, pluralism, and "closeness" on the one hand, and those who dismissively ascribe to it anything from cultural imperialism to economic tyranny to strangulation of individual identities. To what extent globalization, modernization, and commercialization are coterminous with Americanization remains open to debate, but few would fail to notice the saturation of the "modern" and the "global" with expansive U.S. symbols: from Coca-Cola to IBM, from the Academy Awards to actor Leonardo Di Caprio, from the dollar to chairman of the Federal Reserve Board Alan Greenspan's kudos, from Microsoft's invasion (in fact, invention) of most computer desktops to Cable News Network (CNN), and so on.

At the same time, however, the seemingly uncontested and intensifying American hegemony over the world has generated the first signs of a powerful, though once again clumsy, backlash. Unease with the increasing American unilateralism on the political level has often given rise to vocal reactions. Anti-American political platforms are becoming more widespread in European societies, sometimes preaching a form of abstract emancipation from U.S. hegemony but often assuming the form of cultural particularism and insularity. The extension of EU activities from the purely economic to social, political, and cultural fields has provided for some the basis for the construction of an alternative, but has also been interpreted by others as a simple reformulation of the wider "Western" hegemonic creed with a new veneer.

The problem for Europe is that it is at the same time part of this specifically Western globalized code and distinct from the latter's dominant American component. Differences in political, economic, social, and cultural outlook across the Atlantic may seem less fundamental when juxtaposed to what scholar Samuel P. Huntington has called the "clash of civilizations" (for example, Western versus Islamic), but they are not so inconsequential as to be brushed aside as mere minor variations. Disagreements with regard to the role of the state in running the economy, caring for the population, promoting cultural innovation, and acting as an international player have become increasingly evident between Europe and the United States. American unilateralism with regard to international crisis management and legal regulation have recently generated tensions within the Western camp. The U.S. attitude toward institutional channels of the United Nations (UN) and the newly established International Criminal Court have revealed to many Europeans the limits of the American commitment to a pluralistic international order. At the same time, the United States increases its presence in the political sphere, often functioning as an impediment to the development of distinctly European institutions—for example, a military force with a mandate and decision-making powers independent of the North Atlantic Treaty Organization (NATO).

For this and other, similar developments Europeans have only themselves to blame, for the effective filtering of American influence presupposes the existence of a distinct identity, an awareness of its specificity and value, the determination to promote it as an overall project (that is, not in a piecemeal, spasmodic manner), and the mechanisms for generating popular identification with its fundamental components. Uncritical negativity toward, and rejection of, Americanization remains as problematic as the earlier uncritical absorption of its alleged novelty. European culture has already accommodated large segments of American influence and trends, sometimes successfully. A constructive response does not entail a blanket refusal of cultural exchange—idioms do not evolve in separation from, let alone opposition to, each other. A distinct European identity can and should remain receptive to outside influences, which it subsequently distills, adapts, and contextualizes. However, there is absolutely no

point in resorting to rhetorical condemnations or spasmodic outbursts against U.S. influence on Europe without the awareness of a positive distinctiveness and the resolve to promote it in a dialectical relation to Americanization. It was the absence of this momentum within Europe, rather than the strength of American infiltration per se, that resulted in a virtual paralysis of European political, economic, social, and cultural identity in the twentieth century; it is this chronic and disruptive paralysis that constitutes the most fundamental threat to Europe's cultural specificity.

—ARISTOTLE A. KALLIS,
UNIVERSITY OF BRISTOL

Viewpoint:
No. The flow of cultural influences is multidirectional, and American culture legitimately enjoys mass popularity in Europe.

The hegemony that the United States has enjoyed since the end of World War II has not been merely military or diplomatic. In the decades that followed 1945, many Europeans came to fear that their national cultures were threatened by the growing international popularity of American culture. Music, movies, dress, food, attitudes, slang, and other aspects of daily life seemed to be influenced more and more by American values and business. At a time when an enormous amount of political power flowed from Washington, cultural currents seemed to go along with it.

There should be little surprise that Europeans would develop a strong resentment of the growing popularity of all things American. The traditional European perception of the United States portrayed (and sometimes still portrays) it as a semicivilized place, defined by a lack of "real" history and culture, and dominated by a social ethos not far removed from the worst stereotypes of the Wild West. America's emphasis on universal liberty struck many Europeans as naive. Its championing of rugged individualism subverted their hierarchical views of society and departed from their traditional views of community. Its emphasis on personal ambition, achievement, and wealth appeared vulgar and amoral. The new nation's rise as a world power in the early twentieth century looked much like an embarrassment of riches falling into the lap of a spoiled child. Even before World War II, European critics were alarmed by the growing popularity of American cultural idioms in

AMERICANIZATION

Europe. Early Hollywood dominated European cinema with images of cowboys, gangsters, bandits, and flappers. The sensual rhythms of jazz thrilled the young and worried their parents. To its critics, these creations of American culture undermined traditional morality and were beginning to take the place of the "superior" idioms of European culture.

Such critiques intensified after World War II and remain current today. After having made a decisive contribution in ending another world war, America and its people were popular. U.S. soldiers were legendary for their generosity. American financial assistance immediately poured into devastated European economies. If America was a land of wealth, abundance, and opportunity, these characteristics only inspired impoverished Europeans to admire it. Many emigrated there after the war. Yet, other Europeans, including the cultural and political elite, bemoaned the skyrocketing popularity of American culture. Would the product of their civilizations be replaced so quickly and easily by Westerners and Coca-Cola just because America enjoyed a temporary ascendancy? Did the result of World War II entitle "philistine" American culture to dominate European markets and sway the values of the continent's youth?

For all their concern, however, America's perceived threat to European culture and traditions was greatly exaggerated and presented in an obtusely one-sided manner. The driving force of cultural anti-Americanism was intimately connected with politics. America's enhanced position led many Europeans to fear that its influence was there to stay, and to lament that their nations' long periods of international influence were drawing to a close. As the Cold War emerged between the United States and the Soviet Union, many observers, including some Americans, expected that Washington, D.C., was deliberately using its economic power to tether Western Europe to its orbit. If the Americans would use trade, financial assistance, and diplomatic clout to capture European foreign and economic policies, why should they not also attempt to win over the hearts and minds of average citizens, especially impressionable young ones, to their cultural values? From this premise, many European critics deduced that almost any manifestation of American popular culture was part of a larger, calculated plan to saturate their Continent with products and propaganda.

Of course this threat was a myth. There was no vast conspiracy of U.S. businessmen, government officials, and popular-culture figures determined to force the products of American culture down the throats of hapless European consumers. Yet, the idea that America was using culture as another means of extending its hegemony suited many European prejudices. It enabled the European elite to continue to demonize America as the new avaricious power they had traditionally believed it to be. Intellectual critics of capitalism identified American culture as the latest and most virulent manifestation of an ideology that they held to be anathema. Critics of an older generation had something neatly tangible and safely foreign to blame for bewildering and uncomfortable social change. If imperialism was the highest stage of capitalism, then "cultural imperialism" was expected to go along with its political manifestation. For all of these disaffected groups, the popularity of U.S. culture symbolized American hegemony. French intellectuals of the 1950s did not march in the streets against Coca-Cola because they opposed the carbonated soft drink; they protested because it came from a country whose power they resented, whose society they despised, and whose influence they feared.

This fear was totally unjustified. Neither France nor any other European country is "just like us," to quote a typical accusation leveled at alleged American ambitions. French café culture was not displaced by McDonald's, even if *le fast food* is popular. Most European nations have thriving motion-picture industries of international renown that have not disappeared in a flood of trite Hollywood movies. Appreciation of national cultures and identities is at the forefront of European social and political life. Distinctly European habits, attitudes, mores, traditions, and sensibilities are there for all to see. In contemporary Europe, concerns about the perceived consequences of immigration and European integration are much more pressing than the specter of Americanization in discourses of national identity. Even if there had been a plan to ensure American cultural hegemony over Europe, who could say that it has succeeded?

How, then, can one explain the enduring popularity of American culture in Europe? There are simpler explanations than Cold War conspiracies, deliberate cultural imperialism, and rabid international capitalism. First, American culture is legitimately popular in Europe and elsewhere. In a modern world with a faster pace of life, improved communications, and increasing demands for immediate satisfaction, many aspects of the "American way of life" sell themselves. Wide availability, low prices, consumer satisfaction, quality entertainment, and speed are not difficult to imagine as universal values in what is increasingly becoming an interdependent global economy. Who, in any society or culture, would prefer narrow availability,

AMERICANIZATION

high prices, consumer dissatisfaction, uninspired entertainment, and delay when faced with such an alternative, even if it is American in manufacture or inspiration? Why not eat lunch at McDonald's or have coffee at Starbucks if it is fast, easy, tasty, and cheap?

Second, in America's dynamic, success-driven, and technology-oriented economy, many of its consumer products are simply better than those made by foreign competitors. In some sectors, such as computers and telecommunications, there is no foreign competition to certain U.S. products, while other American products are simply cheaper and qualitatively superior to those of foreign competitors. If Europeans like American goods or ingenuity, it is largely for their own sake, not because they are forced to. In a like manner, more-traditional cultural idioms are pervaded by Americans who have requisite talents and skills. America's system of higher education, especially its graduate and professional schools, commands the highest prestige in dozens of fields and professions. It should come as no surprise that many of the top international scholars, scientists, and artists are Americans or American trained. Once again, a concentration of superior resources has resulted in a quality product that other nations cannot equal.

Third, regardless of the reason, many Europeans simply like American movies, television, music, and fashions. Since they are consumers in market economies, they are free to indulge their individual tastes. As French actor Yves Montand, a former communist and anti-American protester, said so simply in the early 1980s, if his countrymen did not like American cultural capital, they would refuse. But free European consumers do buy it. Naturally, there are alternatives, but no one has forced German television to broadcast *The Simpsons,* while subscribers to pay television in France can watch *South Park.* American movie and record industries do not compel European audiences to go out and buy their products. Indeed, when the French government attempted in the early 1990s to place "protectionist" quotas on the number of American movies and television series that could be imported, popular demand, not American imperialists, defeated the initiative. As consumers in free-market economies, Europeans create demands that American producers fill. In the last half of the twentieth century it would be difficult to argue that anyone has been harmed or has become less of who they are. Indeed, there are many cases in which American culture has failed dismally in European markets. When the Walt Disney corporation opened its Euro-Disney theme park outside Paris in the early 1990s, it was a huge failure. European consumers had little familiarity with Disney, and the opening of an American-style theme park did not capture their interest. In the world of sports, soccer has undisputed mass appeal, while American football, baseball, and basketball command little attention outside the United States. In a truly free market, not every product is guaranteed success. Consumers buy what they like and ignore what they do not.

Fourth, even while American culture is popular in Europe, who can deny that European and other cultures are popular in America? Would apprehensive European intellectuals agree that American culture was threatened by the popularity of the Beatles or the Rolling Stones? Probably not. Do Americans who buy Jaguars, Porsches, or Mercedes sacrifice their cultural heritage because they prefer those fine automobiles to Fords or Buicks? In the American free market, consumers love all varieties of ethnic cuisine, from Italian to Vietnamese. The fashion conscious sport Italian suits and English shoes. The host of a party might ask his guests to R.S.V.P., or *répondez s'il vous plaît.* For a time in the 1990s it was chic for young Americans to affect European ("Eurotrash" to its critics) styles of manner and dress. Yet, no one has ever suggested seriously that any of these tastes, styles, and consumer preferences constitute a threat to American culture or identity. Why should the analogous popularity of American products in European countries threaten theirs?

"Americanization" has been a problematic concept for European societies. Despite the fears and insecurities of the elite, who have seen their nations' power and global influence decline in the last century, there is remarkably little to suggest that the popularity of American culture represents a threat. There is no evidence that it was ever intended to displace indigenous cultures and identities, nor has it succeeded in doing so to any important extent. Rather, it has simply been the case that American consumer goods, entertainment, and other cultural products command a loyal purchasing public in Europe, and elsewhere too, just as European culture commands loyal adherents in the United States. In neither case is anyone's culture or identity threatened.

–PAUL DU QUENOY,
GEORGETOWN UNIVERSITY

References

Jean Baudrillard, *America,* translated by Chris Turner (London & New York: Verso, 1988).

Richard Falk, *Predatory Globalization: A Critique* (Cambridge: Polity Press, 1999).

Samuel P. Huntington, *The Clash of Civilizations and the Remaking of World Order* (New York: Simon & Schuster, 1996).

Tony Judt, *Past Imperfect: French Intellectuals, 1944–1956* (Berkeley: University of California Press, 1992).

Richard F. Kuisel, *Seducing the French: The Dilemma of Americanization* (Berkeley: University of California Press, 1993).

Richard H. Pells, *Not Like Us: How Europeans Have Loved, Hated, and Transformed American Culture since World War II* (New York: Basic Books, 1997).

David Strauss, *Menace in the West: The Rise of French Anti-Americanism in Modern Times* (Westport, Conn.: Greenwood Press, 1978).

AMERICANIZATION

BRITAIN AS PART OF EUROPE

Does Great Britain have a national identity culturally distinct from Europe?

Viewpoint: Yes. Great Britain's domestic traditions, geography, and world-view continue to distinguish it from the Continent.

Viewpoint: No. Great Britain's shared history and close economic ties with the Continent have made it an inseparable part of Europe.

Until relatively recently, geographers, historians, government officials, and other authorities have conceived of the British Isles as a separate entity from the European continent that lies little more than twenty miles across the English Channel. Many Britons and foreigners alike argue that the "splendid isolation" policy pursued by the British government in the late nineteenth century has long been the quintessence of British identity. Even the narrow geographic separation from the Continent was sufficient to keep British institutions, worldviews, and culture outside those shared by continental nations. Britain's history as the greatest colonial power and its long "special relationship" with the United States gave it world-power status and an identity that transcended the narrow confines of Europe.

Yet, others doubt the relevance of these factors. Despite them, Britain has long been drawn into European struggles by rulers with interests on the Continent and by an elite who recognized the importance of the European balance of power. In the twentieth century, Britain's decline as a world power and the loss of its colonial empire resulted in greater cooperation and integration with the Continent. In terms of foreign trade, travel, and tourism—and the institutions of the European Union (EU)—Britain's European identity is beyond doubt.

Viewpoint:
Yes. Great Britain's domestic traditions, geography, and worldview continue to distinguish it from the Continent.

England has been invaded time and again—Celts and Romans, Vikings and Normans—but 1066 marked the last time foreign invasion succeeded. The twenty-odd miles of the aptly named English Channel have proved more than a physical barrier; they have been a psychological wall against the culture and politics of the Continent.

England for all practical purposes abandoned its territorial claims on the Continent at the conclusion of the Hundred Years' War (1337–1453). Over the next three centuries France and the other continental powers and would-be powers concentrated on developing their land armies. England, beginning with the reign of Henry VIII (1509–1547), built the greatest navy and naval tradition in the world. After the defeat of the Spanish Armada (1588), the English fleet held sway over the seas for an unprecedented four centuries. The climax of this naval military supremacy came with the rise of Napoleon Bonaparte. A dominant theme in the Wars of the French Revolution was a standoff between the greatest land power and the largest sea power. The sea power prevailed.

In the years following the Congress of Vienna (1815), Europe, in the main, turned its interests and energies inward, consolidating national identities. Prussia incorporated the German states, by war and diplomacy, into a modern, unified Germany. The Austrian Empire strove to tighten its grip on middle Europe, and France concentrated on healing the wounds of a quarter century of revolution. Great Britain, meanwhile, used its navy to expand and consolidate a colonial empire that had spread worldwide. Even after the loss of the American colonies, the new United States remained one of Britain's largest trading partners. Wealth flowed in from all over the world, making Britain by far the wealthiest European state, and, by and large, self-sufficient relative to the Continent. Europe was largely an outlet for British luxury goods, not a source of staples or basics.

With the rise of the Industrial Revolution the economic gap between Britain and Europe continued to widen. With industrialism grew a sense of nationalism, of a distinctive British identity. Nationalism began to sweep Europe as well, especially after the Prussian defeat of Austria (1866) and France (1871). Britain, however, taking full credit for having defeated Napoleon and imposing a formula for peace through the concept of "balance of power," sustained its feeling of insularity and superiority. Britain saw itself as the primary power, if not the hegemon: above the petty frays of the Continent, but able to prevent any one continental country from becoming dominant.

The wooden ships that for three centuries had protected the island against any possible invasion and made the British Empire possible became obsolete the day two American ironclads began their duel in Hampton Roads, Virginia (1862). Britain responded by taking the lead in steam-driven battleships. The young German emperor, Wilhelm II, decided to construct a fleet that would match Britain's. Answering this challenge, Britain embarked on a construction program intended to ensure that its fleet remained larger than the combined fleets of any two countries. This plan was undertaken both to secure the defense of the British Isles and to protect as well the sea-lanes to India, Hong Kong, and elsewhere.

Britain remained active in European politics during the nineteenth century primarily to prevent any grand coalitions or imperiums such as that formed by Napoleon from arising. Its success, in turn, led to the ill-considered belief that diplomacy could solve all differences between civi-

lized nations. This policy worked well for seventy years, when Europe was ruled by an interlocking and interrelated aristocracy, for both the tsar of Russia and the emperor of Germany were kin to Queen Victoria, as were the king of Greece and several minor German rulers. As the Industrial Revolution spread through the Continent, however, the focus of power began shifting to more-dynamic elements who were willing to challenge the status quo. At the same time, industrialization fostered increased interaction between England and the Continent. Germany, Britain's most serious rival, grew precipitously and became its second largest trading partner by 1914.

The British Foreign Office, which had consistently defused potentially serious international crises since mid century, became less confident of its ability to maintain single-handedly the peace that had prevailed over most of the nineteenth century. As Germany and the German navy grew in strength, Britain found it prudent to negotiate diplomatic ententes with France (1904) and Russia (1907). In 1914, as nation after nation activated its automatic mobiliza-

Late-nineteenth-century portrait of Victoria, Queen of the United Kingdom, called the grandmother of Europe. Her children and grandchildren included royalty in Germany, Prussia, Greece, Norway, Russia, Romania, Sweden, and Spain

(Bettmann/CORBIS).

BRITAIN AS PART OF EUROPE

tion plans in reaction to Austria-Hungary's declaration of war against Serbia, Britain's projected deterrent became part of a doomsday machine.

After World War I the combatants retreated to try to heal their grievous wounds. Britain concentrated on restoring the empire to its Edwardian strength. It faced a strong independence movement in India and serious armed rebellion in Ireland. It lost Ireland in 1920 and India, "the Jewel in the Crown," in 1947. At the Washington Naval Conference (1921–1922) Britain officially abandoned the prewar mantra of possessing an equal number of capital ships as the next two largest navies. Under the new ratio Britain and the United States would have an equal number and Japan 60 percent of the number. Britain still saw itself primarily as an island naval power with its fleet as its first line of defense. In World War II the Royal Air Force (RAF) provided defensive power, but the threat of the navy prevented a cross-channel invasion attempt.

World War II deepened the feeling that Britain was not really a part of Europe. The British people took deep retrospective pride in their lone stand against Adolf Hitler's forces. The RAF and Royal Navy performed brilliantly in defending the isle from invasion and defeat. Britain's army saved the vital link of the Suez Canal and participated in the defeat and occupation of Nazi Germany. Above all, Britain established what both Prime Minister Winston Churchill and President Franklin D. Roosevelt liked to call a "special relationship," with the United States emerging as Britain's successor in securing a global status quo. Britain was correspondingly ambivalent about close ties with the Continent. Readily joining the North Atlantic Treaty Organization (NATO) and becoming an active partner in the Cold War, Britain was nevertheless more interested in cultivating its "special relationship" than in becoming part of Europe. In any case, few alternatives existed. Germany was struggling with rebuilding its cities and establishing a viable government. France was initially enmeshed in unwinnable colonial wars, and later followed its own unilateral path by pulling out of NATO in 1966 and developing its own nuclear force.

As general political and economic tendencies on the Continent toward various forms of cooperation increased, Britain remained cautious. The British joined the European Economic Community (EEC), a "common market," only after years of internal debate—involving not only specifics such as protection of British agriculture, but a far more fundamental concern: the loss of national identity. Under serious economic duress, Britain finally joined the EEC in 1973. Yet, even the development of this relationship has remained halfhearted. Under Margaret Thatcher's govern-

ment in 1979–1990, contention over European budgets and agricultural subsidies led to sharp disputes. Jacques Delors, the French president of the European Commission, at one point talked of expelling Britain. Thatcher's successor John Major refused to enter the European Union (EU) Exchange Rate Mechanism (ERM) in 1993, and Britain remains one of only three EU countries that has not converted its currency to the euro, the pan-EU currency introduced in January 1999. Since 70 percent of the population oppose that step, according to public opinion polls, it is unlikely to do so in the future. Finally, under the Labour government of Tony Blair, Britain remains steadfast in its relationship with the United States. Most recently, it has been the most committed foreign nation in supporting the U.S. "war on terrorism," the tactical and strategic steps taken against the terrorist networks that carried out attacks on the United States in September 2001. Britain was the only European nation to commit troops to the U.S. campaign against the Taliban regime in Afghanistan (2001–2002), and was one of the few countries to back the military strike against Iraq in 2003.

For almost a millennium the English Channel has served Britain as both guard and custodian. Long habit and two world wars have kept Britain mindful of its own identity and cautious in accepting the unifying tendencies currently dominating continental European politics. The thought of losing that identity means there is likely to be an England for the calculable future.

—JOHN WHEATLEY,
BROOKLYN CENTER, MINNESOTA

Viewpoint:
No. Great Britain's shared history and close economic ties with the Continent have made it an inseparable part of Europe.

Britain is and has long been an integral part of Europe. Leaving the modern era aside for the moment, ancient Britannia, what is now known as England, became an important province of the Roman Empire after Julius Caesar conquered it in the first century B.C.E. and later developed into an important part of Latin Christendom. England's conquest by William, Duke of Normandy, in 1066 both placed a French-speaking elite in charge of the realm and united it with substantial dynastic landholdings in continental Europe. Expanding and defending these possessions commanded English attention, power, and resources for the next four centuries. England celebrated and participated in Renaissance art and scholarship, embraced the religious reforms of the Protestant Reformation, made substantial intellectual contributions to the Scientific Revolution and the Enlightenment, and became the major force in the colonization of the rest of the world. European politics came to play a major role in English strategic thinking, leading England gradually to establish control over Ireland and to negotiate an enduring dynastic union with Scotland, as well as to maintain a major interest in the politics of continental Europe. Sensitivity to the European balance of power developed at least as early as the sixteenth century, when Queen Elizabeth I sent troops and supplies to battle Spanish hegemony in the Netherlands, a region that the English identified wholly with their nation's security and that they would defend against France in the seventeenth, eighteenth, and nineteenth centuries, and against Germany in the twentieth. With the sole exception of James II's marriage in 1659 to Anne Hyde, before the reign of Edward VIII (1936), who renounced the throne to marry an American divorcée, all of Elizabeth's successors married into the ruling houses of continental Europe. In 1689–1702 the throne was occupied by William III, a Dutch prince (jointly with his wife Mary II until her death in 1694), and in 1714–1901 Britain's reigning monarchs were members of the German Hanoverian dynasty, who until 1837 ruled Britain along with the Kingdom of Hanover. The current dynasty, the Windsors, only have an English family name because they changed it from the original German Saxe-Coburg-Gotha for nationalist reasons during World War I.

If earlier eras fail to convey Britain's "Europeanness," the opening of the twentieth century highlighted the personal connections between the British throne and the rulers of Europe. When Queen Victoria died in 1901, her son and heir Edward VII was an uncle of both the emperor of Germany and the tsar of Russia, as well as a brother-in-law of the kings of Denmark and Greece and a more distant relative of several other sovereigns. European high politics in the era has been described as a family affair, in which Queen Victoria was the recently departed grandmother. Even if family ties could not prevent diplomatic wrangling in the early century or forestall the outbreak of World War I, Britain's role in the conflict was central and decisive. Strategic threats from German power within continental Europe led directly to its involvement, which, even if Britain had traditionally resisted alliances, came only three days after the beginning of hostilities. Nearly 750,000 British troops perished on muddy French and Belgian battlefields to keep the Germans in check, and Britain's economy was, like every other combatant nation's, oriented fully toward winning the war. Britain predicated its participation in the peace settlement and its subsequent interactions with Europe on restraining German power and Soviet influence, a lesser, yet important theme deriving from Britain's traditional resistance to Russia. When these efforts failed with the outbreak of World War II, Britain again became a crucial and, for nearly a year, the only participant in a pan-European war against Germany. The subsequent uneasy peace between the Western Allies and the Soviet Union stimulated yet more active British participation in European affairs. In the immediate aftermath of the war, the great prime minister and Conservative Party leader Winston Churchill, who had fleetingly offered a political union to defeated France in 1940, advocated Britain's full integration into a "United States of Europe." By 1949 the country was a member of several bilateral and multilateral defensive alliances with its neighbors in Western Europe and with the United States, which had adopted a dominant role there.

As Britain's colonial empire contracted and its standing as an independent power in its own right dwindled, its leaders of all political persuasions sought to enhance their country's influence through its inclusion in the trade, politics, defense, and new institutions of what was beginning to develop into a united Europe. In the 1950s Britain adhered to a common European authority for nuclear power, and Prime Minister Harold Macmillan's government (1957–1963) advanced British candidacy for membership in the European Economic Community (EEC), a free economic association established in 1958 among France, West Germany, Italy, Belgium, the Netherlands, and Luxembourg. The unsuccessful outcome of this effort in 1963 did not stop British leaders from making another effort, which failed in 1967, and a third try, which resulted in Britain's accession in 1973. Britain subsequently participated in the EEC's Common Agricultural Policy (CAP) and helped finance subsidies for the EEC's poorer members. It signed and ratified the Maastricht Treaty (1992), an agreement that transformed the EEC into the European Union (EU) and established the broader integration of its member states, including common European citizenship, a common European parliament and commission of ministers, and common European policies and institutions for economic, legal, human rights, and educational matters. An increasing amount of legislation and regulation that impact British law, business, farming, government administration, and daily life come from the European Parliament in

OUR DESTINY IS IN EUROPE

British prime minister Margaret Thatcher delivered a speech in Bruges on 20 September 1988 concerning the place of Britain in Europe:

Europe is not the creation of the Treaty of Rome. Nor is the European idea the property of any group or institution. We British are as much heirs to the legacy of European culture as any other nation. Our links to the rest of Europe, the continent of Europe, have been the dominant factor in our history. For three hundred years we were part of the Roman Empire and our maps still trace the straight lines of the roads the Romans built. Our ancestors—Celts, Saxons and Danes—came from the continent.

Our nation was—in that favourite Community word—"restructured" under Norman and Angevin rule in the eleventh and twelfth centuries.

This year we celebrate the three hundredth anniversary of the Glorious Revolution in which the British crown passed to Prince William of Orange and Queen Mary. Visit the great Churches and Cathedrals of Britain, read our literature and listen to our language: all bear witness to the cultural riches which we have drawn from Europe—and other Europeans from us.

We in Britain are rightly proud of the way in which, since Magna Carta in 1215, we have pioneered and developed representative institutions to stand as bastions of freedom. And proud too of the way in which for centuries Britain was a home for people from the rest of Europe who sought sanctuary from tyranny.

But we know that without the European legacy of political ideas we could not have achieved as much as we did. From classical and mediaeval thought we have borrowed that concept of the rule of law which marks out a civilised society from barbarism. And on that idea of Christendom—for long synonymous with Europe—with its recognition of the unique and spiritual nature of the individual, we still base our belief in personal liberty and other human rights.

Too often the history of Europe is described as a series of interminable wars and quarrels. Yet from our perspective today surely what strikes us most is our common experience. For instance, the story of how Europeans explored and colonised and—yes, without apology—civilised much of the world is an extraordinary tale of talent, skill and courage.

We British have in a special way contributed to Europe. Over the centuries we have fought to prevent Europe from falling under the dominance of a single power. We have fought and we have died for her freedom. Only miles from here in Belgium lie the bodies of 120,000 British soldiers who died in the First World War. Had it not been for that willingness to fight and to die, Europe would have been united long before now—but not in liberty, not in justice. It was British support to resistance movements throughout the last War that helped to keep alive the flame of liberty in so many countries until the day of liberation.

Tomorrow, King Baudouin will attend a service in Brussels to commemorate the many brave Belgians who gave their lives in service with the Royal Air Force—a sacrifice which we shall never forget.

It was from our island fortress that the liberation of Europe itself was mounted. And still today we stand together. Nearly 70,000 British servicemen are stationed on the mainland of Europe. All these things alone are proof of our commitment to Europe's future.

The European Community is one manifestation of that European identity. But it is not the only one. We must never forget that East of the Iron Curtain peoples who once enjoyed a full share of European culture, freedom and identity have been cut off from their roots. We shall always look on Warsaw, Prague and Budapest as great European cities.

. . . The European Community belongs to all its members. It must reflect the traditions and aspirations of all its members.

And let me be quite clear. Britain does not dream of some cosy, isolated existence on the fringes of the European Community. Our destiny is in Europe, as part of the Community. That is not to say that our future lies only in Europe. But nor does that of France or Spain or indeed any other member.

The Community is not an end in itself. Nor is it an institutional device to be constantly modified according to the dictates of some abstract intellectual concept. Nor must it be ossified by endless regulation.

The European Community is the practical means by which Europe can ensure the future prosperity and security of its people in a world in which there are many other powerful nations and groups of nations.

We Europeans cannot afford to waste our energies on internal disputes or arcane institutional debates. They are no substitutes for effective action.

Europe has to be ready both to contribute in full measure to its own security and to compete commercially and industrially, in a world in which success goes to the countries which encourage individual initiative and enterprise, rather than to those which attempt to diminish them. . . .

Source: *Margaret Thatcher, "The Text of the Speech Delivered in Bruges by The Rt. Hon. Mrs Margaret Thatcher, FRS, on 20th September 1988," in "Bruges Revisited," Paper #34, The Bruges Group website <http://www.brugesgroup.com/mediacentre/index.live?article=92#britain>.*

BRITAIN AS PART OF EUROPE

Strasbourg and the European Commission in Brussels. Gestures toward a common European defense and foreign policy indicate a future of integration in these areas, too.

Critics of the integration of Britain into Europe argue that its non-European essence is still upheld by past disagreements with the EEC and EU, the unlikelihood of its future use of the euro (the common European currency introduced in 1999), and certain aspects of cultural identity. None of these factors, however, has nullified or substantially reduced Britain's European identity. Continental, mainly French, opposition to British EEC membership kept Britain out until 1973, but this opposition nevertheless waned in time for Britain to join Ireland and Denmark in the Community's first wave of expansion beyond its six charter members. Subsequent episodes, which included British prime minister Margaret Thatcher's demand that the EEC return what she believed to have been her country's misused CAP contributions and French EEC leader Jacques Delors's later suggestion that Britain be expelled (both in the 1980s), did little to undermine Britain's firm presence within the EEC or stop its participation in the "ever closer union" promised by the EU upon its founding. Britain's withdrawal from the EU's Exchange Rate Mechanism (ERM) in 1993 and substantial domestic opposition to adopting the euro as its currency do separate it in a meaningful way from most other EU nations, but these differences should not be exaggerated. Denmark and Sweden, both EU members, have not adopted the euro, nor may all of the ten East European and Mediterranean nations slated for admission in 2004. None of these nations, along with Switzerland and Norway (neither of which have joined the EU), has raised or will raise questions about their European identity by rejecting the common currency. Why should Britain?

While critics also correctly observe that Britons are among the least likely EU populations to identify themselves as "Europeans" rather than as members of their respective national groups, this point is moot as virtually no EU member state's population contains a majority or even an especially large plurality of citizens who consider themselves "European" rather than French, Irish, Portuguese, or Austrian. Distinct national institutions, including the common law system and monarchy of England (but not Scotland), speak strongly in favor of a distinct British identity, but every EU member state has exceptional national features that persist despite continuing integration. Indeed, six other EU member states (Belgium, Denmark, Luxembourg, the Netherlands, Spain, and Sweden) have heavily symbolic constitutional monarchs whose thrones face no threat from their countries' EU membership, to say nothing of myriad institutional and cultural differences that will not disappear anytime soon. Regardless of abstruse debates about "identity," few Britons, and no major British political party, favor their country's withdrawal from the EU, and there is no appreciable consensus supporting that outcome within or among the other member states.

The idea of the "non-Europeanness" of Britain has also focused on what many have argued to be its special presence in the world. As an imperial power, it held sway over a quarter of the earth's surface in 1900, dominated the seas with the most powerful navy and merchant marine, and developed closer relations with the United States than any other nation. Even the loss of empire and maritime predominance did not dissuade those who argued that Britain's distinct identity would be preserved by its enduring "special relationship" with the United States and its continuing links to its former colonies through the Commonwealth of Nations. Neither of these factors, however, ultimately confirmed a non-European identity for Britain. On one hand, its "special relationship" with the United States, while still strong, has withered in importance. After World War II, Washington took on greater global commitments, which, especially in international trade and relations with the Third World, often superseded its relationship with Britain. In the same era Britain, without its global power, became more introspective, focusing on its progressive integration into Europe and on developing a European welfare state and mixed state and market economy that had less in common with that of the United States. In any case, both advocates and critics of Britain's movement into Europe point out that EU membership has not and probably will not compromise the close Anglo-American partnership. A European Britain seems hardly less reliable or more distant to Washington than a non-European one, and successive U.S. administrations have favored European integration.

Most former British colonies, on the other hand, raised heavy tariffs on British goods as soon as they became independent and diminished trade and other relations with the United Kingdom. Some former colonies, as well as traditionally important areas of British investment such as Latin America, turned to other powers, especially the United States, the Soviet Union, or both, for closer strategic and economic relations during the Cold War. Other former colonies degenerated into civil war, brutal dictatorships, and other political disasters that were not conducive to maintaining strong and

BRITAIN AS PART OF EUROPE

HISTORY IN DISPUTE, VOLUME 17: TWENTIETH-CENTURY EUROPEAN SOCIAL AND POLITICAL MOVEMENTS, SECOND SERIES productive ties with Britain. In only a few cases did sharing the English language, common law, and monarchy have a major political or economic significance. By 2002 Britain conducted well more than half its foreign trade with EU nations, compared to just 18 percent with EEC members in 1962, while destinations in continental Europe accounted for about 75 percent of British tourism. It is hard to dispute that Britain is now "in Europe."

–PAUL DU QUENOY,
GEORGETOWN UNIVERSITY

References

Jeremy Black, *Convergence or Divergence?: Britain and the Continent* (New York: St. Martin's Press, 1994).

Roger Carrick, *Britain and Europe: One Foot In and One Foot Out* (Milwaukee: Center for International Studies, University of Wisconsin-Milwaukee, 1999).

Ennio Di Nolfo, ed., *Power in Europe? II: Great Britain, France, Germany, and Italy, and the origins of EEC, 1952–1957* (Berlin & New York: De Gruyter, 1992).

Sean Greenwood, *Britain and European Cooperation since 1945* (Oxford & Cambridge, Mass.: Blackwell, 1992).

Greenwood, ed., *Britain and European Integration since the Second World War* (Manchester & New York: Manchester University Press, 1996).

Vassiliki N. Koutrakou and Lucie A. Emerson, eds., *The European Union and Britain: Debating the Challenges Ahead* (New York: St. Martin's Press, 2000).

John Milfull, ed., *Britain in Europe: Prospects for Change* (Aldershot & Brookfield, Vt.: Ashgate, 1999).

Ulrike Rüb, ed., *European Governance: Views from the UK on Democracy, Participation and Policy-Making in the EU* (London: Federal Trust, 2002).

BRITAIN AS PART OF EUROPE

Were social class identities important factors in twentieth-century European political life?

Viewpoint: Yes. European politics have been deeply rooted in visible class divisions, and experiments in political leveling have utterly failed.

Viewpoint: No. Class identities were not as important as political ideologies, nationalism, religion, and state power in Europe during the twentieth century.

The communist philosophy of Karl Marx had a great impact on the development of European historical thought, in addition to its obvious influence on political events. Marx theorized that historical change results from a change in the material means of production. According to Marx, economic relations directly determined social and political realities, and these relations were characterized by intense conflict. In other words, conflicts between rival identities of social class were the primary stimuli in historical development.

Marx's ideas have—directly or indirectly—influenced many historians of twentieth-century Europe. In their view major political changes, whether violent and immediate or peaceful and gradual, depended on antagonism between clearly defined social classes in European societies, usually a working class (proletariat) and a possessing class (bourgeoisie). Revolutions, mass movements, protests, and even wars all had a basis in pronounced class division.

A rising generation of historians rejects this interpretation. As European societies evolve, they appear, in the view of these scholars, ever more distant from Marx's theories. In contrast, such other factors as religion, nation, ethnicity, and regional provenance seemed to have meant more to Europeans than social class. Indeed, the definition of social class appears on closer inspection to have been fluid, variable, and arbitrary. The growth of consumerism, the democratization of taste, and other features of contemporary European life appear to have removed class conflict from the political stage.

Viewpoint:
Yes. European politics have been deeply rooted in visible class divisions, and experiments in political leveling have utterly failed.

Over the course of the twentieth century, as the bourgeois and managerial elements of society increasingly dominated the European social landscape, and as educated members of professional and managerial backgrounds permeated the political parties of the Left, some observers concluded that class no longer mattered, and probably never did matter, as a political and social factor. Nothing, however, could be further from the truth. When *class* is mentioned, one usually thinks of the Marxian definition of the term, whereby the sole consideration of ownership of the means of production replaced the older political and social aspects of class. For Europe, however, this definition may well be too narrow, for the weight of history and culture is still felt. Europe remains deeply marked by social and class divisions just like any other society. No society has succeeded in removing the political dimensions of class—experiments to do so in the twentieth century have utterly failed—and it seems exceedingly unlikely that any society will ever be freed of the distinctions of class and their political repercussions.

The most notorious attempt to wipe away the political dimensions of class was the Bolshevik Revolution (1917). Russia's new communist leadership earnestly sought to bring about a Marxist society where the only remaining class would be the proletariat. However, the Bolshevik Party failed to build its utopia exactly as prescribed by German political philosopher Karl Marx's ideology. Marx predicated his model upon industrialized western Europe, which not only differed from his monocausal explanation of human development but also varied widely from Russian society. In 1917 about 80 percent of Russians were still peasants. Forced industrialization, urbanization, and collectivization in the Soviet Union were adopted to counter this situation, but they were notoriously bloody processes rife with corruption, oppression, and injustices. They were also accompanied by the development of a new definition of class. The *nomenklatura,* the privileged elite of the Union of Soviet Socialist Republics (U.S.S.R.), secured for itself whatever (many) privileges and (few) luxuries were available. Political advantage and socio-economic class were more closely and cynically linked under the Soviet model than perhaps anywhere else. This model spread over Eastern and Central Europe after 1945. The attempt to eradicate the link between class and politics proved disastrous.

Another attempt at creating a utopia where class and politics would no longer be linked proved little better. The National Socialists grabbed power in Germany in 1933, promising, among other things, to smash the plutocracy. Though the *Nationalsozialistische Deutsche Arbeiterpartei* (National Socialist German Workers' Party, NSDAP, or Nazi Party) is most famous for its notion of creating a society where the only class of any meaning was that of "race"—the *Volksgemeinschaft* (National Community)—no such social change ever came to be. Germans in the 1930s (and even today, for that matter) remained enthralled with anyone with the aristocratic "von" in front of his name. This fixation even reached comical proportions as Joachim "von" Ribbentrop, a champagne salesman turned Nazi foreign minister, tacked the aristocratic prefix on his name after persuading a childless distant relation, whose branch of the family had been ennobled, to adopt him. The military, as conservative as ever, remained class conscious, with many officers com-

ing from nonnoble upper-class families or bearing the "von" in their names. With the partial exception of the *Luftwaffe* (German Air Force)—which, as a new form of armament representing a twentieth-century modernity, attracted younger officers—old privileges of class remained in place in the military. Across Nazi Germany, princes and counts remained socially revered; even the highest Nazis could be seen to fawn over the hereditary aristocracy. The industrial and financial elite similarly retained their positions of privilege, albeit with new National Socialist trappings.

The National Socialists were acutely aware of the importance of class to the proletariat. Pathologically fearful of the Marxist message, the Nazis liquidated any authentic labor movement in 1933. Organized labor was subsumed in the Nazi "German Labor Front," a body whose control by the Nazis spoke volumes about the actual importance of class to the political arena. The *Gleichschaltung* (coordination) attempted to bring all members of German society into the Nazi fold, and to remove class distinctions, but in fact social structure remained pretty much untouched. When the American and Soviet armies finally crushed the Nazis in 1945, the political parties that emerged in the western zones of divided Germany (political pluralism, of course, being eradicated in the Soviet zone) over 1945–1950 followed the usual pattern of social stratification. Social Democratic and Communist Parties explicitly sought to represent the classic Marxist-defined working class, while liberals sought to represent the free professions and middle classes. Christian Democrats, a revival of the old Catholic Center Party, sought to transcend this class-based vision of society but ended up being little more than a broadly based conservative party.

The party politics of other European countries might have gone through less turmoil than those of Germany, but they too had to confront the issue of class. In World War I and World War II, as nations sought total mobilization, it was hoped that the old class divides would be put aside in the interest of national solidarity. The Socialist International collapsed as the socialist parties of Europe almost all responded to the call to rally around the flag. The German *Burgfrieden* (fortress peace) was an often-cited example of shelving class differences for the good of the war effort, but within two years, this truce was sorely tested. Class tensions in Germany were so strong that in 1918 the strains of war triggered a series of open battles between the socialist Left, part of which embraced communism, and the establishment. The reactionary military and private Right-wing militias were called out in 1918–1919 to put down all kinds of leftist and working-class uprisings. Making matters worse, in the first four years of the peace, the governing elite chose to

CLASS IDENTITIES

deal with economic problems with inflation, a measure that hurt the middle class the most. This policy only further alienated the middle classes from their natural protector, the republican government established at Weimar. When the time came for the Republic to call on its natural defenders, the middle class, to protect it from the attack of the Nazis, the call went unanswered. Class concerns and related economic tensions pounded the final nail in interwar Central European democracy's coffin.

Class and politics also intersected neatly in interwar Europe during France's Popular Front governments (1936–1938) and the Spanish Civil War (1936–1939). Here, working-class identity, in partnership with the intellectual classes, sought to develop a more harmonious political atmosphere between the classes, only to be booted out of power in France and gunned down in Spain. Interwar Britain was hardly less touched by class considerations, as Conservatives held the political landscape in a headlock while the working classes and their political representatives futilely sought to alleviate the suffering of the 1920s and 1930s. This grip of the ruling elite was so tight that it took the strains of twenty years of economic depression and a world war to break it. Labour—a party whose name clearly shows the link between class and politics—finally was able to grab the reins of power for a sustained period in 1945–1951.

Even the case of Scandinavia, identified with more-egalitarian systems, shows how class and politics remain interwoven in European society. Denmark, Sweden, and Norway have remained dominated by the Social Democratic movement since the 1920s. Since that decade Denmark has had non–Social Democratic governments only twice. Considerations of class persist in these countries. An American visitor to Denmark, for example, would be shocked to see that a person's mailing address and even phone-book listing contain the person's occupation, such as "butcher," "carpenter," "bank inspector," or "lawyer." One's social function is important: public knowledge automatically tells one whether the person with whom one is dealing is a social inferior or superior. Social democracy, Scandinavia's perhaps most distinguished and distinguishing political export, also seems to carry class connotations. Although the political class there, and elsewhere in Europe, is increasingly dominated by an educated and legally trained elite, Social Democracy (and its British cousin Labour), still pays a considerable amount of attention to the issues that gave birth to the movement. Working-class interests remain important to the Social Democratic movement.

The assertion that class does not matter any more in Europe resembles similar claims for North America. In North America, however, the claim is (perhaps surprisingly) believed. Most North Americans maintain that they are "middle class," yet those who call themselves middle class can range from a fast-food cook to a bank president. Americans may be oblivious to their class distinctions when it comes to politics, but that does not mean the differences are not there. Nor does it mean that there are no political repercussions from class differences: the American social elite have racked up a series of political advantages. In Europe, assertions that class has faded away are similarly false.

–PHIL GILTNER,
ALBANY ACADEMY

**Viewpoint:
No. Class identities were not as important as political ideologies, nationalism, religion, and state power in Europe during the twentieth century.**

The history of twentieth-century Europe has so often been presented in a context of class conflict that it requires almost a paradigm shift to consider an alternate perspective: class consciousness has on the whole been a false consciousness, to use a Marxist term, far less significant than political ideologies, nationalism, religion, and state power. Beginning with the French Revolution (1789) and continuing through the nineteenth century, Europe's defining social experience was the transformation of subjects into citizens. States, and specifically their military institutions and artifacts, became focal points of individual identities and primary sources of collective pride. Such contemporary alternatives as sports teams—soccer is by far the best example—did not exist; even the revived Olympics in the late nineteenth century, intended as a celebration of individual virtue, was rapidly structured along state lines to represent international competition.

The synergy of states and citizens was in good part achieved through compulsory military service. Especially during the long periods of peace between 1815 and 1914, conscription was an unmistakable way of demonstrating the state's authority. It was also frequently a positive experience for the participants. Standards of living and conditions of labor were no worse, and frequently an improvement, over a civilian experience in increasingly depressed agriculture or growing and unregulated industry. Military service was universally recognized as a male rite of passage, the completion of which secured adult

CLASS IDENTITIES

status. States increasingly became a source of perceived benefits, ranging from disability insurance to postal services. The fin de siècle "package" of social benefits might not seem much by the standards of the twenty-first century, but it was impressive compared to what had gone before. It was also free—or seemed so in an era when states raised most of their income from indirect taxes, rather than direct taxes on income, inheritance, or investment profits.

The blend of services and benefits was more than sufficient to integrate men and women of every income level and social status into the state order. The state's primary rival, Marxian socialism, was most successful when it replicated the state on a smaller scale, providing what amounted to a variant system whose ideological boasts of uniting the human race through the Socialist International did not extend to posing challenges appropriate for an interest group in a plural society.

World War I further reinforced state authority, moral and physical alike. European men lined up, fell in, marched off, and died with a continuing commitment that surprised even the governments that sent them into the trenches. On the various home fronts, states that never before had called for serious sacrifices oversaw regimes of deprivation that at the end approached starvation. The war ended episodically, as one tormented citizenry after another came to hate its government more than it feared its enemies. The resulting reorganizations replicated the old order as opposed to challenging it or to denying it. The new states of eastern and Central Europe were organized along political lines, with nationalism focused—initially at least—on political identity even in such ethnically mixed nations as Poland and Yugoslavia. Class conflicts remained secondary to politics for the socialists and for communist movements that quickly became extensions of a Soviet Union that itself from first to last made a mockery of its "workers and peasants" and internationalist rhetoric in pursuit of domestic and international power for its majority population of ethnic Russians.

The rise of fascism and related Right-wing ideologies between the world wars posed a comprehensive, principled challenge to class conflict by proclaiming it irrelevant in the overarching context of the nation—the usual definition of which in ethnic terms often overshadowed the constructed nature of ethnicity. Even in the Third Reich, Aryan identity was frequently instrumental. What was fundamentally important in Adolf Hitler's Germany, Benito Mussolini's Italy, Francisco Franco's Spain, and their would-be imitators was the individual's acceptance of, and identification with, the political community. Traditional and Marxist-influenced

class distinctions were denied. The worker remained a worker and the boss a boss, but in principle, neither status was as significant as that of belonging to the state. Private property was legally sustained, but its uses were closely monitored and regulated in the context of public welfare. Individual achievement was recognized and glorified in fields from athletic competition to scientific research. Instead of setting himself apart from the community, the hero exemplified the community's best.

World War II further blurred class identities in all European political systems. The common sacrifices and demands of total war generated in Britain, arguably Europe's most class-determined society in 1939, a commitment to equality of condition under the Labour government's socialist order, which emphasized government intervention and regulation over free enterprise and management. First brought into office in 1945, Labour survived a brief challenge in the Margaret Thatcher years and came to dominate European politics by the end of the twentieth century. As it erodes such rights as self-defense and eliminates distinctions of class (witness for example the 1999 abolition of the hereditary aristocracy's right to sit in the House of Lords), it has gone a long way toward transforming its once heterogeneous citizen community into homogenized subjects of what critics call the "nanny state."

Class structures took a similar beating in postwar Western Europe. Characteristic of developments on the Continent was the Socialists' abandonment, whether de jure or de facto, of any but a rhetorical connection with the original ideas of German political philosopher Karl Marx, in favor of the opportunity to participate fully in the political and economic reconstruction facilitated by the American-sponsored Marshall Plan (1947) and its local imitators. The resulting "Economic Miracle" shattered class politics by extending prosperity and homogenizing tastes, not through the redistribution or destruction of wealth, but through the consumerization of the economy and society. An assembly-line worker who owns an automobile and takes annual vacations abroad is a proletarian by courtesy. A Left-wing physician or middle-management executive who identifies with the Viet Cong and the Palestinians, who donates to Greenpeace and votes for the Green Party, is a bourgeois Marx would scarcely recognize. And again, the growing bureaucratization of post-industrial Europe, first country by country and now through the European Union (EU), is reversing historic patterns of citizenship as it makes more and more details of daily life subject to the decisions of unelected, unaccountable bureaucrats. The former Warsaw Pact is a foot-

HOUSE OF LORDS ACT 1999

The following legislation was passed by the British Parliament and ended the hereditary right of the upper class to seats in the House of Lords:

An Act to restrict membership of the House of Lords by virtue of a hereditary peerage; to make related provision about disqualifications for voting at elections to, and for membership of, the House of Commons; and for connected purposes.

[11th November 1999]

BE IT ENACTED by the Queen's most Excellent Majesty, by and with the advice and consent of the Lords Spiritual and Temporal, and Commons, in this present Parliament assembled, and by the authority of the same, as follows:

1. No-one shall be a member of the House of Lords by virtue of a hereditary peerage.

2. (1) Section 1 shall not apply in relation to anyone excepted from it by or in accordance with Standing Orders of the House.

(2) At any one time 90 people shall be excepted from section 1; but anyone excepted as holder of the office of Earl Marshal, or as performing the office of Lord Great Chamberlain, shall not count towards that limit.

(3) Once excepted from section 1, a person shall continue to be so throughout his life (until an Act of Parliament provides to the contrary).

(4) Standing Orders shall make provision for filling vacancies among the people excepted from section 1; and in any case where—

(a) the vacancy arises on a death occurring after the end of the first Session of the next Parliament after that in which this Act is passed, and

(b) the deceased person was excepted in consequence of an election, that provision shall require the holding of a by-election.

(5) A person may be excepted from section 1 by or in accordance with Standing Orders made in anticipation of the enactment or commencement of this section.

(6) Any question whether a person is excepted from section 1 shall be decided by the Clerk of the Parliaments, whose certificate shall be conclusive.

3. (1) The holder of a hereditary peerage shall not be disqualified by virtue of that peerage for—

(a) voting at elections to the House of Commons, or

(b) being, or being elected as, a member of that House.

(2) Subsection (1) shall not apply in relation to anyone excepted from section 1 by virtue of section 2.

4. (1) The enactments mentioned in Schedule 1 are amended as specified there.

(2) The enactments mentioned in Schedule 2 are repealed to the extent specified there.

5. (1) Sections 1 to 4 (including Schedules 1 and 2) shall come into force at the end of the Session of Parliament in which this Act is passed.

(2) Accordingly, any writ of summons issued for the present Parliament in right of a hereditary peerage shall not have effect after that Session unless it has been issued to a person who, at the end of the Session, is excepted from section 1 by virtue of section 2.

(3) The Secretary of State may by order make such transitional provision about the entitlement of holders of hereditary peerages to vote at elections to the House of Commons or the European Parliament as he considers appropriate.

(4) An order under this section—

(a) may modify the effect of any enactment or any provision made under an enactment, and

(b) shall be made by statutory instrument which shall be subject to annulment in pursuance of a resolution of either House of Parliament.

6. (1) In this Act "hereditary peerage" includes the principality of Wales and the earldom of Chester.

(2) This Act may be cited as the House of Lords Act 1999.

Source: "House of Lords Act 1999," Her Majesty's Stationary Office, HMSO Online <http://www.hmso.gov.uk/acts/acts1999/19990034.htm>.

note to these processes: its lesser members could hardly wait to escape. Russia, paradoxically, features several "new classes," especially a criminal/entrepreneurial body that is unusual if not quite unique. Its persistence, however, reflects state weaknesses and the persistence of an old elite. Experience suggests a reorganized Russia, too, will eventually affirm the primacy of state power over the power of class.

–DENNIS SHOWALTER,
COLORADO COLLEGE

References

G. E. Glezerman, *Classes and Nations,* translated by David Fidlon (Moscow: Progress Publishers, 1979).

Mike Hill and Warren Montag, eds., *Masses, Classes and the Public Sphere* (London & New York: Verso, 2000).

Michael Howard and William Roger Louis, *The Oxford History of the Twentieth Century* (Oxford: Oxford University Press, 1998).

Gregory M. Luebbert, *Liberalism, Fascism, or Social Democracy: Social Classes and the Political Origins of Regimes in Interwar Europe* (New York: Oxford University Press, 1991).

Carolyn M. Vogler, *The Nation State: The Neglected Dimension of Class* (Aldershot, U.K. & Brookfield, Vt.: Gower, 1985).

Gordon Wright and Arthur Mejia Jr., eds., *An Age of Controversy: Discussion Problems in 20th Century European History* (New York: Harper & Row, 1973).

CLASS IDENTITIES

COMMUNIST INTELLECTUALS

Were communist intellectuals duped by Soviet propaganda?

Viewpoint: Yes. Taken in by Soviet propaganda, Western intellectuals believed in communism because they were generally ignorant of its true costs and personally alienated from their own governments and societies.

Viewpoint: No. Western intellectuals were throughly convinced that in theory communism offered the best and most promising solutions for humanity's problems and that Soviet failures would be overcome.

Many twentieth-century European intellectuals were drawn to communism. Looking to the works of Karl Marx, Friedrich Engels, and other communist philosophers gave them hope for a better society, one ruled by equality and rationality. When the Bolshevik coup of November 1917 led to the creation of a socialist state in Russia, many Westerners idealized the new regime and remained steadfastly enthusiastic about its promise even when confronted with evidence about the excesses and horrors of communism.

What was the reasoning behind their idealism? It is possible to maintain, as one essay suggests, that communists and their supporters were genuinely proud of their system and were right to claim that it had improved lives, created opportunity, and lived up to much of its promise. "True believers" may have had a point. The other side of the argument, however, points to evidence that intellectuals worked actively to conceal the horrors of communism or were successfully taken in on a mass scale by deliberate deception. All the while many individuals dismissed credible evidence, which only grew in volume over time. Those who continued to defend communism did so at a loss of their honesty and integrity.

Viewpoint:
Yes. Taken in by Soviet propaganda, Western intellectuals believed in communism because they were generally ignorant of its true costs and personally alienated from their own governments and societies.

The defense of communism by Western intellectuals was one of the most disappointing exercises in twentieth-century thought. The sad truth is that legions of writers, professors, artists, journalists, and other Western thinkers ardently defended and extolled an ideology that recent scholarship holds responsible for the deaths of as many as one hundred million people. By the end of the twentieth century an avalanche of evidence proved that almost every attempt to defend communism was founded on ignorance, delusion, and plain dishonesty.

The first communist government, founded in Russia after the Bolshevik Revolution of November 1917, attracted a great deal of sympathy from the Western Left. But what appeared to hold so much promise was in fact the most brutal dictatorship known to modern man. Communist rule in Russia, and later in every nation that mimicked it, depended on a secret police, a network of concentration camps, arbitrary terror to cow real or potential opposition, the elimination of independent civil society, the subordination of nearly every aspect of life to the dictatorial control of the state, and a host of other measures that ran roughshod over the traditional Left's ideals of rights, democracy, and freedom.

Immediately after the Bolshevik coup, however, sympathetic Western observers promoted the new system. Perhaps the simplest explanation for this support during communism's earliest years is that few Westerners, particularly intellectuals, either knew much about Russia or bothered to visit there in the decade after 1917. World War I, which ended a year after the Bolshevik coup, and the ensuing Russian Civil War, which lasted until late 1920 in European Russia and longer in the Far East, proved effective barriers even to those who might have been inclined to visit what was still regarded as an exotic and less civilized land. It was far easier to sit around in Western cafés or university dining halls marveling at news of the transformation of Russia, as did the Cambridge University friends of émigré and future novelist Vladimir Nabokov, than to examine it critically. Academic study of Russia remained scant until after World War II. Practical experience there was limited to the relatively small number of businessmen, diplomats, and travelers who had gone there before 1917, and to the refugees who fled afterward. Since few of these individuals had any sympathy for Bolshevism, it was easy, especially for Western Soviet enthusiasts, to dismiss their unflattering testimony and negative opinions as the personal biases of those with an obvious ax to grind. Indeed, in many intellectual circles, the epithet "anti-Soviet" remained synonymous with "biased," "ignorant," and "reactionary" well into the Cold War and in some cases beyond.

At the same time, many sympathetic intellectuals believed steadfastly that any amount of suffering was acceptable as long as it succeeded in advancing their ideals. French poet Louis Aragon used his verse to praise the Soviet secret police and its use of terror. When American philosopher and sometime communist Sidney Hook asked German communist playwright Bertolt Brecht's opinion of the purges that claimed the lives of thousands of committed Soviet communists in the 1930s—people who were virtually never guilty of the crimes of which they were accused—Brecht replied, "the more innocent they are, the more they deserve to die." As recently as 1994 British Marxist historian Eric Hobsbawm unapologetically affirmed in a television inter-

view that the sacrifice of fifty to twenty million lives would be acceptable if it furthered the happiness of humanity. Admirers still place long-stemmed roses on Stalin's grave.

Leaving these egregious statements aside, one should not ignore that many in the Western Left had reasons to want the Soviet experiment to succeed. Socialists who had experienced decades of frustration in parliamentary politics were cheered by the success of their more radical Russian colleagues, who, whatever their failings, promised to put some of their shared ideas into practice. Progressives who had long decried the excesses of capitalism looked with hope on what they believed to be a new and promising beginning for humanity, even if it experienced what some chose to call "growing pains." Ideologues who remained devoted to what they thought to be the "unfulfilled promise" of the French Revolution of 1789 believed they saw its final unfolding in 1917. Many mainstream Westerners who had been ill disposed toward tsarist Russia were not unhappy to see it replaced by a regime that at least pretended to the language of democracy.

Looking at the "Soviet experiment" through rose-colored glasses blinded these types to many unpleasant and undeniable truths, however. American journalist John Reed, who witnessed the Bolshevik coup and subsequently reported on Soviet Russia, wrote favorably about "Soviet democracy," even as Vladimir Lenin's dictatorship grew more and more repressive. In the process he, too, became a committed communist. Another American visitor, the progressive journalist Lincoln Steffens, declared after visiting Soviet Russia in 1919, "I have seen the future, and it works!," even though the country's urban population had fallen to less than half its pre–World War I figure, famine was ravaging the countryside, and armed resistance to the Soviet government reached its height that year. Why would these noticeable problems escape the attention of such intelligent people? Their desire to see socialism succeed probably had much to do with it, and there is much evidence to suggest that their positive views derived from their preconceptions. Other members of Steffens's traveling party, including future U.S. ambassador to the Soviet Union William C. Bullitt, later alleged that the journalist thought up and practiced declaiming his (in)famous comment before they even got to Russia.

While some of the early enthusiasts reported selectively or deceptively on the Union of Soviet Socialist Republics (U.S.S.R.), in later years the Soviet government took steps to make sure that it received favorable press abroad. Part of its strategy was to minimize its people's contact with foreigners. Within only a few years of the Bolshevik Revo-

COMMUNIST INTELLECTUALS

lution, it became nearly impossible to travel abroad or emigrate. After Josef Stalin consolidated power in the late 1920s, a period when waves of repression eliminated millions of real or perceived enemies of the regime, people with foreign contacts suffered intensely; the government viewed them as potential conduits of bad news. In the terrorized atmosphere of the 1930s, it became dangerous to stay in touch with friends and relatives abroad or, as one unfortunate stamp collector found out, even to appear to have a foreign correspondence. Eliminating those with real or imagined foreign contacts subsided with the post-Stalin leadership's general departure from mass terror, but interacting with foreigners nevertheless remained taboo well into the 1980s. Foreign travel also remained heavily restricted. Only the most-trusted Communist Party members and most-prestigious cultural figures were permitted to go to the West, even if several of them used that privilege to defect. After being forbidden for decades, emigration became possible, if still extremely difficult, because of its growing importance in the U.S.S.R.'s relations with the United States.

If the Soviet government sought to control what its own people could learn about the West or tell the West about the Soviet Union, its control of foreigners was also rigid. During the purges resident foreigners, a category that ironically included many foreign communists who were living in Soviet exile or had settled in the

Soviet Union to help build the utopia, were decimated by arrests and executions. Foreign travel to the U.S.S.R. was heavily regimented by a government tourist agency charged explicitly with isolating tourists from ordinary people. "Study abroad" programs and opportunities for foreign scholars to research in the Soviet Union were not allowed until the 1950s and then were strictly controlled. Secret-police surveillance of foreign residents, often conducted openly with the purpose of intimidating them, remained a standard practice until communist rule began to wane in the late 1980s. Broad sections of Soviet territory, including hundreds of cities and entire regions, were closed to foreigners until the Russian government abolished the restrictions in 1992. Since the government controlled all aspects of political, social, and economic organization, Western investigations of Soviet life encountered a centralized bureaucracy that released piles of documents that naturally only made the Soviet Union look good.

These circumstances threatened to make the manipulation of Western opinion relatively easy. Journalism was subject to particularly strenuous attempts at control, especially in the Stalin years, when state censors read all communications from foreign journalists to their editors, and when journalists were told outright that unfavorable reporting would have major consequences, including, as many found, arrest or expulsion from the country. Well into the 1980s the secret police subjected foreign journalists to varying degrees of harassment, ranging from the standard surveillance that all foreigners had to live with to blackmail about their sex lives. Compliant foreign correspondents, however, could expect excellent treatment, interviews with high-profile figures, and greater access to good material. While many journalists were diligent and took risks to report the truth, others did not. *New York Times* reporter Walter Duranty, who won the Pulitzer Prize in 1932 for a series of articles that denied the existence of a famine that in fact killed several million people, received celebrity treatment for his favorable stories and avoided public exposure in a sex scandal of which the Soviet secret police had evidence. Famous for repeating "I put my money on Stalin," Duranty later became an important adviser on Soviet affairs to U.S. president Franklin D. Roosevelt. When confronted with evidence of the famine by skeptical colleagues, he is reported to have remarked dismissively, "they're just Russians." Reed, who also received the royal treatment for his favorable stories on Soviet Russia, was honored with burial in the wall of Moscow's Kremlin, just behind the future site of Lenin's Mausoleum, after he died of typhus (a disease that the Soviet government refused to acknowledge as a national problem) in October 1920. Sidney Webb and Beatrice Webb, cofounders of the British Fabian Society, a non-Marxist socialist organization, wrote a glowing description of the Soviet Union's social and economic development after visiting in the 1930s. In one passage they praised the officials in charge of Stalin's brutal program of agricultural collectivization, marveling at the strong convictions of those who implemented policies that they knew would cause many deaths.

Despite the ease with which such figures could suspend truth to defend the U.S.S.R., one did not have to experience its flattery and threats firsthand to conceal its horrors. In a rare moment of candor about the communist system in which he professed deep belief, French writer and philosopher Jean-Paul Sartre admitted to a few colleagues that there was indeed a vast network of concentration camps in the U.S.S.R., but condescendingly added that to say so in public would only depress the hopeful and hapless French working class. If admitting that there was oppression threatened the ultimate achievement of utopia, then it was better not to admit that there was oppression.

Duranty's deception has now been so thoroughly exposed that the Pulitzer Board in June 2003 considered stripping him posthumously of his prize (the board ultimately decided not to revoke it). While he and others were consciously deceptive, many Western intellectuals were simply taken in by deliberate Soviet attempts to deceive them. Often already inclined toward socialism, visiting foreign cultural and political figures were invariably treated to luxury travel and accommodations, obsequious receptions, and fulsome praise. In addition to official flattery, the Soviet government organized Potemkin-village–style tours designed to show off its achievements just as much as they were intended to hide its failings. British playwright George Bernard Shaw, another member of the Fabian Society who visited the Soviet Union in the 1930s, expressed his enthusiasm for the Soviet educational system when he found that even the waitresses in his dining car had read all of his plays and were eager to discuss them. Naturally, they were specially trained agents planted on Shaw's train to impress the playwright, who later called Stalin a "good Fabian." When leftist French premier Edouard Herriot visited Kiev in 1932, at the height of the famine that Duranty concealed, he was driven along clean streets filled with happy people and prosperous- looking shops. Of course he never said anything about the famine after being treated to these improbable scenes. African American bass Paul Robeson, who toured the U.S.S.R. with much fanfare in 1935, favorably compared Soviet treatment of ethnic minorities to troubled race relations in his own country, but no one ever told him about the millions of non-Russians who had died or were languishing far away from their homes simply because of who they were. As late as 1984, a time of great shortages and just seven years before the collapse of the U.S.S.R., Left-wing American economist John Kenneth Galbraith could hail the "solid well being" of the people he saw on a trip to Moscow and comment on the city's well-stocked shops. One wonders what else Soviet officials would have shown him. These high-profile visitors may not have been lying about their impressions, but a generous interpretation of them suggests that they were easily fooled. In the less generous opinion of Soviet expert Robert Conquest, they were "suckers." It is worth noting that Robeson suffered a nervous breakdown after Stalin's successors partially exposed the crimes of his regime in 1956.

Even before the collapse of the Soviet Union and other communist regimes exposed the extent to which sympathetic Western intellectuals had defended the indefensible, popular opinion already saw the true circumstances. No amount of campus idealism could silence the growing chorus of dissidents within communist societies, ignore the admonitions of disillusioned former communists, or refute the increasingly damning body of critical scholarship on communism. As early as 1951, German political philosopher Hannah Arendt concluded, in an

NOR IS THAT ALL!

In a study published posthumously, German socialist Rosa Luxemburg made the following comments about Bolshevik agrarian policy:

A socialist transformation of economic relationships presupposes two things so far as agrarian relationships are concerned:

In the first place, only the nationalization of the large landed estates, as the technically most advanced and most concentrated means and methods of agrarian production, can serve as the point of departure for the socialist mode of production on the land. Of course, it is not necessary to take away from the small peasant his parcel of land, and we can with confidence leave him to be won over voluntarily by the superior advantages first of union in cooperation and then finally of inclusion in the general socialized economy as a whole. Still, every socialist economic reform on the land must obviously begin with large and medium landownership. Here the property right must first of all be turned over to the nation, or to the state, which, with a socialist government, amounts to the same thing; for it is this alone which affords the possibility of organizing agricultural production in accord with the requirements of interrelated, large-scale socialist production.

Moreover, in the second place, it is one of the prerequisites of this transformation, that the separation between rural economy and industry which is so characteristic of bourgeois society, should be ended in such a way as to bring about a mutual interpenetration and fusion of both, to clear the way for the planning of both agrarian and industrial production according to a unified point of view. Whatever individual form the practical economic arrangements may take—whether through urban communes, as some propose, or directed from a governmental center—in any event, it must be preceded by a reform introduced from the center, and that in turn must be preceded by the nationalization of the land. The nationalization of the large and middle-sized estates and the union of industry and agriculture—these are two fundamental requirements of any socialist economic reform, without which there is no socialism.

That the Soviet government in Russia has not carried through these mighty reforms—who can reproach them for that! It would be a sorry jest indeed to demand or expect of Lenin and his comrades that, in the brief period of their rule, in the center of the gripping whirlpool of domestic and foreign struggles, ringed about by countless foes and opponents—to expect that under such circumstances they should already have solved, or even tackled, one of the most difficult tasks, indeed, we can safely say, the most difficult task of the socialist transformation of society! Even in the West, under the most favorable conditions, once we have come to power, we too will break many a tooth on this hard nut before we are out of the worst of the thousands of complicated difficulties of this gigantic task!

A socialist government which has come to power must in any event do one thing: it must take measures which lead in the direction of that fundamental prerequisite for a later socialist reform of agriculture; it must at least avoid everything which may bar the way to those measures.

Now the slogan launched by the Bolsheviks, immediate seizure and distribution of the land by the peasants, necessarily tended in the opposite direction. Not only is it not a socialist measure; it even cuts off the way to such measures; it piles up insurmountable obstacles to the socialist transformation of agrarian agriculture.

The seizure of the landed estates by the peasants according to the short and precise slogan of Lenin and his friends—"Go and take the land for yourselves"—simply led to the sudden, chaotic conversion of large landownership into peasant landownership. What was created is not social property but a new form of private property, namely, the breaking up of large estates into medium and small estates, or relatively advanced large units of production into primitive small units which operate with technical means from the time of the Pharaohs.

Nor is that all! Through these measures and the chaotic and purely arbitrary manner of their execution, differentiation in landed property, far from being eliminated, was even further sharpened. Although the Bolsheviks called upon the peasantry to form peasant committees so that the seizure of the nobles' estates might, in some fashion, be made into a collective act, yet it is clear that this general advice could not change anything in the real practice and real relations of power on the land. With or without committees, it was the rich peasants and usurers who made up the village bourgeoisie possessing the actual power in the hands in every Russian village, that surely became the chief beneficiaries of the agrarian revolution. Without being there to see, any one can figure out for himself that in the course of the distribution of the land, social and economic inequality among the peasants was not eliminated but rather increased, and that class antagonisms were further sharpened. The shift of power, however, took place to the disadvantage of the interests of the proletariat and of socialism. Formerly, there was only a small caste of noble and capitalist landed proprietors and a small minority of rich village bourgeoisie to oppose a socialist reform on the land. And their expropriation by a revolutionary mass movement of the people is mere child's play. But now, after the "seizure," as an opponent of any attempt at socialization of agrarian production, there is an enormous, newly developed and powerful mass of owning peasants who will defend their newly won property with tooth and nail against every attack. The question of the future socialization of agrarian economy—that is, any socialization of production in general in Russia—has now become a question of opposition and of struggle between the urban proletariat and the mass of the peasantry. How sharp this antagonism has already become is shown by the peasant boycott of the cities, in which they withhold the means of existence to carry on speculation in them, in quite the same way as the Prussian Junker does.

The French small peasant became the boldest defender of the Great French Revolution which had given him land confiscated from the émigrés. As Napoleonic soldier, he carried the banner of France to victory, crossed all Europe and smashed feudalism to pieces in one land after another. Lenin and his friends might have expected a similar result from their agrarian slogan. However, now that the Russian peasant has seized the land with his own fist, he does not even dream of defending Russia and the revolution to which he owes the land. He has dug obstinately into his new possessions and abandoned the revolution to its enemies, the state to decay, the urban population to famine.

Source: *Rosa Luxemburg,* The Russian Revolution, *translated by Bertram Wolfe (N.p.: Paul Levi, 1922; New York: Workers Age Publishers, 1940); Marxists Internet Archive <http://www.marxists.org/archive/luxemburg/1918/russian-revolution/ch02.htm>.*

analysis that remains relevant and respected, that Soviet communism equaled the insidiousness of German Nazism as a "totalitarian" ideology. Many Western leftists, particularly Americans, appreciated early on that defending communism was an impossible task that would only implicate their moral and ethical foundations, alienate them from the public, and jeopardize the realization of their ideas. Confronted with documents, confessions, mass graves, and other irrefutable evidence, defenders of communism today find themselves more confined to ivory-tower and coffeehouse ghettos of malcontents who are aging, dwindling in number, and ignored. More and more does communism seem to have been "a sad, bizarre chapter in human history" whose last pages have now been written.

—PAUL DU QUENOY,
GEORGETOWN UNIVERSITY

Viewpoint:
No. Western intellectuals were throughly convinced that in theory communism offered the best and most promising solutions for humanity's problems and that Soviet failures would be overcome.

In any mass political movement there are those whose moral convictions are less than pure. Many people are power hungry, cynical, opportunistic, and greedy. History is full of examples of individuals joining mass movements for reasons other than improving the lot of humanity. Not all Nazis joined the party because they shared Adolf Hitler's evil vision of the future. Membership in the Nazi Party provided opportunities for social advancement or could have been the difference in being hired for a particular position. Peer pressure can also influence one's choice; sometimes it is easier to join the National Socialists, Fascists, or Communists than to risk alienating one's friends, colleagues, or community. Self-preservation is also a factor. Over the centuries many mass religious movements have threatened those who would not convert. When faced with a choice between a public conversion to the reigning religious power or losing one's head, many people chose the former. Overall, people join mass movements for many reasons.

Yet, ideological conviction is an important factor in assessing the motives of the leadership or intellectuals of a mass movement. Many communist intellectuals genuinely believed in the goals of their movement. German socialist activist Rosa Luxemburg provides a good example. Although her opinions on the revolutionary spontaneity of the masses differed from Russian communist Vladimir Lenin's vision of an elite group of professional revolutionaries who would bring a clear class-consciousness to the workers, she was dedicated to the international communist movement. She emerged as a leader of the Spartacists in Germany, a faction of Independent Socialists who had split from the German Social Democratic Party during World War I. The Social Democratic leadership's support of German war aims caused many of its members, such as Luxemburg and Karl Liebknecht, eventually to leave the party. Luxemburg's Spartacists later formed the core of the German Communist Party, which was founded in December 1918. None of the evidence indicates that Luxemburg ever became less concerned about the influence of a revolutionary central committee over the international socialist movement. Although she respected Lenin, she disagreed with his means. Nevertheless she remained dedicated to furthering the goals of the proletariat in Germany and in the world. Had she not been murdered during the right-wing reaction to the German revolution in January 1919, she might have been able to lessen the influence of the Bolsheviks over communists within Germany and in the rest of Europe.

Socialist parties in Europe split after World War I, with many members opting for a more peaceful democratic socialism, while others joined the emerging communist parties. One can question the intentions of those who obtained power in these new communist parties. In Germany the deaths of Liebknecht and Luxemburg enabled men such as Ernst Thälmann to rise to power. Thälmann was one of a group of leaders more supportive of "bolshevization." This new group generally supported directives coming from Moscow, including the need to form a united front against the growing fascist threat. However, there were problems. The communist parties were willing to do whatever was necessary to gain power, including fully discrediting the more-moderate democratic socialists. Two groups that shared many ideas about how to solve humanity's problems frequently mistrusted each other more than they did their "bourgeois" and fascist opponents. In Germany this internal conflict made it difficult for the social democrats to unify with the communists against the growing threat from Hitler. By the time they achieved a common platform it was too late.

Much communist activity in the 1920s and 1930s was indeed heroic. For example, communist accounts of this period are replete with self-serving condemnation of their more moderate leftist cousins. By not joining a popular front with the communists against National Socialism, democratic socialists allegedly betrayed the working people of Germany, Europe, and the world. The evidence, of course, questions the communists' sincerity; for example, German communists always ran a separate candidate in the presidential contests of the 1920s. Nevertheless, when Hitler gained power in Germany, the communists rose to the challenge. German communists headed Hitler's enemy list and were the first group he and his followers tried to eliminate. Despite constant pressure during these dark years—including a disastrous initial response in 1934–1935, a betrayal by their Soviet patrons in 1939–1941, and a general ineffectiveness—the surviving communist resisters never wavered in their opposition to Nazi Germany. Self-preservation was part of their motivation during these years. To be a communist meant to risk severe persecution and mortal danger. These men and women who stayed in Germany and maintained the struggle against Hitler were also committed to resisting fascism. Not only did they and their leaders believe that Hitler would lead Germany to ruin, they also were convinced that communism provided the path that everyone should follow.

The former East German Museum for German History provides a good example of how to judge the sincerity of certain communist intellectuals. The museum was founded in 1952 by a committee of East German professors, historians, and writers and was commissioned by the German Democratic Republic (GDR) and governing Socialist Unity Party. Nevertheless the director of the museum, heads of its divisions, and most of those who designed the exhibitions were intellectuals. There were many omissions in the history they displayed, most of which overlooked Soviet shortcomings. Visitors in the 1950s would see some interesting explanations. They were told that the Nazi-Soviet pact of 1939 was an example of how two states with different ideologies could coexist peacefully. The exhibit claimed that the Germans violated this pact; apparently the Soviets were content with it. There were no explanations of the Soviet role in the division of Poland or why the enlarged 1941 Soviet border was more sacrosanct than the 1939 one. Viewers were told that the masses in capitalist countries were responsible for forcing their leadership to join the Soviet-led crusade against fascism. There was no reference to the 1953 strikes against the East German regime, even though the overwhelming majority of visitors must have at least heard of this uprising.

These omissions are difficult to justify, but the overall narrative was genuine. It presented the story of the German people's struggle against oppression. The narrative began with the earliest record of Germanic settlement in Central Europe. It highlighted important events in the people's struggle, including the German Peasants' War (1524–1525), the revolutions in 1848 and 1918–1919, the struggle against National Socialism, and the founding of the GDR (1949). Alfred Meusel, first director of the museum, lived through much of the final struggle against fascism. He experienced the uprisings in Kiel (November 1918) that precipitated the revolution. He was a dedicated communist who had to flee in 1933 when the Nazis came to power. His writings on history contain a mixture of German nationalism and loyalty to the Soviet Union. The museum reflected his vision, one that he and his fellow communists lived before the founding of the GDR. Even if some of the details were included to appease the GDR's Soviet patrons, the overall narrative of struggle was something the museum's leadership genuinely believed.

It is difficult to justify all the activities of European communists after 1920. The "bolshevization" of the national parties, the allegiance to Soviet leader Josef Stalin, and the antipathy toward more-moderate democratic socialists provide reason to suspect the intellectual integrity of the European communist leadership. However, none of the evidence so far has proved that Thälmann, Meusel, or the thousands of communists who remained in Germany to resist Hitler were not convinced that their way provided the best solutions for humanity's problems. Indeed, they could have been personally alienated from their own societies, as many were, and still believed in communism. In fact, Meusel was a dedicated German nationalist. He participated in at least three of the *Deutsche Begegnungen* (German Meetings) of the 1950s, assemblies of West and East German intellectuals who were searching for a means to reunify their country. Although the GDR's vision of reunification was prevalent in Meusel's speeches, he was undoubtedly dedicated to Germany. His example shows how difficult it is simply to dismiss the sincerity of Europe's communist intellectuals. Some of them may have had impure motives. Others may have joined the party for personal gain or to survive in a difficult world. Many, however, believed in their cause, and as the example of the German communists who resisted Hitler shows, were willing to die for their dreams of a better humanity.

–DAVID MARSHALL,
UNIVERSITY OF CALIFORNIA, RIVERSIDE

References

Hannah Arendt, *The Origins of Totalitarianism* (New York: Harcourt, Brace, 1951).

Robert Conquest, *The Great Terror: A Reassessment* (London: Hutchinson, 1990; New York: Oxford University Press, 1990).

Conquest, *The Harvest of Sorrow: Soviet Collectivization and the Terror-Famine* (London: Hutchinson, 1986; New York: Oxford University Press, 1986).

Conquest, *Reflections on a Ravaged Century* (New York: Norton, 2000).

Stéphane Courtois and others, *The Black Book of Communism: Crimes, Terror, Repression*, translated by Jonathan Murphy and Mark Kramer (London & Cambridge, Mass.: Harvard University Press, 1999).

Albert S. Lindemann, *A History of European Socialism* (New Haven: Yale University Press, 1983).

David E. Marshall, "*Das Museum für Deutsche Geschichte*: A Study of the Presentation of History in the Former German Democratic Republic," dissertation, University of California, Riverside, 2002.

Allan Merson, *Communist Resistance in Nazi Germany* (London: Lawrence & Wishart, 1985).

Malcolm Muggeridge, *Chronicles of Wasted Time* (London: Collins, 1972).

Vladimir Nabokov, *Speak, Memory: A Memoir* (London: Gollancz, 1951).

David Remnick, *Lenin's Tomb: The Last Days of the Soviet Empire* (New York: Random House, 1993).

S. J. Taylor, *Stalin's Apologist: Walter Duranty, the New York Times's Man in Moscow* (New York: Oxford University Press, 1990).

Sidney Webb and Beatrice Webb, *Is Soviet Communism a New Civilisation?* (London: Left Review, 1936).

COMMUNIST INTELLECTUALS

CULTURAL WATERSHED

Was World War I a watershed in European cultural life?

Viewpoint: Yes. World War I resulted in major changes and innovations in cultural expression.

Viewpoint: No. Cultural changes and innovations were already in progress before 1914 and continued to develop after 1918.

Historians of twentieth-century Europe often focus on World War I as a watershed in the Continent's cultural development. Four hard years of death, destruction, and trauma appeared to have forever changed the values and tastes that prevailed before 1914. Yet, an ongoing debate, reflected in this chapter, questions whether the conflict's influence on European culture was truly that profound. From one perspective, it certainly was important. Only war, deprivation, and dislocation could have caused the changes in values and attitude that made the 1920s apparently so different from the early 1900s. With traditional modes of authority, social organization, and artistic expression challenged by political events, profound cultural change was unavoidable.

A more nuanced argument suggests, on the other hand, that the roots of Europe's postwar cultural change were already firmly entrenched in the years before 1914. New concepts in art, science, literature, music, dance, fashion, and myriad other media could be observed in experimental stages or in full bloom during those years. From a cultural perspective, the war years were an unpleasant counterpart to continuing trends of cultural transformation—one with deeper roots than the violence of the war.

Viewpoint:
Yes. World War I resulted in major changes and innovations in cultural expression.

Europe has had its share of wars, but no single war has had as great an effect upon Western culture as World War I, which critically undermined Europe's faith in itself and humanity. Prior to the war, Europe was indisputably at the pinnacle of human development. The blight of the early phases of industrialization and urbanization had given way to the model city of Paris, with its spacious boulevards, beautiful parks, public gardens, performing arts, and museums. London was the richest city in the world. European universities were emulated everywhere, as were its science, technology, and government practices. European-ruled empires dominated the world map. The achievement of the rational, scientific Western mind was clear for anyone to see.

Thus, the utterly meaningless, gargantuan slaughter of World War I came as a tremendous shock. If the world was in fact completely rational and knowable, as Western thought had held to be true since the Renaissance and the Enlightenment, then how was the barbaric depravity of the Western Front to be explained? How could one link the stability and respectability of metropolitan France, Edwardian England, or Wilhelmine Germany to the pointless carnage of Verdun (1916) or the Somme (1916)?

Such a question lies at the heart of the cultural change that began in Europe during World War I. The war dramatically undermined faith in humanity and European civilization. Examples of wartime memoirs are well known. Erich Maria Remarque's *All Quiet on the Western Front* (1931) perhaps stands out as the archetypal Great War memoir. Rather than glorifying or celebrating the heroics and camaraderie of the wartime experience, the novel showed how an entire generation had been ruined by the ordeal. Over the course of the work all of the protagonist's friends are killed, and in the end he, too, dies, on a day when the Front was officially "all quiet." Even worse for the established order, Remarque exposed the gap between the expectations of his society and the reality of the war experience, from training to serving on the front lines. Remarque and his generation were completely robbed of their faith in government authority. That veterans were disillusioned perhaps is no great change, but similar works by Siegfried Sassoon, Robert Graves, Wilfrid Owen, Guillaume Apollinaire, Ernest Hemingway, and others in addition to Remarque could fill entire libraries. Literature was only the beginning, for the "lost generation" that wrote it cast its shadow over the next fifty years of European politics, too.

Even those who had no personal experience of the war were affected by the cataclysm. Thomas Mann, for example, had already demonstrated his interest in decay in his prewar *Buddenbrooks* (1901), but his postwar works, the true source of his reputation as a literary master, were colored by the war in their much more explicit bleakness. His magnum opus, *The Magic Mountain* (1924), is packed with a cacophony of art, ideas, history, philosophy, tension, and philistinism all cast against a backdrop of death at a tuberculosis sanatorium high above Europe's troubles in Davos, Switzerland. The pointlessness of existence is explicitly brought forth in the anticlimax of the novel, as Hans Catorp goes off to the war to face his equally certain and random death. The utter senselessness of the path of history is perhaps less clearly, but still allegorically, shown in Mann's metaphorical novel of the ascendancy of Nazism, *Doctor Faustus* (1947), in which the musical genius Faustus descends into complete madness in his quest for greatness.

Others also argued that belief in historical progress was senseless and that Western civilization was on the cusp of its destruction. Oswald Spengler's *The Decline of the West* (1918–1922) may well have posed as a scientific proof of the fall of the West, but in terms of actual content, it may well stand better as an allegory. Although he died in 1924, Franz Kafka's reputation grew dramatically in the 1920s and 1930s. Kafka's works portrayed a world where technology and bureaucracy had ground humanity into senseless, hopeless, and despairing dust. Although there may have remained a kernel of hope in his characters, the outlook for any improvement was bleak. Even the other great Czech literary phenomenon of the era, Jaroslav Hasek's *The Good Soldier: Schweik* (1921–1923), may have been a farce, but he was nevertheless engaged in an unwinnable struggle with a pointless and unthinking bureaucratic civilization. The works of T. S. Eliot, William Butler Yeats, W. H. Auden, and Aldous Huxley all questioned the prewar regime, its values, and its notions of life's meaning and declaimed that they were all irretrievably lost.

The plastic arts (visual arts such as paintings, sculptures, and movies) and performing arts were hardly any more hopeful than literature. Certainly, many of the avant-garde schools of art had their roots in the prewar era—Cubism and expressionism, for example, could trace their origins to the 1890s. The uncertainty introduced into science with the development of the theories of particle physics, whereby matter is not matter and energy is not energy, only reinforced the simple observation that civilization is not civilization. Hence, painter René Magritte's famous painting of a pipe under which is written (in French) "this is not a pipe." Freud's theories of dark, uncontrollable forces governing man's behavior similarly assaulted man's belief in himself. The rational, precise, objective depictions of reality, which had reigned since the invention of perspective in the Renaissance, were correspondingly discarded in favor of emotional expression, attempts at revealing inner essences (not, incidentally, unlike medieval conceptions of art, literature, and truth). Expressionism may have sought to reveal emotional truth by avoiding what appears to be physical objectivity, but Surrealists used symbols that clearly were recognizable to probe the dark, messy, and murky ghosts that linger in man's animalistic psyche. The Surrealists were especially devoid of faith in progress, utterly incapable of love for the "bourgeois" society they lived in. It was an inexplicable crime to them that the same order that had produced World War I should remain in power afterward. André Breton, a leading figure among the Surrealists, despaired so much for his society that he declared that the ultimate Surrealist act would be to walk into a crowded street and open fire upon the crowd.

Similar images of violence, psychological tension, and aberration appear in other artworks of the age, such as the new medium of motion

DADAISM

In a 1922 lecture, Tristan Tzara, a poet and founder of the Dada movement that arose in reaction to World War I, commented:

What good did the theories of the philosophers do us? Did they help us to take a single step forward or backward? What is forward, what is backward? Did they alter our forms of contentment? We are. We argue, we dispute, we get excited. The rest is sauce. Sometimes pleasant, sometimes mixed with a limitless boredom, a swamp dotted with tufts of dying shrubs.

We have had enough of the intelligent movements that have stretched beyond measure our credulity in the benefits of science. What we want now is spontaneity. Not because it is better or more beautiful than anything else. But because everything that issues freely from ourselves, without the intervention of speculative ideas, represents us. We must intensify this quantity of life that readily spends itself in every quarter. Art is not the most precious manifestation of life. Art has not the celestial and universal value that people like to attribute to it. Life is far more interesting. Dada knows the correct measure that should be given to art: with subtle, perfidious methods, Dada introduces it into daily life. And vice versa. In art, Dada reduces everything to an initial simplicity, growing always more relative. It mingles its caprices with the chaotic wind of creation and the barbaric dances of savage tribes. It wants logic reduced to a personal minimum, while literature in its view should be primarily intended for the individual who makes it. Words have a weight of their own and lend themselves to abstract construction. The absurd has no terrors for me, for from a more exalted point of view everything in life seems absurd to me. Only the elasticity of our conventions creates a bond between disparate acts. The Beautiful and the True in art do not exist; what interests me is the intensity of a personality transposed directly, clearly into the work; the man and his vitality; the angle from which he regards the elements and in what manner he knows how to gather sensation, emotion, into a lacework of words and sentiments.

Dada tries to find out what words mean before using them, from the point of view not of grammar but of representation. Objects and colors pass through the same filter. It is not the new technique that interests us, but the spirit. Why do you want us to be preoccupied with a pictorial, moral, poetic, literary, political or social renewal? We are well aware that these renewals of means are merely the successive cloaks of the various epochs of history, uninteresting questions of fashion and facade. We are well aware that people in the costumes of the Renaissance were pretty much the same as the people of today, and that Chouang-Dsi was just as Dada as we are. You are mistaken if you take Dada for a modern school, or even for a reaction against the schools of today. Several of my statements have struck you as old and natural, what better proof that you were a Dadaist without knowing it, perhaps even before the birth of Dada.

You will often hear that Dada is a state of mind. You may be gay, sad, afflicted, joyous, melancholy or Dada. Without being literary, you can be romantic, you can be dreamy, weary, eccentric, a businessman, skinny, transfigured, vain, amiable or Dada. This will happen later on in the course of history when Dada has become a precise, habitual word, when popular repetition has given it the character of a word organic with its necessary content. Today no one thinks of the literature of the Romantic school in representing a lake, a landscape, a character. Slowly but surely, a Dada character is forming.

pictures. While Hollywood turned out light-hearted fare such as the Keystone Kops, Buster Keaton, or Charlie Chaplin, Germany's Babelsberg produced movies such as *The Cabinet of Dr. Caligari* (1920), *Metropolis* (1927), *The Blue Angel* (1930), and *M* (1931), which depicted worlds of violence, mental illness, depravity, and fear. Consider, too, Bertolt Brecht's capitalist villain from *The Threepenny Opera* (1928), "Mack the Knife," who was so removed from a normal life that the only way he could feel alive was to kill. Now a famous song to people around the world, thanks to its having been adopted by American performers of popular music, "Mack the Knife" stands as a much cheerier sounding counter to the more difficult European music and art of the era, which was more often atonal and experimental than composer Kurt Weill's more melodic music.

Perhaps it might be relevant here to mention the oddest artistic movement of the interwar years, Dadaism, which explicitly began as a

Dada is here, there and a little everywhere, such as it is, with its faults, with its personal differences and distinctions which it accepts and views with indifference. We are often told that we are incoherent, but into this word people try to put an insult that it is rather hard for me to fathom. Everything is incoherent. The gentleman who decides to take a bath but goes to the movies instead. The one who wants to be quiet but says things that haven't even entered his head. Another who has a precise idea on some subject but succeeds only in expressing the opposite in words which for him are a poor translation. There is no logic. Only relative necessities discovered "a posteriori," valid not in any exact sense but only as explanations. The acts of life have no beginning or end. Everything happens in a completely idiotic way. That is why everything is alike. Simplicity is called Dada.

Any attempt to conciliate an inexplicable momentary state with logic strikes me as a boring kind of game. The convention of the spoken language is ample and adequate for us, but for our solitude, for our intimate games and our literature we no longer need it.

The beginnings of Dada were not the beginnings of an art, but of a disgust. Disgust with the magnificence of philosophers who for 3000 years have been explaining everything to us (what for?), disgust with the pretensions of these artists-God's-representatives-on-earth, disgust with passion and with real pathological wickedness where it was not worth the bother, disgust with a false form of domination and restriction "en masse," that accentuates rather than appeases man's instinct of domination, disgust with all the catalogued categories, with the false prophets who are nothing but a front for the interests of money, pride, disease, dis-

gust with the lieutenants of a mercantile art made to order according to a few infantile laws, disgust with the divorce of good and evil, the beautiful and the ugly (for why is it more estimable to be red rather than green, to the left rather than the right, to be large or small?). Disgust finally with the Jesuitical dialectic which can explain everything and fill people's minds with oblique and obtuse ideas without any physiological basis or ethnic roots, all this by means of blinding artifice and ignoble charlatans' promises.

As Dada marches it continuously destroys, not in extension but in itself. From all these disgusts, may I add, it draws no conclusion, no pride, no benefit. It has even stopped combating anything, in the realization that it's no use, that all this doesn't matter. What interests a Dadaist is his own mode of life. But here we approach the great secret.

Dada is a state of mind. That is why it transforms itself according to races and events. Dada applies itself to everything, and yet it is nothing, it is the point where the yes and the no and all the opposites meet, not solemnly in the castles of human philosophies, but very simply at street corners, like dogs and grasshoppers.

Like everything in life, Dada is useless.

Dada is without pretension, as life should be.

Perhaps you will understand me better when I tell you that Dada is a virgin microbe that penetrates with the insistence of air into all the spaces that reason has not been able to fill with words or conventions.

Source: Tristan Tzara, "Lecture on Dada," in Dada Painters and Poets: An Anthology, *edited by Robert Motherwell (New York: Wittenborn, Schultz, 1951), pp. 246–251.*

reaction to the madness of the war. Started in neutral Zurich in 1915, the Dada movement, with its deliberately nonsensical name, asserted that the whole of existence and art was pointless. Performances would include such acts as a speech delivered from within a closed diving helmet, or a wall scrawled in chalk while a second performer erased the writing. Plastic arts might be a urinal titled "Fountain" or a collage of completely random clippings called "Clippings from my kitchen table." Here, however, unlike Surrealism, there was a certain playfulness and humor that hinted that humanity was, despite all evidence to the contrary, a positive force in the universe.

All the developments in arts and literature in the interwar years were direct attacks on the prevailing social order of the prewar era, whether they were open assaults like those of the Dadaists or like the German *Bauhaus* movement, which sought a marriage of art and technology. What was clear was that the old order was no longer an adequate structure for humanity. The nineteenth-century belief in the certain benefits of progress, science, and technology had been completely obliterated by the war. World War II only served to reaffirm these notions. It is still uncertain whether Europeans will ever regain their optimism. Developments since the fall of the Berlin Wall in 1989 seem to indicate that Europeans remain cautiously guarded on the idea of progress (they also indicate that Europe is hardly as advanced as it might believe: witness the genocides of the Balkans). Even if the optimism and positivism of the nineteenth century went hand in glove with the hubris that yielded two world wars, it was perhaps not such a bad thing.

–PHIL GILTNER,
ALBANY ACADEMY

Viewpoint:
No. Cultural changes and innovations were already in progress before 1914 and continued to develop after 1918.

World War I was not a turning point in either the direction or the substance of Western culture. The postwar world was not the result of four years of cataclysm but of centuries of European evolution and particularly of the dynamic decades preceding 1914. The appearance of a shattered world is the reflection of personal grief that we have inherited from some of its most notable individuals, such as Ernest Hemingway. This transient period of mourning, while overwhelming in 1920, in retrospect is less influential to the course of the twentieth century than was the Russian Revolution or the Great Depression.

When World War I began, it was greeted with surprising enthusiasm and nationalist fervor, and was even welcomed by many, if not most, Europeans. Nationalist feelings had been on the rise for more than a century, and found expression in overwhelming popular support for the war; support that cut across the political, social, and economic divides within the combatant nations. Why not support a war that would solve the mounting tensions of the previous decades once and for all, and that would be over in a scant three to four months? Everyone knew the troops would be home by Christmas.

The positive attitude of Europeans toward this horrific war seems strange in retrospect. It is important to understand that Europe had experienced a century of amazing progress and technical achievement. Advances were apparent in almost every area of life. Slavery was abolished in the Western world. Popular education had spread, and literacy had increased dramatically. The conditions of the laborer had improved, and the welfare of women and children was being addressed. The suffragette movement gained popularity and drove Europe toward universal suffrage. Democracy in general was no longer a suspect experiment but rather an admirable and achievable goal. Sanitation, transportation, control of disease, and nutrition were all improving. In effect the world had come to resemble the modern one we recognize. People read the newspaper every morning, went for weekend excursions, attended college football games, and drank bottled beer. Advertisers barraged them with descriptions of the newest gadgets and fashions, and the word *movie* entered the American vocabulary for the first time in 1912. Whatever plight modern society had not yet solved, people were sure science would eventually cure. Western society seemed on an unbeatable tide of prosperity.

In the midst of this glorious period of hope, progress, and success the world suddenly plunged itself into chaos, destruction, and carnage. What started as "blowing off of steam," in Theodore Roosevelt's words, turned into "The Great War" or "The War to End All Wars." That same technology and progress that had made so much possible also enabled men to kill each other for months on end on a scale unimaginable. By the time the war concluded many felt that the world itself had ended.

As perhaps might be expected after such a massive trauma, people were apt to react in one of two ways. Following a period of grief they either returned to their old lives in an attempt to restore normalcy, or they tried to distance themselves from the perceived cause of the catastrophe: the culture of the nineteenth century. The latter believed the whole construct of Western society bankrupt and liable for World War I. Thus, they set off to adopt a "new" culture that moved away from the perceived qualities of the old one.

This new culture, characterized by a disaffection from the optimism of the nineteenth century, attacked the decaying aristocracy and elites, questioned the benefits of the industrial revolution, and generally assaulted the old order. It sought for an expression of emotion and inner ideas; an explosion of color and sound; discord and conflict in art, literature, and music. Yet, if we examine the culture of the postwar world, we repeatedly find the genesis of these new cultural aspects or movements in the decades before World War I.

CULTURAL WATERSHED

Perhaps the most important comparison can be made in the fine arts, beginning with painting. If World War I were truly a watershed, it is reasonable to expect that painting before and after the conflict would be greatly different. Or, we would expect the major components of modern art to have arisen following the Great War. Neither is the case. The modern chaos of substance and rejection of traditional forms and perspective came decidedly before the war. Georges Braque and Pablo Picasso began their collaboration in 1908, turning out dozens of works that sought an alternative to "single-point-of-view" perspective, which had dominated painting since the Renaissance. Parisian critic Guillaume Appolinaire dubbed their work "Cubist" because of their use of sharp lines and angles, especially in human portraiture. Henri Matisse met Picasso in 1906; he was already a member and founder of the group of painters known as the Fauves, or "savage beasts," who were inspired by African and other colonial art forms. Matisse painted wild, fantastic animal shapes, disregarding the physical world's limitations of skin and bone. Marc Chagall went further, doing away with all semblance to his subjects' physical forms; his utterly new manner of portraying the world that *might be* rather than the world that *was* led Appolinaire to invent the word *Surrealism* to describe his work. Outside Paris, Eduard Münch had already painted the surreal, haunting figure of "The Scream" in 1893. His approach was a rebellion against the structured, orderly world of the Romantics; it was also a step beyond what the Impressionists had achieved a few decades earlier. Painting was losing its boundaries.

Dance too, continued to expand beyond earlier boundaries. Already by the end of the nineteenth century, classical ballet had become well established. Most of the characteristics we now associate with this art form were evident: dancing on point; the smooth, graceful movement of the whole body; the need to tell a story and evoke emotion through movement; the strong contrast in dance steps between men and women; the skin-colored tights, short skirts, and clinging fabrics were all present in *Sleeping Beauty*, first performed in 1890. By the end of the Edwardian Age, classical ballet would change dramatically. The performance of Igor Stravinsky's *The Rite of Spring* (1911–1913), produced by Sergei Diaghilev, was a leap away from the elegance, flow, and harmony of earlier pieces. The plot was barbaric, the music dissonant, the rhythm pounding, the dance "accentuated by frenetic twists and jerks." This violent work was met by three days of rioting in Paris when it premiered.

The twentieth century would see an increasing cultural contribution from the New World,

especially the United States. Outside the world of ballet, modern dance would be created through the free and unreserved movements of the American dancer Isadora Duncan who shocked Europe with her bare legs and feet, revealing costumes, and suggestive dance. In this newly emerging world, where culture seemed to reflect increasingly the lower classes, a dance craze emerged from the brothels of Argentina— the tango. Its low birth seemed to have no impact on its popularity, and well before the war tango parties and teas were all the rage. The tango was joined by ever more frenetic dances such as the turkey trot, which along with the tango had come via the United States. These trends continued into the 1920s with the dance most associated with the post-war era, the Charleston.

The Rite of Spring caused riots, duels, assaults, and homicides. Tangible battle lines were drawn between those who hailed it as a work of genius and those who felt it to be obscene and degenerate. Yet, a generation of composers saw Stravinsky as the creative father of their work: Maurice Ravel, Sergei Prokofiev, Claude Debussy, Aaron Copeland, Leonard Bernstein, George Gershwin, Frank Zappa, and a host of others celebrated the carefully orchestrated, complex cacophony and dissonance. Stravinsky, himself the product of a decades-spanning movement away from traditional forms of musical expression, was not alone. George Bernard Shaw used the term *abstract* to describe the artists who used music the way the new painters were using canvas. Beginning perhaps with Beethoven, music evoked themes and feelings with sound. No composer sought so deliberately to change the way music was written and performed as the German Richard Wagner. His bombastic operas forced a dramatic conflict between the "music of the word" and the "music of the instruments." His work was being declared "unperformable" long before the famous *Ring* cycle was first produced in 1876. Forty years before the war Wagner wrote volumes on the need for revolution in music and for all art to come together as one to force the revolution and thereby change the world. He was Adolf Hitler's favorite composer.

On the eve of World War I, Stravinsky and other composers became interested in a new form of music that was being imported to Europe from the United States: jazz. It seemed to brim with energy; it was not the carefully controlled energy of their music, but a more natural or inherent rhythmic surge from the heart instead of the brain. One of the earliest fathers of jazz was American pianist and composer Scott Joplin, who published his ragtime music from coast to coast. Perhaps for the first time in American history, because of copyright legislation, national distribution, and technological progress, every dance hall and house with a piano in the country was listening to the same piece of music. Well before World War I, professional music factories existed, where mass-produced popular tunes were turned out at astonishing rates, much as they are today by major record labels. This trend was a radical departure from the world where new popular music was extremely rare; people in England listened to the folk song "Barbara Allen" for more than three centuries, albeit with new verses every few years. So where did this new energy of music come from?

The dynamism of nineteenth-century industrialization and the new urban life forced a collision between white gospel, black spirituals, country folk songs, city orchestras, dance-hall bands, and the new ragtime; the explosive result of that collision was jazz. Just as Wagner's elaborately staged operas consciously sought to combine instruments, voice, acting, prose, lighting, and stage effects to create a unique art form, so, too, did jazz combine music, voice, and dance—although it was not a conscious thing, but a welling up of the impulse to create, to improvise in the moment of performance such that no two recitals of a piece would ever be the same. What drove people toward jazz also drove away many who found only chaos or disorder in the rhythms, much as they had found only noise in Wagner and Stravinsky, and a confusion of color in Picasso and Chagall.

Prefiguring virtually all of modern literature are the works of American Samuel Clemens, known as Mark Twain. His early novels of life on the Mississippi River, especially *The Adventures of Tom Sawyer* (1876) and *Adventures of Huckleberry Finn* (1884), have lost none of their popularity nearly a century and a half later. He was read by vast numbers of people, from every class, all ages and colors, and his work was translated in his lifetime into dozens of languages, from French to Japanese. He reached more people in his era than probably any author since the Apostles. Racism baffled and appalled him; he considered it our greatest failing as a species. He wrote of the dehumanizing trend of industrialization and warned of technology unchecked or rashly used. *A Connecticut Yankee in King Arthur's Court* (1889) centers around a modern man going back in time and bringing his technology with him: the result is a catastrophic war and unparalleled destruction—decades before World War I. His later works have the bizarre imagery and intense empty longing for meaning that make up much of twentieth-century literature. Antiheroes emerge, lost and insane, from the pages of *The Mysterious Stranger* (1905), a work

considered by many on its publication to be blasphemous. Having lived through the crucible of the American Civil War (1861–1865) and seen how horribly *un*-changed society was, it is unlikely Twain would have seen World War I as anything other than a horrible calamity, albeit one he had predicted.

The dominant forms of the late nineteenth century were the staged drama and the novel. Twain had described from his earliest works what Honoré de Balzac called the "little histories" that normal, average humans live out every day. Balzac, Twain, and Charles Dickens served as a prologue for modern literature writing about society from the bottom up. The 1920s and 1930s generation of disenchanted writers were doing nothing different. Referring to the eternal nature and modernity of Dickens's work in comparison with earlier novelists William Thackeray and Anthony Trollope, Shaw wrote, "the England of Thackeray and Trollope is gone, but the England of Dickens is still very much alive." Anyone who has wandered through twenty-first-century city slums is forced to agree; World War I did nothing to change either human nature or a writer's perceptions of it.

Dickens and Twain show sweeping panoramic views of all layers of society. Other authors, however, moved in the opposite direction and examined the most basic elements of society: the individual and the inner workings of his mind. They were influenced by Sigmund Freud and the development of psychology, which had established the existence of the unconscious, over which man had no control. Irrationality, a concept anatema to post-Enlightenment thought, was accepted as the basis of human motivation. Russian author Fedor Dostoevsky wrote of the individual buffeted by the irrational world around him. His most famous character, Raskolnikov from *Crime and Punishment* (1866), finds salvation through the irrational concepts of faith and hope. Dostoevsky can be seen as the herald of the rejection of materialism and rationalism, and his works the first signs of the erosion of faith in progress.

The evolution in literature by 1900 is perhaps nowhere more evident than in Marcel Proust. Like Dickens and Dostoevsky, Proust wrote about the world around him, but the focus was internal, often his own private life. Writing in a cork-lined room so no one would be disturbed as he screamed out the words he penned, Proust finished the draft of *Swan's Way* in 1912. Interrupted by World War I, he picked up where he left off with little sign that he even noticed the war. Elsewhere in France, Emile Zola had written of tortured, comsumptive dancers and poets, dying in garrets abandoned by the modern world. His novel *The Masterpiece* (1886) depicts many artists' unfortunate fate: an outwardly glamorous life in nightclubs such as the Moulin Rouge, and then crawling home to collapse in squalor. The horror of the Parisian slum prefigured the horror of the trenches for many writers.

In dramatic circles, too, the themes of the day could no longer be kept from the stage. Like Wagner, playrights would now use the stage to put across political and social views to the audience. Russian Maxim Gorky wrote *The Lower Depths* in 1902, a play about the poorest and meanest elements of society, people so downtrodden and dispirited they have no hope of ever leading a decent life. In all literature, there is an increasing focus on the plight of the poor, on those neglected or left out of the shining world of steam and steel and a sense of betrayal for the promises unfulfilled.

Even those who were not particularly beaten down by society felt alienated by it. W. Somerset Maugham's novels are riddled with disaffected and somnambulant characters, shuffling through the unpleasant. Hemingway's drunken heroes are of the same type, just as John Steinbeck's dust-covered farmers from *The Grapes of Wrath* (1939) are not far removed in situation or tone from the factory workers in Gorky's novel *The Mother* (1907). The notion that the masses could actually think and feel was what propelled an earlier generation of philosophers toward socialism; the seeds they planted blossomed before World War I in hundreds of novels.

In a similar way the new science of psychiatry drove many writers to consider their own inner garrets. The Irish novelist James Joyce wrote about a series of semiconnected characters engaged in introspective monologue in *The Dubliners,* first published in 1909. While deeply moved by the tragedy of the war, Joyce was not particularly motivated to change either his subject matter or writing style. His postwar works, *Ulysses* (1922) and the impenetrable *Finnegan's Wake* (1939), are perhaps more influenced by his meeting with Proust in 1921 than by the war; both are further explorations of the inner monologue of the human mind as it interacts with the outside world. Czech author Franz Kafka urged the world to read "only the kind of books that wound and stab us" in 1904. He certainly reflects the alienation and turning inward so often associated with postwar writers, but his images are all drawn from the Austro-Hungarian Empire, and its fall at the end of the war had little effect on his writing.

It is unwise, indeed probably impossible, to dismiss the importance of World War I as *subject matter,* but it was more a catastrophic and traumatic event than a cultural watershed. "We are the hollow men, we are the stuffed men," begins T. S. Eliot's 1922 poem "The Hollow Men." Taken by itself it fairly screams of the end of the world as we know it; the final stanza notes, "this is the way the world ends, not with a bang, but a whimper." Eliot was reacting to the war, certainly, but he was reacting in a manner he had already established. His earlier poems reflect a similar introspection and rebellion against tired themes, rhyme, and meter. "The Love Song of J. Alfred Prufrock" was written in Chicago in 1915, two years before America entered the war. Like Picasso and Wagner, Eliot had already abandoned traditional forms. So, too, did the radical poet Ezra Pound. He also was devastated by the war; but he was thirty-four when it ended, and though it altered his political views for life, his work was that of a man formed by the nineteenth century. His cultural reactions were shaped by an earlier revolution: the ideals of the French Revolution and of socialism mattered more to his art than four years of fighting.

The surreal world of Chagall's canvasses might have been used as book covers for the new popular works being produced on the eve of World War I. Science fiction and fantasy, branches of literature more popular today than most others combined, had already produced masterpieces by 1914. H. G. Wells and Jules Verne wrote of time travel, nuclear-powered submarines, lost worlds of dinosaurs, exploring the Moon and Mars, and even of wars destroying all life on earth. Bram Stoker's *Dracula: The Undead* (1897) was already a popular novel, and Joseph Sheridan Le Fanu had created even more horrific vampires of his own. Edgar Rice Burroughs and H. Rider Haggard had published *Tarzan of the Apes* (1912) and *King Solomon's Mines* (1885), respectively—adventure novels involving lost cities and forgotten tombs. Arthur Conan Doyle's drug addict, Sherlock Holmes, became the first world-famous detective in 1888. The popularity of this genre was well established before the rending events of the war, and if it grew even greater in the 1920s and 1930s, it is perhaps more because of the rise of literacy and momentum.

Another example of increasing momentum can be seen in women's fashions. The 1920s will always be remembered as the decade of the flapper. Yet, many of the fashion changes associated with this image occurred before World War I. By the turn of the century the world of fashion had already become recognizable. New styles were promoted in fashion shows and displayed on tall models strolling down catwalks in fancy and elegant surroundings. Knockoffs of haute couture could be purchased in a department store, and increasingly large segments of society were keeping up with the newest trends as advertised in the ever growing number of women's magazines.

In 1908 modern fashion was born, brought into the world by one basic concept: the natural figure. The move had started away from clothing that distorted a woman's shape and hampered her movements. The tailored suit became a symbol of emancipation, and skirt length rose to ankle length and shorter for some activities such as golf. With the suffragette movement, increased education, increasing career opportunities, and interest in sports—above all, the bicycle—women's fashion adapted. Along with slimmer, simpler skirts and wider, freer jackets, the handbag came into being as a necessity to accommodate the increasingly popular makeup and cigarette holders. Long a province of the aristocracy, fashion was not being enjoyed by the middle class. Instead of empresses and kings, style was dictated by actresses and dancers. According to Elizabeth Ewing, the most notable was American Irene Castle, who, with her "bobbed hair and slim, lythe boyish figure, set a new ideal for fashion, [which] amounted to a clean break with everything that belonged to the sunlit Edwardian afternoon of the world. It all happened before 1914, although it was to be the blueprint of the twenties. . . ."

If World War I was truly a watershed, one would look for radically different approaches to political problem-solving, or for new political movements to arise. Such was not the case; liberal, radical and socialist governments did, indeed, sweep into power in Europe, but before the war, not after it. A liberal, Labour-dominated government took power in Britain in 1901. In France the struggles between socialists and military conservatives ended with a fiercely Left-leaning government. Even in imperial Germany the socialists had an effective voice in the Reichstag, and the kaiser's most outspoken critic in the German legislature was a woman, the socialist Rosa Luxemburg.

The political tides following the war were rather flat. Mussolini's fascists were not much more than socialists with strong backing from the Army. Even Hitler's Nazis had a social program similar to Roosevelt's New Deal in the United States, and his well-known racist policies grew out of nineteenth-century social Darwinism and the works of German philosopher Friedrich Nietzche. The real political waves had already crashed, in many places well before the war began. Perhaps the strongest of these was anarchism. In many ways it was the political equivalent of the painters' rejection of "single-point-of-view" perspective. Anarchy was based on the premise that an individual is not locked into the society around him; he is free to make his own assessment and act on his own initiative. To date, there has never been any group as disappointed, disillusioned, and disaffected by Western culture and society as the anarchists. By 1901 they had assassinated many heads of state, including the tsar of Russia, the king of Italy and the president of the United States. Hundreds of lesser political figures met the same fate. Far from revolutionizing the political landscape, the Great War only served to numb people for a few years.

Indeed, little was new to the average person in the 1920s. Louis Sullivan, the great guru of American architecture, had already prophesied one-hundred-story buildings. The Pulitzer Building finished in 1892 was the first to rise above three-hundred feet. The skyscraper trend was well underway by 1900, and the first urban planners were hard at work. Several generations had already captured moments of the world around them with cameras, and with the advent of x-rays, pictures could be taken where no camera could reach. Industry transformed the laboratory from the domain of the amateur scientist to the businessman and made it essentially profitable. Applying that technology was now the realm of the marketer or salesman, like Thomas A. Edison, who spent his life convincing people they needed his inventions. This new market economy made it possible for innovative scientists such as Nicola Tesla of Serbia to find funding for their experiments.

New technology had immediate effects on society. As it had with the telescope and the microscope in earlier centuries, technology once again changed our perspective of distance: the Wright Flyer in 1903 presaged the end of distance for those traveling far, while Henry Ford's Model A automobile, first produced in 1912, greatly reduced it for those traveling closer to home. We had begun the process of lengthening our days and lives, condensing our world, and creating the information superhighway. The introduction of electric power, the evolution of medicine, the endless stream of information from printed matter and then through moving pictures brought the world closer to home and inspired many to use the newest modes of transportation during their growing leisure hours to go places never before possible. Indeed, it was the family car, perhaps more than any single invention, which fueled the rush of cultural changes after the war—changes that were already happening but might have waited much longer without wheels.

War did not destroy the world; it destroyed the *illusion* of the world: the illusion of progress and of prosperity. There were many who already knew it was an illusion, and they were not caught unawares; indeed, they were the sensitive souls creating the underpinnings of the illusion. It is an illusion that does not die an easy death: Western society keeps returning to the pleasant fantasy of comfort, of the inevitability of progress and of some inherent superiority. Moreover, it is an illusion that is shattered repeatedly, and each time there are those who see in the burst bubble the end of the world as we know it, whether they see it in a mushroom cloud or collapsing skyscrapers in Manhattan.

–JULIJANA BUDJEVAC AND
LAWRENCE HELM,
WASHINGTON, D.C.

References

Daniel Boorstin, *The Creators: A History of Heroes of the Imagination* (New York: Vintage, 1993).

Modris Eksteins, *Rites of Spring: The Great War and the Birth of the Modern Age* (Boston: Houghton Mifflin, 1989).

Elizabeth Ewing, *History of Twentieth Century Fashion* (New Jersey: Barnes & Noble, 1986).

Peter Gay, *Weimar Culture: The Outsider as Insider* (New York: Harper & Row, 1968).

Donald S. Gochberg, ed. *The Twentieth Century. Classics of Western Thought,* volume 4 (New York: Harcourt Brace Jovanovich, 1980).

John Peacock, *20th Century Fashion: The Complete Sourcebook* (London: Thames & Hudson, 1993).

Raymond J. Sontag, *A Broken World 1919–1939* (Philadelphia: Harper & Row, 1971).

Barbara Tuchman, *The Proud Tower* (New York: Macmillan, 1966).

Gordon Wright and Arthur Mejia, Jr. *An Age of Controversy: Discussion Problems in 20th Century European History* (New York: Harper & Row, 1973).

CULTURAL WATERSHED

ECONOMIC AND POLITICAL CHANGES

Did economic change in twentieth-century Europe anticipate political change?

Viewpoint: Yes. Industrialization and consumerism determined major political events in twentieth-century Europe.

Viewpoint: No. Economic change more frequently resulted from political events.

German communist philosopher Karl Marx believed that economic relations fundamentally determined the political structure of all human societies. This chapter examines that hypothesis in reference to twentieth-century Europe. As an argument presented here suggests, one does not have to be a Marxist to see the connection between economics and politics. As Europeans came to have a greater voice in government through democratic politics and burgeoning civil life, their concerns about wages, employment, retirement, social welfare, living conditions, and other essentially economic issues arrived at the forefront of political life. Such concerns spurred powerful socialist movements and later moderate governments that presided over a community of increasingly consumerized capitalist societies.

Yet, as the other argument maintains, twentieth-century Europeans saw the development, continuation, or reemergence of many noneconomic factors at the center of political life. A century of frequent conflict and terrible human tragedies proved that nation, religion, memory, and idealism all contributed to the making of Europe at least as much as, if not more than, economics alone.

Viewpoint: Yes. Industrialization and consumerism determined major political events in twentieth-century Europe.

One need not be a Marxist to maintain that economic change has generally preceded political change in nineteenth- and twentieth-century Europe. The two major economic transformations of the last two centuries—industrialization and consumerism—had undeniable and dramatic impacts on European political life.

Perhaps the most important underlying factor in economic change during the modern era was the political democratization of Europe. By 1918 all major European states but Russia had democratic governments elected by universal manhood suffrage, and in Germany and Britain, female suffrage. As average people came to have a greater impact on politics—whether it was through elections, demonstrations, revolutions, or other mass participatory processes—politics tended to become a reflection of their concerns. Since most Europeans worked for a living, worried about feeding their families, and entertained hopes for a materially prosperous future, the structure of national and international economics was of paramount concern. As Bill Clinton's campaign adviser

James Carville crudely explained the motivation of American voters in the 1990s, "it's the economy, stupid."

How did this truth work itself out in the relationship between economic and political change? In many ways the political realities of late-nineteenth- and early-twentieth-century Europe would have been impossible without the massive economic transformation facilitated by the Industrial Revolution. Beginning in Britain in the 1790s and spreading throughout the rest of the Continent over the next century, industrialization had social and political effects that are difficult to overstate. Factories dotting the landscape employed ever larger numbers of the lower classes, who in effect sold their labor to survive. The older pattern of agricultural dependence began to decline as peasants realized that factory jobs—no matter what their disadvantages and hardships and no matter how nefarious their critics have since made them seem—offered steadier and better-paying employment and greater social opportunities than life on the farm. Cities offered not just relatively stable factory jobs but otherwise unavailable access to literacy, education, media, entertainment, and other amenities that promised a better life. Often simply not living in fear of starving after a bad harvest was motivation enough. In some ways the products of the Industrial Revolution made the contrast between city and country all the more clear. Railroads, steamships, refrigeration, and other features of the modern transport sector meant that goods, including agricultural produce, could be shipped at faster speeds and, consequently, lower prices. As a result, agricultural prices went into a tailspin by the 1880s, barely rising again until after World War II. With lower profits from an already hard and increasingly unprofitable life, the number of urban wage earners grew exponentially throughout Europe. By the end of the nineteenth century, the population of almost all of Western Europe (France remaining a notable exception until 1931) was primarily urbanized. To take a couple of examples, Germany went from being one-third urban and two-thirds rural at the time of national unification in 1871 to being two-thirds urban and one-third rural at the beginning of World War I. Russia, despite being the least industrialized European country, nevertheless doubled its urban population between its 1897 census and the revolutionary year of 1917.

What did these drastic economic changes mean for European political life? Even with the appearance of the first factories, European workers began to develop a community of interests. Although historians debate the relevance and applicability of "social class" as a primary collective identity, workers and their sympathizers nevertheless embarked on campaigns to curb the abuses of industrialization and confront the worst consequences of urbanization. In addition to demanding such specific concessions as shorter working hours, legislation banning child labor, the right to unionize and strike, and programs of social insurance, this community of working-class concerns coalesced to form mass movements and political parties to accomplish these and other goals.

While not all supporters of the working class were Marxists, or even socialists, the incendiary call of German political philosophers Karl Marx and Friedrich Engels for workers of the world to unite in *The Communist Manifesto* (1848) formed one of the most important bases of political action over the next century and a half, one with global rather than just European ramifications. Economic dilemmas of industrialization and urbanization thus had direct political consequences. Every major European country developed a powerful socialist movement; all but the British Labour Party were founded on Marxist principles. In the parliamentary systems of Western Europe, socialist parties came to be among the largest and most popular political formations. In the elections of 1912 the German Social Democrats became the largest party in the Reichstag. After 1918 Labour replaced the Liberal Party as Britain's major party of the Left. French socialists entered governing cabinets during World War I, played a central political role in the interwar era, and became the senior partner in a coalition government in 1936. Although most socialists rejected Marx and Engels's call to revolution after 1900, they nevertheless maintained working-class goals at the center of their programs. Before the outbreak of World War II, most of Western Europe adopted many longstanding socialist demands, including the eight-hour workday, government-sponsored health insurance, old-age pensions, progressive taxes on income and inheritance, mandatory vacation time, and state-funded education.

As notable as the achievements of these "revisionist" socialists were, more-radical members of the socialist movement who looked directly to Marx branched off to found communist parties, which advocated violent revolution to secure the full nationalization of industry and its management by the state. In November 1917 the communist Bolshevik Party seized power in Russia and ruled over the land for the next seventy-four years. Unsuccessful communist coups occurred in Germany and Hungary in 1919, while much of the rest of Europe, confronted with what seemed to be a rising red tide, feared more communist coups. In addition to spreading an ideology founded to promote working-class interests, the appearance of communism also stimulated a political reaction that led in part to the rise of

THAT STATE I CALL SOCIALISM

The following excerpt is from the writings of Ramsay MacDonald, British Labour Party leader and prime minister in the early part of the twentieth century:

Under a democratic Parliamentary Government, however, it is practically impossible to maintain a pure and simple Socialist Party—although government by parliamentary groups makes this easier. Even then, as we see in France and Australia, the Socialist Party will have on occasions to co-operate in a *bloc* either refusing or accepting the responsibility of office.

In Great Britain at present, political parties are in confusion, but the lines of division between two great parties are emerging. The mass of the people are prepared to accept the new doctrines not as absolute ideas, as the fully-fledged Socialists do, but as guiding principles in experimental legislation. That is what the rise of the Labour Party means— that is all that it ever need mean, because that is how society develops from stage to stage of its existence. The Manchester school was never more than a tiny nucleus in the political life of the nineteenth century, but it supplied progressive ideas to that century and consequently led it. Nineteenth-century politics without Manchesterism would be a body without a brain. So in the twentieth century, Socialism, which will be infinitely more powerful than Manchesterism was in the nineteenth, will probably fulfil itself by being the creative centre of a much more powerful political movement. This is the position of the Labour Party at present.

The voting strength of this movement will come from the ranks of labour—the organized intelligent workers—the men who have had municipal and trade union experience— the men of self-respect who know the capacity of the people. These men will feel the oppression of the present time, its injustice, its heartlessness. They know their own leaders and have confidence in them. Their concern is that of the man who gives service and sees his reward disappear like water through a sieve. They are to be the constructive agents of the next stage in our industrial evolution. But they are not to stand alone. Socialism is no class movement. Socialism is a movement of opinion, not an organization of status. It is not the rule of the working class; it is the organization of the community. Therefore, to my mind one of the most significant facts of the times is the conversion of the intellectual middle class to Socialism. Those who think that the middle class is to organize against Socialism are to discover that they are profoundly mistaken. To put it on the lowest ground, only part of the interests of the middle class is opposed to Socialism, and against that must be placed the intellectual attractiveness of the Socialist theory. In determining political effort an active intelligence and an awakened idealism are always more powerful than personal interests. To quote *The Communist Manifesto* once more: "Just as, therefore, at an earlier period, a section of the nobility went over to the bourgeoisie, so now a portion of the bourgeoisie goes over to the proletariat, and in particular a portion of the bourgeois ideologists, who have raised themselves to the level of comprehending theoretically the historical movement of a whole."

In the ninth book of *The Republic* Plato discusses the wise man as citizen. "He will look at the city which is within him, and take heed that no disorder will occur in it such as might arise from superfluity or want; and upon this principle he will regulate his property and gain and spend according to his means." "Then, if that is his motive," remarks Glauson, "he will not be a statesman." "By the dog of Egypt, he will," ejaculated Socrates.

So long as Plato's reading of the human heart remains true, men will take up their abode in the city "which exists in idea," and rich and poor alike will labour for the establishment of the State where life alone will be valued as treasure, and the tyranny of the economic machine will no longer hold spiritual things in subjection. That State I call Socialism.

Source: *Ramsay MacDonald,* Ramsay MacDonald's Political Writings, *edited by Bernard Barker (London: Penguin, 1972), pp. 161–163.*

fascism—an ideology largely defined by its opposition to communism—and to moderate leftist political thought that also came to identify itself by what made it different from communism.

It would be difficult to say that these momentous changes in European political life resulted from any other cause but the economic changes of the Industrial Revolution. Without new difficulties in labor and production, there could have been no major socialist movement. Without a socialist movement, there could have been no communist movement, and it is not all that much of a stretch to say that without communism, there would have been no fascism. What two ideologies could be more closely identified with twentieth-century political thought than communism and fascism?

If the Industrial Revolution caused the restructuring of the European political landscape before World War II, the "consumer revolution" that came after 1945 also effected a major change in modern European politics. A major benefit of the Industrial Revolution was that as it systematized production and reduced the costs of goods, more of the population could partake in what it produced. In a related way, the guaranteed wages, leisure time, and other benefits ushered in by the political changes associated with industrialization for the first time enabled even the working class to purchase homes, automobiles, vacations, and other material benefits of the good life. The democratization of taste and entertainment through mass literacy, popular theater, movies, and television both integrated the working class into the mainstream of national and international cultures and inculcated them with consumer values.

The result across the board was a moderation of European political thought. If revisionist socialists and other forces of the moderate Left had secured a decent standard of living for the urban masses and seemed to be working for further progress, why should workers have remained a source of radicalism? Indeed, they almost universally bought into the prevailing system. Socialist parties definitively abandoned revolutionary Marxism as their theoretical basis in the postwar era, often because they realized that the more they clung to it, the more they lost touch with existing political realities and sources of mass support. By the 1990s, British Labourites, French socialists, and German Social Democrats were forced to embrace, or at least appear to embrace, full market economics and probusiness and progrowth economic policies to compete seriously—and in all three cases successfully—for national political power. Socialists embracing capitalism certainly represented a momentous political change, but it was impossi-

ble without the transition to what is increasingly called a postindustrial economy.

Yet, while Western European socialists successfully adapted to changed economic circumstances, radical socialism failed to keep pace and met its doom. Western European communists saw their support shrink to an insignificant following of fanatics and malcontents. Communist regimes in Eastern Europe followed ideological strictures that forced them to reject profit, enterprise, innovation, consumer industry, and the political freedom to call for a change in such attitudes. As a result, the quality of life experienced by the people of the region lagged dramatically behind that of the West. Communist governments rightly came to be seen as archaic, backward, repressive regimes that had to rely on coercion to stay in power and had to deny economic liberty to help do so. As Eastern European masses saw and heard about the consumer prosperity of the West, their attitudes of opposition to their own governments boiled. By 1989 their largely peaceful demonstrations and the evisceration of government led to the collapse of communist rule throughout the region. In the absence of communism, Eastern Europe pursued, with varying degrees of success, the same consumer society that moderated radical politics in the West. Once again, this dramatic change in European politics cannot be separated from an economic basis. If the Industrial Revolution radicalized European masses to effect major political change, consumerism moderated them to effect another.

—PAUL DU QUENOY,
GEORGETOWN UNIVERSITY

Viewpoint:
No. Economic change more frequently resulted from political events.

Few better proofs exist of the axiom that intellectually we all remain Marxists than the survival of the argument that economic change has been the key to political development in twentieth-century Europe. The true catalyst of change has been three interfacing world wars, one (1914–1918) confined to Europe, one (1939–1945) focused on it, and one (1946–1990) decided within its boundaries. These wars essentially had in common, moreover, not the strength but the weakness of their economic aspects.

World War I had its roots in a breakdown of diplomacy. In the decades before 1914, Europe had evolved along common lines of economic

ECONOMIC AND
POLITICAL CHANGES

and social development to a point where conflict increasingly seemed impossible because it was unsustainable. English writer Rudyard Kipling's 1903 allegorical poem "The Peace of Dives," in which peace is kept in the ancient world by the interlocking of commercial relations, was no less compelling because of its obvious ironic twist. Just as the hero of the poem is the rich man of Scripture who spurns a beggar at his door and is condemned to hell, so the often-criticized forces of finance capitalism become the guarantor of peace. British economist Norman Angell made the same point in *The Great Illusion: A Study of the Relation of Military Power in Nations to their Economic and Social Advantage* (1910), arguing that the disruption of international credit by war would gridlock combat within a short period. In social terms, the major concerns of governments and armies when considering war prior to 1914 were which way their citizens in arms—socialists and others—would point their guns when mobilized, and how long they would be able to withstand emotionally the horrors of the modern battlefield. Here and there intellectuals such as French poet Charles-Pierre Péguy derided a world made safe for fat little men with briefcases and dreamed of living large on fields of glory. Ordinary Europeans of all classes and castes, however, looked forward to more mundane plea-sures: buying a bicycle, receiving a pay raise, and enjoying the company of their grandchildren. The enthusiasm that greeted the outbreak of war was febrile, lacking the deep roots so long ascribed to it by mythmakers.

What held the war together from the start was the physical and moral power of the state. Governments organized economies for war, arrested or ignored dissenters as they deemed necessary, and subjugated ordinary men and women to networks of controls unthinkable in the free societies of a prewar period that seemed increasingly idyllic as time passed. Civic identity and patriotism brought men into uniform and kept them there despite the hecatombs of dead whose size the generals never seemed able to diminish. Perhaps the greatest irony of World War I was that states never understood the degree of credibility at their disposal, and in consequence tended to neglect its renewal. The French military mutinies of 1917 represented a consistent process of renegotiating particular social contracts—in this case, an agreement between the soldiers and the state that the war would continue without the bloody offensives of the first three years, but with French victory as its eventual objective. In Germany the abortive program of national mobilization in 1916 generated a similar renegotiation on the home front—a process involving the uneasy sharing of power among capitalists, workers, soldiers, and bureaucrats. As the conflict progressed, however, the room for negotiating such agreements shrank to a point where each combatant's war ended when citizens hated their governments more than they feared their enemies. Class warfare in the Marxist sense, or any other, had little or nothing to do with the process.

That situation was true even in Russia, where the Bolsheviks owed their triumph to military victory over a diffuse set of disorganized and inept opponents, and where the revolution of the proletariat was made after the fact, at gunpoint. Elsewhere, states took stock of their experiences and focused on creating a domestic authority that would enable full mobilization for a total war of indefinite length should that become necessary. Diplomacy after 1919 acquired a sharp edge, becoming war by other means, in an inversion of nineteenth-century German military philosopher Carl von Clausewitz's maxim that war is the extension of politics by other means. In economic contexts the Soviet Union's successive five-year plans were politically directed military operations, with so-called armies of workers and labor fronts, having no significant relationship to Marx's theories of economic development. Fascism, National Socialism, and related Right-wing interwar theories of development emphasized forced mobilization of internal resources in what amounted to a war environment. Societies were structured along political rather than economic lines. Concepts of *Volksgemeinschaft* (people's community) challenged the Marxist model of class struggle by making it irrelevant to a state-centered identity with an ethnic base that in turn was politically defined. Even in the Third Reich the definition of an Aryan could be surprisingly flexible.

The primacy of politics continued during and after World War II. Neither defeat nor victory left much room for economic primacy in a Europe that by 1945 was an economic backwater. In the Soviet Union and the states under its control, economics were put to the service of politics once more: this time a Cold War that eventually became a metastasizing cancer, draining resources into an ultimately counterproductive military establishment. In the West, recovery initially depended on outside aid such as the Marshall Plan (1947). Its continuation was heavily contingent on patterns of economic development that succeeded to the extent that they eschewed economics-based class conflict in both principle and practice. The West German "social market economy" typified and symbolized the

use of domestic political processes to bypass irrelevant class-warfare models. A negative example was provided by Britain's "Old Labour" and its adherence to a value system that held that it was less important if Britain starved collectively than if everyone died in the same time frame: immiserization in the name of Marx that denied Marx's most basic principles.

Both models, however, ultimately depended on the success not only of deterring war but of providing a continuing and credible security umbrella in a conventional as well as a nuclear context. The Soviet Union was constrained to exercise cautious diplomacy because it recognized the heavy cost of going to war with the West—and increasingly as well, the potential advantages of cooperating with such initiatives as the Federal Republic of Germany's conciliatory "Eastern Policy" of the 1970s. The recovery that eventually gave birth to the European Community in the late 1940s and 1950s, like the series of wars that had destroyed old Europe, was essentially a political process, not an economic one. It depended on the extension of U.S. Marshall Plan aid for the explicitly political reason of marginalizing extremist movements and attitudes and developed into a program of continental integration out of the political necessity of preventing further destructive conflict. Politics, not economics, drove these essential developments.

–DENNIS SHOWALTER,
COLORADO COLLEGE

References

Norman Angell, *The Great Illusion: A Study of the Relation of Military Power in Nations to their Economic and Social Advantage* (New York: Putnam, 1910).

Richard A. Comfort, *Revolutionary Hamburg: Labor Politics in the Early Weimar Republic* (Stanford: Stanford University Press, 1966).

Niall Ferguson, *The Cash Nexus: Money and Power in the Modern World, 1700–2000* (New York: Basic Books, 2001).

William I. Hitchcock, *The Struggle for Europe: The Turbulent History of a Divided Continent, 1945–2002* (New York: Doubleday, 2003).

John Markoff, *Waves of Democracy: Social Movements and Political Change* (Thousand Oaks, Cal.: Pine Forge Press, 1996).

ECONOMIC AND
POLITICAL CHANGES

EUROPEAN INTEGRATION

Was the intensified momentum toward European integration after World War II an ideologically driven attempt to limit the power of the nation-states?

Viewpoint: Yes. The trauma of World War II intensified attempts to adapt a federalist European system, abridging state sovereignty to gain increased security.

Viewpoint: No. Integration emerged, with significant pressure from the United States, as the answer to Western Europe's changing strategic requirements and economic needs.

Since 1945 the nations of Europe have been moving steadily toward economic and political integration. As early as 1946, British leader Winston Churchill was talking about a "United States of Europe" that would avoid conflict and share the resources of the continent. Just five years later France, West Germany, Italy, Belgium, the Netherlands, and Luxembourg formed the European Coal and Steel Community (ECSC), an organization that guaranteed free trade in heavy industrial commodities. After less successful talks on a European defense organization, the ECSC nations created the European Economic Community (EEC), a common market for all trade, in 1957. By 1986 the EEC included twelve nations that were in many ways becoming components of a supranational body. In 1992 they formed the European Union (EU), with an elected European Parliament, common legislation outside of economic matters, gestures toward a common foreign and defense policy, a project for a pan-European constitution, and, in 1999, a common currency. After further expansion in 1995, the EU boasted fifteen member states, including all of Western Europe except Switzerland and Norway. In December 2002 it invited an additional ten nations, including several members of the former communist bloc and even three former republics of the Soviet Union, to join in 2004.

Why would Europe, which had been at war with itself for centuries before 1945, have moved so quickly toward integration? From one perspective, it appeared that after the most destructive war in human history, Europe was so materially devastated and psychologically jarred that it naturally decided to reject bloody conflicts such as World War II. A philosophical aversion to conflict and a widespread embracement of pacifism moved the continent forward on the path of cooperation and interdependence.

Another explanation has been that Europe's nations, weakened as they were by World War II, were so overwhelmed by the vast new power of the United States and the Soviet Union that they believed their only hope to act as powers in their own right was to combine their efforts. In an economic world order dominated by American trade and finance and confronted with communist challenges, a competitive European presence seemed to depend on greater cooperation. If France, Germany, Italy, or even Britain was forced to acknowledge that it could no longer play an independent international role, it now seemed all the better to throw in one's lot with past competitors to ensure an influential future. As the EU grows larger, more influential, and more tightly bound, a consideration of how and why it arose is in order.

57

Viewpoint:
Yes. The trauma of World War II intensified attempts to adapt a federalist European system, abridging state sovereignty to gain increased security.

World War II shattered the European continent. It transformed political, military, economic, social, and cultural relations between and within states. Borders were redrawn, political and social institutions collapsed, and economic and social ties were destroyed or significantly altered as Europe experienced temporary de facto unification as a consequence of the Nazi conquests. Most importantly, the fact that almost every state of continental Europe had been ruined or dramatically weakened proved for the Europeans the limits to which the nation-state was able to guarantee security and independence. This harsh experience of national collapse, resettlement of huge masses of people, military actions, and resistance movements that transcended borders (some historians even referred to World War II in Europe as the "European Civil War"), discredited the idea and reality of national sovereignty in the eyes of many Europeans. Moreover, the war itself proved the dangers of unlimited state sovereignty as the prewar European system of national states had fallen so manifestly. As a result, Europeans gained much practical experience in abridging state sovereignty in favor of association of different countries in larger political and economic entities.

The German New Order was built on the enslavement of many European states. The brutality of the Nazi occupation vividly betrayed the cultural cornerstone of the idea of a united Europe. At the same time, however, Nazi visions of postwar Europe, racially defined and Germanized, promoted the view of the Continent as a single political entity. The unfolding war also witnessed an active use of pan-European slogans by the Nazi propaganda machine. The Nazis portrayed the war as a struggle for a "new Europe" and stressed a "common European destiny" in the "crusade against alien forces"—especially Russian Bolshevism and Anglo-American hegemony. These slogans and ideas attracted the attention of many Europeans, creating some sense of Continental solidarity when the German-led coalition went to war against the Soviet Union. As some European historians note, if there was a genuine chance of integrating Europe during the Nazi period, it was certainly between July and November of 1941, when victorious Germany posed as a leader of Europe, united against external foes. As German military fortunes disappeared, the Nazis used the formula of a united Europe and even the term "European union" in political and diplomatic attempts to prevent the disintegration of their empire. In 1942–1943 the German Foreign Ministry prepared several memoranda on European confederation, foreseeing a "European community" of countries that voluntarily embraced "European solidarity" and "European obligations," but these projects had no practical effect.

At the same time the transnational character of the antifascist struggle, the need to counter Nazi pan-European appeals, and the necessity to draw some lessons from the war stimulated interest of many noncommunist Resistance organizations of various countries in the ideas of a united and democratic Europe. In 1941–1944 different Resistance groups developed a federalist design for future Europe to replace the old system of independent states. The pan-European ideas of the Resistance movement elaborated some themes that contributed to the development of future approaches to European integration: a voluntary association open to all European states; the renunciation of absolute sovereignty and exaggerated nationalism; and self-government by the masses. The 1944 Geneva declaration of the Resistance leaders called for a federal Europe with a written constitution and a supranational government directly responsible to the peoples of Europe. Many historians trace the origins of postwar European integration to concepts and ideas of the wartime Resistance.

The German occupation of Europe also left a legacy in terms of unification of the Continental economy. The need to mobilize all resources, irrespective of national boundaries for total war, created, though for a short period of time, a united and centrally controlled Continental economy. This reality emphasized the prominence of economic and administrative approaches to European unification. Many Europeans began to understand that Continental unity should not be sought through political unification in the first instance but through practical economic and administrative steps, such as pooling of various spheres of economic activity—transport, heavy industry, electricity, agriculture, and distribution. There were several projects and plans to reorganize and manage the Continental economy prepared in Germany in 1940–1943, in which specific economic functions were assigned to each country. Nazi planning of a new European economic order paid a great deal of attention to German economic relations with France. In the long-term and broader perspective this orientation emphasized the key role of Franco-

EUROPEAN INTEGRATION

German cooperation within the European integration.

On the Allied side, particularly in Britain, the question of economic integration was discussed widely by governmental agencies, press, and public in connection with plans for the postwar economic reconstruction of Europe. This discussion highlighted the significant potential of Continental economic interdependence, particularly the development of transnational industrial regions, such as mining and coal production in the area stretching from the Ruhr to Lorraine to Luxembourg and eastern Belgium. This goal foreshadowed an idea to unite the European mining and coal industry, which was to emerge as the Schuman Plan (1950) to create the European Coal and Steel Community (ECSC)—a nucleus of a wider European economic integration.

The wartime experience also brought about some ideas on political unification. These initiatives and projects would create regional federations of countries with similar economic and political characteristics, that is, a West European Federation, Central European Federation, Balkan Federation, and so on. A British initiative of 1940 to create the Anglo-French union resulted in a detailed blueprint for close political, military, and economic cooperation useful for postwar discussions on European integration. In 1944 Belgium, the Netherlands, and Luxembourg agreed on a postwar customs union (Benelux) that was a logical step toward the integration of Western Europe.

The Resistance's discussions on European unification during the war had also revealed important issues, as well as national differences, in the approach to the problem of European unification, which were to influence the future. Mainly, these disagreements were on how the European federation should be constituted and the extent to which national sovereignty should be limited. Pan-European activists within the French, German, and Dutch Resistance accepted the necessity of supranational authority and economic union but wanted European states to retain some independence in foreign affairs. While the French viewed the federation as a guarantee against future threats from Germany, the Germans considered European integration as a way to anchor their country in Western Europe. The Italians were the most enthusiastic supporters of federalism, while the Danes and Norwegians were extremely wary of any supranational authority in Europe and hoped for a looser confederation. Discussions within the Resistance, as well as the debates on European problems in Great Britain, had also raised the question whether Britain must be a part of united Europe, reflecting the emerging conflict

between a European and a wider world role of this country.

Some developments during World War II, such as close Anglo-American cooperation, the creation of Allied integrated military administrative machinery, and the existence of multinational formations within the forces of the antagonists (such as in the British armed forces) foreshadowed future approaches to European integration in the military sphere. Additionally, many adherents of a united Europe repeatedly emphasized the necessity of a continental unification to strengthen the weakened European role in the world.

—PETER RAINOW,
SAN MATEO, CALIFORNIA

Viewpoint:
No. Integration emerged, with significant pressure from the United States, as the answer to Western Europe's changing strategic requirements and economic needs.

Was European integration driven by ideological formulations? Was the philosophical dedication to a "United States of Europe" echoed in the Marshall Plan (1947) the reason European leaders were willing to surrender increasing amounts of autonomy? Was federation the motive? An abundance of rhetorical evidence certainly exists to support these claims. Integrationist thought and formulas were at their peak in the aftermath of World War II, and some key figures in this process were acknowledged subscribers to various schools of thought. An entire generation horrified and emotionally exhausted by the destruction of two devastating world wars, followed by revelations of the Holocaust, lent substantial credibility and political currency to anything promising to prevent another such conflagration in Europe. Furthermore, the postwar period is considered by many to represent a crisis in the nation-state as the legitimate primary political unit. Indeed, much of the bloodshed during the twentieth century seemed to accompany the pursuit of the nation-state. It follows then that Europe in the postwar period championed federalist theories and supranational institutional solutions to diminish the role of the nation-state and its ability, even its motivation, to make war.

Though plausible, this explanation does little to reveal the manner in which European integration has proceeded, nor does it account for its timing. Despite a strong current of support, the

King Juan Carlos of Spain presenting euro currency in the Casa de la Moneda el Rey, 1999, three years before its circulation

(© Marcou/SIPA)

EUROPEAN INTEGRATION

first palpable (though also somewhat tentative) attempt at substantive integration did not arrive until several years after the war had ended (the European Coal and Steel Community, ECSC, 1951), and then only six countries (France, West Germany, Italy, Belgium, the Netherlands, and Luxembourg) partook. The Treaty of Rome, which created the European Economic Community (EEC), was ratified in 1957, a full twelve years after World War II ceased, and it went into effect the following year. To explain what drove European integration after World War II and to account for "why then" and "why in this manner," a much more sophisticated answer is required. The origins, as well as successive waves, of increasing European integration have been pursued as answers to Western Europe's shifting strategic requirements and economic needs. The means of integration, moreover, demonstrate that integration has been at least as much of a boost to the nation-state as a source of its deterioration. Indeed, the nation-state has been the agent of integration and has approached "Europe" as a vehicle to achieve aims no longer attainable at the national level.

Following the total defeat of Nazi Germany and its occupation at the hands of the Allies, debate ensued as to the future of Germany as a single state. Various plans were formulated—many aimed to undo the Prussian unification of Germany (1871). The French continued to desire annexation of the Saar and much of the Rhineland. The Germans understood that they might have lost more than the war; their newly defined national identity was also at stake. The German Federal Republic's leadership under Konrad Adenauer recognized that Germany was quite literally "on probation" and needed to demonstrate its Western democratic traits to have any hope of rehabilitation. The problem of integrating Germany into Europe (also known as the "German Question") remains a centerpiece of the European Union (EU).

To the dismay of the French, the British and Americans quickly ceased to demand a permanent division of Germany. In 1946 they combined their zones to be administered as a single economic unit—an entity called "Bizonia." The French remained reluctant to bring their zone into this unit but subsequently changed their stance after the Americans reminded them of the yet undistributed aid of the Marshall Plan. In comparison to the Germany established by the Versailles Treaty (1919), the new Federal Republic must have seemed far less menacing. World War I was fought almost entirely outside the borders of Germany, and when it surrendered, the German military still occupied foreign territory. After World War II, Germany was occupied; its capital symbolically was moved to Bonn, a quiet Rhenish town. Though the weakness of the French position is well known, it is important to understand

THE HOPE OF ALL MEN OF GOOD WILL

At the 31 October 1949 meeting of the Organization for European Economic Cooperation in Paris, Administrator Paul G. Hoffman made the following speech:

It has been fifteen months since I had the privilege of meeting with this Council. In that period Western Europe has made truly amazing progress in restoring its industrial and agricultural production. That progress is the result of work, hard work, on the part of millions of Europeans. That is the human story behind the cold statistics of production increased.

We applaud the success of your efforts. We in the Economic Cooperation Administration, and you in the Organisation for European Economic Cooperation, have come to know each other well. Through working with you toward our common objectives, we have come to hold the O.E.E.C in high esteem, and our feeling toward its members is one of deep friendliness. I am delighted to be here, and I am pleased to note the presence of the representatives of the German Republic as full partners in your organisation. It is as an admiring friend of the O.E.E.C that I speak to you today.

Since 1947 we have confounded both the Communists and the other cynics by proving, first, that together we could successfully start economic recovery in Western Europe; and, second, that we could join in laying the foundations for security against attack upon our Atlantic community. We have seen anxiety give way to hope. Today I am asking you to turn hope into confidence.

The European Recovery Program is now approaching the halfway mark. The time has come to consider carefully what more must be done to hold the ground already gained and to assure the further progress that is vitally needed. We must now devote our fullest energies to this major task.

These tasks are: First, to balance Europe's dollar accounts so that Europe can buy the raw materials and other items which mean employment and better living.

The second—and to say this is why I'm here—is to move ahead on a far-reaching program to build in Western Europe a more dynamic, expanding economy which will promise steady improvement in the conditions of life for all its people. This, I believe, means nothing less than an integration of the Western European economy.

The first of these tasks can be achieved only through vigorous and effective action by this organisation and by every participating government. Unless dollar earnings rise dramatically between now and June 1952, Europe's trade with the Americas will have to be balanced at so low a level that it will spell disaster for you and difficulties for us. The readjustment of exchange rates which occurred in September paves the way for a larger expansion of dollar earnings, but devaluation by itself is obviously not enough.

I want briefly to mention two specific fields of action which seem to me especially relevant to this objective.

One concerns domestic fiscal policy. As was clearly foreseen by your governments, devaluation, essential though it was, gave new impetus to inflation. If, as a result, the past year's efforts at stabilization are undone and your costs and prices are allowed to rise, the potential benefits in dollar earnings will never be realized. This should not be allowed to happen. Unpleasant though it may be, action—particularly budgetary action—to prevent inflation is imperative.

The other field of action I have in mind is the provision of direct incentive to private exporters. Practically all Europe's exports are furnished by private producers. Governments may set targets; they may exhort; but unless sales in dollar markets bring adequate rewards to sellers, the great effort required to enter and hold those markets will never be made.

Urgent as I regard the first major task—that of balancing Europe's trade with the dollar area—its performance will not be meaningful unless we have come to grips with our second —the building of an expanding economy in Western Europe through economic integration.

The substance of such integration would be the formation of a single large market within which quantitative restriction on the movements of goods, monetary barriers to the flow of payments and, eventually, all tariffs are permanently swept away. The fact that we have in the United States a single market of 156 million consumers has been indispensable to the strength and efficiency of our economy. The creation of a permanent, freely trading area, comprising 270 million consumers in Western Europe, would have a multitude of helpful consequences. It would accelerate the development of large-scale, low-cost production industries. It would make the effective use of all resources easier, the stifling of healthy competition more difficult.

EUROPEAN INTEGRATION

Obviously, such a step would not change the physical structure of European industry, or vastly increase productivity overnight, but the massive change in the economic environment would, I am convinced, set in motion a rapid growth in productivity. This would make it possible for Europe to improve its competitive position in the world and thus more nearly satisfy the expectations and needs of its people.

This is a vital objective. It was to this that Secretary Marshall pointed in the speech which sparked Europe to new hope and new endeavour. It was on this promise that the Congress of the United States enacted the E.C.A. act. This goal is embodied in the convention of the O.E.E.C.

I know that the difficulties which stand in the way of its achievement will spring all too readily to mind, but before integration is dismissed as a merely romantic possibility, too remote to have any bearing on practical, immediate decisions, I invite you to weigh the alternative.

Even assuming brilliant success in overcoming the dollar deficit in the next two years, the end of E.R.P in 1952 will at best leave Europe in only a precarious balance with the dollar area. Monetary reserves will be inadequate, and it is plain that dollar shortages will recur in one country or another the first time the European economy is subjected to serious pressure. In the absence of integration, nations would each separately try to protect their dollar reserves. They would attempt to earn dollars from each other by restricting imports. The vicious cycle of economic nationalism would again be set in motion.

The consequences would be the cumulative narrowing of markets, the further growth of high cost protected industries, the mushrooming of restrictive controls, and the shrinkage of trade into the primitive pattern of bilateral barter.

This course spells disaster for nations and poverty for peoples. This is why integration is not just an ideal. It is a practical necessity.

This being so, it is your job to devise and put into effect your own program to accomplish this purpose—just as it was your responsibility, which you carried out so ably,

to take Secretary Marshall's original suggestion and give it life and breath.

In a program designed to accomplish effective and lasting integration, certain fundamental requirements suggest themselves. First, means must be found to bring about a substantial measure of coordination of national fiscal and monetary policies. Trade and payments cannot long continue free among countries in which there are widely divergent degrees of inflationary, or deflationary, pressure. The development of such differences in financial pressures among different countries will inevitably force the reimposition of restrictive controls. Unless individual countries accept the necessity for some coordination of domestic financial policies, the prospects for eliminating even the most restrictive types of controls over international trade will be dim indeed. Coordination of these vital national policies need not result in identity of policy. Coordination need only go so far as to insure that policies will not diverge so drastically as to break down the whole structure of European unity; but it must go at least that far.

Another essential of your plan, I believe, is that it should provide means for necessary exchange rate adjustments, subject, of course, to the general supervision of the International Monetary Fund, where these are the only feasible alternatives to imposing direct exchange controls within Europe. This is necessary because there will be occasions when, either for reasons of policy or as result of circumstances beyond the control of government, prices and costs in one country will diverge from those in other countries too far to be brought into line through internal financial measures alone.

Even when effective means are found to coordinate financial policies and to promote needed exchange rate changes, there are still bound to be temporary disturbances in the flow of trade and payments between countries. Their whole impact should not be allowed to fall upon the gold and dollar reserves of the individual countries. I believe, therefore, that a third essential of any plan you devise must be a means to cushion the effect of these inevitable temporary disturbances.

Fourth, means must be found to insure that severe strains are not imposed upon the maintenance of integration through conflicting commercial policies and practices. Such strains might arise from disguised barriers to trade within an area or from radically divergent policies toward external trade.

This brings me to our final suggestion, which has to do with the path by which this goal of integration may be reached. I have repeatedly referred to the creation of a single European market. Many of the immediate steps that need to be taken toward this goal can, and will, involve the whole group of the participating countries. But there are other arrangements, some already in prospect, involving smaller groups of countries which, I am convinced, will also turn out to be steps toward the same objective. I do not believe that any path toward integration should be left unexplored. It seems to me absolutely essential that arrangements arrived at within groups of two, three, or more countries should be in harmony with wider possibilities of European unity and should, under no circumstances, involve the raising of new or higher barriers to trade within Europe than already exist.

I feel, therefore, that, while pressing forward to the broader objective of economic integration of all the participating countries, we should not slacken our efforts toward establishment of close economic arrangements within one or more smaller groups of countries—always with the intention that these should contribute toward and not be turned against, the integration of the whole of Western Europe and its overseas territories.

I have made a number of references of the urgency of starting immediately on this program of integration. My conviction on this point is based, in the first place, on the acute realization of the very short time still remaining during which American aid will be available to cushion the inevitable short-run dislocations which a program of integration will involve. There is another very important reason for speed. The people and the Congress of the United States and, I am sure, a great majority of the people of Europe have instinctively felt that economic integration is essential if there is to be an end to Europe's recurring economic crises. A European program to this end—one which should show real promise of taking this great forward step successfully—would, I strongly believe, give new impetus to American support for carrying through into 1952 our joint effort toward lasting European recovery.

For all these reasons—but particularly because of the urgency of the need—I do make this considered request: That you have ready early in 1950 a record of accomplishment and a program which together will take Europe well along the road toward economic integration.

By accomplishment I mean really effective action to remove the quantitative restrictions on trade on which you have recently made a start. I also mean the elimination in Europe of the unsound practice of double pricing—that is, maintaining export prices for fuel and basic materials at higher levels than domestic prices. This practice results in higher production costs throughout Europe. It cannot be squared with your pledges of mutual aid.

By a program, I mean a realistic plan to meet the fundamental requirements I have described. Perhaps you will accomplish this through adaptation of existing institutions. Perhaps you will find that new central institutions are needed.

We are together playing for high stakes in this program. The immediate goal is a solidly based prosperity for an economically unified Western Europe—a goal which President Truman reaffirmed to me just before I left Washington. Beyond that lies what has been the hope of all men of good will during your life-time and mine, an enduring peace founded on justice and freedom. That high hope can be realized if we, the people of the free world, continue to work together and stick together.

Source: "The Hoffman Speech (1949)," History of European Integration, website, Historical Institute, Leiden University <http://www.let.leidenuniv.nl/history/rtg/res1/hoffman.htm>.

EUROPEAN INTEGRATION

that other factors allowed the Allies to be flexible in their stance on postwar Germany.

Wider geopolitical developments figured heavily into the decision making of all the agents of integration. In particular, the United States actively sought to foster Western European integration. There is little secret that post–World War II U.S. foreign policy was dominated by its increasing rivalry with the Union of Soviet Socialist Republics (U.S.S.R.). Rebuilding Western Europe and ensuring its prosperity became a cornerstone of Cold War policy (as well as integral to the regimes of Western Europe). Economic success quickly undermined communist movements in Western European countries and solidified the orientation of those countries toward the United States. As other theaters, such as Korea, demonstrated that the United States would need to be engaged globally, the Americans pressured Western Europe to provide a unified front against the Eastern bloc. Those who see the roots of integration in ideology often underplay the role of the United States in fostering European integration.

Although signs of rivalry between the United States and U.S.S.R. were clear even before the end of World War II, the bipolar division of Europe and the world truly began to crystallize around the Marshall Plan. While it has been widely debated how sincere the offer was intended to be, aid was offered to countries already under Soviet influence. After the first major infusion of Marshall aid was delivered in late 1948, a significant precedent was set in the contrasting economic policies of the two blocs. Western European democracies were thus wedded to economic success as a source of legitimacy vis-à-vis the nations of the Soviet bloc.

The Marshall Plan required that participating members cooperate with one another. Payments were distributed by the Organization for European Economic Cooperation (OEEC). Though it is not commonly considered an element of integration, the OEEC's European Payments Union continued to facilitate interstate trade long after the Marshall Plan ceased. The European Payments Union established credit margins for the participating states and allowed them to manage bilateral deficits without renewing or setting up trade restrictions. In other words, one country's deficit with another could be offset by a surplus with still other countries. By mandating cooperation, the United States gave a significant and early push to European integration.

In May 1950 French foreign minister Robert Schuman proposed an economic association that allowed its members to share joint production of coal and steel. These resources were still widely considered essential for making war. With the creation of a "High Authority," control over these important military and strategic resources would no longer reside with national governments. The French proposal was formulated to ensure France's expanded share of postwar steel production (with a large market to peddle its finished products), while also going a long way to safeguarding its security.

At this point, competing versions of "Europe" emerged. The British and Scandinavians, according to scholar David de Giustino, advocated a Europe in terms of "free trade, peaceful relations and human rights; for them, the Council of Europe, representing a family of independent nations, was sufficient." Unlike the Low Countries, France, and Germany, they saw no need to surrender features of national sovereignty. It is not insignificant that this alternate vision of European integration found manifestation in the OEEC and the Council of Europe. The desire and perceived necessity to push European integration into the realm of supranational institutions independent of national governments by the "Six" (France, West Germany, Italy, Belgium, the Netherlands, and Luxembourg), throws into relief the fact that forces beyond ideology were driving these developments. Though ideological discourse raged among the "nationalists," "federalists," and "functionalists," at every turn external impetus in the form of shifting strategic, foreign-policy, or economic concerns, or perceived risks/benefits, can be clearly identified for each nation-state. That Western European leaders formulated their goals vis-à-vis the European project differently from one another, and at different times, undermines the idea that a commitment to integrationist ideology was driving this process.

In 1951 the ECSC came into existence. This event, formulated tentatively and narrowly to ensure equal access to essential natural resources and thereby provide an element of security, effectively cemented the Franco-German axis as the shaping foundation and core of European integration. A model for future integration was thus effectively established. The outbreak of the Korean War (1950–1953) and the insistence by the Americans that Germany be rearmed provided a fresh push. The result of this external impetus and the successful experience of the ECSC was the European Defense Community (EDC, 1950–1954) and European Political Community (EPC). The failure of these arrangements made the successful negotiation of the Treaty of Rome all the more imperative. In fact, the abortive EDC and EPC may have given federal ideologues greater leverage in shaping the terms of the Rome treaty, but agreement to these terms was motivated by strategic, political, and economic calculations.

Many of those who subscribe to the idea that ideology provided the origins of European integration note that World War II left Europeans looking for alternatives to the nation-state. This search, they argue, quickly led to supranational formulations and ideas. Subsequent pursuit of integration was seen as a deterioration of the nation-state as the primary political unit. It is no accident that European nation-states negotiated integration and the forms of its manifestation. During the same period of disenchantment with the nation-state, it is arguable that integration, in the form it has been realized, rescued the nation-state. Furthermore, integration, while also addressing clear and present strategic and economic needs, provided a framework for the rehabilitation of the nation-state as the primary guarantor of security, freedom, and prosperity.

Alan S. Milward, a widely acknowledged expert of European integration and various national archives, has postulated that the ECSC, EEC, and their successor institutions were negotiated by nation-states to serve nation-state objectives. Milward has further suggested that supranational components can be attributed principally to the need to address the German Question, for any other solution would not have gone far enough to prevent possible German domination.

The French strategy is a clear example of a regime transferring itself to a European plane to pursue objectives no longer attainable on a narrowly national basis. As Western Europe became more "America's Europe," France sought another medium through which to engage its neighbors and the world. To put it simply, France as a member of the EEC was greater than France without the organization. The EEC, however, was not greater than France, as French president Charles de Gaulle firmly demonstrated through his use of the national veto when it suited him.

Beyond speeches and preambles, it is difficult to find a clear thread connecting ideological discourse and the manifestations of European integration. What began as a solution to the German Question and a feature of U.S. Cold War foreign policy emerged as a forum for achieving national goals. States carefully negotiated integration to answer a myriad of immediate and long-term needs and aspirations and, in spite of the hopes of the federalists, negotiated integration in such a way as to enshrine the role of the nation-state as primary political agent. Time and again, and on various levels, it is clear that even as ideological discourse clearly influenced integration, it was neither decisive in shaping its outcomes, nor did it provide the original impulse. This model of member-state behavior within European integration will likely continue to shape the EU as it seeks to define its final form.

–SCOTT VARHO,
ARLINGTON, VIRGINIA

References

Howard Bliss, ed., *The Political Development of the European Community: A Documentary Collection* (Waltham, Mass.: Blaisdell, 1970).

Martin J. Dedman, *Origins and Development of the European Union 1945–95: A History of European Integration* (London & New York: Routledge, 1996).

David de Giustino, *A Reader in European Integration* (London & New York: Longman, 1996).

Peter Gowan and Perry Anderson, eds., *The Question of Europe* (London & New York: Verso, 1997).

Alan S. Milward, *The Reconstruction of Western Europe, 1945–51* (London: Methuen, 1984; Berkeley: University of California Press, 1984).

Derek W. Urwin, *The Community of Europe: A History of European Integration Since 1945* (London & New York: Longman, 1991).

EUROPEAN INTEGRATION

EUROPEAN SOCIALISM

Did European socialists abandon their Marxist roots to become a centrist political force?

Viewpoint: Yes. European socialists moved to the Center in the twentieth century largely because they decided to work for their major goals peacefully and democratically.

Viewpoint: No. European socialists became moderate but remained true to their Marxist principles.

Despite Karl Marx and Friedrich Engels's incendiary call to revolution in *The Communist Manifesto* (1848), most European socialists rejected the role of violence as "the midwife of history," to use Marx's expression. So-called revisionist socialists, including Eduard Bernstein and August Bebel in Germany, Jean Jaurès in France, and the leadership of the British Fabian Society (the intellectual predecessor of the Labour Party) instead advocated broad political and social change through elections, popular mandates, and existing democratic structures. Over the course of the century, the European socialist parties they led became relatively moderate political forces that legitimately attracted mass support and formed governments of the Center-Left.

This chapter asks whether twentieth-century socialists could achieve this moderation and yet remain true to their Marxist principles. To many scholars their rejection of revolution suggests that they could not. Moderate politics and working within the existing bourgeois system struck their objective students and communist critics alike as a compromise too great to maintain any real connection to Marxism. Yet to others, moderate socialists' abandonment of revolutionary violence did not change their fundamental devotion to social and economic change. Even if the methods were nonviolent in character, their effects generally remain inspired by Marx's original ideas and visions.

Viewpoint:
Yes. European socialists moved to the Center in the twentieth century largely because they decided to work for their major goals peacefully and democratically.

Given that one of the principles of Marxism is the violent overthrow of the existing bourgeois state and the establishment of a dictatorship of the proletariat, it is difficult to believe that European socialism could have simply become moderate and remained true to its Marxist principles at the same time. If European socialists had tried moderation, this approach would have meant changing their goal to a peaceful transformation of the existing system. This change would not have been that helpful; there still would have been considerable distrust of the Left among the more bourgeois liberal parties, theoretically making work within the system just as difficult. It was also difficult for a party dedicated to a peaceful overthrow of the state to organize foot soldiers for its needs. Therefore, even if European socialism did not move to the absolute Center in the twentieth century, it moved in the direction of the Center. Between 1900 and 1920, the socialist parties in many European states, especially Germany, split between a hardcore group of dedicated Marxists and moderates who accommodated the bourgeois system they had once opposed. What resulted were Social Democrat parties that traveled far from their Marxist origins. Many have remained at least slightly left of Center, while battling with the Center-Right parties within their respective states.

One of the best means to evaluate the decision to abandon Marxism is to consider how the remaining Marxists viewed their more moderate socialist brethren. In 1952 the communist German Democratic Republic (GDR, or East Germany) constructed a museum that would exhibit an elaborate version of German history. The main thread in the Museum for German History's standing exhibition was the people's struggle against oppression. It seemed, however, that the museum was frequently concerned with the Left's struggle against opportunism. Visitors could review extensive details of the fight against the so-called revisionists. The German Social Democratic Party, explicitly Marxist at the time of its founding in 1875, was one of the main enemies. According to the museum, in 1914 the Social Democratic Party betrayed the working people of Germany by supporting the German war effort. In 1918 Social Democratic treachery allegedly continued as the party sided with conservative forces against the more radical German leftists. Indeed, the museum portrayed the Social Democratic leadership as particularly vile for sending paramilitary troops against striking and rebellious German workers. The regime of the Social Democrat president, Friedrich Ebert, was presented as no better than the militarists that had governed the country before 1918; the Social Democrats had become just as oppressive as the monarchists who had once tried to eliminate socialism from the German Empire.

The Museum for German History showed viewers that two groups split from the Social Democratic Party at the end of World War I. The Independent Social Democratic Party was presented more favorably in the GDR. Its leadership was less willing to accommodate the German military and bureaucracy, and was more sympathetic to the demands of the workers. However, the Independent Socialists' efforts were insufficient; only one party fought on behalf of the people against their oppressors. The German Communist Party, formed by the more radical Social Democratic dissenters, assumed the people's struggle at its founding in December 1918. The museum presented them as leaders in the antifascist struggle that would con-

sume Germany through the rise of National Socialism and World War II. The communists were allegedly the first to recognize the dangers posed by Adolf Hitler. They advocated a unified popular front against fascism, eventually under the leadership of the Soviet Union. The Social Democratic leadership not only refused to support the communists' struggle but actively resisted it as well. According to the museum, the Social Democrats' myopia doomed the German people. Because they would not support a popular front with the communists, the Nazis gained power and led Germany into twelve years of suffering, war, and total destruction.

The museum's indictment of the Social Democrats did not end with World War II. After 1945 the same forces that had oppressed the people for centuries reappeared in the West. Whereas the German Social Democrats in the Russian zone combined with the German communists to form the Socialist Unity Party, those in the Western zones remained a separate party. The museum presented West German Social Democrats as part of the imperialist regime that would threaten the newly created GDR. Although the advent of Willy Brandt's *Ostpolitik* would moderate the GDR's presentation of West Germany, the East Germans would never completely forgive the Social Democrats. Through the 1980s, exhibitions in the Museum for German History always presented Social Democratic leadership as having betrayed the German people.

It would be difficult to dismiss the history in the Museum for German History as communist propaganda. The museum's exhibitions reflected the historical perspective of its leadership. Nonetheless, there was a direct connection between the museum's version of history and the historical outlook of the GDR. Moreover, the overall narrative in the East German presentation of history differed little from the perspectives throughout the Soviet bloc. Therefore, it is evident that the most dedicated communists in Central and Eastern Europe, at least when their countries were under Soviet domination, strongly disagreed with the decision of European socialists to move to the Center. Those who did betrayed the working class and were little different from the bourgeois enemies of the proletariat.

It is also evident that after 1945 socialist parties in Western Europe achieved power. For example, after holding power briefly in 1924 and gaining respect by working with the Conservatives in Depression and wartime national coalition governments, the British Labour Party won a mandate to form a new government in 1945. Although Labour never completely socialized the means of production in Britain, the party

GERMAN SOCIAL DEMOCRATIC PARTY

The loss of support suffered by the governing Social Democratic Party (SPD)-Greens coalition in their first year in office is unique in post-war German history. Disastrous losses in the European, state and local elections, and weeks of demonstrations in the new capital of Berlin by public service workers, pensioners, the unemployed and farmers, have shown the enormous degree to which the government has discredited itself in just a few months.

What are the causes of this? Is it a conjunctural development, or does it express a long-term tendency? Does the end of the twentieth century, dubbed by some the "social democratic century", also mean the end of social democracy?

Attempts to attribute the problem merely to the "outward appearance" of the government can hardly be taken seriously. Such assessments come from journalists, economic spokesmen and politicians who last year enthused about SPD Prime Minister Gerhard Schroeder's talk of a political "neue mitte" (new center), and were subsequently offended to find that the government won its victory mainly due to promises of social reform. Since then they have tirelessly denounced the government for not having broken its election promises quickly enough. They regard the voters as a stupefied, infinitely pliable mass and reduce every political question to a problem of public relations.

Those who say it is the disappointment of the voters, who had hoped for greater social justice from the new government, which is responsible for the decline of the SPD and Greens are closer to the truth. Since his resignation as SPD party chairman, Oskar Lafontaine has appointed himself the spokesman of such a view. He accuses his successor, Schroeder, of leading the party along the wrong path, and insists that Schroeder does not understand "how and why we won the federal elections". Lafontaine finds it hard to explain, however, why he supported Schroeder for so long and why his only reaction has been to resign his political posts.

The fact that Lafontaine has, nevertheless, raised a sore point is shown by a study of the Allensbach Institute, which is politically close to the Christian Democrats. It concludes that there can be no talk of "classical social democratic ideas being out of fashion in the population. A strong welfare state, a social network and ideals of equality are highly valued within the general population. . . . A relative majority is convinced that a country can develop better, not only when equality of opportunity is afforded, but when equality of outcome is also sought. The growing criticism of the government cannot be attributed to the fact that classical social democratic concepts have lost their attraction in the population."

In the end, Lafontaine's statements do not explain the deeper causes for the decline of the Social Democrats. He implies that a return to the SPD's election promises of last year, or to the policies of the government's first months in power, would resolve the crisis. He limits the problem to a defense of the SPD program, presenting himself as its guardian, while accusing Schroeder of defecting to the camp of neo-liberalism. For Lafontaine, the question of how far Schroeder himself is a product of the social democratic program does not

arise at all. If one considers the crisis of the SPD in the light of its history, it soon becomes clear how fallacious Lafontaine's conceptions are.

At the end of the last century the SPD was shaken by a controversy that proved to be decisive for its further development. It went down in history as the "revisionism debate". It concerned the question of whether the function of social democracy consisted (in the words of Rosa Luxemburg) of "the futile attempt to mend the capitalist order" or "a class struggle *against* this order, to abolish it".

Theoretically, the revisionists, who argued for a reconciliation with the existing social order, were in the minority. They were regularly outvoted at party congresses. But the practice of the party operated in their favor, and finally they won the upper hand.

The practice of the SPD moved inevitably within the framework of the existing order. The opportunity to overturn an obstacle in a stormy assault or conquer a hostile position never arose in Kaiser Wilhelm's empire. The Social Democrats limited themselves to extending the influence of the party by dogged, detailed work. This shaped the character, and, above all, the psychology of its rapidly growing body of functionaries.

When in 1914 the outbreak of the First World War suddenly confronted the SPD with the alternative of either defending its political principles and taking a stand against the war, or adapting to the pro-war euphoria, it decided for the latter—and voted in parliament to grant the Kaiser his war credits. The parliamentary group justified this with the words: "The culture and the independence of our own country must be guaranteed. In the hour of danger, we will not abandon the Fatherland."

The "culture" was at that time the Prussian military boot; "independence" meant a hatred of the French and a desire for colonial possessions; the "Fatherland" was Krupp, AEG and the Deutsche Bank.

Sobered by the war, millions of workers broke with the SPD in the following years and turned to the German Communist Party (KPD), which they expected to abolish the capitalist order. They were bitterly disillusioned when the KPD was sucked into the degeneration of the Soviet Union and then, under the increasing influence of Stalinism, pitifully failed in this task.

The SPD, for its part, did not desist from demanding the "defence of the Fatherland". From then on its face was shaped by a mixture of patriotism, trust in authority, and love of order, combined with an hysterical fear of any intervention from below by the masses. They reacted far more strongly to the accusation made by the conservative right that they had "stabbed" the German army in the back, than to the indignation of the hungry masses. They went so far as to form a pact with the *Reichswehr* (imperial army) and the reactionary *Freikorps* (volunteers) to defeat the revolutionary uprisings of the post-war period and, in 1919, murder the revolutionary leaders—Rosa Luxemburg and Karl Liebknecht. Their social base was composed of government officials, administrative staff and better-off workers, who identified with state and Fatherland, and regarded any danger to the existing order as a threat to themselves.

EUROPEAN SOCIALISM

The SPD responded to the rise of the Nazis by clinging even more strongly to the state. They supported Bruening's emergency decrees and the election of Hindenburg as *Reichspraesident,* who in turn appointed Hitler as chancellor. "A mass party, leading millions, holds that the question as to which class will come to power in present-day Germany, which is shaken to its very foundations, depends not on the fighting strength of the German proletariat, not on the shock troops of fascism, not even on the personnel of the Reichswehr, but on whether the pure spirit of the Weimar Constitution (along with the required quantity of camphor and naphthalene) shall be installed in the presidential palace," wrote Leon Trotsky, characterizing the attitude of the SPD.

The party discredited itself so badly that after the Second World War even the Allies considered its renewed ascent improbable. "Many German workers obviously blame the Social Democrats' policy of appeasement during the Weimar Republic for the ascent of the Nazis, and for this reason do not seem to welcome their return to power," an American government document noted in 1944.

However, the Allies had not counted on the obstinacy of the SPD, embodied particularly in the person of Kurt Schumacher, the party's first post-war chairman. An invalid whose health was broken by 10 years in the concentration camps, Schumacher sacrificed his life for the reconstruction of the party. A passionate patriot and anticommunist, Schumacher understood himself to be the guardian of German interests against the Allies. He contributed crucially to re-establishing the German state after the war, salvaging as much of the old *Reich* as possible. He prevented any rapprochement between the SPD and KPD, opposed shifting the Polish/German border west to the line formed by the rivers Oder and Neisse, and argued for a "strong, central state power".

The initial beneficiaries of his efforts were the conservatives, who provided the first three federal chancellors—Konrad Adenauer, Ludwig Erhard and Kurt Georg Kiesinger. Only in the 1960s was the SPD carried into government for the first time, on a wave of youth and working class protest. In 1966 they became junior partners in the "grand coalition" headed by the Christian Democratic Union/Christian Social Union. Then, in 1969, Willy Brandt became the first SPD chancellor in the "small coalition" government with the Free Democratic Party.

In the Brandt era the SPD came closest to realizing its espoused goal of a "social market economy", i.e., a reformist policy of placing certain constraints on the capitalist market in the interests of class peace and social consensus. Wages and social security benefits rose, government programs in the areas of education, social welfare and health were expanded. The rebellious youth found work in the public services and broader social layers gained access to the universities. But even in this period, concerns over state authority and order dominated the thinking of the SPD. This was shown in their support for emergency laws and the *Berufsverbot* decree, which banned the employment of "radicals" in the public service.

In retrospect, this period in many ways represented an exception. The improvement of the social position of the bottom social layers was attributable less to the initiatives of the SPD than to an international offensive of the working class, which even more conservative governments in other countries were unable to oppose. Moreover, this period corresponded to the end of a post-war boom, which had above all profited big business. Without directly endangering the functioning of the capitalist economy, there was a certain room for maneuver in the distribution of society's wealth.

With the onset of an international recession at the beginning of the seventies, the calls for an end to these policies grew ever louder, to which the SPD adapted itself. Brandt, who had proved unable to restrain the expectations which the broader electorate placed in him, was replaced by Helmut Schmidt as SPD leader and chancellor in 1975. Schmidt adopted a course of harsh austerity measures, driving up unemployment. This policy was continued by his successor, Christian Democratic leader Helmut Kohl, from 1982 onwards. The results today are over 4 million unemployed and the impoverishment of broad social layers, with the accumulation of scandalous levels of wealth at the pinnacle of society.

Under Oskar Lafontaine's chairmanship, the SPD was again able to channel the widely felt need for social justice to its own benefit, culminating in last year's election victory for the SPD. But from the beginning, expectations that the elections meant a return to the reformist politics of the early 70s were built on sand. The entire international framework has changed fundamentally since the Brandt era. Economic life is controlled by transnational corporations and financial establishments, which stamp political life with their mark.

Traditional social-democratic reformist politics are unable to oppose this concentrated power of capital. In order to stand up to this, it is necessary to mobilize the mass of the population against the prevailing structures of power and ownership. A party like the SPD, which for decades has defended bourgeois order, is neither able nor willing to undertake such a struggle.

The present crisis of the SPD expresses the fact that the course it took 85 years ago has reached its end. Lafontaine raises many justified criticisms against Schroeder, but his own conceptions lie completely within the bounds of traditional social democratic policy. What drives him, as he writes, is the fear that "radical parties may gain ground" if the social democratic governments of Europe do not provide an alternative policy to neo-liberalism.

For the working class, the decline of the SPD places on the agenda the construction of a new political party based upon the internationalist and socialist principles which the SPD abandoned nearly one hundred years ago.

Source: Peter Schwarz, "The Decline of the German Social Democratic Party," 12 November 1999, World Socialist website <http://www.wsws.org/articles/1999/nov1999/spd-n12.shtml>.

EUROPEAN SOCIALISM

translated its electoral gains into a wide range of reforms. The party's program, including its social welfare state, would influence British politics for the next three decades, facing its first serious challenge after the rise of Margaret Thatcher in 1979. Tony Blair would restore Labour's fortunes in the 1990s, creating a platform that would enable him to win at least two parliamentary elections, and work well with American presidents Bill Clinton and George W. Bush. The British Left may be currently in power, but they have moved far into the Center to capture and hold this power.

Although the German Social Democratic Party allegedly betrayed the proletariat, receiving the wrath of the East Germans in the process, they have been able to compete with the German Christian Democrats since 1945, and periodically hold power (in a coalition in 1966–1969 and by themselves in 1969–1982 and since 1998). The party's Bad Godesberg program of 1959 enabled it to move into the mainstream by explicitly renouncing Marxism and revolution and accepting market incentives and private ownership of the means of production. The party became even more acceptable after its participation in the "Grand Coalition" of 1966–1969. By cooperating with the Christian Democrats the party showed German voters it could govern at the national level, leading to electoral victory in 1969. The Social Democrats remained in the opposition until 1998, when Gerhard Schroeder led the party back to victory. Although Schroeder has had difficulty working with George W. Bush on international issues, he was close to Bill Clinton, and his party remains firmly in the center of German politics.

In 1981 François Mitterrand led the French Socialist Party to electoral victory in that year's presidential elections. His party had already moved to the Center in 1968; like the German Social Democrats, the French had renounced Marxism in favor of a more market-based approach to France's economic problems. The communists were part of socialist coalition governments from time to time, but moderate socialists were in control. Because of this situation there was no rush to socialize France's means of production. Legislation to nationalize certain industries passed, along with measures to increase the minimum wage, create more government jobs, and expand retirement benefits. In its earlier years, Mitterrand's France resembled its Social Democratic neighbors far more than it did any state in the Soviet bloc. France's capitalists may have preferred a Gaullist, but they were not living in a communist or really even a socialist society.

Although the move to the Center by Europe's socialists caused considerable criticism

from the Continent's remaining Marxists, the decision produced positive results. Socialist parties throughout Western Europe gained power. Since 1945 the fortunes of these various parties have varied. The governing British Labour and the German Social Democratic Parties are in good health, while France and Italy's socialists were weakened by scandal in the 1990s. Nevertheless, almost all of Europe's moderate socialist parties were able to gain and maintain power on their own through democratic means. It is difficult to believe that these parties would have remained successful if they had remained Marxist, especially during the Cold War. The end of the Cold War and the collapse of the Soviet Union have provided an opportunity to see if the more Marxist socialists can compete with their moderate cousins. Results from Germany have been mixed. The Party of Democratic Socialism (PDS), successor to the East German Socialist Unity Party, has competed in elections since 1990. PDS has had some success; it has sent delegates to the Bundestag and been the junior partner in various coalition governments in Germany's regional parliaments and in the Berlin city council since December 2001. However, the PDS has remained a regional party restricted mostly to the former GDR. The evidence since 1990 has shown that the moderate German Social Democrats have done much better against their more Marxist competitors, and that when German voters have chosen a Left-wing alternative to the Social Democrats, they have favored the environmentally oriented Green Party over the PDS.

–DAVID MARSHALL,
UNIVERSITY OF CALIFORNIA, RIVERSIDE

Viewpoint:
No. European socialists became moderate but remained true to their Marxist principles.

Although most European socialists have abandoned the revolutionary aspect of Karl Marx's ideology, many of his ideas, goals, and categories of analysis continue to resonate on the Continent's political Left. Especially in the years since the collapse of the Soviet Union (1991), the label *Marxist* has become somewhat taboo in mainstream Western society. Yet, the fact remains that many Western leftists, including centrist socialist and social democratic political parties, still have much common ground with important aspects of Marxist ideology; many tacitly

EUROPEAN SOCIALISM

acknowledge this situation by describing themselves as "post-Marxist" or "neo-Marxist."

The most essential commonality is the Western Left's continuing belief in the primacy of the state. Few leftists advocate armed revolution or government by Marx's "dictatorship of the proletariat," but the fundamentally Marxist notion that the state is the best and most rational organ to govern economies and societies lives on. Western socialists did not act on this dictum with the immediacy and thoroughness of communists and unabashed Marxists in other places, but over the course of the twentieth century their tenure in power, almost always resting on democratic foundations, resulted in the vast expansion of state authority. The mixed economies of Western Europe have placed a substantial number of industries under government control, to the point where the state-administered portion of the economy approaches 40 to 50 percent of the Gross Domestic Product. Usually this reach includes vital economic sectors, such as transportation, communications, power, health care, education, banking, and, in some cases, heavy manufacturing—sectors with which virtually all private businesses and individuals must interact and upon which almost all depend. Political opposition has largely prevented the further expansion of government roles in European economies, but many mainstream socialist parties and political figures have nevertheless favored such expansion. In the late 1940s Brit-

ain's Labour government nationalized not just the "commanding heights" of the economy, but also mining, trucking, steel production, and other more ordinary industries. Although the Labour Party had not been founded on Marxist principles, its expansion of state economic authority moved them sharply toward their goal of eliminating "exploitative" private management in industries where it was thought to be at its worst. The subsequent Conservative government reversed many of these nationalizations, while later Labour governments lacked the strength and ambition to restore them. In 1984 France's socialist government nearly implemented a measure that would have eliminated private schools, most of which were operated by the Catholic Church. In addition to completing the state's monopoly on education, the measure would have diminished the influence of organized religion and eliminated the supposed social inequalities that were alleged to accompany private education—both long-standing Marxist goals. Only the largest protest demonstration in French history stopped the measure in its tracks. Domestic critics and some leftist foreign analysts of post-Soviet Russia's economy have advocated the renationalization of recently privatized industrial and natural resource assets. The reasons are not because the critics believe state management would be better (indeed, most observers agree that it would be worse), but because they share the Marxist belief that remov-

French Socialist Party secretary François Mitterrand standing on the Mount of Olives, Israel, October 1976

(Richard Melloul/CORBIS SYGMA)

EUROPEAN SOCIALISM

ing those assets from private hands will somehow ameliorate rising social inequality and ensure a "fairer" distribution of wealth.

In the realm of social and cultural life, moderate socialists have by no means abandoned the Marxist goal of creating a "classless" society. Indeed, their persistence in using raw economic data (for example, salaries, net worth, and real estate values) to categorize people and evaluate their attitudes and motivations is a direct inheritance from Marx. So, too, is their unceasing defense of progressive taxes on income and inheritance—two of Marx's major social as well as economic goals—which levy proportionally heavier burdens on increasing sums. Top marginal tax rates in Western Europe reached as high as 70 percent of a person's income and inheritance before recent reductions across the region. The rationale for these mammoth taxes was and is not simply generating revenue, but a deliberate attempt to equalize the net income and worth of all citizens and families. The revenue itself pays, at least theoretically, for Europe's vast social welfare states—another Marxist dream—in which the government plays the principal role in subsidizing education, health care, payments to the poor and unemployed, and other social services. To the moderate socialist mind, just as to the minds of the most doctrinaire Marxists, these goals, despite being far from realized and facing serious challenges in execution, outweigh the corresponding discouragement of initiative and encouragement of rising tax evasion and emigration.

The limitations of the more traditional Marxist approach have not discouraged moderate socialists from attempting to create classless societies, but have instead led them to other more creative and sometimes bizarre means to that end. After the Austrian Republic was created in 1918, its moderate socialist leaders outlawed and subsequently punished the use of aristocratic titles and the noble *von* particle in family names, taking a cue from Russia's Bolshevik government, which had abolished titles of nobility in December 1917. In both cases the ruling Marxist party could not abide enduring social distinctions, no matter how symbolic titles had become in democratic states and even under those countries' prerevolutionary regimes. In the 1980s socialist French president François Mitterrand's government sponsored the construction of the drab Opéra Bastille, Paris's new principal theater for opera and ballet, with the "socially conscious" yet incredibly condescending purpose of building a simple, utilitarian structure where France's lower classes were expected to feel "less out of place" than in the opulent settings of a more traditional opera house. The audience of the ugly theater remains one of the most elite in the world, and the overwhelming majority of Frenchmen have never attended a performance there, but it was born in an attempt to democratize high culture in a way of which Marx would probably not have disapproved. In Britain the governing Labour Party recently attempted to democratize the country's historic honors system, first by removing hereditary peers from the House of Lords and then by opening the distribution of honors, including life peerages (which still carry the right to sit in the Lords), to popular nomination. An earlier Labour government created a precedent of no longer awarding hereditary peerages, which has been kept with just three exceptions since 1965. The cumulative effect of these measures was to diminish visible social hierarchies and reduce the perception of exclusivity that surrounded those who enjoyed government recognition, both steps toward the social homogenization long advocated by Marxists. Finland's socialist government assesses fines for traffic violations according to the perpetrator's income: in February 2004 one business executive was fined the equivalent of more than $200,000 for speeding. It is hard to doubt that redistributing wealth is one of the main reasons for this law, in which fines are extracted from each according to his means.

In the years after World War II, finally, moderate socialists ceased to fear open political cooperation with communist parties. Doing so before the war had been a virtual impossibility in most countries, for socialists and communists, despite the ultimate similarity of their goals, remained divided on political tactics and the use of violence. The one major case of such cooperation, in Spain in 1936–1939, precipitated a bloody civil war and drew forth the now largely substantiated accusation that the communists were using their partnership with the socialists to sabotage the Spanish Republic to their own advantage. Yet, after 1945 the old mantra of "no enemies on the Left" returned in force, and West European communists and socialists often agreed to cooperate to advance their complementary visions of a progressive society. In France socialists willingly accepted communists as junior partners in coalition governments immediately after World War II and again in the early 1980s and late 1990s. Italian communists frequently cooperated with their country's powerful Center-Left socialist movement. West German Social Democrats, forming their first national government in 1969, were eager to promote good relations with the communist regime in East Germany, despite having officially shed Marxism as their party's theoretical basis ten years earlier. After national reunification in 1990, local governments dominated by moderate socialists had no problem maintaining many of the symbolic monuments and street names created and assigned by the East German communists. These include a prominent socialist realist monument to no less important figures than Marx and Friedrich Engels themselves in the center of Berlin, a city that despite its brutal Cold War partition came to be ruled in December 2001 by a coalition of Social Democrats and members of the successor to the former East Germany's ruling Socialist Unity Party. The enduring Marxist roots of moderate European socialism are there to be seen.

–PAUL DU QUENOY,
GEORGETOWN UNIVERSITY

References

Peter Hitchens, *The Abolition of Britain: From Winston Churchill to Princess Diana* (San Francisco: Encounter, 2000).

Kate Hudson, *European Communism since 1989: Towards a New European Left?* (New York: St. Martin's Press, 2000).

Albert S. Lindemann, *A History of European Socialism* (New Haven: Yale University Press, 1983).

David E. Marshall, "*Das Museum für Deutsche Geschichte:* A Study of the Presentation of History in the Former German Democratic Republic," dissertation, University of California, Riverside, 2002.

Gerassimos Moschonas, *In the Name of Social Democracy: The Great Transformation, 1945 to the Present* (London & New York: Verso, 2002).

Lawrence Wilde, *Modern European Socialism* (Aldershot, Hants, U.K., & Brookfield, Vt.: Dartmouth, 1994).

EUROPEAN SOCIALISM

EXISTENTIALISM

Was existentialism the expression of a generally held sense of displacement due to the chaotic conditions of twentieth-century European life?

Viewpoint: Yes. The sense of meaninglessness and alienation that influenced mid-twentieth-century philosophers derived from a common reaction to the horrors and disappointments of total war, hypocrisy, and social divisions.

Viewpoint: No. Existentialist philosophy was produced by intellectual malcontents who were self-absorbed, were alienated from their societies, and could find no rational purpose in their own lives.

Existentialism was one of the main philosophical schools of the twentieth century. Encompassing literature, drama, politics, and social thought in addition to philosophy, existentialists argued that human life and experience acquire meaning and definition only through one's own free choice of actions and moral imperatives. "Existence," their quintessential dictum held, "precedes essence." Drawing from the works of the philosophers Soren Kierkegaard, Friedrich Nietzsche, and several other important nineteenth-century cultural figures, twentieth-century existentialists emphasized the perceived meaningless of life and the sole power of one's consciousness to overcome that meaninglessness. Belief in absolute truth, objective conceptions of beauty, guiding principles in the universe, and the presence of a Supreme Being had no place in their worldview.

Some students of the existentialist movement have argued that it arose from the chaotic conditions of twentieth-century European life. Earlier thought had been influential, but the tremendous disasters and losses of the two world wars and related traumas appeared to prove the existentialist point. Mass violence, destruction on an industrial scale, the randomness of millions of individual fates, and other ugly faces of modernity added authority to the tenets of the philosophy. Detractors of the philosophy have argued, however, that this authority was fleeting. Existentialist writers and philosophers were, on closer inspection, malcontented individuals who were dissatisfied with the structures and values of their societies, especially as they entered a period of major change. To proponents of this argument, existentialists seem more isolated from the world around them, caught in a futile attempt to rationalize their own shortcomings by denying the meaning of anything other than their own self-absorption.

**Viewpoint:
Yes. The sense of meaninglessness
and alienation that influenced
mid-twentieth-century philosophers
derived from a common reaction
to the horrors and disappointments
of total war, hypocrisy, and social
divisions.**

France at the end of World War II suffered less from physical desolation than moral ruin. Its armies had been defeated in a few weeks, and its leaders collaborated with the enemy. Nearly everyone else had made personal, private terms with the German occupation in order to stay at work, feed his family, and avoid the growing fear of the knock on the door that heralded one's disappearance into the concentration-camp world of "night and fog." An exception to this pattern of fear and compliance was the underground, a loose network of Resistance fighters and their supporters that grew to sizable strength as the occupation ground on. Among the leading symbols for those men and women was Jean-Paul Sartre, the founder of French existentialism.

Existentialism was born in the nineteenth century in the philosophies of Soren Kierkegaard and Friedrich Nietzsche. The former found God; the latter envisaged man as God. Twentieth-century existentialism, best represented in Germany by Martin Heidegger, who paused in his philosophical career to make the choice to become a Nazi, found its focus in France. Critics dismissed it as a set of attitudes that legitimated the alienation natural to young adults. Existentialism as a philosophy, presented by its two most influential spokesmen, Sartre and Albert Camus, centered around the proposition that there was no essential human nature. Instead, our nature develops over the history of our existence.

This postulate developed along several related lines. Atheistic existentialism, as presented by Sartre, was the most logical and the most coherent. It stated that if God does not exist, there is at least one being in whom existence precedes essence, who exists before he can be defined by any concept. This being is man, who defines himself by the process of action. If man, as the existentialist conceives him, is indefinable, it is because at first he is nothing. Only afterward will he be something, and he himself will have made what he will be. Thus, there is no human nature, since there is no God to conceive it. Not only is man what he conceives himself to be, he is also only what he wills himself to be after this thrust toward essence.

It is difficult for people today to place themselves in the minds of Europeans in the years immediately after 1945. Germany was physically destroyed and divided between East and West. The country was defeated militarily and politically and suffered humiliation, shame, and guilt. Within months rebuilding began—at least in the Western zones. Yet, as the Germans climbed over the piles of bricks that had once been the cities of their pride, they had little time for philosophical musings. In Britain, deprivations continued as well, with rationing and other wartime regulations remaining well into the 1950s.

The French for their part embarked on a wave of denunciations and recriminations over who collaborated with the Germans. In attempting to purge their collective soul, they found there was no exit for their angst. Into this fertile ground stepped Sartre, a prolific writer of plays and novels, a spokesman for a philosophy that offered not an explanation for the horrors and ambiguities of the occupation years, but rather a view of the world that could place a perspective on events.

Sartre found himself the literary and intellectual lion of his age. He dominated literature and theater for at least twenty years, in a country that prizes literary and intellectual prowess and sets correspondingly demanding standards. He became a leading member of the ultimate establishment club—the French Academy. He became rich while the rest of the country was struggling in poverty. Not only was he the idol of the literati, but as a self-proclaimed communist, he also became a hero of labor.

Sartre earned his laurels, including a Nobel Prize in literature in 1964, which he refused as being too bourgeois, by developing existentialism as a way to isolate the individual from the world, and at the same time asserting a concept of self-responsibility that separates the individual from social responsibility. Since the individual man does not have commonality with the rest of humanity, the best one could do was seek freedom from the corrosive influences of society and concentrate on the creation of one's own nature. Neither God nor reason existed as guides to behavior. Instead, the freedom existentialism offered, and the necessity for choice it imposed, would combine first to carry man beyond the despair of meaninglessness, and then to nurture an engagement that would bring about the radical transformation of bourgeois society. It was this political dimension that distinguished French existentialism from its German counterpart—and which made it attractive in Europe, and in the West, seeking to escape the apparent dead end of collectivism.

THE NIGHT OF TRUTH

During World War II, the French philosopher Albert Camus served with the Resistance and edited the Parisian daily Combat. *After the war he became a leading exponent of disillusionment, nihilism, and morality. The following is an article that he wrote celebrating the liberation of Paris.*

While the bullets of freedom are still whistling throughout the city, the cannons of the liberation are entering the gates of Paris amid shouts and flowers. In the most beautiful and hottest of August nights, the eternal stars over Paris mingle with the tracer bullets, the smoke of fires, and the colored rockets of a mass celebration. This unparalleled night marks the end of four years of monstrous history and of an unspeakable struggle in which France came to grips with her shame and her wrath.

Those who never despaired of themselves or of their country find their reward under this sky. This night is worth a world; it is the night of truth. Truth under arms and in the fray, truth sustained by force after having so long been empty-handed and unprotected. It is everywhere this night when people and cannons are booming simultaneously. It is the very voice of the people and the cannons; it wears the exhausted face of the street fighters, triumphal under their scars and sweat. Yes, it is indeed the night of truth, of the only truth that matters, the truth that is willing to fight and conquer.

Four years ago men rose up amid ruins and despair and calmly declared that nothing was lost. They said we had to carry on and that the forces of good could always overcome the forces of evil if we were willing to pay the price. They paid the price. And, to be sure, that price was heavy; it had all the weight of blood and the dreadful heaviness of prisons. Many of these men are dead, whereas others have been living for years surrounded by windowless walls. That was

the price that had to be paid. But those same men, if they could, would not blame us for this terrible and marvelous joy that sweeps us off our feet like a high tide.

For our joy has not broken faith with them. On the contrary, it justifies them and declares that they were right. United in the same suffering for four years, we still are united in the same intoxication; we have won our solidarity. And we are suddenly astonished to see during this dazzling night that for four years we have never been alone. We have lived the years of fraternity.

Harsh combats still await us. But peace will return to this torn earth and to hearts tortured by hopes and memories. One cannot always live on murders and violence. Happiness and proper affection will have their time. But that peace will not find us forgetful. And for some among us, the faces of our brothers disfigured by bullets, the great virile brotherhood of recent years will never forsake us. May our dead comrades enjoy by themselves the peace that is promised us during this panting night, for they have already won it. Our fight will be theirs.

Nothing is given to men, and the little they can conquer is paid for with unjust deaths. But man's greatness lies elsewhere. It lies in his decision to be stronger than his condition. And if his condition is unjust, he has only one way of overcoming it, which is to be just himself. Our truth of this evening, which hovers overhead in this August sky, is just what consoles man. And our hearts are at peace, just as the hearts of our dead comrades are at peace, because we can say as victory returns, without any spirit of revenge or of spite: "We did what was necessary."

Source: *Combat, Paris, 25 August 1944.*

In that sense Sartre's communism was an anomaly, and in fact he broke with the Party relatively early, in the aftermath of the Hungarian Revolution in 1956. That he continued to identify with communist ideas and causes reflected his abiding hatred for the values and policies represented by a United States he regarded as the final, overripe embodiment of capitalism, militarism, and every other obstacle to the realization of the future. It was not an intellectual process, but its appeal was strong to a genera-

tion of European youth who perceived themselves facing the rubble of two millennia of history, with only their hands to clean it up and only their minds to make sense of the catastrophe.

Eventually, existentialism would be undone by its own abstract nature. In the early postwar years Camus warned *what* one chose was as important as *that* one chose. This apparent indirect acceptance of values external to the individual was initially uncongenial to the majority of those who identified with existentialism. What happened in consequence, however, was a growing indifference to the facts of any real-world issue. What was important was the position one was expected to take: a position of protest, a position outside the bourgeois frameworks that structured inauthenticity. The eventual result was existentialism's devolution to a movement that was more about style than substance—and a search for choices in new contexts that included pure aestheticism, Third World Romanticism, and a fresh paradigm known as poststructuralism.

-JOHN WHEATLEY,
BROOKLYN CENTER, MINNESOTA

Viewpoint:
No. Existentialist philosophy was produced by intellectual malcontents who were self-absorbed, were alienated from their societies, and could find no rational purpose in their own lives.

The familiar aphorism of the 1970s, "the personal is political," had its roots in an existentialist movement whose influence reflected the emergence before World War II of a generation of intellectual malcontents who sought to universalize the meaninglessness of lives rendered empty by inaction in the face of the century's greatest challenge: totalitarianism. Existentialism thrived on dismissing the world as absurd, and on presenting consciousness as adrift in chaos. It was popularly identified with the experience of the French Resistance: in a time when whirl was king and established ideals proved hollow, true humanity depended upon making personal choices and living—or dying—by them, preferably with a certain je ne sais quoi flair. In that context resisting the Nazis was not a matter of affirming France; it was not even a matter of affirming right and justice. Resistance, according to this aspect of the existentialist myth, was an affirmation of self, from which in turn it became possible to restructure the universe.

The Cartesian roots of the Resistance imagery were reinforced by extensive borrowings from Friedrich Nietzsche, in particular his insistence on the importance of ego-based action even after one perceived the artificial nature of external values and the absolute indifference of the universe. Existentialism's German roots went even deeper. In the years after World War I a young Lutheran intellectual, Karl Barth, drew on the work of Danish philosopher Soren

Kierkegaard in developing a theology that denied divine support for secular progress. In the late 1920s Martin Heidegger and Karl Jaspers each built on Georg Hegel's *Phenomenology of Spirit* (1807) and its description of consciousness becoming self-aware in the context of imposing intellectual order on what is otherwise a formless mass, to assert the centrality of the integrated human spirit in an identity otherwise characterized by anxiety. To understand this centrality, moreover, was to act on it. Heidegger in particular emphasized the difference between "unauthentic," that is, unaware and uncritical participation, and the "authentic" existence based on constant self-analysis. At the least, however, passivity represented denial of existence. Johann Faust's cri de coeur, "*am Anfang war die Tat*" (in the beginning was the deed), was also the beginning of awareness.

Early German existentialism was basically an elitist response to the politics and culture of a mass age, and as such tended to isolate the self-defined and self-realized individual. Also, particularly in Heidegger's version, best presented in *Being and Time* (1927), the *fact* of action was privileged over the *nature* of action. Thus, Heidegger, confronted with the rise of National Socialism, wound up as a registered party member, rector of the University of Freiburg, and a spokesman for Hitler's New Order. Jaspers, after briefly considering the prospects of using National Socialism as an instrument of academic reform, sought to establish the university as a self-governing center of elite thought, free of second-rate minds and exempt by virtue of its institutional self-awareness from the *Gleichschaltung* (coordination) imposed on the Reich's other subaltern institutions.

Jaspers never fell under Nazism's spell; Heidegger's overt enthusiasm lasted a matter of months. It did not matter. Rather than being incorporated into the system, they and their followers were rapidly shifted out by a regime despising abstract intellectual activity in any form and specifically scorning the lofty detachment of the existentialists as parasitic. After the war both Jaspers and Heidegger developed substantial national and international reputations. Underlying—and to a degree undermining—them, however, was the question of whether the existentialists' critique of objectivity and their privileging of choice had fostered the Germans' acceptance of the vitalist ideology of National Socialism.

Arguably more to the point, critics argued, the German existentialists' definition of action as a thing in itself, not requiring any particular this-world behavior, had merely cloaked their use of relatively influential and privileged positions as backdrops for personally defined virtue. The

HISTORY IN DISPUTE, VOLUME 17: TWENTIETH-CENTURY EUROPEAN SOCIAL AND POLITICAL MOVEMENTS, SECOND SERIES   **77**

EXISTENTIALISM

French philosopher Jean-Paul Sartre in Luxor, 1967

(Bettmann/CORBIS)

were otherwise occupied. He nevertheless became a French household word, as opposed to a Parisian aphorism, after the liberation, when a wartime generation of intellectuals sought to catch up on developments since June 1940. His major philosophical text, *Being and Nothingness* (1943), was popularized by a successful play, *No Exit*. First presented in May 1944, it invited parsing in terms of a German occupation, addressed with the insouciant cleverness in the face of doom that the French wished they were offering in real life.

Collective wish became collective myth in a postwar France, where attitude took the place of faith on both Left and Right. Even for active Resistance members, the occasions for facing ultimate questions and abiding by single decisions had in fact been few and far between. For Voltaire's "moderately sensual men"—and women—the war and the occupation had been a study in shades of gray. However, not until Marcel Ophuls released his scathing motion picture *The Sorrow and the Pity* in 1969 would France have to confront its banality. Meantime, it was flattering to remember in terms of knife-edge choices made with panache, and Sartre rode the process to the top. Existentialism became international shorthand for a view of life as without any meaning except that created by action undertaken in a climate of desperation. Only when standing alone, stripped of excuses and supports, could a human being recognize that he had no nature, no identity except the one he created by the deed. Heidegger's denunciation of humanism and its implied extension of man's power over nature only encouraged an inward focus that amounted to solipsism.

Whether authenticity was its own reward or whether, as Jaspers argued, certain existential situations could offer an intimation of transcendence, the central principle was choice. Existentialism, however, continued to eschew assisting its disciples in the matter of what to choose. That fact was highlighted in the ongoing debate between Sartre, whose espousal of communism arguably reflected sheer contrariness, and Albert Camus. Unlike Sartre, Camus had actual experience in the Resistance, and a corresponding conviction that what one did mattered as much as the doing itself. Camus's key contribution to existentialist doctrine—at times it seems appropriate to use religious rather than philosophical terminology—was his insistence that choice and commitment must be limited by respect for others. Yet, in an imperfect world, particularly the world produced by World War II, it seemed the best that could be done in that respect was to apply the principle of double effect: will and work to minimize the harm that seemed inevitably done by real-world choices.

decisions they made proved in the event irrelevant even for the immediate participants—and set no public example of virtue in its original sense, in a time when such example was badly needed. Heidegger's response was his postwar "Letter on Humanism," with its sweeping denunciation of that concept as no more than a euphemism for the materialistic exploitation of nature. Reaffirming the existentialist's role as a "shepherd of Being," it guided German existentialism ever deeper into what the Romantic poet Heinrich Heine called the airy empire of dreams.

The ideas of Jaspers and Heidegger were, however, by no means confined to Germany. Well before the war Jean-Paul Sartre had begun developing his own version of a philosophy of action, where deeds and not words or ideas determined character. The German occupation chafed a temperament that was already anarchic and impatient of external restriction. Yet, in a direct inversion of what might be expected, Sartre's Resistance was a thing of mind, spirit, and rhetoric alone. The risks and rewards of the warrior in darkness were not for him, nor were the risks of writing to defend Jews summoned for deportation, or to remind waverers that there would be an eventual reckoning. Sartre's own career flourished—not least because better men

For the existentialist, that was thin gruel indeed. As a consequence, existentialism in the 1960s increasingly evolved toward a set of individualized attitudes that left a corresponding philosophical vacuum to be filled by poststructuralists who found surprisingly little intellectual resistance to their ideas.

–DENNIS SHOWALTER,
COLORADO COLLEGE

References

William Barrett, *Irrational Man: A Study in Existential Philosophy* (Garden City, N.Y.: Doubleday, 1958).

Tony Judt, *The Burden of Responsibility: Blum, Camus, Aron, and the French Twentieth Century* (Chicago: University of Chicago Press, 1998).

Judt, *Past Imperfect: French Intellectuals, 1944–1956* (Berkeley: University of California Press, 1992).

Robert C. Solomon, *From Rationalism to Existentialism: The Existentialists and Their Nineteenth-Century Backgrounds* (Atlantic Highlands, N.J.: Humanities, 1978).

Robert Wicks, *Modern French Philosophy: From Existentialism and Postmodernism* (Oxford: Oneworld, 2003).

Richard Wolin, *The Politics of Being: The Political Thought of Martin Heidegger* (New York: Columbia University Press, 1990).

EXISTENTIALISM

THE FAR RIGHT AFTER 1945

Are the various post–World War II extreme Right-wing political organizations the descendants of fascism?

Viewpoint: Yes. Movements such as Jean-Marie Le Pen's National Front and Jörg Haider's Freedom Party have perpetuated the tenets of European fascism.

Viewpoint: No. The post-1945 extreme Right arose from grassroots concerns about local problems and in response to new issues such as immigration and European integration.

The leader of France's far-Right National Front, Jean-Marie Le Pen, was persecuted for a 1987 remark in which he trivialized the Holocaust as "a mere detail" of history. Fifteen years later he placed second in the French presidential election. In 2000 Jörg Haider's controversial far-Right Freedom Party entered a coalition government in Austria after a resounding victory at the polls, despite its leader's earlier praise for aspects of Nazi Germany. The following year Italy's center-Right Christian Democrats formed a governing coalition with the far-Right National Alliance Party, even though its leader, Gianfranco Fini, thought Benito Mussolini was the best politician of the twentieth century.

Many critics and observers have wondered how closely related Europe's new far Right is to its fascist tradition, widely believed to have been discredited after the defeat of Nazi Germany and fascist Italy in World War II. To some, the policies, platforms, positions, and statements of the new far-Right are undeniably fascist, rooted in the national chauvinism, xenophobia, anti-Semitism, extreme traditionalism, and discretely Left-wing social policies advanced by Mussolini, German leader Adolf Hitler, and other fascists of two generations ago. To others the new far Right is only a marginal phenomenon that draws most of its success from "protest voters" who feel disenchanted with the current system and cast ballots as a function of their personal and local concerns.

Viewpoint:
Yes. Movements such as Jean-Marie Le Pen's National Front and Jörg Haider's Freedom Party have perpetuated the tenets of European fascism.

Fascism is a broad concept and is subject to many definitions and interpretations, but several modern European political movements perpetuate at least some of its tenets and can trace their ideological ancestry to undeniably fascist political parties and figures. Whether they use or accept the fascist label—and most do not because of the dubious history and connotations of the term—these strains of European political thought derive in a more or less straight line from the fascist movements of the second quarter of the twentieth century.

Although fascism is commonly identified with the extreme Right of the political spectrum, one of its more singular characteristics was its claim to transcend traditional political divisions between Right and Left and to bridge fractures among social classes, as they were perceived in the Marxist sense. The formal name of the Nazi Party, the National Socialist German Workers' Party, for example, combined the nomenclature of both the Right (*National*) and the Left (*Socialist* and *Workers'*). Part of the reason for this oddity was that its leaders wanted to appeal broadly to many segments of German society in order to win support, but it also underlined their emphasis on forging a unified "national community" under their leadership. The same idea was espoused by Italian and French fascists, many of whom were former socialists who wanted to use the power of the state to create a uniform society free from social conflict. Employing a largely artificial and arbitrary definition of *nation*, based on supposed ethnic and historical continuities and usually defined by the exclusion and ostracism of an "other" (meaning a nonmember of the "nation"), was their means to this goal.

This idea continues in what is commonly called the *far Right* in modern European politics and is an especially present factor in countries that had a substantial fascist past. France's National Front and its leader Jean-Marie Le Pen have often used the slogan "Neither Right Nor Left, But France" to describe their ideology, which is both strongly nationalist and bitterly antiestablishment. Its strongest expression is a xenophobic concept of citizenship and national belonging directed at the exclusion of outsiders, who are regarded as disruptive or burdensome in their relation to French culture and identity. Its most public target is the large and mainly non-integrated Muslim population, but it also includes Jews, non-Muslim Asians, the forces of European integration, American popular culture, and political figures and institutions that support or tolerate their assimilation. Not coincidentally, these same groups and phenomena were the chief targets of French fascists in the 1920s and 1930s. Both have favored exclusionary policies in the interests of "protecting the national community," and both have articulated them publicly with provocative statements, threatening behavior, and an undisguised and even flaunted contempt for the prevailing political order. Strikingly, the National Front's xenophobic nationalism has also been paired with support for a strong welfare state, subsidies for the underprivileged (at least the native French underprivileged), and generally broad government involvement in the economy—positions normally identified with the Left and with the socialist ideology that, though few modern leftists care to admit it, was shared by fascism's earli-

est proponents. Although the earlier generation of French fascists never managed to win national political power, the National Front has enjoyed relatively more success. In the first round of France's 2002 presidential elections, Le Pen placed second, capturing nearly one out of every five votes cast and displacing the sitting center-left prime minister, Lionel Jospin, on the final second-round ballot.

Italy, which had a fascist government under Benito Mussolini from 1922 to 1943 (and until 1945 in the German-occupied northern regions), is another notable case of persisting fascism. Its National Alliance Party is in fact the direct organizational descendent of Mussolini's Italian Fascist Party, which mutated into the Italian Social Party after World War II and then into the modern National Alliance. Although its rhetoric is less strident than that of its predecessors, much of the contemporary party's ideology, especially its approach to economics, immigration, and crime, has come down in a more or less straight line from the 1920s. In 1994 National Alliance leader Gianfranco Fini called Mussolini "the greatest politician of the century." In recent years the deposed and executed dictator's image has been making a discrete recovery among Italians who are nostalgic for what they believe to have been his regime's ability to ensure law and order and "make the trains run on time." The National Alliance has benefited at the polls. In 2001 it entered government for the first time, forming a coalition with Italy's center-right Christian Democrats. Although Fini, who became deputy prime minister, subsequently distanced himself and the party from his and its rather undisguised fascist origins, the connections and continuities are there for the world to see and wonder about. In a particularly idiosyncratic expression of the party's ancestry, Mussolini's granddaughter Alessandra sat as one of its members of parliament from 1992 to 2003.

While Germany's Nazi past was so horrible and traumatizing that fascist politics could not be revived on any great scale there, it does have some far-Right groups that have perpetrated violent attacks on immigrants—especially in economically depressed areas of the former East Germany—and self-consciously aspire to imitate Nazi rhetoric and symbolism. The far-Right National Republican Party has largely avoided direct associations with Nazism, and stringent laws against publicly praising or advocating Nazism, fascism, and racism have kept potential revivals in check, confining them mostly to its underground "skinhead" subculture. Neighboring Austria, which had its own Nazi Party before its absorption by Germany in 1938 and was an integral part of Nazi Germany until 1945, offers more evidence of persisting fascism, however.

HOW SEVERE A THREAT IS HAIDER?

In a 2000 sermon Rabbi Emeritus Samuel H. Stahl, who serves the Temple Beth-El in San Antonio, Texas, commented on the rise of Jörg Haider in Austria:

In recent weeks, I have been encouraged by the moral outrage of many countries at bringing the ultra-right wing Freedom Party, led by Jorg Haider, into the new government coalition of Austria.

Almost immediately after the Austrian elections the nations of the 15-member European Union swiftly imposed severe sanctions on Austria. They have courageously insisted that any country violating the principles of liberty, democracy, and respect for human rights must be excluded from their association. In fact, they may soon expel Austria from the Union.

Other countries also have reacted decisively. Israel withdrew its ambassador to Vienna. United States called home its ambassador for consultations. Huge masses of protestors assembled on Vienna streets to voice their abhorrence at this disturbing turn of national events.

Jorg Haider ran on a frightening platform. He expressed his admiration for Hitler and the Nazi party. He not only praised it for its orderly employment policies, he also lauded members of the Waffen SS. Haider fulminated against immigration with warnings of "over-foreignization," a term used by the Nazis. He told potential voters that the hordes of Eastern European and Third World refugees were threatening the economy and the ethnic composition of Austria. In short, Haider effectively played on the fears and insecurities of the Austrian people. As a result, his radical Freedom Party received 27% of the vote. It was the second largest number of votes in this recent election.

But we must ask ourselves: How severe a threat is Haider? Haider himself is not necessarily a racist nor an anti-Semite. He is basically a slick and conniving political opportunist. He will spout whatever lines are necessary to win an election.

He expends excessive energy on cultivating his public image. As a child, he grew up as an overweight son of a poor cobbler in Austria. However, by his 20's, he became fascinated by both politics and fashion. He now drives a bright blue Porsche, sports a tan the year around, and owns a wardrobe with an endless supply of designer suits.

He tailors his accents to the particular constituency that he is addressing. When he is speaking to the masses, he uses a lower class dialect. However, his speech becomes considerably more polished and cosmopolitan when he is with the middle class.

Haider is such an opportunist that, earlier this week, he resigned as a member of the present government. He explained that he wanted [to] ease the pressure that the opponents of the new coalition have brought upon the government. This is pure bunk!

Political pundits believe that the real reason that he resigned is that he wants to distance himself from the unpopular tax increases that the present government is planning. These tax boosts could be an impediment to his ultimate desire to become the Chancellor of Austria.

We have even more evidence of his ambitious nature. The day after the election, having run on a racist ticket, he joined his coalition partners in signing an anti-racist declaration. In it, they affirmed that "Austria accepts a responsibility arising out of the tragic history of the 20th century and the horrendous crimes of the National Socialist regime. Our country is facing up to the light and dark sides of its past and to the deeds of all Austrians, good and evil, as its responsibility."

Haider's signing this document was a gross act of hypocrisy. In fact, the statement itself is a blatant lie. The fact is that Austria still has not overcome its sordid, blemished history. Its traditional antipathy toward Jews has been like a cancerous growth for the past 100 years.

Occasionally, the cancer goes into remission, but more often it spreads its poisons throughout the nation. Austria has always been rife with anti-Semitism. In the early 1900's Karl Lueger, the rabid anti-Semite, served as the popular mayor of Vienna. Austria was also the birthplace of Adolf Hitler, a fact of which some Austrians are immensely proud. Furthermore, as German troops triumphantly marched into Austria in early 1938, throngs of Austrian citizens greeted them with flowers and with welcoming shouts of, "*Sieg Heil.*"

Then, in 1986, experts brought convincing proof that Kurt Waldheim had served in the Nazi regime during W.W.II. Soon thereafter, his popularity soared and the Austrian people elected him President of their country. Austria justifiably has earned notoriety as the most pro-Nazi, anti-Semitic country in Central and Western Europe, even more than Germany itself.

Let us recall that Vienna alone claimed 200,000 Jews before 1938. Most unfortunately perished in the death camps. Today, only 7,000 Jews remain in all of Austria. Austrian anti-Semitism persists to such a degree that since the recent election, violent verbal and physical assaults against Austria's Jews have increased ten times.

Thus, the coalition statement accepting responsibility for Austria's disgraceful past is empty rhetoric. Austria has never really done genuine *teshuvah*, has never fundamentally repented, for its gross atrocities.

Source: *Samuel M. Stahl, "Austria's Newest Moral Blight," sermon, 3 March 2000, Temple Beth-El, San Antonio Texas, website <http://www.beth-elsa.org/ be_s0303.htm>.*

After a sudden swell of popular support, the country's far-Right Freedom Party emerged with nearly 28 percent of the vote in 1999 parliamentary elections and subsequently entered a coalition government. Its campaign featured a commitment to stringent restrictions on immigration, a strong antiestablishment tone, nationalist anti-European Union (EU) rhetoric, and a revaluation of Austria's mainstream social and political values. Its leader Jörg Haider, a charismatic populist who has been unfavorably compared to earlier far-Right populist leaders in twentieth-century Europe, has made many alarming remarks that have suggested an affinity for his country's—and Germany's—fascist past. In one widely condemned public comment, he praised Adolf Hitler's employment policies. In another he honored the memory of members of Nazi Germany's Waffen SS, the military arm of the vast security apparatus that administered the Nazi police state and had responsibilities for its concentration camps and the implementation of the Holocaust.

Post-Soviet Russia also offers a case of modern fascism. In the confusion and social strain that accompanied the collapse of the Soviet Union, the far-Right (and quite wholly misnamed) Liberal Democratic Party emerged as a virulently nationalist, xenophobic, and anti-Semitic force in Russian politics. Its leader Vladimir Zhirinovsky has publicly praised Hitler and German Nazism, gotten into fistfights with other members of the new Russia's parliament, openly threatened nuclear attacks on Germany and Japan, and demanded the return of Alaska from the United States, among a host of other bombastic, violent, and extremist comments and actions, none of which are out of character with the European fascist tradition. Playing off economic crisis, the shock of losing world-power status, and other social and political convulsions—the same factors that benefited fascist movements after World War I—his party has captured significant percentages of parliamentary votes. In the December 1993 elections the Liberal Democrats won the second-largest number of seats. Ten years later, in parliamentary elections that were substantially manipulated in favor of a political party loyal to President Vladimir Putin, Zhirinovsky's party captured nearly 12 percent of the popular vote, more than Russia's two main prodemocracy parties combined. Tellingly, one of the Liberal Democrats' main slogans— "We are for the Russians, We are for the Poor"— fits the general fascist pattern, combining strident nationalism with a traditionally leftist claim to represent the disadvantaged. A secondary and rather more marginal political formation, the National Bolshevik Party (again combining the Right's *National* with the Left's *Bolshevik* in its

name and ideology), is even more overtly fascist. Its leaders advocate violent resistance to the prevailing political order and even parade around in uniforms made to resemble those of Nazi storm troopers—brown military outfits and caps, with a red armband containing a black hammer and sickle instead of the now-taboo black swastika.

Fascism has little chance of "coming back" as a major force in twenty-first-century Europe. In the absence of major wars or economic crises, and tainted by the stigma of past fascist regimes, the European far Right remains decidedly marginal, and nowhere is it likely to command a majority or leading plurality of popular support. Le Pen's astonishing capture of 18 percent of France's 2002 presidential vote was counterbalanced by President Jacques Chirac's reelection by an astounding 82 percent in the second round of the contest. Even when parties that have associations with past fascist regimes and movements have entered government—as in the recent cases of Austria and Italy—fears that they would try to subvert democracy or impose a new version of authoritarian government have been largely unjustified by their actions and policies. Indeed, as both the Austrian and Italian cases have shown, becoming junior partners in coalition governments seems to moderate extremists who have to deal with the practicalities of day-to-day administration rather than engage in the maverick politics of attack and rebellion. Nevertheless, fascism's impact on European politics has been more lasting than many would like to believe, and it is difficult to deny its continuing presence.

–PAUL DU QUENOY,
GEORGETOWN UNIVERSITY

Viewpoint:
No. The post-1945 extreme Right arose from grassroots concerns about local problems and in response to new issues such as immigration and European integration.

Fascism was a product of its times. Although this ideology had its roots in European thought, it needed the right set of conditions for its proponents to gain power after World War I. In Germany, for example, there were disturbing signs before the war—the existence of Right-wing authoritarian organizations, anti-Semitic groups, militaristic societies, and a leadership that was antiliberal. France had several rightist organizations that originated in reaction to the liberal, individualistic, egalitarian

attitudes that had developed throughout the nineteenth century. Nonetheless, World War I and the health of liberalism were crucial in whether the fascist movements in either nation would gain power. In Germany the newly created Weimar Republic, the nation's first serious experiment in democracy, was stigmatized by defeat in World War I. In addition, the onset of the worldwide Depression in 1929 aided the rise of fascism in Germany. Had it not been for this economic collapse, the Weimar Republic might have survived and German fascism would have been a footnote in history. In France, liberalism was much stronger, and the country had been on the winning side in World War I. Although sudden defeat in 1940 caused the country to turn rightward, the French faced a government that was more a part of the traditional conservative Right than the spawn of fascism. Fascism governed in Nazi Germany and Italy, and there were elements of it in Spain, Portugal, Romania, and Hungary. This ideology clashed with Bolshevism during World War II and was thoroughly defeated.

Although the total defeat of fascism in 1945 rendered it virtually powerless in Europe, the extreme Right did not disappear. It adjusted to new realities. For example, movements that appeared after the war existed in stronger, more stable states. Although France and Germany have experienced turmoil since 1945, the Federal Republic and French Fifth Republic (founded in 1958) have remained stable. Liberalism and democracy succeeded in these important countries. The stresses in Western Europe in the past few decades have differed from what troubled the region before World War II. Immigration is one example while the growth of the European Union (EU) is another. Since 1945, Europe has experienced a steady stream of immigration from all over the world. It should surprise no one that France, Germany, and Britain have not adjusted completely to newer faces in their societies. The EU has created even more serious concerns among a significant minority of the population, centralizing in Brussels many decisions that used to be the prerogative of the nation-state. Not only does Europe have a common defense framework, it has had a single currency since January 1999. These and other steps toward a more federalized EU have often been made without much feedback from the public. In France and Germany, for example, political parties from the Left and Right have tended to agree about Europe, leaving voters with fewer means to express dissent, which has provided an opening to parties such as Jean-Marie Le Pen's National Front in France and Jörg Haider's Freedom Party in Austria. Although the leadership of these parties has expressed some ideas disturbingly similar to interwar fascism, their appeal is

Russian political cartoon from *Izvestia* showing Right-wing candidate Vladimir Zhirinovsky leaping over the opposition, 13 December 1993

(Courtesy of Izvestia, © *1993)*

based more upon current realities. Most voters who enabled Le Pen to place second in the first round of the 2002 presidential elections were not looking for a return to either Vichy or something worse. Le Pen provided an alternative to the parties that had allegedly failed the French electorate; the vote for him was more in protest of the mainstream parties than in support of his positions. Indeed, in the second round of voting, the center-Right incumbent Jacques Chirac won easily with more than 82 percent of the vote.

Stanley Payne, who has devoted much of his career to examining fascism, has argued that one should not apply a rigid definition of fascism to various historical phenomena, nor should one deny that many movements had some fascist characteristics. There were similarities across Europe's extreme Right-wing movements during the interwar period, and there were distinct differences. There were even varieties of fascism: movements in Italy, Germany, Spain, Hungary, and Romania all had distinct national characteristics, with National Socialism being the most extreme. Payne constructed a typology of fascism, describing three main aspects of these movements. This generic description of fascism, however, was meant to help students understand these phenomena, while not applying to every regime or movement with these tendencies. Fascists were antiliberal, anticommunist, and even anticonservative, meaning that fascist groups were willing to align with movements from other sectors in order to gain power. Their objectives included the creation of a nationalist authoritarian state, the organization of an integrated national economic structure, a radical change in the nation's relationship with other powers, and the promotion of an idealist program that would realize some new form of a modern, self-determined, secular culture. Fascists emphasized style. Their meetings were replete with romantic and mystical symbolism, and were highly choreographed. They concentrated on the mobilization of the nation; the objective was to create a mass party militia. They stressed the masculine principle, along with male dominance, and they espoused an organic view of society. They exalted youth above all other stages in life, and at least initially emphasized the conflict of generations. Finally there was a specific tendency toward an authoritarian, charismatic, personal style of leadership.

Fascist parties needed allies to obtain power; neither German dictator Adolf Hitler nor Italian leader Benito Mussolini could have prevailed without outside assistance. The Nazis were aided by several factors. Not only was the Weimar Republic stigmatized by accepting Germany's defeat in World War I, its liberal parties had collapsed by 1932. The German Democratic Party, which had never been strong during the republic, almost disappeared in 1932. Many of its voters gravitated toward the rising National Socialist German Workers' Party (Nazis), which was using the parliamentary system to gain power. The Nazis had allied parties who opposed the system. Even their mortal enemies, the German communists, wanted to destroy the young parliamentary democracy. Hitler gained power because of scheming and manipulation by conservatives, and he consolidated his power with the compliance of most of the other political parties. Although the communists protested in 1933, their struggle was eventually silenced. Some neighboring countries were probably apprehensive when the Nazis obtained control of Germany, but there was little they could or would do. Through working the political system and turbulent times to his advantage, Hitler was in power until Germany's total defeat in World War II.

The examples of Haider and Le Pen provide more evidence of how Europe's extreme Right has faced new realities since 1945. It is unfortunate that Haider's party was able to enter Austria's governing coalition in February 2000. Because Austria never confronted its Nazi past the way Germany did, it was far less willing to prevent anyone such as Haider from gaining power. Nevertheless, Haider had to moderate his message in order for his party to succeed at the ballot box. Voters heard him praise Hitler far less and bash the EU, immigration, and the Austrian status quo much more. Even though Haider had addressed issues that resonated across the continent when he entered the government, the rest

of the EU turned Austria into a pariah state. France has not yet risked being ostracized from its European neighbors. In the past two decades, the National Front has been able to enter the French parliament, albeit with only a few seats at the most. Clearly, its role is only as a protest party. France's two-round system of elections enables voters to "scare" their leaders by voting extreme in the first round and moderating their choices when determining which candidates win seats in the parliament.

Fascism has been destroyed in European politics, and the era that gave rise to these movements is dead. It is best to consider Le Pen, Haider, and their followers as responding to local concerns in a marginal way. The evidence has shown that Le Pen will never receive more than a protest vote. The news from Austria is becoming more encouraging. Haider's party lost considerable support after entering a governing coalition, faded dramatically in November 2002 parliamentary elections, and now appears to have been little more than a party of protest against the system.

–DAVID MARSHALL,
UNIVERSITY OF CALIFORNIA, RIVERSIDE

References

Thomas Childers, *The Nazi Voter: The Social Foundations of Fascism in Germany, 1919–1933* (Chapel Hill: University of North Carolina, 1983).

William I. Hitchcock, *The Struggle for Europe: The Turbulent History of a Divided Continent, 1945–2002* (New York: Doubleday, 2003).

Lothar Höbelt, *Defiant Populist: Jörg Haider and the Politics of Austria* (West Lafayette, Ind.: Purdue University Press, 2003).

Maurice Larkin, *France since the Popular Front: Government and People, 1936–1996*, second edition (Oxford & New York: Clarendon Press, 1997).

Jonathan Marcus, *The National Front and French Politics: The Resistible Rise of Jean-Marie Le Pen* (Washington Square: New York University Press, 1995).

Stanley G. Payne, *Fascism: Comparison and Definition* (Madison: University of Wisconsin Press, 1980).

Harvey G. Simmons, *The French National Front: The Extremist Challenge to Democracy* (Boulder, Colo.: Westview Press, 1996).

THE FAR RIGHT AFTER 1945

FRENCH AND RUSSIAN REVOLUTIONS

Are there useful comparisons to be made between the French Revolution of 1789 and the Russian Revolution of 1917?

Viewpoint: Yes. The violent use of state power to achieve order after revolutions displaced incompetent governments, common to both the French and Russian Revolutions, is a meaningful study with applications to contemporary situations.

Viewpoint: No. The French and Russian Revolutions had fundamentally different ideologies, and comparisons between them are inaccurate.

When revolution erupted in Russia in 1917, many of its leaders self-consciously identified their situation with the turbulent era of the French Revolution (1789). Events, trends, individuals, groups, and ideologies either took on or were assigned identities that mirrored previous occurrences in revolutionary France. Bolshevik war commissar Lev Trotsky was compared to French revolutionary general and later emperor Napoleon Bonaparte. Trotsky's great rival, Josef Stalin, who was accused of reversing revolutionary ambitions as he rose to power, was said to have ushered in a "Thermidorian Reaction," an allusion to the restrained period that followed the most radical phase of the French Revolution.

Are these comparisons valid, and do the two revolutions represent a case of history repeating itself? One argument agrees with the self-conscious interpretation endorsed by members of the early Soviet government. France before 1789 and Russia before 1917 shared many of the same problems: governments of questionable competence, wide social divisions, turbulent capitalist economies replacing stagnant agrarian ones, and ambitious middle groups that felt entitled to greater power. It was only natural that these similarities of cause should lead to similarities of result: a period of limited reform followed in turn by a radical phase of terror; a restrained climb down; and a relatively stable period of authoritarian rule, albeit worse in both cases than what had come before.

To other scholars these comparisons seem self-fulfilling and overstated. No matter what Russia's revolutionary leaders thought, their ideology was fundamentally different from that of their French predecessors, as were their attitudes toward law and order, economics, foreign policy, military affairs, and a host of other issues. The causes of 1917 seem more rooted in World War I, while the causes of the French Revolution were rooted in state financial crisis and contentious disputes over modernization. Accordingly, the two revolutions were different and are too complex to be subject to the simplifications of a general comparison.

**Viewpoint:
Yes. The violent use of state
power to achieve order after
revolutions displaced incompetent
governments, common to both the
French and Russian Revolutions,
is a meaningful study with
applications to contemporary
situations.**

Historians of the twentieth century have
been intrigued by the links between the French
Revolution (1789) and the Russian Revolution
(1917). At first glance, visions of the French and
Russian people fighting to overthrow unjust,
corrupt monarchies dominate the imagination.
However, this simple interpretation fails to
explain why some historians have insisted (until
the fall of communism in 1989) that the Russian Revolution marked the continuation, if not
the fulfillment, of the democratic and egalitarian promises of 1789. At the same time, other
scholars perceived 1789 as an unfortunate blueprint for 1917, in that regicide, coupled with
violence on the part of the masses, led to a tearing of the social and political fabric of Russia
that paved the way for Josef Stalin's dictatorship, much in the same way that excesses of the
French Revolution allowed Napoleon Bonaparte
to usurp power. In addition, historians in the
tumultuous twentieth century remained divided
over several key questions: why did the legacy of
1789 inspire Vladimir Lenin and Lev Trotsky;
were they trying to complete the "unfinished"
work of 1789; and did the French Revolution
provide the foundation for the abuse of state
power that marked the Russian Revolution?

A superficial analysis of the two revolutions
reveals that they had certain traits in common.
Revolutionaries in France and Russia attempted
at first to craft moderate, democratic political
orders that ultimately failed, with a resulting
"radicalization." In France in 1791 a constitutional monarchy was inaugurated that forced
Louis XVI to share power with the National
Assembly. It failed after Louis attempted to
escape from France following a lukewarm
embrace of the new political order. In 1792 the
revolution made a radical turn after the
Jacobins took control of the legislature and
declared a republic, thereby paving the way for
the execution of the king. In 1917 the Provisional Government in Russia attempted to stabilize the nation and build democratic
institutions. The pressure of Russia's involvement in World War I and the government's
inability to quell unrest at home allowed the
Bolsheviks to capitalize on these weaknesses

and to seize control of the government in
November 1917. The result of each radicalization was the elimination of both monarchs.
Louis XVI was placed on trial and executed in
January 1793, followed by his wife, Marie Anto-
inette, later that same year. In July 1918 the Bolsheviks executed Tsar Nicholas, his wife,
Alexandra, and their children without the benefit of trial. Finally, the model for the "ruthless
revolutionary," often celebrated by the Left and
excoriated by the Right during the twentieth
century, emerged in France with the appearance
of Maximilien Robespierre and in Russia with
the entrance of Lenin onto the world stage.

Many Russians in the early twentieth century, including Lenin and Trotsky, viewed their
revolution as a continuation of the unfinished
political and social battles of 1789. French revolutionaries wanted to build a new world based
on the ideals of the Enlightenment and radical
political principles of popular sovereignty, representative government, individual rights, and
social and political equality. The power of their
dream came from their belief that these principles were "universal." In addition, their insistence that the social and political environment
of a particular nation could be reconfigured in
accordance with these principles has had a great
impact on revolutionary movements all over the
world, including Russia, China, and Cuba. The
oppressive Russian imperial state resembled the
one that existed in France before the revolution
and, therefore, was ready to be overthrown by
force. Not only would the Bolsheviks destroy
the social and political system of Russia, Lenin
and Trotsky argued, they would establish a new
sociopolitical order based on socialist ideology
that would bring economic, political, and social
equality. Their ideological mentor was German
political philosopher Karl Marx, who wrote
that the French Revolution was an important
step toward socialist society in that it inaugurated a new world based on private property
and capitalism. Therefore, Lenin and Trotsky
believed that they would provide the final reckoning with capitalism, the result being the realization of the new world envisioned by the
French revolutionaries.

Institutionalized violence was a pervasive
part of both revolutions. Why do revolutionaries, who insist on the principle of popular sovereignty, often rely on violence to further their
"democratic" goals? The Law of 22 Prairial,
Year II (10 June 1793) is a good example. It prevented individuals accused of certain crimes
from gaining access to an adequate defense
before the courts. The creation of the Committee of Public Safety signaled the wish of the
Jacobins to root out enemies, and those who
were convicted were often victims of trials that

were a mockery of justice. In Russia, after the Bolsheviks seized power, the Cheka, a secret police, was established, first as a means for keeping order, but soon it was employed in seeking out potential enemies of the state. In both cases countless lives were lost, or at the least, severely disrupted.

The problem of revolutionary violence profoundly affected twentieth-century French intellectual history. After Adolf Hitler came to power in Germany in 1933, intellectuals in France were forced to consider the legacy of the Russian Revolution, especially as political violence between Left and Right escalated dramatically in the 1930s. As the 150th anniversary of the French Revolution approached in 1939, intellectuals on the Left championed the violence of 1917 as necessary to bring the egalitarian promises of 1789 to fruition; those on the Right believed the success of Bolshevism marked the birth of a dangerous new dictatorship that used socialist and humanitarian ideals as an excuse to consolidate power in the hands of an elite. The Soviet defeat of the Nazis during World War II further complicated historical interpretations, as the onset of the Cold War forced historians to choose political and methodological sides.

Historians of France and Russia defined themselves in two major ways, which in some cases was driven by Cold War allegiances. Specifically, historians generally turned to either the *thèse de circonstances* or *thèse du complot* to explain the revolutions. The *thèse de circonstances* approach favors the view that revolutions shape the actors more than the actors shape their respective revolution, and is favored by those with leftist political views. For example, French historian Georges Lefebvre held that despite the best intentions of the revolutionaries to establish a democratic order, the fear of aristocratic plotting against the Revolution and the war with Europe distorted these goals and helped provide the mentality that produced the Reign of Terror. Revolutionaries often employed violence in reaction to real threats. Russian and Soviet scholar Moshe Lewin views the need of the Bolsheviks to stabilize the economy after years of world war and civil war as the central issue driving debates within the party and for giving the new Soviet state its bureaucratic foundation. Ideology is secondary to the revolutionaries' need to respond to internal and external events.

The *thèse du complot* approach emphasizes the role of ideology and how revolutionaries consciously shaped events. This view appeals to those on the political Right who view 1789 and 1917 as breeding grounds for dictatorship. François Furet and Richard Pipes, historians of France and Russia, respectively, employ this approach. For Furet, the revolutionaries of 1789 did not understand the power of the ideas they were unleashing, especially that the people, not the monarch, should form the basis of the nation. The power of this idea justified revolutionary violence and in the end distorted whatever positive outcome the revolution promised. For Pipes, Lenin and the Bolsheviks used terror to establish a Communist state and shaped the revolution to fit their own ideological ends.

Despite the polarizing effects of these two approaches, historians nonetheless opened new avenues for research into areas such as the development of the French and Soviet state in the wake of revolution and the use of political symbolism by the revolutionaries. In France, the Jacobins used state power to control grain prices in an attempt to stave off starvation and solidify their political base with the sansculottes and the poor. In addition, the French Revolution was the harbinger of modern politics, as revolutionaries sought to gauge public opinion by contrasting the Marianne (the idealized image of woman as the Republic) with the corrupt Old Regime. In the spring and summer of 1918 the Bolsheviks, faced with widespread food shortages, used state power to seize grain from the peasants, while controlling industry and financial institutions to jump-start the economy. The new Soviet regime quickly learned the power of public opinion and employed propaganda and slogans to gain support for the revolution. In the 1920s literacy campaigns and the push to bring electricity to the countryside were meant to include each Soviet citizen in the new socialist utopia.

In conclusion, the connection between the French Revolution and the Russian Revolution cannot be denied. Simple historical comparisons distract historians from determining how the two revolutions have left their imprint on twentieth-century European history. Understanding why revolutionaries use state-sponsored violence as a means to achieve "humanitarian" ideals might shed light on totalitarian movements on the Left, including the Soviet Union, and on the Right, including Nazi Germany. If historians are to understand how politics and historical methodology are related in French and Russian historiography, it is necessary to look at the connection between the two revolutions in light of World War II and the Cold War, when the *thèse de circonstances* and *thèse du complot* approaches forced historians into methodological straitjackets. Only then can one begin to understand the power that the legacies of 1789 and 1917 represent.

–LAWRENCE H. DAVIS,
SALEM STATE COLLEGE

FRENCH AND RUSSIAN REVOLUTIONS

THE TASK AT HAND

In 1905 Russian Communist leader Vladimir Lenin commented on two previous major European revolutions:

In other words, are we to have a revolution of the 1789 type or of the 1848 type? (We say *type* in order to dispose of the preposterous idea that there can be any repetition of the irrevocably vanished social, political, and international situations of 1789 and 1848.)

That a Social-Democrat must want and *work for* the former, of this there can hardly be any doubt.

Yet Martynov's way of stating the issue reduces itself wholly to a tail-ender's desire for a more modest revolution. . . . In this case Social-Democracy will unavoidably remain "in opposition"—even *to the revolution;* this indeed is what Martynov wants—to remain in opposition even to the revolution. . . .

In favour of type I we have: (1) An immeasurably greater store of resentment and revolutionary feeling among the lower classes in Russia than there was in the Germany of 1848. With us the change is *sharper;* with us there have been no intermediate stages between autocracy and political freedom (the Zemstvo does not count); with us despotism is Asiatically virginal. (2) With us a disastrous war increases the likelihood of a *severe* collapse, for it has involved the tsarist government completely. (3) With us the international situation is more favourable, for proletarian Europe will make it impossible for the crowned heads of Europe to help the Russian monarchy. (4) With us the development, of class-conscious revolutionary parties, their literature and organisation, is on a much higher level than it was in 1789, 1848, or 1871. (5) With us the various nationalities oppressed by tsarism, such as the Poles and Finns, provide a powerful impulse to the attack on the autocracy. (6) With us the peasantry is in particularly sorry plight; it is incredibly impoverished and has absolutely nothing to lose.

Of course, all these considerations are by far not absolute. Others may be contraposed to them: (1) We have very few survivals of feudalism. (2) The government is more experienced and has greater facilities for detecting the danger of revolution. (3) The spontaneity of a revolutionary outburst is complicated by the war, which creates problems that have no bearing on the revolution. The war demonstrates the weakness of the Russian revolutionary classes, which would not have had the strength to rise without it (cf. Karl Kautsky in *The Social Revolution*). (4) Other countries provide no stimulus to a revolution in ours. (5) The national movements towards the dismemberment of Russia are likely to tear the bulk of the Russian big and petty bourgeoisie away from our revolution. (6) The antagonism between the proletariat and the bourgeoisie with us is much deeper than it was in 1789, 1848, or 1871; hence, the bourgeoisie will be more fearful of the *proletarian* revolution and will throw itself more readily into the arms of reaction.

Only history, of course, can weigh these pros and cons in the balances. Our task as Social-Democrats is to *drive* the bourgeois revolution onward as far as it will go, without ever losing sight of our *main* task—the independent organisation of the proletariat.

This is where Martynov gets muddled. The complete revolution means seizure of power by the proletariat and the poor peasantry. *These classes,* once in power, *cannot* but strive for the *socialist* revolution. *Ergo,* seizure of power, from being at first a step in the *democratic* revolution, will, by force of circumstances, and against the will (and sometimes without the awareness) of its participants, *pass into* the socialist revolution. *And here failure is inevitable.* If attempts at the socialist revolution are bound to end in failure, we must (like Marx in 1871, when he foresaw the inevitable failure of the insurrection in Paris) *advise* the proletariat *not to rise,* but to wait and organise, *reculer pour mieux sauter.*

Source: V. I. Lenin, "A Revolution of the 1789 or the 1848 Type?" in Lenin Miscellany V *(1926), from* Lenin Collected Works, *volume 8 (Moscow: Foreign Languages Publishing House, 1962), pp. 257–259; translated by Bernard Isaacs and Isidor Lasker, V. I. Lenin Internet Archive <http://www.marxists.org/archive/lenin/works/1905/apr/00.htm>.*

FRENCH AND RUSSIAN REVOLUTIONS

Viewpoint:
No. The French and Russian Revolutions had fundamentally different ideologies, and comparisons between them are inaccurate.

Historical comparisons are especially tricky when it comes to such important events as the French (1789) and Russian (1917) Revolutions. Much depends on what exactly is being compared, at what period of history, and for what purpose. After all, in 1917 two events in Russia merited the term *revolution:* first, the establishment of the Provisional Government following the Tsar's abdication in February/March and second, the overthrow of that government by the Bolsheviks in October/November. All revolutions are immensely complex events born from various factors, and they produce unforeseen and long-lasting effects. One is reminded of Chinese communist premier Zhou Enlai, who, when asked what he thought of the gains of the French Revolution, nearly two centuries afterward, answered: "It is too early to tell."

Both the French Revolution and the Russian Revolutions ran a course that can be divided into initially moderate, then radical, and finally reactionary stages. In the case of the first revolution, it is difficult to say when it ended: 1794, 1799, 1815, 1830, 1848, 1851, 1871, 1940, or 1968? It is clear, however, that in each of these years the forces set in motion in the 1790s let themselves be known. No wonder it was said in the nineteenth century: "When France sneezes, Europe catches a cold." Indeed, Russia was not immune to the French germ, and symptoms began appearing immediately after the defeat of Napoleon Bonaparte as the Russian officers, almost all of them perfectly fluent in French, came back to Russia. The result was the Decembrist Uprising (1825), which failed in its immediate goals of creating a constitutional government in Russia, but was a milestone in the birth of the Russian intelligentsia and marked the first serious rift between society and the tsarist government on the issue of reforms. With the exception of the Polish uprising (1830–1831) and Russia's intervention in the Hungarian uprising (1848–1849), the revolutionary events of 1830 and 1848 largely bypassed Russia. Yet, something not readily apparent, although more important, was taking place as the Russian intelligentsia internalized the clashes on the European barricades. This process greatly contributed to what later became an extremely variegated and complex tradition of opposition. In the absence of political rights, the Russian intelligentsia dis-

cussed religious, political, economic, and social problems in works of literature and, especially later in the century, in journalism. The French Revolution was a constant reference point, and the Russian opposition movement was divided in its views of it. Russian intellectuals saw what they wanted to see in the French Revolution, creating multiple versions of it. The ahistorical and highly politicized nature of Russian perceptions is a valuable reminder that the French Revolution was a mirror for thinkers and activists of almost all political shades in all countries.

In the mid nineteenth century, Slavophiles and Westerners dominated the debate regarding Russia's place in relation to Western Europe. Some of the most prominent Slavophile thinkers were Ivan Kireevskii, Konstantin Aksakov, Nikolai Danilevskii, Iurii Samarin, and Aleksei Khomiakov. They shared the belief that the French Revolution was a peculiarly Western phenomenon. Kireevskii formulated the principal tenets of Slavophilism in 1839. According to these scholars, three crucial historical periods constituted Western civilization: Christianity; the reign of the barbarians who destroyed Rome; and the classical heritage. The fall of Rome was a blessing because the Romans excelled at law but ignored the organic ties of society and made the state an abstract principle, which bound but did not unite its individual subjects. Later, the mechanism of industrial production came to govern this soulless, logico-technical civilization. According to Khomiakov, Russian Orthodoxy stood above this situation because it contained the idea of *sobornost* (conciliarism), individualism, and the necessity to restrain it through coercion. Aksakov regarded all forms of legal and political relations as inherently evil. Internal truth was the voice of conscience enshrined in religion, tradition, and customs that the French Revolution aimed to destroy and replace with what the Slavophiles perceived as artificial and external truth. They maintained that a rationalistic society developed much faster than a truly Christian one because material progress was always easier to achieve than spiritual purity. Hence, for the Slavophiles, Peter the Great's Westernizing reforms put Russia on a dangerous (French) track, and the country had to turn back to its native roots.

Some conservative thinkers such as Ivan Aksakov and Konstantin Pobedonostsev saw the Revolution as a potentially dangerous precedent that produced terror, anarchy, and dictatorship as a result of flawed revolutionary ideology based on rationalism, secularism, and individualism. Misguided utopianism misfired in its attempts to enthrone Man and Reason in the place of King and God. Fedor Dostoevsky, Vladimir Soloviev, and Konstantin Leontiev saw

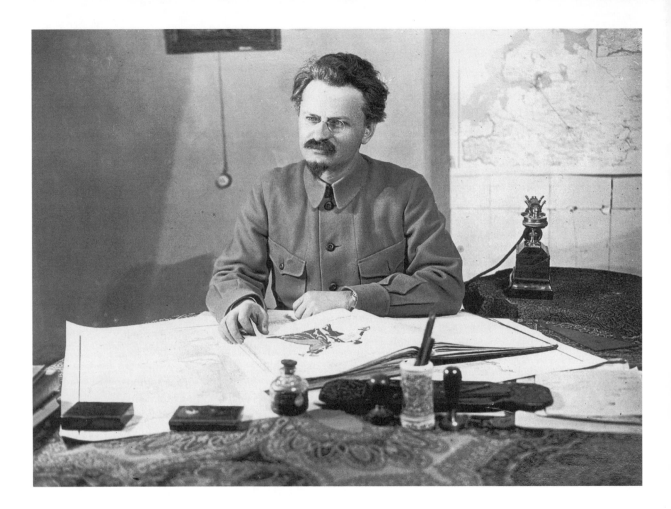

the French Revolution not just as a product of
Western hubris but also as satanic delusion.
According to Soloviev, the Antichrist would be
the most perfect of all human beings—the universal genius combining all artistic, moral, political,
and religious gifts. He would also attempt to
build the kingdom of God on Earth and try to
accomplish everything that Christ failed to do in
his first coming: to grant material well-being and
peace to humanity. This activity would inevitably
result in chaos and bloodshed proving the absur-
dity, futility, and destructiveness of revolutions
against the established order.

Liberals of the Great Reform Era (1860s
and 1870s) took a more pragmatic view of Western changes and saw Russia as a potential beneficiary of Western knowledge and practices if they
were adapted to native conditions. Aleksandr
Herzen's ideas formed the basis of the Populist
movement, but his interpretations of the Revolution were various and often contradictory. More
concerned with socialism than with a bourgeois
revolution, he identified the Russian peasant
commune as the model of the future society and
saw Russia as the birthplace of the freedom,
equality, and brotherhood that the French pursued but failed to achieve. For radical Russian
revolutionaries such as Petr Zaichnevsky, Petr

Tkachev, and members of the radical People's
Will, the Reign of Terror was a lesson in the
moral value, necessity, and cathartic qualities of
political violence.

Moderate liberals such as Petr Struve and
Pavel Miliukov depicted the French Revolution
as the unfortunate result of Bourbon resistance
to overdue reforms and implied that the revolution's main lesson for the tsarist government was
that it should reconcile itself with its liberal
opponents and cooperate with them in developing and implementing reforms. Some moderate
leftists such as Evgenii Tarle and Georgii Plekhanov argued that French and Russian societies
were uncannily similar and that a Russian revolution would repeat the main stages of its historical
predecessor, while other moderate leftists such
as Aleksandr Amfiteatrov claimed that Russia
would not follow the French path because the
Russian bourgeoisie, unlike the French, was too
weak to confront the autocracy.

The political group that paid most attention
to the French precedent was the Bolshevik faction of the Social Democratic Party, but even
here the interpretations were widely divergent.
However, they are well worth examining in some
detail since the Bolshevik interpretation of the
French Revolution left the deepest impression

on both sides of the Iron Curtain as a result of the ideological battles of the Cold War.

For Vladimir Lenin and other Marxist leaders, power struggles within the Jacobin hierarchy paralleled their own competition for influence in the Social Democratic Party, which split into two factions (Bolshevik and Menshevik) in 1903. The Jacobin dictatorship anticipated the Bolsheviks' centralized organization, and Lenin greatly appreciated French revolutionary leader Maximilien Robespierre's manipulation of ideology for personal ambition and power.

Yet, the Bolsheviks did not always see the French Revolution as directly relative to the Russian situation and were more than willing to use it as a tool in the political struggle when it suited their purposes. Lenin saw the French Revolution through the prism of Marxism, of course, which he modified into Marxism-Leninism to validate the Bolshevik coup, even though it did not fit into the Marxist framework. Lenin realized the differences between the French situation of the 1790s and the Russian circumstances of the 1910s. The collapse of the Jacobin government yielded valuable lessons on how to retain political power and prevent a rollback of revolutionary gains. Lenin wrote in a letter to a German socialist in July 1918: "Despite the worst weeks, we will not allow the 'usual' (1794 or 1849) path of revolutions and will win over the bourgeoisie." In Lenin's mind, the Russian Revolution would be successful because of the new international, or rather transnational, atmosphere in which it was expected to happen. In the closing speech of the Russian Socialist Democratic Workers' Party (RSDWP) Congress in 1906, he said that the Russian Democratic Republic had only one reserve—the socialist proletariat in the West— which was "in arms on the eve of the last engagement with the bourgeoisie." Since Russia was not surrounded by feudal or semifeudal states, the news of a Russian Revolution would cause the workers of Europe to rise against their own bourgeoisie. In a brochure published the same year, Lenin argued that small-scale business and trade were the reserves of a Russian reaction. He feared that the Revolution, even if victorious, risked losing its fruits and its inertia. Thirteen years later, in 1919, in a speech at the Soviet Congress of Unions, Lenin congratulated the Russian proletariat for holding out until the awakening of the West European workers: "In this sense, comrades, we can already say that we are many times more fortunate than the figures of the French Revolution, which was defeated by an alliance of monarchical and other countries."

Of course, the most common use of French Revolutionary rhetoric was to defend the political violence of the Red Terror. Lenin's attitude toward his political opponents among the Social Democrats and Liberals and his intransigence toward the tsarist and Provisional governments anticipated his views on violence as a method of persuasion. No other subject inspired such vociferous rhetoric from him as the application of the Jacobin Terror to the Russian situation. He wrote that proletarian historians saw in Jacobinism, not a fall, but one of the "highest *upsurges* of an oppressed class in their struggle for liberation." The Jacobins gave France its "best examples of a democratic revolution."

Contrary to Marx, Lenin also believed that the peasantry, which Marx believed to be an essentially traditional and conservative class, could be a political force if properly indoctrinated and mobilized. Indeed, the French example demonstrated that insufficient consideration and misuse of the peasantry could derail an otherwise successful urban revolution: "All European revolutions ended in failure precisely because the village did not know how to deal with its enemies. The workers in the towns of England and France executed their tsars a hundred years ago (we are the ones who fell behind with our Tsar); nevertheless, old ways were established again after a while."

In the end, Lenin's views of the French Revolution were so contradictory that it is simply impossible to coherently answer "How did Lenin conceive of the French Revolution?" Every supposition meets with several exceptions. Lenin clearly looked to the French example as a test case—but how and what did he learn from it? Codifying his conclusions yields little in the way of structure, but the nature of his learning process and how he applied his conclusions give a clearer answer. One prominent feature of Lenin's thinking was the pervasive desire to go "beyond" the French Revolution. He read appropriate meanings and values into it, always with the intention of exceeding what had been "achieved" by it. This approach was completely different from the conservatives' desire to avoid it altogether or the moderate liberals' intention of studying it in order to avert its most egregious excesses.

In the memory of Western liberals and Russian moderate reformers, the excesses of the French Revolution were suppressed in favor of the gains of the bourgeoisie. The Bolsheviks emphasized the failure of the Jacobins to establish the democracy they had pursued. They posed as "heirs" to the French Revolution's ideals and as modern agents of its unfulfilled promises. During the Cold War, Soviet and Western Marxist historiography emphasized the latter view while conservative and liberal approaches focused on the former. Since facts are multifaceted in their nature, the accuracy or inaccuracy of comparison depends more often than not on the point of view from which it is made. To ask about the accuracy of comparisons between the two revolutions is to ask for a simultaneous view of a three-dimensional figure in time. The question of self-consciousness, however, is historically much more fruitful. All comparisons are self-conscious, but that does not make them inaccurate. Factual errors do. Understanding this difference forces historians to examine themselves in the process of examining facts, and once again resurrects the eternal issue of the relationship between the perceiver and the perceived, turning history back into a meditation on humanity in the world, not on the world encasing humanity.

–ANTON FEDYASHIN,
GEORGETOWN UNIVERSITY

References

Marvin R. Cox, ed., *The Place of the French Revolution in History* (Boston: Houghton Mifflin, 1998).

William Doyle, *The French Revolution: A Very Short Introduction* (Oxford & New York: Oxford University Press, 2001).

Sheila Fitzpatrick, *The Russian Revolution* (Oxford & New York: Oxford University Press, 1982).

François Furet, *Interpreting the French Revolution,* translated by Elborg Forster (Cambridge & New York: Cambridge University Press, 1981; Paris: Editions de la Maison des sciences de l'homme, 1981).

Furet, *The Passing of an Illusion: The Idea of Communism in the Twentieth Century,* translated by Deborah Furet (Chicago: University of Chicago Press, 1999).

Jack A. Goldstone, ed., *Revolutions: Theoretical, Comparative, and Historical Studies* (San Diego: Harcourt Brace Jovanovich, 1986).

Georges Lefebvre, *The French Revolution,* volume 2, *From 1793 to 1799,* translated by John Hall Stewart and James Friguglietti (New York: Columbia University Press, 1964).

Moshe Lewin, *The Making of the Soviet System: Essays in the Social History of Interwar Russia* (London: Methuen, 1985).

Arno J. Mayer, *The Furies: Violence and Terror in the French and Russian Revolutions* (Princeton: Princeton University Press, 2000).

Mary Nolan, "Ideology, Mobilization, and Comparison: Explaining Violence in *The Furies,*" *French Historical Studies,* 24 (Fall 2001): 549–557.

Richard Pipes, *The Russian Revolution* (New York: Knopf, 1990).

Dmitri Shlapentokh, *The Counter-Revolution in Revolution: Images of Thermidor and Napoleon at the Time of Russian Revolution and Civil War* (New York: St. Martin's Press, 1999).

Shlapentokh, *The French Revolution and the Russian Anti-democratic Tradition: A Case of False Consciousness* (New Brunswick: Transaction Publishers, 1997).

Shlapentokh, *The French Revolution in Russian Intellectual Life, 1865–1905* (Westport, Conn.: Praeger, 1996).

Theda Skocpol, *States and Social Revolutions: A Comparative Analysis of France, Russia, and China* (Cambridge & New York: Cambridge University Press, 1979).

John M. Thompson, *A Vision Unfulfilled: Russia and the Soviet Union in the Twentieth Century* (Lexington, Mass.: Heath, 1996).

FRENCH AND RUSSIAN REVOLUTIONS

GENOCIDE

Were twentieth-century genocides the product of age-old hatreds?

Viewpoint: Yes. The Holocaust and other genocides resulted from ancient ethnic and religious tensions that were facilitated by modern technology.

Viewpoint: No. Twentieth-century genocides resulted from new ideologies, coldly rational political strategies, and technological developments.

Perhaps the saddest feature of twentieth-century Europe was its affliction by genocide—a crime that targets an entire racial, ethnic, or religious community. The prime example, of course, was the Holocaust in Nazi Germany. Committed to an anti-Semitic ideology, Adolf Hitler's regime decided to make its "final solution" of the "Jewish question" the extermination of Europe's Jews. It also pursued policies that targeted the Slavic and Gypsy (Roma) populations of Eastern Europe. The communist government of the Soviet Union similarly targeted "suspect" nationalities and other social groups, which were subjected to great persecution and loss of life. Even after these horrific examples, at the end of the century the leaders of Yugoslavia and the Serbian component within its former republic of Bosnia-Herzegovina stood accused of genocidal policies and actions against Bosnia's Muslim population and against the Albanian population of the Kosovo region. Genocidal incidents in the African state of Rwanda, Cambodia, and Saddam Hussein's Iraq command world attention at the turn of the twenty-first century.

This chapter investigates why genocide only came about in the twentieth century. On the one hand, it appears to have been the product of age-old hatreds. Religious, ethnic, and other antagonisms built over centuries to explode in the twentieth century's context of unprecedented violence and total war. Yet, as the second contributor argues, modernizing societies, especially those that knew great political and social instability, could quickly and easily approach ethnic or religious "others" as threats, scapegoats, or coldly bureaucratic problems to be solved. From this perspective, age-old hatred and sentiments paled in comparison to the twentieth century's special combination of bureaucracy and technology.

**Viewpoint:
Yes. The Holocaust and other
genocides resulted from ancient
ethnic and religious tensions that were
facilitated by modern technology.**

Three waves of ethnic conflict and genocide occurred in the twentieth century. These
catastrophes were precipitated by World War I,
World War II, and the end of communism.
During and after World War I, the Ottoman
Empire perpetrated the first large-scale genocide in the century against its Armenian minority. Two decades later the Nazis tried to
annihilate Jews, Gypsies, and other "undesirable" groups in Europe. At the end of the century, Serbs worked to cleanse large parts of the
non-Serb populations in Bosnia. Scholars have
long sought to determine the causes of these
recent conflicts and how populations—often
after living together peacefully for centuries—
could turn violently against each other. Several
schools of thought have attempted to explain
genocide in the twentieth century: age-old ethnic tensions and nationalism; new technologies
that facilitated mass mobilization and murder;
and new institutions that allowed politicians to
harness the former and the latter simultaneously. Ethnic tension and nationalism are the
most important factors because they explain
how genocide occurred in societies regardless of
their political institutions and cultural or technological development.

Genocide is different from mass killings,
which have been occurring for millennia.
According to the United Nations (UN), genocide is defined as:

> Any of the following acts committed with the
> intent to destroy, in whole or in part, a
> national, ethnical, racial, or religious group, as
> such: a.) killing members of the group; b.)
> causing serious bodily or mental harm to
> members of the group; c.) deliberately inflict-
> ing on the group conditions of life calculated
> to bring about its physical destruction in
> whole or in part; d.) imposing measures
> intended to prevent births within the group;
> e.) forcibly transferring children of the group
> to another group.

Using this definition, one can see that
genocide is the calculated attempt to destroy a
community of people solely on account of its
ethnic, religious, or national identity. Even if
the attempt to destroy the group fails, the act is
still considered to be genocidal by virtue of the
original intent. Equally important is that the
goal does not have to be to destroy the group as
a whole; the intention to destroy part of a
group is also genocide.

This type of mass murder first occurred in
the twentieth century between 1915 and 1923
in present-day Turkey. This genocide was
rooted in the social structure of the Ottoman
Empire, in which Christian Armenians were tolerated but were considered inherently inferior
to Sunni Muslims. It also was connected to
events in the politics of the Ottoman Empire in
the late nineteenth century. At that time Sultan
Abdulhamid tried to counter disruptive forces
of liberalism, nationalism, and constitutionalism in the empire by appealing to Muslim solidarity and emphasizing the traditional and
Islamic character of his reign. This pan-Islam
movement was also a result of the empire
becoming more Asiatic and Muslim after the
loss of several Balkan provinces in 1878 and
increasing Muslim resentment of Christians. At
the same time, Russian expansion along the
Black Sea and in the Caucasus region caused
many Muslims to migrate to the Ottoman
Empire to be in a Muslim state and to escape
Russia's brutal tactics of conquest.

These problems were compounded by the
increasing nationalism among the Armenians
and the empire's different communities. In the
late 1880s some nationalist organizations began
to call for Armenian independence, even
though the broader Armenian community
wished to remain within the empire. Istanbul
reacted by forming *Hamidiye* (irregular regi-
ments) made up of Kurds in the Armenian areas
of the empire. In the autumn of 1894 the
Hamidiye massacred Armenians in Sasun. In
1895 and 1896 an estimated three hundred
thousand Armenians were killed after a group
of Armenians occupied the Ottoman Bank and
threatened to blow it up.

Although many Armenians were massacred, there was no systematic plan to destroy
the whole population until the rise of the
Young Turks in the early twentieth century.
The Young Turks deposed the Sultan in 1909
and thereafter pursued increasingly pro-Turkish
national policies at the expense of other peoples of the Ottoman Empire, including the
Armenians. The events of World War I, in
which Russia offered the Armenians a state in
exchange for their support of Russian war aims,
fit perfectly within the Young Turks ideological
program. When some Armenians joined the
Russian military, deserted the Ottoman army,
and engaged in guerilla warfare, the Ottoman
government relocated many Armenians to Zor
in the Syrian desert. Special squads incited villagers along the way and killed them. The few
Armenians who reached Zor were either killed
outright upon arrival or left there to die. By
February 1915 the remaining Armenians in the
empire were forced into labor battalions and

GENOCIDE

Muslim man holding his granddaughters at a United Nations refugee camp at Kladanj, Bosnia-Herzegovina, 1995

(David Turnley/CORBIS)

were worked to death or killed, in some cases after being forced to dig their own graves. Between 1915 and 1918, one-half to three-quarters of the Armenian population of the Ottoman Empire were destroyed, an estimated one million to two million deaths.

What caused the genocide in 1915, while in 1894 the violence did not develop into genocide? One reason is that in 1915 Russia invaded Anatolia, and the Armenians, who composed a large minority (about 40 percent) in six eastern provinces, were sympathetic to the Russian side. Naturally, the Turks saw the Armenians as a fifth column and said that deportations were necessary in a time of war. However, the Armenians countered that not all of them were sympathetic to the Russians and that the actions of a minority of the community certainly did not justify wholesale deportation and slaughter, especially since many had been loyal citizens of the Ottoman Empire for centuries.

The Armenian genocide was ultimately a result of postcolonial struggles of landownership, statehood, and the search for a new Turkish identity as the Ottoman Empire was breaking up. The identity aspect is important because as Christians and non-Turks, the Armenians did not fit into the definition of what it was to be a legitimate member of the Young Turks state. Geographically they also separated the Turkish population of Anatolia from the Turkic peoples of present-day Azerbaijan and

Central Asia, whom the Young Turks wished to incorporate into a pan-Turkish state. To deal with these problems, the Turks wanted to expunge the Armenians from the country and from their history. In order to achieve this goal, the Turks harkened back to past disloyalties of the Christian Armenians, and looked to the massacres of 1894 and 1896 as a precedent for the inferior group to be driven from their land. In 1915 the Turks used telegraphs and newspapers to help develop and publicize their strict form of nationalism. Using these new tools, they manipulated historical religious and ethnic hatreds, proclaimed "holy war" against "the infidels," and stirred "Muslim fanaticism" to justify the genocide against the Armenians.

Almost two decades later Adolf Hitler perpetrated the next genocide: the murder of nearly six million European Jews and as many as ten million others. Some scholars see the Armenian genocide as a direct precedent for Hitler's genocide. While talking to his top government officials before the Holocaust, Hitler asked, "who still remembers today the annihilation of the Armenians?"

The German genocide was also rooted in long-standing religious animosities. Beginning in the thirteenth century, Jews were expelled from German cities and forced to endure many other humiliations. After 1800, racism, and not religious prejudice, became the basis of anti-Semitism. In 1873 Wilhelm Marr came up

GENOCIDE

with the term *anti-Semitism,* which he defined as prejudice against the Jews based on their race. This change was important because while Jews could previously convert to Christianity to escape religious prejudice, they could not change their ethnic or "racial" heritage. German anti-Semites wanted to undo the progress that the Jews had gained in their status during the reign of Frederick the Great (1740–1786), and they hoped to curtail what they saw as damaging Jewish influence on the German nation. In 1881 German anti-Semites circulated a petition calling for a special census of the Jews, limited Jewish immigration, and the continued "Christian character" of schools and state authority positions. The petition, which contained both racist and Christian language, received 265,000 signatures.

Although anti-Semites remained on the fringes of German politics, their frequent rhetoric made it more and more acceptable to denigrate Jews. Not surprisingly, Adolf Hitler belonged to an anti-Semitic party. In his earliest political writings he wrote that Jews were a race, not a religion, and that one needed to go farther than earlier forms of violence: "the final aim of a modern anti-Semitic policy . . . must be the uncompromising removal of the Jews altogether." Five years later while in jail in Munich for trying to seize power illegally, Hitler began writing *Mein Kampf* (My Struggle, 1925–1927), in which he elaborated on this idea.

In January 1933 Hitler was named Chancellor of the German Republic. Upon taking office, he destroyed the opposition and consolidated power. Hitler used a classic identity-building process—splitting people into "us" and "them." The Jews' status in Germany quickly declined under Hitler's rule. His government orchestrated a boycott of Jewish stores and slowly implemented segregation in hotels, clubs, restaurants, movie theaters, and other public places. Many Germans even pretended that they did not know their Jewish friends. The Nuremberg Laws, passed in 1935, further marginalized Jews by revoking their citizenship on account of their non-Aryan racial status and by prohibiting sexual contact and marriages between Jews and non-Jews.

These legal prohibitions were reinforced by the events of 9 November 1938, known as *Kristallnacht,* or the "night of the broken glass." During *Kristallnacht,* Hitler's storm troopers destroyed and looted Jewish-owned stores, ransacked Jewish homes, and set fire to synagogues throughout Germany. Approximately one hundred German Jews were killed, and thirty thousand Jewish males aged sixteen to sixty were arrested and sent to concentration camps. Despite the government's assertion that *Kri-*

stallnacht was a spontaneous act, most of the population did not support the violence; mostly there was indifference toward the Jews on the part of German citizens. The night of broken glass was followed by more-restrictive measures, such as curfews, bans from public transportation and certain public spaces, forced labor, and confinement to "Jewish Houses." The pace of discrimination against the Jews quickened when World War II began. Starting in September 1941 all Jews over six years of age had to wear a yellow Star of David, and beginning in October, the Germans began the first large-scale deportations of the Jews to ghettos, labor camps, or concentration camps. Ninety percent of the German Jews deported died. German civilians and members of the German army watched the mass killings of Jews and did nothing.

Like the Armenian case, the German genocide occurred under the cover of war. Also similar to the Armenians, the Germans were trying to create a new, "pure" identity. This goal would have been hard to achieve since the Jews had been in Germany for a long time. To avoid this problem the Germans decided to cleanse their country, and the historical record, of the Jews. They did so through genocide. In order to justify the action to the German people, many of whom knew about it and were involved in some way, Hitler and the Nazis used age-old prejudice against the Jews. Among the peasantry, the Nazis used traditional religious anti-Semitism, while to those living in the city they portrayed Jews as capitalists. The main point of Nazi anti-Semitism was to prove that Jews were racially inferior and were contaminating the pure, superior Aryan German race, and were therefore not worthy of life. As a result, the Nazis attached the adjective *Jewish* to the evils that they attacked. This propaganda provided a justification for the increasingly repressive and violent behavior toward Germany's Jews and led to the Holocaust.

Almost fifty years later, Bosnian Serbs and Serb paramilitary units perpetrated genocidal acts against Bosnian Muslims that bore a striking resemblance to those of the Nazis against Jews in the 1940s. During the 1991–1995 war in Bosnia-Herzegovina, the Serbs massacred, raped, interned, expelled, and tortured Bosnian Muslim civilians. Part of the Serbs' military plan was ethnic cleansing, which included rounding up all of the Muslim men in Bosnian villages and cities and either killing them or sending them to concentration camps. Yugoslav soldiers also forced Muslim families out of their houses and burned Muslim villages to the ground. The assault on Srebrenica (a Bosnian Muslim UN-protected zone) was illustrative of this policy. In Sre-

GENOCIDE

brenica, Serb forces killed about 2,000 prisoners of war and expelled the entire Muslim population of the town. Between 145,000 and 250,000 people died during the war and genocide, and 2.5 million Bosnians were displaced. What was particularly striking about the Bosnian genocide was that the perpetrators often knew their victims and had lived side by side with them.

As in the previous two cases, the Bosnian genocide occurred during wartime, although in this case it was a civil war. Also similar to the other two cases, Serbs were trying to build a new Serb country and identity that did not include Muslims. To accomplish this task the Serbs embarked upon a deliberate campaign to rid their territories of Muslims. Ethnic cleansing was necessary given the demographics of Bosnia, in which 31.3 percent of the population were Serbs. In order to build this new identity and exclude the Muslims, the Serbian leader, Slobodan Milosevic, turned to virulent nationalism and pitted the Serbs against the Muslims and Croats by selectively using history to create nationalist myths.

Serbian nationalists also effectively utilized the memory of the fierce interethnic fighting and massacres that took place in occupied Yugoslavia during the 1940s. Most of the worst fighting occurred in Bosnia, part of independent Croatia, which was a satellite of Germany. Although some Bosnians collaborated with the Ustasha (a Croatian independence movement created in 1929, which came to prominence during World War II) and a small group joined the SS, many Muslims fought with the partisans against the Axis. Nevertheless, these facts did not stop Milosevic from invoking nationalist and religious myths in order to mobilize crucial popular support for the 1990s conflict.

In all three abovementioned cases, nationalists selectively used history and manipulated religious and ethnic prejudices to justify genocide, which was used as a method of changing identities as states were forced to face new realities during and after wartime. Yet, not every nation seeking to change its identity resorts to genocide. Perhaps one of the factors that pushed these cases over the edge was demography. All three incidents of genocide took place in multicultural societies with minorities that had made significant contributions to the identities and histories of their states. In trying to remake their identity, the majorities saw these strong minorities as threats to their new, pure identities. In order to discredit the minority the majority did what it was historically predisposed to do—demean and disgrace the minority.

–KERRY FOLEY,
WASHINGTON, D.C.

Viewpoint:
No. Twentieth-century genocides resulted from new ideologies, coldly rational political strategies, and technological developments.

Genocide, the annihilation of an ethnicity, religious community, or social group, is a phenomenon inextricable from the modern age. Genocide was only committed in the past century, although it had its roots as far back as the French Revolution. Developments in political thought, technology, and bureaucratic organizations were the essential preconditions to executing mass murder on a systematic scale. Ancient hatreds between peoples, religions, and civilizations were at best secondary explanations for such barbaric acts.

First and foremost, genocide was a product of totalitarian ideologies. These ideologies began to take shape during the French Revolution, whose supporters were committed to overthrowing Europe's dominant political order in the name of social justice and modernity. The revolutionaries' emphasis on unconditional loyalty to the French Republic reflected their concern with eliminating those who were likely to oppose their goals. The Republican authorities encouraged the notion that the Catholic Church and wealthy aristocrats were responsible for oppressing the French people. The state tried to eliminate popular sympathy for these internal enemies by enacting a series of laws against the Church. These efforts culminated in Maximilien Robespierre's campaign of terror, which failed in its goal to eliminate the French nobility and clergy. Nevertheless, the Committee of Public Safety had been the first attempt in history to carry out an act of genocide.

Napoleon's conquests in Europe and his espousal of French nationalism contributed to later ideological developments. The imposition of the Napoleonic Code on conquered foreign territories such as the Rhineland and other German territories fostered the desire by new subjects to emulate the French national model. On the one hand, many European reformers believed that the French Republic represented the dominant form of government; on the other hand, they were angered by Napoleon's chauvinistic acts, such as the enforcement of a continental blockade against British products, which hurt most European markets. In their eyes, new nations needed to counter the French threat. Though these early practitioners of nationalism did not try to adopt genocide as part of this new policy, they adopted many of the same principles of modernization and social upheaval that had

KILL THAT SCUM

In 1992 Rezak Hukanovic, a Muslim from the Bosnian town of Prijedor, was arrested and placed in a concentration camp, where hundreds of prisoners were tortured and killed, all part of Serbian "ethnic cleansing." In his memoir, Hukanovic recounts a series of brutal beatings:

The souls of those on the inside whom the beasts outside hadn't yet devoured bore the same marks. Fate had been anything but generous to them. Their bodies looked as if they had risen from the grave even as the earth still came thudding down against the planks above them. Beating and cursing, cursing and beating, and constant humiliation, the most painful wound that can be inflicted on a human being. It was as if even the slightest kindness had been put under lock and key.

The Serb jailers—treading on their own promises with combat boots and piercing them with daggers, for no benefit to themselves or their tribe—were playing some strange game. But in that game, prisoners perished. The game was becoming a way of life, a daily routine. Anyone in his right mind knew that a game starting out with such low odds couldn't end well.

And where on earth was the poisonous game conceived? In the head of that blood-thirsty lyricist, the mad psychiatrist from Sarajevo, Radovan Karadzic. Years before, clearly spelling out the evil to come, he had written, "Take no pity let's go / kill that scum down in the city." It was he who formed the sham government, a shadow of the powers centered in Belgrade. It was he who roused Serbs to a hatred that they used to fortify the dim byways of their souls, invigorating them with violent, merciless, and implacable power. Would they ever sober up from their intoxicated, anything but naive revelry?

The prisoners—seized against their will and humiliated at every turn, the smiles gone forever from their withered lips, exhausted and sick, starving to death, staring absently with glassy eyes—were made of the same substance, were born under the same sky, and had lived on the same soil as their jailers. . . .

"In front of me," the guard ordered, pointing to the White House. On the way over he ranted and raved, cursing and occasionally pounding Djemo on the back with his truncheon. The hot, heavy air made everything even more unbearable. Djemo cast one more dull glance backward, into the distance, almost stopping. The guard pushed the barrel of his rifle hard into Djemo's back, until he felt a sharp pain and beads of sweat gathered on his face.

An overwhelming desire came over Djemo. He was on the verge of turning to spit in the bearded creature's face and punch him right in the middle of his ugly, drunken snout. But no—the voice of his son resounded in his ears like a seal ripped open within his torn heart. Defiantly, Djemo raised his head high above his shoulders and kept walking. The guard took him to the White House, to the second room on the left. (There were no prisoners in the White House then; they were only brought in later.) The next second, something heavy was let loose from above, from the sky, and knocked Djemo over the head. He fell.

Something flashed across his eyes, and everything became blurry. Blistering heat scorched his face and neck. He couldn't open his eyes. Half-conscious, sensing that he had to fight to survive, he wiped the blood from his eyes and forehead and raised his head. He saw four creatures, completely drunk, like a pack of starving wolves, with clubs in their hands and unadorned hatred in their eyes. Among them was the frenzied leader of the bloodthirsty pack, Zoran Zigic, the infamous Ziga whose soul, if he had one at all, was spattered with blood. He was said to have killed over two hundred people, including many children, in the "cleansing" operations around Prijedor. He took barely enough time between slaughters to put his bloody knife back into its sheath. Scrawny and long-legged, with a big black scar on his face, Ziga seemed like an ancient devil come to visit a time as cruel as his own. Anyone who came close to him also came close to death.

"Now, then, let me show you how Ziga does it," he said, ordering Djemo to kneel down in the corner by the radiator, "on all fours, just like a dog." The maniac grinned. Djemo knelt down and leaned forward on his hands, feeling humiliated and as helpless as a newborn. Just then they brought three more prisoners in from his dorm: Asaf, Kiki, and Bego. Being the last, Bego was immediately taken to the room across the way by Nikica, the youngest of the group of murderers. The sounds of beating and screaming soon reached the room Djemo was in. Asaf had to take the same position as Djemo, only at the other end of the radiator.

The tallest of the guards, another local murderer, named Duca, ordered Kiki to lie down on his back in the middle of the room. Then he jumped as high as he could and, with all his 250-odd pounds, came crashing down on Kiki's stomach and ribs. Another wild man wearing a headband came up to Asaf and started hitting him with a truncheon made out of thick electrical cable. Ziga kept hitting Djemo the whole time on the back and head with a club that unfurled itself every time he swung it to reveal a metal ball on the end. Djemo curled up, trying to protect his head by pulling it in toward his shoulders and covering it with his right hand. Ziga just kept cursing as he hit, his eyes inflamed by more and more hatred. The first drops of blood appeared on the tiles under Djemo's head, becoming denser and denser until they formed a thick, dark red puddle. Ziga kept at it; he stopped only every now and then, exhausted by his nonstop orgy of violence, to fan himself, waving his shirttail in front of his contorted face.

At some point a man in fatigues appeared at the door. It was Šaponja, a member of the famous Bosnamontaza soccer club from Prijedor; Djemo had once known him quite well. He came up to Djemo and said, "Well, well, my old pal Djemo. While I was fighting in Pakrac and Lipik, you were pouring down the cold ones in Prijedor." He kicked Djemo right in the face with his boot. Then he kicked him again in the chest, so badly that Djemo felt like his ribs had been shattered by the weight of the heavy combat boots. He barely managed to stay up on his arms and legs, to keep himself from falling. He knew that if he fell it would be all over. Ziga laughed like a maniac. Then he pushed Šaponja away and started hitting Djemo again with his weird club, even more fiercely than before.

The strange smell of blood, sweat, and wailing that enveloped the room only increased the cruelty of the enraged beasts. Djemo received another, even stronger kick to the face. He clutched himself in pain, bent a little to one side, and collapsed, his head sinking into the now-sizable pool of blood beneath him. Ziga grabbed him by the hair, lifted his head, and looked into Djemo's completely disfigured face: "Get up, you scum, and get out, everybody out," he shouted. Pulling Djemo up by the hair, Ziga raised him to his feet. Djemo could barely stand up, but he managed to take one step and then another, with Asaf and Kiki following.

"On all fours, I said—like dogs!" Ziga bellowed, like a dictator. He forced the three men to crawl up to a puddle by the entrance to the White House and then ordered them to wash in the filthy water. Their hands trembling, they washed the blood off their faces. "The boys have been eating strawberries and got themselves a little red," said Ziga, laughing like a madman before he chased them all back into the White House.

Source: Rezak Hukanovic, The Tenth Circle of Hell: A Memoir of Life in the Death Camps of Bosnia, *translated by Colleen London and Midhat Ridjanovic, edited by Ammiel Alcalay (Oslo: Sypress Forlag, 1993; New York: Basic Books, 1996), pp. 55–56, 60–64.*

once led to Robespierre's police state. The seeds of state terror were sown for future generations.

The idea to annihilate whole groups of people matured in the twentieth century. By 1900 social Darwinists posited the idea that only dominant nations deserved to survive. The Germans in particular stressed rapid military and colonial expansion as a means for a people to achieve greatness in the emerging power struggle in Europe. By World War I international relations had become a zero-sum game, where the absolute victory of a rival nation or alliance of nations over the other(s) became the formula for civilizational success. The mass mobilization of human and material resources during the conflict was only one part of the equation. Some radical German nationalists such as Adolf Hitler spread the idea that the Jews and Bolsheviks had stabbed Germany in the back in order to implement a Jewish-dominated world order. This great lie was essential to the Nazis' success in annihilating over two-thirds of European Jewry, the most dramatic example of genocide in our time.

Genocide became the primary means for totalitarian movements to maintain control over society. As Hannah Arendt argued, death camps became the focal point for totalitarian regimes like Nazi Germany and the Soviet Union to demonstrate their absolute control over society. The fact that these regimes could strip a person at any

GENOCIDE

moment of his or her legal identity terrorized society to the point that no one would dare question the government's authority over who would live or die.

Without proof that it had successfully liquidated its target group, a totalitarian movement could no longer show that it exercised absolute control over humanity. Hitler organized the slaughter of Jews in the demented belief that this was Germany's great contribution to the world. By using genocide, the Nazis wanted to show that they alone could predict and execute great historical decisions. The Nazis were even more desperate to pursue this goal in the final years of the war, when military defeat was inevitable. Likewise, Josef Stalin's Soviet Union punished "class enemies," particularly the kulaks, or wealthier peasants, with much the same logic. The simple fact of their existence as a social group threatened communism, and the state's willingness and ability to destroy them demonstrated its power to reshape humanity and society. The state-manufactured famine that afflicted Ukraine in 1932–1933 contained genocidal overtones, as Stalin spoke of his desire to harm the Ukrainians as a people for alleged unreliability. The collective punishment meted out to minority nationalities accused of cooperating with the Germans was also genocidal in nature. The Chechens, whose plight had created an enduring problem for Russia, lost more than one-half of their number because of the repressive policies of the Soviet government.

The death camp was also used to break down the individual's moral identity. While most of the prisoners in Auschwitz were sent straight to the gas chambers upon arrival, others were thrust into a contest of survival with other prisoners. It was not uncommon for prisoners to betray their friends, comrades, and even family members in order to avoid immediate death. The Nazis hoped thereby to strip their victims of their innocence before they were forced to succumb to the inevitable.

Genocide also required a modern bureaucratic structure. The early modern state may have at times instigated massacres on a large scale, but it did not have the ability to murder systematically. For instance, the conquistadors of the sixteenth century were guilty of enslaving and killing many innocent Native Americans in the name of the Spanish Crown and the Catholic Church. While it has been estimated that 90 percent of the population of Central and South America was wiped out in the first century of colonial rule, the Spanish state did not plan to eliminate the population. Rather, diseases that the Spanish and other Europeans brought with them killed the vast majority of Native Ameri-

cans. Thus, the annihilation was an unintended effect of the discovery of America.

Even if the Spanish had intended to kill all of the Native American population, they lacked the ability to identify, gather, and execute all members of the target group. Above all, one needed a government that was aware of the origin, social standing, and location of all its subjects in order to accomplish such a task. The authorities would need constant censuses, painstaking statistical analyses, a legal code to legitimize all state decisions, and a nationwide net of local police who could enforce them. These administrative prerequisites would not come truly into being until the turn of the twentieth century, when technological developments like the telegraph, electrification, the railroad, and the popularization of yellow journalism made it possible for governments to mobilize their human and material resources.

Modern media also played a fundamental role in generating sufficient popular support to carry out genocide. Hitler and his minister of propaganda, Joseph Goebbels, were pioneers in using radio and film to convey the evil idea that the extermination of the Jewish race was a great service to humanity. The Nazis often began these efforts on the false pretext that the Jews and other enemies planned to murder Germans. One of the most blatant uses of such propaganda came immediately before the invasion of Poland in September 1939, when Hitler asserted that the Poles were systematically killing their German minority. More than three million Poles died as a result of the invasion and the subsequent German occupation.

As late as the 1990s, Serbian television claimed that Croatian and Bosnian Serbs were the victims of a new holocaust. Popular Serbian outrage against the Croats and Bosnian Muslims for these perceived crimes against humanity was matched by their resentfulness toward Europe and the United States for ignoring "genocide." Yet, the media itself was key to building up popular support for a government policy of genocide against Bosnian Muslim civilians. The majority of the Serbian population, which had no regular access to alternative points of view, supported Slobodan Milosevic until the opposition began to threaten the propaganda stranglehold.

In brief, genocide has only flourished within the context of the past hundred years. The true pioneers of genocide were the Nazis and Stalinists, who could develop a totalitarian mind-set that would mobilize its population to carry out genocide and intimidate its citizens and all potential victims to accept the pointlessness of resisting. Genocide required not only death camps like Auschwitz but also ever-pervasive police forces like the KGB or Gestapo, which

GENOCIDE

could seize their victims at a moment's notice, and demonstrate the ability of the state to control every aspect of public and private life. Such totalitarian movements also were the only ones capable of turning new mediums of communication like radio, movies, and television to propagate the aims and legitimacy of genocide.

-YORK NORMAN,
GEORGETOWN UNIVERSITY

References

Hannah Arendt, *The Origins of Totalitarianism* (New York: Harcourt Brace Jovanovich, 1973).

Zygmunt Bauman, *Modernity and the Holocaust* (Ithaca, N.Y.: Cornell University Press, 1989).

Frank Chalk and Kurt Jonassohn, *The History and Sociology of Genocide: Analyses and Case Studies* (New Haven: Yale University Press, 1990).

Bogdan Denitch, *Ethnic Nationalism: The Tragic Death of Yugoslavia* (Minneapolis: University of Minnesota Press, 1994).

Sarah Gordon, *Hitler, Germans and the "Jewish Question"* (Princeton: Princeton University Press, 1984).

Eric Hobsbawm, *The Age of Extremes: A History of the World, 1914–1991* (New York: Pantheon, 1994).

Tim Judah, *The Serbs: History, Myth and the Destruction of Yugoslavia* (New Haven: Yale University Press, 2000).

Carole Rogel, *The Breakup of Yugoslavia and the War in Bosnia* (Westport, Conn.: Greenwood Press, 1998).

Helmut Walser Smith, ed., *The Holocaust and Other Genocides: History, Representation, Ethnics* (Nashville, Tenn.: Vanderbilt University Press, 2002).

GENOCIDE

GERMAN CULTURAL FIGURES

Were radical German cultural figures such as Richard Wagner and Friedrich Nietzsche influential in the development of Nazism?

Viewpoint: Yes. Friedrich Nietzsche's notions of the "will to power" and the *Übermensch* (Superman) and Richard Wagner's anti-Semitism were key components of Nazi ideology.

Viewpoint: No. A legacy of anti-Semitism, the surge in German nationalism after World War I, and the economic crises of the 1920s and 1930s were the forces that shaped Nazism. Wagner's music and Nietzsche's philosophy were tools the Nazis perverted to promote their ideology.

Adolf Hitler's Germany tried assiduously to propagandize itself as a modern representative of long-standing themes in German and European culture. Among the most preferred individuals lionized by the Nazi regime were nineteenth-century composer Richard Wagner and philosopher Friedrich Nietzsche.

If, as many cultural critics have argued, these figures' ideas could so easily be adapted to fascism or Nazism, should they not bear some responsibility for the evil of those ideologies? According to some observers, Wagner's operas contain stereotypes that were self-consciously both created and perceived to be anti-Semitic, and employ characters who are imbued with greed, envy, treachery, and other evil motivations. By reinforcing these negative depictions in the popular imagination, Wagner fertilized the German mind for the growth of Nazism. In a similar fashion, the argument maintains, Nietzsche's ideal of a "Superman" who could stand strong in his rejection of Christian ethics and democratic values only lent itself to Nazi ideals of a revolutionary "new man" who belonged to a "master race" fit for world domination.

The counterpoint to this argument suggests that Wagner's and Nietzsche's works and beliefs were victims of twisted Nazi interpretations. Since both men died decades before Hitler came to power in 1933, it is difficult to maintain that they would have endorsed his policies or relished the notion that they had inspired the horrors of his regime. Just as some critics point to allegedly proto-Nazi ideas in their works, other interpretations can just as credibly present anti-Nazi messages. Wagner's powerful themes of achieving redemption through love and reaching salvation through faith seem to reject the most central tenets of Nazi ideology. Nietzsche may have believed in the "Superman," but since he never argued that Germans or "Aryans" were the only legitimate candidates for that philosophical construction, and since he never excluded Jews, Slavs, or other Nazi targets from it, his association with Nazism becomes dubious. As both Wagner and Nietzsche remain popular subjects of study and interest, evaluating their connections to one of the major political and philosophical movements in the twentieth century is a worthwhile exercise.

**Viewpoint:
Yes. Friedrich Nietzsche's
notions of the "will to power" and
the *Übermensch* (Superman) and
Richard Wagner's anti-Semitism
were key components of
Nazi ideology.**

Friedrich Nietzsche was one of the most accomplished of all German writers. His philosophical writing was exceptional in its brilliance and its powerful imagery, but he was perhaps best known for his ability to design clever epigrams and metaphors of many different or even conflicting persuasions. Since he was a post-Hegelian dissenter, Nietzsche eschewed metaphysical systems of whatever type. In Nietzsche's mind, systematizers lacked integrity, and their example, if given universal application, could well restrict a philosopher's ability to examine controversial issues that otherwise might be ignored. Nietzsche was a genius at creating dynamic aphorisms that captured not only scholarly minds but the hearts of hopeful "true believers" as well. Creative expressions such as "the will to power," *Übermensch* (Superman), "beyond good and evil," "God is dead," and others seemed to flow from his pen. In Nietzsche's ideas there was, and still is, something for everyone, except perhaps, for the fainthearted. If the concepts of Immanuel Kant's categorical imperative and Georg Hegel's dialectical reasoning were not easily accessible to the average person, there was always something in Nietzsche's pronouncements that excited even the most boorish philistine.

It was precisely Nietzsche's untraditional approach that attracted the National Socialist German Workers' Party (Nazis) to his work. Historically, there can be no question that Nazi officials clearly approved of and touted Nietzsche's ideas—at least as the Nazis chose to interpret the meaning of his thoughts. For the most part, Nazi officials and propagandists regarded Nietzsche to be a harbinger of twentieth-century totalitarianism, and thus they often directly borrowed—out of context or not—many of Nietzsche's statements, titles, and aphorisms, and converted them into powerful Nazi slogans.

Nothing could be more typically perplexing in this regard than Nietzsche's "will to power" and his invention of the *Übermensch*. These two ideas are closely related, since they sprang from Nietzsche's thoughts about an inner power to affirm one's self. The *Übermensch* is an ideal human being who possesses the will to power that allows him to marshal his inner strength in such a way that he is able to accomplish anything

he sets out to do. Nietzsche believed that mankind could literally "will" itself a new image, if not a new essence. Mankind could transform itself by means of a transmutation of all values on its way to becoming a race of supermen.

In the bold hyperbole of the Superman and the will to power, the Nazis saw immense opportunity. Nietzsche said: "What is good?—Everything that heightens the feeling of power in man, the will to power, power itself." The temptation to steal such opportunistic statements, albeit at the expense of deeper philosophical meaning, was far too great for the Nazis to resist. Naked power was something that even the most boorish storm trooper could understand. Ultimately, critics argued that Nietzsche's will to power became Hitler's will to kill, at the expense of millions of peoples' lives, even if Nietzsche was misunderstood. Though Nietzsche never would have condoned genocide, he might have argued that the interpretation of his—or anyone else's—words should always be strictly subjective. Like many later intellectuals, Nietzsche believed that knowledge was always shaped by one's perspective and particularly by the place and time in which one lives.

Another aspect of Nietzsche's work that the Nazis eagerly adopted was his exaltation of war. Of course, this idea was related to Nietzsche's admiration of energy and power. The metaphor that he chose for an ideal society was that of an ancient warrior class. The warrior's code that he extolled was built upon ruthless vitality tempered with the obligations of honor and loyalty. Nietzsche held great admiration for Homeric Greeks, knightly deeds, and powerful, clever Renaissance princes. Nietzsche valued strong—even immoral—personalities who were impulsive and energetic. He believed that the will to dominate is always preferable to weakness and compassion. Yet, oddly enough, one would think that Nietzsche, in glorifying both war and power, would have loved the Germany of Chancellor Otto von Bismarck, in which he lived, but such was not the case. Nietzsche much preferred poetry and philosophy, believing that Germany had become far too politically conscious at the expense of traditional virtues.

Nietzsche's break with the past included his rejection of bourgeois society in general, together with liberalism, socialism, democracy, egalitarianism, and the Christian ethos. From Nietzsche's perspective, these ideas eat away at the "institutions, traditions, guardianship of the upper classes." Anything that tends to equalize human beings is undesirable, since equality inhibits mankind's progression toward the will to power. Nietzsche believed that equality, and certainly Christianity, nullified important virtues such as pride, courage, and wisdom. He felt that

1930s portrait of Adolf Hitler as a Teutonic knight from medieval literature, defaced by American troops at the end of World War II

(U.S. Army)

pandering to the weak was only an excuse for mankind to justify its failure to seize its true destiny, which could only be realized through strength. In all of this argumentation, the Nazis saw great utility. Nietzsche thought Christian morality to be nihilistic because it refuses to accept human nature as it really is. Even Nietzsche's "God is dead" pronouncement was viewed by the National Socialist horde as positive, since anything that lessened the power of the Church increased the power of the Nazi Party. After all, pious Christians became squeamish when asked to participate in genocide and were unwilling to give in to the dictates of a totalitarian state.

Perhaps the most controversial issue is whether Nietzsche was an anti-Semite. Nietzsche was fond of speaking out against religion in general, including Judaism, but his interest in Judaism principally lay in trying to understand what role the Jews might have played in the development of Western morality—one that he generally eschewed. The truth is that if Nietzsche thought that something was seriously wrong with Jewish people, it was the fact that in one sense they were responsible for the advent of Christianity!

Without getting into the relationship between Wagner and Nietzsche—a most complicated and controversial series of events—it should be pointed out that in one sense there is a profound similarity between the two men. Both spent a good part of their lives searching for myths that could best reveal the power and even the nuances of their work. Nietzsche's ancient warriors and Wagner's legendary protagonists were cut from the same cloth. Nietzsche was a philosopher and Wagner an artist. Nietzsche's conflicting writings were one thing, but insofar as Wagner is concerned, the principal issue is whether there is anything in Wagner's art that suggests his work was instrumental in the creation of National Socialism.

It has been argued that the Nibelung dwarves Mime and Alberich, and Alberich's son Hagen—characters in *Der Ring des Nibelungen* (The Ring of the Nibelung) operatic tetralogy—are nothing more than odious anti-Semitic stereotypes because of their greed, treachery, and lust for power. The seductive Kundry in the opera *Parsifal,* who uses her charms to tempt Christian knights, is supposed to be a rare female Semitic stereotype, as she is a reincarnation of the Hebrew woman who mocked Christ on the cross. Beckmesser in the opera *Die Meistersinger von Nürnberg* (The Mastersingers of Nuremberg) is jealous, suspicious, dishonest, pedantic, and irritating—all traits that nineteenth-century audiences identified as anti-Semitic. The Flying Dutchman of *Der fliegende Holländer* sails the seas in an eternal and elusive search for redemption. Of course, opera is by nature often excessively dramatic, but Wagner did not create these characters without a measure of sympathetic understanding. Alberich is, at first, nothing more than lustful until his advances are rejected by the teasing Rhine Maidens. His later desire for material wealth and power was, symbolically, a kind of "default position" in his life, it being impossible to attract women of his choice. So Alberich renounces love, steals the Rhine Maidens' treasure, fashions from it a ring that gives its bearer all power, has the treasure stolen from him, and then spends the rest of the tetralogy trying to retrieve the treasure. Alberich's brother Mime is malicious and cunning but not inhuman. He raises the hero Siegfried for ulterior motives, but the dwarf possesses the normal fears and concerns that other more "noble" human beings experience. Kundry and the Dutchman both achieve salvation in redemptive death.

That Wagner was to some extent anti-Semitic is a proven fact. Wagner's essay *Das Judentum in der Musik* (Judaism in Music) is his permanent testimony in this regard. The essay has not so much to do with music as with his perceptions of the influence of Judaism upon contemporary European society and culture. It has been said that the closing paragraph suggested that Judaism per se would have to perish if Jew and Gentile would ever be reconciled. Presumably, such reconciliation would require the conversion of the Jews. Wagner's most hostile critics have argued that this paragraph is

anti-Semitic and, therefore, was instrumental in Hitler's decision to implement the Final Solution. Yet, later, in alluding to the struggle between Christianity and Judaism in a letter to Hungarian composer Franz Liszt, Wagner stated, "I believe in human beings and—need nothing further!" Wagner never mentions the word *race.* However, for the most part, scholars agree that while Wagner's art may be subject to "anti-Semitic tendencies," Wagner did not believe in using art in any manner except for the sake of art. It should also be pointed out that Wagner's anti-Semitism did not necessarily reveal itself in day-to-day practice. Though Wagner encouraged conductor Hermann Levi to convert to Christianity, he nevertheless insisted that Levi conduct the first performance of *Parsifal* in Bayreuth. In addition, Wagner entrusted a Jew, Angelo Neumann, with the responsibility of directing an extensive European tour of The *Ring of the Nibelung.* It is also a well-known fact that Wagner refused to sign an 1880 petition to restrict Jewish civil rights.

On what grounds did Hitler appropriate Wagner as an figure of National Socialism? Obviously, it could not have had anything to do with the typical Wagnerian protagonist's search for redemption, usually through the love of women. One is left to conclude that Hitler must have thought he could use Wagner's music to resurrect the Germanic glory so often erroneously associated with the Holy Roman Empire. In Wagner's music Hitler thought he had rediscovered German glory together with the essence of the "German spirit." The brilliance of the music was overwhelming, and since the operas were often fleshed out in Germanic mythical garb, Hitler appropriated Wagner's whole repertoire in the name of the Third Reich.

–RAY HANNA,
WASHINGTON, D.C.

**Viewpoint:
No. A legacy of anti-Semitism, the surge in German nationalism after World War I, and the economic crises of the 1920s and 1930s were the forces that shaped Nazism. Wagner's music and Nietzsche's philosophy were tools the Nazis perverted to promote their ideology.**

Although elements of anti-Semitism were found in the works of nineteenth-century cultural German figures, the ideals or cultural influences of Germany's past did not cause or foreshadow Nazism. However, certain individuals may have indirectly, although quite significantly, influenced several top Nazis, including Adolf Hitler. Nevertheless, despite what links can be made with artistic paradigms and the rise of Nazism, German cultural figures were not critical in the development of Nazism—the increase of German nationalism after World War I, combined with a legacy of centuries of anti-Semitism, was more critical than any particular figure.

As one of their major goals, the Nazis planned to ensure that all areas they conquered in Europe, as well as any other territories around the world, would be Jewish-free. Their racist agrarian-oriented ideology dictated this need to purify their race by killing all Jews and others deemed undesirable by Nazi philosophy. Thus, they needed a way to spread their message of hate in a way to which the German people would relate. The Nazis, who espoused romantic, ultra-nationalistic sentiment, utilized many concepts borrowed from German cultural figures to meet this goal. By co-opting examples of anti-Semitism from popular culture, the Nazis were able to make their ideology much more palatable to the populace. They borrowed from the works of cultural figures such as composer Richard Wagner and philosopher Friedrich Nietzsche ideals that advocated the destiny of the individual and racial separation and inspired fervent German nationalism. Overall, several factors, when combined, were responsible for the critical development of Nazism, including the revival of Teutonic heroism. Consequently, the same factors all made it much easier for German citizens to accept the total dehumanization of Jews and others.

The Nazis used—and in some cases, reinterpreted—selected German works of art and philosophy, including music and literature, to fit their ultranationalistic, racist-based propaganda. They especially excerpted, or drew comparison to, works that revived pagan Teutonic mythology, invoked German patriotism, or predicted the rise of a Germanic master race as embodied in an elite Aryan feudal warrior. This case was especially true in the work of Wagner, who was one of Hitler's favorite personal figures. Wagner personified the warrior myth in several of his operas; as a result, he gave legendary status to the Germanic warrior whose destiny belonged to his country. Hitler took many of these concepts and applied them to National Socialism, including co-opting of Wagner's Teutonic warrior for the symbolization of the *Schutzstaffel* (Protective Echelon, SS). However, while Wagner's music may have influenced Hitler, his compositions did not give rise to Nazism. Hitler coopted ideals expressed in Wagner's writings and music that promoted anti-Semitism and noble sacrifice. Wagner's music and written essays were, in many cases, anti-Semitic, but at no time did his works ever advocate total, mass genocide of Jews and others marked unsuitable for life according to Nazi *Weltanschauung* (ideological world outlook). Instead, Hitler and other top Nazis chose to co-opt Wagnerian musical and dramatic themes as a form of identification for the Party.

Hitler was a rabid Wagner devotee and continually sought ways to incorporate Wagner's music into the development of his political aspirations. He repeatedly used the composer's works for both personal and political reasons and even cultivated a serious relationship with Wagner's family. Some of Wagner's most important works focused on Germanic myths, which Hitler found especially appealing. The music evoked Germanic heroism, which Hitler identified with and sought to emulate. He viewed Wagner as an important cultural figure, a "renaissance man," who inspired the German nation to achieve even greater cultural heights for future generations. It was this same Wagnerian expectation that Hitler believed the Jews had robbed Germany of. Much like a figure in one of the composer's romantic operas, Hitler viewed himself as a heroic character selected by destiny who would rescue Germany, as well as restore the Germanic cultural greatness of previous generations. However, despite Hitler's attempts to the contrary, there exists no tangible link between Wagner and the rise of Nazism, other than Hitler's personal preference for the composer's work.

There exists, however, one critical, undeniable link to the development of Nazism connected with Wagner: Houston Stewart Chamberlain, a British subject. A staunch anti-Semite who advocated racial separation, Chamberlain married one of Wagner's daughters. In developing his personal ideology, which he later published, Chamberlain incorporated centuries of European anti-Semitism with racial thinking that ultimately influenced Hitler. Combined with what Hitler adopted from Wagnerian thought, Chamberlain's philosophy may have contributed to the formation of Hitler's *Weltanschauung*. Hitler greatly admired Chamberlain's ideology; from 1923 until Chamberlain's death in 1927, the two corresponded and occasionally met. Thus, it remains a strong possibility that more so than any German cultural figure, Chamberlain's form of racial anti-Semitism was critical in the development of Nazism.

Nazism originated as an ideology and a political party in the early twentieth century. At first, virulent anti-Semitism, while part of its doctrine, was not a central focus of its philosophy, nor was the Party alone in its views. Other political parties had also earlier adopted anti-Semitism as one of their tenets, following other movements that sought to separate Jews from Euro-

GERMAN CULTURAL FIGURES

THIS ENRAPTURED HOUR

August Kubizek, a former school friend of Adolf Hitler, describes their attendance at a Wagner opera around 1905–1906 in Linz, Austria:

It was the most impressive hour I ever lived through with my friend. So unforgettable is it, that even the most trivial things, the clothes Adolf wore that evening, the weather, are still present in my mind as though the experience were exempt from the passing of time.

Adolf stood outside my house in his black overcoat, his dark hat pulled down over his face. It was a cold, unpleasant November evening. He waved to me impatiently. I was just cleaning myself up from the workshop and getting ready to go to the theatre. *Rienzi* was being given that night. We had never seen this Wagner opera and looked forward to it with great excitement. In order to secure the pillars in the Promenade we had to be early. Adolf whistled, to hurry me up.

Now we were in the theatre, burning with enthusiasm, and living breathlessly through Rienzi's rise to be the Tribune of the people of Rome, and his subsequent downfall. When at last it was over, it was past midnight. My friend, his hands thrust into his coat pockets, silent and withdrawn, strode through the streets and out of the city. Usually, after an artistic experience that had moved him, he would start talking straight away, sharply criticising the performance, but after *Rienzi* he remained quiet a long while. This surprised me, and I asked him what he thought of it. He threw me a strange, almost hostile glance. "Shut up!" he said brusquely.

The cold, damp mist lay oppressively over the narrow streets. Our solitary steps resounded on the pavement. Adolf took the road that led up to the Freinberg. Without speaking a word, he strode forward. He looked almost sinister, and paler than ever. His turned-up coat collar increased this impression.

I wanted to ask him, "Where are you going?" But his pallid face looked so forbidding that I suppressed the question.

As if propelled by an invisible force, Adolf climbed up to the top of the Freinberg. And only now did I realise that we were no longer in solitude and darkness, for the stars shone brilliantly above us.

Adolf stood in front of me; and now he gripped both my hands and held them tight. He had never made such a gesture before. I felt from the grasp of his hands how deeply moved he was. His eyes were feverish with excitement. The words did not come smoothly from his mouth as they usually did, but rather erupted, hoarse and raucous. From his voice I could tell even more how much this experience had shaken him.

Gradually his speech loosened, and the words flowed more freely. Never before and never again have I heard Adolf Hitler speak as he did in that hour, as we stood there alone under the stars, as though we were the only creatures in the world.

I cannot repeat every word that my friend uttered. I was struck by something strange, which I had never noticed before, even when he had talked to me in moments of the greatest excitement. It was as if another being spoke out of his body, and moved him as much as it did me. It wasn't at all a case of a speaker being carried away by his own words. On the contrary; I rather felt as though he himself listened with astonishment and emotion to what burst forth from him with elementary force. I will not attempt to interpret this phenomenon, but it was a state of complete ecstasy and rapture, in which he transferred the character of *Rienzi* without even mentioning him as a model or example, with visionary power to the plane of his own ambitions. But it was more than a cheap adaptation. Indeed, the impact of the opera was rather a sheer external impulse which compelled him to speak. Like flood waters breaking their dykes, his words burst forth from him. He conjured up in grandiose, inspiring pictures his own future and that of his people.

Hitherto I had been convinced that my friend wanted to become an artist, a painter, or perhaps an architect. Now this was no longer the case. Now he aspired to something higher, which I could not yet fully grasp. It rather surprised me, as I thought that the vocation of the artist was for him the highest, most desirable goal. But now he was talking of a *mandate* which, one day, he would receive from the people, to lead them out of servitude to the heights of freedom.

It was an unknown youth who spoke to me in that strange hour. He spoke of a special mission which one day would be entrusted to him, and I, his only listener, could hardly understand what he meant. Many years had to pass before I realised the significance of this enraptured hour for my friend.

Source: *August Kubizek,* Young Hitler: The Story of Our Friendship, *translated by E. V. Anderson (London: Wingate, 1954), pp. 64–66.*

pean society. However, although anti-Semitism was prevalent in Europe and had been for centuries, it was not until Hitler took over the leadership of the National Socialist German Workers' Party (Nazi Party) that anti-Semitism became a core part of its philosophy, with the result that Jewish persecution later developed into state-sanctioned, industrialized mass murder. Indeed, from 1929 until 1933 the importance of Germany cultural figures in the development of Nazism was the aggressive application of music and philosophy to help make its anti-Semitic policies more palatable to the German people.

If one event can be assigned blame for the development of Nazism, it was the advent of worldwide depression in 1929. Because of this severe economic crisis, Hitler was finally able to reach the masses, who were looking for a leader they could identify with. Hitler attempted to present himself as a heroic figure, much like a character in a Wagnerian opera, who promised a return to economic prosperity as well as the assurance of a renewal of German culture. Hitler used every opportunity to express his goal of a nationalistic renewal to the German people and promised that Germany would never again suffer at the hands of its enemies. Hitler applied a variety of references to Germany's cultural past. Nazism developed for many reasons, including Germany's disastrous failure at war, along with a rise in extreme anti-Semitic nationalistic movements that appealed to the economically and socially dispossessed. The aggressive ideology of Nazism promised a future for Germans who believed that they had none. Certainly, the collective works of Wagner and others may have possessed elements of anti-Semitism, and directly influenced Hitler in his thinking, but in no way were cultural figures of the nineteenth century, or their bodies of work, entirely accountable for Nazism. The possible exception, of course, remains Wagner, but the guilt of association was with Hitler, not the composer.

However the Nazis or their sympathizers may have used Nietzsche, his contribution as a precursor to Nazism has been widely overstated. In no way did he directly contribute to the development of Nazism. Unlike many other cultural writings of the nineteenth century, Nietzsche's work did not possess elements of anti-Semitism. Instead of Jews, his contempt was for Christianity and for a segment of humanity that he identified as possessed by a "slave morality." Nietzsche disregarded the concept of a supreme godhead entirely, and denounced any regimented religious practices where the group was emphasized over the individual. He also virulently criticized nineteenth-century German society for having been enslaved by traditional Christian values and denounced what he felt were bourgeois corrup-

tive elements that emphasized group conformity over individual achievements. Nietzsche's philosophy focused on one critical element that the Nazis co-opted: his conception of the ideal individual as an all-powerful *Übermensch* (Superman). This concept was Nietzsche's antidote to human conformity. A person who denounced traditional societal mores, the Superman was an individual liberated from bourgeois values who also sought freedom from traditional societal expectations via his own personal achievements. The Superman was not denigrated by society, nor was he content to conform or follow the masses. He was an idealized self-governing figure, a moralistic thinker who used his independence from traditional religions to contribute to society in several different ways, including through the arts. The concept of the *Übermensch* was co-opted by the Nazis to fit their idealization of the master race. Although there are links between Nietzsche's idealization of the human race and Nazi eugenics, in no way was it Nietzsche's intention that the Superman be characterized as a German or as a member of any other race or ethnicity. His philosophy, no matter how the Nazis misrepresented it, simply would not have advocated mass genocide of the Jews. The Nazis instead adopted the Superman as a paradigm for the Aryan Nazi man. Consequently, attempts such as these, along with continued co-option by the Nazis of his philosophy, gave Nietzsche the unjust reputation of having been responsible for the critical development of Nazism. For centuries, anti-Semitism had been prevalent in Europe. It was this legacy of hatred of Jews that developed into Nazism.

The anti-Jewish sentiment expressed so violently by the Nazis can be traced back to biblical times when Jews were blamed as "Christ killers." Persecution of Jews occurred throughout early modern Europe. Jews were expelled from England in the thirteenth century and remained banned from that country for hundreds of years. Other countries followed England's example; European governments continually persecuted Jews. Obvious anti-Semitic influences are found in the works of Shakespeare. In Europe, the late nineteenth century exploded with politicians, writers, and other cultural figures advocating anti-Semitism, but Jewish persecution already existed, on varying scales. There was no one particular source for this hatred. Several factors merged that were critically responsible for the development of Nazism, including the strong surge in German nationalism after the defeat in World War I and the tremendous economic crises of the 1920s and 1930s.

The philosophy of Nietzsche, music of Wagner, and works of others were used by the Nazis to develop and propagate their worldview. They

GERMAN CULTURAL FIGURES

did not cause this worldview to come about. The shameless co-option of these works helped validate the aggressive expansionist, militarist, and racist measures that the Nazis implemented. The development of Nazism was influenced by centuries of anti-Semitism and cannot be pinpointed as having critically developed because of the ideals of nineteenth-century cultural figures.

—WENDY MAIER, CHICAGO

References

Karl Dietrich Bracher, *The German Dictatorship: The Origins, Structure, and Effects of National Socialism,* translated by Jean Steinberg (New York: Praeger, 1970).

Ernest K. Bramsted, *Germany* (Englewood Cliffs, N.J.: Prentice-Hall, 1972).

Bramsted, *Goebbels and National Socialist Propaganda, 1925–1945* (East Lansing: Michigan State University Press, 1965).

Roselle K. Chartock and Jack Spencer, eds., *Can It Happen Again?: Chronicles of the Holocaust* (New York: Black Dog & Leventhal, 1995).

Eugene Davidson, *The Trial of the Germans: An Account of the Twenty-two Defendants Before the International Military Tribunal at Nuremberg* (New York: Macmillan, 1966).

James M. Glass, *Life Unworthy of Life: Racial Phobia and Mass Murder in Hitler's Germany* (New York: Basic Books, 1997).

Jacob Golomb and Robert S. Wistrich, eds., *Nietzsche, Godfather of Fascism?: On the Uses and Abuses of a Philosophy* (Princeton: Princeton University Press, 2002).

Ian Kershaw, *Hitler, 1889–1936: Hubris* (London: Lane, 1998).

Kershaw, *Hitler, 1936–1945: Nemesis* (London: Lane, 2000).

Berel Lang, *Act and Idea in the Nazi Genocide* (Chicago: University of Chicago Press, 1990).

Barry Millington, *Wagner* (London: Dent, 1984).

Raymond Phillips, ed., *Trial of Josef Kramer and Forty-Four Others: The Belsen Trial* (London: Hodge, 1949).

Richard Wagner, *Judaism in Music and Other Essays,* translated by William Ashton Ellis (Lincoln: University of Nebraska Press, 1995).

GERMAN CULTURAL FIGURES

GERMAN ECONOMIC CRISES

Was the economic instability of Germany after World War I caused by the victors' demand for unreasonable reparations?

Viewpoint: Yes. Germany's economic troubles were caused by a high reparations burden, harsh trade discrimination, and destructive intrusions into German economic life.

Viewpoint: No. Germany's economic difficulties were caused by the failed policies of its own government, especially its overreliance on high inflation, heavy borrowing, and fiscal austerity.

Germany's loss in World War I was followed by two major economic crises. In 1921–1924 the country suffered from severe economic dislocation and hyperinflation. Like most of the world in 1929–1932, it was crippled by the Great Depression. Both crises had serious political consequences. During the first period there were armed uprisings by both the extreme Left and extreme Right, while the second spawned rising electoral popularity for German communists and for the Right-wing Nazi Party. On 30 January 1933 Nazi leader Adolf Hitler was named chancellor of Germany. Many historians believe that the economic instability of the post–World War I era was an instrumental factor in his rise.

Historians disagree on who was responsible for these German economic crises. A traditional argument long blamed the western powers that had emerged victorious in World War I. Motivated by a desire for revenge, they forced Germany to sign a punitive peace treaty that included an enormous reparations bill. When the bill was presented in 1921, it took capital and resources out of the German economy. Provisions that made the debt more manageable and solved the first crisis in 1924 only made the health of the German economy dependent on foreign capital, which dried up in the wake of the Great Depression. Throughout the period, the argument maintains, responsibility for both crises lay with the Allied governments.

Revisionist historians argue that this theory is flawed. Reparations were nothing new in European diplomacy, and the decision to try to eliminate them through hyperinflation belonged wholly to an irresponsible German government. Its insistence on harsh austerity measures during the Great Depression, its fostered dependence on foreign capital to finance economic prosperity, and its failure to raise revenue through taxation or other necessary but unpopular means created the economic dilemmas that led directly to Hitler's rise.

**Viewpoint:
Yes. Germany's economic troubles
were caused by a high reparations
burden, harsh trade discrimination,
and destructive intrusions into
German economic life.**

At the end of World War I, Europe was in shambles. Millions had died in the fighting, and millions more perished from starvation and disease in the months that followed the armistice. The peace treaty that ended the conflict between Germany and the Entente, the "Carthaginian Peace," as it became known, locked its signatories into an unavoidable course toward economic instability and eventual war.

Germany's two interwar economic crises were the result of external pressures and controls imposed by the victors. The greatest pressure placed upon Germany came directly from its western neighbor. While its culpability in the economic crises that riveted Germany from 1921 through 1924, and then again in 1929 through 1932, cannot be denied, France was under tremendous pressure from its allies—the British and the Americans. France and Britain came out of the war with £3,703,500,000 of accumulated debt of which £2,965,250,000 was owed to the United States. Any suggestions of forgiving the debts or maintaining the wartime system of economic controls fell on deaf ears. Faced with an enormous bill, accompanied by a devastated countryside and industrial base, France transferred its problems onto Germany, thereby saddling it with a greater burden than could be handled. Unwilling and unable to increase domestic taxation, the French government needed the reparations just as French industrialists needed access to German coal, coke, and ores.

Despite Berlin's best efforts, the German obligation to pay for the damages of World War I remained unchanged, and France's finances became inextricably linked to the war reparations. France continued to take an economic hard line with Germany in part because of British and American reluctance to enter a military alliance with France. This stance prompted France to reach out to smaller countries in eastern Europe. The lack of assurances from Britain or the United States to provide aid in the event of resurgent German militarism created an atmosphere in which keeping Germany in a weakened state through reparations became France's primary means of defense.

While the loss of life to all sides in the conflict had been equally severe, Germany managed to escape any physical damage. Its factories and cities were untouched by the war. Those factories that had produced war materials could be retooled to produce nonmilitary products. While Germany was still in fiscal hot water, it was by no means worse off than France. The German army had destroyed the French coal mines in the north and west of the country, and the use of heavy artillery over much of eastern France had resulted in damage estimated at an enormous £2.2 billion. The amount of German reparations was the topic of much heated debate among the Great Powers that met in Paris to settle the peace. The French, having suffered the most physical destruction, pushed for greater reparations as well as access to German natural resources. The British had suffered tremendous casualties and a heavy debt. There was also a strong political need to hit Germany with a large bill, which was exacerbated by Allied newspapers, and to name the sum at a later date since popular opinion in Britain and France seemed intent on declaring any named amount too low. In April 1921 the Allies set the reparations at 132 billion marks ($33 billion) plus interest. Germany had to pay $2 billion in fixed annual annuities plus 26 percent of the value of its exports. The majority of the reparations were to be paid in cash.

When the Germans first saw the reparations bill, they knew all too well that the sum was beyond their ability to pay. Moreover, they risked revolution and upheaval at home since many citizens felt that Germany was being treated like a defeated power although no battles had been fought on German soil. Despite their misgivings, payments began. The German government eventually responded to this tremendous fiscal burden by initiating inflation, which spun out of control in 1922, devaluing the German mark to record lows.

It has been suggested by historians that economic mismanagement by the Weimar government was to blame for the economic crises that followed. While there is reason to identify certain domestic economic policies as key factors in the two crises, a closer look at Allied intervention in German affairs implies that Weimar was merely taking a reactive stance to constrictive controls imposed upon it. Aside from France's reclamation of the disputed territory Alsace-Lorraine, which surprised no one, the Allies also redistributed control of Germany's colonial holdings. The cost of the separation of Germany from raw materials and markets in these developing areas is not easily calculated but clearly curtailed economic recovery. In October 1921 Upper Silesia, an industrial area rich in coal, was severed from Germany and given over to the newly re-created

REPARATIONS

In The Economic Consequences of the Peace *(1919), English economist John Maynard Keynes noted the German response to Allied demands for reparations following World War I:*

The German counter-proposals were somewhat obscure, and also rather disingenuous. It will be remembered that those clauses of the reparation chapter which dealt with the issue of bonds by Germany produced on the public mind the impression that the indemnity had been fixed at £35,000 million, or at any rate at this figure as a minimum. The German delegation set out, therefore, to construct their reply on the basis of this figure, assuming apparently that public opinion in Allied countries would not be satisfied with less than the appearance of £35,000 million; and, as they were not really prepared to offer so large a figure, they exercised their ingenuity to produce a formula which might be represented to Allied opinion as yielding this amount, whilst really representing a much more modest sum. The formula produced was transparent to anyone who read it carefully and knew the facts, and it could hardly have been expected by its authors to deceive the Allied negotiators. The German tactic assumed, therefore, that the latter were secretly as anxious as the Germans themselves to arrive at a settlement which bore some relation to the facts, and that they would therefore be willing, in view of the entanglements which they had got themselves into with their own publics, to practice a little collusion in drafting the treaty—a supposition which in slightly different circumstances might have had a good deal of foundation. As matters actually were, this subtlety did not benefit them, and they would have done much better with a straightforward and candid estimate of what they believed to be the amount of their liabilities on the one hand, and their capacity to pay on the other.

The German offer of an alleged sum of £35,000 million amounted to the following. In the first place it was conditional on concessions in the treaty ensuring that 'Germany shall retain the territorial integrity corresponding to the armistice convention, that she shall keep her colonial possessions and merchant ships, including those of large tonnage, that in her own country and in the world at large she shall enjoy the same freedom of action as all other peoples, that all war legislation shall be at once annulled, and that all interferences during the war with her economic rights and with German private property, etc., shall be treated in accordance with the principle of reciprocity'; that is to say, the offer is conditional on the greater part of the rest of the treaty being abandoned. In the second place, the claims are not to exceed a maximum of £35,000 million, of which £31,000 million is to be discharged by 1 May 1926; and no part of this sum is to carry interest pending the payment of it. In the third place, there are to be allowed as credits against it (amongst other things): (a) the value of all deliveries under the armistice, including military material (e.g. Germany's navy); (b) the value of all railways and state property in ceded territory; (c) the pro rata, share of all ceded territory in the Germany public debt (including the war debt) and in the reparation payments which this territory would have had to bear if it had remained part of Germany; and (d) the value of the cession of Germany's claims for sums lent by her to her allies in the war.

The credits to be deducted under (a), (b), (c), and (d) might be in excess of those allowed in the actual treaty, according to a rough estimate, by a sum of as much as £32,000 million, although the sum to be allowed under (d) can hardly be calculated.

If, therefore, we are to estimate the real value of the German offer of £35,000 million on the basis laid down by the treaty, we must first of all deduct £32,000 million claimed for offsets which the treaty does not allow, and then halve the remainder in order to obtain the present value of a deferred payment on which interest is not chargeable. This reduces the offer to £31,500 million, as compared with the £38,000 million which, according to my rough estimate, the treaty demands of her.

This in itself was a very substantial offer—indeed it evoked widespread criticism in Germany—though, in view of the fact that it was conditional on the abandonment of the greater part of the rest of the treaty, it could hardly be regarded as a serious one. But the German delegation might have done better if they had stated in less equivocal language how far they felt able to go.

In the final reply of the Allies to this counter-proposal there is one important provision, which I have not attended to hitherto, but which can be conveniently dealt with in this place. Broadly speaking, no concessions were entertained on the reparation chapter as it was originally drafted, but the Allies recognised the inconvenience of the indeterminacy of the burden laid upon Germany and proposed a method by which the final total of claim might be established at an earlier date than 1 May 1921. They promised, therefore, that at any time within four months of the signature of the treaty (that is to say, up to the end of October 1919), Germany should be at liberty to submit an offer of a lump sum in settlement of her whole liability as defined in the treaty, and within two months thereafter (that is to say, before the end of 1919) the Allies 'will, so far as may be possible, return their answers to any proposals that may be made.'

This offer is subject to three conditions. 'Firstly, the German authorities will be expected, before making such proposals, to confer with the representatives of the Powers directly concerned. Secondly, such offers must be unambiguous and must be precise and clear. Thirdly, they must accept the categories and the reparation clauses as matters settled beyond discussion.'

The offer, as made, does not appear to contemplate any opening up of the problem of Germany's capacity to pay. It is only concerned with the establishment of the total bill of claims as defined in the treaty—whether (e.g.) it is £37,000 million, £38,000 million, or £310,000 million. 'The questions', the Allies' reply adds, 'are bare questions of fact, namely, the amount of the liabilities, and they are susceptible of being treated in this way.' If the promised negotiations are really conducted on these lines, they are not likely to be fruitful. It will not be much easier to arrive at an agreed figure before the end of 1919 than it was at the time of the conference; and it will not help Germany's financial position to know for certain that she is liable for the huge sum which on any computation the treaty liabilities must amount to. These negotiations do offer, however, an opportunity of reopening the whole question of the reparation payments, although it is hardly to be hoped that at so very early a date, public opinion in the countries of the Allies has changed its mood sufficiently.

I cannot leave this subject as though its just treatment wholly depended either on our own pledges or on economic facts. The policy of reducing Germany to servitude for a generation, of degrading the lives of millions of human beings, and of depriving a whole nation of happiness should be abhorrent and detestable—abhorrent and detestable, even if it were possible, even if it enriched ourselves, even if it did not sow the decay of the whole civilised life of Europe. Some preach it in the name of justice. In the great events of man's history, in the unwinding of the complex fates of nations, justice is not so simple. And if it were, nations are not authorised, by religion or by natural morals, to visit on the children of their enemies the misdoings of parents or of rulers.

Source: *John Maynard Keynes,* The Economic Consequences of the Peace *(London: Macmillan, 1919) <http://socserv2.socsci.mcmaster.ca/~econ/ugcm/3ll3/keynes/peace.htm#Ch5>.*

Poland. The consequences of this seizure weakened the German government and contributed to even higher levels of inflation.

In December 1922 French finance minister Charles de Lasteyrie proposed the creation of a separate Rhineland currency in the event of a collapse of Germany's currency. This proposal was based on the presupposition that the Rhineland would be severed from Germany and turned into a buffer state. The German government reacted by funding an enormously costly supporting action for the mark.

Throughout the interwar period Germany was buffeted with constant threats of seizures by France for failure to make good on the payment of war reparations. France sought British aid in its attempt to impose sanctions on Germany in March 1921 by creating a separate customs zone for the Rhineland. In January 1923 a more forceful intervention led to a Franco-Belgian occupation of the industrial Ruhr region. Reacting to a violation of its sovereignty, the German government subsidized passive resistance among workers in the region. Gaining nothing financially and enjoying no international backing, the French backed down and withdrew their forces in September 1924. Germany's inflation problem only worsened during the crisis, however.

In an attempt to ameliorate the economic downturn in Germany, a committee of U.S. and British bankers chaired by American financier J. P. Morgan met to discuss a long-term loan of 200 million marks. Despite the small size of the loan, the proposal was indefinitely tabled because the French would not reduce their reparations claims. This refusal reduced Germany's credit rating and subsequently made it harder to secure much-needed funds from foreign lenders. Eventually, German economic stabilization was only brought about by an American-led debt restructuring program, the Dawes Plan (1924), which reduced Germany's reparations burden and made payments more manageable.

The next economic crisis, coming after the crash of the American stock market in October 1929, resulted in a collapse in German heavy industrial output. In the same year the Paris Experts Committee met to renegotiate German reparations. It was feared that the committee would be unable to reach an agreement, and although a new debt restructuring plan designed by American financier Owen Young reduced German payments further, the economy began to react negatively. The unexpected withdrawal of American finance capital from German industry created further problems, including high unemployment. In 1931 an announcement by the government that it could no longer pay war reparations created a panic that led people to pull their money out of banks. At this point, Germany's money supply had already contracted by 17 percent because of a combination of inflation and poor bank management. Banks often fell victim to panics that cost them in liquidity and contributed to their instability.

Viewing the trouble that the reparations burden had caused Germany, U.S. president Herbert Hoover declared a moratorium on reparations payments in 1931, on the understanding that the British and French would be absolved from further payments on their World War I debt. Despite that measure, however, American economic interests had successfully lobbied for a high import tariff, the Smoot-Hawley Tariff, in 1930. It was the highest import tariff in American history. Germany, like other nations, saw its exports to the United States fall dramatically. In retaliation, Germany followed the general international reaction to Smoot-Hawley and immediately increased its own import tariffs. Losing a sizable amount of its export trade and seeing imports decline, Germany's already troubled economy sank further.

The war reparations placed on Germany were to blame for much of the economic turmoil that plagued the Weimar Republic. Rene-

gotiations and reinterpretations of the terms of Versailles often translated into bank panics and hyperinflation. America's early obstinacy in rejecting the possibility of debt relief and Great Britain's refusal to provide assurances of security contributed to France's determination to saddle Germany with an unbearable fiscal burden, making it all but impossible for the Weimar Republic to achieve financial prosperity. The persistent threat to create a separate Rhineland state to serve as a buffer between Germany and France, together with the occupation of the Ruhr, was the source of great tension between the neighboring countries. Both France and Germany expended a sizable amount of revenue toward winning over the citizens of the Rhineland, while Germany's economy was saddled by its attempts to frustrate the occupation of the Ruhr in 1923–1924. So long as the Allies maintained the authority to impose sanctions, reparations, and occupation on Germany, the German government could not hope to provide its citizens with economic stability.

–CRAIG ROMM,
CENTER FOR STRATEGIC AND
INTERNATIONAL STUDIES

Viewpoint:
No. Germany's economic difficulties were caused by the failed policies of its own government, especially its overreliance on high inflation, heavy borrowing, and fiscal austerity.

Economists and scholars have argued since the interwar years that the hyperinflation of 1921–1924 and high unemployment of 1929–1932 were the result of the international situation after the German loss in World War I. Doubtless, the demands of the victorious powers for reparations from Germany and control over key banking and spending policies had negative consequences for the German economy. The crises in international trade during the interwar years also aggravated the situation. The German government, however, exaggerated the impact of these factors to alleviate the terms of the Versailles Treaty (1919). Scholars have often accepted these arguments as proof that French, British, and American policies toward Germany eventually brought Adolf Hitler to power by 1933. In fact, there is a variety of factors that show the German government and its policies were largely responsible for both eco-

GERMAN ECONOMIC CRISES

HISTORY IN DISPUTE, VOLUME 17: TWENTIETH-CENTURY EUROPEAN SOCIAL AND POLITICAL MOVEMENTS, SECOND SERIES

Workers dismantling the Krupps automotive plant in the Ruhr Valley, circa 1923

(Hulton-Deutsch/CORBIS)

nomic crises. Ultimately, the Weimar Republic's failure to adopt realistic economic and fiscal policies led to its demise.

Historians have often claimed that reparations imposed on Germany at Versailles were an unbearable burden that forced the newly formed republican government to inflate its currency to meet these demands. These scholars have claimed that the initial demand of approximately 431 billion gold marks (a gold mark was the value of the German mark in 1913, before the onset of wartime inflation) to pay for damaged buildings and infrastructure in northern France and Belgium, pensions for Allied veterans, and compensation for wounded war veterans and widows, was totally unreasonable. Renowned economist John Maynard Keynes argued that this figure was more than ten times the amount he thought that the German economy could bear. In his eyes, any amount greater than approximately 41 billion gold marks would devastate the German economy and plunge Europe and the world into political and economic chaos. Thus, Keynes also rejected the revised figure of 132 billion gold marks ($33

billion) that the Allies agreed to after extended negotiations in London in 1921.

In actuality, the cost of reparations was lower than the above figures indicate. Although on paper the reparations debt was initially set at 132 billion gold marks, the German government was not required to pay 82 billion until after its economy had recovered. In other words, the Weimar Republic immediate burden was only 50 billion gold marks, a figure only slightly higher than Keynes's estimate of the amount the German economy could bear.

The Allied governments loaned enormous sums to rescue the German economy. Indeed, the amount of net capital to flow into Germany between 1919 and 1931 reached approximately 27 billion gold marks, while the Germans only paid 19.1 billion in reparations. Much of the rest was invested directly into economic development and used to buttress government spending. An important reason why the victorious powers took such actions was that they realized that the German national debt of nearly 85 billion gold marks was a far greater burden than the reparations. The Allied demand that Germany give up its colonies and severely reduce its military spending helped economically, although the restrictions wounded German national pride.

Admittedly, the French occupation of Germany's industrial Ruhr Valley in January 1923, in reaction to the Weimar government's default on its reparation payments, disrupted the German economy. The resulting strikes by workers in the valley only worsened this situation. The German government whipped up patriotic sentiments by calling for passive resistance against the "invaders" but lost international credibility and increased its debts. Since the government in effect paid Ruhr workers to strike against the French occupiers, inflation was exacerbated.

The real reason the Weimar Government inflated its currency, however, was to cover costs for its own ambitious domestic agenda. Instead of pushing for an austerity program for its people, the government sought broad popular support by expanding welfare and other social programs for the working class and unemployed. The Social Democratic Party (SPD) that led the Weimar Republic from its inception until 1923 had lived up to its party program. Moderate politicians and German industrial leaders, fearing that the radical Left would seize power, agreed to SPD trade-union leader Carl Legien's demand for an eight-hour workday on 15 November 1918. This agreement signaled the beginning of a long period of cooperation between the SPD and big business on labor issues. Nevertheless, the cost of expanded social programs between 1923 and 1928 has been estimated at more than 525 billion marks—four times the total amount of the reparations bill (132 billion), and more than 26 times the amount that the Germans actually paid (19.1 billion). These costs led to huge debts.

Having reached this point, the Social Democratic leadership made a reckless gamble. In 1923 the leadership embarked on a hyperinflationary monetary policy to continue social spending. It avoided responsibility by making patriotic statements to the electorate accusing the Allies and not themselves for the debt, a fiction that its domestic political opponents helped perpetuate by criticizing the government and its leaders for having ended the war on "dishonorable" terms. The Social Democrats claimed that hyperinflation would deny the Allied governments their reparations and make German exports more competitive, thus helping industry and the economy as a whole. These arguments were far from the truth. Beyond convincing foreign investors that the German economy was too risky, inflation eliminated individual and private assets. The impoverished middle class soon realized that the republican

government was at least partly responsible for its woes. They were suspicious that hyperinflation was just a backhanded way for the SPD to expropriate the rich and create a "classless society."

The second crisis, 1929–1932, was different from that of the early 1920s in several major respects. The change in political climate was obvious. On one hand, the SPD lost a considerable amount of influence among the public at large and had to compete actively with the Communist Party and growing Nazi Party for working-class votes. On the other hand, the bourgeoisie and rural population shied away from both the Socialists and Communists. As a result, the Right and Center parties won the majority of the Reichstag in 1928.

Chancellor Heinrich Brüning, a moderate Right-wing politician, reacted to the stock market crash (29 October 1929) in New York by trying to keep the German mark stable and to balance the budget. Gone were the days of inflation and protecting the German working class. Instead, the German government chose to cut social spending and salaries in order to build up its credit rating and rejuvenate its collapsed bond market. Despite these measures, unemployment soared, reaching 20 percent by 1932. Cuts in welfare spending only alienated the unemployed. Severe deflation also set in, strongly increasing the value of the mark between October 1929 and February 1932. A strong mark made reparation payments more difficult and convinced international analysts that Germany was not a stable market.

One may claim that the American stock market crash was responsible for the disaster. Indisputably, this event wreaked havoc on the German economy, as indeed it did in many other nations, yet the German government bore primary responsibility for worsening the crisis. If Brüning had not made such drastic cuts in social spending, allowed the government to go into debt, and taken the currency off the gold standard (as Britain did in 1931 and the United States would do in 1933), he might have ameliorated the situation. Brüning needed to borrow money or raise taxes to counteract unemployment. The chancellor, counting on middle-class support, refused to do either and only proposed more cuts in government spending.

In brief, the failure of German governments during the Weimar era to come to grips with economic realities was a major contributing factor to the rise of Hitler and the destruction of the republic. One might argue that the reparations catalyzed the crisis of 1921–1924 and that the American stock market crash caused the economic downturn of 1929–1932. Nevertheless, one cannot deny that the government had a

GERMAN ECONOMIC CRISES

chance in each case to maintain the loyalty of both the working and middle classes. Instead, persistent social strife paved the way for political revolution.

–YORK NORMAN,
GEORGETOWN UNIVERSITY

References

David Abraham, *The Collapse of the Weimar Republic: Political Economy and Crisis* (Princeton: Princeton University Press, 1981).

Theo Balderston, *The Origins and Course of the German Economic Crisis: November 1923 to May 1932* (Berlin: Haude & Spener, 1993).

Gerald Feldman, *The Great Disorder: Politics, Economics, and Society in the German Inflation* (New York: Oxford University Press, 1993).

John Hiden, "Hard Times–From Weimar to Hitler," *Historical Journal,* 32 (December 1989).

Harold James, "The Causes of the German Banking Crisis of 1931," *Economic History Review,* new series 37 (February 1984).

Ian Kershaw, ed., *Weimar: Why Did German Democracy Fail?* (London: Weidenfeld & Nicolson, 1990).

Walter A. McDougall, "Political Economy versus National Sovereignty: French Structures for German Economic Integration after Versailles," *Journal of Modern History,* 51 (March 1979).

Alan Sharp, *The Versailles Settlement: Peacemaking in Paris, 1919* (New York: St. Martin's Press, 1991).

Steven B. Webb, "Fiscal News and Inflationary Expectations in Germany after World War I," *Journal of Economic History,* 46 (September 1986).

Webb, *Hyperinflation and Stabilization in Weimar Germany* (New York: Oxford University Press, 1989).

GERMAN ECONOMIC CRISES

GREAT DEPRESSION

Was the Great Depression in Europe a product of unrestrained capitalism?

Viewpoint: Yes. The global financial crisis following the 1929 New York Stock Market crash was caused by risky business practices and unregulated capital markets resulting from unsound fiscal leadership at the national level.

Viewpoint: No. The Great Depression resulted from excessive government intervention in the international financial system and domestic economies.

When the New York stock market collapsed in October 1929, much of the industrial world felt its effects in a worldwide economic depression. The United States and much of Europe found themselves caught in a spiral of failing banks and businesses and mass unemployment. Many of the effects lasted for years, ending only with World War II.

This chapter examines the reasons for this catastrophic collapse, focusing mainly on the question of government involvement in economic matters. One argument, traditionally advanced by historians and economists, suggests that several national governments, especially those of the major powers, failed to take any proactive steps to solve their countries' economic problems. Whether they did not believe philosophically in a government role in the economy or whether they feared political opposition to new policies, they lacked the fortitude to act. Another argument suggests the opposite: that poor economic conditions resulted from excessive government intervention. Central banks, legislatures, and other national bodies charged with fiscal responsibility manipulated tax structures, credit schemes, investment policies, and international trade to the point where the healthy economic climate of the 1920s took a turn for the worse. Since the role of government in the economy remains a contentious issue in the twenty-first century, these essays highlight the relevance of the Great Depression.

Viewpoint:
Yes. The global financial crisis following the 1929 New York Stock Market crash was caused by risky business practices and unregulated capital markets resulting from unsound fiscal leadership at the national level.

The international financial crisis that followed the collapse of the New York stock market in October 1929 was largely the result of unregulated economies and occurred in the absence of sound fiscal leadership from national governments. Investment bubbles, unstable loan structures, harmful austerity measures, and a general unwillingness to take controversial measures that may have led to practical solutions bedeviled Europe's economic life and wrought havoc with its political stability.

Many of Europe's troubles derived from the unsatisfactory settlement of World War I. Germany, the principal defeated power, had been forced to accept full responsibility for the conflict and was obliged to pay a heavy reparations bill. Although the country's hyperinflation of 1923 was only a temporary situation, Berlin's willingness to print more money to defeat attempts to collect the full amount of the reparations mandated an international solution. After France and Belgium ended their occupation of the Ruhr—a measure taken in a vain attempt to collect the reparations directly—American loans, extended as part of the Dawes Plan (1924) and the Young Plan (1929), provided capital for a long-term structured payment of Germany's debt.

Yet, the lesson provided by easy American finance was not lost on the German government and business sector. Much of the German economy's recovery in the 1920s was also financed by foreign, and especially American, capital. While accepting foreign investment was not intrinsically irresponsible, in the German case it was so pronounced that much of the country's prosperity became dependent on foreign credit. In the absence of a comprehensive banking authority, private banks, investment firms, and other businesses made the situation worse by offering to borrow at high interest rates. This advertisement of competitive returns on investment in Germany created a bubble: the more the Germans accepted foreign loans at inflated interest rates, the more money they would have to pay back at some future time.

Naturally, this situation would only be possible if prosperity were permanent. Yet, economies fluctuate, and in Germany's case, after 1929 the future of its economic health depended on events in a foreign country. After the bubble of America's own unregulated economy burst in the stock market crash, Germany suffered for its shortsightedness when the loans upon which it had grown dependent dried up. To make matters worse, when American banks tried to recall their loans, the uncontrolled manner of their use in Germany made them impossible to repay. German business had used the borrowed capital to modernize and expand industry by buying new equipment, improving infrastructure, and paying wages. Little of what the enterprises had done could be transferred back into liquid capital to return. Further, the government, rather than investing in profitable ventures, had used foreign loans to make reparations payments and to finance spending on salaries, pensions, and public assistance—spending that offered no returns, even if it did guarantee a modicum of political and economic stability for some segments of German society. One outcome of this situation was that the American banks that had financed Germany's economic recovery, reparations, and government spending tanked once the volume of their missing capital

was discovered. As the American economy descended into depression, Germany ceased to receive its regular infusion of loans, partly because its borrowers' credit was ruined and partly because its fiscal mismanagement had helped bankrupt many of its lenders across the Atlantic.

Of course this spelled disaster. The extent of the government's reliance on foreign capital effectively prevented it from helping industry, which could only close its doors on an unprecedented scale. Successive German governments failed to respond in any meaningful way. The centrist and Right-wing politicians who dominated the leadership in the early 1930s strenuously resisted tax increases and refused to reduce subsidies to politically powerful but economically unprofitable constituencies like the country's large landowners. Their preferred solutions abjured interventionist measures to promote employment, bail out bankrupt industries, or tap underutilized sources of revenue. Rather, the governments implemented austerity measures, often relying on the emergency executive powers of Weimar Germany's presidency to sidestep potential opposition from the Reichstag. These measures included comprehensive wage and salary cuts for government employees; cuts in pensions and other benefits to the poor, elderly, and infirm; and—incredibly, given the growing number of unemployed Germans—a reduction in the number of government jobs.

These measures, however, had only a marginal effect. While the government did reduce spending somewhat, the economy still plummeted. Reductions in salaries, benefits, and jobs resulted in a corresponding decline in consumer spending. Together with the loss of foreign capital, revenue from domestic spending also began to disappear. As German industry lost more and more income, it produced less, creating an economy of scarcity, which caused resurgent inflation. Confronted with immiserization from government austerity measures and inflated prices from industry, German consumers continued the cycle by buying still less. In the absence of interventionist government policies, by 1932 more than 6 million Germans—20 percent of the work force—were unemployed. Unsound and irresponsible economic policies had created this situation, and Germans registered their dissatisfaction at the polls and in the streets. Adolf Hitler's extremist Nazi Party, which offered broad economic recovery as the centerpiece of its program, overcame political marginalization and surged in popularity. The Nazis moved from returning just 12 members to the Reichstag in 1928 to returning 107 in the elections of September 1930 and 230 in those of July 1932. The last results made them

French Premier Léon Blum at a Front Populaire peace rally, September 1936

(Bettmann/CORBIS)

the legislature's largest political party; Hitler was appointed chancellor six months later. The German communists, who offered their own radical solutions to economic difficulties, did comparatively less well, but still increased their percentage of the parliamentary vote by 50 percent in the same period. The distance between a do-nothing government and an impoverished electorate willing to embrace radical solutions was indisputably great.

Britain also suffered during the Great Depression, though its lesser degree of reliance on American capital and more stable political system moderated its effects. Still, neither the Labour government of 1929–1931 nor the coalition government that followed did much to prevent the economy from sinking or to promote its recovery. Like the ineffectual German governments that preceded Hitler's rise to power, no major British political force implemented or supported the implementation of sweeping interventionist measures. Labour had lost support because of alleged subversive communist activity—the cause of the fall of its first and short-lived government from power in 1924—and did not want to antagonize the coun-

try by pursuing higher taxation or other policies too closely associated with socialism. The Conservatives, who shared power with Labour during the National Government of 1931–1935, objected to government intervention as a matter of principle.

As a result, the British governments of the Depression era adopted many of the same austerity measures that the Germans had put into practice, and they experienced the same effects. Indeed, the formation of the coalition National Government in 1931 resulted directly from Labour prime minister Ramsay MacDonald's failure to secure his party's support for nearly £100 million of cuts in social spending, much of which was carried out by the coalition. Industry declined and unemployment grew. The devaluation of the pound in 1931 was intended to make British exports cheaper and therefore more competitive abroad, but it also reduced the value of savings, pensions, investments, wages, and salaries at home. Britain's lack of dependence on American capital spared it a fate as bad as Germany's, but its government's absent leadership nevertheless did not help. In addition, although there was no British

Hitler, the 1930s were the height of British political radicalism—Sir Oswald Moseley's British Union of Fascists attracted some 50,000 members by the middle of the decade, while the British Communist Party succeeded in returning a member of Parliament in 1935.

France, with a large agricultural sector, did not immediately experience the effects of the Depression, mainly because the franc had already been devalued during a currency crisis in 1926 and because the tenuous nature and high turnover of its interwar governments precluded the formulation of any consistent economic policy. Nevertheless, as the rest of the world industrial economy suffered, France could not escape. However, just like every other major European government, successive French governments were paralyzed by the Right's resistance to state intervention in economics and by the Left's fear that broad intervention would be labeled communism. Even after the election of a Left-wing coalition "Popular Front" government in 1936, Prime Minister Léon Blum made only modest gestures, such as guaranteeing the forty-hour workweek, introducing paid vacations for workers, sponsoring wage negotiations between labor and management, and partially nationalizing the Bank of France and the armaments industry. Recovery remained elusive, while Blum's critics suspected that even his moderate economic policies portended revolution. Significant political threats grew from a variety of fascist groups and from a strengthened Communist Party, which had won a million and a half votes and seventy-two seats in parliament in the elections of 1936. France only began to show signs of growth in the months leading up to World War II.

Of the major European powers, Germany, Britain, and France were the worst hit by the Great Depression. In each case national governments failed to respond to the economic crisis with any coherent or effective policy. Even Left-wing governments and politicians shied away from doing anything that might have appeared controversial or been tainted by association with communism. In the absence of decisive measures, all of the countries suffered growing impoverishment, noticeable (if varying) degrees of political radicalism, and mounting economic weakness. In Germany the untended economic difficulties played a major role in the rise of Nazism to national government. Germany's economic recovery depended to an extent on Hitler's broad intervention in the economy, especially his regime's massive increases in military spending, vast public-works projects, and assault on the rights of the working class to organize independently of the state. Britain and France plodded on with

struggling economies until the challenges of World War II exposed their continuing weaknesses. More interventionist policies may have enabled them to withstand those challenges better.

–PAUL DU QUENOY,
GEORGETOWN UNIVERSITY

Viewpoint:
No. The Great Depression resulted from excessive government intervention in the international financial system and domestic economies.

The worldwide growth of large-scale governments with both mandates and propensities for large-scale intervention in domestic economies is usually linked to the Great Depression, which began in 1929. That development reflected the depth and endurance of the economic collapse: its apparent resistance to less potent remedies. Government shares of nonmilitary employment, spending, and Gross National Product increased steadily. Governments became involved in almost every area of their economies, both as participants and regulators. Yet, perhaps the most decisive development was the tectonic shift in public opinion on the subject. The seeming failure of private enterprise in particular led broad sectors of the public to consider state intervention sensible. The question was no longer whether public authority should be involved, but why it should not.

That mind-set persisted for decades after the Depression gave way to, in many cases, unprecedented levels of growth and prosperity. Government presence was considered de rigueur as a guarantor of fairness, a source of wisdom, and a security blanket: "always keep ahold of nurse / for fear of finding something worse." When in the middle of the Cold War, Western intellectuals like Daniel Bell became enamored of the theory of "convergence" (the idea that the West and the East were coming together institutionally and behaviorally), one of the centerpieces of the new wisdom was the certainty that "managed economies" would be a dominant feature of the new global order.

In the context of events since 1990 this situation sounds almost quaint. Yet, only in recent years have scholars begun investigating the structure's roots and questioning whether government involvement in economic and financial systems might have contributed to the Depression's origins as well as its alleviation. The line of

THE DESPAIR OF TODAY

At the Lausanne Conference in 1932, German chancellor Franz von Papen gave a speech outlining his country's economic woes:

Nothing can prove more clearly the catastrophic upheaval which has occurred during this period than a comparison between the world as it was, to all appearances at any rate, in 1929 and the situation today.

In those days there existed a system of international credit which appeared to function without friction and an active and fruitful exchange of capital from one country to another. Commercial relations between almost all countries seemed to be regulated on a solid basis by a clear and well-organized system of commercial treaties. Competent authorities, governments, parliaments, economic circles and public opinion were unanimous in recognizing as unreasonable and in condemning any policy of isolation. Every country was ready to welcome the goods of other countries in well-ordered exchanges. Industry worked at a profit. Agriculture, if not in Germany, at any rate in the majority of other countries, could live. The world opened itself wide to commerce. Banks evidenced a spirit of enterprise and granted credits to foreign countries. Investors were disposed to entrust their savings to foreign governments. In the majority of countries unemployment was still at that time an unknown problem. Those were the characteristic features of the period during which the Young Plan was conceived.

What an abyss between the glowing optimism of those days and the pessimism and despair of today! None of the promises of that period have been realized.

The desperate situation which prevails today is evidenced by the number of 25 million unemployed. . . . In Germany this state of things has most strongly shaken the confidence of the masses in the good functioning of the capitalist system.

A certain number of states have already found themselves obliged to suspend their payments abroad. This constitutes a grave warning not to delay taking the necessary measures in order that other great countries may not find themselves in the same position. I need not describe what would be the repercussions, the disastrous results on the world crisis of such further steps. In the present uncertainty there is no need to be surprised that the international circulation of capital and credit is, for the time, almost entirely arrested. The capitalists of wealthy countries, far from collaborating in a reasonable distribution of such capital, think only of withdrawing as rapidly as possible the credits which they have granted, and do so even though in their own countries capital can no longer find remunerative investment. The employer is often obliged, in order to make up his losses, to live on his capital. The capital which is in existence, and is destined to form the basis of fresh prosperity, shrinks steadily.

On the other hand, as a consequence of the increase in the value of gold, or as a result of the fall in prices, debtors are obliged to pay from 40 to so per cent more, and in this connection private debtors and debtor States are in exactly the same position. If an improvement of the situation does not speedily occur, we must expect a general adjustment of debts to become inevitable.

There remain two facts of a general character which I would also like to deal with.

The world has had to pass through crises in the past. . . . In one essential point, however, the present crisis is different from earlier ones. Formerly we had to deal with crises resulting from a lack of equilibrium between production and consumption, and a period of two to three years was generally sufficient to re-establish equilibrium. But upon the present crisis of international exchange there has been superimposed a second crisis—an unprecedented crisis of credit. This credit crisis has causes peculiar to itself. The most important are the public international debts and political payments, which are contrary to all sound or reasonable economic principles. The crisis of international exchange will not be surmounted unless the credit crisis is also overcome, and the latter cannot be overcome unless the specific cause from which it results is ruthlessly swept aside. That is the first point.

The second point is this. Under the influence of political debts a complete displacement has taken place between debtor and creditor countries in the repartition of gold on the one hand and the exchange of merchandise on the other. Gold has accumulated in the two national economic systems which are creditors under the system of international debts, whereas Germany is today the only debtor country which is almost entirely lacking in gold. In the creditor countries gold has become sterile, and in Germany the absence of gold is causing a growing paralysis of the economic machinery.

GREAT DEPRESSION

On the other hand, the commercial balance of Germany has become favourable during the last two years, under the pressure of its external debt, which is closely linked with the political debts, whereas in former decades it was always unfavourable. In the same period a development in the contrary direction has taken place in the creditor countries. . . .

The German problem is the central problem of the whole of the world's difficulties.

The German situation is characterized by the following:

1. The high level of interest, which crushes agriculture and also industry;

2. The burden of taxation, which is so oppressive, in the opinion of the Special Advisory Committee, that it cannot be increased, but has yet been increased, in order to assure the very existence of the State, by the imposition of fresh taxes within the last few days;

3. The external debt, the service of which becomes ever more difficult by reason of the progressive diminution of the surplus of exports; and

4. Unemployment, which is relatively more widespread than in any other country whatever. . . .

What is particularly fatal is that an ever-growing number of young people have no possibility and no hope of finding employment and earning their livelihood. Despair and the political radicalization of the youthful section of the population are the consequences of this state of things. . . .

The former reserves of the Reichsbank are exhausted. The reserves in gold and foreign currency of which the Reichsbank can freely dispose are no more than 390 million marks for a fiduciary circulation of 3,800 million marks, which means that the legal cover for the currency circulating in the country, which should be 40 per cent, is now no more than about 10 per cent. If in the next few weeks we are to fulfil our obligations, this small cover will become even more insufficient. . . .

The foreign trade of Germany closed in 1931 with an excess of some 3 milliards of marks. . . . The forced development of this favourable balance has led in all countries to protective measures against German imports, with the consequence that the excess of exports rapidly diminished in 1932.

In view of the fact that the prices of all goods have fallen by 50 per cent as compared with the prices of 1928–1929, the loan charges on private German debts abroad have alone reached almost to the level of the normal annuity contemplated by the Dawes Plan.

Germany could not by herself arrest this development. No international decision has been taken up to now by the responsible statesmen to arrest this development. The very wise initiative of President Hoover in June 1931 was inspired by the idea of giving the world a respite destined to produce a solution of the most urgent economic problems. This goal, nevertheless, has not been reached. Sufficient account has not been taken of the reality of economic laws. . . .

The external debt of Germany, with its very heavy interest charges, is, for the most part, attributable to the transfers of capital and the withdrawals of credits which have been the consequences of the execution of the Treaty of Versailles and of the reparations agreements. Thus, the Special Advisory Committee finds that the 18 milliard marks which were borrowed by Germany from other countries after the stabilization of her currency have been counterbalanced by an exodus of more than 10 milliard marks under the heading of reparation payments alone. At the present time, when we are beginning to convert into goods the value of money obligations, it is almost impossible to form an idea of the importance of the payments which have been made by Germany. I do not want to enter into a discussion of the question of what may have been the real value of those payments to the creditor countries which received them. It is natural that when goods to the value of several milliards are thrown on the market, there is not only a fall in prices, but there is also a non-economic utilization of those goods in the countries which receive them. Therefore, the profit realized by those who receive the goods is considerably inferior to the loss suffered by those who provide them. . . .

GREAT DEPRESSION

It is often said that Germany would become a formidable competitor with other countries if she were freed from her political debts. I am firmly convinced that those fears are based on absolutely erroneous considerations. The lightening of the budget charges produced by inflation, through the reduction of the service of internal debts, only constitutes an apparent alleviation of the burden. Inflation has also destroyed private fortunes and savings; indeed, the whole of the resources in capital which the German economic system had at its disposal. The lightening of the budgetary burden was therefore illusory. A comparison between the fiscal charges in Germany and in other countries is problematical, because such a complete confiscation of fortunes as has taken place in Germany has not occurred elsewhere.

Inflation has, therefore, lessened the capacity for competition of the entire German economic system. The State and private economy have lost their reserves. The destruction of those reserves of capital was followed by the contracting of fresh debts too rapidly and on too large a scale. The consequences became intolerable to the national economy. Agriculture and industry found themselves faced with the impossible task of meeting interest rates of 10 per cent and more for short-term credits, and only very little less for long-term credits. In addition, they are both crushed under the burden of taxation and fiscal charges. The present high level of public expenditure is to a large extent made necessary by social service obligations. On the other hand, the economic depression has automatically confronted the State with obligations which formerly fell upon private shoulders. The State has only assumed those obligations in view of its duty to prevent social distress and violent disturbances of public order which such distress threatens to bring about. For all these reasons, the German Government has gone to the very limit in the utilization of its resources and reserves. Public and private economy are today once more at the point where they found themselves after the inflation, that is to say they are devoid of any reserves and find themselves faced with an unemployment problem unprecedented in history. It is obvious that an industrial debtor country devoid of reserves, as Germany is now, could not constitute for a long time to come a menace to its competitors.

Source: Documents on British Foreign Policy, 1919–1939, *second series, volume 3 (London: H.M. Stationary Office, 1938–1939), pp. 197–201.*

investigation dates to World War I. Events between 1914 and 1918 encouraged the development of command economies in all the belligerents: to allocate resources, to encourage production in certain areas, and increasingly to control distribution. The degree of effectiveness achieved was unremarkable by later standards. It was, however, not merely encouraging but exhilarating to a new generation of bureaucrats loath to surrender the power they had gained, and to a new generation of soldiers firmly committed to preparing for the next major conflict.

The apparent success of Vladimir Lenin's Bolsheviks in the new Soviet Union further encouraged devotees of state management. Lenin's doctrine of faith, that political authority could be the catalyst of economic development, turned Karl Marx on his head. Though its initial applications in the 1920s were hardly promising, the vision was powerful. Combined with the legacy of the Great War, it generated among economists an ideological shift from laissez-faire to interventionism well before the outbreak of the Great Depression.

The new order was far from a theoretical construct. The German inflation that began in World War I as a device to finance the conflict was continued as a matter of policy after 1918 as a means of transferring funds, domestically and internationally, without any of the traditional and awkward legalities like applying for loans. The Soviet Union's repudiation of tsarist Russia's debts was another sign of the new times—and it is indicative of the cooperation and the complaisance of other governments and their financial structures that the Soviet Union's international credit did not vanish entirely. On a more benign note, the war's human costs created unprecedented demands for relief—medical care, pensions, housing subsidies, and unemployment benefits—that continued so long after the guns stopped that they became permanently incorporated into public budgets with neither precedents nor fund-raising structures for such increases. In addition, the new states of southern and eastern Europe created by the Versailles system imposed controlled economies on ethnically and politically divided societies, at the price of alienating farmers and the lower middle classes and deepening urban-rural tensions. Administrations not competent to manage even marginally developed economies handicapped new governments in acquiring domestic legitimacy and establishing international confidence.

That last point, indeed, became universal as the 1920s progressed. The politicization of economics and the postwar tendency to make diplomacy the conduct of war by other means created a near-Hobbesian state of affairs, requiring only a single push to cause an implosion. That push was provided by the United States. America's economy had assumed such significance during and after the Great War that Europe's economies depended on its health and stability. The slump of 1929 would have had serious consequences had it been solely an economic problem. Instead, government intervention exacerbated its consequences in two crucial areas.

The first one was essentially domestic. The monetary policies pursued by the Federal Reserve system are generally described as disastrous. Between 1930 and 1933 America's money supply and its price level fell by a third. Real interest rates reached double digits. Bank failures reached such epic proportions that a bank holiday was among the first major actions of the Roosevelt Administration. The explanations for the catastrophe fall under two categories. One describes a deliberate "contractionary policy" for the sake of bureaucratic objectives; the other depicts policy failures as the product of honest mistakes in judgment. In both cases the crucial subtext is the presence, and the application, of government power to an economic problem—with results analogous to doing brain surgery with a chainsaw.

As America's domestic economy spiraled into ruin, the government sought to help in a second way. The Smoot-Hawley Tariff (1930) was not a direct response to the Great Depression. Planning for tariff revision began in 1928 in response to the economic crisis facing agriculture, and there is no real proof that the new and higher tariff rated directly led to a down-

turn in the domestic business cycle. What did happen, however, was a 40 percent decline in U.S. foreign trade, the poisoning of international trade relations, the widespread adoption of similar tariffs in Europe and Asia, and the fostering of a sense that no country could be trusted, however deep the diplomatic or cultural links might be, if economics were involved. The Smoot-Hawley Tariff, more than any single policy initiative, transformed a serious recession into the Great Depression.

The consequences of government involvement in domestic economies and the international financial system continued to impact world economic and political systems until the collapse of the Soviet Union discredited intervention on the Marxist model, while the simultaneous boom enjoyed by market systems lent weight to the argument that even democratic elections do not guarantee universal expertise in government. The exact balance between states and economies remains subject to debate. Yet, continuing research into the roots of the Great Depression is likely to substantiate in even more detail the workings of that "Law of Unintended Consequences," which emerged time and again during the 1920s and 1930s when governments tried to be helpful and were not.

–DENNIS SHOWALTER,
COLORADO COLLEGE

References

Patricia Clavin, *The Great Depression in Europe, 1929–1939* (New York: St. Martin's Press, 2000).

John A. Garraty, *The Great Depression: An Inquiry into the Causes, Course, and Consequences of the Worldwide Depression of the Nineteen-thirties, as Seen by Contemporaries and in the Light of History* (San Diego: Harcourt Brace Jovanovich, 1986).

Thomas E. Hall and J. David Ferguson, *The Great Depression: An International Disaster of Perverse Economic Policies* (Ann Arbor: University of Michigan Press, 1998).

Michael Howard and William Roger Louis, *The Oxford History of the Twentieth Century* (Oxford: Oxford University Press, 1998).

GREEN PARTIES

Have the Green parties had a significant impact on European politics?

Viewpoint: Yes. European Green movements have gathered major electoral support and seriously influenced national policies on energy, environmental protection, and other issues.

Viewpoint: No. Green movements have been of only marginal influence; although they raise concerns about government policies, their overall effectiveness has been minimal.

The development of organized environmental movements on a large scale was a novel feature in European politics after World War II. Arising within the growing parameters of civil society, stimulated by new scientific concerns about the consequences of pollution and industrialization, and fostered by the rebellious mood of the 1960s, "Green" parties became a force in nearly every nation in Western Europe.

How influential were these movements, however? As one argument in this chapter maintains, Green parties grew steadily in the public eye, successfully drawing mass support, influencing governments, and promoting legislation. Leading Green figures have risen to positions of national prominence and entered national governments. Environmental issues are a mainstay of modern electoral politics.

Yet, despite their visibility, some observers question the true strength of the Greens. Few organized Green movements can compete with mainstream political parties, often because their positions and tactics alienate moderate electorates. Their successes at national levels have largely depended on marriages of convenience. Many of their demands have been brought to fruition by other politicians, often without Green influence. As concerns about the health of the global environment capture more headlines, a consideration of the strength and relevance of Green politics in Europe adds perspective.

Viewpoint:
Yes. European Green movements have gathered major electoral support and seriously influenced national policies on energy, environmental protection, and other issues.

Concern about environmental protection has grown dramatically in virtually all advanced industrialized democratic societies since the 1960s. Environmental movements that emerged in that decade, initially assuming the form of nongovernmental organizations, have gradually attracted considerable support and have effectively exerted significant pressure upon Western European governments. Since the early 1980s political parties specifically concerned with environmental issues, so-called Green parties, have also played an important role, entering national parliaments and bringing their concerns to the legislative agenda. However, the prominence of Green parties in specific European countries is by far not the only indicator of the impact of environmentalism. Under the growing pressure of popular environmental movements, many traditional political parties have successfully incorporated "Green" issues into their platforms, as they came to the realization that failure to address such issues might seriously jeopardize their chances to achieve electoral success. European integration, which has gradually gained momentum during the second half of the twentieth century, has led to the increasing coordination and harmonization of environmentalists in the different member countries of the European Union (EU) and resulted in the creation of a common environmental policy endorsed and carried out by the EU's central legislative and executive bodies. At present, the protection of the environment and the solution of environmental problems are integral parts of the general political and socio-economic development of Western Europe. Many legislative measures have been adopted to limit pollution in its various forms and to ensure that various consumer products are environmentally safe. Naturally, this situation has affected whole industries and economic sectors, such as metallurgy, power production, and manufacturing, which have to comply with environmental safety regulations.

The birth of the modern environmentalist movement in the 1960s and its subsequent dramatic growth have been conditioned by two major factors. First, new environmental problems experienced in advanced, industrialized, democratic societies, such as toxic waste, acid rain, nuclear power, and garbage disposal have generated concern among the general public in these countries. Second, the growth of environmentalism also reflected a critique of modern society and its insatiable materialism, excessive consumerism, and obsession with economic growth. In the early 1960s the World Wildlife Fund, an international environmental group with branches in several European countries, began promoting conservation and the protection of endangered species. Rachel Carson's *Silent Spring* (1962) and other books drew public attention on both sides of the Atlantic to many unresolved problems related to pollution, such as the indiscriminate use of the insecticide DDT. Meanwhile, the youth protest movement quickly spread over Western Europe and readily embraced the ideas and concerns of environmentalist activists. Increasing public awareness of the menace posed by uncontrolled pollution and resource depletion soon prompted, and was in turn stimulated by, governmental actions. The Council of Europe declared 1970 as the "European Conservation Year" in an effort to attract public attention and stimulate discussion on

environmental issues. The general political climate thus became conducive to the rise of environmentalist activism, and in the 1970s many international ecological movements emerged. Friends of the Earth (founded in 1969 in the United States) and Greenpeace (founded in 1971 in Canada) established branches in many European countries—West Germany, Ireland, France, Italy, Spain, Sweden, Switzerland, and others—during the 1970s and early 1980s. These organizations challenged the dominant social paradigm of Western industrial democracy; claimed that big business had thwarted control mechanisms; and argued that nuclear waste, along with various other forms of pollution and resource depletion, presented a clear danger to humanity's well-being. National ecological groups that came to prominence at this time include the Small Earth Society in the Netherlands and the Foundation for Alternative Life in West Germany.

During the 1970s Green issues gradually became part of electoral politics in Western Europe. This situation was conditioned by the transition to a postindustrial social organization in which most individuals can satisfy a fairly broad range of economic needs and are protected from economic depredations by effective social insurance systems. Only in this climate of security and affluence could people broaden their range of political and social demands and attribute greater importance to issues that go beyond the agenda of economic growth. In France, Belgium, Germany, and Austria, Green parties that emphasized issues related to environmental protection established solid presences in political life. In the 1980s the Greens in Germany won an average of 5.1 percent in parliamentary elections, 6 percent in Belgium, and 4 percent in Austria. In many other European countries, environmental issues were incorporated into the agenda of Left-libertarian parties, such as the Socialist People's parties in Denmark and Norway and the Pacifist Socialist Party in the Netherlands. Even more important, as a result of the successful popularization of environmental issues by broad civic activist organizations such as Friends of the Earth and Greenpeace, ecological concerns began to be addressed by traditional political parties with broad electoral support all over Western Europe. In 1998 the German Green Party entered national government as a coalition partner of the German Social Democrats.

In the 1980s virtually all countries in Western Europe created their own environmental ministries, which have imposed controls over a variety of economic activities in the spheres of industrial development, construction, and agriculture. Industry has modified production technology to comply with new environmental

GREENPEACE VICTORIES

2002

Brazil declares a moratorium on export of Mahogany following revelations of the extent of illegal logging and timber trade. Greenpeace actions around the world help enforce the ban.

2002

The European Union, followed by Japan, ratifies the Kyoto Protocol on climate change. Intensive Greenpeace lobbying must continue because, for the protocol to enter into force, 55 parties to the convention must ratify it.

2002

Greenpeace helps defeat a major drive by pro-whaling nation Japan and its supporters to re-introduce commercial whaling through the International Whaling Commission. The re-introduction would have been disastrous for whales, which are now protected under the 1982 commercial whaling ban.

2001

Greenpeace turns 30 years old in September. The environmental group has grown from a small band of inspired volunteers to an international environmental organization with offices in 30 countries. As always, Greenpeace thrives on committed activism and widespread, growing public support.

2001

After years of negotiations and pressure from Greenpeace, a global agreement for the elimination of a group of highly toxic and persistent man-made chemicals (Persistent Organic Pollutants or POPs), became a reality in May 2001 when a UN Treaty banning them is adopted.

2001

A historic agreement with logging companies is reached on the conservation of Canada's remaining coastal rainforest and approved by the government of British Columbia. This follows years of campaigning by Greenpeace, most recently targeting the trade and investments of companies involved in logging the endangered Great Bear Rainforest.

2001

Greenpeace lobbying, together with earlier expeditions to the Southern and Atlantic Oceans exposing flag of convenience (FOC or "pirate") vessels, are instrumental in the adoption of an "international plan of action" to combat illegal fishing in international waters.

2000–2001

An ever increasing and significant number of European retailers, food producers, and subsidiaries of multinational companies guaranteed to keep genetically engineered ingredients out of their products due to consumer pressure. Thanks to its consumer networks in 15 countries, Greenpeace tests products, collects information about food products and policies and exposes contamination cases.

2000

Further to Greenpeace's April–May expedition exposing pirate fishing in the Atlantic, an import ban is adopted on all bigeye tuna caught by FOC vessels in the Atlantic.

2000

Turkey's plans to build its first nuclear reactors at Akkuyu as part of a larger project to construct 10 reactors by the year 2020, is finally cancelled in July after eight years of campaigning by Greenpeace and others. The only remaining market for all major western nuclear companies is China.

2000

The Biosafety Protocol is adopted in Montreal, Canada. It aims to protect the environment and human health from risks of Genetically Modified Organisms (GMOs) by controlling international trade of GMOs. Greenpeace has campaigned to stop the irreversible release of GMOs into the environment and to protect biodiversity from genetic pollution since 1995.

1999

Nine countries ban the use of harmful phthalates in polyvinyl chloride (PVC) toys for children under three and the EU introduces an "emergency" ban on soft PVC teething toys.

1999

Japan is ordered to stop "experimental" fishing of Southern Bluefin Tuna by the International Law of the Sea Tribunal.

1998

The Environmental Protocol to the Antarctic Treaty comes into force.

1998

A historic accord, the OSPAR Convention, bans the dumping of offshore installations at sea in the North-East Atlantic. The Convention also agrees on the phasing-out of radioactive and toxic discharges, as proposed by Greenpeace.

1998

The oil company Shell finally agrees to bring its infamous offshore installation, the Brent Spar, to land for recycling. Greenpeace campaigned since 1995 to persuade the oil company not to dump disused installations in the ocean.

1998

After 15 years of campaigning by Greenpeace, the EU finally agrees to phase out driftnet fishing by its fleets in EU and international waters by the end of 2001. France, Italy, the UK and Ireland, continued driftnetting in the North-East Atlantic and Mediterranean after Japan, Taiwan and Korea stopped driftnet fishing on the high seas when the worldwide ban came into force at the end of 1992.

1998

Logging giant MacMillan Bloedel announces it will phase out clearcut logging activities in British Columbia, Canada.

1997

After campaigning for urgent action to protect the climate since 1988 by Greenpeace and others, ministers from industrialized nations adopt the Kyoto Protocol agreeing to set legally-binding reduction targets on Greenhouse gases.

1997

Greenpeace collects the UNEP Ozone Award for the development of Greenfreeze, a domestic refrigerator free of ozone depleting and significant global warming chemicals.

1996

The Comprehensive Nuclear Test Ban Treaty (CTBT) is adopted at the United Nations.

1995

Following a high profile action by Greenpeace, and public pressure, Shell UK reverses its decision to dump the Brent Spar oil platform in the Atlantic Ocean.

1995

Greenpeace actions to stop French nuclear testing receive wide international attention. Over seven million people sign petitions calling for a stop to testing. France, UK, US, Russia and China commit to sign the CTBT.

1995

Following a submission made with Greenpeace support, UNESCO designates Russia's Komi Forest as a World Heritage Site.

1994

After years of Greenpeace actions against whaling, the Antarctic whale sanctuary, proposed by France and supported by Greenpeace, is approved by the International Whaling Commission.

1994

Greenpeace actions exposing toxic waste trade from Organization for Economic Cooperation and Development (OECD) to non-OECD countries culminate in government negotiation of the Basel Convention banning this practice.

1993

The London Dumping Convention permanently bans the dumping at sea of radioactive and industrial waste worldwide.

1992

France cancels this year's nuclear tests at Moruroa Atoll, following the Rainbow Warrior visit to the test zone, and vows to halt altogether if other nuclear nations follow suit.

1992

Worldwide ban on high seas large-scale driftnets comes into force.

1991

The 39 Antarctic Treaty signatories agree to a 50-year minimum prohibition of all mineral exploitation, in effect preserving the continent for peaceful, scientific purposes.

1991

Major German publishers go chlorine-free after Greenpeace produces chlorine-free edition of Der Spiegel as part of campaign against chlorine-bleaching.

1989

A UN moratorium on high seas large-scale driftnets is passed, responding to public outrage at indiscriminate fishing practices exposed by Greenpeace.

1988

Following at sea actions, and submissions by Greenpeace, a world-wide ban on incinerating organochlorine waste at sea is agreed by the London Dumping Convention.

1985

French nuclear testing in the South Pacific again becomes the subject of international controversy, particularly following the sinking of Greenpeace's ship, the Rainbow Warrior, by the French Secret Services.

1983

The Parties to the London Dumping Convention call for a moratorium on radioactive waste dumping at sea. As a result of Greenpeace's repeated actions against ocean dumping, this is the first year since the end of the Second World War where officially no radioactive wastes are dumped at sea.

1982

After at sea actions against whalers, a whaling moratorium is adopted by the International Whaling Commission.

1982

EC bans import of seal pup skins in response to public criticism triggered by Greenpeace actions in Canada.

1978

Greenpeace actions halt the grey seal slaughter in the Orkney Islands, Scotland.

1975

France ends atmospheric tests in the South Pacific after Greenpeace protests at the test site.

1972

After the first Greenpeace action in 1971, the US abandons nuclear testing grounds at Amchitka Island, Alaska.

Source: Greenpeace Internet Page <http://www.greenpeace.org/international_en/victory/>.

GREEN PARTIES

standards. The use of artificial fertilizers is strictly monitored. Car manufacturers have been pressed to limit automobile emissions in newly designed vehicles. The presence of hazardous substances has been considerably limited in various consumer products, ranging from foodstuffs and clothing to furniture. Nuclear power plants have adopted comprehensive safety measures, and the transportation and disposal of toxic waste have been subjected to strict regulations.

European integration further accentuated the prominence of environmental policies in Western Europe. The Single European Act (1987), the most important purpose of which was to facilitate the creation of a single European market, also explicitly recognized the improvement of environmental quality as a legitimate objective in its own right. The European Parliament, which also has its own Green parliamentary group, has passed several legislative measures harmonizing the environmental policies of all member countries. As a result, any industrial company, construction firm, power plant, or agricultural producer in any EU member country has to comply with strict environmental standards in order to be competitive in the common market.

In Eastern Europe environmental problems had been largely neglected by communist regimes until 1989. Public discussion of such issues was suppressed. Rapid industrialization in the absence of viable environmental regulations has led to high levels of pollution, which directly threatened the well-being of people in many regions. Continuous neglect of environmental problems was probably the chief factor that brought about the Chernobyl ecological catastrophe in the Soviet Union in April 1986. Understandably, the fall of communist governments in 1989 and the transition of Eastern European countries to democracy and free-market economics dramatically changed the situation. However, environmental concerns themselves were an important catalyst of democratic reforms and played a major role in the region's dissent movement. Environmental organizations, which emerged often in response to crises in specific regions such as the Halle-Leipzig industrial area in the former East Germany or the city of Russe in Northern Bulgaria, not only contributed significantly to heightening the general public's awareness of environmental problems but also combined their specific ecological concerns with demands for overall democratization. In some cases, such as in East Germany, Poland, Hungary, Ukraine, Slovenia, and Bulgaria, environmental groups were among the most influential actors in bringing down the communist system. In other countries, such as Czechoslovakia, Armenia, and

Romania, environmental problems themselves directly contributed to the fall of the totalitarian regimes.

After 1989, environmental issues in Eastern European politics quickly attained a prominent place. Furthermore, Eastern European countries' aspirations to become full members of the EU mandated a rapid harmonization of their environmental legislation and policies with those of the organization. For example, the shutting down of nuclear power plants in Slovakia, Bulgaria, and Lithuania is considered to be an unavoidable requirement that such countries will have to fulfill in order to qualify for EU membership.

–YORK NORMAN,
GEORGETOWN UNIVERSITY

Viewpoint:
No. Green movements have been of only marginal influence; although they raise concerns about government policies, their overall effectiveness has been minimal.

The development of Green parties has had a minimal impact on European political life. Although they receive much media attention and advocate ideas that resonate broadly in some European electorates, their strength as a major political force compares only with other small, marginal parties.

A recapitulation of some recent statistics will illuminate the situation. In the first round of the 2002 French presidential election, the Green candidate Noel Mamère captured barely 5 percent of the vote. In 1997 his party captured a mere 7 seats in France's 577-seat National Assembly. Even the most noted case of Green party involvement in politics, in Germany, illustrates its limitations more than its strengths. In the 1998 parliamentary elections it polled just 6.7 percent of the electorate, a figure that rose slightly to 7.4 percent in the elections of September 2002. Although the Greens formed a coalition government with Chancellor Gerhard Schröder's moderate-Left Social Democrats, and their leader Joschka Fischer became the country's foreign minister, these developments were more the result of the Social Democrats' ability to form precarious majorities than an appreciation of the Greens' strength. In Britain in 2001 and Italy in 2002, the national Green parties won less than 3 percent of the vote in parliamentary elections. Nowhere in Europe has a Green party scored higher than 10 percent.

Why are the Greens so weak? Part of the reason lies in their self-defined focus on environmen-

tal policies. In complex modern societies facing many other important issues, the Green parties' singular orientation has naturally limited their appeal. Although they do take stances on other issues, mainly to garner more mainstream support, their major focus remains the environment. Most Europeans care about their environment, yet that concern cannot compete with issues relating to economic development, social welfare, foreign policy, and other areas that they see as more directly relevant to their lives. That other, more broadly based "umbrella" parties should attract more attention and support should not come as much of a surprise.

Another crippling factor for Green parties is that their stances on nonenvironmental issues tend to be too radical for mainstream European electorates. Many national Green parties emerged from the far Left's protest movements of the late 1960s, while newer ones have sought self-consciously to emulate the actions and views of the more established movements. In recent decades the radical tradition has alienated more European voters than it has attracted. The Green parties that have sprung from it espouse views and policies well to the left even of Europe's mainstream socialist parties. As European society became less defined by class, more integrated commercially, and less motivated by ideology, support for the extreme Left waned. Even the center Left has had to abandon most of its more radical positions to attract support. The so-called third way to which

British prime minister Tony Blair, German chancellor Gerhard Schröder, and, to a lesser extent, former French prime minister Lionel Jospin have appealed (in more or less conscious imitation of U.S. president Bill Clinton's centrist "New Democrat" image) has successfully adopted many long-standing beliefs of the political Right. These beliefs have included a firm faith in market economics, support for a reduced role for government in the economy and society, vigilant anticrime measures, and other policies. Only in this modified form have traditional parties of the Left found respectability and trustworthiness in the eyes of Europeans comparable to that enjoyed by the British Conservatives or the German Christian Democrats (and the American Republicans) in the 1980s. In such an environment, Green parties stand with other parties of the extreme Left as homes for marginalized radicals, disgruntled intellectuals, and protest voters who object to corruption or apathy in the mainstream Left-wing parties. As European election figures have shown with consistency, neither these groups nor voters who place environmental concerns above all others make up a significant percentage of national electorates.

The perceived radicalism of Green environmental policies has also contributed to the movement's weakness. True to its radical origins in the 1960s, many Green parties advocate grass-roots-based direct action, including protest marches, street demonstrations, and other confrontational

Chernobyl Nuclear Power Station, Ukraine, site of the world's worst nuclear power accident on 25–26 April 1986

(Yann Arthus-Bertrand/CORBIS)

GREEN PARTIES

tactics with government and industry. Although the activists believe that these measures impact government policy, alter business practices, raise general awareness, and produce tangible results, they nevertheless upset the sensibilities of many voters who favor using the established political process to effect change. Green policies calling for such measures as the abolition of nuclear power, stricter pollution standards, and more government environmental regulation are believed to threaten commercial prosperity, material quality of life, individual freedom, and productive employment. Societies that embrace these values on a long-established philosophical basis are hardly likely to support parties that they believe may place limitations on them.

In addition to their other limitations, Green parties are fairly redundant in contemporary European political landscapes. Postwar Western Europe still developed the world's most far-reaching and stringent laws to protect the environment without any major reliance on the Greens. Governments of both the center Right and the center Left campaigned on platforms that addressed environmental policy comprehensively and have implemented these policies without needing Greens to help them. In the opinion of European electorates, the centrist parties have more-sensible environmental policies than the Greens and are more experienced and trustworthy in the handling of environmental issues.

In addition to their poor electoral performance, limited appeal, and redundancy, Green participation in government has been a small affair and to little effect. Only two Green parties have ever entered a major national government: in France in 1997–2002 and in Germany since 1998. Media attention has highlighted their successes in these cases, but the major point is not that Green parties are influential, but rather that these cases were unprecedented and exceptional. While the French Green Party leader Dominique Voynet became the environment minister in Jospin's cabinet in 1997, his party only had seven parliamentary deputies. Jospin nevertheless wanted their support to strengthen his precarious majority, but the coalition that he had already formed with the French Communist Party did not at all depend on Green participation. In addition, Jospin's tenure as prime minister showed this weakness. Voynet nearly resigned over disagreements with the government in 1999, and no progress was ever made on the Greens' central issue, reducing France's dependence on nuclear energy. The country still produces a staggering 78 percent of its electricity in nuclear power plants.

The German Greens fared little better. Green-led protests against the deployment of American cruise missiles in West Germany in the early 1980s—missiles deployed after the signing of an agreement between Washington and Helmut Schmidt's Social Democratic government—were totally ineffectual. Although Schröder desperately needed a coalition to form a Social Democratic government in 1998—enough to appoint a Green foreign minister—the German Greens have had only a marginal influence over state policy. Schröder has shown no sign of fulfilling his initial promise to make Germany free of nuclear energy, and he has received considerable support from big business. Much to the Greens' consternation, the Social Democratic majority in the coalition categorically overruled their objections to the use of German military forces in Yugoslavia since 1999 and in Afghanistan since 2001. Although the September 2002 elections reaffirmed Schröder's need for his Green coalition partners, their continued participation in the government, however ineffectual, was a lesser evil than a Right-wing government or the loss of a national platform from which to advertise their views.

Green parties and movements have been of little effectiveness in Europe. Their environmental focus, political radicalism, and confrontational tactics have turned off many voters. More moderate and mainstream alternatives have reflected European environmental sensibilities with greater accuracy and considerable effect. The Continent's Greens continue to languish in single-digit poll numbers, widespread suspicion, and—even when they have entered national government—in ineffective and marginal roles on national stages.

–PAUL DU QUENOY,
GEORGETOWN UNIVERSITY

References

Rachel Carson, *Silent Spring* (Boston: Houghton Mifflin, 1962).

Daniel Coleman, *Ecopolitics: Building a Green Society* (New Brunswick, N.J.: Rutgers University Press, 1994).

Brian Doherty and Marius de Geus, eds., *Democracy and Green Political Thought: Sustainability, Rights, and Citizenship* (London & New York: Routledge, 1996).

Michael O'Neill, *Green Parties and Political Change in Contemporary Europe: New Politics, Old Predicaments* (Brookfield, Vt.: Ashgate, 1997).

Dick Richardson and Chris Roots, eds., *The Green Challenge: The Development of Green Parties in Europe* (London & New York: Routledge, 1995).

Douglas Torgerson, *The Promise of Green Politics: Environmentalism and the Public Sphere* (Durham, N.C.: Duke University Press, 1999).

GREEN PARTIES

INTERNATIONAL FASCISM

Was fascism widespread in the 1920s and 1930s?

Viewpoint: Yes. Significant fascist movements appeared in several European nations besides Germany and Italy.

Viewpoint: No. Although sympathizers could be found outside of Germany and Italy, few fascist movements achieved power in other European nations.

This chapter debates whether fascism, like communism, captured enough popularity in the 1920s and 1930s to deserve consideration as a true international phenomenon. One argument suggests that it was indeed pervasive. Although the success of fascist ambitions was confined to Germany and Italy, fascists or their sympathizers in other European nations, as well as the Middle East, the United States, and Russian émigré circles, formed mass movements and political parties that had a discernible impact on national governments and ideologies of power. If even Ireland could have a serious fascist movement (the "Blue Shirts") with tens of thousands of members and if leaders like the Norwegian Vidkun Quisling self-consciously imitated Adolf Hitler and Benito Mussolini, who could deny that fascism was international?

Yet, this statement can be refuted. As the counterpoint essay in this chapter makes clear, a precise definition of what constitutes fascism remained, and has remained, somewhat elusive. Disparaging a tendency to "see fascism everywhere," this argument suggests that many Right-wing or authoritarian political formations departed from German Nazism and Italian fascism, and even that those two ideologies were too widely divergent to be considered the same. The failure of fascism to take root outside Germany and Italy, furthermore, damages the claim that it was a major phenomenon abroad. Even if small fascist groups did proliferate throughout Europe and the world, it was precisely their inability to come to power that made them irrelevant, and that made international fascism a chimera.

Viewpoint:
Yes. Significant fascist movements appeared in several European nations besides Germany and Italy.

International fascism certainly existed. In the years between World War I and World War II, fascism spread beyond its home country of Italy and its second home, Germany (whose National Socialism was a modified version of fascism), to take root in more than a dozen states. The evidence shows that many interwar political movements adopted (and adapted) fascist ideology and symbols; that such movements had significant followings; that they maintained connections with each other; and that a few intellectuals took steps toward creating a formal international organization to link them.

Most people would agree that fascism includes the following characteristics: strong nationalist feelings that may involve racism and

Norwegian prime minister and Nazi collaborator Vidkun Quisling, 19 August 1945, the day before he was tried for war crimes and high treason. He was executed on 24 October

(Bettmann/CORBIS).

anti-Semitism; belief in authoritarianism, violent action, and the primacy of the state over the individual; opposition to communism and liberalism as well as the communist and liberal views of history; and a predilection for uniforms, parades, and symbols (often inspired by national history) evoking power and might. Italian philosophy professor Camillo Pellizzi defined fascism in 1922 as "the practical negation of historical materialism and, still more, the negation of democratic individualism, of the rationalism of the Enlightenment—fascism is the affirmation of the

principles of tradition, hierarchy, authority, and individual sacrifice in view of a historical ideal."

Not everyone agrees with this formulation, but attempts to replace or discredit it have been unsuccessful. Eugen Weber distinguishes fascism, in which ideology is merely a means to acquire power, from National Socialism, in which ideology dictates what that power will be used for. By Weber's definition, though, a power-hungry Nazi could be a fascist rather than a National Socialist, and an idealistic Italian fascist would really be a National Socialist, despite all his protests to the contrary. Gilbert Allardyce insists that "the word fascismo has no meaning beyond Italy. . . . The so-called fascist parties are too mixed, diverse, and exceptional to be collected into such a general typology." His pronouncement disregards interwar perceptions of fascism and leaves many self-proclaimed fascist parties out in the cold. The word *fascist* must be broad enough to match the observations of the British fascist Oswald Mosley and the one-time communist Arthur Koestler, both of whom saw fascism facing off against communism in a Europe-wide struggle for dominance. It must be broad enough to include the All-Russian Fascist Party (established by émigrés in Manchuria and the United States in 1934), the Faisceau (established in France in 1925), Mosley's British Union of Fascists, and the Bulgarian Natsionalna Zadruga Fashisti.

Such groups may have drawn on different national traditions and personal beliefs to create fascisms that suited them, but they were fascist nonetheless. For example, Mosley's British fascists, who sported Italian-style black shirts, German-style anti-Semitism, and aggressive "Britain First" nationalism, agitated for a corporate state free of political parties and social classes. The Bulgarian fashisti openly looked to Benito Mussolini's Italy for ideological inspiration. Other movements denied any connection with fascism or Nazism—staunch nationalists were understandably reluctant to associate themselves with rival nations. Yet, according to the Spaniard José Primo de Rivera and the Hungarian Ferenc Szalasi, the movements simultaneously rejected communism and liberalism in favor of fascist corporate states "in which all individuals and classes are integrated" in a "most perfect totality" under "the direction and guidance of the Hungarian (or Spanish, or Latvian) people."

In interwar Europe, fascist groups were almost everywhere: Britain, where the British Union of Fascists attracted nearly 50,000 members at its height in 1933 and remained popular in London's East End until it was outlawed in 1940; Spain, whose Falange adopted the colors red and black; Belgium, where another red-and-black party, the Rexists, earned 21 parliamentary seats in 1936 and coexisted uneasily with a small but militant group of club-wielding Flemish nationalists called the Verdinaso; Yugoslavia, where 2,000 gray-uniformed Ustasha demanded that Bosnia- Herzegovina be given to Croatia, while sympathetic historians tried to prove that Croatians descended from Goths; Bulgaria, where the Natsionalna Zadruga Fashisti had about 8,000 members; Hungary, where the National Socialist Party and various other fascist/national socialist parties together received 750,000 of 2,000,000 votes in a 1939 election; Romania, where new members of the Iron Guard received sacks of Romanian earth and vowed to "struggle against Jewish Communism"; Lithuania, where the Iron Wolf Party came to power in 1926 and implemented authoritarian rule; Latvia, where the Thunder Cross called their leader "Führer" and copied Nazi iconography; Estonia, where Freedom Fighters carried clubs and sang of "Manly Spirit"; Norway, where "Forer" Vidkun Quisling's brown-shirted National Union Party waited for the world fascist revolution until Adolf Hitler installed him in power in 1940; and Finland, where members of the People's Patriotic League wore armbands depicting a man, armed with a club, riding a bear. Meanwhile, across the Atlantic, immigrants and home-grown Right-wingers joined the anti-communist and anti-Semitic Silver Legion of America, the Italian American Black Shirts, and the German American Bund, the last of which attracted anywhere from 20,000 to 100,000 members.

Informal connections between these groups existed. The Freedom Fighters in Estonia inspired the Thunder Cross in Latvia. Italian fascists donated money to Belgium's Rexists, whose leader would later receive the German Iron Cross for his courageous service on the Eastern Front. The Romanian Iron Guard sent volunteers across Europe to fight for the Nationalist side in the Spanish Civil War (1936–1939), while party members who stayed at home wore their uniforms openly when it was rumored that Hitler had admired their movement.

For some scholars, however, informal connections are not enough. By their definition, *international fascism* exists only when a single fascist party draws members from all over Europe and coordinates actions across national lines. In other words, they demand a fascist equivalent to the Communist International, the Moscow-dominated organization of national communist parties founded in 1919. Yet, this strict definition is far too limited. No one demands that the 1848 "Springtime of the Peoples" produce a board of directors and an official platform in order to be certified as an international movement. Moreover, an international Renaissance began in fifteenth-century Italy and spread across Europe without the benefit of a single monthly meeting. Although international fascism may be a less pleasing contribution to human history than the two above-mentioned examples, it lacks nothing in terms of organization.

Nevertheless, an organization did exist that fits the strict definition of international fascism. It began in the late 1920s in Italy, where a group of intellectual fascists felt the need for an authoritative description of the philosophy of fascism. This theory of *fascismo universale* (universal fascism) would, they felt, lead to a complete spiri-

INTERNATIONAL FASCISM

tual and political transformation of Italy and the world. Their efforts culminated in a conference held at Montreux, Switzerland, in 1934, where representatives of thirteen countries (not including Germany) attended. The Congress of Montreux foundered, mostly because its members were unable to come to an agreement on the issue of anti-Semitism. (Some wanted a doctrine free of the idea of racial superiority; others insisted that racism was a fundamental part of fascism.) However, according to Allardyce, the delegates did manage to agree on several key "articles of faith": "the monolithic state, economic corporatism, something called the 'national revolution,' and above all else, the proposition that each nation must solve its own problems in its own way"—the last tenet a kind of United Nations in reverse.

International fascism as represented by the Congress of Montreux was to be short-lived. The movement faded away after Mussolini and Hitler joined forces, and it never became a world revolution. It did, however, knit together many strands of informal cooperation between fascists—the loose connections of international fascism—into one small knot.

—CATHERINE BLAIR,
GEORGETOWN UNIVERSITY

Viewpoint:
No. Although sympathizers could be found outside of Germany and Italy, few fascist movements achieved power in other European nations.

Aside from what occurred in Germany and Italy, few major fascist movements developed in Europe in the 1920s and 1930s. Despite the fact that many links can be seen in the ideology of these groups, as they largely were opposed to liberal democracy, materialism, Marxism, feminism, egalitarianism, bourgeois civilization, and individualism, one cannot speak of "international fascism." In describing several small fascist groups that appeared across Europe in the interwar period, one is repeatedly forced to analyze the reasons for each group's failure, an indication of their lack of influence and significance. Some groups suffered from the lack of a charismatic leader. Others cropped up in countries that were not socially, politically, or economically ripe for widespread support of fascism. Finally, in part because of the lack of a universal doctrine of political philosophy, several groups were crippled by their inability to align with other

like-minded groups to create larger coalitions with broader domestic and international support. Although a few did gain sizable memberships or briefly exercise power, to argue that this is evidence of international fascism is to characterize these political and social movements mistakenly.

An examination of fascist groups in several countries will further elucidate this point. British fascists were plagued by many problems. First, the British Union of Fascists (BUF), the most popular group, was fractured. The British people were not supportive of anti-Semitism or the type of violence espoused by such a group. The British government was able to act decisively to curb the activities and influence of the BUF, especially in light of the BUF's support of Adolf Hitler into the late 1930s. British fascism never became a significant political force.

Irish fascist sympathizers were known as "Blue Shirts." Although the movement had forty-six thousand members in 1934, this popularity was short-lived. Similarly, although the Blue Shirts had many of the superficial trappings of fascist groups, most obviously the shirts, they differed ideologically from most other fascists. The Blue Shirts supported democracy; did not endorse violence; and seemed uninterested in racism, anti-Semitism, or anticommunism. Thus, it is not possible to suggest the Blue Shirts as evidence of an international fascist movement.

A few fascist groups developed in Portugal, but the socio-economic conditions did not exist there for fascism to flourish. World War I and the subsequent depression did not affect Portugal as directly as it was still a predominantly agricultural country. Although some observers have characterized Antonio Oliveira Salazar and his movement to be fascist, it is most accurately described as authoritarian. His rightist government did not even really include fascists in political roles.

Despite fertile ideological ground for fascism in France, a country with a history of anti-Semitism, anti-intellectualism, authoritarianism, and various other intellectual currents, fascism did not take hold of French politics. Like Portugal, France was less industrialized and more agrarian than Germany and bore less of the brunt of the economic dislocation of the 1920s and 1930s, providing less opportunity for fascist ideology to take root in France. In France, fascists could not support a single leader or organize a single group. Groups such as Action française and Croix de Feu/Parti Social Français were on the extreme Right, but not necessarily fascist—or even antifascist—an important distinction to bear in mind when looking at the broader European stage.

INTERNATIONAL FASCISM

ITS OWN BEST ARGUMENT AGAINST ITSELF

In response to a meeting of members of the fascist-leaning German-American Bund at Madison Square Garden on 20 February 1939, the New York Times *printed the following editorial:*

There is no occasion to worry about what happened in and around Madison Square Garden on Monday evening. The German-American Bund, exercising the right of free speech which its German allies long ago suppressed, hired a hall. It pledged "undivided allegiance" to the flag, deplored the "campaign of hate" of which it believes itself to be the innocent victim, endorsed the Golden Rule and listened to speeches denouncing the National Administration, the city administration and a number of eminent and respected private citizens.

Seventeen hundred policemen kept an unsympathetic outside crowd of between 10,000 (Commissioner Valentine's estimate) and 100,000 (Chief Inspector Costuma's estimate) in reasonable order. Several fights took place outside the hall. But for so large a meeting of so insolent a character the occasion passed off pretty peaceably. The police demonstrated that the uniformed strong-arm squad maintained by the Bund was unnecessary, as it is totally out of keeping with the atmosphere of a public meeting in a democratic country.

We need be in no doubt as to what the Bund would do to and in this country if it had the opportunity. Unless its attitudes and utterances are greatly misleading, it would set up an American Hitler. It is an outspoken enemy of the traditions of the American democracy, including those upheld by George Washington, whom it insulted by pretending to honor. In spite of these facts, its members are entitled to free speech and to the protection of the other constitutional guarantees so long as they keep within the laws which bind all of us. We cannot deny these rights and still call ourselves a democracy. It would be folly to deny them, for the Bund, functioning freely, is its own best argument against itself.

To some observers Monday's spectacle was ominous because it resembled the Nazi demonstrations in Germany which preceded Hitler's rise to power. To such observers toleration seems a dangerous weakness. But the attitude of the police, of the city government and, as we think, of the public generally was evidence of confident strength, not of weakness.

We are not, to state the case mildly, afraid of the Bund. The limits to which this or any other group, including the Communists, may go are definite. If any group attempts to overpass those limits, ample and legal force exists to put them down—and let them have no doubt of the outcome: they will be put down.

Source: *"The Bund Meeting,"* New York Times, 22 February 1939, p. 20.

It is best to imagine fascists sprinkled across Europe in small, unconnected groups, rather than forming a large-scale movement. For example, there were fascists in Norway. Vidkun Quisling established the *Nasjonal Samling,* or National Union Party, in 1933. Yet, neither Quisling nor the National Union Party achieved great political success. Its designation as the only legal party in 1940 was due to Nazi occupation, not an indication of domestic support for the party, its leader, or its agenda. There were Finnish fascists as well, although their appeal lay mostly in strong nationalism. Ultimately, Finnish fascism came to be publicly identified with German National Socialism. That identification, along with economic improvement and parliamentary reforms, stymied the rise of fascism in Finland.

Some Russian expatriates in Manchuria and the United States became fascists as well, forming the All-Russian Fascist Party in 1934. This party was diametrically opposed to the Soviet Union. It wanted to create a state based on "God, Nation, and Labor." The party, however, split less than a year after it was founded and disappeared entirely by the outbreak of war between Germany and the Soviet Union.

Secret societies in Hungary developed into fascist political parties in the 1930s. The parties adopted some of the symbols of fascism, including wearing green shirts with an arrow cross symbol. (The Arrow Cross Party was formed in 1936 and had around two hundred thousand members at the end of 1939.) Although none of these parties enjoyed success on the scale of Italy or Germany, the Hungarian government did adopt some of their reforms, and Ferenc Szalasi, the leading proponent of "Hungarianism," held power briefly in 1944 until the Soviet arrival. Even this modest success, however, is far from an indication of the existence of a larger movement.

Circumstances were not ripe for fascism in Czechoslovakia, either. Those groups that did develop were marginal, without significant followers. In Slovakia, however, there was more attraction to fascism due to religious and nationalist feelings of domination from Prague. When Slovakia became a German protectorate in 1939, these parties lost any chance for political authority, as Hitler's puppet, Monsignor Josef Tiso, exerted the real power.

In Belgium, there were at least eight rightist movements in the interwar period that could be at varying degrees linked to fascist ideology, affectations, or behavior. None of these groups, however, really gained widespread support. Belgium, like Portugal and France, did not experience extreme social and economic change and was less susceptible to fascism. Belgium's religious and linguistic divisions meant that it was difficult for any party to gain widespread support. None of the extreme Right-wing parties captured the population's imagination with a charismatic leader or compelling political program.

To speak of fascism in Poland in the first part of the twentieth century is also somewhat of a misnomer. The best way to describe important Polish political movements that developed characteristics similar to those described as fascist elsewhere in Europe is as extreme Right or, more moderately, as Right of Center. The history of rightist movements in Poland is not particularly neat; it can be more accurately described as an evolutionary process. Over time different movements emerged, often subsuming previously prominent groups. Yet, despite the creation of new groups (or at least of differently named groups), the movements of the Polish Right were not fascist themselves. The extreme Right in interwar Poland was highly nationalistic, anti-Semitic, opposed to democratization, initially anticlerical, and had youth and paramilitary organizations. Yet, there were significant points on which the two movements diverged. Specifically, Roman Dmowski criticized Italian fascism and German Nazism for personality cults, the militarization of politics, an obsession with industrialization, and a disregard for the rule of law. He opposed what historian Andrzej Walicki describes as "right-wing totalitarianism," instead favoring a tradition-based conservative movement in a time of European upheaval.

Owing to links between Italian and Austrian fascists—Benito Mussolini supported Austria's protofascist party, the Heimwehr, financially—one could attempt to see a larger connection between fascist movements. Yet, Mussolini was motivated by fears of rising National Socialism, a move that indicated the splits even between fascist Italy and Nazi Germany at the time. The Heimwehr did gain significant political support, but it was subsumed by Austrian chancellor Engelbert Dollfuss into his Fatherland Front movement and by the mid 1930s ceased to exist as an independent party. Alongside this group, an Austrian Nazi Party developed, but it was patterned on Hitler's model in Germany and did his bidding.

Nevertheless, there were some fascist successes. Like the Austrian fascists, the Yugoslavian Ustasa directly benefited from external assistance. German and Italian aid proved essential to the rise of the Ustasa to power in Yugoslavia. Fascists also existed in Romania, known there as the League of the Archangel of Michael. In the 1937 elections, the League secured the second-largest share of the voting.

In the United States, similar small fascist groups appeared, many of which were tied to their respective European homelands. By 1924 Rome was directing the Italian American Black Shirts' operations. Their popularity, as well as that of other Italian American fascist groups, was tied to Italian patriotic sentiment. It rose in the mid 1930s, a time of Italian foreign-policy successes, but fell in the 1940s in an effort to appear to have undivided loyalty to the United States. In addition to the Italian American fascist groups in the United States, the Nazi party in Germany inspired the creation of extreme Right groups. The most prominent example, the German-American Bund, was a Nazi organization intimately connected with the Ausland-Organization of the German National Socialist Worker's Party (NSDAP). Its mission was to convince German Americans that ethnic links should be stronger than those of citizenship. Estimates at Bund membership vary from twenty thousand to one hundred thousand, signifying the group's prominence; however, it declined in 1939 predominantly owing to the Nazi-Soviet Pact, which stimulated significant ideological disputes and precipitated a decline in Bund membership. Bund members drilled in paramilitary uniforms and adopted much of the Nazi regalia for their own ceremonial uses. The federal government took the seditious nature of the Bund so seriously that it was under scrutiny from the House Un-American Activities Committee beginning in the fall of 1938, and it was subject to similar treatment from state and local governments. Its enemies charged that the Bund was nothing more than a front for German intelligence.

A further indicator of the extent of the fractures within fascist groups in Europe in the interwar period was the failed efforts by some to found a "Fascist International," an organization that would roughly correspond to the Communist International established in 1919. The Congress of Montreux in 1934 was intended to create such an organization, but it collapsed due to disagreements between national delegates and shifts in the foreign policies of Mussolini's Italy and Hitler's Germany. This failure is further confirmation of the absence of an international fascist movement.

–SARAH SNYDER,
GEORGETOWN UNIVERSITY

References

Gilbert Allardyce, "What Fascism is Not: Thoughts on the Deflation of a Concept," *American Historical Review,* 84 (April 1979): 367–388.

F. L. Carsten, *The Rise of Fascism* (Berkeley: University of California Press, 1967).

Martin Conway, "The Extreme Right in Inter-War Francophone Belgium: Explanations of a Failure," *European History Quarterly,* 26 (April 1996): 267–292.

Charles F. Delzell, ed., *Mediterranean Fascism, 1919–1945* (New York: Harper & Row, 1970).

Roger Griffin, ed., *Fascism* (Oxford: Oxford University Press, 1995).

Walter Laqueur and George Mosse, eds., *International Fascism 1920–1945* (New York: Harper & Row, 1966).

Michael Arthur Ledeen, *Universal Fascism: The Theory and Practice of the Fascist Interna-tional, 1928–1936* (New York: H. Fertig, 1972).

Nicholas Nagy-Talavera, *The Green Shirts and the Others: A History of Fascism in Hungary and Rumania* (Stanford, Cal.: Hoover Institution Press, 1970).

Stanley G. Payne, *A History of Fascism, 1914–1945* (Madison: University of Wisconsin Press, 1995).

Hans Rogger and Eugen Weber, eds., *The European Right: A Historical Profile* (Berkeley: University of California Press, 1965).

Robert Soucy, *French Fascism: The First Wave, 1924–1933* (New Haven: Yale University Press, 1986).

Soucy, *French Fascism: The Second Wave, 1933–1939* (New Haven: Yale University Press, 1995).

Zeev Sternhell and others, *The Birth of Fascist Ideology: From Cultural Rebellion to Political Revolution,* translated by David Maisel (Princeton: Princeton University Press, 1994).

Bela Vago, *The Shadow of the Swastika: The Rise of Fascism and Anti-Semitism in the Danube Basin, 1936–1939* (Farnborough, Hants, U.K.: Saxon House for the Institute of Jewish Affairs, 1975).

Eugen Weber, *Varieties of Fascism: Doctrines of Revolution in the Twentieth Century* (Princeton: D. Van Nostrand, 1964).

Zvi Yavetz, "An Eyewitness Note: Reflections on the Rumanian Iron Guard," *Journal of Contemporary History,* 26 (September 1991): 597–610.

INTERNATIONAL FASCISM

INTERNATIONAL JUSTICE

Has the concept of international justice been effectively adopted in contemporary Europe?

Viewpoint: Yes. International justice has been highly effective in punishing and deterring war criminals and other violators of human rights and international law.

Viewpoint: No. International justice has been ineffective, because it rests on arbitrary legal foundations and has failed to punish many of those guilty of international crimes.

A major response to the horrors of the twentieth century was a series of attempts to create a system of international justice—an infrastructure of ethical values, law codes, and judicial institutions that the community of nations would share. Ideas for a world court began to circulate just after World War I when, with limited success, representatives of the Allied powers attempted to enforce clauses of the peace settlement that pertained to the prosecution of war criminals. After World War II a much more comprehensive system of justice was imposed on German and Japanese war criminals, with international courts and prosecutors leading the way. The newly created United Nations (UN) drafted a law code that defined previously unrecognized and unpunished "international crimes" such as genocide, aggressive warfare, and other transgressions against human rights and world peace. By the 1990s new international tribunals were designated to prosecute crimes in Cambodia (although UN negotiations with that government failed by 2002) and the former Yugoslavia. At the turn of the twenty-first century, talks were being held on the creation of a permanent International Criminal Court (ICC).

The concept of international justice has provoked much debate about its effectiveness. To some observers it has appeared to be arbitrary in its application. The Nuremberg trials (1945–1946) of German war criminals, for instance, rested on prosecutions for newly defined crimes that did not exist at the time of their perpetration and ignored existing German laws that could just as effectively have meted out justice. Questions have also arisen about the ability of international judicial bodies to carry out their mandates. If a national government refuses to cooperate, the international body is powerless to act. In their current form, international courts broadly lack the powers of arrest and prosecution that would make them meaningful.

A different argument suggests that despite its shortcomings, international justice has become conceptually and practically well grounded. International statutes and judicial bodies have deterred potential criminals and have won, as arbiters of disputes, the respect and recognition of many nations. On a practical level the successful prosecution of German and Japanese war criminals and subsequent investigations and prosecutions of crimes against international law produced tangible results by punishing the guilty, establishing precedents for the future, and besting the alternative of doing nothing. As nations continue to negotiate the structures and powers of the planned ICC, the past effectiveness of international justice stands as a paramount subject of investigation.

Viewpoint:
Yes. International justice has been highly effective in punishing and deterring war criminals and other violators of human rights and international law.

In the course of the "long twentieth century," Europe was the theater of some of the most heinous crimes in history, which necessitated new, unparalleled definitions of human brutality and revived a wider debate about universal responsibility vis-à-vis such extreme acts. The century started with the direct and indirect annihilation of large sections of the Armenian population within the boundaries of the Ottoman Empire (1915–1916), continued with the devastating World War I, experienced the widespread use of biological weapons in the Italo-Ethiopian war (1935–1936), reached a horrifying climax with World War II and the "Final Solution," and resuscitated old nightmares in the multiple crises of the former Yugoslavia (Bosnia-Herzegovina and Kosovo) in the 1990s. While the fundamental causes of these acts were of minimal novelty—their unprecedented scale and exceptional cruelty shook the foundations of modern civilization and cast a grave shadow on the future of any belief in human progress. It became painfully apparent that modernity had not succeeded in shielding humanity from the excesses of violence, repression, persecution, and murder. States, with their sophisticated repressive apparatuses, dominant groups, armies, paramilitary organizations, and secret polices, were now even more capable of embarking upon crimes against humanity with increased "efficiency" and a limited sense of moral or political obligation to global standards of conduct.

In the aftermath of World War I, when the devastating human and material cost of the conflagration became apparent to contemporary observers, the need to redress the balance between the wielding of arbitrary power by the state and the rights of individuals or groups within its jurisdiction was articulated with renewed urgency. This situation had been predicated on the consequences of the Great War. In the postwar conference for restoring a viable peace and stability in the shattered continent, U.S. president Woodrow Wilson capitalized on his nation's aura of representing a "new" world (and with it a sense of international morality untainted by the excesses and perversions that had burdened European great-power behavior). Against the unbridled anarchy of competing state jurisdictions, Wilson campaigned with energy and enthusiasm for the creation of the League of Nations. This organization was intended to be an international supreme body representing a higher order of authority and morality for regulating conflicts. The significance of this proposal was perhaps not evident during the Paris Peace Conference, where Britain, France, and Italy had upheld their familiar old diplomatic quid pro quo as de facto arbiters of international justice and morality. Instead, the League of Nations was supposed to supply an extra level of international power beyond the traditional "great powers" versus "smaller states" with decidedly democratic procedures of crisis resolution and conflict management through collective decision making. The concept of collective security aspired to redraw the boundaries of responsibility for actions both within and across the jurisdiction of the states, providing clear procedural, political, and ethical standards against which the behavior of individual agents could be judged and confronted.

Since then the proponents of international justice have experienced both agonizing defeats and resounding (albeit never unopposed) triumphs. From the beginning it became apparent that the novelty of this new arrangement, aimed at mitigating the erstwhile supreme and unchecked power of the sovereign state in the international system, could and would be fiercely contested. The refusal of the U.S. Congress to accept Wilson's experiments in Paris overshadowed the hopes and expectations for a new, more layered and balanced international order. Even new European states—created through the series of treaties (Versailles, Trianon, and St. Germain) after World War I—reacted negatively to the restriction of what they perceived as their uncontested sovereign power. For example, the League's clauses for protecting minorities within states were opposed because they were seen as incursions into the domain of state jurisdiction.

Undoubtedly, interwar stability in the 1920s nurtured hopes: Germany and, later, the Soviet Union were integrated into the League; the Locarno Pact (1925) promised peace in western Europe; and international initiatives produced unprecedented agreements, such as the Kellogg-Briand Pact (1928) for the renunciation of war. This interlude, however, was followed by a series of failures of the international justice system that weakened its political and moral foundations to the point of virtual paralysis. The invasion of Ethiopia by Benito Mussolini's Italy provided a testing ground for the League's ability to act effectively—but the verdict was damning, both for the institution and for the states that were supposed to act as guardians of the new order. Gaps in the system,

INTERNATIONAL JUSTICE

RESOLUTION 827

In 1993 the United Nations Security Council passed Reso-lution 827 concerning the punishment of war criminals in the former Yugoslavia:

The Security Council,

Reaffirming its resolution 713 (1991) of 25 September 1991 and all subsequent rele-vant resolutions,

Having considered the report of the Secretary-General (S/25704 and Add.1) pur-suant to paragraph 2 of resolution 808 (1993),

Expressing once again its grave alarm at continuing reports of widespread and flagrant violations of international humanitarian law occurring within the territory of the former Yugo-slavia, and especially in the Republic of Bosnia and Herzegovina, including reports of mass kill-ings, massive, organized and systematic deten-tion and rape of women, and the continuance of the practice of "ethnic cleansing", including for the acquisition and the holding of territory,

Determining that this situation continues to constitute a threat to international peace and security,

Determined to put an end to such crimes and to take effective measures to bring to jus-tice the persons who are responsible for them,

Convinced that in the particular circum-stances of the former Yugoslavia the estab-lishment as an ad hoc measure by the Council of an international tribunal and the prosecution of persons responsible for seri-ous violations of international humanitarian law would enable this aim to be achieved and would contribute to the restoration and main-tenance of peace,

Believing that the establishment of an international tribunal and the prosecution of persons responsible for the above-mentioned violations of international humanitarian law will contribute to ensuring that such violations are halted and effectively redressed,

Noting in this regard the recommenda-tion by the Co-Chairmen of the Steering Committee of the International Conference on the Former Yugoslavia for the establish-ment of such a tribunal (S/25221),

Reaffirming in this regard its decision in resolution 808 (1993) that an international tribu-nal shall be established for the prosecution of persons responsible for serious violations of international humanitarian law committed in the territory of the former Yugoslavia since 1991,

Considering that, pending the appoint-ment of the Prosecutor of the International Tri-bunal, the Commission of Experts established pursuant to resolution 780 (1992) should con-tinue on an urgent basis the collection of infor-mation relating to evidence of grave breaches of the Geneva Conventions and other viola-tions of international humanitarian law as pro-posed in its interim report (S/25274),

Acting under Chapter VII of the Charter of the United Nations,

1. *Approves* the report of the Secretary-General;

2. *Decides* hereby to establish an interna-tional tribunal for the sole purpose of prosecut-ing persons responsible for serious violations of international humanitarian law committed in the territory of the former Yugoslavia between 1 January 1991 and a date to be determined by the Security Council upon the restoration of peace and to this end to adopt the Statute of the International Tribunal annexed to the above-mentioned report;

3. *Requests* the Secretary-General to submit to the judges of the International Tribu-nal, upon their election, any suggestions received from States for the rules of procedure and evidence called for in Article 15 of the Statute of the International Tribunal;

4. *Decides* that all States shall cooperate fully with the International Tribunal and its organs in accordance with the present resolu-tion and the Statute of the International Tribu-nal and that consequently all States shall take any measures necessary under their domestic law to implement the provisions of the present resolution and the Statute, including the obli-gation of States to comply with requests for assistance or orders issued by a Trial Cham-ber under Article 29 of the Statute;

5. *Urges* States and intergovernmental and non-governmental organizations to con-tribute funds, equipment and services to the International Tribunal, including the offer of expert personnel;

6. *Decides* that the determination of the seat of the International Tribunal is subject to the conclusion of appropriate arrangements between the United Nations and the Nether-lands acceptable to the Council, and that the International Tribunal may sit elsewhere when it considers it necessary for the efficient exer-cise of its functions;

7. *Decides also* that the work of the Inter-national Tribunal shall be carried out without prejudice to the right of the victims to seek, through appropriate means, compensation for damages incurred as a result of violations of international humanitarian law;

8. *Requests* the Secretary-General to implement urgently the present resolution and in particular to make practical arrangements for the effective functioning of the International Tribunal at the earliest time and to report peri-odically to the Council;

9. *Decides* to remain actively seized of the matter.

Source: "Resolution 827 (1993)," United Nations: International Criminal Tribunal for the Former Yugo-slavia Website <http://www.un.org/icty/basic/statut/S-RES-827_93.htm>.

INTERNATIONAL JUSTICE

commencing with the isolationism of the United States and aggravated with the departure of fascist states from the organization (Germany in 1933 and Italy in 1937), meant that the League could never claim the status of a normative order accepted by all constituent elements of the international system.

Infinitely worse was still to come, though. The Geneva Conventions, attempting to introduce rules for the conduct of war, proved impossible to enforce and were a dead letter long before the world was plunged into another major conflagration. The League of Nations, having failed to prevent or resolve localized conflicts in the 1930s, virtually collapsed as the European states embarked upon the most catastrophic and brutal "total" war that history had ever recorded. The Nazi "New Order" became a horrifying euphemism for the mass murder of "life unworthy of life" throughout Europe. Jews primarily, but also Sinti/Roma, Slavs, disabled/mentally ill people, and other groups that displayed "non-normative" behavior became targets of a widespread campaign of total elimination, under the same perverted guise of state jurisdiction that collective security had failed to restrict.

The quantitative extent and qualitative radicalization of mass murder created a new reality that outlived the collapse of Adolf Hitler's regime in 1945. Authorities realized that a more effective and stable concept of international justice had to be devised to address extreme crimes such as those experienced during the war. The operation of the International Military Tribunal in Nuremberg provided the legal and political milieu in which the crimes of 1933–1945 were exposed and punished in a symbolic way. Even during the proceedings, former Reichsmarschall Hermann Goering repeated the conventional argument in favor of unmitigated state jurisdiction by stating that one "seems to forget that [Nazi] Germany was a sovereign state, and that her legislation within the German nation was not subject to the jurisdiction of foreign countries." However, the die was cast—with all their failings, the Nuremberg trials provided a genuine turning point by extricating certain actions from the protective shield of "state jurisdiction" and establishing them as the legitimate concern of international justice, with legally grounded precedents for intervention and punishment. By the end of the 1940s "genocide" and "crimes against humanity" had been clearly entrenched in the vocabulary of international law as valid foci of collective concern and action, in accordance with the new legal framework.

At the same time, the strengthening and elaboration of existing international law pro-vided further ammunition to the cause of superimposing a level of authority above the previously uncontested domain of state politics. The creation of the United Nations (UN) rearticulated the need for an international collective authority—with the power to prevent, intervene, and punish—and provided a significantly more elaborate mechanism of international involvement. Furthermore, the UN statute provided for the operation of special tribunals to deal with specific instances of human-rights violations. These initiatives promoted a legal declassification of war as a domain of nonnormative behavior where conventional moral conduct cannot always be expected.

The polarized atmosphere of the Cold War was by no means an auspicious testing ground for such institutional arrangements. International justice suffered immeasurably under the political manipulation of loopholes in the system. Faced with new cases of infringement of international law, public opinion was divided between two major schools of thought. On the one hand, realists argued that there was no possibility of erecting a viable form of authority above that of sovereign states, as the latter operated in an essentially anarchic world and represented the highest form of legally normative power. On the other hand, liberal institutionalists underlined the advances in collective responsibility, not simply for legal regulation but, perhaps more importantly, in creating an international "public opinion" with an increasing awareness that certain acts should and could be subject to scrutiny. Although the realist argument proved extremely hard to overcome, upholding the traditional concept of a monopoly of states' jurisdiction in their "internal" affairs, the ongoing elaboration of the legal and political apparatus of international justice won converts and rendered the system significantly more legitimate. What has also been achieved is the cultivation of a strong impression that while the mechanisms of international justice might have proved less effective than expected or desired, there is always a global ethical/legal dimension even in the exercise of state sovereignty. By making matters of previously exclusive domestic jurisdiction objects of international concern and, potentially, responsibility, the system of international justice demolished the belief that violations of human rights and law perpetrated under the pretext of state orders were unpunishable. Furthermore, since the Nuremberg trials (and similar proceedings against war criminals in other European countries after 1945) the idea that leaders were de facto exempted from persecution has been shattered.

The realist approach claimed vindication in the absence of major crises from 1945 to

1989 and in the stabilizing effect of bipolarity as an ethical and political deterrent. Liberal institutionalism, the argument goes, proved unable either to avert or to resolve tensions, let alone to erode the power of state jurisdiction over internal affairs. The escalation of ethnic conflict and the revival of old nightmares in the former Yugoslavia after 1989 supplied further legitimacy to the realist claim that liberal institutionalism is no viable alternative to the "anarchic" international system and to the entrenched position of sovereign states. It is true that international political/diplomatic mediation in the two major crises in Yugoslavia (Bosnia-Herzegovina and Kosovo) failed to forestall the disintegration of civic order and genocidal policies. This result may be a factually accurate depiction of the most serious crisis that Europe has witnessed since World War II: after all, it was only after military intervention that international justice was able to function, without any evidence that the liberal institutionalist agenda discouraged criminal behavior in either case.

Such an assessment, however, does not do justice to a recent determination to extend the scope of international jurisdiction. The establishment of the International Criminal Court (ICC, 2002) represents another crucial turning point in the history of promoting global standards for making individual and official perpetrators of heinous crimes accountable. In conventional legal practice, there is little margin or justification for preventive or preemptive justice. Deterrence of future crimes is promoted through punishment and through clear procedures that outline the implications of specific acts. The establishment of the International Criminal Tribunal for the Former Yugoslavia (ICTY) has received a crucial boost after the handing over of such a high-profile figure as former Yugoslavian president Slobodan Milosevic to international authorities. Beyond Europe similar tribunals (for example, in Rwanda) are performing similar tasks, displaying a determination to overcome procedural problems and a still deeply embedded culture of unrestricted sovereignty in the handling of domestic affairs.

Paradoxically, the failures of international justice have been caused by the resistance of the old rationale of state unaccountability. Those who criticize the record of the UN have deliberately failed to note that shortcomings are rooted in the refusal of states to do away with the final say in the handling of international matters. To use a much-debated recent example, the ICC began with a seriously limited capacity for normative international jurisdiction—the result of opposition from the United States primarily, but also from other major states such as

China and Israel, to the principle of accountability for actions otherwise authorized by legitimate governments.

The concept of international justice has gradually altered the notion that there can be no meaningful regulation or assessment of human behavior in circumstances of war, internal conflict, or collapse of civic order. Its political record will continue to lag behind the increasing sophistication (but limited coercive function) of its legal apparatus. It is a great achievement, however, that international justice in the twentieth century managed to challenge the notion that there is nothing above state sovereignty and domestic law; that there is no responsibility burdening actions of alleged *raison d'état;* that leaders can claim impunity from any form of persecution beyond the boundaries of their state; and that perpetrators can seek refuge in the argument that their acts were authorized through "legal" means and committed under the guise of such legality. The belief that sovereignty is not an unconditional privilege but a reversible condition in clearly outlined circumstances is, and should continue to be, the basis for the advancement of a more democratic, ethical, and sensible framework for human and state conduct. In this domain, international justice has offered invaluable services that the world should cherish and build upon.

—ARISTOTLE A. KALLIS,
UNIVERSITY OF BRISTOL

Viewpoint:
No. International justice has been ineffective, because it rests on arbitrary legal foundations and has failed to punish many of those guilty of international crimes.

War crimes and genocide are not new occurrences; they have been occurring for centuries. Yet, the horrors of two world wars, including the use of chemical agents, machine guns, trench warfare, long-range artillery, and airplanes plus the mass killing of Armenians, Jews, and others, caused nations to advocate the creation of new guidelines for the conduct of war. These principles included the prevention of war and better treatment of combatants and civilians. It also led to the formation of new mechanisms of justice, to transcend the potential biases of national courts, that took the form of international criminal tribunals: the International Military Tribunal in Nuremberg

(IMT), the International Criminal Tribunal for the Former Yugoslavia (ICTY), and the International Criminal Tribunal for Rwanda (ICTR).

Yet, to date, few alleged criminals have been brought to justice, even though substantial laws, norms, and institutions exist to help prevent and punish their crimes. In the twentieth century the concept of international justice has been ineffective because it has rested on arbitrary and vague legal foundations, relied on the cooperation of both the international community and the societies in which the crimes were committed, and failed to punish many of those guilty.

One of the most vexing problems is that international law is inherently vague and often does not spell out who is responsible for carrying out its provisions. A good example is the Convention on the Prevention and Punishment of the Crime of Genocide (1951), which does not specify penalties, only stating that contracting parties should enact legislation needed "to provide effective penalties for persons guilty of genocide." The type of legislation countries or the international community should adopt is not even discussed. The statute for the ICTY (created to try war crimes committed during the Balkans wars in the early 1990s) only states that penalties are limited to imprisonment. This inadequacy contrasts with the IMT, set up to try Germans for their war crimes after World War II, which stipulated that the death penalty could be imposed.

International law does not delineate enforcement mechanisms. Countries are simply instructed that they should cooperate with tribunals and United Nations (UN) resolutions. Beyond this level, the tribunals' charters do not add enforcement mechanisms. For example, the UN mandate does not give the ICTY power to arrest, but only to try, war criminals in the former Yugoslavia. Obviously, this provision limits who can be brought to trial and means that the apprehension of indicted war criminals depends on other agencies. This limitation is a problem because the North Atlantic Treaty Organization (NATO), which is engaged in peacekeeping in Bosnia, has no explicit mandate to arrest indicted war criminals. Among NATO ranks there is confusion as to exactly what their policy is, in particular regarding the question of whether they can actively search for war criminals.

The ad hoc nature of international tribunals also affects the success of international justice. They were established only to try a restricted number of crimes during a specific time frame, and a new tribunal cannot be set up to investigate every instance of war crimes. Each time a court is set up there is a significant start-up period that gives war criminals time to hide and avoid apprehension. After World War I—while Britain, France, and the United States were arguing over what type of international justice to pursue—German emperor Wilhelm II, who was implicated in war crimes, lived a quiet life of exile in the Netherlands. Similarly, Bosnian Serb president Radovan Karadzic and commander-in-chief of the army Ratko Mladic utilized international inaction in hunting war criminals to form armed security forces to ensure a bloody confrontation if the international community attempted to seize them. The fact that ad hoc tribunals need to be established by the UN Security Council to try individuals for violations of international law adds an arbitrariness about which crimes will be tried in international courts and injects international politics into justice. For example, why were courts set up to try crimes in Germany, Bosnia, and Rwanda, but not in Iraq, Sierra Leone, or Cambodia? Benjamin Ferencz, a prosecutor at the Nuremberg trials, wrote that "temporary courts created à la carte on a selective basis are not good enough. To be respected, international law must apply equally to everyone, everywhere."

Even if international law was not vague and was applied to everyone equally, domestic and international resolve would still be crucial for international justice to succeed. Because international courts do not have the power to arrest, their success depends on the international community and domestic cooperation in order to investigate, apprehend, and mete out punishments. Both domestic and international cooperation are rarely present at these important stages, complicating the success of international justice.

In cases in which the world community has shown the will to act, international justice has succeeded. This result can be clearly seen in the Nuremberg IMT of 1945–1946, created to try German war criminals for their crimes, which included aggression against citizens and genocide during World War II and the Holocaust. This case was exceptional, however. Britain, France, the Soviet Union, and the United States occupied Germany. The Allies were able to gather evidence easily and detain the indicted, many of whom were already prisoners of war. High-level Nazi officials were tried in Nuremberg, and lesser-known suspected war criminals were tried in the four occupied zones of Germany. Nineteen high-level Nazis were convicted, and so Nuremberg is considered an important precedent toward establishing an effective system of international criminal justice.

INTERNATIONAL JUSTICE

Unfortunately, the Nuremberg trials stand alone, and the international community seems to have lacked the full determination to take a decisive stand against violators of international law in other cases. The abortive trials after World War I are a good example. The end of the conflict sparked an international debate about what type of justice should be created for war criminals. Britain and France clamored for an international tribunal, with France calling for the creation of a permanent tribunal to try war crimes, while the United States pushed for each nation's military tribunals to prosecute cases that occurred in their countries. To bring an end to this impasse, in 1919 the international community created the Committee of Enquiry into Breaches of the Laws of War, which urged an international criminal court to try heads of state and top military leaders. The report also detailed hundreds of war crimes and named hundreds of war criminals. Sections 227 to 230 of the Versailles Treaty (1919) mandated an international war crimes tribunal and required countries to cooperate with investigations and trials. The international community continued to wrangle about the creation of the international tribunal, but made it known that it would not enforce these sections. Allied pleadings for the Netherlands to give up the former German emperor for trial were to no avail. This difficulty, in addition to American unwillingness to force Germany to hand over indicted individuals who remained in the country, meant that few war criminals were apprehended and that international trials could not occur. After failing to secure an international tribunal after World War I, the Allies agreed to allow Germany to try a few cases domestically. Domestic courts either acquitted Germans accused of war crimes or gave them light sentences, saying that the indicted were just following orders. Out of 900 identified war criminals tried by Germany's supreme court, 888 were acquitted or had their charges dismissed. This outcome destroyed the credibility of the trials and left the impression that justice had not been meted out. British officials called these trials a "scandalous failure of justice."

Bosnia provides another good example of the need for international will to carry out trials once a tribunal is created. In this case, the international community's guilt about its lack of action during the Serb genocide against Muslims resulted in the establishment of the ICTY. However, the international community's will seems to have stopped at this point; it has for the most part failed to enforce the ICTY statute. Even though the Dayton Accords (1995), the treaty ending the war, say that the International Peacekeeping Force (IFOR, the UN force in Bosnia) should arrest war criminals, international troops have in large part failed even to arrest war criminals they have come across, let alone hunt for them. NATO has taken a strict interpretation of its mandate in Bosnia, to keep the peace, and is concerned that if it were to start hunting and apprehending war criminals, it would provoke attacks on its soldiers. After much publicity about the failure of peacekeepers to arrest war criminals, the forces acted a few times and some arrests were made. Despite these actions by NATO, several high-ranking indicted Bosnian Serbs remain free. Two high-profile cases are those of Mladic, who is living in Serbia, and Karadzic, who is moving around the Serb-controlled part of Bosnia-Herzegovina, to avoid capture. NATO enforcement actions seem to be tied to bad publicity and do not necessarily show the will to act. This inaction highlights the inconsistent support for the apprehension of war criminals.

The Serbian case is perhaps the most egregious example of domestic noncompliance with international law. Both the ICTY statute and Dayton Accords placed primary responsibility for the apprehension of indicted war criminals on the states in which they reside. Most of the war criminals resided in Serb-controlled Bosnia, with a few thought to be living in Serbia proper. Neither of these entities has made serious attempts to arrest war criminals. Furthermore, many war criminals continued to hold positions of power and to move freely. There is one big exception—the arrest of Slobodan Milosevic in April 2001. It is important to note that this arrest came at a time of discord within the Serbian opposition parties. Vojislav Kostunica, Yugoslavia's nationalist president, was embroiled in a bitter political battle with Zoran Djindjic, Serbia's democratic prime minister, who favored handing Milosevic over to the Hague. What finally made the difference was the U.S. refusal to participate in the international aid donor's conference until there was evidence of more Yugoslav cooperation on arresting war criminals, and the European Union's similar conditional policy for honoring its pledges made at the conference. Serbia, still reeling from the devastating economic effects of the Balkans wars, was forced to hand Milosevic over to the ICTY for prosecution. What really tipped the scale in the Milosevic case was the international community's strong position and resolve. As of November 2000, ninety-six people have been publicly indicted by ICTY for war crimes, with another three publicly acknowledged as having been indicted under sealed

indictment. But only thirty-four of these ninety-nine indicted individuals entered custody in the Hague, and a vast majority were low-ranking actors in the war.

Western governments, which came under heavy fire for their inaction in Bosnia, tried to deflect criticism by saying that the Balkan governments have not acted. But if NATO is not fulfilling its mandate to arrest war criminals, how can it expect Balkan governments to do the same? This finger-pointing is able to occur because of the vagueness of the Dayton Accords and the ICTY statute, allowing all parties to claim that it is not their mandate to apprehend and extradite war criminals.

In the twentieth century the international community has made progress in bringing violators of international law to justice. Despite the lack of international trials after World War I, debate led to the adoption of the principle that punishment of war crimes is the proper action, as opposed to the previously practiced amnesty. The aborted trials also marked the development of the principle of individual criminal responsibility for war crimes. The success of the Nuremberg trials showed that when international and domestic will are both present, international justice can be achieved. The trials also set a precedent; aggressive war was condemned as an international crime for the first time, and was codified in the Nuremberg Principles. The ICTY added to international law as well. For the first time, rape was established as a crime against humanity.

What is really needed to ensure the effectiveness of international justice (the indictment and trial of more war criminals) is a permanent international court that would be able to hunt war criminals almost immediately and investigate crimes, without having to form a last-minute staff. After World War I the French demanded a permanent international tribunal to try war criminals. At that time, there was not enough international will to set up even an ad hoc tribunal, let alone a permanent one. In the wake of the Nuremberg trials, an international court was pondered, but Cold War antagonisms prohibited its creation.

Yet, successful tribunals created the environment and precedent for the establishment of the International Criminal Court (ICC). After trying for most of the century, on 17 July 1998, at the conclusion of weeks of intensive negotiations, a draft treaty establishing the ICC was passed and later went into effect after sixty countries formally ratified it. Only time will tell if the ICC will be successful where ad hoc international tribunals have failed. The fact that the United States put enormous resources into making sure that ICC courts would not apply to Americans signifies that Washington thinks that it will have a major influence in world affairs and that ICC rulings will be enforceable. Given Washington's current influence in world affairs, U.S. actions indicate that international justice will play an even greater role in the twenty-first century than it did in the twentieth century.

–KERRY FOLEY,
WASHINGTON, D.C.

References

Michael E. Brown and others, eds., *Nationalism and Ethnic Conflict* (Cambridge, Mass.: MIT Press, 1997).

Alexis Heraclides, *The Self-Determination of Minorities in International Politics* (London & Portland, Ore.: Cass, 1991).

Radha Kumar, *Divide and Fall?: Bosnia in the Annals of Partition* (London & New York: Verso, 1997).

Thomas D. Musgrave, *Self-Determination and National Minorities* (Oxford: Clarendon Press, 1997; New York: Oxford University Press, 1997).

Mortimer Sellers, *The New World Order: Sovereignty, Human Rights, and the Self-Determination of Peoples* (Oxford & Washington, D.C.: Berg, 1996).

Patrick Thornberry, *International Law and the Rights of Minorities* (Oxford: Clarendon Press, 1991; New York: Oxford University Press, 1991).

Susan L. Woodward, *Balkan Tragedy: Chaos and Dissolution after the Cold War* (Washington, D.C.: Brookings Institution, 1995).

INTERNATIONAL JUSTICE

LENINISM v. STALINISM

Is there a meaningful distinction between Leninism and Stalinism?

Viewpoint: Yes. Vladimir Lenin's regime was much milder and less authoritarian than Josef Stalin's.

Viewpoint: No. Although Josef Stalin killed more Russians than Vladimir Lenin, the structures and mentalities of his regime were inherited from Lenin and had broad precedent in the earlier incarnation of the Soviet state.

Josef Stalin ruled the Soviet Union with an iron fist from the late 1920s to 1953. Many scholars have identified Stalinism with the totalitarian model of government, in which the state controls, or at least aspires to control, all aspects of society. Stalin's adaptation of this concept included a vast system of terror managed by a secret police, a network of concentration camps, the suspension of justice, arbitrary arrests, and the generalized fear that one could always be arrested, tortured, and killed.

Did Stalin's use of terror and creation of a totalitarian system develop on its own, or did it only build on existing trends in the political life of the Soviet state? A traditional argument, favored by those more sympathetic to the ideals of the Russian Revolution (1917), has posited that Stalin's rise to unchecked power in the late 1920s marked a definitive break with the rule of his predecessor, Vladimir Lenin. According to these scholars, Stalin's regime brought an end to permitted degrees (however limited) of political and economic freedom and social and artistic experimentation. Stalin, in effect, ended the most promising aspects of the Revolution and thwarted its best ideals.

A counterargument, which has existed since 1917 but has recently been revisited by scholars making use of new sources, holds that Stalin inherited the foundation of his regime directly from Lenin. Although Stalin certainly caused more deaths and arguably greater suffering, proponents of this alternate view suggest that the ideology of totalitarian rule was inherent in Lenin's system of government and political thought. The infrastructure that Stalin made use of, they maintain, also made its appearance during Lenin's leadership and soon after the Bolsheviks came to power.

Viewpoint:
Yes. Vladimir Lenin's regime was much milder and less authoritarian than Josef Stalin's.

There are grounds to argue that Soviet leader Josef Stalin's policies of social transformation displayed continuity from Vladimir Lenin's precedents. When the Bolsheviks came to power in October 1917, they had an ideological commitment to establishing the system of state-regulated society, with little space left to local initiatives or market forces. Capitalism and its principles had no place in the future Soviet society, and many Bolsheviks sincerely believed that this project was what German political philosopher Karl Marx would have wanted them to implement. In foreign policy, Lenin and Lev Trotsky were committed to spreading the "ideals of October" to Europe and the rest of the world. This commitment had deep roots in Lenin's theory of imperialism, which argued that there would be a chain reaction of revolutions across the globe once one link was loosened. Lenin saw Russia as such a "weak link in the chain" and believed it would set the example and transform the entire world of "imperialist exploitation." Illusions of the approaching world revolution were only reinforced by the extremely volatile international context. Consumed by World War I, European powers were experiencing serious domestic unrest. Germany, where Social Democrats were especially influential, seemed to Lenin and Trotsky particularly close to experiencing a revolution.

The ideas of a totally regulated society ("military communism") and world revolution were soon abandoned by Lenin and others in the Bolshevik leadership, however. Tight discipline and centralized rule were easier to justify during the bloody civil war of 1918–1921, but the post-civil-war condition was an entirely different matter. Lenin admitted that although the extension of the military-communism model had been a product of the Bolsheviks' ideological beliefs, it constituted a political defeat, one that was indeed all too evident. As a result of horrendous violence committed by both the Red and White armies, millions of people were killed. Horrific famines added millions more to the dead. A March 1921 revolt at the Kronstadt naval base, in which sailors demanded better economic conditions and democratization, was but a final reminder that without radical change, the Bolsheviks' days in power might be numbered.

Having admitted that "we have failed," Lenin proposed a principally different approach to reviving the postwar economy and reforming society. At the Tenth Party Congress (March 1921), he first formulated the New Economic Policy (NEP), which was based on different philosophical assumptions than those of military communism and world revolution. At home, Lenin argued for granting greater freedom to the peasantry and for introducing "elements of capitalism" to stimulate rapid economic revival. Although he insisted on the preservation of control of political life and the "commanding heights" of the economy, he did not see this innovation as a capitalist restoration. Externally, Lenin rethought the idea of world revolution and instead put forward the thesis of "temporary stabilization of capitalism," arguing the need for "peaceful coexist-

ence" between Soviet Russia and the Western world. This argument, of course, had implications for the domestic economy; Lenin realized the urgent need for foreign investment, which was impossible without revising the previously established confrontational view of the Western world. Despite initial resistance from the Party to such radical revisions of early Bolshevik ideology, Lenin insisted that NEP should be "for real and for a long time."

After Lenin's death in January 1924, his argument was continued most consistently by Nikolai Bukharin, a brilliant theoretician and, to use Lenin's own words, "the favorite of the entire Party." Lenin's evaluation of Stalin was not as encouraging. In his political will, he characterized Stalin as "too rude" and someone "who has concentrated in his hands too much power," of which Stalin would unlikely be able to "make good use." Having begun as a loyal supporter of military communism, Bukharin underwent a revolution in his views and emerged as a major advocate of more socially democratic principles in domestic and foreign policies.

Unlike Bukharin, Stalin never had a reputation as a serious theoretician and, during the early 1920s, preferred to stay away from theoretical debates. Instead, Stalin was working to transform his bureaucratic job as Party general secretary into a meaningful political platform for concentrating power. When Lenin was still alive, the politically clever Stalin revealed no principled objections to NEP. However, when an opportunity presented itself, he used one of Lenin's polemical characterizations of NEP as a "temporary breathing space" in order to introduce radically different domestic and foreign policies and, in effect, to return to the earlier principles of military communism and external confrontation.

Stalinist projects for reforming the system were those of a socialist autocracy, rather than socialist democracy, an approximation of which was advocated by Bukharin. The 1928 food crisis presented Stalin with an opportunity to impose his autocratic policies of collectivization. In Stalin's view the fact that the peasants were no longer willing to sell bread to the state at below market prices implied the need to extort bread by force. Otherwise, city workers would starve and industrialization would become impossible to continue. This assertion was a pretext, as Stalin had far more ambitious plans. In one of his better-known speeches, Stalin announced in 1929 that "NEP went to hell" and openly advocated a rapid and forceful industrialization, especially in the military sector, justifying such an economic great leap forward by appeals to national survival.

SCREAMS IN THE CORRIDOR

In his memoirs Polish Jew Janusz Bardach, who had volunteered to serve in the Soviet army and was later convicted of treason, recalls some of his experiences in a gulag:

Elia was one of the large number of political prisoners known as "jokers." All had been sentenced for one thing—telling a political joke. Jokes about Stalin or any other member of the Politburo were considered subversive and punished with three- to ten-year sentences.

"I finished my five-year term four months ago," Elia continued, "but now I'm being investigated again. My poetry got me in trouble. Several of my poems were stolen. The next time I saw them they were on the interrogator's desk."

. . .The nights at Petropavlovsk reminded me of the night in the prison in Gomel, lying on the bare floor, swathed in the body heat and communal odor of my cellmates, smelling the putrid breath of the person behind me and feeling the sweat, hair, and dirt of the prisoner in front. I felt weary and hostile. Gone were my timidity and revulsion.

That night Elia squeezed in next to me to sleep. His body was trembling. In the middle of the night I was awakened to a guard's voice calling out names. Elia's was among them. The men were ordered to go into the corridor. Elia went stiff, then got up. It was just as he had anticipated. I began shaking, as though I had been ordered to rise myself. In the morning the door opened, and Elia and another prisoner were shoved into the cell and crumpled to the floor. Their eyes were bruised and swollen. Blood stained their shirts. "I signed everything," Elia whispered as I tried to make a place for him next to the wall. "And they still wouldn't let up on me." His voice sounded as though it came through a tunnel—hollow, faint, far off.

The NKVD had elevated beating to an art. If political prisoners didn't confess quickly enough to suit the interrogators, guards burned them with cigarettes, inserted needles under their nails, or pulled their nails out altogether. Those who resisted were clubbed, kicked in the genitals, or beaten until their bones were broken. Interrogations could last for days and nights without end, with bright lamps shining in the prisoners' eyes to keep them awake. Some said that the sleepless nights, when they were forced repeatedly to tell their story, were as torturous as the savage beatings. Any mistake or inconsistency was followed by an interrogator's rage. "You're

lying! Yesterday, you told me you met Jakovlev in December 1935. Now you tell me you knew him since September 1933. So you were already plotting for two years, and now you're trying to deceive me."

Sometimes prisoners I hadn't seen before entered the cell alone and at odd hours. They looked half-alive and could hardly walk. Weak, emaciated, mumbling nonsense, sometimes crying, they were returning from the isolator, a special punishment chamber reserved for serious crimes and infractions.

I'd never forget the beatings I received after my attempted escape. The experience was so fresh in my mind, I was afraid the authorities would find some reason—or no reason—to do it again. I became obsessed with the thought that with every opening of the door, my name would be called. I tried to reason with myself that since I had already been sentenced and that unless I did something wrong, I wouldn't be interrogated. But it was impossible to rid myself of the fear, especially hearing the muffled screams in the corridor. I obsessed that somehow my attempted escape would be brought to someone's attention and interrogation would begin. I'd be accused again of treason and sentenced to death.

Each day after breakfast we were taken for a walk in the inner yard. We walked briskly in single file with our hands clasped behind our backs, our heads hanging to avoid looking at the watchtowers, guards, and German shepherds. Talking was forbidden during the two laps around the yard and in the corridor. Sometimes after the walk prisoners didn't return to the cell. For a while the disappearances were a mystery. Then one day a rumor circulated that there were informers.

Three times a day we were taken to the bathroom, a large room at the end of the corridor. It had an antechamber with ten sinks and faucets. The inner sanctum had ten holes in the cement floor. The guards remained outside, and so the bathroom became the social hub and market for the prisoners. In the cell we could not talk too loudly for fear of being overheard. But in the unsupervised toilet prisoners could talk, scheme, trade food and tobacco, and plot or take out revenge.

Source: *Janusz Bardach and Kathleen Gleeson,* Man is Wolf to Man: Surviving the Gulag *(Berkeley: University of California Press, 1998), pp. 160–162.*

LENINISM v. STALINISM

In foreign affairs Stalin consistently advocated an image of the Soviet Union being "encircled" by imperialist enemies and spies. A major revision of Lenin's principles of "peaceful coexistence" and "learning from capitalism," the image served to justify total political and economic control over society. It justified Stalin's thesis of "inevitable intensification of class struggle" under the conditions of a transition to socialism and mass terror in the Party and outside. Although Stalin rapidly collectivized peasant households, the proportion of them increasing from 1.7 percent in 1928 to 93 percent in 1937, and built an elaborate military-industrial complex, the costs were mass terror, fear, repression of creative thought, and elimination of the incentive of the rural sector's development.

Bukharin's plan, which followed much of Lenin's thinking, was principally different. Instead of rapid and forceful industrialization at the price of extorting bread from the peasants, Bukharin advocated the maintenance of market-based relations between urban and rural areas. Industrialization would continue, he insisted, but under the conditions of a dual economy in which the state would implement strategic planning and control heavy industry, foreign trade, banking, and transportation. A private sector should be preserved, in Bukharin's vision, for smaller enterprises and peasant farming. Such policies, in his view, would develop necessary trust between the peasantry and the state and therefore prevent future food crises. Bukharin further argued that Stalin's "military-feudal exploitation of the peasantry" would be "leading to civil war."

Externally, following Lenin's ideas of "peaceful coexistence" with the West, Bukharin advocated closer political relations with European social democratic parties and was behind the idea of collective security in Europe in order to stop the rise of Nazi Germany. That stand, too, was a world of difference away from Stalin's militant separation from European social democratic parties (whom at one point, he referred to as "social-fascists") and his collaboration with German leader Adolf Hitler, which ended only in Hitler's unexpected attack on the Soviet Union on 22 June 1941. Although Lenin did not live to see the development of the Bukharin-Stalin debate, his own perspective would have been closer to Bukharin's ideas of cooperation with European social democrats and gradual industrialization, than to Stalin's forceful industrialization, mass terror, and cooperation with Nazi Germany.

–ANDREI P. TSYGANKOV,
SAN FRANCISCO
STATE UNIVERSITY

**Viewpoint:
No. Although Josef Stalin killed more Russians than Vladimir Lenin, the structures and mentalities of his regime were inherited from Lenin and had broad precedent in the earlier incarnation of the Soviet state.**

One of the greatest enduring myths of twentieth-century European history is that Josef Stalin's Soviet Union was a singular horror, unconnected with the revolution begun by his predecessor Vladimir Lenin and far out of step with the intentions of his associates. A "bad" Stalin, in other words, subverted what an essentially "good" Lenin had started; a terrorist dictatorship spoiled "promising" initial movement toward a socialist society. As Russian archives are explored and old evidence is reexamined, however, the truth of the matter seems to be that Stalin merely inherited the mechanisms, ideological grounds, and will to carry out massive horrors. By the time Lenin died in January 1924, the basis and mentalities of Stalin's regime were already firmly in place.

The most nefarious feature of Stalinism was the dictator's use of mass terror to enforce his will over both the ruling Bolshevik Party and the country at large. Particularly in the 1930s, Stalin used a secret police, concentration camps, genocidal deportations, censorship, and show trials to destroy opposition to his rule. Each and every one of these means had a direct precedent in the years of Lenin's rule (1917–1924). Lenin's government founded the Soviet secret police, the Cheka, just six weeks after the Bolsheviks seized power in their November 1917 coup d'état. It immediately employed terrorist methods, including many instances of brutality against real or perceived enemies of the new government. Historians have calculated that more people were executed for political crimes in the first four months of Bolshevik rule than the tsars had executed in the last ninety-two years of the Russian Empire. In one of the most effective measures taken to spread Bolshevik rule, the Leninist secret police was charged with taking hostages to cow potential opponents into submission. Secret police measures extended to all classes of society and all sources of opposition. Cheka agents executed Tsar Nicholas II and other members of the imperial family and tsarist government, as well as factory workers (for whom the Bolsheviks were supposedly fighting) who went on strike for higher wages and better rations and peasants who did not like having their grain confiscated

Poster celebrating one of Josef Stalin's Five Year plans and "the victory of socialism," circa 1930

(from T. C. W. Blanning, ed., The Oxford Illustrated History of Modern Europe, 1996)

LENINISM v. STALINISM

by the new government. The Cheka dealt in a like manner even with socialist critics of the new regime. The Menshevik wing of the Russian Social Democratic Party, which included some of Lenin's old associates, was persecuted mercilessly for suspected disloyalty, as was the Socialist Revolutionary Party, some of whose members had even participated in Lenin's early government. Secret police measures were also used to maintain discipline in the Red Army. Political commissars were appointed to watch military commanders for signs of disloyalty; the families of tsarist officers were held as virtual hostages, lest their sons defect to the anti-Bolshevik White forces or simply not perform to expectations. Although the Cheka went through a series of name changes in the 1920s, its organization and much of its early personnel were still at Stalin's disposal in the 1930s.

Some scholars have argued that unlike Stalin, Lenin was unwilling to use terror within the Bolshevik Party itself (as if using it only against the rest of the population somehow made him better), yet there were several instances in which he subjected his acolytes to dictatorial discipline and violent coercion. Indeed, Lenin's leadership of the Bolshevik faction of the Russian Social Democratic Party had derived from his insistence on the Party's acknowledgment of his unchallengeable and highly disciplined leadership authority. During Lenin's tenure in power he directly threatened Party leaders who favored a more participatory socialist system and greater rights for labor. He forced them to recant their views publicly or face punishment. In March 1921 Lenin brutally suppressed a rebellion by revolutionary sailors at the Kronstadt naval base who demanded a more democratic political system. After defeating them in a military operation, soldiers systematically executed hundreds of prisoners, while survivors who escaped to nearby Finland were shot after returning home under promises of amnesty. Finally, in the years just before Lenin's death, the Party was subjected to a purge that removed hundreds of thousands of members from its ranks. This purge may have been bloodless, but Stalin's use of purges as a method of control in the 1930s was simply an adaptation of Lenin's threats and actual uses of violence to impose discipline.

Stalin has also been justly vilified for dispatching huge numbers of his people, most of them innocent of any crime and sentenced without any real trial, to concentration camps in remote parts of the Soviet Union where they were forced to perform difficult labor. With survival rates of less than 10 percent, confinement in these camps, known collectively as the gulag (the abbreviation of *Glavnoye Upravleniye*

Ispravitelno-trudovykh Lagerey or Chief Administration of Corrective Labor Camps), was a virtual death sentence. Stalin did not invent them, however. The first camps in the system were actually founded on Lenin's orders as early as August 1918. Even before that, the confinement of "class enemies" as hostages had necessitated their detention in a variety of locations, including open spaces surrounded by barbed wire and guard towers. The labor component of detention in the Soviet state was also an early Leninist innovation, with "class enemies," "social parasites," and other "undesirable" people drafted into forced-labor brigades from which they often did not return. By the time of Lenin's death, tens of thousands of people were held in these conditions. Although the camps consumed millions of victims under Stalin, the "legal" ability to send people there, the license to work and starve them to death, and in some cases the physical construction of the facilities for their detention, all dated to the years immediately after the Revolution, when Lenin was still in charge.

Another of Stalin's heinous crimes was the perpetration of genocidal deportations of "class enemies" and minority ethnic groups for purposes of state. At the beginning of his drive to collective Soviet agriculture, Stalin victimized "kulaks," peasants who were considered well-off, even though the definition remained deliberately elastic so that one could never be sure whether one's self or one's neighbor might be considered a "class enemy," and so that anyone who opposed the regime for any reason could easily be labeled an enemy. This campaign resulted in the deportation of at least several hundred thousand people, yet it had undeniable roots in Lenin's earlier calls for "class war in the countryside," incitements to violence against precisely the same group of peasants, who were either slightly better off or just opposed his regime.

While some scholars have emphasized the relative freedom that ethnic minorities enjoyed in the 1920s, Lenin nevertheless sanctioned extreme cases of collective brutality against certain groups to punish the actions of individual members. In 1919–1920 the Don Cossacks, an ethnically mixed warrior society that enjoyed a distinct identity under the tsars, were brutally suppressed because they tried to revive their autonomous identity and because some of their number supported White forces operating in their home territories. Lenin's solution was to kill tens of thousands of them and forcefully relocate possibly as many as five hundred thousand more to ensure that they would no longer be a threat. In Central Asia in February 1918, Lenin sanctioned the use of extreme force against the civilian population of the Muslim city of Kokand, where the indigenous peoples had established a provisional government for their region. More than fourteen thousand people were killed in a brutal sacking and burning of the city, while a sustained campaign against Central Asia's Muslim nationalities continued in response to resistance throughout the 1920s. There were also sustained campaigns with ethnic overtones in Chechnya, which Stalin would later victimize more thoroughly, and neighboring Daghestan. In Ukraine, where a series of autonomous and independent governments held power in 1917–1920, Bolshevik troops and secret police executed people for simply speaking Ukrainian or identifying with a non-Soviet Ukrainian state. One of Stalin's first acts after rising to full power in the late 1920s was the elimination of Ukraine's remaining intelligentsia and much of its indigenous peasantry in a state-manufactured famine. Since Stalin had been the commissar for nationalities in Lenin's government, the continuity from Lenin's treatment of ethnic minorities to his own should come as no surprise.

Stalin's regime also relied on total state control of not only print journalism but book publishing, the intellectual arena, artistic endeavors, and the emerging film and radio media. Lenin's rule was too early for radio and the early Soviet state was too impoverished to sustain an impressive film industry, but the other media were subject to equally thorough state control and censorship. Only one day after the November 1917 coup, Lenin's government shut down the newspaper presses of opposition parties. This policy was extended through the following year, by which time all opposition parties, including other socialist parties, had lost their presses. Nonpolitical journalism also suffered under Lenin, as privately owned media outlets were expropriated along with all other venues of private enterprise. Newspapers were subordinated to Bolshevik editorial control, and the only main organs of daily news were the Party's old paper, *Pravda,* and the official paper of the Soviet government, *Izvestiia.* The book publishers' industrial plant was confiscated, and the state took over decisions about publication and distribution. Independent intellectual activity was thoroughly repressed by Lenin. Some intellectual opponents of Lenin's regime, such as anti-Bolshevik poet Nikolai Gumilev, were executed, and many others, representing some of the best and most renowned minds in Russian philosophical, historical, religious, artistic, literary, and scientific thought were forcibly expelled from the country in the early 1920s or pressured to emigrate on their own. Others committed suicide in the face of state pressure. Stalin may have

killed or exiled more intellectuals in the 1930s, but he was only following a precedent that Lenin had set.

Another salient feature of Stalin's dictatorial system was his reliance on public "show trials" to discredit opponents and promote his consolidation of power. Although the vast majority of his victims received no public trials, seventy members of the Soviet leadership were tried publicly in 1936–1938. Most were condemned to death and executed after delivering false confessions to crimes of which they were almost certainly innocent. This totalitarian technique also had firm roots in Leninism. One of Lenin's first steps upon gaining power was to abolish the existing justice system and replace it with "people's courts" guided by a "socialist legal consciousness." Naturally, these informal proceedings, often formed by little more than angry mobs of revolutionary-minded lower classes, were intended for public consumption and purposes of class propaganda. Formal proceedings against people from privileged backgrounds and officials of the tsarist and provisional governments were strongly imbued with moralizations that reflected and advertised the ideology of the new regime. Lenin even planned a public show trial of Tsar Nicholas II, in which Lenin's associate Lev Trotsky dreamed of being the prosecutor, but a sudden advance by anti-Bolshevik forces that might have rescued the tsar and his family necessitated their execution.

Clearly, Stalin carried on the Marxist-Leninist tradition of radical socialist government by whatever means necessary. According to Lenin's theoretical writings, Russia was too far behind to follow German political philosopher Karl Marx's original prescriptions for revolutionary action—that is, to allow a prolonged "bourgeois-democratic" phase of development to precede the establishment of socialism. Russia's revolutionary leaders had to overcome this precarious position by "forcing the hand of history" and acting with extreme and ruthless practicality toward any obstacle they faced. Even if Stalin transformed the Soviet Union on a greater scale and at a greater cost than Lenin, both leaders appealed to the same ideological justification, which Lenin had invented. Whatever most immediately served the interests of the state took priority over any other consideration—not just pleasantness, convenience, or sentimentality, but justice, rights, and even human life itself. Both men were dictatorial murderers for the same reason. Stalin justified the human cost of agricultural collectivization in the 1930s by declaring, "you can't make an omelette without breaking eggs." He meant that the socialist society could not be achieved without major sacrifices. Lenin, with his creation of secret police, concentration camps, genocidal

violence, censorship, and show trials, only anticipated his top lieutenant's statements and actions.

–PAUL DU QUENOY,
GEORGETOWN UNIVERSITY

References

Anne Applebaum, *Gulag: A History* (New York: Doubleday, 2003).

Stephen F. Cohen, *Bukharin and the Bolshevik Revolution: A Political Biography, 1888–1938* (New York: Knopf, 1973).

Cohen, *Rethinking the Soviet Experience: Politics and History since 1917* (New York: Oxford University Press, 1985).

Stéphane Courtois and others, *The Black Book of Communism: Crimes, Terror, Repression,* translated by Jonathan Murphy and Mark Kramer (Cambridge, Mass. & London: Harvard University Press, 1999).

Orlando Figes, *A People's Tragedy: The Russian Revolution, 1891–1924* (New York: Viking, 1997).

David M. Kotz and Fred Weir, *Revolution from Above: The Demise of the Soviet System* (London & New York: Routledge, 1997).

Iver B. Neumann, *Russia and the Idea of Europe: A Study in Identity and International Relations* (London & New York: Routledge, 1996).

Richard Pipes, *The Russian Revolution* (New York: Knopf, 1990).

Pipes, ed., *The Unknown Lenin: From the Secret Archive* (New Haven: Yale University Press, 1996).

Richard Sakwa, *The Rise and Fall of the Soviet Union, 1917–1991* (London & New York: Routledge, 1999).

Robert Service, *Lenin: A Biography* (Cambridge, Mass.: Harvard University Press, 2000).

Ronald Grigor Suny, *The Soviet Experiment: Russia, the USSR, and the Successor States* (New York: Oxford University Press, 1998).

Lev Trotsky, *The Revolution Betrayed* (Garden City, N.Y.: Doubleday, Doran, 1937).

Robert C. Tucker, *The Marxian Revolutionary Idea* (New York: Norton, 1969).

MASS EDUCATION
AND CULTURE

Did universal education and the promotion of mass culture stem from altruistic motives?

Viewpoint: Yes. Universal education and mass culture resulted from the general desire to create an active, educated, and involved citizenry.

Viewpoint: No. European governments promoted universal education to extend control over their citizenry by systematically instilling basic beliefs that served the purposes of the state.

One of the greatest achievements in twentieth-century Europe was near-universal literacy and at least rudimentary education. The ideals behind this achievement, the philosophical roots of which go back to the Enlightenment, seem self-evidently positive. Educated and literate citizens could participate fully in democratic societies and at last have their own say in how they were ruled. At the same time their quality of life, cultural awareness, and general welfare were elevated to unprecedented levels.

A more cynical analysis, however, maintains that increasingly powerful governments sought to educate their peoples to serve the purposes of the state. Regardless of the benefits, mass education disseminated official versions of history and politics, while literacy made traditionally autonomous populations easier to control and simpler to manipulate. Mass culture, including sports, popular theater, daily newspapers, and other media, helped create national values and impart patriotic messages.

Viewpoint:
Yes. Universal education and mass culture resulted from the general desire to create an active, educated, and involved citizenry.

Mass participation in government and society demanded an informed and well-integrated citizenry. Although cynical scholars of nineteenth- and twentieth-century Europe have argued that mass education and culture were merely the tools of oppressive governments that sought to use them to establish and perpetuate control over their societies, the democratization of knowledge and the creation of a participatory citizenry was one of the highest ideals of the European reformers. In several ways, literacy, universal education, daily newspapers, popular theaters, and other attributes of mass culture reduced the power of government and created actualized civil societies that embraced and demanded democracy and reform.

The importance of education was expressed as early as the eighteenth century. Philosophers of the Enlightenment, a tradition of social and political thought founded upon reason, empiricism, science, pragmatism, and secularism, were outspoken in their condemnation of ignorance and united in their calls for universal education. Control was plainly not their game. According to

MASS EDUCATION AND CULTURE

the ideals of Enlightenment thinkers, the best and most rationally organized polity would be one in which all people, or at least all males, were sufficiently literate and informed to play a meaningful role in the management of government and society. This ideal was perhaps most prominently echoed in the American revolutionary and third president Thomas Jefferson's deep conviction that a well-educated citizenry was essential for the success and survival of democracy, but it is impossible to ignore his debt to the eighteenth-century European intellectual tradition that he adapted to American conditions and to which he in turn contributed. The earliest attempt to introduce Enlightenment ideals as the basis of European national government—in France after the Revolution of 1789—included an impressive array of educational reforms designed to replace corrupt and anachronistic practices (such as selling university degrees) with stricter and more effective pedagogy. The centralization of France's educational system under Napoleon was designed to ensure that the greatest possible number of students received the same high degree of academic competency. It is interesting to note that the major opponents of these reforms during Napoleon's rule and thereafter—reactionary politicians and clergy—opposed them precisely because they threatened to break the monarchy and the Catholic Church's traditional and

monopolistic control of educational life under the Old Regime. The promoters of mass education, and their ideological ancestors, favored that goal precisely because it promised to break the power of authoritarian political and social structures and liberate the general population from their control.

Another consistent belief of Enlightenment thinkers and their successors in the nineteenth and twentieth centuries was that mass education and, later, cultural integration would automatically induce the newly educated masses to embrace their political beliefs. Perhaps it was an arrogant way to approach the issue, but many modern European pedagogues believed (and still believe) that support for reactionary or conservative political philosophies derived (and still derive) either from fundamental ignorance or from inadequate education. Many educators, scholars, journalists, and others committed to public enlightenment sincerely believed that if the masses were educated, they would surely see the light and abandon the older traditions, attitudes, and customs that seemed at the worst backward and at the best incompatible with the reformist and revolutionary Left's ideals of modernity. It should not be surprising that the socialist publicists Karl Marx and Friedrich Engels included free universal education among their ten major objectives in *The Communist Manifesto* (1848).

In a less ideologically specific sense, a strong consensus among European elites of all political persuasions maintained that education would make better citizens. Observing the consequences of mass industrialization and urbanization, elite opinion was shocked at rising crime rates, decaying family values, squalid living conditions, poor hygiene, and the spread of disease. In these circumstances a new socially modish view reversed the older notion that poverty was caused by moral and physical turpitude and that the lower classes were naturally condemned to their baleful existence. Instead, the absence of education suggested itself as a major cause of the horrible conditions in European cities, and finding ways to solve these problems almost always involved dreams of universal literacy and greatly expanded and improved educational systems. Education was believed to be a critical element in raising the masses out of poverty. General education would give them productive employment as an alternative to crime or precarious hand-to-mouth existence. The resulting economic improvement, it was presumed, would lead to greater stability in families and communities. In times of economic depression, schooling was an alternative to unemployment for adolescents who were old enough to work but still young enough to go to school: enrollment in French secondary schools, for example, doubled between 1931 and 1939, when France latently suffered the effects of the Great Depression. Spreading knowledge about proper nutrition and personal hygiene—a goal that remained elusive until the eve of World War II in many parts of Europe—was expected to improve health and increase the material quality of life. Literacy, of course, was the key to all of these goals, and activists and government officials of all political persuasions embraced it as a major objective. Literacy also became one of the principal enterprises of private charities by the turn of the twentieth century. To cite one striking example, the autocratic government of tsarist Russia committed itself to achieving universal primary education and made great strides in that direction, but it was the communist government of the Soviet Union—made up of the tsarist regime's most determined opponents—that accomplished that goal in the 1920s and 1930s. Although neither regime was democratic and both had very different ideas about the meaning of citizenship, each pursued universal literacy because its leaders believed it would benefit the people and the country. In an even more striking irony, both the tsars and the Soviet bodies charged with educational matters referred to education as "enlightenment."

The development of mass cultural life at the end of the nineteenth century complemented the dissemination of literacy and knowledge. Rather than mobilizing cultural events and products to control their peoples, European governments usually found themselves playing reactive games. The growth of an accessible mass-circulation media—"mass" in large part because of growing literacy but also because of high-volume industrial production and distribution techniques—presented existing regimes with a great proliferation of news reports and expressions of opinion that came to influence politics and society in unprecedented ways. Governments could only react—generally with limited success—with the imposition of various forms of censorship. Over time, however, increasingly democratic polities and governments removed or restricted this power to the point at which most of Europe enjoyed a free press that appealed to millions of people and often adopted ideological views and positions on particular issues that registered their strong opposition to the government. Since media was, by and large, free of government control and even influence after a certain point, it is entirely correct to speak of it as a pillar of civil society, an organic social structure that existed and evolved independently of traditional institutions of authority. The growth of a mass circulation press resulted in a democratization of knowledge, in a diversity of opinion, and in the creation of a civic consciousness that only truly repressive regimes like Nazi Germany and the Soviet Union could seek to control to their own advantage.

Mass culture also manifested itself in leisure activities. The growth of theater as a nonelite form of entertainment was particularly vital in this regard. Many reformers, such as the radical French man of letters Romain Rolland, believed that it was naturally accessible to the great mass of people, for, they presumed, one did not need literacy to comprehend the social, moral, and political messages of the stage. As theatrical censorship declined in Europe, growing urban masses had access to affordable theaters, cabarets, vaudeville acts, and, later, movies and other forms of popular entertainment that bound them culturally and intellectually to wider developments in national debates and movements. Although conservatives and reactionaries sometimes feared the popularization of political and social messages through popular entertainment, even many of them nevertheless believed that a respectable popular culture would reduce the masses' perceived abuse of drink, overindulgence in prostitution, and attraction to other morally questionable activities.

The twentieth century saw the advent of universal literacy and education throughout Europe and the full development of a democratized mass culture available to almost anyone who wished to consume it. The result of these

LITERACY RATES IN 2000

EUROPE	% Literate	OTHER NATIONS	% Literate
Albania	97.8	Algeria	88.5
Belarus	99.8	Bangladesh	48.4
Bulgaria	99.7	Benin	53.1
Croatia	99.8	China	97.7
Cyprus	99.8	Cuba	98.8
Estonia	99.7	Ethiopia	55.0
Greece	99.8	Ghana	91.1
Hungary	99.8	Haiti	64.4
Italy	99.8	India	72.6
Latvia	99.8	Lebanon	95.2
Lithuania	99.8	Mali	36.1
Malta	98.6	Mexico	97.0
Poland	99.8	Peru	96.7
Portugal	99.8	Pakistan	57.0
Republic of Moldova	99.8	Puerto Rico	97.5
Romania	99.6	Senegal	50.7
Russian Federation	99.8	Rwanda	83.4
Slovenia	99.8	South Africa	91.3
Spain	99.8	Syria	87.2
Ukraine	99.9	Vietnam	95.2

Source: "Literacy rates, aged 15-24, both sexes, per cent (UNESCO)," United Nations, Department of Economic and Social Affairs <http://unstats.un.org/unsd/mi/mi_series_results.asp?rowId=656>.

developments was not the augmentation of state authority over powerless masses. Rather, they accelerated the Continent's movement toward democratic government and open societies. For the first time, interested citizens of any class or background could voice concerns, participate in affairs of state, and openly express opinions about their societies.

—PAUL DU QUENOY,
GEORGETOWN UNIVERSITY

Viewpoint:
No. European governments promoted universal education to extend control over their citizenry by systematically instilling basic beliefs that served the purposes of the state.

The extension of education and culture during the Enlightenment began as a private affair. From coffeehouses and lending libraries to Masonic lodges and scientific societies, the focus was on individual development in voluntary contexts. Not until the French Revolution did successive French governments begin using the media, broadly defined, to publicize and legitimize their behaviors. Napoleon made "spin-doctoring" an art form, using his bulletins, proclamations, and dispatches to create what sometimes became an alternate reality. Among his opponents, the British and the reformed Prussian governments followed a similar course, Prussia especially seeking connections with the German media to spread the word of a new order whose benefits were not projected as being confined to a single state.

Education witnessed a similar development. Napoleon needed administrators and placed corresponding emphasis on expanding and systematizing the secondary and higher schools that produced them. Other continental states followed suit. Prussia, with its legally defined *Abitur* (school-leaving examination) as the link between *gymnasiums* (secondary schools) and universities, set the common central European pattern for institutionally linking states and schools. As bureaucracies expanded in the nineteenth century, state service became a major rival to private enterprise, business, and the free professions of law and medicine in attracting graduates. It might take longer to become fully established, but the risks were less, and the rewards were surer. Combined with the cliché, almost as prevalent on the Continent as in Britain, that there was no substitute for experience in the business world, the result was to steer generations of young, capable, and ambitious men into government service–which they in turn came to define as public service.

The nineteenth-century state had in principle only limited spheres of responsibility. Its accepted duties were to provide security from external threats and to limit domestic tensions. Both came to be seen as a common matrix: the integration of a state's people into a public structure whose claims to loyalty and identity would override all others. The Prussian reform movement originally spoke of "making subjects into citizens." As the century progressed, the challenge became making everybody into citizens first and anything else, religion, occupation, or social class, a distant second.

Education seemed a beginning common denominator–not least because most bureaucrats were themselves the products of educational systems–and understood their potential value in socializing individuals. A significant difference existed, however, between the elite systems, products of the Enlightenment and the Napoleonic era, and the mass educational structures that emerged during the second half of the nineteenth century. In their ideal form these expanded systems strongly resembled the factories developed by the Industrial Revolution, using large bureaucratized institutions to turn out a mass product: in this case a socialized and literate workforce. In its defense it should be said that the factory was the tropic, defining institution of the century, and as such a natural model for organizing other institutions including libraries and department stores. Moreover, it was the first time in history a state had attempted to finance permanently any mass institution. Courts, prisons, tax offices, and even barracks had particular and limited "constituencies." Schools took in everybody. At the turn of the century about 10 percent of the national budgets of the developed great powers, Germany, France, and Britain, were devoted to public education–not a shabby figure even the standards of a later century–and a major change in traditional budget structures.

States expected something for their money. The main avowed function of primary education was national integration. It was accomplished by a broad spectrum of academic and socializing devices, ranging from textbooks

with patriotic constructions, no matter the subject, to institutional environments stressing identification with the state as a manifestation of the home country, however differently the latter might be defined in France or Austria-Hungary.

At the same time, the government schools challenged existing orders by providing nontraditional opportunities to an increasing number of children whose parents had historically been outside the loop of such opportunities. That pattern was enhanced as more teachers entered the profession from the peasant, working, and lower-middle classes of Europe. Far from challenging the system, most of these new arrivals supported it enthusiastically as a stepping-stone for their own children, and often from principle as well. The nationalism of French and German elementary teachers, in particular prior to 1914, was proverbial and did not need to be forced. Among the best evidence is architectural: the confrontational arrangement of the main square in small-town France, with the church facing off against the town hall and the school–sometimes in the same building.

Those who completed the elementary schools of continental Europe in turn found themselves with choices. There were jobs, many of them at lower levels of the bureaucracy: on the railways and the streetcars; in the post offices and the burgeoning network of agencies that issued officially stamped paper. Banks and department stores, shipping lines and insurance companies, all depended on paper trails. Service positions like nursing incorporated increasing demands for literacy. Russian folk wisdom called the illiterate conscript soldier "a doomed man," condemned to little more than his share of latrine cleaning and potato peeling.

Mass culture followed the same pattern. As literacy spread, churchmen, conservatives, and literati deplored and denounced what they described as the mind-numbing trash that shaped and dominated popular taste. The Left uttered similar complaints, at times denouncing mass culture as an "establishment" plot to corrupt the proletariat and distract it from its historical mission of introducing a new society. The rise of popular newspapers, popular music, popular humor–and the music halls and vaudeville theaters that nurtured and spread them—were accompanied by their growing respectability. By the turn of the century, "mass" culture was evolving into "popular" culture–in good part by shedding its rougher edges. Motion pictures, initially an entertainment for the rougher sort of men, by the end of World War I had evolved into arguably the dominant form of family outing. Mass sports, such as soccer in Europe and baseball in the United States, similarly shed their rougher edges—in the American game, as part of a conscious effort to increase its fan base and thereby its profits. Characteristic of the development of any aspect of mass culture, however, was its entertainment aspect. At the expense of uplift and improvement, men and women of the new civic orders wanted to have fun in their off-hours.

What emerged by the end of the nineteenth century was a positive synergy between the needs of the state and the desires of its citizens. The so-called bourgeois virtues—hard work, self-discipline, cleanliness, and impulse control—were as necessary to the successful day-to-day operation of a school as they were to the running of a factory. Yet, they also brought not only intrinsic gratifications but also the opportunity of choice—of becoming something other than one's parents. The organized Left recognized this situation almost immediately and sought to establish its own educational structures to inculcate what were deemed specifically working-class virtues. The irony was that in practice those qualities differed little from their middle-class equivalents. They produced

good people, good citizens, and good soldiers—all without much conscious effort once the system was in place.

−DENNIS SHOWALTER,
COLORADO COLLEGE

References

James Smith Allen, *In the Public Eye: A History of Reading in Modern France, 1800–1940* (Princeton: Princeton University Press, 1991).

Louise McReynolds, *The News under Russia's Old Regime: The Development of a Mass-Circulation Press* (Princeton: Princeton University Press, 1991).

E. Anthony Swift, *Popular Theater and Society in Tsarist Russia* (Berkeley: University of California Press, 2002).

Eugen Weber, *Peasants into Frenchmen: The Modernization of Rural France, 1870–1914* (Stanford, Cal.: Stanford University Press, 1976).

MASS EDUCATION AND CULTURE

Was nationalism consistently important in Europe during the twentieth century?

Viewpoint: Yes. Nationalism had a profound impact on European political, cultural, and economic developments throughout the twentieth century.

Viewpoint: No. By the late twentieth century, nationalism had lost its importance as the countries of Europe engaged in greater economic and political cooperation.

It would be difficult to argue that modern Europe has not been characterized by rampant nationalism. As new states coalesced and old states revived, European political life was imbued with a relatively new form of collective identity, one based on commonalities in culture, language, and the fact or perception of a shared history. A surge in national pride, national antagonisms, theories of ethnic superiority, powerful central governments, and emerging high technology set off a tinderbox of conflict.

One particularly salient aspect of the history of nationalism in twentieth-century Europe has been its durability. At the cusp of a new century and new millennium, scholars debate whether nationalism endured as an important force in European political life or declined markedly between 1900 and 2000. Were the catastrophes of the two world wars sufficient to bury the most potent of national antagonisms, or have such events as the civil war in Bosnia and the continuing problems in Corsica, the Basque region of Spain, and Northern Ireland merely confirmed them? In an era when Europe is moving toward greater political and economic unity, the trajectory of twentieth-century nationalism remains an important topic for consideration.

Viewpoint:
Yes. Nationalism had a profound impact on European political, cultural, and economic developments throughout the twentieth century.

Nationalism is an ambiguous concept. While political leaders and regimes have continuously used it to further their objectives and manipulate public opinion, the general public has often regarded it as an emotional attachment to a mythical or perceived identity. Furthermore, the term has been applied to a variety of phenomena that may be related to, but are different from, nationalism—patriotism, chauvinism, xenophobia, racism, and popular sentiment. Although such concepts are limited manifestations of nationalism, they have consistently been perceived as expressions of both popular imagination and concrete policies pursued by governments. Europe's historical experience throughout the twentieth century has demonstrated that it is difficult to disentangle the role of nationalism from that of other political, cultural, and economic influences. The solution of various economic and social problems has continuously been linked to the stability of the nation-state.

Nationalism has manifested its presence in twentieth-century European history in many ways, although its history may be broadly divided into four periods. From the beginning of the century to the end of World War I, nationalism was a continuation of processes that developed in Europe during the late nineteenth century. It was marked by the triumph of self-determination, nation building, imperial rivalry, and colonial expansion—all of which contributed, in one way or another, to the outbreak of World War I. During the period between the two world wars, isolationism and autarky emerged. This movement culminated in the rise of extreme nationalist regimes such as Nazi Germany and fascist Italy. Even in the communist Soviet Union, Josef Stalin used nationalism in his policy of "socialism in one country." Many scholars argued that nationalism was profoundly discredited in Western Europe and severely repressed in the Soviet Union and communist-controlled Eastern Europe during the next period: the Cold War. However, the nation-state remained the major building block and ultimate basis for the legitimization of power in European politics. The nationalist appeal was invoked on many occasions in both Eastern and Western Europe as a means to mobilize popular support or divert attention from other problems. Finally, at the end of the Cold War in 1989 there was an upsurge of nationalism, especially in Eastern Europe, as it led to the disintegration of multinational states such as the Union of Soviet Socialist Republics (U.S.S.R.), Yugoslavia, and Czechoslovakia, and to the formation of new nation-states along the principle of self-determination. European integration and the enlargement of the European Union (EU) provoked the rise of Right-wing movements all over Western Europe that defended the preservation of national identity.

Nationalism in the last three decades of the nineteenth century and the first two decades of the twentieth century differed from that of the preceding period in several major aspects. First, the "threshold" principle, which postulated that only peoples with a long historical tradition of statehood (for example, the French, Russians, British, and Spanish) had enough viability to establish a nation-state, was essentially abandoned. Many other peoples claimed the right to self-determination and a nation-state. This movement was further emphasized in U.S. president Woodrow Wilson's doctrine of self-determination in the "Fourteen Points," presented to Congress in January 1918 and elaborated in the Paris Peace Settlement (1919). Second, with the multiplication of "unhistorical" nations, ethnicity and language became central to national identity, largely following the example of the two most successful national movements—Germany and

Italy. Third, national sentiments within existing nation-states were marked by a sharp shift to the political Right. Nationalism acquired a more exclusive, separatist character as opposed to its inclusive, expansionist nature before 1870. This shift was helped by the development of racialist theories and social Darwinism, which stimulated such exclusivism. By the beginning of the twentieth century the slogan "survival of the fittest" was increasingly evoked to justify not merely the European-dominated global system as a whole but even a drive for supremacy within that system. Social Darwinists were not content with the concept of a single white "race." Instead, they "discovered" among whites a whole assortment of races (for example, Slavic, Aryan, and Teutonic), which were all, naturally, engaged in a struggle for survival. Such a contest, ultimately, could only be decided by war. World War I could be viewed as the combined result of rivalries among the Great Powers and the quest for self-determination on the part of smaller European peoples, especially in the Balkans, which actually provided the trigger for war.

The end of World War I was marked by the disintegration of multiethnic empires and the emergence of the Soviet Union. Possibly as a reaction to the latter, the Wilsonian principle of self-determination was upheld in Western Europe, which led to further redrawing of national maps. The incorporation of separate nations within ideal national boundaries, however, was a mirage. The development of autarkic tendencies and the rise in importance of national economies during the interwar years was bolstered by economic protectionism. Disillusioning economic experiences in the 1920s were among the major factors that fueled the development of extreme rightist nationalist movements and led to the establishment of fascist and Right-wing authoritarian regimes in several countries in Europe, notably in Germany, Italy, Spain, Portugal, Hungary, and Romania. These regimes, in turn, promoted extreme forms of nationalism, which emphasized notions of racial superiority and exclusivism.

On the other hand, the rise of fascism prompted the development of antifascist nationalism, which combined resistance and people's awareness of the need for social transformation. In this process, leftist movements successfully incorporated nationalist and social elements in their programs. While the Soviet Union had in the early days of its existence turned its back on Russia's past and sought to eradicate all traces of nationalism as incompatible with communist internationalism, Stalin's strategy of "socialism in one country" brought a change in attitude. In the mid 1930s, while the term *national* was still being shunned, Soviet patriotism was now

NATIONALISM

encouraged in a way akin to nationalism. Drawing examples from the achievements of the tsars as successful defenders of Russia from foreign aggression, Soviet patriotism acquired special importance in the context of the emergence of Nazism as a threat to the U.S.S.R. in the late 1930s and during World War II. Furthermore, Soviet propaganda exerted considerable efforts to promote the special mission of Russians as forerunners of a new world order and way of life.

During most of the Cold War many observers believed that the great age of nationalism had passed and that nationalism consisted of a set of obsolescent, dangerous, and objectionable ideas. However, nationalism was far from dead; it persisted in popular attitudes and in appeals made by politicians for support. In the 1960s and 1970s minorities in Western Europe reasserted their claims for nationhood. Basques and Catalans in Spain, Corsicans in France, Slovenes in Austrian Carinthia, Catholics in Northern Ireland, and Germans in northern Italy posed difficult problems for central governments and became threats of varying intensity to the existing constitutional order. In Eastern Europe most of the Soviet satellites exploited national sentiments as a way to mobilize popular support and divert attention from economic and social problems, provided that nationalist rhetoric did not challenge Soviet supremacy. Anticommunist movements in Hungary, the German Democratic Republic, Czechoslovakia, and Poland emphasized national identity and the necessity to do away with Soviet domination. All in all, despite the beginning of integrative processes in Western Europe and the professed internationalism of the communist regimes in the U.S.S.R. and its satellites, the nation-state continued to be the major basis of legitimization of power, and nationalism did not appear to be incompatible with Cold War universalism.

After the collapse of communist regimes in Eastern Europe, which brought the end of Cold War confrontation and opened new prospects for European integration, many analysts were quick to proclaim the end of the age of nations and nationalism. Yet, bitter and violent disputes exploded in the 1990s in the former Yugoslavia and the former U.S.S.R. These conflicts were largely fueled by the aggressive reassertion of national identity on the part of separate national communities. While many observers blamed the eruption of such conflicts on socio-economic backwardness and the lack of democratic traditions in these countries, the last decade of the twentieth century was also marked by a revival of nationalism in parts of Europe. For one thing, minority separatism gained new strength. The Irish, Basque, and Corsican questions flared violently, while popular sentiment began to favor

the "devolution" of government power to regions within nation-states. The reestablishment of a separate Scottish parliament in 1999 and the creation of separate assemblies for Wales and Northern Ireland that same year granted increased authority to the non-English nationalities of the United Kingdom. A separatist movement in northern Italy also gained steam. These developments were accompanied by the growing concern of some smaller European states about the preservation of their national identity in the context of European integration. Norway voted against EU membership in 1994. Denmark, Sweden, and Britain have all declined to take part in the European monetary union, which began on 1 January 1999, and are unlikely to do so in the near future. In addition, the prospects of EU enlargement and the growing number of immigrants from Eastern Europe and other parts of the world stimulated the revival of Right-wing nationalist parties and movements all across Western Europe. Such political formations became especially prominent in the sociopolitical life in France, Germany, Austria, Italy, and even the Netherlands, whose society has long been known for its tolerant attitude toward immigrants and its endorsement of diversity. Despite energetic measures taken by the EU to curb such tendencies, nationalist political leaders such as Jörg Haider in Austria and Jean-Marie Le Pen in France continue to enjoy considerable popularity. Partly as a reaction to this situation as well as to persistent problems related to the transition from socialist, state-planned to free-market economy, similar political movements have gained prominence in Eastern Europe too, their most eminent representative being Vladimir Zhirinovsky in Russia.

–YORK NORMAN,
GEORGETOWN UNIVERSITY

Viewpoint:
No. By the late twentieth century, nationalism had lost its importance as the countries of Europe engaged in greater economic and political cooperation.

Many observers state that a resurgence of nationalism occurred in Europe during the 1990s. The collapse of communist regimes and the end of the Cold War supposedly lifted the lid on long-suppressed and unfulfilled nationalisms, giving rise to the competing claims of national groups for recognition and statehood, with disastrous consequences in places.

SLOVENIAN DECLARATION OF INDEPENDENCE

25 June 1991

On the basis of the fundamental principles of natural law, i.e. the right of the Slovene nation to self-determination, on the principles of international law and the Constitution of the Republic of Slovenia, and on the basis of the absolute majority vote in the plebiscite held on December 23, 1990, the people of the Republic of Slovenia will no longer be part of the Socialist Federal Republic of Yugoslavia. On the basis of an unanimous proposal by all parliamentary parties and group of delegates and in compliance with the plebiscitary outcome, the Assembly of the Republic of Slovenia adopted the Constitutional Act on the sovereignty and independence of the Republic of Slovenia at the sessions of all its chambers on 25 June 1991.

I. Prior to the plebiscite on sovereignty and independence, Slovenia proposed, jointly with the Republic of Croatia, a draft agreement proposing to the other Yugoslav republics an alliance or a confederacy of sovereign states, according to which the present member of the Yugoslav federation would continue to cooperate in the spheres of economy, of foreign policy and in other areas. The Assembly of the Republic of Slovenia voted in favour of a sovereign and independent Republic of Slovenia. Slovenia notified the other Yugoslav republics and the Yugoslav public of the actions which Slovenia was required to take on the basis of the plebiscitary outcome. These messages included the resolution of the Proposal for a Multilateral Dissolution of the Socialist Republic of Yugoslavia and other initiatives. Slovenia also proposed to Yugoslavia and the Yugoslav republics, as the constitutive entities of the Federation, a bilateral dissolution, which would create two or more sovereign states, which would acknowledge each other's status as a legal, international entity. Slovenia repeatedly voiced its readiness to come to an agreement on the permanent and institutionalized forms of cooperation, including the arrangement of interrelations in the event of a Yugoslav confederative or economic community, or some other suitable form of association which would benefit all its nations and citizens. The proposal for a bilateral dissolution and the formation of sovereign states was not accepted within the reasonably allotted time, except by the Republic of Croatia. The Republic of Slovenia was thus compelled to pass the Constitutional Act of the Sovereignty and Independence of the Republic of Slovenia.

II. The Republic of Slovenia has proclaimed its sovereignty and independence and has thereby assumed actual jurisdiction over its territory. Consequently, Slovenia as an international, legal entity, in the full sense of the term, and in conformity with the principles of the unification of sovereign states in Europe, seeks association with other states, membership in the United Nations Organization, membership in the European community and participation in other alliances of states or nations. The sovereignty and the independence of the Republic of Slovenia must be understood as a condition for entering into new integrational processes within the framework of the former Yugoslavia and within the European framework. Moreover, the Republic of Slovenia will strictly adhere to the Founding Document of the United Nations, to the Declaration and other acts of the Conference on European Security and Cooperation, as well as to other international treaties. The establishment of a sovereign and independent state of Slovenia on the basis of the right to self-determination is not an act against any political entity of Yugoslavia or any other foreign political unit. Slovenia recognizes the right to self-determination of the other republics, nations and nationalities of Yugoslavia. Slovenia wishes to exercise its right to sovereignty and to association with other sovereign states in a peaceful manner by mutual agreement, through talks and dialogue, in conformity with the standards of the international community, which means that the future relationships on the territory of former Yugoslavia should stand on democratic principles, without changing the external and internal borders of Yugoslavia.

III. The Republic of Slovenia as a sovereign and independent state hereby proclaims:

• that the Constitution of the Social Federal Republic of Yugoslavia is no longer in force on the territory of the republic of Slovenia. The Republic of Slovenia is continuing with the procedure of assuming actual rule on its territory. The procedure will be carried out gradually and in agreement with the other republics of former Yugoslavia, without encroaching on the right of other republics;

• that it is prepared to continue negotiations regarding the possible forms of association with the states which will be constituted on the territory of former Yugoslavia. On the basis of mutual recognition, the Republic of Slovenia is prepared immediately to initiate talks in order to reach an agreement on an association of sovereign states on the territory of former Yugoslavia.

Within this association, the member states would be free to pursue their joint economic, political, international and other interests. The reaching of such an agreement, or at least a joint declaration of the desire to reach such an agreement, would guarantee that the process of assuming authority in the newly founded states and the process constituting an association of these states would not cause undue conflict. On the contrary, these processes would be mutually stimulating and would facilitate the process of self-determination in all Yugoslav nations, the right of Albanians in Kosovo and the development of democracy in the alliance of sovereign states on the territory of former Yugoslavia;

• in compliance with the decision of the Sabor of the republic of Croatia, Slovenia recognizes the Republic of Croatia as a sovereign state and an international legal entity. The mandate of the Slovene delegates to the Federal Chamber of the Assembly of the SFR Yugoslavia and the delegations of the Republic of Slovenia to the Chambers of the Republics and Provinces of the Assembly of the SFR of Yugoslavia is terminated by the proclamation of the Declaration of Independence. The Assembly of the Republic of Slovenia shall elect a new 12-member delegation, which will be authorized to participate in negotiations regarding the dissolution of Yugoslavia at the Assembly of former Yugoslavia, in the solving of current issues during the transition period and negotiations regarding the possible formation of an association of sovereign states on the basis of approval by the Assembly of the Republic of Slovenia. The Republic of Slovenia appeals to the other Yugoslav republics to delegate such authority to their respective delegations. The Assembly of the Republic of Slovenia also expects the Federal Executive Council to participate in this process.

The Assembly of the Republic of Slovenia authorizes its present Member of the Presidency of the SFR of Yugoslavia to represent the Republic of Slovenia, in conformity with the guidelines of the Assembly of the Republic of Slovenia, in the Presidency of the SFR of Yugoslavia. All outstanding issues such as the status of the Yugoslav people's Army in the Republic of Slovenia, competencies in the sphere of international relations and the issue of the division of common property will be dealt with in a special agreement jointly reached by the Republic of Slovenia and the corresponding bodies of former Yugoslavia.

IV. In its capacity as an international and legal entity, the Republic of Slovenia pledges to:

• respect all the principles of international law and, in the spirit of legal succession, the provisions of all international contracts signed by Yugoslavia and which apply to the territory of the Republic of Slovenia. In conformity with the anticipated agreement on the assumption of the rights and obligations of former Yugoslavia, the Republic of Slovenia will honour its share of international financial obligations towards other states and international organizations, and ensure the free flow of goods, services and people across its borders, and also ensure the uninterrupted flow of transport and communication on its territory;

• endeavour to gain the approval of the international community regarding the proclamation of the sovereign and independent Republic of the sovereign and independent Republic of Slovenia and to improve economic, cultural, political, financial and other ties with the international community. Furthermore, Slovenia seeks legal recognition from all countries which respect democratic principles and the right of all nations to self-determination. Slovenia also anticipates that the international community will use its influence to contribute to the shaping of the alliance of sovereign states on the territory of former Yugoslavia and thus contribute to the bilateral and peaceful implementation of the decision to create the sovereign and independent state of the Republic of Slovenia.

V. The Republic of Slovenia is a legal entity and a social state, whose environment is suitable for market economy. Slovenia pledges to observe human rights and civil liberties, the special rights of autonomous nationalities, as well as the European achievements of industrial democracy (above all socio-economic rights, the rights of the employed to take part in decision-making processes and independent unions), the inviolability of property and the freedom of association in a civil society. Slovenia pledges to guarantee multiparty democracy and local, or regional, self-rule. Slovenia guarantees that political or other form of persuasion will not be used as a basis for instigating inequality or discrimination of any kind. It further pledges to solve all contentious internal and external issues in a peaceful, non-violent manner and to strive to improve cooperation, on an equal footing, with all nations and citizens of Europe where the people, regions, nations and states are free and equal.

Source: "Declaration of Independence," Government of the Republic of Slovenia, Public Relations and Media Office website <http://www.uvi.si/10years/path/documents/declaration/>.

NATIONALISM

Lithuanians demonstrating for independence from the Soviet Union, 1989

(Peter Turnley/CORBIS)

If one takes nationalism, as defined by Ernest Gellner, one of the foremost theorists on the subject, to be "primarily a principle which holds that the political and national unit should be congruent," then even a cursory glance at a map of Europe as it stood at the end of the 1990s would indicate how ascendant nationalism has been over the past century. Territorially, Central and Eastern Europe bear little or no resemblance to those of 1914. Where there were once vast, sprawling multinational empires—German, Austro-Hungarian, Ottoman, and Russian—there are now a host of smaller nation-states. Almost every national group has a state, and every state contains, predominantly, one national group. If a national group does not have a state or lies outside the borders of the nation-state, then it aspires to statehood or association with the nation-state with which it identifies. Given this high level of congruence between national and political units, it would seem that the rise of nationalism over the course of the twentieth century has been inexorable; its political importance has been incontestable.

During the Cold War it was fashionable to argue that nationalism had been superseded by other issues; ideological rather than national differences were supposed to have divided the Continent into two as opposed to a multitude of parts. The wars of secession in the former Yugoslavia were therefore a wake-up call. Was Europe ominously reverting to the exclusivist and aggressive nationalism of the mid century? Nationalism in the 1990s, however, did not tear Europe apart. History was not repeated. For every Yugoslavia, there was a Czechoslovakia: a "velvet divorce" that peacefully bifurcated the country. The disintegration of the Soviet Union into its constituent republics was not accompanied by widespread bloodshed as prophesied. In the opposite direction, Germany reunified, less to the detriment of its neighbors' security than to the functioning of its own economy. Nor was ethnic cleansing in the former Yugoslavia a pattern repeated across the Continent. Sizable national minorities, Hungarian and Russian in particular, remained in several countries. There was no equivalent of Srebrenica (the massacre of more than seven thousand Muslims by Bosnian Serb troops in July 1995) in Estonia or Transylvania. Above all, postcommunist nation-states lined up to join organizations such as the European Union (EU) and the North Atlantic Treaty Organization (NATO), steps that entailed a diminution of hard-won national sovereignty.

By the 1990s the international context in which nationalisms operated had radically changed from the mid century, as had the nature of these nationalisms. The creation of supra- and international organizations after

1945, themselves a reaction to the virulent and destructive variant of nationalism that was widely seen as having contributed to the disaster of two world wars, helped define the parameters in which nationalism was legitimate and acceptable. At the end of the twentieth century it did not take a Euro-enthusiast to recognize that the unprecedented level of economic and political cooperation among an increasing number of European states over the past half century had profound ramifications for the role of the nation-state within the framework of what became the EU, as well as for relations among the member states and the manner in which national differences were articulated and reconciled. Even if one follows scholar Alan S. Milward's argument that European integration in fact "rescued" the nation-state, strengthening it economically and legitimizing it in the eyes of its population, it is still evident that the content and nature of nationalist discourse among member states of the EU has altered significantly since the end of World War II. Notwithstanding the likes of Jörg Haider in Austria and Jean-Marie Le Pen in France, or the periodic breast-beating of successive Greek governments, atavistic forms of nationalism in Western Europe are now for the most part confined to the soccer field rather than the battlefield. When it comes literally to the battlefield, European nation-states have partly delegated control over their armed forces to the supranational military command structure that is NATO. "The national state is no longer the primary locus of armed force," Anthony D. Smith remarked in *Nations and Nationalism in a Global Era* (1995), a development that midcentury nationalists would have viewed with horror. The contrast with the interwar period is, indeed, striking. The logic of nationalism in the 1930s and 1940s, when taken to its extreme, led to autarkic economic policies and crippling national-defence budgets and was ultimately self-destructive. By the end of the twentieth century, nation-states had learned to become interdependent in order to remain independent.

States, both old and new, that emerged from the communist bloc in the 1990s did so into an established system in which economic, and increasingly political and military, sovereignty was pooled. For smaller nation-states, such as Estonia, Slovakia, and Slovenia—all with little or no prior experience of independent statehood—the existence of this state system, and the prospect, real or distant, of integration into it, was a guarantee of their viability. Paradoxically, the emergence of these nation-states, taken as a sign of resurgent nationalism, was accompanied by a parallel widening and deepening of the process of European integration, which underscored increasing interdependence

and the obsolescence of narrow and exclusivist nationalism of the past. Indeed, those states that have been identified with this strain of nationalism—most notably Serbia (post-1992 Federal Republic of Yugoslavia), and to a lesser extent Slovakia, because of its treatment of Roma and Hungarian minorities—were treated either as pariahs or kept at arm's length by the rest of Europe.

Widely dispersed national minorities presented a further paradox in the history of European nationalism. These minorities were invariably the focus and/or source of nationalist agitation and territorial revisionism. Over the course of the twentieth century, however, their numbers dramatically decreased from the combined effects of expulsion, extermination, and the redrawing of frontiers. The increased national homogeneity resulting from this repression, particularly in Eastern Europe, coincided with a reduction in expansionist and/or irredentist nationalism. Having achieved a high level of congruence between national and political units, nationalisms became, in a sense, sated or fulfilled within existing state borders. The adage "good fences make good neighbors" is therefore equally applicable to nationalism: good borders make good nationalists. Those "fences" that were erected at the end of World War I, and adjusted after 1945, were not moved in the aftermath of the Cold War. New states that resulted in the 1990s from the breakup of federations such as Yugoslavia, Czechoslovakia, and the Soviet Union did so along internal borders that remained unchanged. Whether this relative territorial stability in Europe since World War II can be taken as a sign of a general decline in nationalism, it is at least evidence as to a diminution of a variant of nationalism that seeks to expand the political unit of the nation at a neighbor's expense.

Where national minorities remained after World War II, their treatment reflected both the strength and character of nationalism among the majority. West European states reacted to the post-1960s renaissance of minorities with relative tolerance, partly because the political goals of these movements were limited and did not pose a real threat to the existence of the nation-state. By the 1990s, regionalism became the new buzzword in the EU, suggesting that perhaps the nation-state was no longer the most suitable unit of political organization. The increasing polyethnicity of older nation-states such as France and Britain, brought about as a result of mass non-European immigration (a development seen, though to a lesser extent, elsewhere in Europe), has inevitably led to a reevaluation of national identity within these countries. That the racist political move-

NATIONALISM

ments that oppose nonwhite immigration past and present are labeled *nationalist* is a further reminder that the term remains a pejorative and forever linked with the excesses of the mid century that Europe has spent the last half century trying to distance itself from.

It would be rash to claim that the nation-state has or will become redundant, that supranationality has replaced national identity, or that nationalism itself has been eclipsed as a political force. Nationalism persists, but it has been modified in the second half of the twentieth century to the extent that, on the whole, it no longer possesses the destructive capacity it once had and has, by necessity, become self-limiting. Any discussion of decline is, of course, relative, and compared to the central role that it played in transforming and shaping Europe from the French Revolution to the end of World War II, nationalism today, as Eric J. Hobsbawm has argued, against the grain of conventional wisdom, "is simply no longer the historical force it was."

–MATTHEW FRANK,
OXFORD UNIVERSITY

References

Malcolm Anderson, *States and Nationalism in Europe since 1945* (London & New York: Routledge, 2000).

Ernest Gellner, *Nations and Nationalism* (Oxford: Blackwell, 1983; Ithaca, N.Y.: Cornell University Press, 1983).

Eric J. Hobsbawm, *Nations and Nationalism since 1780: Programme, Myth, Reality,* second edition (Cambridge & New York: Cambridge University Press, 1992).

Brian Jenkins and Spyros A. Sofos, eds., *Nation and Identity in Contemporary Europe* (London & New York: Routledge, 1996).

Alan S. Milward and others, *The European Rescue of the Nation State,* second edition (London & New York: Routledge, 2000).

Martijn A. Roessingh, *Ethnonationalism and Political Systems in Europe: A State of Tension* (Amsterdam: Amsterdam University Press, 1996).

Anthony D. Smith, *Nations and Nationalism in a Global Era* (Cambridge: Polity Press, 1995).

NATIONALISM

NAZISM AND COMMUNISM

Were there ideological similarities between Nazism and Soviet communism?

Viewpoint: Yes. Nazism and Soviet communism converged in many significant ways, including their philosophical origins and the ways in which they impacted on government and society.

Viewpoint: No. Nazism and Soviet communism were widely divergent ideologies that had fundamentally different origins and significantly dissimilar effects.

Soviet leader Josef Stalin told his fellow World War II leaders during the February 1945 Yalta Conference that his secret-police chief Lavrentii Beriia was "our [Heinrich] Himmler," referring to the head of Nazi Germany's notorious SS and Gestapo. This comment captures a thriving academic debate about the comparability of fascism and communism. Observers of the "totalitarian school" have argued that these ideologies, traditionally identified with the extreme Right and the extreme Left, respectively, had a great deal in common.

This chapter assesses the merits of this argument. As one essay suggests, both types of regime were characterized by a ruthless police state, a rigid one-party system of government, and an ideological promise to create a utopian society. Yet, as the counterargument maintains, fascism and communism had significant differences that the first argument overlooks. Indeed, fascism and communism largely defined themselves by their mutual opposition and fought determinedly to destroy each other. Valid comparisons between the two appear to be limited to specific comparisons between Nazi Germany and the Soviet Union under Stalin, leaving widely divergent avenues of inquiry and a much broader comparative perspective unexplored. Many nonfascist and noncommunist regimes and leaders, moreover, also shared several of the important characteristics that suggest the comparability of fascism and communism.

Viewpoint:
Yes. Nazism and Soviet communism converged in many significant ways, including their philosophical origins and the ways in which they impacted on government and society.

In the last American presidential elections of the twentieth century, the two major political parties, Democrat and Republican, referred to the valiant veterans of World War II and the heroic struggle that America and its allies fought against Nazi Germany, personified by Adolf Hitler. Indeed, now into the early years of the twenty-first century, *Nazi* is still the generic term used whenever it is necessary to portray a man or a country as the "bad guy." Often in the context of political rhetoric, the essence of the term is forgotten. Conversely, Soviet communism, which

German troops at the Nazi
Party convention held in
Nuremberg, September
1934

(© Getty/FPJ Historical Selects)

forced a generation of Americans to "duck and cover" in fear of nuclear annihilation, was the bogeyman of the seemingly distant past, quickly fading from memory. Sharing a short space in history, these two ideological forces, embodied in the two barbarous states, characterized for many people the twentieth century itself.

While the ideologies and systems created to further them had many differences, the world has inherited their similarites as a new and frightening phenomenon. They are also a warning to future generations of the horrors of which man is capable of perpetrating.

Ideology is defined in *Webster's Dictionary* as "the assertions, theories, and aims that constitute a political, social and economic program." From an historical perspective it is more useful to compare not only the ideologies of German National Socialism and Josef Stalin's Soviet communism, but the systems and actions of the two political movements that espoused these ideologies. Their "assertions, theories, and aims" were neither immutable, consistent, nor achieved, and are thus less relevant.

Nazi Germany is defined as Germany under the Nazi Party's control, after Hitler was appointed chancellor, from 1933 through 1945. *Soviet communism* is more difficult, as it morphed

over time as theories gave way to practical concerns, but is here limited to Stalin's regime, roughly 1924 through 1953. Although there is no evidence to suggest Vladimir Lenin was less capable of evil than Stalin, he died before the Communist Party had achieved total control of the Soviet Union; it fell to Stalin to institute the brutal terror policies that characterized communist rule. More than a space in time, Nazism and communism share a common origin and similar "outcomes."

The two ideologies evolved from Western philosophical thought, specifically from the Enlightenment forward. It is difficult, if not impossible, to judge exactly which thinkers influenced specific elements of ideological development. Even Karl Marx, on whom Lenin and Stalin relied heavily, combined in his writings the works of many earlier writers, from Martin Luther through Voltaire to Georg Hegel and Charles Darwin.

The one thing both National Socialism and communism gained from the entire body of post-Enlightenment thought was a belief in societal progress (though they differed as to who was worthy to be included in their new society). Followers of both ideologies believed in the relentless march of this progress and that they could speed it along through political action. To the Nazis, the laws of nature, corrupted from Darwin, would lead the Aryan race to rule a glorious New World Order. It was the duty of the Nazi Party to encourage and facilitate nature. For the Soviets, the laws of history, as described by Marx, would inevitably lead to a distant (and hazy) Communist utopia. In this utopia their chosen people, the proletarian class, would inherit the earth: the last would be first. To hasten the outcome, the Communist Party of the Soviet Union was charged to use any means necessary.

Both ideologies led to the formation of political parties, eventually ruled by one man, who directed the self-destruction of the current society in order to assist the progress of nature/ history toward a new, better world. The current European society was described as bourgeois parliamentary democracy: the enemy of both Nazism and communism. Both also believed that bourgeois democracy had spawned the other ideology, which made Nazism the natural enemy of communism, and vice versa. Often this enmity between them led to the one trying to distance itself from the other as much as possible. Yet, as Hitler himself proclaimed, "There is more that binds us to Bolshevism [communism] than separates us from it. . . . There is, above all, revolutionary feeling." This revolutionary fervor was necessary, for it was only through violence that the old order could be "transformed." Violent action was at the heart of both Nazism and communism.

Where communism and Nazism most clearly resembled each other was in practice. The political system that evolved to bring about the bright new future has been called totalitarianism. This system was unique to the twentieth century and one limited, at the time, to Nazi Germany and the Soviet Union.

First and foremost in Nazi Germany and the Soviet Union there was one official state ideology, and one political party to promote this ideology. The party, made up of a minority elite, was hierarchically structured and controlled, ultimately, by one man. The new elite class was drawn from the ranks of radicals, heretofore excluded from power. Through the party the dictator controlled the state, and the state controlled life. Both Communists and Nazis made use of symbols, parades, ceremonies, uniforms, and huge, staged rallies; there was an almost religious nature to their gatherings, and both parties took on many characteristics of a cult.

The Party had a supervisory role in all government organizations, including the military. As time went on and the systems evolved, all organizations became government organizations. Under this system, the state controlled education, had a monopoly on arms, and directed centrally planned economies where production goals were set, resources allocated, wages determined, and distribution of production decided. Decisions were based on the needs of the state and the needs of the collective strength with no regard for the individual. In this environment everything was a political matter: there were no private concerns.

The accoutrements of representative government—a constitution, legislature, justice system, and so forth—existed in both states but were irrelevant and largely for show. They were totally subservient to the Party and served only to proclaim and enable decisions made by the Party, not to debate or influence them.

Both systems were characterized by increasingly vast bureaucracies. The size of the central government apparatus grew dramatically as the party, through the state, sought to enter and control all aspects of life. In both societies the party provided hope and a sense of belonging and purpose, but at the same time one could easily lose oneself in the drama, pageantry, and slavish devotion required of Party members. Even the most private family matters, marriage, child bearing, and child rearing, became targets for state interference and control. Both parties gave out medals to women who bore more than ten children; they also sought to orchestrate who could marry whom.

There was no dissent tolerated within either party, or within society at large. Dissidents, or potential dissidents, were dealt with ruthlessly. The public was actively encouraged to participate in policing thoughts and actions. Control was exercised through means of mass terror, conducted by a small but brutally efficient secret police. Their presence was everywhere; most civic clubs and organizations had a Gestapo or KGB infiltrator, and no one could be sure who it was. Enemies of the party became enemies of the state, and the definition of *enemy* was deliberately fluid: "he who does not stand with us stands against us," said Lenin. It became the guiding principle of both parties.

Resistance to the party-controlled forces of terror was extremely rare, and almost always fatal. Gulags and concentration camps dotted the European landscape, filled to capacity not with foreign prisoners at first but with "domestic enemies." The Soviets instituted the first firearm registration, which led to a systematic firearm confiscation. The Nazis followed suit after they came to power. It was largely through gun control that the Nazis and Communists were able to force their will on the majority of the population in the beginning, before they had consolidated power. Both could effectively mobilize large numbers of people and target specific individuals and groups for violence. Domestic terror was more than an unfortunate by-product; rather, it was actively promoted by the two states, and the public motivated to join in beatings, looting, even mass murder of opponents of the party.

Modern technology made this new reign of terror possible in a way unimaginable to prior history's most despotic governments. It enabled an unprecedented invasion of privacy and an iron control. Everyone could be photographed and fingerprinted, their movements tracked, and their conversations recorded. Everyone could have a file sitting in Gestapo or KGB headquarters. Technology also provided the state with the ability to spread its message as never before, through a monopoly on all communications. The new state could teach you what to believe, control the news you heard, direct your actions, and show you your enemies through print, radio, and most importantly, motion pictures. Culture became yet another tool of the state.

Art, literature, music, movies, even architecture had to glorify the state and promote its aims. Nazis and Communists sought not only to remake society but to remake mankind itself. The New Man (a phrase used extensively by both ideologies) was depicted through "socialist realism" as unfettered by old, outmoded moral and ethical concerns. He was solely motivated by service to the state and its ideology. There was "simply no higher ethical authority" than the state.

Propaganda to this end was ceaseless: the New Man could be found plastered on billboards, inserted into textbooks, marching across countless recruitment posters, and pointing toward the future in statuesque granite, steel, and concrete. Grandeur and size were the style of the day. Monstrous statues, imposing neoclassical buildings, and huge rallies and marches served to remind Germans and Soviets alike that they were heading toward this glorious future en masse.

Space does not permit a complete list of similar or identical institutions within the two states; literally thousands of examples remain, from agricultural collection methods to foreign-policy implementation to policy toward youth. While differences between the two ideologies and the systems they engendered certainly existed, the results of Nazi and communist rule for the peoples who lived through them were remarkably similar. On paper the differences may appear significant at times, in practice much less so, and (perhaps most important) for the people ruled there were none at all.

The legacy of Nazi Germany and Stalin's communism is one of total state domination, ideological supremacy over life itself, and, ultimately, terror. As scholar Ernst Nolte explains, it is a legacy of "moral disease . . . the result of man's revolt against God in secularized society."

Yet, it is also a lesson we can learn from, if we desire to avoid repeating its mistakes.

–JULIJANA BUDJEVAC AND
LAWRENCE HELM,
WASHINGTON, D.C.

Viewpoint:
No. Nazism and Soviet communism were widely divergent ideologies that had fundamentally different origins and significantly dissimilar effects.

Most of those who argue that fascism and communism converged point to what they believe to be the two ideologies' common origins, especially their roots in the eighteenth-century Enlightenment, a long and diverse period of inquiry into almost every aspect of the human experience, and the maturation of these roots in the Romantic era of the nineteenth century, which questioned some Enlightenment assumptions while affirming many others. Fascist and communist quests for the perfectibility of man and society, faith in science to solve all problems, pretensions to the mastery of reason and nature, and rejection of the Old Regime's social and political structures appear to recommend their comparability. What proponents of this view fail to admit, however, is that the Enlightenment gave birth to virtually all the "isms" that inhabit the universe of modern politics and society. Conservatism, nationalism, internationalism, liberalism, socialism, capitalism, republicanism, constitutionalism, humanism, feminism, atheism, and just about anything else apart from reactionary monarchism (and even it, by defining itself in opposition to certain Enlightenment ideas) all claim Enlightenment descent and identify important eighteenth-century European and American intellectual figures as their progenitors. Naturally, all of the above have major differences, but all of them, and not just fascism and communism, share both origins in the first blossoming of modern social, political, and economic thought and the ambition of proving beyond dispute their suitability to meet the needs of mankind. European history since the eighteenth century has largely been a tale of struggle among these worldviews, a struggle in which fascism and communism played notable, but not similar, parts.

While it is true that both extreme ideologies emerged in response to political and social crises associated with World War I, they did so in markedly different ways. The growth of Left-

BEWARE THE MARXIST

Below is an excerpt from Mein Kampf *(1925–1927) in which Adolf Hitler condemns Marxism:*

Marxism will march along with democracy until by indirect means it succeeds in getting for its criminal aims the very support of that national intellectual world which it has marked for extermination. But if it became convinced today that in the witches' cauldron of our parliamentary democracy a majority might suddenly be brewed which would furiously go after Marxism—even if only on a basis of a numerical majority entitling it to legislate—the parliamentary thimble rigging would be over with in an instant. Instead of appealing to the democratic conscience, the standard-bearers of the Red International would then send out a fiery summons to the proletarian masses, and their struggle would move at one jump from the stuffy air of our Parliament-chambers into the factories and on to the streets. Democracy would be done for at once; and what the intellectual ability of these apostles of the people had failed to accomplish in the Parliament, the crowbar and sledgehammer of excited proletarian masses would achieve in a flash, just as in the fall of 1918: they would teach the bourgeois world with crushing force the madness of imagining that one can resist the Jewish world-conquest with the methods of Western democracy.

As aforesaid, it requires a devout spirit, when faced with such an opponent, to bind oneself to rules which for him exist only as an imposture and for his own profit, and are thrown overboard the moment they are no longer to his advantage.

In all parties of so-called bourgeois orientation the whole political struggle actually consists only of a scramble for individual seats in Parliament, in the course of which attitudes and principles are thrown overboard like sand ballast as expediency dictates; naturally their platforms are also arranged accordingly, and their strength measured—though in reverse—by that scale. They lack that great magnetic attraction which the great masses will follow only under the irresistible impression of great and outstanding principles and of the convincing force of unqualified faith in these, along with the fanatical fighting courage to be answerable for them.

At a time when one side, armed with all the weapons of a world-concept, even though it be criminal a thousand times over, prepares for onslaught on an existing order, the other side can successfully resist only if it garbs itself in the form of a new (and in our case political) faith, and exchanges the catchword of weak and cowardly defense for the battle-cry of bold and brutal attack. If, therefore, someone, particularly one of the so-called nationalist-bourgeois

Ministers, let us say a Bavarian Centrist, casts up at our movement the brilliant reproach that it is working for an "upheaval," there is but one possible answer to such a political Tom Thumb: Right you are; we are trying to make good what you in your criminal stupidity omitted to do. You and your principles of parliamentary cattle-dealing helped to drag the nation into the abyss: we, however, will attack; by setting up a new world-concept and fanatically, unshakably defending its principles we shall build the steps upon which our people will be able one day to ascend again to the Temple of Freedom. . . .

The ordinary present-day conception of our political world depends generally upon the notion that while the state in itself has creative and cultural vigor, it has nothing to do with racial essentials, but is rather a product of economic necessities, or at best the natural result of a political urge to power. This view, developed to its logical conclusion, leads not only to a misconception of racial forces, but to an undervaluing of the individual. For negation of the variation of the different races in respect to their general culture-developing powers must perforce carry this great error over into the evaluation of the individual person. This assumption of the likeness of races leads to a similar attitude toward peoples, and then toward individual men. And consequently international Marxism itself is but the transference by the Jew Karl Marx of an attitude and a world-concept already long in existence into the form of a definite political profession of faith. Without the underlying foundation of such a generally pre-existing poisoning, the amazing political success of this doctrine would never have been possible. Among the millions, Karl Marx was really the one man who, with the sure eye of the prophet, recognized the essential poisons in the slough of a slowly decaying world, and segregated them, in order, like a black magician, to make a concentrated solution for the quicker destruction of the independent existence of free nations on this earth—all this in the service of his race.

Thus the Marxist doctrine is the concentrated intellectual essence of today's universal world-concept. Even for that reason alone any struggle against it by our so-called bourgeois world is impossible, nay ridiculous, because even the bourgeois world is essentially impregnated with all these poisons, and is devoted to a world-concept which in general differs from the Marxist one only in degree and in personalities. The bourgeois world is Marxist, but believes in the possibility of the domination of certain groups of men (bourgeoisie), while Marxism itself systematically tries to deliver up the world to the hands of Jewry.

Source: *Adolf Hitler,* Mein Kampf *(New York: Stackpole Sons, 1939), pp. 364–366, 369–370.*

wing radicalism throughout Europe was fueled by economies of increasing scarcity and increasingly desperate populations caught in the worst conflict humanity had experienced until that time. In Russia, rising discontent and incompetent national leadership boiled over in a successful communist coup d'état in November 1917. Although the nascent Soviet regime barely survived and could only sustain itself through state-sponsored terror, widespread passivity, the weakness and disorganization of its opponents, and major ideological compromises, its success inspired the formation of communist parties throughout the world, almost always out of an existing socialist party or movement.

It was the threat that the rising popularity of communism posed that led to the development of European fascism as an organized political force after World War I, even if there were some "proto-fascist" philosophical currents brewing in earlier times. Scholars who compare the two ideologies are hard-pressed to explain how fascism and communism were alike if one rose in opposition to the other, but that is, in effect, what happened in the 1920s and 1930s. Horrified by tales of communist excesses in Russia and confronted at home with militant communist movements and coup attempts that were controlled from Moscow and sought to imitate it, initially obscure fascist leaders, promising order, national honor, and vigilant anticommunism, succeeded in gaining mass support, as well as the support of important business, military, religious, and aristocratic elites, all of whom knew that they were among the communists' first targets. As the historian Ernst Nolte has noted, anticommunist themes were of paramount importance in fascist ideology and propaganda, to the extent that fascism took on a primary identity both among its leaders and in popular perceptions as the political force that stood most resolutely against communism. This impression played a crucial role in helping fascist parties throughout Europe gain mass support and, in Italy and Germany, rise to national power, largely on the votes of those who favored stability and tradition and saw communism as the greatest threat to their way of life. The success of fascism, in other words, resulted directly from its self-conscious differentiation from and opposition to communism. In the same way, communists came to identify themselves as the greatest opponents of fascism. The Soviet Union at least pretended to support collective security against Nazi Germany in the 1930s. It described its own socialist opponents as "social fascists" to demonize and differentiate them, and in the aftermath of World War II used the label *fascist* to describe almost any government or attitude that opposed it.

Another unsustainable part of the convergence argument holds that since fascists and communists sometimes opposed the same government policy or voted the same way when they were not in power, their compatibility was evident and they became political bedfellows, however strange. Some measures in Weimar Germany's parliament, for example, were defeated with the support of both Nazi and communist members. Yet, comparing the two extremes in this way belies their great mutual antagonism. When they did vote or act in the streets together, it was not because they agreed on something or had found a new cooperative spirit, but because both parties had the same strategy of immobilizing or destroying the status quo in order to promote their own rise. All they shared was the fanaticism and ruthlessness to use any means to reach their different ends, along with the practical realization that their best chance to achieve power would emerge if the existing government were thrown into crisis. Both parties aspired to create an extremist regime, but their plans were incompatible and mutually exclusive. Indeed, once one party succeeded in taking national power, its first measure was to annihilate the other, which consistently placed first among its opponents. After Adolf Hitler became chancellor of Germany in January 1933, one of his first actions was to wipe out the German Communist Party; its leaders were among the first prisoners in Nazi concentration camps. Likewise, when the Soviets marched into Eastern Europe at the end of World War II, fascists and people associated with fascism were the first to be eliminated. In these cases, the enemy of one's enemy was definitely not one's friend.

A final flawed point of the convergence argument rests on direct comparisons of the structures and methods of Nazi Germany and the Soviet Union, especially under Josef Stalin's rule (1924–1953). While there are many valid commonalities between these two regimes, including a cult of personality centered on the leader, a pervasive one-party state, and strikingly similar apparatuses of terrorist rule (secret police, concentration camps, and so on), the comparison is deceptive within the parameters of this chapter. Hitler and Stalin may both have had sweeping dictatorial powers, broad sway over the lives of their people, and personal appetites for cruelty, but so have many other leaders who were neither fascist nor communist. Leadership cults, for example, have emerged in many polities where institutionalized weakness led to a central authority of exaggerated magnificence, including France (the "Sun King" Louis XIV and later Napoleon Bonaparte, who tried to emulate him), modern Turkey (its first president, Kemal Atatürk, whose image is still in every government building and on every denomination of currency), Japan before 1945 (the reigning emperors, who were officially regarded as divine), and Iraq (Saddam Hussein, a noncommunist admirer and emulator of Stalin's methods). Conversely, both fascist and communist regimes have existed without them. Italian dictator Benito Mussolini, the first fascist leader to come to power (1922) and the first major politician to use the word *fascism*, never developed a personality cult to the level of Hitler's. Even in the Soviet Union, Stalin's successors denounced his personality cult after his death and did not create a new one. Although sweeping state power, concentration camps, and secret-police networks certainly do go hand in hand with both fascism and communism, they, too, have nevertheless appeared in many other states that fit neither ideology. European monarchs aspired to absolutism centuries before fascism or communism; Spanish and British colonial authorities were the first to use concentration camps; and police forces charged with fighting political crimes have been known all through modern history. Basing one's comparison of fascism and communism on the methods of just one of each ideology's leaders—methods which were not new and which were shared with many nonfascists and noncommunists—is not the most promising exercise in a broader perspective. While it is instructive to compare the anatomies of the Nazi and Soviet regimes, it fails to address the origins and development of fascist and communist ideology, which were in fact different.

–PAUL DU QUENOY,
GEORGETOWN UNIVERSITY

References

Gilbert Allardyce, "The Place of Fascism in European History," in *The Place of Fascism in European History*, edited by Allardyce (Engelwood Cliffs, N.J.: Prentice-Hall, 1971).

Hannah Arendt, "Fascism as Totalitarianism: Ideology and Terror," in *The Place of Fascism in European History*, edited by Allardyce (Engelwood Cliffs, N.J.: Prentice-Hall, 1971).

Carl Cohen, ed., *Communism, Fascism and Democracy: The Theoretical Foundations* (New York: Random House, 1962).

Robert Conquest, *Reflections on a Ravaged Century* (New York: Norton, 2000).

Carl J. Friedrich and Zbignew Brzezinski, "Fascism as Totalitarianism: Men and Technology," in *The Place of Fascism in European History*, edited by Allardyce (Engelwood Cliffs, N.J.: Prentice-Hall, 1971).

François Furet, *Fascism and Communism* (Lincoln: University of Nebraska Press, 2001).

David E. Ingersoll and Richard K. Matthews, *The Philosophic Roots of Modern Ideology* (Engelwood Cliffs, N.J.: Prentice Hall, 1991).

Gregory M. Luebbert, *Liberalism, Fascism, or Social Democracy: Social Classes and the Political Origins of Regimes in Interwar Europe* (New York: Oxford University Press, 1991).

Ernst Nolte, *Three Faces of Fascism: Action Française, Italian Fascism, National Socialism* (New York: Holt, Rinehart & Winston, 1966).

Stanley Paine, "Who Were the Fascists?" in *Who Were the Fascists: Social Roots of European Fascism*, edited by Stein Ugelvik Larsen and others (Bergen: Universitetsforlaget / Irvington-on-Hudson, N.Y.: Columbia University Press, 1980).

Raymond J. Sontag, *A Broken World 1919–1939* (New York: Harper & Row, 1971).

Zeev Sternhell, *Neither Right Nor Left: Fascist Ideology in France*, translated by David Maisel (Princeton: Princeton University Press, 1996).

Gordon Wright and Arthur Mejia Jr., eds., *An Age of Controversy: Discussion Problems in 20th Century European History* (New York: Harper & Row, 1973).

ORIGINS OF FASCISM

Was fascism an immediate product of World War I?

Viewpoint: Yes. Fascism was an authoritarian Right-wing reaction to the radical leftist movements that arose in the turmoil caused by World War I.

Viewpoint: No. Although it only coalesced and developed into a mass political movement after World War I, fascism developed from strains of thought that can be traced throughout Western civilization.

Fascism was a major ideology in twentieth-century European political and social thought. Emphasizing the creation of a new society by the authority of a fanatical party or state with control of virtually every aspect of life, fascist ideals are now entirely discredited. Nevertheless, in the first half of the century fascists commanded a great deal of attention, support, and admiration, not only from malcontents and fanatics but also from intellectuals, the elite, foreign observers, and millions of ordinary Europeans. Without that support, German leader Adolf Hitler and Italian dictator Benito Mussolini could never have ruled, and other fascists could not have hoped to rule.

One of the major debates among students of European fascism has focused on its origins. Its appearance as a mass movement after World War I seemed to be almost as sudden as its disappearance after World War II. A conventional argument has suggested that fascism was an immediate product of European social and political conditions after World War I. Masses who were weary after what had been by far the bloodiest conflict on the Continent were amenable to a powerful state that pretended to know all the answers to their problems. Communism had such pretensions, but the specter raised by the Bolshevik Revolution (1917) in Russia and subsequent, if less successful, communist uprisings in Germany and Hungary made Europeans so fearful of the extreme Left that they willingly embraced the ideology and tactics of the extreme Right. In government and society, fascism was their reaction and their answer.

Another, more subtle, argument finds, however, that fascism represented much continuity from earlier innovations in European political and philosophical thought. Rather than cropping up because of World War I or specifically responding to communism, fascists drew from existing strains in irrationalist thought represented by philosophers such as Henri Bergson, Friedrich Nietzsche, and Georges-Eugène Sorel; from the revolutionary violence advocated by early socialist thinkers; and from the French Enlightenment's emphasis on the perfectibility of man and society through the offices of a powerful state. The times that followed World War I merely allowed the fusion of these earlier developments into a new ideology that soon played a major role on the Continent. A consideration of how and why such a major and ultimately destructive political movement could come about offers important lessons for the future.

Viewpoint:
Yes. Fascism was an authoritarian Right-wing reaction to the radical leftist movements that arose in the turmoil caused by World War I.

Fascism did not originate in a vacuum; it had obvious antecedents in European political and philosophical thought. The extreme leftist movements that developed after World War I, most notably in Russia, also had European intellectual predecessors. Yet, it is not accurate to claim that these movements had deep origins in the European past. Fascism was not inevitable; there were many factors necessary for it to become a mass movement after 1918 and to gain power in Germany and Italy. Disruptions caused by World War I, along with the Great Depression, were crucial for the appeal of fascist movements. Had there been no war, those movements that became fascist might have easily been transformed into something else. Other Right-wing conservatives or radical rightist organizations could have prevailed in Germany and Italy in the 1920s and 1930s. Instead, because of circumstances arising from the end of war, Benito Mussolini gained control of Italy and Adolf Hitler gained control in Germany.

Although the tsar probably could not have maintained power indefinitely in Russia, World War I accelerated the fall of the Russian imperial system. Vladimir Lenin's Bolsheviks gained power and installed a regime that proved hostile to liberal states throughout the Continent. In 1919 the German Left split, with more moderate elements attaining power in the nation's first experiment with democracy, while extreme factions attempted to lead a revolution. A German communist party was formed in December 1918; it was identified with the radical revolutionary forces that carried out mass strikes across the country. In the opinions of Social Democratic leaders Friedrich Ebert and Gustav Noske, the Bolshevik threat in Germany was real. They felt it necessary to align with the Right and stabilize the country and were responsible for creating the paramilitary units that suppressed the radical groups. These *Freikorps* (volunteer paramilitary units) were anticommunist and antiliberal, and many of their members gravitated toward the more radical rightist movements in postwar Germany, including the Nazis.

It is obviously dangerous to argue that fascism was merely a reaction to the extreme leftist movements that developed after 1918. One runs the danger of using the rise of Bolshevism to justify the fascist reaction. That conclusion is of course absurd. There is no justification for anyone to have ever turned toward a Hitler, a Mussolini, or any of the other Right-wing authoritarian leaders. Alternatives did exist, especially in France and Germany. Nevertheless, the Germans had a radical leftist communist party, which had no love for the new democracy. Although German communists participated in the Parliament and maintained a relatively stable percentage of votes throughout the existence of the republic, they advocated the end of this system. The rest of the electorate knew this sentiment; conservatives were afraid of the Left, and the Nazis manipulated these fears. The fate of Russia remained in the background; no one in power wanted to repeat this revolution in Germany. Support of the communists was actually growing in the early 1930s; in the final free election of the Weimar period, the communists received 16.9 percent of the vote. Hitler gained power in early 1933 because of the conservatives' attempt to use him against a growing threat from the Left. His power solidified in part because of the electorate's fears of the far Left. Although there were many reasons why the Nazis gained power in Germany, their ability to manipulate fears of Bolshevism was indeed an important factor.

Anyone attempting to argue that fascism had deep origins in European political and philosophical thought would have to at least link this movement to the French Revolution. In *The Origins of Totalitarian Democracy* (1952), historian J. L. Talmon sought to understand the genesis of the movements that killed millions in Germany and the Soviet Union. He contrasts the Anglo-American tradition of liberal democracy with the European "political messianism" that had originated from the French Revolution. The latter school was far more dangerous; in fact, it resulted from a national group's desire for "salvation," leading to highly centralized and often dangerous political entities. Political messianism was an outgrowth of the thought of Jean-Jacques Rousseau, whom Talmon presented as influencing the first French Revolutionary dictator, Maximilien Robespierre, and generations of European intellectuals. Karl Marx's socialism and German romantic conservatism developed from ideas that originated during the French Revolution. The obvious conclusion from Talmon's work is that these ideas grew throughout the nineteenth century and needed only minor alterations to be transformed into Marxism and fascism.

A problem with Talmon's analysis is that despite the existence of fascist movements in France in the first part of the twentieth century, no fascist gained power. In *Fascism: Comparison and Definition* (1980), Stanley G. Payne indi-

ORIGINS OF FASCISM

cated that many of the ideas that were found in fascist movements and Nazism first appeared in France. Nonetheless, movements in France that meet Payne's criteria for a fascist party appeared after World War I and were relatively weak. Despite all the troubles its Third Republic encountered, especially in World War I, France's liberal democracy survived. Radical and conservative rightist parties later had a greater appeal, culminating in the establishment of the Vichy regime (1940). Vichy France was more than a simple puppet regime; conservative forces attempted to reorganize French society to their liking. Nonetheless, this regime depended heavily on German support. Once the Germans occupied all of France, the government of Philippe Pétain lost any hint of legitimacy it might have had.

Payne also argues how one could mistakenly conclude that the roots of movements that either became fascist parties or demonstrated some fascist characteristics lay in the initial reactions to the Enlightenment and the French Revolution. The problem with this argument, according to Payne, is that the early movements were more concerned with a return to traditionalism and with avoiding the modernization of society associated with the Industrial Revolution and rise of liberalism. These forces were not strong enough to counter the effects of liberalism, enabling it to consolidate its hold in western Europe and even to appear in Germany and Russia. Rightist reactionary forces that appeared in the late nineteenth century tried to come to terms with modernism, and instead of simply advocating a return to an earlier time, argued for an authoritarian liberalism more manageable by the state. Payne presents this movement as one of the precursors of fascism, showing that these forces were forward looking and able to present a more effective alternative to the liberal states that had been consolidated in Europe.

According to Payne, the forces that coalesced into Right-wing authoritarian movements after 1914 were greatly influenced by the so-called cultural crisis of 1890–1914. Although this crisis did not affect Europe as a whole, central Europe, especially its intellectual elite, experienced a noticeable change in attitude during this period. There was a growing hostility toward liberal parliamentary democracy, bureaucracy, and the sense of "equality" that had been developing since the Enlightenment. A new scientism that encouraged doctrines of race, elitism, hierarchy, and the glorification of war and violence replaced the old nineteenth-century scientism that had been far more democratic, liberal, and egalitarian. Social Darwinism was in full vogue at this time; this theory influenced the new pseudoscientific studies that were taken

seriously in fascist doctrine. There was also a search for unity in nature, one that reinforced the conceptualization and appeal of nationalism and stressed order, authority, and discipline within society rather than individualism and self-indulgence. All of these new ideas created a different climate among Europe's elite in 1914, one that would be far more receptive to Right-wing authoritarian and fascist movements after the war.

Although many scholars have tried, it has been difficult to define fascism. There were many Right-wing movements in Europe with some fascist aspects in the first part of the twentieth century; however, only a few of them could be convincingly designated as fascist. There were different kinds of fascism in different countries, with the most extreme version appearing in Germany. The evidence shows that none of these parties would have gained power had it not been for a complex series of factors. One of these factors was the growing appeal of communist parties. The rise of fascism was not predetermined, and without the results of World War I and the Great Depression, this movement might have been a mere footnote in history. Therefore, it is not possible to argue that fascism had deep roots in European political and philosophical thought. Fascism's origins cannot be found in 1789; 1890 is far more plausible. It is better then to argue that fascism was more of a Right-wing reaction to the extreme leftist movements caused by the dislocations of World War I, while recognizing that the roots of fascism were planted at the end of the nineteenth century.

–DAVID E. MARSHALL,
UNIVERSITY OF CALIFORNIA, RIVERSIDE

Viewpoint:
No. Although it only coalesced and developed into a mass political movement after World War I, fascism developed from strains of thought that can be traced throughout Western civilization.

Although historians have viewed fascism as a phenomenon related to political and economic developments after World War I, one needs to look at its philosophical roots in European thought. Fascism—an ideology that emphasizes the supreme sovereignty of the state to the detriment of individual rights and the importance of a leader to guide his state in a struggle against other nations—was a reaction against the "humane" aspects of Christian tradition and the rational principles of "decadent" bourgeois liberalism. It certainly developed in connection to events of its day. The resentment of those countries that felt cheated by the Paris Peace Conference (1919), the instability of ethnic groups who felt the need to mobilize in order to secure their interests, the economic hardships that affected the middle and working classes during the 1920s and 1930s, and the great charisma and political skills of leaders such as Italian dictator Benito Mussolini and German leader Adolf Hitler, were all critical to fascism's formation as a full-fledged political ideology. Nevertheless, one cannot look at the movement in an historical vacuum. Fascism developed from strains of philosophical thought that can be traced throughout the history of Western civilization.

The idea of the individual's absolute submission to the state can be identified in the ancient traditions of the Greek city-state of Sparta. Citizens of Sparta coordinated all of its physical and intellectual activities in the corporate interests of the city-state. Their military discipline and absolute obedience to the "spirit" of the polity contrasted sharply with the Athenians' belief in the individual and skeptical outlook on life. For later fascist thinkers, Sparta's eventual victory over Athens demonstrated the superiority of the earliest manifestation of the "Fascist spirit" over that of "ancient Democracy."

Sixteenth-century Italian philosopher Niccolò Machiavelli's advice to the ruler of Florence introduced the idea of the absolute, secular ruler. Looking to the ancient Greeks and Romans for inspiration, Machiavelli saw the "modern ruler" as one who upheld virtue. He defined virtue as the ability of a great man who, after having calculated the needs of his kingdom, was willing to use every means at his disposal to carry out the interests of his state. Christian morality—and its condemnation of sin and promotion of the ethical individual—did not apply to politics. Rather, the prince could manipulate his people or go to war with anyone if he truly acted for his kingdom's purpose. Machiavelli pioneered the idea that the leader of a polity should seek inspiration in ancient times in order to justify itself against "traditional" Christian thought, which had sought to constrict his actions by canonical law and ecclesiastical authority.

Early modern thinkers also made important intellectual contributions to the roots of fascism. The most important of these intellectuals was the seventeenth-century Englishman Thomas Hobbes, who saw sovereignty as absolute, towering over the rights of those who had granted it in the first place. God alone stood above the ruler. A firm believer in the Reformation, Hobbes also argued that the ruler had authority over both religious and civil law. The king also had the right to determine the religion of his subjects (a common notion at this time of religious warfare).

Georg Hegel, the greatest philosopher of German Romanticism, was more inspirational. In his idea of reason, Hegel described the development of the world as one of a struggle among states, nations, and civilizations in progressive ages of human history. The historical development of an age was most often defined as a conflict between two rival states, which were themselves the concrete embodiment of ideal forms of government. One state triumphed over the other by borrowing certain aspects from its rival and later led history to a new stage of development. Hegel saw the present-day manifestation of this dialectical model in the eventual victory of a fully modernized Prussian monarchy over Napoleon Bonaparte's French Republic. Fascist ideologues shared this interpretation of history as a combat between nations, a zero-sum game where one state benefits at the expense of another.

Hegel also took the next step in defining the state's relationship to religion. Whereas Machiavelli and Hobbes viewed the state's interests as distinct from religious authority, Hegel argued that the state embodied religion. In other words, the progress of the state as an idea in history was the true purpose of religion. Just as religious authority was identical with state sovereignty, so too was the Christian duty of every subject to obey his ruler. God, religion, and the church only remained captive to the temporal historical process. This philosophy was only a step away from renouncing God as superfluous.

Finally, Hegel saw no place for the individual outside of acting on behalf of the state. There were only two prototypes in this regard. One was the common subject, who obeyed his ruler and carried out the acts that were commanded of him. The second case, the hero, had a much higher purpose. He could, if given the opportunity, undertake a great courageous act that would significantly advance the cause of his state. Once this act was completed, however, the hero had no meaning in history. The state could eliminate him if it served its own self-interest, as seen for example in the murder of Roman ruler Julius Caesar by Marcus Junius Brutus. Hegel's idea was that the individual was a mere cell in the body politic. To discard a person whose function had ended was completely natural and right: humanitarian principle had no place.

Later German thinkers elaborated on aspects that became central to fascist doctrine. Friedrich Nietzsche has been recognized for his contempt of Christian morality. He advocated the unique role of the individual as a "superman" to act

BOTH PRACTICE AND THOUGHT

The following excerpt comes from Italian dictator Benito Mussolini's "The Doctrine of Fascism," an article published in the Italian Encyclopedia in 1932:

1. Like every sound political conception, Fascism is both practice and thought; action in which a doctrine is immanent, and a doctrine which, arising out of a given system of historical forces, remains embedded in them and works there from within. Hence it has a form correlative to the contingencies of place and time, but it has also a content of thought which raises it to a formula of truth in the higher level of the history of thought. In the world one does not act spiritually as a human will dominating other wills without a conception of the transient and particular reality under which it is necessary to act, and of the permanent and universal reality in which the first has its being and its life. In order to know men it is necessary to know man; and in order to know man, it is necessary to know reality and its laws. There is no concept of the State which is not fundamentally a concept of life; philosophy or intuition, a system of ideas which develops logically or is gathered up into a vision or into a faith, but which is always, at least virtually, an organic conception of the world.

2. Thus Fascism could not be understood in many of its practical manifestations as a party organization, as a system of education, as a discipline, if it were not always looked at in the light of its whole way of conceiving life, a spiritualized way. The world seen through Fascism is not this material world which appears on the surface, in which man is an individual separated from all others and standing by himself, and in which he is governed by a natural law that makes him instinctively live a life of selfish and momentary pleasure. The man of Fascism is an individual who is nation and fatherland, which is a moral law, binding together individuals and the generations into a tradition and a mission, suppressing the instinct for a life enclosed within the brief round of pleasure in order to restore within duty a higher life free from the limits of time and space: a life in which the individual, through the denial of himself, through the sacrifice of his own private interests, through death itself, realizes that completely spiritual existence in which his value as a man lies.

3. Therefore it is a spiritualized conception, itself the result of the general reaction of modern times against the flabby materialistic positivism of the nineteenth century. Anti-positivistic, but positive: not sceptical, nor agnostic, nor pessimistic, nor passively optimistic, as are, in general, the doctrines (all negative) that put the centre of life outside man, who with his free will can and must create his own world. Fascism desires an active man, one engaged in activity with all his energies: it desires a man virilely conscious of the difficulties that exist in action and ready to face them. It conceives of life as a struggle, considering that it behooves man to conquer for himself that life truly worthy of him, creating first of all in himself the instrument (physical, moral, intellectual) in order to construct it. Thus for the single individual, thus for the nation, thus for humanity. Hence the high value of culture in all its forms (art, religion, science) and the enormous importance of education. Hence also the essential value of work, with which man conquers nature and creates the human world (economic, political, moral, intellectual).

4. This positive conception of life is clearly an ethical conception. It covers the whole of reality, not merely the human activity which controls it. No action can be divorced from moral judgment; there is nothing in the world which can be deprived of the value which belongs to everything in its relation to moral ends. Life, therefore, as conceived by the Fascist, is serious, austere, religious: the whole of it is poised in a world supported by the moral and responsible forces of the spirit. The Fascist disdains the "comfortable" life.

5. Fascism is a religious conception in which man is seen in his immanent relationship with a superior law and with an objective Will that transcends the particular individual and raises him to conscious membership in a spiritual society. Whoever has seen in the religious politics of the Fascist regime nothing but mere opportunism has not understood that Fascism besides being a system of government is also, and above all, a system of thought.

6. Fascism is an historical conception, in which man is what he is only in so far as he works with the spiritual process in which he finds himself, in the family or social group, in the nation and in the history in which all nations collaborate. From this follows the great value of tradition, in memories, in language, in customs, in the standards of social life. Outside history man is nothing. Consequently Fascism is opposed to all the individualistic abstractions of a materialistic nature like those of the eighteenth century; and it is opposed to all Jacobin utopias and innovations. It does not consider that "happiness" is possible upon earth, as it appeared to be in the desire of the economic literature of the eighteenth century, and hence it rejects all theological theories according to which mankind would reach a definitive stabilized condition at a certain period in history. This implies putting oneself outside history and life, which is a continual change and coming to be. Politically, Fascism wishes to be a realistic doctrine. . . . To act among men, as to act in the natural world, it is necessary to enter the process of reality and to master the already operating forces.

7. Against individualism, the Fascist conception is for the State; and it is for the individual in so far as he coincides with the State, which is the conscience and universal will of man in his historical existence. It is opposed to classical Liberalism, which arose from the necessity of reacting against absolutism, and which brought its historical purpose to an end when the State was transformed into the conscience and will of the people. Liberalism denied the State in the interests of the particular individual; Fascism reaffirms the State as the true reality of the individual. And if liberty is to be the attribute of the real man, and not of that abstract puppet envisaged by individualistic Liberalism, Fascism is for liberty. And for the only liberty which can be a real thing, the liberty of the State and of the individual within the State. Therefore, for the Fascist, everything is in the State, and nothing human or spiritual exists, much less has value, outside the State. In this sense Fascism is totalitarian, and the Fascist State, the synthesis and unity of all values, interprets, develops and gives strength to the whole life of the people.

8. Outside the State there can be neither individuals nor groups (political parties, associations, syndicates, classes). Therefore Fascism is opposed to Socialism, which confines the movement of history within the class struggle and ignores the unity of classes established in one economic and moral reality in the State; and analogously it is opposed to class syndicalism. Fascism recognizes the real exigencies for which the socialist and syndicalist movement arose, but while recognizing them wishes to bring them under control of the State and give them a purpose within the corporative system of interests reconciled within the unity of the State.

9. Individuals form classes according to the similarity of their interests, they form syndicates according to differentiated economic activities within these interests; but they form first, and above all, the State, which is not to be thought of numerically as the sum-total of individuals forming the majority of the nation. And consequently Fascism is opposed to Democracy, which equates the nation to the majority, lowering it to the level of that majority; nevertheless it is the purest form of democracy if the nation is conceived, as it should be, qualitatively and not quantitatively, as the most powerful idea (most powerful because most moral, most coherent, most true) which acts within the nation as the conscience and the will of a few, even of One, which ideal tends to become active within the conscience and the will of all—that is to say, of all those who rightly constitute a nation by reason of nature, history or race, and have set out upon the same line of development and spiritual formation as one conscience and one sole will. . . .

10. The higher personality is truly the nation in so far as it is the State. It is not the nation that generates the State, as according to the old naturalistic concept which served as the basis of the political theories of the national States of the nineteenth century. Rather the nation is created by the State, which gives to the people, conscious of its own moral unity, a will and therefore an effective existence. The right of a nation to independence derives not from a literary and ideal consciousness of its own being, still less from a more or less unconscious and inert acceptance of a *de facto* situation, but from an active consciousness, from apolitical will in action and ready to demonstrate its own rights: that is to say, from a state already coming into being. The State, in fact, as the universal ethical will, is the creator of right.

11. The nation as the State is an ethical reality which exists and lives in so far as it develops. To arrest its development is to kill it. Therefore the State is not only the authority which governs and gives the form of laws and the value of spiritual life to the wills of individuals, but it is also a power that makes its will felt abroad, making it known and respected, in other words, demonstrating the fact of its universality in all the necessary directions of its development. It is consequently organization and expansion, at least virtually. Thus it can be likened to the human will which knows no limits to its development and realizes itself in testing its own limitlessness.

12. The Fascist State, the highest and most powerful form of personality, is a force, but a spiritual force, which takes over all the forms of the moral and intellectual life of man. It cannot therefore confine itself simply to the functions of order and supervision as Liberalism desired. It is not simply a mechanism which limits the sphere of the supposed liberties of the individual. It is the form, the inner standard and the discipline of the whole person; it saturates the will as well as the intelligence. Its principle, the central inspiration of the human personality living in the civil community, pierces into the depths and makes its home in the heart of the man of action as well as of the thinker, of the artist as well as of the scientist: it is the soul of the soul.

13. Fascism, in short, is not only the giver of laws and the founder of institutions, but the educator and promoter of spiritual life. It wants to remake, not the forms of human life, but its content, man, character, faith. And to this end it requires discipline and authority that can enter into the spirits of men and there govern unopposed. Its sign, therefore, is the Lictors' rods, the symbol of unity, of strength and justice.

Source: *Michael Oakeshott,* The Social and Political Doctrines of Contemporary Europe, *third revised edition (Cambridge: Cambridge University Press, 1942; New York: Macmillan, 1942), pp.164–168.*

ORIGINS OF FASCISM

Truck carrying Nazi supporters, 1924

(By permission of Roger-Viollet)

beyond the bounds of Christian morality in order to enjoy true happiness. Christianity was the religion of the meek that poisoned vulnerable minds with the ideas that mercy and democracy were virtues. Fascists lauded him for his glorification of the ruthless individual, a prototype for a party leader as a "man of action" who opposed the decadent masses. Oswald Spengler shared these sentiments but emphasized the social Darwinist idea of a struggle of nations for world dominance.

French and Italian circles also made key contributions. For instance, French socialist Georges-Eugène Sorel emphasized the importance of irrational myths to motivate a violent social movement. Mussolini rallied his followers, the Black Shirts, to revive his "Roman Empire" with their fists. The Nazi emphasis on Germany's barbaric past was another concrete example. Italian politi-

cal scientist Gaetano Mosca proposed in the years before 1914 that conquering "groups" who needed to dominate the weaker were central to sociology. Several key contemporaries connected race to this concept and the need for its "group" to be dominant over weaker "ones." Others, such as French sociologist Gustave Le Bon, emphasized the ability of political leaders to tap into the emotions of a crowd's subconscious in order to override individual rational thought.

One must conclude that European thought before World War I had a deep impact on the fascist movements that emerged during the interwar years. Most of the basic ideas behind the new ideology were borrowed from philosophers and writers of the decades and centuries that preceded the interwar years. Fascists were inspired by Hobbes and Hegel's emphasis on the absolute sovereignty of the state over the individual, Machiavelli's advocacy of a ruthless leader guided by state interest, and Nietzsche's ideal of the superman and his denunciation of Christian tradition. The ancient Spartans' absolute discipline, Hegel's utter disregard for the individual outside of his service to the state, Spengler's social Darwinist struggle of nations, Sorrel's rejection of rational enlightenment thought, Mosca's thinly veiled sociology of race, and Le Bon's emphasis on crowd psychology were other ideas that did not fall on deaf ears. From this morass of ideas, Mussolini and Hitler were able to mold a fascist worldview. The intellectual debts that Mussolini owed to Sorrel and Le Bon—as Hitler did to Spengler, Nietzsche, and the Hegelian tradition—cannot be ignored. These demagogues reformulated these concepts into pure intellectual dynamite: thrown into the worst political and economic crisis in the twentieth century, most Europeans never knew what hit them.

–YORK NORMAN,
GEORGETOWN UNIVERSITY

References

Hannah Arendt, *The Origins of Totalitarianism* (New York: Harcourt, Brace, 1951).

Carl Cohen, ed., *Communism, Fascism, and Democracy: The Theoretical Foundations,* third edition (New York: McGraw-Hill, 1997).

Colorado University Department of Philosophy, *Readings on Fascism and National Socialism* (Chicago: Swallow Press, 1952).

Aristotle A. Kallis, ed., *The Fascism Reader* (London & New York: Routledge, 2002).

Stanley G. Payne, *Fascism: Comparison and Definition* (Madison: University of Wisconsin Press, 1980).

J. L. Talmon, *The Origins of Totalitarian Democracy* (London: Secker & Warburg, 1952).

S. J. Woolf, ed., *The Nature of Fascism* (New York: Random House, 1969).

ORIGINS OF FASCISM

PACIFISM

Was pacifism an important factor in diplomacy between the two world wars?

Viewpoint: Yes. Pacifists exerted a major influence over governments, societies, and diplomacy in the interwar period.

Viewpoint: No. Though popular, pacifism was a relatively weak political force that had little impact on decision making and ultimately failed to stop World War II.

An important feature of the period following World War I was the growth of pacifism in Europe's public sphere. Shattered by the horrors and losses of the conflict, many Europeans believed that war could no longer be a solution to international disputes. Veterans' groups, women's organizations, political movements of both the Right and the Left, the literary world, religious societies, and a variety of other formations in civil society lobbied governments, protested in the streets, and worked to influence the general public to oppose war. German author Erich Maria Remarque's *All Quiet on the Western Front* (1929), the quintessential antiwar novel, became a best-seller, with millions of copies printed in every country in Europe. Even the rise of the belligerent Adolf Hitler in Germany in January 1933 failed to change pacifist views. The following month, the Oxford Union, Britain's premier university debating society, resolved never "to die for King and Country."

Some have argued that pacifism was instrumental in influencing governments in the 1930s. This situation was particularly true in Britain and France, which tried to appease Nazi Germany rather than risk confrontation. Faced with potentially hostile citizenries, European politicians took popular pacifism seriously into account when they made decisions about foreign policy and the use of military force.

In counterpoint, however, one can argue that pacifism was of marginal significance. Despite all the agitation and marching, pacifist ideals rarely penetrated government. Remarque's own land put Hitler into power just four years after his pacifist novel appeared. Other nations ruthlessly suppressed pacifist movements, while even the British and French policy of appeasement was influenced by such other factors as an appreciation of their military weakness and a realistic belief that Hitler could be stopped by shrewd diplomacy rather than war.

Viewpoint:
Yes. Pacifists exerted a major influence over governments, societies, and diplomacy in the interwar period.

The main course of international affairs as determined in the capitals of the great European powers was profoundly altered by World War I. One of the results of the conflict was that government leaders became more receptive to the public outcry for pacifist policies. The creation of the League of Nations, an organization established for the sole purpose of avoiding another catastrophic war, testifies strongly to the change in diplomacy's wider goal. Yet, with the ascension of Adolf Hitler and the Nazis, many pacifist organizations throughout Europe pulled back from their doctrinaire positions. Indeed, by the late 1930s only in Britain was the influence of pacifism upon foreign affairs still discernible.

Another interwar development that arose from the belief that differences between states could be negotiated was appeasement, which unfortunately became one of the most derided of public policies in the twentieth century. According to the commonly held view, a craven fear of war, arising from the horrors of World War I, motivated Britain's leadership, in particular Prime Minister Neville Chamberlain, to seek a peaceful accommodation with Hitler at all costs. This policy, the argument follows, led directly to the outbreak of World War II.

This view of appeasement is rather simplistic, however. For one thing, appeasing the dictators was a goal predicated upon the assumption that it was better to negotiate than to fight. Of course, one cannot simply dismiss public opinion, either. The Paris Peace Conference (1919) and the following diplomatic conferences of the 1920s and 1930s were all held with an eye toward the public, in the spirit of U.S. president Woodrow Wilson's wildly popular promise of "open covenants, openly arrived at." Yet, to claim that there is a clear and direct link from revulsion at the World War I experience to pacifism to appeasement to World War II is a glaring generalization. Governments seldom act only upon a single factor. Appeasement was also rooted in the hard economic, military, and financial facts that World War I created for Britain. The war created a crushing debt that was never fully overcome, and the military cost of empire was considerable. Troop deployments away from Europe were quite large. On 1 January 1938, for example, there were sixty-four British battalions in the home islands (including Ireland), while some seventy-eight battalions were deployed overseas—forty-five in India alone.

Nevertheless, British public opinion influenced government policy (which, incidentally, explains why Winston Churchill and his jingoism were rejected by the political establishment and the voting public before the war as well as right after its end). Even after the emergence of Hitler and the stridently aggressive Nazi Party, Britons still expressed a strong pacifistic slant. For example, in February 1933, a month after Hitler's ascension to power, the assembled students of the Oxford Union, a university debating forum representing the cream of British society, resolved two-to-one that "this house in no circumstances would fight for King & Country." Churchill, incidentally, denounced this resolution immediately as the expression of the "basest elements" expressing themselves among some "foolish boys," while German diplomat Joachim von Ribbentrop putatively reported to Hitler that the resolution was irreconcilable proof that Britain would never fight. Both men misinterpreted the resolution, however, as it certainly was colored by antijingoistic and anti-imperialistic sentiments among the students. One cannot, of course, forget that such an expression was also a rejection of parental values by young students, a phenomenon of Western traditions of individualism. Either way, the resolution certainly grabbed Britain's attention, and several other universities and debating societies passed similar declarations.

The Peace Ballot of 1935 was another famous case of widespread pacifistic sentiment in Britain. Coming two years after the "King and Country" resolution, this event also stood out against the backdrop of two years of Nazi, and Italian Fascist, bellicosity. The Peace Ballot reflected the sentiments of a broad cross section of the entire country. The League of Nations Union, a private British group supporting the League of Nations, sponsored a nationwide political event where ordinary Britons were invited to cast their ballot on a series of questions relating to the League and to disarmament in general. Some eleven million Britons responded and overwhelmingly approved of the League of Nations, disarmament, prohibition of military and naval aircraft, and abolition of weapons manufacture by the private sector. Not every element of the Peace Ballot received a near-unanimous endorsement, however. Only six million endorsed the idea that military force should not be used by Britain to punish military aggression.

That the Peace Ballot influenced British diplomacy can be seen in Prime Minister Stanley Baldwin's 1936 response to Churchill's parlia-

PACIFISM

WORKING FOR PEACE

On 10 December 1926 Peace Laureate Fridtjof Nansen delivered the presentation speech for the Nobel Peace Prizes in Oslo. He honored the 1925 recipients (English foreign secretary Sir Austen Chamberlin and American diplomat Charles Gates Dawes) and 1926 recipients (French prime minister Aristide Briand and German minister of foreign affairs Gustav Stresemann), all for their efforts to preserve peace in Europe.

We still remember it vividly, that event of over eight years ago. For four long years the world had resounded with the fearful din of the battlefields, the piercing cries of the dying, the forlorn laments of parents and widows over the bloody corpses of their sons and husbands.

Then suddenly the terrible nightmare faded, the roar of the cannons was stilled; the unbelievable had really happened—the world war had ended!

Europe breathed again, raised its head, gazed out over the disconsolate fields of battle, over the endless mounds of smoldering ruins, toward the horizon and the breaking day. But the day would not be hurried. Dark clouds gathered from all sides and spread from country to country; stormy skies cast their menacing shadows first in one place, then in another. It was as if everyone was waiting for a dawn which would not come. Now insidious doubt seeps into men's minds, breeding a melancholy uneasiness. Fear takes hold, and the powers of darkness gain sway. Suspicion and distrust grow between nations, between classes, and only thistles prosper in such soil. Hatred grows; increasing insecurity and fear paralyze all initiative, opening the way to every kind of blunder. There is talk of another war. It is as if the world, which had once before hovered on the brink and peered down into the abyss but which had at the eleventh hour dragged itself onto safer ground, is once again in perilous darkness being drawn back into the depths.

What is wrong? What is missing? It is the good human qualities that can grow only in the light of day: forbearance, confidence, compassion, the sincere desire for full cooperation in rebuilding the world. . . .

But if we do not get rid of war, if we do not put a complete end to it, if Europe does not reduce and limit its armaments, then we shall have no reforms and no progress of any significance.

We can be certain that in the future, just as in the past, armament will call forth counterarmament, alliances and counter-alliances; it will engender suspicion and distrust, bringing fear to men's hearts; it will lead to international crises; it will lead to war, perhaps to small local wars at first, but, finally and inescapably, it will bring down upon us a great world war no less frightful than the last.

If the work for disarmament which the League of Nations has now begun does not produce results, if the level of armaments is maintained, then war will result. It seems to me that all our past experience shows this to be incontrovertible. But do not take my word for it. Listen to what more qualified authorities have to say.

Lord Grey, foreign minister of Great Britain at the outbreak of the war, has said, and he has said it time and time again, that it was Europe's steadily increasing armaments which led to the war in 1914. He has warned us that if armaments in Europe are maintained, if the nations of the world embark on a new contest in military preparedness, we will bring upon ourselves anew war as inevitably as we did the last one. And he has told us that a new war will mean the end of our civilization as we know it today.

Who will question Lord Grey's authority to speak on this subject? Many other leading statesmen have uttered the same sentiments on several occasions. Let me mention just one. As recently as January of this year, Mr. Baldwin, the present prime minister of Great Britain, said: "A new war in the West and the civilization of our era will collapse in a fall as great as that of Rome."

These men I have mentioned are not fanatics, indeed not even pacifists; they are responsible statesmen who have exercised or who will in the future exercise great power in the leadership of the world. If they mean their statements seriously, then it seems to me to follow that there is scarcely any other political problem worth discussing until the problem of the next war is resolved.

Let us pause for a moment to consider what they have said. It may seem fantastic to state that our civilization can be obliterated.

We have a sense of vitality and strength, a feeling that a great future lies ahead of us. But let us not forget that civilizations have been wiped out before. Powerful nations, which seemed as strong then as the most powerful states of our time seem to us now, have vanished. The Roman Empire, which ruled Europe for a period hundreds of years longer than the lifetime of our modern Western civilization, was swept away by the invasion of barbaric hordes.

You have no sense of any impending disaster, you are too conscious of the forces of life around you. I feel the same. I too feel these forces. But I also sense that the last war inflicted upon our civilization a terrible wound, a painful wound that is still far from healed. It was as if the very foundations shook under Europe. And, worst of all, most Europeans still do not understand the true nature and significance of the last war. They are already about to forget it before they have learned the lesson it should teach them. They are forgetting their dead.

Of course, there are still millions of people in practically every country of Europe who cannot forget the horrors of the war. The carnage of the battlefields, once seen, is not easily forgotten. These people can tell of the merciless slaughter on the lovely countryside of France; of the agony of mind, the terror inspired by the big bombardments and the ceaseless rattle of gunfire in a modern offensive; of the inconceivable suffering of wounded and broken men hanging perhaps for days on barbed wire, crying out for the death which they themselves had not the strength to inflict. Of such horrors and worse can these people tell, and if Europe would only heed them, if all its people would only remember the war's bestiality, its barbaric cruelty, they would see to it that war would never occur again.

But there are other aspects of war which I, perhaps more than most people, have had the opportunity to observe. For more than six years now, it has been my task, on behalf of the League of Nations, to investigate and as far as possible to alleviate the terrible aftereffects of war. During all these years I have had to deal with hundreds of thousands of prisoners of war, with famine, with refugees—frightened refugees, each with his own story of endless heartrending tragedy, the old, the women, the little helpless children left alone because of the vicissitudes of war, and all of them lost, plundered, bereft of everything of value in this world.

I wish I could give you a picture of what I have seen and experienced. I wish I could just for one moment make you feel what it is to see a whole nation fleeing in wild terror along the country roads; or to travel among a people struck down by famine; to enter huts where men, women, and children lie still, no longer complaining, waiting only for death in countries where corpses are dug up out of their graves and eaten, where maddened mothers slay their own children for food. But no, I cannot attempt it now.

All this endless misfortune, all this misery and incredible suffering, these hundreds of thousands of forsaken prisoners of war, these famines, these millions of helpless refugees—they are all, directly or indirectly, the results of the war. But, believe me, all these calamities cannot occur without undermining our entire social system; they sap the vitality of nations and they inflict wounds so deep that they will take a long time to heal, if they ever do.

And still, even still, people talk about the probability of another war. Do we not stop to think what this would mean? Even if the next war is no worse than the last, I believe it will destroy our European civilization. But of course the next war will not be like the last. It will be incomparably worse.

I shall not weary you by going further into that. It is enough to say that in the event of a new war we face the threatening fact that our civilization can be annihilated, just as other civilizations have been annihilated in the past. But we also have the means to avert this threat. War does not come unless we wish it upon ourselves. War is not the result of some uncontrollable catastrophe of nature; it is the result of man's will. It is his own shame. And truly, with reasonable policies, it would be comparatively easy to put an end to war.

PACIFISM

Let me suggest the course which I believe can lead us forward. The governments of Europe must unite around and stake their all on what I shall, for the sake of brevity, call the League of Nations policy.

Do not misunderstand me here. The League of Nations is no longer a remote or abstract idea. It is a living organism. Its institutions are now an essential part of the machinery of world control. If we can put the full force of the combined power of individual governments behind these institutions, behind the policy of disarmament, behind all the policies pursued by the League, then we shall put an end to war.

But the governments, whether of large countries or of small, must stake everything on this policy without reservations. There must be no clinging to ancient rights to wage private wars. There must be no secret hopes that, if the League is weak in certain areas, it can be made to serve private interests.

We must follow the new road in international politics mapped out at Locarno, and we must burn behind us the bridges that lead back to the old policies and the old systems which have failed us so tragically. It has always been my conviction that, in the great things of life, it is of decisive importance to have no line of retreat—a principle which certainly holds good here.

By the very nature of things, progress will depend essentially on the actions of the great powers. But small nations like our own can also do much. For the large states must take into account such a variety of factors, such a multitude of conflicting interests, that their leaders may often find it difficult to follow their own convictions, assessing all the time, as they must, the political currents among their electorates, the national self-interests of their countries, not to mention the complex intrigues which frequently surround them. All these circumstances can often restrict their freedom to act.

Small nations and their leaders enjoy greater latitude in this respect; they have fewer conflicting interests, and for them a policy of peace without restrictions or reservations is a natural one. If all the small nations will work together resolutely and systematically in the League of Nations to lay the ghost of war, they can achieve much, greatly strengthening the League in the process.

Certainly, it cannot be denied that the great powers can give and on occasion have given the impression of acting somewhat arbitrarily and without proper consideration for the views of the other members of the League. But the small nations have ample opportunity to state their case if they will just confidently take it. And when they fail to do so, the blame falls chiefly on themselves. As Briand said in his splendid speech to the last Assembly, there must in future be no more resorting to "methods of negotiation which are inconsistent with the true spirit of the League of Nations", and "the League's work shall in future take place in the full light of day and with the collaboration of all its members."

It is, then, the duty of all members, and not least of the small nations, to unite in the task of abolishing war, to participate positively in this work, not to wait passively but to act.

If we really want to put an end to war, if we want to be rid of heavy armaments, the governments must, as I have said, stake everything upon the policy of the League of Nations without thinking about any lines of retreat. They must work in every way and at every opportunity to build up the power and strength of the League. If they do so and if their peoples support them in the same spirit, then shall the evil monster of war be felled and our future secured for the work of peace, that of building, not tearing down.

Source: Fridtjof Nansen, "No More War," 10 December 1926, Nobel e-Museum <http://www.nobel.se/peace/laureates/1926/presentation-speech.html>.

mentary question as to why Britain was not arming in the face of the Nazi and Fascist threat:

Supposing I had gone to the country and said that Germany was rearming and that we must rearm, does anyone think that this pacific democracy would have rallied to that cry at that moment? I cannot think of anything that would have made the loss of the election from my point of view more certain.

Pacifism cast a long shadow, not just over the interwar decades but over the entire twentieth century. Wilson's pledge of a newer, more open form of diplomacy was predicated upon the notion that international affairs would be inherently more peaceful. Both Wilson and pacifists believed that wars were caused by deviations from an absolute moral right and that morality in international affairs was sorely lacking. The League of Nations, Kellogg-Briand Pact (1928) to outlaw war, United Nations, and various other forays into international cooperation that characterized the twentieth century were all expressions of this sentiment. International liberalism and leftism both embraced this idea as their own. Though it is not widely recognized, World War I, in its alteration of the concept of war in the public eye, permanently changed attitudes toward international affairs.

–PHIL GILTNER,
ALBANY ACADEMY

Viewpoint:
No. Though popular, pacifism was a relatively weak political force that had little impact on decision making and ultimately failed to stop World War II.

In the years following the peace conference at Paris (1919), the European continent became fractured after only a few short years of peaceful coexistence. After the rise of the Nazi Party and the remilitarization of the Rhineland, Great Britain and France reacted to a revitalized Germany with overwhelmingly antiwar policies. While this reaction may be considered to have been motivated by pacifism, it is far more likely that other, less pure motivations were at the heart of European antiwar policies.

Pacifist sentiment during this period was certainly a factor in public rhetoric. Most of the leaders during this time achieved political office by speaking out against war as a means to an end. The activities of these same governments, however, suggest that a different attitude was prevailing. In France, a desperate government struggled

to maintain peace through strategic alliances with Germany's eastern neighbors, while hiding behind its own defenses. Great Britain emerged from the Paris Peace Conference with a guilty conscience and a struggling economy, which was only exacerbated by France's continuing hostility toward Germany. Both countries were badly affected by the Great Depression and were poorly prepared for a remilitarized and aggressive Third Reich. Though the motivations for each country were different, all of them originated at Versailles.

As Germany's most vociferous antagonist at Versailles, France pushed through many humiliating and punitive sections of the peace treaty. France's attitude at the peace conference and in the years immediately following it only served to alienate its chief allies, namely, the United States and Great Britain.

The United States had become increasingly isolated from Europe after the war, due largely to President Woodrow Wilson's declining political standing at home. The U.S. Senate took offense at Wilson's unilateral dealings with postwar Europe. The Republican-controlled Congress worked to undermine Wilson's idealistic crusade by refusing to ratify the Treaty of Versailles or to join the League of Nations. The Great Depression also contributed to American isolation. International trade became sluggish as countries sought to protect their own injured industries.

Great Britain also came away from Versailles with a less than perfect feeling. France's punitive actions toward a defeated (if not beaten) Germany made Versailles more about revenge than peace. Britain subsequently refused to endorse French efforts at punishing Germany for failure to deliver on many of the conditions of the postwar settlement, including seizing Ruhr coalfields or attempting to establish a Rhenish buffer state. Great Britain also refused to provide any assurances of military support to France should Germany again threaten the stability of Europe. France therefore sought defensive treaties with Eastern European countries. The "Little Entente," as these arrangements came to be called, however, failed to promote the feeling of security that France required.

Between the two world wars France neglected to modernize its military. Much of its air force was surplus from World War I, and its navy and army were poorly maintained. The impact of the Great Depression made military budgets leaner in most countries, but French military expenditures were either cut or allocated to ineffective projects, such as the defensive—and ultimately unfinished—Maginot Line. France's emphasis on a defensive barrier generated little confidence from its eastern allies as they correctly deduced that French forces were unlikely

PACIFISM

Nobel Peace Medal, the international award first given in 1901 for achievements in physics, chemistry, medicine, literature, economics, and peace

(Bettmann/CORBIS)

to emerge from behind it. Ultimately, the Maginot Line provided little deterrence to Germany, as its forces successfully went around it in 1940. French policies and military plans suggested a posture based more on fear than pacifism.

On 7 March 1936, the day after the French Senate ratified a new Franco-Soviet pact, the German army entered the demilitarized Rhineland. This blatant disregard for the Versailles Treaty and subsequent international agreements catapulted the French government into chaos even though the move had been anticipated. French premier Albert-Pierre Sarraut's weak cabinet, an interim government holding power between elections, was unable to reach a consensus on what was to be done. The British explicitly told his foreign minister that they would not support a military response. The Americans did not care, and since France had not itself been attacked, none of its eastern allies was obliged to do anything. Isolated, France only brought the treaty violation to the attention of the League of Nations Council.

Great Britain had not suffered the physical destruction endured by France during World War I, nor did it share a border with Germany, and therefore London maintained a different attitude toward German culpability. Though the casualties suffered by the British were high, the notion of laying blame for the entire war at the feet of the Germans did not sit well with the less aggrieved Britons. While there was a great deal of demand for war reparations, many felt the French had gone too far and that the Germans had been dealt with unfairly. As trade and contact between former enemies was reestablished, the punitive measures that Germany was forced to endure only reinforced the guilt that many politicians in Britain felt.

Even as early as 1922, efforts were made to redress the mistakes of Versailles. A committee of American and British bankers, chaired by U.S.

financier J. P. Morgan, met to discuss a long-term loan of 200 million marks. The proposal was indefinitely tabled because the French would not reduce their reparations claims. Subsequent financial negotiations reduced the sum Germany was required to pay and stretched out its payments.

When the Nazis took power in Germany in 1933, Britons were slow to react to any possible threat from Adolf Hitler's regime. Robert Hadow, first secretary of the Foreign Office from 1931 to 1939, supported the revision of the peace treaty. He felt, as many did, that a destitute Germany benefited no one, especially Britain. Hadow sought to revise the "catastrophic stupidity" of the "uncomprehending Chancelleries" and "crass ignorance among the so-called Statesmen" of the Versailles Conference. It was felt that European recovery necessitated Britain's assistance of Germany in acquiring raw materials and providing political assistance.

Avoiding the mistakes made prior to World War I was precisely what the British elite had in mind. Eager to avoid what they saw as overly provocative alliances that threatened to fuel external conflicts, Britain instead sought to become an honest, yet interested, broker. British prime minister Ramsay MacDonald sought to end reparations through negotiations in the summer of 1932. France offered to cancel the German debt and then reissue it through German railway bonds. The exact figures were unresolved, which of course raised MacDonald's suspicions. He, however, approved of the idea in principle and conveyed the offer to the Germans, who ignored it. Hitler renounced further reparations payments shortly after coming to power.

As Hitler's annexation of the Sudetenland from Czechoslovakia followed the annexation of Austria in 1938, the British still felt that appeasement was in order, rather than the use of military force. British foreign policy indicated a motivation of making amends for the mistakes of Versailles rather than a great sense of pacifism.

The role of pacifism in the interwar period was small. Although some public interest groups, especially veterans organizations, supported pacifism and abjured war, their impact on government was minimal. In France organized pacifists were largely philosophical rather than religious. The most organized were leftist and humanitarian. They felt that modern warfare had reached a scale that threatened the existence of civilization, and they therefore opposed war in any form. They held deep reservations against the war-guilt clause and the notion of defensive war. After the 1938 conference in Munich, which conceded the Sudetenland to Hitler, one of the leaders of the larger pacifist groups, René Gerin, wrote, "Courage, comrades! The treaties are being revised without war! This is indeed what we have been demanding in our propaganda. But we never dared to hope that we would be listened to so soon." It can be inferred from this statement that even the most organized of pacifist movements felt that their message was being ignored. As actual motives behind the appeasement of Hitler are reviewed, it becomes evident that they had more to do with realist politics than with philosophical pacifism.

-CRAIG ROMM,
CENTER FOR STRATEGIC AND
INTERNATIONAL STUDIES

References

Arthur H. Furnia, *The Diplomacy of Appeasement: Anglo-French Relations and the Prelude to World War 1931–1938* (Washington, D.C.: University Press, 1960).

Lindsay W. Michie, *Portrait of an Appeaser: Robert Hadow, First Secretary in the British Foreign Office, 1931–1939* (Westport, Conn.: Praeger, 1996).

Gustav Schmidt, *The Politics and Economics of Appeasement: British Foreign Policy in the 1930s,* translated by Jackie Bennett-Ruete (Leamington Spa, U.K. & New York: Berg, 1986).

Alan Sharp, *The Versailles Settlement: Peacemaking in Paris, 1919* (New York: St. Martin's Press, 1991).

PACIFISM

PUBLIC INTELLECTUALS

Did the public intellectual have an influential role in twentieth-century European thought?

Viewpoint: Yes. Public intellectuals substantively shaped the political and social debates of modern Europe.

Viewpoint: No. In an age of mass politics, mass media, and professional specialization, the public intellectual ceased to exercise any serious political influence.

The phenomenon of the public intellectual is a relatively new one in European life and thought. Deriving an income and livelihood from one's ideas and intellectual actions led both to a profusion of academic activity in the interests of society and to the emergence of a professional group defined by its ability to express ideas of broad social interest. In many ways public intellectuals have been thought of as a nineteenth-century phenomenon. Political and social debates centered on literacy and emerged from print media—books, journals, and letters—accessible only to the minority of Europeans who could read and write. Such topics as political change, social reform, and philosophical development evolved in these venues.

The fate of public intellectuals in the twentieth century has been the subject of much consideration. In an age of mass-circulation newspapers, radio, television, film, broad public opinion, and near universal literacy, how has the image and influence of the European public intellectual endured? One answer is that the public intellectual is dead. A consequence of democratized knowledge and opinion—a major goal of many public intellectuals—is that academics, philosophers, critics, and others who establish themselves through the articulation of ideas are of increasingly marginal influence and speak to an ever declining audience. Additional factors such as the increased specialization of knowledge, within the academy in general as well as in particular fields, has left fewer and fewer intellectuals who can speak with confidence or authority on subjects outside of their immediate interests.

Another argument posits, however, that throughout the twentieth century, men and women of conscience were always able to speak out and develop ideas that resonated with broad segments of the public and carried a great deal of influence on governments. Whether they were commenting on prevailing social values or expressing opposition to a particular policy or event, figures such as Sigmund Freud, Jean-Paul Sartre, Simon de Beauvoir, Albert Camus, Jürgen Habermas, Andrei Sakharov, Pierre Bourdieu, and many others achieved fame, notoriety, and popularity for the breadth of their ideas. In this way, the public intellectual survived and retained a major presence in European cultural life.

Viewpoint:
Yes. Public intellectuals substantively shaped the political and social debates of modern Europe.

Public intellectuals substantively shaped the debates that defined European history in the twentieth century. Born in the struggles of the Dreyfus Affair (1894–1906) in France, intellectuals were leaders of the Russian Revolution (1917), played a key role in the reorientation of European culture in the aftermath of World War I, defined the political ideology of fascism and defended the principles that opposed it, dissented against the ossification of the world into two competing powers in the Cold War, valiantly advocated decolonization during the breakup of European empires, and continued into the twenty-first century after the fall of the Berlin Wall (1989) as the conscience of their nations and of European civilization. Their social role has been concurrent with the rise of mass politics, mass media, and professionalization; while the majority of intellectuals may not follow their precepts and dictates, they nevertheless continue as a vital force, defining the significance of the changes in the world and acting as visionaries for the next millennium.

The word *intellectual* was introduced into every language and culture from the French *intellectuel*, which was first given widespread use at the height of the Dreyfus Affair, an event that philosopher and historian Hannah Arendt called "the dress rehearsal of the twentieth century." The case of Alfred Dreyfus, a Jewish captain who was a member of the French General Staff falsely accused of treason and found guilty by a military tribunal in 1894, erupted into a bloodless civil war by 1898. After a long and unsuccessful campaign to exonerate Dreyfus, famous naturalist writer Emile Zola published an open letter addressed to the president of the Republic on 13 January 1898 in Georges Clemenceau's newspaper *L'Aurore* (The Dawn) under the huge headline: "J'Accuse" (I Accuse). The letter indicted the military, with the complicity of the Catholic Church, in perpetuating a grave injustice against an innocent citizen, and demanded a revision of the verdict in the name of truth and justice. The next day a group of university professors, scientists, and writers published a "manifesto of the intellectuals" supporting Zola, thus giving common currency to a previously arcane word. Intervention by these intellectuals resulted in rioting in the streets and a long battle between the Dreyfusards and anti-Dreyfusards. It was another episode in a continuing "Franco-French" war

between Republicans versus Monarchists and Bonapartists; liberals and socialists versus conservatives; secularists versus clericalists, the Right, and the military; and the Church's desire for an organic, hierarchical, Catholic, traditional social order versus the Republic's recasting of the egalitarian, democratic values of the French Revolution, including fraternity, equality before the law, and the rights of the individual.

Dreyfus was vindicated and democratic values enthroned with their advocates, henceforth known as intellectuals, as a major new social actor. The intellectuals of the Dreyfus Affair became the archetype of the public intellectual, consolidating the role of the ancient philosopher; the monks of the middle ages; the *clercs* of the seventeenth century; the *philosophes* and *hommes de lettres* of the eighteenth century; and the Romantic prophets, *savants* (scientists), and publicists of the nineteenth century. This group identity was formed in networks of recruitment (for example, in educational institutions, journals, societies, circles for discussion, and publishing houses), and their opinions have framed debates through the dissemination of their ideas in the mass media (newspapers, magazines, books, radio, and television). Intellectuals stand as witnesses of the cultural conscience and representatives of the highest values of humanity. They are poised to speak in the name of truth against those they perceive as blocking the achievement of justice. Their cries are constituted through the use of a polemical discourse (Left versus Right, good versus evil, moral versus immoral, and truth versus illusion). Finally, intellectuals speak against the dominant voices of power on behalf of the oppressed and marginalized.

The Russian intelligentsia were particularly active social critics of the tsarist state, condemning its backwardness, ignorance, and violence against the downtrodden masses. This opposition was especially true in the circles surrounding political philosopher George Plekhanov and economist Peter Struve, who were inspired by the writings of German political philosopher Karl Marx and other international socialists. One of Plekhanov's allies and supporters was Russian communist leader Vladimir Lenin, who admired him as the founder of Russian Marxism and sought to expand the revolutionary activity and party building he had begun. When Russian troops were decimated in World War I, mass protests arose leading to the abdication of the throne by Tsar Nicholas II in March 1917. A Provisional Government ruled with the Soviets (worker's councils) until Lenin and another revolutionary intellectual, Lev Trotsky, orchestrated the Bolshevik coup d'état and assumed power. Only a small group of the Russian intelligentsia gave the October Revolution an uncritical welcome. After a brief phase of extraordinary utopian experimentation in the arts and culture, following the brutal civil war that defeated forces opposed to the revolution, dissenting intellectuals were repressed. In 1922 dozens of Russia's greatest intellectual minds were expelled.

The end of World War I and the success of the Russian Revolution expanded and transformed the modernist cultural revolution that ushered in the new century. "You know how greatly the general economic situation has been disturbed, and the polity of states, and the very life of the individual," Paul Valéry, French writer and poet, pronounced after World War I; "you are familiar with the universal discomfort, hesitation, apprehension. But among all these injured things is the Mind. The Mind has indeed been cruelly wounded; its complaint is heard in the hearts of intellectual men; it passes a mournful judgement on itself. It doubts itself profoundly." This crisis was sutured by a phase of amazing creativity in art, literature, philosophy, music, and science. The cultural revolution carried out by intellectuals had a profound impact upon society, however, challenging the values that had led to the trenches, transforming gender roles, altering aesthetic tastes and sensibilities, changing the conception of human consciousness by introducing the unconscious, and criticizing the philistine desires for comfort and uniformity of the new bourgeoisie that came with the prosperity of the 1920s. The masses now had access to these new cultural forms and values as a result of the spread of mass-circulation daily newspapers, radio, motion pictures, and public education.

With the crash of the American stock market (October 1929) and the ensuing world economic depression, reactionary modernists, calling themselves fascists, most successfully manipulated the new culture industry to their ends. In the wake of World War I, there was already a deep disaffection with liberalism: a sense that it was not democratic enough because representative government led only to the rule of vested interests. As German cultural critic Arthur Moeller van den Bruck put it, "not the form of the state makes a democracy, but the participation of the people in the state."

The role of ideology was important to the fascist revolution, and therefore so were intellectuals, with no better example than in Italy, the first state to put a fascist regime in power. Disaffected by the peace settlement ending World War I, fiery poet Gabriele D'Annunzio led a force of war veterans in 1919 to take over the city of Fiume—to the jubilation of Italian nationalists, who brilliantly used mass festivals as a new art form to weld myth and symbols, hymns, sacred fires, and flags into a new secular and national liturgy in the name of the people. The same year, Benito Mussolini launched the first fascist party with the support of Italian futurists, a group of artists who maintained that they would "glorify war—the world's only hygiene—militarism, patriotism, the destructive gesture of freedom bringers, beautiful ideas worth dying for." When Mussolini became leader of the first fascist state, his minister of education for a time was philosopher Giovanni Gentile, and his minister of justice was Alfredo Rocco, author of *The Political Doctrine of Fascism* (1926), who each argued that the fulfillment of the individual could only take place with their full integration into the nation. Antagonistic to liberal democracy and parliamentary government, opposing capitalism in the name of the little man, contending in Mussolini's words that "fascism [is] the complete opposite of Marxian Socialism, the materialist conception of history," they proposed a viciously anticommunist, spiritual revolution that glorified action and heroism and promised to build the new man through the national socialist state. An inspiration to intellectuals across the continent—including English poet T. S. Eliot and American poet Ezra Pound, who became a propagandist for the regime—the fascist antinomies resulted in a polarization that placed benighted liberals, but most prominently socialists and their fellow travelers, in a war of ideas that was ultimately settled on the battlefields of Europe and around the world between 1939 and 1945.

In Poland, where the population faced either total subjugation or extermination, those intellectuals who survived the first roundups invariably joined the underground resistance against Nazism, eventually establishing the largest clandestine press in Europe. When the liberating forces of the Soviet Union erected an "Iron Curtain" that descended across Eastern Europe, intellectuals kept alive cultural distinctiveness, a national consciousness, and a revisionist approach to socialism that opposed Stalinism. Soviet leader Josef Stalin's death in 1953 resulted in an efflorescence of subversive doctrines and dogmas that were crushed by Nikita Khrushchev's ongoing repression, which drove thousands of intellectuals such as philosopher Leszek Kolakowski and poet Czeslaw Milosz into Western exile. Those who remained formed discussion clubs for music, sculpture, and film appreciation; student theater and satirical reviews mushroomed across the country. In an "Open Letter to the Party" (1965), Jacek Kuron and Karol Modzelewski denounced the repression of the intelligentsia by the bureaucrats.

By 1968 it became clear that the vehicle for change was not going to come from within the

Alfred Dreyfus, circa 1894, a Jewish French army captain convicted of treason and publicly defended by the novelist Emile Zola, who was convicted and imprisoned for libeling the army and subsequently exonerated

(Harlingue Viollet)

PUBLIC INTELLECTUALS

state and the Party, and Polish dissident intellectuals began to foster direct links with the Polish working class, ultimately producing the ten-million-strong independent trade union *Solidarnosc* (Solidarity), which survived the martial law designed to repress them after 1980 and eventually formed the Solidarity government in 1989 that was erected when the Berlin Wall came crashing down. Vaclav Havel, a writer and dissident playwright, led the opposition in Czechoslovakia and became both the first postcommunist president and the first president of the new Czech Republic in 1993. As these cases make manifest, intellectuals were often in the avant-garde of those refusing to capitulate to the dogmatism and debauchery of Stalinism, while still remaining critical of capitalist states, the promotion of aggressive individualism at the expense of community, the economic exploitation of the Third World, and the repression of movements of national independence.

While in jail Adam Michnik, one of the leaders of Solidarity, had studied the work of German philosopher Jürgen Habermas, whose *Structural Transformation of the Public Sphere* (1962) played an important part in Poland, Hungary, and other Eastern European states in helping to define the character of civil society. Habermas's role as a public intellectual serves as an example of the ongoing importance that intellectuals have in defining the terms of debate throughout Europe. Having grown up with the Nazi regime, he was fifteen when the bombs stopped exploding in 1945. He had served as a member of the Hitler Youth and was sent in the last months of the war to "man the western defenses"; he was encouraged by a father who was a "passive sympathizer" with Nazism. When the Nuremberg war-crimes trials brought to light the devastation of the concentration camps, the leitmotiv of Habermas's future work (as well as that of many postwar intellectuals) was revealed: vigilance against such criminal behavior.

This goal had already emerged as central to the concerns of the "Frankfurt School," a group of primarily Jewish philosophers and social thinkers, including Theodor Adorno and Max Horkheimer, whose interdisciplinary investigations, grouped under the rubric of "critical theory," revolutionized a diverse number of fields from their headquarters at the Institute of Social Research at the University of Frankfurt. Habermas became Adorno's assistant in 1956 and took over Horkheimer's chair in 1964, from which he engaged in a systematic defense of the principles and values of the Enlightenment as an incomplete, but ongoing, project of modernity. This stance led him into political conflicts: with the Right, who accused him of fostering the ideas behind the New Left in the 1960s, and the Left, who thought that he was not radical enough; with those who urged German reunification with East Germany in the name of nationalism, rather than republican and democratic principles; with those who are indifferent to the problems of poverty and intolerant toward minorities and immigrants; and most famously with German revisionist historians, who have attempted in his words "to make Auschwitz unexceptional" by comparing it with other twentieth-century massacres. "He's a public figure," Peter Glotz, a leader of Germany's Social Democratic Party has remarked. "His writings don't influence masses of blue-collar workers, but they are read by a lot of German party officials and journalists and so on. In this way he is very influential."

While sharing the same desire as Habermas to end political oppression and moral myopia, postmodern critical theorists, such as French philosopher Jean-François Lyotard, have argued that "at the finish of this century, after the enormous massacres we have experienced, no one can any longer believe in progress, in consensus, in transcendent values. Habermas presupposes such a belief." Instead, following in the footsteps of the icons of the public intellectual, Jean-Paul Sartre, the most recognized existentialist, and his lifelong companion, Simone de Beauvoir, the *mater familias* of postwar feminism, Lyotard and his cohort of postmodern French intellectuals have excavated the archaeology of Western rationality to determine how so much devastation could be done in the name of development and ratiocination, thereby hewing closely to the investigations of Habermas's mentors. Lyotard proposed that the role of intellectuals should not be the defense of so-called universal precepts, but rather the task of illuminating the irreconcilable differences among competing conceptions of truth, justice, and liberty.

These principles are debated daily by intellectuals in Europe on the cultural pages of newspapers, in weekly magazines and monthly journals, over the radio, and on television. In France until recently, Bernard Pivot hosted a television show each Friday night at prime time that pitted leading intellectuals against one another in a discussion about their recently published books. The vignettes presented here demonstrate that the debate about the values that underlie European civilization and the means to achieve them have taken place in France, Russia, Italy, Poland, Germany, and across Europe through the twentieth century. As cultural arbiters, intellectuals have thus played and continue to play a major role in European society and politics.

—JONATHAN JUDAKEN,
UNIVERSITY OF MEMPHIS

Viewpoint:
No. In an age of mass politics, mass media, and professional specialization, the public intellectual ceased to exercise any serious political influence.

As British historian Stefan Collini warned, "it is always difficult to distinguish fact from fiction in narratives of cultural decline." This warning is particularly helpful when evaluating the issue of the decline of the influence of public intellectuals. There is clearly a nostalgic, even defensive, position inherent in critics who mourn the loss of a "golden age" of public intellectuals. However, the nostalgia inherent in many of these narratives of decline should not detract attention or serious analysis from historically rooted political, social, and cultural changes that led to the decline of the influence of public intellectuals in twentieth-century European thought.

While historians continue to debate the term *public intellectual* and have not reached consensus, Richard A. Posner's qualified definition provides some parameters. The public intellectual "writes for the general public, or at least for a broader than merely academic or specialist audience, on 'public affairs'—on *political* matters in the broadest sense of the word, a sense that includes cultural matters when they are viewed under the aspect of ideology, ethics or politics." As an ideal type, most European historians identify the first half of the twentieth century, from the Dreyfus Affair (1894–1906) through the immediate post–World War II period, as the heyday of public intellectuals. They point to such prominent Western European intellectuals as Emile Zola, Max Weber, L. T. Hobhouse, John Maynard Keynes, Karl Mannheim, Marc Bloch, George Orwell, Hannah Arendt, and Albert Camus, among others. While these public intellectuals represent a wide variety of intellectual traditions and political or social positions, they all have in common the ability to move readily from the world of ideas, theory, or disciplinary knowledge to social and political criticism on public affairs. For example, British sociologist Hobhouse actively used his sociological theory and professional standing to shape the progressive "New Liberal" social program of the Liberal government from 1906 to 1914. Camus used his popularity and standing as an existentialist philosopher, playwright, and novelist toward political and social criticism of public affairs ranging from the political direction of the French Communist Party to French policy in Algeria.

With such powerful examples in twentieth-century European history, the question of the decline of the influence of public intellectuals more often becomes, what happened to public intellectuals in the tradition of Hobhouse and Camus? Has the quality and number of authentic public intellectuals simply declined over the course of the late twentieth century? Have intellectuals abandoned social and political criticism of public affairs to work for narrow ideological interests or for professional and personal status as tenured faculty in research universities and policy institutes? In short, why is there such a dearth of great public intellectuals in European public life, and what caused this condition?

The question is far more complex than simplistic narratives would suggest. The historical social and cultural context has changed, not the quality of intellectuals themselves. It is the nature of the production and distribution of knowledge that has changed, and not intellectual disengagement from public affairs. This observation can be demonstrated in three distinct but related areas: the professionalization and specialization of knowledge, the democratization of the public sphere, and the transformed nature of the creation and distribution of public opinion.

The professionalization and specialization of knowledge is one of the seismic shifts in the intellectual history of twentieth-century Europe. Beginning in the late nineteenth century and accelerating to the present day, knowledge has been increasingly subdivided into ever more refined disciplines, specialties, and areas. Knowledge producers—intellectuals, writers, academics, scientists, and theorists—have both contributed to this specialization and responded to it. On the one hand, more and more knowledge producers are needed to mine deeper into disciplines and specialties. The dramatic growth in the number of universities and think tanks in both Europe and the United States during the second half of the twentieth century and the number of academics working in them are a testament to this development. On the other hand, the specialization of knowledge has created opportunities and careers for experts within a discipline. Graduate programs are training ever more specialized students to work in ever more specialized fields, attend conferences and symposia, and ultimately publish in journals or presses aimed at specific audiences.

The acceleration of specialization worked against the influence of public intellectuals. To return to Posner's definition, public intellectuals write for a general public and hope to influence ideas, politics, and policies in general terms understood by that public. To do so, they must write and speak in the general language

MANIFESTO OF THE 121

In a document called "Proclamation of the 121, Declaration on the Right to Insubordination in the Algerian War," issued on 6 September 1960, a group of public intellectuals protested the French position in Algeria:

A very significant movement is developing in France, and it is necessary that French and international opinion be better informed about it, as a new turning point in the Algerian War forces us to see, not to forget, the depth of the crisis which began six years ago.

More and more, French people are pursued, imprisoned, condemned, for refusing to participate in this war or for coming to the aid of Algerian combatants. Misrepresented by their adversaries, but also diminished by those who should have the duty to defend them, their reasons remain generally misunderstood. However, it is not enough to say that this resistance to the authorities is simply honorable. The protest of these men, their honor and righteous view of the truth attacked, has a significance that surpasses the circumstances under which it has taken place, and this significance is important to reassess, whatever the outcome of events.

For the Algerians, the continued fight, either by military means, or by diplomatic means, is unambiguous. It is a war of national independence. But for the French, what does it mean? It is not a foreign war. Never has the territory of France been threatened. There is more: the war is carried out against men whom the State chooses to regard as French, but who fight precisely to cease being so. It would not even be enough to say that it is a war of conquest, an imperialist war, accompanied by added racism. There is that in any war, and the ambiguity persists.

In reality, by a decision that constituted a fundamental abuse, the State first mobilized whole classes of citizens for the sole purpose of performing what it itself designated as the work of a police force against an oppressed population, which has only revolted out of a concern for basic dignity, demanding to be finally recognized as an independent community.

Neither a war of conquest, nor a war of "national defense," nor a civil war, the Algerian war has slowly become an action of the army and of a caste that refuses to surrender in the face of an uprising of which even elected officials, aware of the general collapse of colonial empires, seem ready to recognize the meaning.

Today, it is mainly the will of the army that maintains this criminal and absurd combat, and this army, by the political role that many of its top representatives make it play, sometimes acting openly and violently without legal authority, betraying the objectives with which the country entrusts it, compromises and is likely to pervert the nation, by its orders forcing citizens into complicity with a factious and degrading action. Should it be recalled that, fifteen years after the destruction of Hitler's program, French militarism, as a result of the requirements of such a war, has succeeded in re-establishing torture and making it once again an institution in Europe?

It is under these conditions that many French people have come to question the meaning of traditional values and duties. What is civic duty, when, under certain circumstances, it becomes shameful obedience? Are there not times when refusing to serve is a sacred duty, when treason signifies courageous respect for the truth? And when, by the will of those who use it as an instrument of racist or ideological domination, the army is confirmed in a state of open or latent revolt against democratic institutions, does not revolt against the army take on new meaning?

The question of conscience has been posed from the very start of the war. As this war prolongs, it is normal that this question of conscience be resolved concretely by increasing acts of insubordination, of desertion, as well as of protection and aid to the Algerian combatants. Free movements that have developed apart from all official political parties, without their assistance and, ultimately, in spite of their disavowal. Once again, in the absence of frameworks and pre-established slogans, a resistance has been born, from a spontaneous awakening, seeking and inventing forms of action and means of fighting commensurate with a new situation of which politicians and newspapers of opinion agree, whether by inertia or doctrinal timidity, or by nationalist or moral prejudices, to not recognize the true meaning and demands.

The undersigned, considering that each person must come to a conclusion about acts which it is no longer possible to present as isolated and random events, considering that they themselves, in their own way and according to their means, have the duty to intervene, not in order to advise those who must decide for themselves when confronted with such serious problems, but to ask those who judge these men to not let themselves be taken by the ambiguity of words and values, declare:

* We respect and deem justified the refusal to take arms against the Algerian people.

* We respect and deem justified the actions of the French people who consider it their duty to provide aid and protection to the Algerians oppressed in the name of the French people.

* The cause of the Algerian people, which contributes in a decisive way to the downfall of the colonial system, is the cause of all free men.

Source: "Proclamation of the 121," DISSI-DENT.INFO <http://www.dissident.info/ resistance%20statements/Proclamation%20of%20the%20121.htm>.

and terms of "universal knowledge"—a common set of culturally shared and agreed-upon truths that cut across disciplines, specializations, and areas of knowledge. In modern European history, this ability is the inheritance of the Enlightenment. Public intellectuals in the eighteenth and nineteenth centuries could refer to commonly accepted universal ideas of truth, freedom, rights, progress, science, beauty, culture, and so on. They may have debated the ways for society to reach these ideals, but they and their elite, educated public understood what the ideals meant and had a common reference point to debate the means. During the twentieth century, specialization and specialists demolished the universality and common language that public intellectuals require to influence public affairs. For example, during the 1870s, public intellectuals such as English poet Matthew Arnold could define *culture* and get almost universal assent from Europe's intellectuals and elite reading public. Today, there are literally hundreds of definitions of culture provided by thousands of cultural theorists writing in specialized journals devoted explicitly to culture. Generalist public intellectuals wielding universal knowledge on public affairs are increasingly rare in European society and culture. Most intellectuals today only have authority before specialized readers who share their training, language, terminology, goals, and interests. They have no similar authority in the general public. In French philosopher Michel Foucault's terms, *universal* (public) intellectuals have been replaced by *specific* (specialist) intellectuals. The specialization and professionalization of knowledge demands it.

Emerging simultaneously with specialization and equally detrimental to the influence of public intellectuals was the democratization of the public sphere. According to prominent German critical theorist Jürgen Habermas, the Enlightenment, bourgeois ideal of the public sphere—an elite, unitary public sphere of rational-critical citizens debating political and social issues toward consensus—declined throughout the twentieth century in Europe. While the causes and effects of this development are complex, recent scholarship has argued that the enfranchisement of previously excluded groups, including the working classes and women, created and empowered new heterogeneous, multiple-public spheres that explicitly challenged the idea and practice of a unitary public sphere and the dominance of an elite, educated public. Generally, these emergent democratic publics sought out their own leadership, intellectuals, and spokespeople who focused on specific political and social issues relevant to their lives, experience, and future. For example, in most European nations throughout the twentieth century, socialist and working-class organizations, movements, and mass political parties generated their own intellectuals and working-class public sphere—often simultaneously against the bourgeois intellectuals and bourgeois public sphere. Increasingly in France, Great Britain, Italy, and Germany it became unrealistic for public intellectuals to speak for "all" citizens on public affairs or to assume commonalities among different and competing publics. This condition of intellectual life is precisely what French intellectual Julien Benda identified and railed against in his famous *Treason of the Intellectuals* (1927). Yet Benda, like most critics of the decline of public intellectuals, saw the crisis in terms of intellectuals abandoning their mission and responsibilities. In fact, the mission and responsibilities abandoned the public intellectual. The rise of multiple publics and politicized interest groups in interwar Europe undercut the conditions for public intellectuals and made way for other types of intellectuals and public spokesmen, including demagogues such as Adolf Hitler and Benito Mussolini.

Since the interwar years in Europe the fragmentation of the public sphere and the associated decline of the influence of public intellectuals has continued, and even accelerated. In the postmodern condition of the late twentieth century—the dissolution of absolute truths, the rise of identity/interest politics, and an expansion of the notion of the political—the idea of elite public intellectuals wielding universal ideas aimed at consensus is antiquated at best and hegemonic at worst.

Finally, the transformed nature of the creation and distribution of public opinion inherent in the democratization of the public sphere worked against the influence of public intellectuals. As late as the 1890s in Europe, public opinion was generally produced by an elite group of intellectuals, politicians, writers, and reviewers; shaped by high-profile newspaper editors; and distributed to middle- and upper-class readers in a few well-known daily or weekly papers in each nation. The revolution in the print press at the turn of the century transformed the style and dramatically lowered the price of dailies. The rapid expansion of the reading public resulting from mandatory elementary education throughout most of Western Europe exploded the traditional press marketplace. New dailies such as Alfred Harmsworth's *Daily Mail* in England (1890) catered to working-class and lower-middle-class tastes and interests and the demands of a growing mass consumer culture. Sections focusing on comics, entertainment, sports, gambling, gossip, health, and crime expanded while sections devoted to public affairs and literary reviews contracted—a trend that continues steadily to the present day. European public intellectuals, who traditionally wrote on public affairs for an educated reading public who shared their educational background and cultural reference points, were marginalized in the process.

The advent of television, available to most European consumers after 1960, further accelerated the decline of public intellectuals and their influence on public opinion. Television, creating and reflecting mass consumer culture, provided less opportunity for intellectuals for sustained political and cultural criticism than the traditional print press of the first half of the twentieth century. While "serious" newspapers and journals continue to exist throughout Europe, the remarkable growth of American-style soap operas, serials, talk shows, and "family entertainment" on European television transformed what the public sees, reflects upon, and considers important. In the face of these developments, public intellectuals are in a double bind. On one hand, the rational-critical public they once wrote for has been transformed from a "culture debating" to a "culture consuming" public, to use Habermas's terms. On the other hand, European media conglomerates and corporations, ever conscious of market share, consumer tastes, and public relations, have increasingly limited valuable airtime for public intellectuals or serious political debate. Public intellectuals who do find airtime on national news shows or special-interest talk shows increasingly compete for public notoriety with other media celebrities and become what French sociologist Pierre Bourdieu called *le Fast Talker*. The American equivalent would be the ever growing number of paid "experts" or political commentators appearing regularly on network and cable news shows. This group includes credentialed historians such as Michael Beschloss and Doris Kearns Goodwin or former political appointees such as William Bennett and James Carville.

The decline of the influence of public intellectuals in European thought is not absolute. In 1960 a group of public intellectuals around Jean-Paul Sartre, including Simone de Beauvoir, André Breton, Simone Signoret, and many others, protested against the war in Algeria with a "Manifesto of the 121." This important political and social position by public intellectuals drove French public opinion against the war. In 1987 German historians and public intellectuals involved in the *Historikerstreit* (historian's controversy) over the place of National Socialism and the Holocaust in German national identity and history dominated the mainstream press and polarized mass public opinion. These events demonstrate the potential of public intellectuals to remain relevant to contemporary European social, political, and cultural thought.

However, these rare moments aside, the influence of public intellectuals in European thought has significantly declined during the course of the twentieth century. The contemporary European public sphere and public opinion are no longer commanded by independent, yet politically engaged, public intellectuals. There are intellectuals in the tradition of Eduard Bernstein, F. T. Marinetti, Arthur Koestler, Benda, and Sartre, but the world in which they exercised their influence and wielded their universal authority is gone.

–CHRISTOPHER E. MAURIELLO,
SALEM STATE COLLEGE

References

Zygmunt Bauman, *Legislators and Interpreters: On Modernity, Post-Modernity, and Intellectuals* (Cambridge: Polity Press, 1987; Ithaca, N.Y.: Cornell University Press, 1987).

Pierre Bourdieu, *Acts of Resistance: Against the Tyranny of the Market,* translated by Richard Nice (New York: New Press, 1998).

Stefan Collini, "Lament for a Lost Culture: How the Twentieth Century Came to Mourn the Seriousness of the Nineteenth," *TLS: The Times Literary Supplement* (19 January 2001): 3–5.

Venita Datta, *Birth of a National Icon: The Literary Avant-Garde and the Origins of the Intellectual in France* (Albany: State University of New York Press, 1999).

David Drake, *Intellectuals and Politics in Post-War France* (Houndmills, U.K. & New York: Palgrave Press, 2002).

Michel Foucault, *Language, Counter-Memory, Practice: Selected Essays and Interviews,* edited by Donald F. Bouchard, translated by Bouchard and Sherry Simon (Ithaca, N.Y.: Cornell University Press, 1977).

Jürgen Habermas, *The Structural Transformation of the Public Sphere: An Inquiry into a Category of Bourgeois Society,* translated by Thomas Burger with the assistance of Frederick Lawrence (Cambridge, Mass.: MIT Press, 1989).

Jeremy Jennings and Anthony Kemp-Welch, eds., *Intellectuals in Politics: From the Dreyfus Affair to Salman Rushdie* (London & New York: Routledge, 1997).

James Joll, *Three Intellectuals in Politics* (New York: Pantheon, 1960).

Jonathan Judaken, "Bearing Witness to the *Différend:* Jean-François Lyotard, The Postmodern Intellectual and 'the jews,'" in *Jews and Gender: The Challenge to Hierarchy,* edited by Jonathan Frankel (Oxford & New York: Oxford University Press, 2000), pp. 245–264.

Christopher Lasch, *The Revolt of the Elites and the Betrayal of Democracy* (New York: Norton, 1995).

P. K. Lawrence, ed., *Knowledge and Power: The Changing Role of European Intellectuals* (Aldershot, U.K. & Brookfield, Vt.: Avebury, 1996).

Jean-François Lyotard, *Tombeau de l'intellectuel: et autre papiers* (Paris: Editions Galilée, 1984).

Oskar Negt and Alexander Kluge, *Public Sphere and Experience: Toward an Analysis of the* *Bourgeois and Proletarian Public Sphere,* translated by Peter Labanyi, Jamie Owen Daniel, and Assenka Oksiloff (Minneapolis: University of Minnesota Press, 1993).

Stanley Payne, *A History of Fascism* (Madison: Wisconsin University Press, 1995).

Richard A. Posner, *Public Intellectuals: A Study in Decline* (Cambridge, Mass.: Harvard University Press, 2001).

Bruce Robbins, ed., *Intellectuals: Aesthetics, Politics, Academics* (Minneapolis: University of Minnesota Press, 1990).

Edward W. Said, *Representations of the Intellectual: The 1993 Reith Lectures* (New York: Pantheon, 1994).

Michael Walzer, *The Company of Critics: Social Criticism and Political Commitment in the Twentieth Century* (New York: Basic Books, 1988).

PUBLIC INTELLECTUALS

PUBLIC OPINION

Was public opinion influential in twentieth-century political decisions?

Viewpoint: Yes. In an age of democratic politics and mass information, public opinion was an essential factor in political decision making.

Viewpoint: No. Politicians, skillful at manipulating public opinion, more frequently used it as an excuse for their policies than as a guiding force.

Conventional views of the journalistic profession and its increasing variety of media—print journalism, television reportage, twenty-four-hour cable news, and so on—hold it to be so powerful that it forms a "Fourth Estate." This metaphor, which alludes to the three-estate system of government that defined prerevolutionary France, conveys the perceived power of organized public opinion and suggests that it had achieved importance and authority nearly equal to that of established government.

One essay in this chapter, which seeks to evaluate the relevance of public opinion in twentieth-century Europe, holds that the importance of media and its ability—both technological and political—to elaborate public opinion remained profound and important. A more sinister view, however, turns this argument on its head. It suggests that throughout the twentieth century, governments were both more willing and more able to manipulate public opinion to their own ends. Even in democratic societies, propaganda, censorship, coercion, and other forms of control succeeded in warping public opinion more often than public opinion influenced government.

Viewpoint:
Yes. In an age of democratic politics and mass information, public opinion was an essential factor in political decision making.

There can be little doubt that public opinion has informed and indeed determined government policies in twentieth-century Europe. As democracy spread, mass education and media grew, and communications technology increased in sophistication, the public's ability to make its views known and relevant evolved into an unavoidable feature of political life.

Europe's democratization during the twentieth century was the most essential factor in elevating the importance of public opinion. Although this process was uneven and differed from country to country, over the course of the century almost all European nations adopted representative democratic political systems in which citizens chose their leaders in mass participatory elections. Critics can point to cases of electoral manipulation, low voter turnout, the persistence of undemocratic structures and institutions within ostensibly democratic governments, and other imperfections, but it is impossible to deny that the for-

Italian riot police
clashing with
demonstrators
protesting a European
Union conference, Rome,
October 2003

(Ruben Sprich/Reuters/CORBIS)

tunes of almost all of the Continent's political leaders have become inseparable from their ability to satisfy the demands of the public, which makes the most powerful and direct statement of its views in regular elections. Guaranteed freedom of opinion, conscience, and expression ensure that these demands can be articulated without limitation, while universal, direct, equal, and secret balloting ensures that all voices are heard without interference. If democratic governments fail to satisfy their electorates, they can be, and often are, voted out of office. If they win public approval for their policies and actions, they can be, and often are, kept in power. Since holding power rises and falls on the outcome of democratic elections, political legitimacy can rightly be said to derive from a freely and peacefully expressed "popular mandate" rather than force, tradition, religious authority, and other bases that have in the past proved divisive and created instability.

To contemporary European political elites, therefore, favorable public opinion equals not simply power, but the legitimacy to justify its being held and wielded. In modern societies, governments, political parties, interest groups, and media outlets conduct almost daily polls to measure public opinion. Assessing the public's views of political and social issues, economic conditions, individual politicians, and other relevant subjects commands the attention of elites, who are now often accused of governing in accordance with what will make or keep them

popular with voters rather than with what they truly feel to be right. Who can discount the importance of public opinion if it is widely perceived to be not merely a justification for leadership but actually a replacement of it? An entire industry is now devoted not simply to collecting polling data but also to improving the accuracy of the process and interpreting its results with greater precision. Statistical analysis, probability laws, and interrogative logic have all taken on major functions in the political process, specifically because they help elites understand and interpret the public mood. Governments, leaders, and political parties who ignore popular opinion do so at their peril.

Even undemocratic states have shown and continue to show sensitivity to public opinion. Cynics often point to its manipulation by undemocratic governments, particularly the extreme variants that existed in Nazi Germany and the Soviet Union, but this manipulation underlines two important points. First, both the Nazis and the Bolsheviks had to pay a modicum of attention to public opinion in their formative years and could only abuse, manipulate, and suppress it after they were firmly in power. The Nazis did so by participating in Weimar Germany's free parliamentary elections after the failure of their paramilitary putsch in November 1923. Appealing to public opinion in a time of national defeat, cultural uncertainty, and economic crisis, they simply won enough votes to gain national political power. Undemocratic

PUBLIC OPINION

abuses of that power followed, but the Nazis' ability to perpetrate them initially rested with courting public opinion as it was expressed at the polls. In the Soviet case the so-called October Revolution of 1917 was in reality a coup d'état that the Bolshevik regime attempted to justify by claiming that it had acted to defend democracy from supposed threats. Although the Bolsheviks' actions quickly undermined any pretense to democratic government and obliterated the illusion that they represented popular opinion, they carefully cultivated the image of being widely popular and broadly representative. When even the Bolsheviks' blatant coercion and ruthless terrorism failed to eliminate opposition, they again played up to public opinion by introducing a limited market economy (the New Economic Policy of the 1920s) and stepping back, however briefly, from the worst of their repressive policies. The regime backtracked on these concessions, but only when it had accrued enough power and authority to do so without jeopardizing its position. However antidemocratic both regimes were, in both cases, appealing to public opinion was a crucial first step in creating totalitarianism.

Second, these regimes and their elites took great pains to control and manipulate public opinion to their own advantage. The Soviet government began closing opposition newspapers immediately after the Bolsheviks seized power in 1917 and quickly established state hegemony over the entire public sphere. The Nazis did largely the same thing between their arrival in power in 1933 and the outbreak of World War II in 1939. Both governments (and those that mimicked them) persecuted critics, imprisoned or expelled dissidents, censored public media, and took steps to limit uncontrolled foreign sources of information. Their secret police services were charged with monitoring public opinion, detecting potentially subversive messages in "approved" or ostensibly apolitical modes of expression, and investigating and punishing even private statements that criticized the regime. What drove these policies was not the belief that public opinion was just another malleable raw material for the state to mobilize to its own ends but the acute fear that freedom of expression and the ramifications of free public opinion would undermine the authority of those regimes. Along with this fear went the arrogant assumption that politically and ideologically ascendant elites were fitter to govern nations than freely chosen representatives of the public.

Ultimately, the Nazis, the Soviets, and Europe's other authoritarians were incapable of maintaining control of information and mastering the views of the public. Military defeat and the deprivations of war effectively disproved Nazi claims of military invincibility and cast doubt on their promises of a destiny of national greatness. Instead, they encouraged swelling domestic opposition to the Nazi regime sometime before its final destruction in 1945. In July 1944 elite opponents nearly succeeded in assassinating Adolf Hitler—after several prior attempts going back to 1938—and in deposing the Nazi government. Their failure and the regime's horrific retribution were nevertheless followed by open acts of defiance in the last months of the war, when civilians began to fear and despise their government, and when many important state and military officials engaged in clandestine peace negotiations, directly disobeyed Hitler's orders to carry out a scorched earth policy, and sanctioned mass surrenders of troops to the Western allies. The Soviet government never faced military conquest, but keeping the lid on its crimes and other failings became impossible. Under Josef Stalin's rule tens of millions of people were brutalized by the state, imprisoned in its vast concentration-camp network, or simply made to disappear. Even without open discussion or direct acknowledgment of what was happening, few could not see that the regime relied on terror to maintain control. Within three years of Stalin's death even his own successors—not a democrat among them—condemned aspects of what had happened, at least to the limited audience of the party elite (though the content of their discussion was leaked and became publicly known). Revealingly, many of them feared exposing too much information about Stalin's regime or freeing too many unjustly imprisoned people because they rightly believed that once those steps had been taken public opinion would turn irretrievably against them. Indeed, it did. Securing full government acknowledgment of what had happened under Stalin remained a focal point for the Soviet Union's growing dissent movement, and after Mikhail Gorbachev's regime began to allow open discussion of it in the late 1980s, popular rage turned decidedly against the government and its ideology. Continuing government attempts to deny that its elite was grossly privileged compared to average citizens, to fool its people into thinking that they were better off than Westerners, to mask unavoidable shortages of basic commodities, and to ignore obvious cases of great environmental harm were no less important in tarnishing the regime's public image. Once Gorbachev liberalized freedom of expression to the point where these problems could be discussed, the house that he hoped to rebuild fell down forever.

In any society that one wishes to study, finally, the latter half of the twentieth century brought innovations that created a surge in public opinion's power and relevance. Building on an already vast public space defined by daily newspapers, mechanized printing plants, near universal literary and primary education, and the quick processing of information via telegraph, telephone, and radio, the advent of television, satellite communications, personal computers, tape and video recorders, the Internet, widespread higher education, and a host of similar innovations made the flow of information too difficult for even the most determined government to control. Even less-developed nations, including the Soviet Union and its communist client states, experienced a surge in uncontrollable media once the requisite technology became available. Carbon paper, typewriters, and tape recorders were essential, if now relatively primitive, tools for dissidents who spread ideas and information secretly and thereby played a major role in the downfall of communism. And even authoritarian regimes that managed to survive into the twenty-first century are hard-pressed to stop their citizens from logging on to the Internet, calling each other on cell phones, and interacting digitally with the rest of the world. As these regimes tarry with their attempts to remain in the past, most European societies have learned that possessing a well-informed, articulate, and opinionated citizenry is not only an unavoidable reality but also an undeniable benefit that has helped them place among the world's most prosperous nations.

–PAUL DU QUENOY,
GEORGETOWN UNIVERSITY

Viewpoint:
No. Politicians, skillful at manipulating public opinion, more frequently used it as an excuse for their policies than as a guiding force.

The twentieth century frequently has been described as an age of mass politics: an era when the "common man" shaped public decisions, whether by direct action in the streets or by influencing governments unwilling to act against the demands of their constituents. What is surprising, given the familiarity of the cliché, is its limited validity. From World War I to the Kosovo campaign of 1999, the weight of evidence is that states have been successful to an unprecedented degree in mobilizing public support behind policies governments consider desirable, and sustaining that support well beyond rational-actor paradigms.

To a degree that success reflected the nineteenth-century establishment of nationalism as the fundamental public loyalty, transcend-

ing claims of class, church, clan, and family. At the least it reflected governments' increasing ability to deliver more than they demanded. Prior to 1914 the modern state was a service institution, providing everything from mail service to old-age pensions, paying for most of it through indirect taxes that did not bite deeply enough to generate consequent protest. That situation was in sharp contrast to the other institutions mentioned, which either depended on promises such as socialism and religion, or like clan and family made concrete demands on individuals just beginning to enjoy the pleasures of self-actualization. Even the obvious exception, compulsory military service, was a blood tax only in theory until the Great War.

By the time the guns went off in 1914, then, governments had a reservoir of goodwill. Recent research has demonstrated the shallowness and volatility of the often-cited enthusiasm for war in all the belligerent countries. Anything but an irresistible primal force, its effect depended on its being harnessed and focused through increasingly comprehensive national mobilizations. As the costs of war deepened, public opinion was cited in Europe's foreign ministries as a major obstacle to peace. That assertion, however, was more self-deception than anything else. A state's ability to keep fighting depended ultimately on its ability to sustain what became the wasting asset of public morale, by some combination of victories, promises, and lies. In each case the end came when the people loathed their government more than they feared their enemies.

That fact was not lost even on the democratic states that survived the war or emerged from it. The 1920s and 1930s were characterized in France and Britain by significant efforts to mobilize political opinion behind domestic policies and initiatives. Assent was no longer enough; participation became the ideal. Its absence was usually processed as a sign of government failure, as in France, Poland, or Yugoslavia. That reaction was to a degree influenced by the rise of states ostensibly based on ideologized public opinions. Fascist Italy, Nazi Germany, and Communist Russia had in common propaganda machines that could change lines at the will of their respective governments and security systems that specialized in removing dissidents. They prided themselves on being able to mobilize the masses behind anything from war with Abyssinia to the genocide of the Jews to the Five-Year Plans.

One of the distinguishing characteristics of World War II was in fact the persistent strength of belligerent morale. Between 1939 and 1945, defeat was a military, not a moral matter. Even France went down not from lack of moral fiber; it sued for peace only when its military resources were at the point of exhaustion. Italy left the war

PUBLIC OPINION

IN THE PEOPLE'S COURT

In the summer of 1944 a group of German military leaders attempted to assassinate Adolf Hitler. Their goal was to seize control of the government and to arrange a favorable peace settlement with the Allies. Hitler, however, miraculously survived the bombing at his field headquarters in East Prussia on 20 July, and the conspirators were quickly identified and apprehended. The subsequent trials were showcases of Nazi propaganda, intended to demonstrate the will of the German people and the righteousness of the Third Reich. In the end, about two hundred people were executed. The following is a report given by Erich Stoll, a cameraman assigned to make newsreels of the court proceedings and executions:

One day the camera people of the Deutsche Wochenschau (German newsreel) received an order from the then Reich film superintendent, Hans Hinkel, to make films of the court proceeding of July 20, 1944; it was allegedly to be shown in the newsreel.

We were taken to the People's Court, and there we were told to make sound-film takes and close-up shots of the proceedings, as inconspicuously as possible. We installed temporary lighting, and set up our sound camera behind the doors, so as to make the shots through a hole. One camera-man was to make close-up shots and shots of the general atmosphere in the court-room.

The then Reich film superintendent chose which of the camera-men was to make which shots. He also noted the number of feet of film used for each sequence, so that he was sure every bit of footage was handed over to him. The president of the People's Court, Dr. Freisler, consented enthusiastically to the idea of films being made, and agreed that by all means everything was to be shot.

The footage began with the defendants being led in, their handcuffs being taken off, and their seats assigned to them. Then came the judges under the chairman court president, Dr. Freisler, and the trial started. Every major defendant had to be filmed with the sound camera.

During the first recess, the film superintendent, Hans Hinkel, and the president of the People's Court asked how the pictures had turned out. We had to inform the president that he had shouted too loud at the defendants, so that it was not possible for the sound-modulation man to get a balance between the shouting voice and the low voices of the defendants. Unfortunately, the president of the court continued his shouting at the other sessions, so that what was taken must be called technically inadequate.

The camera-man Sosse, one of the camera people who had to film the executions, described this event:

"The building, which must have been heavily damaged previously by air raids, had been put together again in a make-shift way. The room was about 13 feet wide and 26 feet long. A black curtain divided this room in two. Only a little daylight came in through two small windows. Immediately in front of these two windows were eight hooks in the ceiling, and from these the convicts were to be hanged. There was also a contrivance in the room for beheading.

"The former General was the first prisoner to be led through the black curtain into the room. Two executioners brought him. Previously, the prosecutor had once more read the death sentence to the condemned men, in the ante-room, with the words: 'Defendant, you have been sentenced by the People's Court to death by hanging. Executioner, perform your function.'

"The defendant went to the end of the room with his head high, although urged by the hangmen to walk faster. Arrived there, he had to make an about-face. Then a hemp loop was placed around his neck. Next he was lifted by the executioners. The upper loop of the hemp rope was attached to the hook on the ceiling. The prisoner was now dropped with great force, so that the noose tightened around his neck instantly. In my opinion, death came very quickly.

"After the first sentence had been carried out, a narrow black curtain was drawn in front of the hanged man, so that the next man to be executed would not be aware of the first one. Immediately afterward, the second condemned man arrived. He also took his last steps with assurance. After each execution, a narrow black curtain was drawn in front of the hanged man, so that no condemned man could see those who had gone before him. The executions were carried out in very rapid succession. Each doomed man walked his last steps erect and manly, without a word of complaint.

"I also know that these and other executions, as well as all trials in the People's Court were filmed by press photographers of the Heinrich Hoffmann firm.

"Only the most important of the remaining trials were filmed, again on order of the then Reich film superintendent. Nine cameramen took turns in making the films. This was because every camera-man disliked the assignment. Further filmings of the executions were refused, as I declared that I could not expect my camera-men to film any more of such cruelties. All the cameramen were with me on that. . . ."

A further report is based on the statement of a prison warden. If the macabre details of the execution appear here, it is only because they typify the satanic cruelty of the man who ordered them. The prison warden first describes the place of execution:

"Imagine a room with a low ceiling and white-washed walls. Below the ceiling a rail was fixed. From it hung six big hooks, like those butchers use to hang their meat. In one corner stood a movie camera. Reflectors cast a dazzling, blinding light, like that in a studio. In this strange, small room were the Prosecutor General of the Reich, the hangman with his two assistants, two camera technicians, and I myself with a second prison warden. At the wall there was a small table with a bottle of cognac and glasses for the witnesses of the execution.

"The convicted men were led in. They were wearing their prison garb, and they were hand-cuffed. They were placed in a single row while the hangman got busy. He was known in his circles for his 'humor'. No statement, no clergymen, no journalists.

"One after another, all ten faced their turn. All showed the same courage. It took, in all, 25 minutes. The hangman wore a permanent leer, and made his jokes unceasingly. The camera worked uninterruptedly, for Hitler wanted to see and hear how his enemies had died. He was able to watch the proceedings that same evening in the Reich Chancellery. That was his own idea. He had had the executioner come to him, and had personally arranged the details of the procedure: 'I want them to be hanged, hung up like carcasses of meat.' Those were his words."

Source: "Spectacle of Horror—Reports of the cameramen and prison warden," The German Conspiracy to Destroy Hitler, 1938–1944 <http://www.joric.com/Conspiracy/1V-Horror.htm>.

by the decision of its government, not from the war-weariness of its citizens. Richard Overy stresses the importance of Allied victory to a sense that the war was a just conflict on the side of progress—however differently the sentiments may have been presented in the United States, Britain, and the Soviet Union. Nazi Germany surrendered only when its cities lay in ruin and most of its territory was occupied. After two atomic bombs the people of Japan still did not take to the streets, ropes and knives in hand, to hunt their rulers.

Yet, at the same time, morale was rendered effective by state-generated focusing. The Soviet Union, for example, added religion and nationalism to the communist focus of its ideology, then stirred in a measure of xenophobia to produce the moral blend that drove the Red Army from the gates of Moscow to the center of Berlin. In the aftermath of Pearl Harbor and Bataan, U.S. wrath focused almost totally against Japan was put at the service of a "Germany first" strategy developed before the war by the Roosevelt administration in secret negotiations with the British. National Socialist propaganda took advantage not only of the Allies' overt demand for unconditional surrender but also of a growing, albeit unacknowledged, awareness of what the German Reich was doing "in the name of the German people" to nurture a last-stand mentality. Organized terror from above was applied to frontline combat units. Germany put its teenagers in ditches with rocket launchers and festooned its streets with the corpses of soldiers hanged for "defeatism." As for the Japanese, they surrendered and accepted defeat when the emperor told them to. A people whose soldiers at times ate their own dead rather than give up began acculturating to their conquerors almost from the beginning of the occupation. All they needed was permission.

The Cold War manifested an essentially similar pattern. To speak of a "creation" of public opinion is too strong—certainly neither the United States nor the U.S.S.R. invented their positions from whole cloth in the style of George Orwell's *1984* (1949), with its ever-present "memory holes." Nor were their Ministries of Information, official and otherwise, nearly that powerful, despite the insistence of the West's anti-American Left that U.S. mass media and mass culture were global agents of "false consciousness." Governments were, however, again successful in focusing their respective public opinions. Even the major failure in that regard, the Vietnam War, did not in the long run change America's essential attitudes and orientations. The Carter administration lasted only a single term and paved the way for twelve years of more engagement in the Cold War. Popular opinion was even less significant in the final years of the U.S.S.R.—especially compared to the popular exhaustion that emerged once the system slacked its reins.

In general, then, the evidence of the twentieth century suggests that public opinion by itself is likely to have little direct impact even on core issues. On the other hand, it cannot be created from whole cloth, by either ideology or fiat. Nor can it be manipulated at will. What most often happens is a process in which governments focus and structure civic opinion, using it to facilitate and legitimate policies that are at least negatively acceptable to their citizens—that is, not so far removed from existing values and attitudes that

they are received with shock or disbelief. More synergy than dialectic, it is a pattern likely to persist into at least the first years of the next century.

–DENNIS SHOWALTER,
COLORADO COLLEGE

References

Martin Ebon, *The Soviet Propaganda Machine* (New York: McGraw-Hill, 1987).

Walter Lippmann, *Public Opinion* (New York: Free Press, 1997).

Richard Overy, *Why the Allies Won* (New York: Norton, 1996).

David Remnick, *Lenin's Tomb: The Last Days of the Soviet Empire* (New York: Random House, 1993).

David Welch, *The Third Reich: Politics and Propaganda* (London & New York: Routledge, 1993).

PUNISHING FORMER COMMUNISTS

Were there justifiable reasons for the failure to prosecute former communist leaders for criminal abuse of power?

Viewpoint: Yes. In the nations of Eastern Europe and the former Soviet Union, deep examinations of the past and the prosecution of former communist leaders have been seen as stumbling blocks to national reconciliation and stable political transitions.

Viewpoint: No. Most former communists have escaped punishment because they used their continuing political influence to secure legal immunity and to obscure or conceal the records of what happened under the regimes they served.

The largely peaceful collapse of communism in Eastern Europe (1989) and the Soviet Union (1991) created difficult social and legal dilemmas. Among these problems was the fate of former communist leaders and officials in the emerging new societies. As hard evidence of communist crimes became available, many wondered whether the surviving perpetrators should be investigated and brought to trial. In most cases they were not. At the turn of the twenty-first century, many of these individuals continued to hold positions of power and authority, while others used advantages accrued under the old system to become wealthy and successful. Only a small number were tried for their actions, and most of those condemned received light sentences.

Was it wise not to pursue criminal charges against former communist leaders? On one hand, avoiding the horrors of the past and leaving old injustices aside may have been a crucial step in ensuring an orderly and effective transition to democracy. Upsetting already tense social conditions with far-reaching investigations and contentious sensational trials might have been counterproductive to that goal. In their effort to control every aspect of political and civil life, communist governments created huge bureaucracies that employed armies of officials and relied on the compliance and complicity of legions of ordinary citizens. If these bureaucracies caused their operators and those who interacted with them to commit crimes, then a fair judicial assessment of postcommunist societies could potentially have involved the prosecution of hundreds of thousands—if not millions—of people.

On the other hand, some observers argue that these factors were largely irrelevant and that the failure to prosecute former communists was a mistake. In addition to denying justice to the victims, in many cases the perseverance of the former communist elite in positions of power retarded or even turned back processes of liberalization and democratization. Many former communist nations remain poor, fragmented, and outside the community of prosperous nations because their leaders still possess old mentalities and practices or thinly veiled adaptations of them. The post–World War II trials of Nazi criminals and associated collaborators throughout Western Europe, moreover, long stood as a reasonable model of justice for punishing guilty officials of a former regime. The continuing transition of former communist states to modern, reformed democracies suggests the value of considering the fate of their former elite.

Viewpoint:
Yes. In the nations of Eastern Europe and the former Soviet Union, deep examinations of the past and the prosecution of former communist leaders have been seen as stumbling blocks to national reconciliation and stable political transitions.

From the perspective of moralists and legalists alike in the Western world, the collapse of the Soviet system offered unparalleled possibilities. Since 1945 successive attempts to establish a basis for dealing with abuses of power, other than the exercise of greater power, had failed. The Nuremberg trials (1945–1946) were tainted with the sense of "victor's justice"; the Tokyo trials (1946–1948) had long since been dismissed as nothing but near-random exercises in payback. The Cold War, combined with the continued strength of national sovereignty, had frustrated attempts such as those made during the Vietnam War (ended 1975) to place rulers in the dock on any but a theatrical basis: they were gestures with nothing supporting them.

At the end of the twentieth century a near-ideal situation to prosecute such crimes emerged. An old order collapsed, for practical purposes without violence. Its successors made their cases for legitimacy essentially by denouncing the human-rights violations of the communist system. Wherever one looked—Poland, Czechoslovakia, Romania, and the former German Democratic Republic—the pattern was the same: communism stood indicted of internal crimes ranging from election fraud to torture. This realization removed the inconveniences that more ephemeral issues such as "crimes against peace" and "waging aggressive war" had posed in 1945. There was no need for external intervention. Instead, new governments could bring their old governors before their own courts—frequently, indeed, on charges of violating their own laws, on the books but never enforced, for such things as illegal imprisonment. Most prospective defendants were still living within the appropriate jurisdictions. The records on which to base prosecutions were almost entirely intact. It only seemed necessary to walk through a wide-open door to establish systematic, unchallengeable precedents for calling administrations to account for their misdeeds, not merely in the name of often-ephemeral international law and poorly defined concepts of human rights, but by the authority of the people victimized.

Yet, the new governments of Eastern Europe from the beginning proved reluctant to pursue that initiative. Even Germany, whose Federal Republic had periodically promised a day of reckoning with the "tyrants" of East Germany, was slow to act. Vaclav Havel, Czechoslovakia's new president and a man whose credentials were unchallengeable, spoke for what seems an overwhelming majority of his countrymen and their counterparts elsewhere when he called for judging men and women on what they will do tomorrow rather than by what they may have done yesterday. Havel's recommendations became de facto policy for an entire region. Each country had a few exceptions: there were some trials of perpetrators ranging from senior officials to border guards. Those proceedings, however, almost never received the kind of publicity their advocates expected. Nor did they generate any groundswell of demands for further waves of trials designed to purify the community.

The wisdom and morality of that approach remains subject to debate. Critics argue that it allowed the old order's *nomenklaturas* (the elite) not merely to evade punishment and to maintain themselves in place, but to aggrandize themselves by taking insider advantage of the privatization processes that transformed economies everywhere east of the Elbe and south of the Danube. The efflorescent corruption accompanying that process is frequently described as a consequence of an ethos of avoiding embarrassing questions that accompanied a decommunization more institutional than psychological.

More serious, especially to the intellectual community, has been the absence of closure. South African reconciliation tribunals are frequently cited as positive examples of that cathartic process. Even if confession is not accompanied by sanction, the argument runs, at least truth has become part of the public process. In the background of the issue, though cited less often than might be expected, is the alleged negative example of the Federal Republic of Germany, whose unwillingness to come directly and completely to terms with its Nazi experience in both individual and institutional contexts represents a corresponding betrayal of victims of the Third Reich. Not, the point is usually emphasized, that West Germany and a reunited Germany have not made significant efforts—but that neither has been willing to go all the way in mastering their past. By implication the former, largely Slavic, Communist client states should do better.

It was not quite that easy. In practical terms, the major problem was that the deposed governments involved large numbers of people—much greater than recognized during their existence, and in many more ways than had been understood. The issue was not being able to replace compromised "former people," but where the line should be drawn for a system that, in good part for the practical sake of full employment, had fragmented and decentralized every aspect of its apparatus. A line drawn too high meant accusations of randomness—and the elite could hire expensive lawyers. Few trials of leading figures were conducted; fewer still produced anything like cathartic results. Extending downward the list of the hopelessly compromised produced another kind of problem. If these people were lustrated, forbidden to hold elective office, or simply dismissed from the posts they held, what was to be done with them? In a public climate predicated on cradle-to-grave security, dismissing them without compensation was certain to cause a fundamental anxiety among the survivors—as well as prompting the question of who would be next. In practical terms, moreover, where were the pensions and gratuities to come from in economies already beginning to unravel?

An even more essential problem in finding and punishing the old order's guilty functionaries was posed by the comprehensive networks of informers generated by state security organizations, themselves suffering from overstaffing and underemployment. Routine investigations for par-

ticular reasons tended with time to overlap, to a point where it was possible in any Eastern bloc country to make a case against almost anybody who had not consciously and deliberately withdrawn from public involvement—and that kind of withdrawal itself engendered suspicion!

The end result, interestingly, was not a group of suspects but a group of informers. East Germany's *Staatsicherheit,* or Stasi, the most notorious of the security agencies, set the pattern. To complete a file on a particular individual, they asked questions of close associates: spouses, relatives, and colleagues. Reluctance was met with judicious revelations from the recalcitrant person's own record. Eventually, about one-third of the population had informed on or was informing on everyone else—and the system was so overloaded that the data it contained was virtually useless for intelligence purposes, since it could neither be retrieved nor correlated.

What it could and did do was create a structure of active complicity in the system. That was what Havel meant when he reiterated that a communist system produced few heroes in the long run and when he warned against inquiring too closely into anyone's past. The question became "where do we stop?" The all too probable answer was when the possibilities of a democratic public life had been poisoned beyond recovery, not by mutual suspicion but by mutual evidence of complicity in the former order.

—DENNIS SHOWALTER,
COLORADO COLLEGE

Former communist Slobodan Milosevic after assuming the presidency of Yugoslavia in 1997

(Reuters/Peter Kujundzik/archive photos)

PUNISHING FORMER COMMUNISTS

**Viewpoint:
No. Most former communists have escaped punishment because they used their continuing political influence to secure legal immunity and to obscure or conceal the records of what happened under the regimes they served.**

The decision not to prosecute former East European and Soviet communists for the crimes they perpetrated while in power was a poor one. Critics of lustration, or the full exposure of what happened under communist rule, argue that prosecutions would have damaged national reconciliation, created ambiguity about who was guilty and who should be punished, and paralyzed national government. No matter what had been done, they suggest, it was better to leave the past in the past. Yet, for a variety of reasons, these criticisms have little basis either in logic or historical experience.

The most obvious consequence of the failure to investigate and prosecute former communists is that they have persisted in positions of power and influence throughout Eastern Europe and the former Soviet Union. Even if former communist societies were determined to punish them, their continuing tenure can effectively block attempts to do so. As the social and economic development of these nations has generally shown over the first postcommunist decade, tolerating this situation might not have been the best course. All too often, former communists who were left untouched by the law and untainted by the stigma of their pasts merely reorganized themselves into a corrupt elite. Many of their actions bear comparison to those of organized crime in the West, complete with tactics of violence, intimidation, and coercion that they had opportunities to witness, and in some cases employ themselves, during the communist era. Civic freedom in many of the involved countries has faced challenges from the same means. In many places the fundamentals of the democratic process have either been ignored altogether or seriously manipulated to the advantage of the old elite.

The counterargument to this point is that some former communist nations—particularly Poland, Hungary, and the Czech Republic—have undergone relatively easy transitions, partially eased by their toleration of their former rulers. Although these "fast adjusters" may have experienced smoother transitions to democracy, they are exceptional among former communist nations, for these three countries were undergoing transitions before the fall of communism. All

three were exceptional in the relative economic liberalization that their governments had pursued before 1989, and all three had major dissent movements that commanded mass support. By the time the communist apparatchiks were sidelined, they had substantive noncommunist or anticommunist figures prepared to take power. East Germany could also be added to this list, for it received massive investment from the West after national reunification in 1990, and its political structures were largely taken over by Westerners. Although some former communists remained in positions of power and influence in these countries, there were enough noncommunists to ensure the viability of market economies and open political systems. To take the case of Poland as an example, the Solidarity movement, which started as a labor organization of dockworkers, expanded in the early 1980s into a mass party with several million members. Without the nerve or Soviet support to destroy the movement, Poland's communist government had little choice but to tolerate it uneasily until it consented to partially free elections in 1989. Solidarity candidates defeated all 161 communist candidates for contestable seats in the lower house of parliament, while 99 out of 100 communist candidates lost contestable seats in the upper house. Solidarity leader Lech Walesa was elected president in December 1990. Governing with a Solidarity-led coalition in parliament, Poland's path to democratic government and market economics was assured under his leadership.

Not all former communist nations have been so lucky, however. Romania, Bulgaria, Slovakia, and the states of the former Yugoslavia overturned communism's monopoly on power, but the communist-era elite remained in place and, although they sang a new tune, hindered the development of market economies and the movement of their governments toward democracy. Some turned to radical nationalism. In Yugoslavia former communist leader Slobodan Milosevic's regime precipitated destructive conflicts involving neighboring Croatia and Bosnia-Herzegovina and the ethnic Albanian population of the Kosovo region. These conflicts had genocidal overtones and necessitated several attempts at intervention by the European Union (EU), United Nations (UN), United States, and finally by the North Atlantic Treaty Organization (NATO), which carried out a military campaign against Yugoslavia in 1999. The conflict precipitated the collapse of Milosevic's regime in October 2000 and its replacement by an uneasy democracy. At this writing Milosevic and several members of the provisional Bosnian Serb government are being tried in an international court for crimes again humanity (some have already been convicted), while others are wanted. If Milosevic and his henchmen had been removed at an earlier time, the region might have been spared much bloodshed.

Milosevic's Balkan neighbors may not have suffered a catastrophe as big as the former Yugoslavia's, but the continuing shortcomings of their societies have nevertheless caused major civil strife and political crises. Weak economies and unstable governments have alienated badly needed foreign investment and made international financial bodies wary. For the same reason, the EU invited only Slovakia (which rid itself of its former communist president in 1998) and the one peaceful former Yugoslavian state of Slovenia to join its ranks in its 2004 expansion. One of the main arguments against including Slovakia, Romania, Bulgaria, and former Yugoslavian countries in NATO (which Poland, Hungary, and the Czech Republic joined in 1999) has been that their meager economic resources cannot meet the costs of military modernization, while their political institutions are not sufficiently democratic to accommodate the alliance's criteria. Free and empowered former communists have not helped solve these problems.

The former Union of Soviet Socialist Republics (U.S.S.R.) offers worse examples of the consequences of the persisting communist elite. With the exception of Lithuania, Latvia, and Estonia, which explicitly rejected communism as a legacy of Russian hegemony after independence, all of its former republics experienced major problems in developing democracy. Most of the newly independent states of Central Asia, as well as Belarus and Azerbaijan, are ruled by authoritarian dictatorships presided over by high-ranking former officials of the Soviet Communist Party. President Saparmurat Niyazov of Turkmenistan took power for life in 1999, adopted the title *Turkmenbashi* (Father of Turkmen), and revived not only the worst features of the late Soviet Union (he was party boss of the Turkmen Soviet Socialist Republic in 1985–1991) but the totalitarian personality cult associated with Josef Stalin and discredited even by subsequent Soviet leaders. In addition to Stalinesque statements, practices, and uses of public space, in 2002 Niyazov personally renamed the months of the year and days of the week, a bizarre measure that included renaming January "Turkmenbashi," after himself. In Azerbaijan, Gaidar Aliev, a former KGB general, Soviet Politburo member, and Azeri Soviet Socialist Republic party leader in 1969–1987 (he was removed for being too hard-line), returned to power in 1993 and ruled in a corrupt and authoritarian manner until he stepped down for reasons of ill health ten years later. A rigged election handed the succession to his son, despite serious rioting. In November 2003 Georgia's authoritarian pres-

ident Eduard Shevardnadze—another former Soviet Politburo member, Georgia's Communist Party boss (1972–1985), and Soviet foreign minister (1985–1990 and 1991)—was forced from power in a bloodless coup after eleven years of rule.

Russia, Ukraine, and Moldova are less extreme examples, but all three nevertheless have major problems related to the persistence of their communist elite. A 2002 survey estimated that 60 percent of Russian business, government, and administrative leaders are holdovers from the Soviet elite. Former president Boris Yeltsin, yet another former member of the Soviet Politburo, provoked a military confrontation with Russia's nascent elected parliament in October 1993, an episode that resulted in sharp limitations on the legislature's powers. In the 1996 presidential election, ostensibly the first free election for an executive in Russian history, Yeltsin used his powers to monopolize the media and manipulate the voting to ensure his victory. His successor, Vladimir Putin, a former KGB officer and high-ranking post-Soviet secret-police official, has continued and augmented many of Yeltsin's methods, particularly in controlling Russia's influential television media, which ceased to be independent of the state in the first years of his presidency. Independent observers have accused government organs of manipulating the December 2003 parliamentary elections, which handed nearly half the seats to a newly formed political party with no program other than loyalty to Putin. Ukrainian president Leonid Kuchma, whose job before 1991 was managing a Soviet missile factory, has relied on similar measures and has, with no legal or political consequences, been directly implicated in the murder of an opposition journalist. Controversial legislative and judicial decisions in December 2003 will permit him to run for a third presidential term, despite the Ukrainian constitution's two-term limit.

Former communist officials have also done much to harm the former Soviet Union's economy. In the 1990s many used their power and influence to buy up vast state assets in rigged and legally questionable privatization deals that left much wealth in the hands of an elite, and largely former communist, few. Many also siphoned off billions of dollars in Western aid and investment intended for more productive uses than shopping sprees in New York, villas on the French Riviera, and fat private bank accounts in Cyprus. At a time when Russia badly needed foreign aid and investment, the net flow of capital actually went out of the country for much of the 1990s. By August 1998 Russia's financial situation had become so problematic that Yeltsin tried to solve it by defaulting on his country's debts to the

PUNISHING FORMER COMMUNISTS

CRIMES AGAINST THE PEOPLE

In 1989 deposed Romanian communist ruler Nicolae Ceauçescu and his wife, Elena, were tried by a military tribunal, which handed down a verdict of death. The following is a portion of the court transcript:

CHIEF PROSECUTOR: Esteemed chairman of the court, today we have to pass a verdict on the defendants Nicolae Ceausescu and Elena Ceausescu who have committed the following offenses: Crimes against the people. They carried out acts that are incompatible with human dignity and social thinking; they acted in a despotic and criminal way; they destroyed the people whose leaders they claimed to be. Because of the crimes they committed against the people, I plead, on behalf of the victims of these two tyrants, for the death sentence for the two defendants. The bill of indictment contains the following points: Genocide, in accordance with Article 356 of the penal code. Two: Armed attack on the people and the state power, in accordance with Article 163 of the penal code. The destruction of buildings and state institutions, undermining of the national economy, in accordance with Articles 165 and 145 of the penal code. They obstructed the normal process of the economy.

PROSECUTOR: Did you hear the charges? Have you understood them?

CEAUSESCU: I do not answer, I will only answer questions before the Grand National Assembly. I do not recognize this court. The charges are incorrect, and I will not answer a single question here. . . .

PROSECUTOR: This situation is known. The catastrophic situation of the country is known all over the world. Every honest citizen who worked hard here until 22 December knows that we do not have medicines, that you two have killed children and other people in this way, that there is nothing to eat, no heating, no electricity.

Elena and Nicolae reject this. Another question to Ceausescu: Who ordered the bloodbath in Timisoara? Ceausescu refused to answer.

PROSECUTOR: Who gave the order to shoot in Bucharest, for instance?

CEAUSESCU: I do not answer.

PROSECUTOR: Who ordered shooting into the crowd? Tell us!

At that moment Elena says to Nicolae: Forget about them. You see, there is no use in talking to these people.

PROSECUTOR: Do you not know anything about the order to shoot?

Nicolae reacts with astonishment.

There is still shooting going on, the prosecutor says. Fanatics, whom you are paying. They are shooting at children; they are shooting arbitrarily into the apartments. Who are these fanatics? Are they the people, or are you paying them?

CEAUSESCU: I will not answer. I will not answer any question. Not a single shot was fired in Palace Square. Not a single shot. No one was shot.

PROSECUTOR: By now, there have been 34 casualties. . . . Please, make a note: Ceausescu does not recognize the new legal structures of power of the country. He still considers himself to be the country's president and the commander in chief of the army.
Why did you ruin the country so much: Why did you export everything? Why did you make the peasants starve? The produce which the peasants grew was exported, and the peasants came from the most remote provinces' to Bucharest and to the other cities in order to buy bread. They cultivated the soil in line with your orders and had nothing to eat. Why did you starve the people?

CEAUSESCU: I will not answer this question. As a simple citizen, I tell you the following: For the first time I guaranteed that every peasant received 200 kilograms of wheat per person, not per family, and that he is entitled to more. It is a lie that I made the people starve. A lie, a lie in my face. This shows how little patriotism there is, how many treasonable offenses were committed.

PROSECUTOR: You claim to have taken measures so that every peasant is entitled to 200 kilograms of wheat. Why do the peasants then buy their bread in Bucharest?. . . We have wonderful programs. Paper is patient. However, why are your programs not implemented? You have destroyed the Romanian villages and the Romanian soil. What do you say as a citizen?

CEAUSESCU: As a citizen, as a simple citizen, I tell you the following: At no point was there such an upswing, so much construction, so much consolidation in the Romanian provinces. I guaranteed that every village has its schools, hospitals and doctors. I have done everything to create a decent and rich life for the people in the country, like in no other country in the world.

PROSECUTOR: We have always spoken of equality. We are all equal. Everybody should be paid according to his performance. Now we finally saw your villa on television, the golden plates from which you ate, the foodstuffs that you had imported, the luxurious celebrations, pictures from your luxurious celebrations.

ELENA CEAUSESCU: Incredible. We live in a normal apartment, just like every other citizen. We have ensured an apartment for every citizen through corresponding laws.

PROSECUTOR: You had palaces.

CEAUSESCU: No, we had no palaces. The palaces belong to the people.

The prosecutor agrees, but stresses that they lived in them while the people suffered. . . .

PROSECUTOR: Mr. Chairman, we find the two accused guilty of having committed criminal actions according to the following articles of the penal code: Articles 162, 163, 165 and 357. Because of this indictment, I call for the death sentence and the impounding of the entire property of the two accused.

The counsel for the defense now takes the floor and instructs the Ceausescus once again that they have the right to defense and that they should accept this right.

COUNSEL FOR THE DEFENSE: Even though he—like her—committed insane acts, we want to defend them. We want a legal trial. Only a president who is still confirmed in his position can demand to speak at the Grand National Assembly. If he no longer has a certain function, he cannot demand anything at all. Then he is treated like a normal citizen. Since the old government has been dissolved and Ceausescu has lost his functions, he no longer has the right to be treated as the president. Please make a note that here it has been stated that all legal regulations have been observed, that this is a legal trial. Therefore, it is a mistake for the two accused to refuse to cooperate with us. This is a legal trial, and I honor them by defending them.

At the beginning, Ceausescu claimed that it is a provocation to be asked whether he was sick. He refused to undergo a psychiatric examination. However, there is a difference between real sickness that must be treated and mental insanity which leads to corresponding actions, but which is denied by the person in question. You have acted in a very irresponsible manner; you led the country to the verge of ruin and you will be convicted on the basis of the points contained in the bill of indictment. You are guilty of these offenses even if you do not want to admit it. Despite this, I ask the court to make a decision which we will be able to justify later as well. We must not allow the slightest impression of illegality to emerge. Elena and Nicolae Ceausescu should be punished in a really legal trial. The two defendants should also know that they are entitled to a counsel for defense, even if they reject this. It should be stated once and for all that this military court is absolutely legal and that the former positions of the two Ceausescus are no longer valid. However, they will be indicted, and a sentence will be passed on the basis of the new legal system. They are not only accused of offenses committed during the past few days, but of offenses committed during the past 25 years. We have sufficient data on this period. I ask the court, as the plaintiff, to take note that proof has been furnished for all these points, that the two have committed the offenses mentioned. Finally, I would like to refer once more to the genocide, the numerous killings carried out during the past few days. Elena and Nicolae Ceausescu must be held fully responsible for this. I now ask the court to pass a verdict on the basis of the law, because everybody must receive due punishment for the offenses he has committed. . . .

PROSECUTOR: It is very difficult for us to act, to pass a verdict on people who even now do not want to admit to the criminal offenses that they have committed during 25 years and admit to the genocide, not only in Timisoara and Bucharest, but primarily also to the criminal offenses committed during the past 25 years. This demonstrates their lack of understanding. They not only deprived the people of heating, electricity, and foodstuffs, they also tyrannized the soul of the Romanian people. They not only killed children, young people and adults in Timisoara and Bucharest; they allowed Securitate members to wear military uniforms to create the impression among the people that the army is against them. They wanted to separate the people from the army. They used to fetch people from orphans' homes or from abroad whom they trained in special institutions to become murderers of their own people. You were so impertinent as to cut off oxygen lines in hospitals and to shoot people in their hospital beds. The Securitate had hidden food reserves on which Bucharest could have survived for months, the whole of Bucharest.

Whom are they talking about, Elena asks.

PROSECUTOR: So far, they have always claimed that we have built this country, we have paid our debts, but with this they bled the country to death and have hoarded enough money to ensure their escape. You need not admit your mistakes, mister. In 1947, we assumed power, but under completely different circumstances. In 1947, King Michael showed more dignity than you. And you might perhaps have achieved the understanding of the Romanian people if you had now admitted your guilt. You should have stayed in Iran where you had flown to.

In response, the two laugh, and she says: We do not stay abroad. This is our home.

PROSECUTOR: Esteemed Mr. Chairman, I have been one of those who, as a lawyer, would have liked to oppose the death sentence, because it is inhuman. But we are not talking about people. I would not call for the death sentence, but it would be incomprehensible for the Romanian people to have to go on suffering this great misery and not to have it ended by sentencing the two Ceausescus to death. The crimes against the people grew year by year. They were only busy enslaving the people and building up an apparatus of power. They were not really interested in the people.

Source: *"Transcript of the Closed Trial of Nicolae and Elena Ceausescu," 25 December 1989, Coup d'etat of 1989 <http://www.timisoara.com/timisoara/rev/trialscript.html>.*

PUNISHING FORMER COMMUNISTS

International Monetary Fund (IMF) and devaluing the ruble. The results were substantially increased impoverishment and a marked, albeit temporary, decline in foreign investment. Despite an economic boom in subsequent years, perceived political opposition under Putin led to the attempted prosecution of two of Russia's wealthiest businessmen, Boris Berezovsky and Vladimir Gusinsky, who fled into exile with their fortunes, and in the October 2003 arrest of the country's richest man, oil and banking tycoon Mikhail Khodorkovsky. After the last episode the Russian state further demonstrated its prowess to would-be opponents by seizing a controlling stake in Khodorkovsky's oil company.

Perhaps it should be no surprise that recent opinion polls and election results have shown that Russians and other former Soviet populations are losing confidence in democracy and market economics. Their experience of that system of government has been under an elite rooted predominantly in the communist past, one that has used its advantages to perpetuate its long presence as the ruling class and to oppress and intimidate others who would like to share it. In the dubious Russian parliamentary elections of December 2003, political parties committed to further democratization won just 7 out of 450 legislative seats. The presidents of several former Soviet republics have been routinely reelected with more than 90 percent of the vote. If the region's communist elite had been marginalized, ostracized, and punished when appropriate after 1991, democracy and market economics may have enjoyed better credentials in the eyes of its citizens.

Another major factor that would have legitimated the punishment of communist criminals after 1989 was that there were well-established international precedents for prosecuting the criminal elite. After World War II the Western occupation zones of Germany were thoroughly de-Nazified, with a series of judicial tribunals investigating not only government officials but army officers, business leaders, doctors, the police, the judiciary, and others responsible for the crimes of the Nazi regime. The Federal Republic of Germany, established in 1949, continued this process with orderly criminal investigations and prosecutions that still continue. Some opponents of lustration in contemporary Eastern Europe and the U.S.S.R. have argued that prosecutions and other judicial proceedings would lead effectively to mass lynching, but the German case is instructive. In the Western zones, Nazi officials were classified by their actions. The worst offenders were tried and punished when found guilty, while lesser offenders were dismissed. Officials who had simply done a competent job without committing crimes were often either not fired or quickly rehired. The only destabilizing mass purge of German society occurred in the Soviet occupation zone, where de-Nazification involved neither justice nor moderation. West Germany's experience proved, however, that punishing the truly guilty was indeed possible without degenerating into ambiguity, crushing the innocent, or wreaking havoc with government and society.

The postwar pattern of retributive justice in West Germany was generally followed throughout liberated Western Europe. In France nearly 100,000 people were formally tried for acts of collaboration under German occupation and the Vichy regime. Yet, more than half were acquitted, while many of the guilty were punished only with a deprivation of civil rights, designed to exclude them from public life for a fixed period of time or permanently, or with light prison sentences. Of more than 4,000 people sentenced to death, only 757 were executed, and most of these individuals had worked directly for the German occupying authority in some nefarious capacity. As in Germany, organized and disciplined French investigations and criminal proceedings continued well into the 1980s and 1990s, including the prosecution of the German SS officer Klaus Barbie, Vichy police officials René Bousquet and Paul Touvier (though Bousquet was murdered shortly before his trial), and Vichy administrative official Maurice Papon. While these processes involved an unusually large number of people, France and most other West European countries carried them out free of negative consequences for their general social stability. In all likelihood the implications of trying war criminals, executioners, bloodstained officials, and other creatures of dictatorship who "just followed orders" were positive for contemporary Europe.

Even while the Western media hailed the more recent of these prosecutions as a final settling with the past and argued that the advanced age of these defendants (Papon was ninety when he was sentenced to ten years in prison) should be no safeguard, few comparable arguments have been applied to former communists, many of whom committed similar or worse crimes. Indeed, functionaries whose guilt for terrible crimes against humanity has been established by documentary records and other compelling evidence—crimes that were punished on the gallows in other countries after World War II—were still alive after 1989. Lazar Kaganovich, an intimate of Stalin whose official duties in the 1930s involved issuing tens of thousands of death sentences against innocent people, lived in quiet retirement until his death in 1996. Vladimir Kriuchkov, who led the KGB during violent crackdowns on dissent in the late Gorbachev era and then participated in the August 1991 coup against Mikhail Gorbachev, is still alive and free. Former Polish president Wojciech Jaruzelski was recently excused from prosecution for the deaths of Solidarity demonstrators at the hands of troops under his command in 1980–1981. Former East German leader Erich Honecker successfully evaded prosecution for reasons of ill health. His secret police chief Erich Mielke, who personally ordered East German border guards to shoot people trying to flee to the West, also successfully used ill health to evade prosecution for crimes in office. In a bizarre application of justice, a German court nevertheless tried and convicted him for the 1931 murder of two Berlin police officers. He was sentenced to four years in jail and served two. Other communist officials have been tried for manslaughter, corruption, and other lesser crimes that have carried lighter punishments than they almost certainly deserved, but even these cases have been few and far between. The execution of Romanian leader Nicolae Ceauçescu on Christmas Day 1989 and the Afghan Taliban's execution of their country's former president in 1997 were the only cases in which former communist leaders received the death penalty. At this writing only Cambodia has announced its intention to begin prosecuting former communist officials, who, in that country's case, are responsible for the deaths of nearly two million innocent people.

The failure to punish former communist officials has created many more problems than its apologists claim to have solved by not punishing them. The continuing political, social, and economic retardation of much of Eastern Europe and the former U.S.S.R. has been directly related to the continued presence of former communist officials in elite positions, along with their authoritarian mentalities, contempt for ordinary citizens, corrupt practices, and selfish love of privilege. They have held up the growth of market economics and true democracy in most of the countries concerned.

They launched the bloodiest conflict Europe has seen since World War II. Moreover, in several places they continue to oppress the same people they were oppressing before 1989. Functioning means and structures for their punishment existed, and exist, within plain sight in Western Europe and at the discretion of international bodies, which continue to function in the twenty-first century, even as former communists continue to evade prosecution, enrich themselves from the resources of their countries and peoples, and wield positions of power and authority to make sure that the situation does not change.

–PAUL DU QUENOY,
GEORGETOWN UNIVERSITY

References

John Borneman, *Settling Accounts: Violence, Justice, and Accountability in Postsocialist Europe* (Princeton: Princeton University Press, 1997).

Neil J. Kritz, ed., *Transitional Justice: How Emerging Democracies Reckon with Former Regimes* (Washington, D.C.: United States Institute of Peace Press, 1995).

Martha Minow, *Between Vengeance and Forgiveness: Facing History after Genocide and Mass Violence* (Boston: Beacon, 1998).

Tina Rosenberg, *The Haunted Land: Facing Europe's Ghosts after Communism* (New York: Random House, 1995).

Michael P. Scharf, *Balkan Justice: The Story Behind the First International War Crimes Trial since Nuremberg* (Durham, N.C.: Carolina Academic Press, 1997).

Susan L. Woodward, *Balkan Tragedy: Chaos and Dissolution after the Cold War* (Washington, D.C.: Brookings Institution, 1995).

RUSSIA AS PART OF THE WEST

Is Russia part of the West?

Viewpoint: Yes. Despite the divergences of Russia's remote past, in modern times Russia has unequivocally become a Western state and a fully integrated part of Europe.

Viewpoint: No. What has been called Russia's Westernization was only a series of superficialities that have been unable to mask distinctly un-European patterns of culture, politics, tradition, and interests.

British statesman Winston Churchill once famously referred to Russia as a "riddle wrapped in a mystery inside an enigma." The consternation expressed in his statement at least partly derived from the question of Russia's identity as a nation. For many observers, Russia is undeniably part of the West. A Christian nation since the conversion of its people in 988, Russia has been intimately tied to Europe by culture, trade, and diplomacy, as well as by faith. The basis for its laws and social organization, from the tsars through the communists to its current leaders, has shared many commonalities with the West. The development of its art, science, and philosophy had pronounced Western influences and went a long way toward influencing the West itself.

Yet, at the same time, other students of Russian history deny the country's Western identity. Despite its Christian faith Russia stood apart from the West. In many respects its political culture derived from the steppe empires of Asia. Its monarchy remained far more powerful than its Western counterparts until it was overthrown, and the communist dictatorship that replaced it also bore impressive comparison to what some scholars have termed "Oriental despotism." Lacking Western concepts of individual rights, private property, and representative government, Russia has remained separate from the West. As post-Soviet Russia looks toward redefining its world role, its identity as part of or in distinction to the West is an important question.

Viewpoint:
Yes. Despite the divergences of Russia's remote past, in modern times Russia has unequivocally become a Western state and a fully integrated part of Europe.

The *West* has traditionally been a term of self-identification created in opposition to a nebulous *East*. The Latin expression *ex Oriente lux, ex Occidente lex*—meaning from the East, light (religion and philosophy), from the West, law (Roman-inspired order with personal liberty and private property)—expressed well the common notion that the specifics of Western civilization contrasted with a less specified and less tangible East. In cultural and historical studies, the West has stood for the Greco-Roman world in antiquity, the Roman Catholic world in the

The Kremlin, Moscow, seat of government power in Russia, exhibits eastern and western architectural influences

(Jos Fuste Raga/CORBIS)

Middle Ages, and subsequently modern Europe and the "New Europes" created by overseas colonization. As the West has come in modern times also to be identified with industrial capitalism and political democracy, so some observers have added Japan to this "West."

In brief, several features suggest that Russia is indeed an integral part of the West. Russia's ethnolinguisitic basis is Slavic, a western branch of the Indo-European family of languages. Russia's Byzantine inheritance in religion (Orthodox Christianity and Roman law) is essentially Greek and Roman. Russia's political structures have been variants of common European types, including medieval kingship, absolute monarchy, constitutional monarchy, socialism, dictatorship, and, after the collapse of the Soviet Union in 1991 and at least in form, parliamentary democracy. Capitalism and communism, Russia's two forms of economic organization since at least the 1880s, are Western developments built on theories of political economy that originated within Western philosophical thought. Adam Smith's capitalism was the product of the Scottish Enlightenment, just as Karl Marx's communism emerged from elements of the German philosophical tradition and from Smith's

observations about economics. Russia's cultural modernization has been thoroughly Western since the reign of Peter the Great (1682–1725) and had some roots that were even older.

The Slavs originated in what is now Poland, Belarus, and western Ukraine, and their closest Indo-European linguistic and cultural cousins are the Baltic and Germanic families. Such key Slavic words as the equivalents of *iron, plow, bread,* and *prince* come from ancient Germanic, and those few such as *bog,* meaning "god," which derive from Iranian roots, were picked up from Sarmatians living in the Roman zone. The greatest affinities of customary and early Slavic law were with neighboring Germanic peoples, whose system of laws inspired the common-law tradition still prevalent throughout the English-speaking world. Russia's Cyrillic alphabet originated as a phonic modification of the Greek alphabet.

The standard terminology of the Greek and, hence, Russian Churches as Eastern Orthodoxy has created the misconception that they alone represent Eastern Christianity. To the contrary, "real" Eastern Christianity is found in the breakaway Syrian, Armenian, and Coptic (Egyptian and Ethiopian) Churches, which adhere to the Nestorian and

HISTORICAL BACKWARDNESS

Below is an excerpt from one of Lev Trotsky's articles on the historical character of the Russian Revolution in which he indicates his belief that Russia is more of a Western entity than an Eastern one:

The development of Russia is characterized first of all by backwardness. Historical backwardness does not, however, signify a simple reproduction of the development of advanced countries, with merely a delay of one or two centuries. It engenders an entirely new "combined" social formation in which the latest conquests of capitalist technique and structure root themselves into relations of feudal and pre-feudal barbarism, transforming and subjecting them and creating a peculiar interrelationship of classes. The same thing applies in the sphere of ideas. Precisely because of her historical tardiness, Russia turned out to be the only European country where Marxism as a doctrine and the Social Democracy as a party attained powerful development even before the bourgeois revolution. It is only natural that the problem of the correlation between the struggle for democracy and the struggle for socialism was submitted to the most profound theoretical analysis precisely in Russia.

Idealist-democrats, chiefly the Narodniks, refused superstitiously to recognize the impending revolution as bourgeois. They labelled it "democratic" seeking by means of a neutral political formula to mask its social content—not only from others but also from themselves. But in the struggle against Narodnikism, Plekhanov, the founder of Russian Marxism, established as long ago as the early eighties of the last century that Russia had no reason whatever to expect a privileged path of development, that like other "profane" nations, she would have to pass through the purgatory of capitalism and that precisely along this path she would acquire political freedom indispensable for the further struggle of the proletariat for socialism. Plekhanov not only separated the bourgeois revolution as a task from the socialist revolution—which he postponed to the indefinite future—but he depicted for each of these entirely different combinations of forces. Political freedom was to be achieved by the proletariat in alliance with the liberal bourgeoisie; after many decades and on a higher level of capitalist development, the proletariat would then carry out the socialist revolution in direct struggle against the bourgeoisie.

"To the Russian intellectual it always seems that to recognize our revolution as bourgeois is to discolor it, degrade it, debase it. . . . For the proletariat the struggle for political freedom and for the democratic republic in bourgeois society is simply a necessary stage in the struggle for the socialist revolution."

Monophysitic doctrines. These doctrines were condemned at the Third and Fourth Ecumenical Councils in the fifth century. Nestorianism denied the eternality of human nature of Christ and hence downgraded the significance of the Virgin Mother of God. Monophysitism denied Christ's human nature altogether. The differences between Roman Catholicism and Russian Orthodoxy, which also calls itself "Catholic," are trivial and mostly hierarchical. The split between these two branches of the Christian faith, which dates from 1054, had to do with the Byzantine (and Russian) Church's refusal to recognize the authority of the bishop of Rome, the Roman Catholic pope, as the supreme pontiff. Yet, the British Anglican Church broke away from Rome in the sixteenth century for largely the same reason. They also restored one of the key Orthodox practices, which Catholicism abandoned in the late Middle Ages—the married parish clergy.

Once one grasps how close Orthodoxy and Catholicism are in relation to the other Christian Churches, one has no trouble understanding why the fundamental outside cultural influences on Russia, besides the Greek and Balkan Orthodox Slavic, were from Catholic Europe. With the Ottoman conquest of Byzantium and the Balkans in the fifteenth century, they became almost totally European—even in church matters. In the eighteenth century, Russia moved from simply borrowing from Europe to contributing to it as an active member. Peter the Great, for example, inspired Frederick the Great of Prussia to take a personal interest in architecture.

In the political realm, early, pagan Russia (Rus) took its basic structures and ideas from Scandinavians. Riurik, the semilegendary founder of the Russian state, and his brothers and retainers were of the same Viking stock that emerged from the

"Marxists are absolutely convinced," he wrote in 1905, "of the bourgeois character of the Russian revolution. What does this mean? This means that those democratic transformations which have become indispensable for Russia do not, in and of themselves, signify the undermining of capitalism, the undermining of bourgeois rule, but on the contrary they clear the soil, for the first time and in a real way, for a broad and swift, for a European and not an Asiatic development of capitalism. They will make possible for the first time the rule of the bourgeoisie as a class. . . .

"We cannot leap over the bourgeois democratic framework of the Russian revolution," he insisted, "but we can extend this framework to a colossal degree." That is to say, we can create within bourgeois society much more favorable conditions for the future struggle of the proletariat. Within these limits Lenin followed Plekhanov. The bourgeois character of the revolution served both factions of the Russian Social Democracy as their starting point.

It is quite natural that under these conditions, Koba (Stalin) did not go in his propaganda beyond those popular formulas which constitute the common property of Bolsheviks as well as Mensheviks.

"The Constituent Assembly," he wrote in January 1905, "elected on the basis of equal, direct and secret universal suffrage—this is what we must now fight for! Only this Assembly will give us the democratic republic, so urgently needed by us for our struggle for socialism." The bourgeois republic as an arena for a protracted class struggle for the socialist goal—such is the perspective.

In 1907, i.e., after innumerable discussions in the press both in Petersburg and abroad and after a serious testing of theoretical prognoses in the experiences of the first revolution, Stalin wrote: "That our revolution is bourgeois, that it must conclude by destroying the feudal and not the capitalist order, that it can be crowned only by the democratic republic—on this, it seems, all are agreed in our party." Stalin spoke not of what the revolution begins with, but of what it ends with, and he limited it in advance and quite categorically to "only the democratic republic." We would seek in vain in his writings for even a hint of any perspective of a socialist revolution in connection with a democratic overturn. This remained his position even at the beginning of the February revolution in 1917 up to Lenin's arrival in Petersburg.

Source: Lev Trotsky, "The Character of the Russian Revolution," 1940, Lev Trotsky Internet Archive <http://www.marxists.org/archive/trotsky/works/1940/1940-russia.htm>.

north and shaped lands as distant as Normandy, England, and Sicily. The Byzantine contribution included some Roman notions of law and concepts of monarchy and tyranny that derived from classical Greece. The Russian state of Novgorod, one of Muscovy's main rivals until the late fifteenth century, was associated with the German Hanseatic League and had a rudimentary city-state democracy. Muscovy's monarchical structure, despite Mongol influences, had a host of similarities with contemporary European lands. In the late seventeenth century Russian political thought came under the direct influence of Europe. Starting with Peter the Great, who embarked on a long, far-reaching tour of Europe in 1698, Russia started to borrow entire institutions from Europe, such as Sweden's collegiate system of government, a precursor to the modern use of ministries. Catherine the Great completed the Europeanization of Russia's nobility, which Peter had begun. Enforced

Western standards of dress and taste complemented Peter's borrowing of court and aristocratic titles, such as *Graf*, the German equivalent of *count*. Alexander I copied France's ministries of state and military general staff, and Napoleon's civil code was a model for Russia's Law Code of 1833. This process intensified to the point that after a period of revolutionary disturbance in 1905–1906, Russia adopted a version of the Prussian 1850 constitution. German economic theory inspired Russian state industrialization policies in the 1880s and 1890s. German revolutionary theory, especially that developed by Karl Marx, provided the intellectual basis for much of Russia's socialist movement, including the most successful revolutionaries—Vladimir Lenin's Bolsheviks, who took power in 1917.

Before 1917 Russian nationalism and that of the minorities within its empire—also copied from Western movements—proved to be the most important rival revolutionary competition to the Marxists. Earlier, German Romantic nationalism had inspired Russia's Slavophiles and French utopian socialism. All of the communists' goals were those of Western visionaries, socialist and nonsocialist. Communist means were analogous to European fascism and Nazism, and they both inspired and were inspired by Western totalitarianism. The entire range of dissidence against the Soviet Russia regime, except for religious movements among Muslims, was Western in origin and content. Post-Soviet Russia has made major strides in developing Western-style capitalism and democracy, including legally protected private property and representative parliamentary government. In January 2003 it revived the thoroughly Western institution of trial by jury, which had also been in place between the tsarist government's judicial reform of 1864 and the Revolution of 1917. Although its government still has semi-authoritarian features at the turn of the twenty-first century, it is well on the path to further reform and liberalization. Russia has been and remains mostly Western.

–DAVID GOLDFRANK,
GEORGETOWN UNIVERSITY

Viewpoint:
No. What has been called Russia's Westernization was only a series of superficialities that have been unable to mask distinctly un-European patterns of culture, politics, tradition, and interests.

The *East* is a nebulous term in historical, geographical, and cultural studies. For the Ancient Greeks, the *East* was literally east of what was then Greece–hence the historic name *Anatolia* for present-day Turkey-in-Asia. Because of the Ottoman Turkish conquests, however, Europe's historic terms *Near East* and the *Eastern Question* applied to Greece, the Balkans, and Black Sea regions–hardly Asia from a modern point of view. Within the world of Christianity, the original core lands of the "Eastern (Orthodox) Church" included Greece, as well as Anatolia, Syria, Judaea, and Egypt. In political theory, "Eastern" or "Oriental" has often been coupled with the notion of "despotism." In modern times, communism has been considered an "Eastern" phenomenon, the *Communist East* being a common expression, often used to express the idea that the Soviet Union was a new version of "Oriental despotism." Russia's geography, stretching across Siberia to the Pacific and including historic steppe lands once dominated

by the Mongol Empire, is nearly two-thirds Asian. Russia's national religion is Eastern Orthodox Christianity. Russia's historic tsarist system fit despotic patterns. As Russia modernized, it created twentieth-century communism, which also represented despotism, and at the turn of the twenty-first century, post-Soviet Russia retains despotic features.

At first glance, Russia's Orthodoxy, as a branch of Christianity, might appear Western, but this is not really the case. Orthodoxy's insistence upon the sanctity of ancient traditions and its blend of mysticism and rationalism render it more akin to Eastern religions than to Roman Catholicism or Protestantism. The Orthodox hierarchy's historic deference to state power and rulers is also in many ways a direct consequence of its origins in the Byzantine Empire. The hesychastic system of breath-control prayer, which medieval Russian monks acquired from their Greek counterparts, was itself an Orthodox borrowing from Indian practices. The characteristic Russian notions of self-identity, developed by the Slavophile thinkers in the 1830s and 1840s and emblematized by such terms as the *Russian soul* or *Russian idea*, have as their core an affirmation of Orthodox traditions in direct opposition to the Catholic and Protestant West. This school of thought and later philosophical developments posited Russia as a messianic entity poised to lead the spiritual regeneration of a world dominated by a "decadent" West. Much of this thinking, it should be noted, found its way into communist notions of the rebirth and reshaping of man and society. Moreover, the second religion of Russia has been Islam since the conquest and incorporation of Kazan in 1552.

In the Kievan, late-Imperial, and post-Soviet periods, the Russian state has appeared similar to Western counterparts, but such appearances may be deceptive, hiding deeper structural divergences. Early Russia (then Rus) arose as a tribute-collecting realm, replacing the earlier steppe-Turkic Khazar Khanate centered in the lower Volga. The notion that the mass of subject peoples were tributary—with goods, money, and labor—to the ruling classes and their state, was present from the start and barely gave way to notions of participatory citizenship in the late empire before communism reimposed labor obligations on most of the population. As state power, taxation, and labor conscription developed in the Mongol period and the Muscovite tsardom, so did the collective responsibility of villagers and townsmen for obligations. By the late 1500s, most Russians were tied down to their domiciles and service to the state. If the nobility and townsmen acquired some real liberties after 1762, the bulk of Russians who were peasants, even after emancipation from serfdom in the 1860s, remained bound to their villages down to 1907, when their obligations were abolished after revolutionary events. Peasants—the vast majority of the Russian population—remained subject to corporal punishment until 1904. The state dominated commerce and industry into the late eighteenth century and remained powerful in the latter down to 1917. Typically for a despotism, Russian commerce and industry did not develop so dynamically as those of the nondespotic West or Japan. The structure of this state being despotic, even without the conscription-manned waterworks of the classical Oriental despotisms of Egypt, Mesopotamia, India, and China, wielders of supreme state power, such as Ivan IV (the Terrible) and Peter the Great, realized the potential for either unlimited, paranoiac, vindictive personal tyranny or the massive mobilization of people and resources for construction projects and warfare.

Theoreticians of despotism often neglect the social and economic value to villagers of their strong communal structures, the traditional prop of the system, but the Russian peasants showed such understanding both during the Revolution of 1917 and after the collapse of the Soviet Union in 1991. In 1917 they appropriated all land for the communal ownership of villages. Since 1991 their descendants have refused to decollectivize agricultural land, and trade in it remains illegal at the beginning of the twenty-first century. Communism was, in the eyes of the "father" of Russian Marxism, Georgii Plekhanov, an "Asiatic restoration," and the leader of the Bolshevik Revolution, Vladimir Lenin, himself recognized that the parasitic tsarist bureaucracy would survive the Revolution, just as the Soviet bureaucracy largely survived the fall of communism. Under the communist regime in the Soviet Union, the degree of state control over labor, property, and the economy surpassed that of any great historic "Oriental despotism," while Josef Stalin's personal tyranny dwarfed that of the most vicious of despots. The post-Soviet Russian transition has created a hybrid polity with similarities to non-Western real and quasi-dictatorial regimes, which use state power over economic interests and employ the press to control the people, and where the alternative to public authority is not a vigorous civil society but a multitude of little

despotisms represented by criminal gangs, the monopolies they enforce, and the tribute (protection money) they collect through threats of violence. Concepts of individual rights, private property, and representative government, all the staple of Western government, society, and philosophy, were long absent from Russia and are only in their infancy there at the present time. Russia has been and remains mostly Eastern.

–DAVID GOLDFRANK,
GEORGETOWN UNIVERSITY

References

Perry Anderson, *Lineages of the Absolutist State* (New York: Schocken, 1974).

David J. Dallin and Boris I. Nicolaevsky, *Forced Labor in Soviet Russia* (New Haven: Yale University Press, 1947).

Steven Handelman, *Comrade Criminal: Russia's New Mafiya* (New Haven: Yale University Press, 1995).

Steven G. Marks, *How Russia Shaped the Modern World: From Art to Anti-Semitism, Ballet to Bolshevism* (Princeton: Princeton University Press, 2003).

Richard Pipes, *Russia under the Bolshevik Regime* (New York: Knopf, 1994).

Pipes, *Russia under the Old Regime* (New York: Scribner, 1974).

Donald Treadgold, *The West in Russia and China: Religious and Secular Thought in Modern Times,* volume 1, *Russia, 1472-1917* (Cambridge: Cambridge University Press, 1973).

Andrzej Walicki, *Marxism and the Leap to the Kingdom of Freedom: The Rise and Fall of the Communist Utopia* (Stanford, Cal.: Stanford University Press, 1995).

Karl Wittfogel, *Oriental Despotism: A Comparative Study of Total Power* (New Haven: Yale University Press, 1957).

Melvin C. Wren, *The Western Impact upon Tsarist Russia* (Huntington, N.Y.: Robert E. Krieger, 1971).

RUSSIA AS PART OF THE WEST

SHORT TWENTIETH CENTURY

Is it appropriate to view the period 1914 to 1991 as a "short twentieth century"?

Viewpoint: Yes. The outbreak of World War I and the collapse of the Soviet Union mark a distinct historical period during which colonialism and empire building gave way to liberal democracy and capitalism.

Viewpoint: No. Viewing the period 1914 to 1991 as a short twentieth century ignores important continuities in European warfare, diplomacy, and politics.

Traditional historians of modern Europe have found it useful to describe the period from the outbreak of the French Revolution in 1789 to the outbreak of World War I in 1914 as "the long nineteenth century," the implication being that events between those two dates had more in common than with what came before and after. A more recent argument suggests that it might be equally apt to conceptualize the period from 1914 to the collapse of the Soviet Union in 1991 in the same terms. As one argument suggests, the political extremities of communism and fascism fell neatly into this period, as did both world wars, the defining conflicts of the twentieth century. Yet, as a counter-argument suggests, long-term continuities at both ends of the chronology blur the distinctions that the two dates suggest.

Viewpoint:
Yes. The outbreak of World War I and the collapse of the Soviet Union mark a distinct historical period during which colonialism and empire building gave way to liberal democracy and capitalism.

Scholars have always had difficulty defining historical periods. Eric Hobsbawm's definition of a "short twentieth century," which began with the outbreak of World War I in 1914 and ended with the dissolution of the Soviet Union in 1991, is no exception. Objections can be raised to either of these events defining the end points of an historical era. One may argue that political, economic, cultural, and technological developments in the fifty years before the

outbreak of World War I were inseparable from defining the significance of the event. Likewise, one can easily exaggerate the importance of the collapse of the Soviet Union. Francis Fukuyama, for instance, argued that this event signaled "the end of history," the total victory of liberal democracy and capitalism on a global scale. The terrorist attacks of 11 September 2001 cannot be written off as a minor aberration to this trend. Still, the historical importance of developments during this period outweighs the fact that there are trends that overlap both dates.

The choice of World War I as the beginning of the short twentieth century has drawn the most criticism. One may argue, for example, that political liberalism, which began to flourish in Western Europe and America in the second half of the nineteenth century, was central to understanding the significance of the war and the years that followed it. Certainly, the development of mass politics, the rise of a politically articulate middle class, and a literate print culture during this time cannot be denied. The trend toward greater political participation, which led to universal male enfranchisement, was crucial to mobilizing the populations of the warring powers to engage in the first great total war. One must also admit that the successful protests by women for the right to vote in the years immediately following the war culminated this process.

Nevertheless, the war initiated a crisis in liberalism that would not be overcome for the rest of the short twentieth century. The estimated thirty-seven million casualties in the war touched all of the belligerent populations and turned their enthusiasm at the outset of the war into a deep sense of alienation from world events. For the French, British, and Americans, there was an overriding conviction that the price of confronting nondemocratic governments was too high. Meanwhile, nondemocratic governments in the form of Bolshevik Russia, fascist Italy, Nazi Germany, and authoritarian regimes throughout Eastern Europe and in Japan thrived. The reaction in the West was predictable. Appeasement, not confrontation, was the diplomatic response of the day.

The popularity of nondemocratic governments was largely confirmed by the events of World War II and the Cold War that followed it. Despite the emphasis by British and American historians on the importance of the Battle of Britain (1940) and D-Day (1944), victory would not have been possible without the participation of the Soviet Union and the communist resistance in Europe. Just as Josef Stalin's ruthless leadership and the great sacrifices of the Red Army overcame the bulk of the German Wehrmacht, the communist partisans in Italy, Yugoslavia, France, Greece, and other Eastern European and east Asian states were central to the Allied strategy. Even though Stalin sought to suppress many of these movements immediately after the war, it was no mistake that communist takeovers soon occurred in China, Yugoslavia, and other nations without the presence of Soviet bayonets. The failure of the Americans to defeat communism in North Korea, Cuba, and South Vietnam proved that the world's greatest economic power had definite international limitations. These defeats, and Soviet propaganda about the "success" of planned communist economies, encouraged others outside the Western world to look to nonliberal models as their key to modernization.

Many of the Western political economies were dependent upon colonialism, a system that had begun to crack after the outbreak of World War I. The warring powers mobilized all the manpower and material resources they could from their colonies. The price for the colonies' sacrifices was a call for home rule, a demand that the British, French, and Americans could not ignore. The Germans were forced to give up their colonies completely as a result of losing World War I. The victors were able to absorb some of these lands, but only temporarily. In the aftermath of World War II, British, French, Dutch, Belgian, and Portuguese colonial holdings dwindled to the point of extinction. The reluctance of these powers to give up these lands only helped spur native insurgents to embrace nonliberal forms of government. Eurocentrism was on the wane.

Further, one may also look at economic and technological developments as an important factor before and after 1914. Admittedly, industrial development, especially from 1870 onward, unified and expanded world markets as never before. Mass production of cheap consumer goods and the transportation of formerly unavailable bulk goods by rail and steamship had a huge impact on the lives of Western middle and working classes, not to mention the foreign populations who provided much of the raw material for factory products. Governments could achieve greater power across the globe by harnessing the trends and advancing further technological developments.

Yet, one can only argue with difficulty that these trends in the world economy continued unabated in the interwar period. Although one might point to the American boom in the 1920s, west European countries such as France and Germany encountered major economic hardships after the war. Britain, too, recovered slowly, its economy picking up by the 1930s only with massive government spending. Soon, the crash of the American stock market in October 1929 would overturn economies throughout the world. For the first time a global economic crisis would threaten the existence of the capitalist system itself. Increasingly, governments would be forced to act in a way contrary to the logic of classical liberal thinkers. Social welfare for the masses and government intervention in the economy would become a political necessity for any regime to survive. The seemingly greater efficiency of totalitarian governments to meet these needs appeared to many as the "wave of the future." Newly developed media, such as radio and film, helped to propagate these ideas.

One may also question the overall importance of the collapse of the Soviet Union in 1991. In particular, one may doubt that it signaled the victory of liberal democracy and capitalism as the model for all countries to embrace. Although nascent democratic movements and

THE GREAT WAR

Many people consider World War I to be a defining moment in the twentieth century. At the time it was the most destructive conflict in human history, with more people killed in that war alone than in all the European wars over the previous eight centuries combined.

Country	Total Mobilized	Dead	Wounded	Prisoners & Missing	Total Casualties
Allied Powers					
Russia	12,000,000	1,700,000	4,950,000	2,500,000	9,150,000
France	8,410,000	1,357,800	4,266,000	537,000	6,160,800
British Empire	8,904,467	908,371	2,090,212	191,652	3,190,235
Italy	5,615,000	650,000	947,000	600,000	2,197,000
United States	4,355,000	126,000	234,300	4,500	364,800
Japan	800,000	300	907	3	1,210
Romania	750,000	335,706	120,000	80,000	535,706
Serbia	707,343	45,000	133,148	152,958	331,106
Belgium	267,000	13,716	44,686	34,659	93,061
Greece	230,000	5,000	21,000	1,000	17,000
Portugal	100,000	7,222	13,751	12,318	33,291
Montenegro	50,000	3,000	10,000	7,000	20,000
Total	**42,188,810**	**5,152,115**	**12,831,004**	**4,121,090**	**22,104,209**
Central Powers					
Germany	11,000,000	1,773,700	4,216,058	1,152,800	7,142,558
Austria-Hungary	7,800,000	1,200,000	3,620,000	2,200,000	7,020,000
Turkey	2,850,000	325,000	400,000	250,000	975,000
Bulgaria	1,200,000	87,500	152,390	27,029	266,919
Total	**22,850,000**	**3,386,200**	**8,388,448**	**3,629,829**	**15,404,477**
Grand Total	**65,038,810**	**8,538,315**	**21,219,452**	**7,750,919**	**37,508,686**

Source: "Casualties: First World War," *Encyclopedia of the First World War* <http://www.spartacus.schoolnet.co.uk/FWWdeaths.htm>.

capitalist reforms took root throughout much of Eastern Europe and Russia, anti-Western and xenophobic nationalist sentiment soon resurged. As the recent electoral success of the reformed communists of Poland, Hungary, and Romania reveals, many people long for the social services they had under the previous communist regime as they have felt the brunt of liberal austerity measures. Former communist apparatchiks often blamed outside interference as the cause behind the troubles, and some, like Slobodan Milosevic, sought to blame the "enemy within."

The ongoing crisis in the Middle East also demonstrates that the Western model of development is not always in vogue outside of Europe and the United States. Much of the Islamic world, including many key regional allies of the United States such as Egypt and Saudi Arabia, resist adopting democracy and the capitalist way of life. Indeed, the international fallout from the terrorist attacks of 2001 has shown that many Muslims see the West as a threat not only politically and economically but culturally as well.

However, one must point out that the end of the Soviet Union did mark the end of empire as a means of forcefully holding peoples together in a single polity. The breakup of the Soviet Union into the various republics that constituted it revealed that the actions of the central government, which ignored local interests, could no longer function. Moreover, Western corporate powers and political interests have globalized to the point where they can work with the former Soviet republics in spite of Moscow's protests. Increased Western ties to Eurasian oil, the spread of Western consumer goods, Anglo-American rock music and youth culture, and active American missionary work are illustrations this trend.

Overall, the "short twentieth century" is a durable concept. Though one cannot understand the overall significance of the outbreak of war in 1914 without examining global developments before it, the event did indeed initiate the crisis of liberalism in both its economic and political forms. The end of colonial rule by the once mighty nations of Europe preceded the fall of the Soviet Union, the last great multiethnic empire. Liberal democracy and capitalism are still disputed throughout the world, both in Russia and Eastern Europe as well as in the Middle East. Yet, new opportunities for success or failure have emerged since the day that Marxist-Leninism died.

—YORK NORMAN,
GEORGETOWN UNIVERSITY

Viewpoint:
No. Viewing the period 1914 to 1991 as a short twentieth century ignores important continuities in European warfare, diplomacy, and politics.

Describing the twentieth century as an essentially "short" seventy-seven-year period beginning with the outbreak of World War I in 1914 and ending with the collapse of the Soviet Union in 1991 is a simplification that both belies important continuities and ignores notable breaks. In many ways 1914 did not mark the beginning of a new period in European history. The industrialization of warfare, the factor identified most directly with the conflict, was already under way and had been experienced and commented upon for at least half a century. The American Civil War (1861–1865), the Franco-Prussian War (1870–1871), the Boer War (1899–1902), and the Russo-Japanese War (1904–1905) all included new weaponry, tactics, home-front mobilization, propaganda, and resource management commonly regarded as World War I innovations. Machine guns, barbed wire, trench warfare, compulsory military drafts, demonizing the enemy, and orienting whole economies toward conflict were not new in 1914. The nature of government and society had also begun to change meaningfully in earlier decades. The powers and responsibilities of the modern bureaucratic state were already on the rise once the requisite developments in communications and information technology had occurred. World War I may have accelerated this tendency toward coordination and organization, but as soon as censuses, railroads, telegraphs, mechanized printing, mass literacy, and other technological innovations became available—all in the

nineteenth century—they were employed without reluctance.

The Great War did even less to transform international politics, for it did not signal an end to the centuries-old tradition of European great power diplomacy. Despite the conflict's unprecedented destructive scale, it was basically a struggle between alliances of the same European powers—Britain, France, Germany/Prussia, Austria-Hungary/Habsburg Empire, Italy/Piedmont-Sardinia, the Ottoman Empire, and Russia—that had been major players since the seventeenth century. Their basic motivations for going to war in 1914 were unchanged: the desire for territorial and economic expansion (Germany, Austria-Hungary, Russia, and Italy); the defense of existing strategic interests and security requirements (Britain, Russia, and Austria-Hungary); and the hope of regaining territory lost in previous conflicts (France, Italy, and the Ottoman Empire). So, too, was the result of the war: a major international peace conference. Like all of its predecessors since the Peace of Westphalia in 1648, the 1919 Paris Peace Conference codified the punishment of the losers, legitimized the aggrandizement of the victors, and established an international system to manage the new status quo. The so-called New Diplomacy, identified with U.S. president Woodrow Wilson and centered on political democratization, national self-determination, multilateral disarmament, and transparency in international relations, failed to inspire conventional European leaders, who either disregarded those concepts altogether or used them as new tools in their old game of great power politics. Indeed, Wilson left the conference prematurely out of frustration, and the United States declined to play a major role in defending Europe's heavily traditional peace settlement.

If post-1914 European war and diplomacy continued to reflect pre-1914 origins and patterns, developments in and since 1991 have represented in many ways broad continuity with earlier decades. The year 1991 (or, more properly and adding still more ambiguity, the period 1989–1991) did see the collapse of the Soviet Union and the definitive end of its hegemonic power over Eastern Europe, but movement toward these events had already been pronounced. Communist ideology, which defined the Soviet state and was the guiding principle of all of its satellites, was long past its prime when the Soviet Union finally fell. Having peaked at the end of World War II, its prestige in Europe tumbled as postwar recovery eliminated material want and spiritual doubt. The Soviet Union's invasions of Hungary (1956), Czechoslovakia (1968), and Afghanistan (1979), sponsorship of authoritarian communist regimes, massive mili-

SHORT TWENTIETH CENTURY

tary, bellicose rhetoric, and calls to armed struggle to its ideological confederates proved to the world that communism could only win through force and coercion and strongly suggested that it would collapse without them. That realization discredited the Soviet government in the eyes of most of the rest of the world, including not only its World War II enemies but also its wartime allies, previously neutral nations, much of the noncommunist Third World, other alienated and resentful communist governments, its own dissatisfied population, and, finally, reformist members of its elite who, despite their continuing commitment to communism, introduced political and economic reforms that totally destroyed the underpinnings of their rule. Long before 1991, communism had lost its debate with capitalism and liberal democracy, and its highest political expression, the Soviet state, had irrevocably become what it had always feared: an isolated pariah surrounded by a world committed either to its permanent isolation or its ultimate destruction.

The collapse of the Soviet Union in 1991, moreover, did not solve the continuing problem of defining Russia's role in international politics. Although it officially shed its communist ideology and lost direct political control over the defunct Soviet empire, its nuclear arsenal, conventional military, influence in many former Soviet republics, and pretensions to world power status all survived. Russia's diplomatic interven-

tion on behalf of Yugoslavia in 1992–2000 and Iraq in 2002–2003, continuing military presence throughout the former Soviet Union, and attempts to challenge NATO expansion in Eastern Europe indicated that the fall of communism was not accompanied by the complete disappearance of Russia's great power ambitions. Only recently has Moscow realized, and then only partly, that modernization and long-term domestic stability depend on Western, and especially American, goodwill, favorable economic and financial relationships with the rest of the world, and major military reform. None of these goals can be attained without Russia's transition to regional power status. Given the country's reluctance to adopt that role for more than a decade after 1991, that year's usefulness as a watershed is limited.

Western Europe's history is even less connected with the year 1991, which had little impact on the region's long progress toward political and economic integration. The development of defensive alliances, limited multinational organizations, and the European Economic Community (EEC) in the late 1940s and 1950s emerged in direct response to the outcome of World War II. Finding in integration a lasting solution to conflicts between nation-states and an alternative to those states' decline as individual great powers, Europe's diplomatic landscape was transformed. Historical competitors eliminated economic barriers, ended arms races, and abandoned political antagonisms to work for a common future. In geographic terms Europe's emerging unity created a peaceful whole unseen since the Roman Empire—a polity that was easily the antithesis of Europe in the thousand years before 1945.

Although the EEC did not develop into the more comprehensive European Union (EU) until 1992, the event, accomplished by that year's Maastricht Treaty, was the result of decades of conceptualization and years of careful negotiation and planning. The ideas and motivations behind it developed relatively early in the postwar era and unfolded largely in isolation from the events of 1991—events that few politicians or scholars anticipated in any case, and for which even fewer had planned. The timing was purely coincidental. So, too, was the introduction of the euro, the common currency adopted by most EU member states in 1999—once again after a long period of negotiation and planning unconnected to the events of 1991. A projected EU military force, common EU defense and foreign policies, and a European constitution are the next likely steps on a path that began long after 1914 but long before 1991. The collapse of communism was merely an auspicious backdrop to the forward motion of these achievements.

Expanding the scope of European unity was also largely unrelated to the events of 1991. Broadening the EEC's membership had been one of the original members' initial goals since the 1950s, and the organization added three members (Britain, Ireland, Denmark) to its original six (France, West Germany, Italy, Belgium, the Netherlands, Luxembourg) in 1973, and three more (Spain, Portugal, Greece) in 1986. The events of 1989–1991 did increase the number of potential candidates for membership but nevertheless failed to influence the timing of their accession. Austria, Sweden, and Finland—Cold War neutral nations with the requisite political and economic institutions in place—only entered the EU in 1995 (Norway, an integral part of the Western alliance, rejected EU mem-

bership at the same time). Eight former communist bloc nations—Poland, Hungary, the Czech Republic, Slovenia, Slovakia, Lithuania, Latvia, and Estonia—as well as Malta and Cyprus, remained out until 2004, a full thirteen years after the collapse of the Soviet Union. Romania, Bulgaria, Albania, the former Yugoslavian states save Slovenia, non-Baltic former Soviet republics, and Turkey still await invitations to join, leaving the 2004 expansion only a partial measure, large though it may have been. Inclusion in NATO, now redefined as the West's generic guarantor of peace and security, was also a relatively slow process. Poland, Hungary, and the Czech Republic joined in 1999, while a broader second round of NATO expansion—to bring in Lithuania, Latvia, Estonia, Slovenia, Slovakia, Romania, and Bulgaria—was also completed only in 2004.

Identifying 1991, or even 2004, as the year in which Eastern Europe was integrated or reunited (if it had ever been united) with the West is as unsatisfactory as identifying 1914 as the year in which Europe left one era for another. For most practical purposes, it would appear more reasonable either to speak of Europe in pre-1945 and post-1945 terms or look at its history as a long, unfolding tale than to imagine a "short twentieth century."

–PAUL DU QUENOY,
GEORGETOWN UNIVERSITY

References

Francis Fukuyama, *The End of History and the Last Man* (New York: Free Press, 1992).

Eric Hobsbawm, *The Age of Extremes: A History of the World, 1914–1991* (New York: Pantheon, 1994).

Jay Winter, Geoffrey Parker, and Mary R. Habeck, eds., *The Great War and the Twentieth Century* (New Haven: Yale University Press, 2000).

SPANISH CIVIL WAR

Was the Spanish Civil War a struggle to safeguard democracy from the threat of fascist tyranny?

Viewpoint: Yes. While the causes were complex, the Spanish Civil War was reduced to an ideological struggle between the Left and the Right.

Viewpoint: No. The Spanish Civil War resulted from the Nationalists' attempt to impose order on a country paralyzed by anarchy and to replace a Republican government directed by communists who were just as tyrannical as the fascists.

After a prolonged period of repressive dictatorship, Spain overthrew its monarchy in 1931. The Republican government that rose in its place faced many pressing problems, few of which were solved in a lasting and decisive way. The election of a Left-wing Popular Front government in early 1936 antagonized many of the Republic's growing number of opponents into action. On 17 July of that year rebellious army units began a Right-wing coup d'état against the government in Madrid. Eventually coming under the command of General Francisco Franco, the insurrection turned into a civil war that the Republican forces seemed more and more likely to lose. By March 1939 Madrid had fallen to the rebels, and Spain settled into a dictatorship that lasted until Franco's death in 1975.

The Spanish Civil War captured international attention on a grand scale. Beginning at a time when fascism and authoritarianism were in the ascendancy throughout Europe, the battlefields of Spain appeared to be proving grounds for the political Left's ability to contain the new ideologies of the Right. Thousands of sympathizers poured into Spain to defend the Republic, while fascist Germany and Italy aided the Right-wing rebels. The war was frequently seen as a test case of freedom versus tyranny and an important precursor to World War II.

There are, however, other perspectives on the Spanish Civil War. A growing counterargument impugns the nature of the Spanish Republic, suggesting that it was a weak entity prone to the use of terror and to increasing reliance on indigenous communists and their sponsors in Moscow. Franco's forces may not have been as saintly as rebel propaganda portrayed them to be, but the flaws of the Republic seemed to tarnish its democratic image, weaken its claims to legitimacy, and undermine its pretensions to moral superiority. To supporters of this argument, the civil war looked more like a contest of two objectionable regimes battling for supremacy rather than a simple tale of good and evil.

Viewpoint:
Yes. While the causes were complex, the Spanish Civil War was reduced to an ideological struggle between the Left and the Right.

Like most major conflicts, the Spanish Civil War (1936–1939) had many causes. Inefficient patterns of landholding, an impoverished and thoroughly disenfranchised workforce, a nervous elite intent upon maintaining order, a Catholic Church accustomed to holding significant wealth and social influence, a top-heavy and distrustful military, strong regional autonomy movements, and a government uncertain of how and whether to achieve reform all helped destabilize the country and contributed to the outbreak of war. Yet, from the outset, the complexity of the Spanish Civil War was subsumed beneath a rhetoric that depicted the fighting not so much as the outcome of many political, social, economic, and cultural problems that had long festered in Spain, but rather as a simple black-and-white battle of democracy (or in some cases, communism) versus fascism, freedom versus tyranny, and good versus evil.

The war began when a small group of high-ranking military officers attempted to overthrow the Spanish government in July 1936. That action was only the spark, however, and the true origins of the war—the causes that led those officers to attempt the coup in the first place—have been the subject of considerable historiographic debate. Historians have located the roots of the Spanish Civil War in different historical moments: in the attempts to modernize the Spanish economic and political system in the late nineteenth and early twentieth centuries; in the disentailments of Church land in the early 1800s; and even in the landholding patterns established during the Reconquista (the Reconquest, a series of military campaigns that liberated the Iberian Peninsula from Moorish rule), which ended in 1492. Others have argued that the actions of the Republican government that came to power in 1931 doomed Spain to war, though these same historians—like Spaniards at the time—often disagree over whether the Republic went too far in its reforms.

The reasons for the war, then, are tremendously complex. Yet, from the outset, this complexity was lost in the polarizing rhetoric of the "sides." Within Spain, supporters of the Republic (known collectively as Loyalists or Republicans) included regional autonomists, professional middle classes sympathetic to a centrist liberalism, and most of the industrialized and agricultural working classes, many of whom were members of socialist and anarchist trade unions. Supporters of the insurgents (known as Nationalists) included the landowning elite, industrialists, large parts of the military, the Catholic Church, and the *Falange Española* (Spanish Phalanx or Spanish Fascist Party). To Loyalists, the rebels seemed intent upon replacing Spain's fledgling democracy with an authoritarian government and protecting the privileges of those elite groups that had long profited at the expense of the common people. To Nationalists, supporters of the Republic were intent on destroying the traditions and heritage that had made Spain great, and they were plunging the nation into chaos. When anarchist and socialist groups seized upon the outbreak of war as the moment to initiate revolutionary activity—establishing both agricultural and industrial collectives, taking control of public utilities in Barcelona, and abolishing many forms of hierarchy—this polarization became even more stark. Now the motivation to fight was greater; not only were Loyalists protecting their nascent representative government, but they were also ushering in an age of true liberation from the social, political, and economic restraints that had oppressed the Spanish working classes for centuries. Many Nationalists, on the other hand, looked at such revolutionary activity and saw a country jumping headlong into "godless" and bloody communism.

Propaganda fed the polemic. Graphic posters and tracts that demonized the enemy first appeared during World War I, but propaganda was produced on an unprecedented scale in the Spanish Civil War. New technologies widened the range of media; propaganda included not only posters and pamphlets but also radio, photomontage, and sound cinema. Indeed, so crucial had persuading the hearts and minds of the Spanish citizenry become to the war effort that both sides dedicated considerable resources to producing propaganda, treating it as yet another weapon. On the Republican side, for example, the *Confederación Nacional del Trabajo–Federación Anarquista Ibérica* (National Confederation of Labor-Iberian Anarchist Federation, CNT–FAI) turned out posters that showed virile peasants suffocated by the "snake" of fascism, while Nationalists depicted their leader, General Francisco Franco, as a noble medieval crusader, his image superimposed on a map of Spain that was clawed to pieces by bloodthirsty "Reds."

This kind of binary rhetoric was in many ways a typical by-product of war. What transformed the Spanish Civil War into more than a conflict featuring nasty propaganda—and turned it into a battle over the grand ideas of "freedom" on one hand and "tyranny" on the other—was the international context in which it took place.

1936 poster of the
communist Popular
Front in Spain during
the Spanish Civil War

(Salmer, Barcelona)

To many observers worried about the advance of fascism on the European continent, the war in Spain could not be separated from tensions building elsewhere. To many, the war indeed came to look like a "dress rehearsal" for larger conflicts that loomed ahead.

For supporters of the Republic, it was easy to link Nationalist forces with the larger international threat of fascism. Franco drew support from the *Falange*. Forcibly merged with another extreme Right-wing party, the monarchist *Tradicion Española*, it became the sole legal party within the Nationalist zone. Its leader, José Antonio Primo de Rivera, was executed in a Republican prison on 20 November 1936 and became a martyr of the Nationalist cause. More significant was the aid that Franco received from both Italy and Germany. Franco and his liaisons approached both Italian dictator Benito Mussolini and German leader Adolf Hitler within the first few days of the military uprising, and arranged the transfer of ships, weapons, planes, advisers, and troops. Indeed, Italian and German airplanes helped airlift Nationalist troops across the Mediterranean from Spanish Morocco, ensuring that the rebellion reached mainland Spain. The support continued until the end of the war: Italian Blackshirts fought in the Battle of Guadalajara (8–18 March 1937), and the German Condor Legion, an elite air unit, bombed the militarily unimportant (but, for the Basques, symbolically sacred) town of Guernica (26 April 1937), killing hundreds in the first purposeful airplane attack on a civilian population. It was easy for Republican supporters to look at Franco's army and see international fascism not only at work, but as the driving force of the war itself. Some historians concur: eminent scholar Paul Preston states that "Mussolini and Hitler turned a coup d'etat gone wrong into a bloody and prolonged civil war."

The Western powers were far less eager to enter the conflict than Germany or Italy. France and Great Britain led an effort to prevent other nations from intervening in the Spanish Civil War, and the resulting Non-Intervention Agreement (August 1936)—which was signed by Germany, Italy, and the Soviet Union but flouted by all three—effectively prevented the Republic from receiving war matériel it desperately needed. The one major power that came to the aid of the Loyalists was the Union of Soviet Socialist Republics (U.S.S.R.). Although reluctant to involve itself at first, the Soviet Union began contributing aid slowly in August 1936 and then signaled its full-fledged assistance in October by delivering planes, tanks, and weapons in exchange for the transfer of Spanish gold reserves.

Soviet aid did not come without strings attached. Certainly, the Soviets used their status as sole supplier to the Republic to win both military and political influence within Spain. The anarchist, socialist, and *Partido Obrero e Unificacion Marxista* (Party of Marxist Unification, POUM) militias were suppressed in favor of a unified People's Army, and positions within the government, eventually including the premiership itself, went to communists or communist sympathizers. Some historians have suggested that these tactics reveal that Soviet leader Josef Stalin had imperialist goals in mind with Spain. Yet, others have used recently released archival material to argue that Stalin instead was attempting to bring the democracies into a collaborative effort against fascism. Certainly the propaganda disseminated internationally by the newly organized Ministry of Propaganda on the Republican side, as well as outright appeals by Soviet diplomats and Spanish politicians, portrayed the Loyalists as defenders of democracy and the Nationalists as fascists. Although some may see Stalin's rhetorical strategy as a ruse, Soviet planes and tanks certainly played a critical role in the Republican defense of Madrid in the fall of 1936, for example, and most historians agree that without Soviet aid, the Spanish Republic would have collapsed long before 1939.

Equally influential in promulgating the view of the war as a fight for freedom were the international volunteers who came to the aid of the Republic. Drawn by a mix of political commitment and romantic idealism, sixty thousand men and women from some fifty countries came to Spain, often at great risk to themselves, to take up arms in defense of the Republic. Many were drawn by reports of the revolutionary activity in Spain; British novelist George Orwell described as "queer and moving" the days in Barcelona when even shops and cafés were collectivized and everyone, dressed in working-class clothes, greeted each other familiarly. His sentiment that "I recognized it as a state of affairs worth fighting for" is one that would have been echoed by many a volunteer. Others came because they were worried about fascism in their own countries or elsewhere and believed that Spain was the place to stop it in its tracks.

Most of the volunteers were at least sympathetic toward, if not actual card-carrying members of, the Communist International, and it was the Comintern that organized the International Brigades, helping smuggle volunteers into Spain and training them at a base in Albacete. Although some, such as Orwell (who fought in a POUM militia), became disillusioned with the Communist Party's suppression of leftist dissident parties and unions, the vast majority of volunteers were less concerned by charges that the U.S.S.R. was attempting to gain control of Spain than they were eager to join forces with the one major power willing to do something for the Republic. It is true that the training at Albacete included long hours of political indoctrination, overseen by a commissar whose job was to ensure that all Brigadiers toed the Party's ideological line and whose tactics, it must be said, included violence. It is also true that for many members of the International Brigades, any displeasure felt over the Comintern's strategies was outweighed by a larger sense of purpose. American volunteer John Tisa, for example, described the hours spent in political "training" as a "sensible recognition by the army and the government that if men and women were being asked to lay down their lives . . . they should at least have the right to know the reasons."

Not all foreigners who participated in Spain's Civil War did so by taking up arms, however. A remarkably large number of artists, writers, filmmakers, and photographers produced work specifically designed to sway opinion regarding the war. Although a few writers, such as American poet Ezra Pound and English novelist Evelyn Waugh, supported the Nationalists, the vast majority sided with the Republicans, and it is to them as well that the representation of the war as a battle of freedom against tyranny can be traced. From Ernest Hemingway's novel *For Whom the Bell Tolls* (1940) to Joris Ivens's movie *The Spanish Earth* (1937) to Pablo Picasso's gripping painting *Guernica* (1937), artistic production was enlisted in the Republican cause. The introduction to the pamphlet *Authors Take Sides on the Spanish War* (1937) summed up the sense of political urgency that many artists felt:

> This is the question we would have you answer: "Are you for, or are you against Franco and fascism? Are you for or are you against the legal government and the people of Republican Spain?" For it is impossible any longer to take no side.

Many artists and writers agreed; blurring the line between art and propaganda, their work reflected this mandate to "take sides."

If some current scholars continue to see the Spanish Civil War as a fight between freedom and tyranny, it is in large part because of what happened after the Republic's surrender. Just a few short months after Franco marched triumphantly through the streets of Madrid, Hitler's tanks rolled through Poland, and the Allied forces could no longer afford to follow a policy of appeasement that was already in effect in July 1936. For veterans of the International Brigades (many of whom went home to be accused of "premature anti-Fascism") the outbreak of World War II must have come as a painful and tragic vindication of their belief in the dangers of advancing fascism. Franco's government kept the hatreds of the Civil War alive, imprisoning and

executing those suspected of fighting for the Republic, publishing works that presented the Civil War as a Christian crusade against barbaric communism, and turning the date of the Nationalist victory (and Republican surrender) into a public holiday. At the same time, opponents of the regime outside Spain could find easy evidence of Franco's continuing tyranny: concentration camps, years of starvation, autarkic economic policies, suppression of regional cultures, and censorship. It comes as no surprise, then, that much of the historical writings on the war supports this polemic. Within Franco's Spain, all historical accounts had to agree with the regime's depiction of the war; historians such as Eduardo Comín Colomer blamed the war on Soviet machinations, while the more scholarly Ricardo de la Cierva presented it as the result of leftist extremism. Outside Spain, a liberal historiography that began with Gerald Brenan's *The Spanish Labyrinth: An Account of the Social and Political Background of the Civil War* (1943) and continued with Gabriel Jackson's now classic *The Spanish Republic and the Civil War, 1931–1939* (1965) depicted the Republican loss as tragedy. Other scholars, such as Stanley Payne and Hugh Thomas, attempted to present the war more objectively and to that end focused on the failings of the Second Republic, but their work was happily and publicly embraced by Nationalist officials and thus enlisted as well in the polemic. Only in recent historical writing has the influence of this binary ideology begun to diminish, as scholars shift their focus from laying blame to attempting to understand the complexities of the war and its rhetorical legacy.

–LISA ABEND,
OBERLIN COLLEGE

Viewpoint:
No. The Spanish Civil War resulted from the Nationalists' attempt to impose order on a country paralyzed by anarchy and to replace a Republican government directed by communists who were just as tyrannical as the fascists.

Almost all aspects of the Spanish Civil War (1936–1939), including its causes and ultimate significance, have been subjects of hot debate. If one author claims that the war was a struggle between freedom and tyranny, another maintains that it was fundamentally a Soviet attempt to export its brand of communism to Western Europe, and a third argues that it was at heart a social revolution. How can one event produce

CARRY ON BOYS

In a 29 July 1937 letter to his family, Harry Fisher describes the bravery of his comrades in the Abraham Lincoln Brigade, a group of U.S. volunteers who served on the Republican side in the Spanish Civil War:

What I want to do in this letter is to write some incidents about some of our comrades. It is the thought of these comrades that makes you willing to face again the hell you have already faced.

First about Comrade Oliver Law. When I first came to Jarama, he was commander of the Tom Mooney machine-gun company. He was a good-looking, well-built negro. Later he was promoted to adjutant of the battalion, and about a month ago he became commander. Now a battalion commander is not supposed to lead his men over the top—he should be a few hundred yards behind. But on July 6th, when we went over the last hill and charged under heavy machine-gun fire, Law was right up in the front, urging us on. When we were forced to drop, he was still up, looking around to see that we were all down. Then he dropped. How he missed being hit that day, I'll never understand.

On July 9, we went over again. It so happened that the fascists had attacked too. We were about a thousand meters apart, each on a high hill, with a valley between us. The Gods must have laughed when they saw us charge each other at the same time. Once again Law was up in front urging us on. Then the fascists started running back. They were retreating. Law would not drop for cover. True, he was exhausted as we all were. We had no food or water that day and it was hot. He wanted to keep the fascists on the run and take the high hill. "Come on, comrades, they are running," he shouted. "Let's keep them running." All this time he was under machine-gun fire. Finally he was hit. Two comrades brought him in in spite of the machine guns. His wound was dressed. As he was being carried on a stretcher to the ambulance, he clenched his fist and said, "Carry on boys." Then he died.

I was in battalion headquarters that morning before the attack. Law was there too. Everyone seemed sentimental. They were talking about home. Law spoke about his wife, how he missed her, how some day he would see her again. Later, the subject was changed. We began telling jokes.

Then there was a company commander [Paul] Burns, an Irish comrade from Boston. I was his runner at the time. While out in front on the same day, he received a thigh wound. He was in awful pain while being dragged in, but he wouldn't utter a sound. While his wound was being dressed, he insisted on loading machine-gun bullets.

Comrade D. [John Deck] was a German American. He had an easy job behind the lines, but refused to stay there. He insisted on being with the boys in the front. He joined the same section I was in while still in Jarama. I used to listen to his stories for hours. He loved to talk, but he was one fellow I never got sick listening to.

On July 7 our battalion was maneuvering around, looking for the fascists. He was the lead scout, always in advance of the battalion, and in the most danger. That night we slept on the slope of a hill. Bullets were whizzing over the hill. The observer notified headquarters that there was a house about 800 meters away, where the bullets were coming from. D. volunteered to go out with bombs and blow up the house. Just as he was ready to go, we got word that we were to go some other place in the morning, so Law refused to let D. go. He was shot in the head at about the same time Law got hit. He was way out in front, a grenade in his hand, ready to throw. He died instantly.

Source: *Cary Nelson and Jefferson Hendricks, eds., Madrid 1937: Letters of the Abraham Lincoln Brigade from the Spanish Civil War (London & New York: Routledge, 1996), pp. 187–188.*

SPANISH CIVIL WAR

such wildly divergent interpretations? Is there any way to reconcile them?

Authors of books (more than fifteen thousand now exist) about the Spanish Civil War have focused on different parts of the war, so that where one sees "the last great cause," another sees "the conquest of Red Spain," and a third sees a religious "crusade." To complicate things further, Spaniards who lived through the war, international volunteers who fought in it, and postwar scholars bringing their own experiences and beliefs to bear on their research, usually have a vested interest in portraying the war a certain way. It is left to readers to sort through their descriptions and to identify the most important motivations. A proper analysis of the Spanish Civil War must acknowledge that it was planned, fought, and influenced by dozens of political organizations and thousands of individuals. Each participant's words and deeds contributed something to the overall significance of the war.

Francisco Largo Caballero, prime minister of the Republic from September 1936 to May 1937, stated in press releases that his government was fighting for democracy and that its main goal was "to maintain the parliamentary regime of the Republic as it was set up by the Constitution which the Spanish people freely assumed." Leading members of the Communist International, hoping to persuade Britain and France to support the Republic, set aside their usual rhetoric of revolution to echo Caballero's statements, while Spanish communists such as Dolores Ibarurri—known by the pseudonym La Pasionaria (The Passionflower)—"never raised the question of socialism during the war, only the question of the defense of the Republic and democracy," according to scholar Burnett Bolloten. Meanwhile, outside Spain, groups such as the Friends of Spanish Democracy formed to show support for the Republic, and would-be members of the International Brigades could read the Republican newspaper Volunteer for Liberty. Postwar titles such as John Dos Passos's The Theme is Freedom (1956) and Lawrence A. Fernsworth's Spain's Struggle for Freedom (1957) continued to stress the idea that the Republic had fought valiantly against a tyrannical opponent. Certainly the Republican government was far more democratic, both in form and content, than the repressive Nationalist government that succeeded it. Thus, historian Helen Graham has justification for her assertion that "the Republic's fundamental aim [was] genuinely to enfranchise the excluded majority by making political democracy an irreversible social and economic reality."

Were the Nationalists really tyrants? When the war began, they could not agree among themselves how Spain should be ruled. The Alphon-sine and Carlist factions of the monarchist movement wanted that institution, which had been overthrown in 1931, to be restored, but they preferred different pretenders as monarch. Falangists (members of the Falange Española, Spanish Phalanx or Spanish Fascist Party) wanted to create an authoritarian, corporate state that would be free of class distinctions and under their supervision. There were even, in the words of General Emilio Mola, "fools who believe that agreement is possible with the representatives of the masses under control of the Popular Front." The one thing they agreed on was the need to restore order to Spain—and that was, in the context of current unrest, not a call for ruthless dictatorship but an understandable political goal. In the few months after the Popular Front came to power in 1936, replacing a government run by the Center and the Right, Spain experienced a series of disruptive strikes, acts of retribution against conservative landowners and industrialists, and attacks on political figures.

True, Falangists were responsible for a good deal of the violence, but they were not responsible for all of it. After the police thwarted an attempted military rebellion in Barcelona in May, residents set fire to churches, convents, and "the homes of well-known rightists and other private buildings," according to Bolloten. Two months later, men connected to the government and driving a government vehicle lured respected monarchist José Calvo Sotelo out of his house, drove him some distance away, and executed him. Seeing the government unable or unwilling to put an end to the unrest, many ordinary Spaniards joined monarchist Fernando Suárez de Tangil in thinking that "we cannot coexist with the protectors and moral accomplices of [Sotelo's assassination] a moment longer. We do not want to deceive the country and international opinion by accepting a role in a farce that pretends that a civilized and normal state exists, whereas, in reality, we have lived in complete anarchy since 16 February." To them, a strong, conservative ruler represented peace and freedom, not tyranny. Thus, if the Republican side had popular support and patriotic justifications, so did the Nationalists. Just as the Republicans did not have a monopoly on righteousness, the Nationalists did not have a monopoly on tyrannical behavior. For example, Bolloten reports that a Catalan anarchist admitted the possibility that "our victory resulted in the death by violence of four or five thousand inhabitants of Catalonia who were listed as rightists and were linked to political or ecclesiastical reaction"; he added unrepentantly, "But this shedding of blood is the inevitable consequence of a revolution." In the first six weeks of the war, Republicans executed seventy-five thousand individuals. Official executions were quick; unofficial killings usually were not. Later in the war, the government restricted civil liberties to an extent that one colonel in their own military forces felt to be harmful. It created interrogation chambers and procedures for prisoners that Minister of Justice Manuel de Irujo, shortly before his resignation from the government, called "cruel and inhuman . . . [a] system of fascist cruelty." The Spanish Socialist Party argued that what opponents called "despotism in government" was "what loyalist Spain demands: a government that governs, not one that must ask permission every day of the ungovernables," according to Bolloten. "A government that governs" was, of course, what the Nationalists had demanded before the war began. The Republican side had grown to resemble its enemy.

Should one then believe the Nationalist version of events rather than the Republican one? The Nationalists claimed they were freeing Spain from the throes of anarchy and the infiltration of evil-minded communists who would turn Spain into a Soviet satellite. In the statement of victory issued on 1 April 1939, Francisco Franco even referred to his vanquished opponent as "the Red army."

The Nationalists executed approximately forty thousand individuals during the war, and Franco's government imprisoned and killed tens of thousands more after the war ended. Those numbers, let alone the aid Nationalists accepted from Nazi Germany and fascist Italy, disqualify the Nationalist side for the role of Spain's savior. However, their worries about anarchy were well grounded. So were their fears of communist infiltration and socialist revolution. The Republicans were as much revolutionaries as they were democrats, if not more so. In the first few weeks of the civil war, a social revolution occurred. Whole industries were collectivized in cities such as Barcelona, while rural laborers formed their own collectives. As the war continued, newspapers reminded readers that "the thousands of proletarian combatants at the battlefronts are not fighting for the 'democratic Republic' . . . [but] to make the Revolution," as quoted in Bolloten. Spain boasted a population of more than one million anarchists, few of whom wanted to miss the chance to eliminate the central government and to rule themselves. Anarchist leaders joined the Republican government only with the utmost reluctance.

Many communists, too, wished to do away with the "bourgeois" system of doing things. They saw no need for the freedom offered by democracy when they could have the freedom offered by socialism. Members of the *Partido Comunista de Espana* (Communist Party of Spain, PCE) saw otherwise. Their viewpoint prevailed in large part because they had Soviet power behind them. It did not begin the war, but the Soviet Union played a substantial role in deciding Republican government policy and prolonging the Republic's survival. Keeping in mind its need for the goodwill of Britain and the United States, the Soviet Union urged Spanish communists to remember that they should fight to support a "bourgeois" democracy. It provided tanks, airplanes, artillery, ammunition, advisers, and soldiers (in exchange for Spanish gold given to Moscow from the treasury "for safekeeping"). It encouraged the formation of the International Brigades (many of whose members, as they later told interviewers, volunteered to defend democracy in the hopes of eventually implementing communism). Jesús Hernández later remarked that "those of us who 'directed' the Spanish Communist party acted more like Soviet subjects than sons of the Spanish people. It may seem absurd, incredible, but our education under Soviet tutelage had deformed us to such an extent that we were completely denationalized."

At the same time, to say that the Republic was a Soviet satellite, as some Nationalists did, was to ignore the hundreds of thousands of patriotic Spaniards who fought for it. It was also to ignore the sectional and religious feelings that motivated many participants on both sides of the conflict. Nationalists wanted a unified Spain. Basques and Catalans wanted autonomy. Carlists defended Catholicism from atheistic communists. Republicans, such as government official Fernando Valera, proclaimed their adherence to "the fraternity of Christ" in the struggle against "the tyranny of the Church." They also exhumed the corpses of nuns and forced rosary beads into monks' ears in order to avenge the oppressive institution of the Church—while their allies, the Basques, continued faithfully to attend Mass. As historian Hugh Thomas wrote, the civil war created "not two Spains but two thousand," each with its own set of motive forces. The Spanish Civil War brought Juan Negrín, prime minister of the Republic for most of the war, to the conclusion that "everyone, absolutely everyone, Socialists, Communists, Republicans, Falangists, Francoists, all of them, are equally contemptible." Perhaps in a moment of despair, his own cynicism led him to see cynicism in everyone else. Can the desire for freedom and order—as well as Catholic fervor, love of one's own region, communist principles, and fascist sentiments—combine to produce nothing more than bloodshed and contempt?

–CATHERINE BLAIR,
GEORGETOWN UNIVERSITY

References

Burnett Bolloten, *The Spanish Civil War: Revolution and Counterrevolution* (Chapel Hill: University of North Carolina Press, 1991).

Franz Borkenau, *The Spanish Cockpit: An Eyewitness Account of the Political and Social Conflicts of the Spanish Civil War* (London: Faber & Faber, 1937).

Gerald Brenan, *The Spanish Labyrinth: An Account of the Social and Political Background of the Civil War* (Cambridge: Cambridge University Press, 1943; New York: Macmillan, 1943).

George Esenwein and Adrian Schubert, *Spain at War: The Spanish Civil War in Context, 1931–1939* (London & New York: Longman, 1995).

Ronald Fraser, *Blood of Spain: An Oral History of the Spanish Civil War* (New York: Pantheon, 1979).

Helen Graham, "The Spanish Civil War," *Historical Journal,* 30 (December 1987): 989–993.

Gabriel Jackson, *The Spanish Republic and the Civil War, 1931–1939* (Princeton: Princeton University Press, 1965).

George Orwell, *Homage to Catalonia* (London: Secker & Warburg, 1938).

Paul Preston, *A Concise History of the Spanish Civil War* (London: Fontana, 1996).

Preston, ed., *Revolution and War in Spain, 1931–1939* (London & New York: Methuen, 1984).

Ronald Radosh, Mary R. Habeck, and Grigory Sevostianov, eds., *Spain Betrayed: The Soviet Union and the Spanish Civil War* (New Haven: Yale University Press, 2001).

Hugh Thomas, *The Spanish Civil War,* third edition (London: Harper & Row, 1986).

John Tisa, *Recalling the Good Fight: An Autobiography of the Spanish Civil War* (South Hadley, Mass.: Bergin & Garvey, 1985).

SPANISH CIVIL WAR

STALIN'S ECONOMIC POLICIES

Was Josef Stalin's reorganization of the Soviet economy a successful endeavor?

Viewpoint: Yes. Though brutal, Stalin's crash program of industrialization saved the U.S.S.R. from German conquest in World War II and transformed it into a superpower thereafter.

Viewpoint: No. Stalin sacrificed agriculture to industry and free enterprise to nationalism. In the process he starved millions of his people to death and created a dysfunctional economy that was bound to fail.

A public-opinion poll conducted in early March 2003, on the occasion of the fiftieth anniversary of Soviet leader Josef Stalin's death, found that 52 percent of Russians still viewed him as a positive force in the history of their country. This chapter analyzes the relative benefits of one of the most important themes in Stalin's government: his thorough transformation of the Soviet Union's economy. Within just a few years after Stalin assumed full power in the late 1920s, virtually all economic activity was concentrated in the hands of the Soviet state. Centrally drafted five-year plans governed all management, distribution, resources, and labor; private agriculture was replaced by state managed collective farms; and the tolerated private economy of the New Economic Policy (NEP) era of the 1920s was eliminated.

To some observers, including many of the Russians who continue to believe in Stalin's great role as a national leader, the balance sheet of the economic transformation was positive. Whatever the domestic costs—and few deny that they were horrible—the full mobilization of resources in the 1930s placed the Soviet Union on a strong enough footing to prevail in the challenges of World War II and to last afterward as a major world power. Failure to do so, they argue, would have imperiled the nation's survival and that of its people. Yet, in the longer duration, many, including the nearly half of Russians who do not think of Stalin in positive terms, see little practical benefit from the creation of a command economy. Millions of innocent people died as the result of state mismanagement and repression linked to economic imperatives, while many of the supposed achievements in industry were far from perfect. More than anything else, Stalin's transformation of the Soviet economy left it bereft of initiative and innovation and doomed it to the relative backwardness that it experienced in the decades after his death.

Viewpoint:
Yes. Though brutal, Stalin's crash program of industrialization saved the U.S.S.R. from German conquest in World War II and transformed it into a superpower thereafter.

On the surface it appears that Soviet dictator Josef Stalin's economic policies were deeply flawed. "De-kulakization" and the collectivization of agriculture cost millions of lives and devastated the Soviet Union's farming sector for at least a generation. Crash urbanization and industrialization were often haphazard, harmful to the environment, and warped by policies that sacrificed sound management for political and ideological expediency. Several important industries that developed under Stalin depended on vast armies of forced laborers, whose imprisonment cost far more than the value of their labor. Over the long term, Stalin's concentration of all legal economic activity in the hands of the state left the Soviet Union sluggish domestically and uncompetitive internationally, two factors that played important roles in the state's later decay and ultimate collapse. Yet, Stalin's economic policies, despite their problems and limitations, can be described as a necessary evil. The positive side of their balance sheet included the Soviet Union's rapid transformation from one of Europe's weaker major powers into one of the world's biggest industrial economies and its development of a heavy industrial base large enough to function as a war machine of tremendous power. Whatever their costs, these feats were crucial factors in enabling the Soviets to defeat Nazi Germany in World War II and last for several decades thereafter as the only major international competitor of the United States.

By the time Stalin rose to full power in the late 1920s, no one could doubt that the Soviet Union stood as heir to one of the weakest world powers. Imperial Russia won its last war against a modern rival when it participated in the victory over Napoleonic France in 1814. Its embarrassing defeats in the Crimean War (1853–1856) and the Russo-Japanese War (1904–1905) stimulated important periods of reform, but these attempts failed to bridge the industrial, technological, and commercial gaps between it and its rivals. Although Russia could fight and win against other underdeveloped powers, its confrontation with Germany in 1914–1918 was a disaster. In addition to losing every battle and campaign against Germany—most of whose resources were in any case deployed on the Western Front—for Russia, the conflict's political and economic strains were the most severe experienced by any major combatant. By February 1917 the tsarist government collapsed, having lost control of its capital and the loyalty of its army. The weak democratic regime that replaced it fared no better and quickly spent its legitimacy. In the growing vacuum of authority, a coup d'état replaced it with a ruthless communist regime, led by Vladimir Lenin, which concluded a draconian peace settlement with Germany and struggled for several years against major domestic opposition and the humiliating occupation of significant portions of its territory by foreign troops. Realities abroad quickly demolished the communist leaders' expectation and hope that their revolution would touch off a pan-European or global revolution. The Soviet state that emerged in the early 1920s suffered from a devastated economy, a traumatized society, and the knowledge that its survival had only been guaranteed by Germany's defeat in World War I and the conflict's exhaustion of the Western Allies to the point where they could not contemplate ousting Russia's communist regime.

As Stalin consolidated control of the Soviet government in the mid to late 1920s, his priorities were informed by a profound sense of Russian backwardness relative to the major powers. He and other Soviet leaders often repeated the clichéd observation that Russia's development had historically lagged fifty to a hundred years behind that of the West, and that the gap needed to be closed if the state and its revolutionary ideals were to survive. Communists who believed in socialism's inherent superiority to the "irrationality" of capitalism and other economic systems maintained that their system would prove itself by accomplishing that goal. In official propaganda and the cultivation of his personal following, Stalin styled himself as a modern-day Peter the Great (reigned 1682–1725), the Russian tsar who attempted with much success to modernize Russia and make it into a competitive European power.

Ideology added urgency to this process. Soviet ideologists, looking to Karl Marx's conceptions of inevitable class conflict and Lenin's emphasis on the connection between international conflict and opportunities for revolution, argued that the "contradictions" of international capitalism would make another major war unavoidable and postulated various Soviet roles in it, ranging from active, idealistic participation to a cynical waiting game followed by the advancement of revolutionary activity and Soviet interests at the expense of the exhausted warring parties. The Great Depression, consequent conflicts in international trade and finance, and the related rise of European fascism convinced them that they were right and that a major war among capitalist powers was on the way. Stalin himself

Soviet worker in a metal factory in Dnepropetrovsk, an important industrial center during the Stalinist era, 1952

(Yevgeny Khaldei/CORBIS)

predicted at a February 1931 Communist Party function that the Soviet Union would have to fight a major war ten years later. Although far more complicated forces and far less predictable actions and events led to the outbreak of World War II, Stalin turned out to be prescient. In June 1941 more than three million German troops invaded his country, made astonishing advances, and won tremendous victories. But despite the Germans' formidable challenge, Soviet arms prevented them from achieving their major objectives in 1941, inflicted major defeats on them at Stalingrad and Kursk in 1942–1943, and drove them back across Eastern Europe to Berlin in 1944–1945.

This victory, the high point of Soviet power, could not have been achieved without the high pace of industrialization of the country under Stalin's rule in the late 1920s and 1930s. Indeed, the expectation of war gave the entire process a military character. Soviet leaders and economic planners thought in terms of economic "fronts," ordered the formation of labor "armies," and identified production norms as "objectives." Firm state control of resources, labor, capital, management, and planning meant that these factors could be oriented fully toward its strategic goals and needs. Harsh discipline (including death sentences for "sabotage" and long labor camp sentences for absenteeism and even tardiness), the use of official terror, outlandish proregime propaganda, and an artificial atmosphere of xenophobia and fear convinced many to work hard and remain loyal. So, too, did Stalin's introduction of (albeit relatively minor) material incentives and social privileges—strictly taboo to orthodox Marxists—to induce higher performance. Brutal and thoroughgoing control of agriculture allowed the Soviet government to export maximum quantities of its leading domestic commodity to finance imports of the latest machinery and production techniques from the West. Domination of the public sphere by the state and the Communist Party, which reached its greatest extent under Stalin, ensured that no one could criticize these policies or protest their human and environmental effects without facing severe punishment. Denial of basic political freedoms and democratic processes guaranteed that there would be no change in government and no sudden alteration of state economic priorities. In most meaningful ways, in other words, the Soviet Union had a dictatorial war economy for more than a decade of peacetime, one that no other nation was developing and the extent of whose power was not reached by any other World War II combatant with the possible exception of Nazi Germany in its last two or three years.

The Soviet government used its militarized economy in several wise ways. The most obvious was its emphasis on heavy manufacturing, which included industries vital for war production (coal mining, steel production, machine manufacturing, and so on). Tremendous strides forward were made in these industries, surpassing not only the Soviet Union and Russian Empire's past production figures, but also threatening, at least in raw figures, to overtake those of West European economies. Most new industrial plants were designed either explicitly for military purposes or for civilian purposes that could easily be converted to military ones (Soviet tractor plants, for example, were easily convertible into tank factories). Impressive achievements in the development of the Soviet communications, transportation, and energy infrastructure were built purposely to supply these plants and connect them more efficiently to central networks and major cities. Although a substantial amount of wartime production was made possible by shipments of American raw materials and finished product under the Lend-Lease program, the Soviets had already built the industrial base, assembled the workforce, and established the militarized institutional culture necessary to turn those shipments into battlefield hardware. New industrial plants and even altogether new cities, furthermore, were often situated in the deep recesses of the Russian heartland. This situation had the double benefit of locating industry closer to newer sources of raw materials in the Urals, Siberia, and the Russian north and of moving much of it beyond the easy reach of invading armies and their arsenals of long-range bombers. The Soviets' defense in depth meant that despite the impressive German advances in 1941, a serious amount of their productive capacity remained far beyond the reach of the invaders. Since Germany's entire national territory and that of all of its allies and conquests came completely within Allied bomber range by 1943, the relative security of Soviet factories and infrastructure was a major wartime advantage. The Soviets' production figures indicated, accurately according to most experts, that their war machine turned out thirty thousand tanks and forty thousand planes in 1943–1945 alone, figures that rank with those of the United States and Germany as the war's highest. Soviet land forces did the bulk of the fighting in the conflict's European theater, not only before but after, the Allied invasion of Normandy in June 1944, and inflicted an estimated 80 percent of Germany's total battlefield casualties. This impressive performance would have been hard to achieve had Stalin not prepared his country for it with rapid industrialization.

Was winning World War II worth the tremendous deprivations and human costs of industrialization and related policies? The alternatives to a Soviet victory over Nazi Germany would almost certainly have been bleaker. The well-documented record of Nazi occupation policies in and future plans for Poland and the territories of the Soviet Union that came under their control indicate that a German victory would have transformed the entire region into a vast slave empire, in which the "subhuman" Slavic population would have existed only to service the German war economy before facing extermination or deportation to make way for German settlement of its lands. During the war several million of the region's people were sent as slave laborers to German mines and factories, while most of its large Jewish population was exterminated by mass gassings or roving firing squads. Millions of Slavs were also killed or allowed to die from starvation and neglect, while hundreds of thousands of others were forcibly relocated to clear space for German settlers, who tentatively began to arrive as the war in the East was still being fought. Even a permanent stalemate or negotiated peace (the latter being a more realistic possibility than many have supposed) would have been a disaster, for the Germans would still have dominated, exploited, and depopulated a huge region inhabited by tens of millions of people. Either variant would have left the German war machine free to deploy the millions of troops otherwise held down by the Soviets to the West, where they might have proved decisive in the war against Britain and prevented or frustrated large-scale American military involvement in Europe. As terrible as Stalin's industrialization and related policies were, the specter of German con-

STALIN'S ECONOMIC POLICIES

quest and Germany's probable long-term domination of Europe were worse.

−PAUL DU QUENOY,
GEORGETOWN UNIVERSITY

Viewpoint:
No. Stalin sacrificed agriculture to industry and free enterprise to nationalism. In the process he starved millions of his people to death and created a dysfunctional economy that was bound to fail.

Josef Stalin's economic leadership was a disaster for the Soviet Union and its people. In only a few years, roughly between 1928 and 1933, his policies reversed the limited successes of the New Economic Policy (NEP), wrecked the Soviet agricultural sector, and imposed blind ideological controls on most aspects of economic life. Many of the enduring problems of the Soviet Union's economy, which left it unprepared for World War II, made it uncompetitive internationally thereafter, and led to its collapse in 1991, had their origins in Stalin's tyrannical and unreasoned policies.

One of the most backward and unproductive aspects of Stalin's economic policies was its reliance on coercion. In no sector of the Soviet economy was this truer than in agriculture. After the painful revolutionary years of forced grain requisitioning and peasant massacres, the New Economic Policy had allowed for a limited and temporary free market in foodstuffs. Peasant resistance to Soviet power largely ceased, and recovery to prewar levels of agricultural production seemed likely. Stalin's introduction of agricultural collectivization in 1929–1930—which forced independent farmers to join state-managed collective farms—destroyed this progress and created long-term problems for Soviet agriculture. One of this policy's first measures involved the murder, arrest, or internal exile of "better off" peasants and anyone else who could potentially lead the countryside against, or independently of, the central government. Labeled with the term *kulak,* a categorization that remained deliberately vague so that it could be applied to anyone who might be a threat, nearly one million of the Soviet Union's most industrious and successful farmers were removed from the fields and sent to their graves, prison camps, or marginal, unproductive lives in Siberian or Central Asian exile settlements. Many preferred to destroy their produce, livestock, and homes rather than allow them to be confiscated. So, too, did many less-

well-off peasants, who rarely entered collective farms voluntarily and usually resented the replacement of their traditional way of life by inefficient state management, omnipresent government control over their lives, and the low daily wages they now received for their labor. The immediate economic result was a marked decline in every index of agricultural productivity—the natural outcome of the state's elimination of any incentive to work hard combined with the widespread slaughter of livestock and burning of crops. Another result was active resistance, which interfered with cultivation and distribution and demanded substantial state resources to suppress its proliferation, including in some cases the Red Army and paramilitary units of the secret police. One expert has calculated that there were more than 13,000 cases of armed insurrection against the government, involving some 2.5 million people. When the Germans invaded the Soviet Union in 1941, many of the peasants they encountered greeted them as liberators.

Resistance and other practical dilemmas caused Stalin to slow the pace of collectivization, but its broad accomplishment by 1933 ended private agriculture in the Soviet Union. Stalin only worsened the situation in the countryside by accelerating his crash program of industrialization and urbanization. Lacking the domestic capital and resources to build new plants, update technology, and import late-model foreign machinery, the Soviets had to rely on the massive export of their only major internationally marketable commodity, grain. Although profits and foreign credits from surging grain exports did help facilitate rapid industrialization, the price was heavy. Marshaling the maximum quantity of produce for export meant that the state-controlled agricultural sector had to squeeze the peasants as much as it could. Frequently, this situation involved confiscating their grain by force, often leaving them without seed to plant for the following season and, especially in the winter of 1932–1933, without enough sustenance to keep them alive. The Soviet government and its apologists methodically suppressed evidence of famine in the 1930s, but emerging statistical data and other information have led historians to estimate that four to ten million people, mostly farmers, died as a result of state economic policy, while millions more were weakened and malnourished.

The Soviets themselves and their foreign defenders tried to dismiss these traumas as the "growing pains" of a new society or as some other kind of "necessary evil" (Stalin repeated the cliché "you can't make an omelet without breaking eggs" when addressing the human costs of collectivization), but Soviet agriculture never recovered from them and experienced long-term

WE ARE TO BLAME

Below is a portion of a speech given by Josef Stalin at the Joint Plenum of the Central Committee and the Central Control Commission of the C.P.S.U.(B.) on 11 January 1933 in which he describes the problems with Soviet agricultural production.

Comrades, I think that the previous speakers have correctly described the state of Party work in the countryside, its defects and its merits—particularly its defects. Nevertheless, it seems to me that they have failed to mention the most important thing about the defects of our work in the countryside; they have not disclosed the roots of these defects. And yet this aspect is of the greatest interest to us. Permit me, therefore, to express my opinion on the defects of our work in the countryside, to express it with all the straightforwardness characteristic of the Bolsheviks.

What was the main defect in our work in the countryside during the past year, 1932?

The main defect was that our grain procurements in 1932 were accompanied by greater difficulties than in the previous year, in 1931.

This was by no means due to the bad state of the harvest; for in 1932 our harvest was not worse, but better than in the preceding year. No one can deny that the total amount of grain harvested in 1932 was larger than in 1931, when the drought in five of the principal areas of the north-eastern part of the U.S.S.R. considerably reduced the country's grain output. Of course, in 1932, too, we suffered certain losses of crops, as a consequence of unfavorable climatic conditions in the Kuban and Terek regions, and also in certain districts of the Ukraine. But there cannot be any doubt that these losses do not amount to half those we suffered in 1931 as a result of the drought in the north-eastern areas of the U.S.S.R. Hence, in 1932 we had more grain in the country than in 1931. And yet, despite this circumstance, our grain procurements were accompanied by greater difficulties in 1932 than in the previous year.

What was the matter? What are the reasons for this defect in our work? How is this disparity to be explained?

1) It is to be explained, in the first place, by the fact that our comrades in the localities, our Party workers in the countryside, failed to take into account the new situation created in the countryside by the authorization of collective-farm trade in grain. And precisely because they failed to take the new situation into consideration, precisely for that reason, they were unable to reorganize their work along new lines to fit in with the new situation. So long as there was no collective farm trade in grain, so long as

there were not two prices for grain—the state price and the market price—the situation in the countryside took one form. When collective-farm trade in grain was authorized, the situation was bound to change sharply, because the authorization of collective-farm trade implies the legalization of a market price for grain higher than the established state price. There is no need to prove that this circumstance was bound to give rise among the peasants to a certain reluctance to deliver their grain to the state. The peasant calculated as follows: "Collective-farm trade in grain has been authorized; market prices have been legalized; in the market I can obtain more for a given quantity of grain than if I deliver it to the state—hence, if I am not a fool, I must hold on to my grain, deliver less to the state, leave more grain for collective-farm trade, and in this way get more for the same quantity of grain sold. . . ."

2) The second reason for the defects in our work in the countryside is that our comrades in the localities—and not only those comrades—have failed to understand the change that has taken place in the conditions of our work in the countryside as a result of the predominant position acquired by the collective farms in the principal grain-growing areas. We all rejoice at the fact that the collective form of farming has become the predominant form in our grain areas. But not all of us realize that this circumstance does not diminish but increases our cares and responsibilities in regard to the development of agriculture. Many think that once we have achieved, say, 70 or 80 per cent collectivization in a given district, or in a given region, we have got all we need, and can now let things take their natural course, let them proceed automatically, on the assumption that collectivization will do its work itself and will itself raise agriculture to a higher level. But this is a profound delusion, comrades. As a matter of fact, the transition to collective farming as the predominant form of farming does not diminish but increases our cares in regard to agriculture, does not diminish but increases the leading role of the Communists in raising agriculture to a higher level. Letting things take their own course is now more dangerous than ever for the development of agriculture. Letting things take their own course may now ruin everything. . . .

3) The third reason for the defects in our work in the countryside is that many of our comrades overestimated the collective farms as a new form of economy, overestimated them and converted them into an icon. They decided that since we have collective farms, which represent a socialist form of economy, we have

everything; that this is sufficient to ensure the proper management of these farms, the proper planning of collective farming, and the conversion of the collective farms into exemplary socialist enterprises. They failed to understand that in their organizational structure the collective farms are still weak and need considerable assistance from the Party both in the way of providing them with tried Bolshevik cadres, and in the way of guidance in their day-to-day affairs. But that is not all, and not even the main thing. The main defect is that many of our comrades overestimated the strength and possibilities of the collective farms as a new form of organization of agriculture. They failed to understand that, in spite of being a socialist form of economy, the collective farms by themselves are yet far from being guaranteed against all sorts of dangers and against the penetration of all sorts of counter-revolutionary elements into their leadership; that they are not guaranteed against the possibility that under certain circumstances anti-Soviet elements may use the collective farms for their own ends. . . .

4) The fourth reason for the defects in our work in the countryside is the inability of a number of our comrades in the localities to reorganize the front of the struggle against the kulaks; their failure to understand that the face of the class enemy has changed of late, that the tactics of the class enemy in the countryside have changed, and that we must change our tactics accordingly if we are to achieve success. The enemy understands the changed situation, understands the strength and the might of the new system in the countryside; and because he understands this, he has reorganized his ranks, has changed his tactics—has passed from frontal attacks against the collective farms to activities conducted on the sly. But we have failed to understand this; we have overlooked the new situation and continue to seek the class enemy where he is no longer to be found; we continue to apply the old tactics of a simplified struggle against the kulaks at a time when these tactics have long since become obsolete. . . .

5) Finally, there is one other reason for the defects in our work in the countryside. This consists in underestimating the role and responsibility of Communists in the work of collective-farm development, in underestimating the role and responsibility of Communists in the matter of grain procurements. In speaking of the difficulties of grain procurement, Communists usually throw the responsibility upon the peasants, claiming that the peasants are to blame for everything. But that is absolutely untrue, and certainly unjust. The peasants are not to blame at all. If we are to speak of responsibility and blame, then the responsibility falls wholly upon

the Communists, and we Communists alone are to blame for all this. . . .

One may ask: What have the peasants to do with it?

I know of whole groups of collective farms which are developing and flourishing, which punctually carry out the assignments of the state and are becoming economically stronger day by day. On the other hand, I know also of collective farms, situated in the neighborhood of the first-mentioned, which, in spite of having the same harvest yields and objective conditions as these, are nevertheless wilting and in a state of decay. What is the reason for this? The reason is that the first group of collective farms are led by real Communists, while the second group are led by drifters—with Party membership cards in their pockets, it is true, but drifters all the same.

One may ask: What have the peasants to do with it?

The result of underestimating the role and responsibility of Communists is that, not infrequently, the reason for the defects in our work in the countryside is not sought where it should be sought, and because of this the defects remain unremoved.

The reason for the difficulties of grain procurement must be sought not among the peasants, but among ourselves, in our own ranks. For we are at the helm; we have the resources of the state at our disposal; it is our mission to lead the collective farms; and we must bear the whole responsibility for the work in the countryside.

These are the main reasons for the defects of our work in the countryside.

It may be thought that I have drawn too gloomy a picture; that all our work in the countryside consists exclusively of defects. That, of course, is not true. As a matter of fact, alongside these defects, our work in the countryside shows a number of important and decisive achievements. But, as I said at the beginning of my speech, I did not set out to describe our achievements; I set out to speak only about the defects of our work in the countryside.

Can these defects be remedied? Yes, unquestionably, they can. Shall we remedy them in the near future? Yes, unquestionably, we shall. There cannot be the slightest doubt about that.

I think that the Political Departments of the machine and tractor stations and of the state farms represent one of the decisive means by which these defects can be removed in the shortest time.

Source: J. V. Stalin, Problems of Leninism *(Peking: Foreign Languages Press, 1976), pp. 631–649.*

languor. During World War II the country could not feed itself, and its war effort depended on nearly four million tons of food sent from the United States under the Lend-Lease program. In the postwar era, agriculture failed to benefit from years of peace, and only reached 1913 production levels in the 1960s, in part because the government eased restrictions on the trade of produce from small private plots. By that time the Soviet Union, which had inherited some of the world's richest farmland and Imperial Russia's traditional economic role as Europe's breadbasket, was reduced to a net importer of foodstuffs. At the height of the Cold War, it even had to suffer the embarrassment of importing grain from its capitalist archrival, the United States, just to feed its people.

Despite the surge in industry that the agricultural sector's misfortune allowed, the Soviet Union did not benefit from it over the long term. Much of the industrial growth was in any case illusory, for Stalin reasoned that in order for the Soviet Union and its revolutionary ideals to stay afloat and gain influence, it would have to convince both domestic and foreign public opinion of the success of doctrinaire Marxist economics. Since Marxism fundamentally rejected free markets and private enterprise, small businesses which had existed under the New Economic Policy—mostly in the service and craft industries and light-manufacturing sector—were eliminated in the late 1920s by nationalization decrees and draconian tax increases.

Increased state authority over the urban economy did not augur improvement, however. Official production indices did show unbelievable growth in many industries, often recording increases of five or even ten times between the implementation of the first state-directed Five Year Plan in late 1928 and its premature "fulfillment" in 1932. The plan's completion in four years rather than five was itself put forward to show the world that the Soviets had exceeded even their own high expectations. Yet, many of the claims that supported this propaganda were simply made up, often by foremen, managers, statisticians, and low-level party members who feared for their jobs or lives if they were seen to be underachieving. Falsification was also a common practice among party higher-ups who assumed that no one outside the leadership would ever know the real figures, which were considerably lower, and believed that exaggerated ones would serve the interests of the state in propaganda form. Many who lived through the time recalled their all too understandable difficulty in reconciling official reports of fantastic economic strides forward and a real economy of chronic shortages. Other figures were literally correct but meaningless in reality. Glass factories,

for example, exceeded their production quotas, which were set according to weight, by manufacturing huge glass blocks. The blocks served no practical purpose, but were easier and faster to produce than windowpanes or other useful articles and still allowed the responsible state economic planning agency to claim them as legitimate finished product. In a like manner chandelier factories exceeded their quotas (also in weight) by constructing massive chandeliers that no ceiling could support. The product was useless but was nevertheless factored into the impressive official production figures. Similar examples abounded.

Ideological considerations compelled Stalin to damage his country's economy further by moving for the replacement of so-called bourgeois experts with authentic proletarians. This measure involved a sweeping state-enforced social transformation that removed from their positions and often resulted in the death or imprisonment of most of the remaining prerevolutionary managers, engineers, technicians, teachers, and skilled craftsmen, people who had remained respected and employed under the New Economic Policy despite their "suspect" origins in the capitalist past. Trained "proletarians," workers selected on the basis of their low socio-economic background, received crash courses in management and higher technical disciplines and took over responsibilities in many industries. Stalin did this partly to "prove" that the working class could do important jobs as well as or better than the old "bourgeoisie," but mainly to create a new class of people in prominent positions who owed to him alone their professional advancement and personal loyalty. Indeed, many of the men "promoted from the workbench" joined the Communist Party, replaced the "Old Bolsheviks" (Communists who had joined the Party before the revolution and did not owe personal loyalty to Stalin) when most of them were purged in 1934–1938, and in some cases reached positions of major government responsibility. The last category included the next two Soviet leaders after Stalin, Nikita Khrushchev (ruled 1953–1964) and Leonid Brezhnev (ruled 1964–1982), as well as dozens of future government ministers and party leaders. In economic terms, however, this policy was a disaster, no matter how much "social mobility" its working class beneficiaries experienced. In the absence of the well-trained experts who had facilitated Imperial Russia's dynamic economy and the Soviet Union's recovery from the turbulent revolutionary era, there appeared tens of thousands of newcomers who often had no qualifications apart from their perceived political reliability and their usually deficient crash courses. Many even lacked a complete primary education, to say nothing of the sophisticated literacy and mathematics skills that good managers, engineers, architects, and draftsmen need to do their jobs. The results can still be seen in the former Soviet Union today in the poor infrastructure, crumbling buildings, inferior designs, and unsafe conditions, mostly left over from any time after about 1930. Many Soviet technical achievements, including its impressive World War II productive capacity, its nuclear weapons and space programs, and the development of its postwar oil industry, depended on the purchase, theft, or other acquisition of foreign know-how. One should not forget that "proletarian" engineers trained in the Stalin era built Chernobyl, the nuclear power plant that was the site of a catastrophic meltdown in April 1986—perhaps the world's worst manmade environmental disaster—as well as the more prosaic collapsing apartment buildings, leaking sewage systems, unsafe submarines, and other late-industrial-age monstrosities that did much more harm than good.

Over time it became more difficult to conceal the shortcomings of the fully centralized, state-planned economy ushered in by Stalin and the corruption and ineptitude of its increasingly uninspired and geriatric personnel. Neither the putative fulfillment and overfulfillment of successive Five Year Plans, nor victory in World War II, nor the postwar era's maladroit emphasis on consumer industry could ultimately convince the Soviet people that the state was capable of providing for their needs. They also ceased to believe that an economy of deprivation, scarcity, and disincentives was a necessary sacrifice for the ever more elusive promise of a bright utopian future. Indeed, even as Khrushchev promised to overtake the West's standard of living by 1970 and bring about the full development of communism by 1980, new developments in mass media and eased restrictions on foreign visitors revealed to the Soviet people that their material quality of life lagged far behind that of the capitalist West and that the gap was only widening. A vast underground popular culture that prized anything Western and a growing dissident movement that pointed out the shortcomings of the entire Soviet system undermined the pretensions of government ideologues who dragged out the same tired old propaganda slogans to extol what were becoming undeniably meaningless Soviet achievements. News of the Soviet Union's stagnant economy and dispirited citizenry energized the country's international opponents, who successfully exposed and exploited its weaknesses to their own ideological and geopolitical advantage, and discredited communism throughout most of the world in the process. As soon as the disgruntled Soviet people had the opportunity to express themselves freely in the late 1980s and early 1990s, they rejected communism so thoroughly that its political strength evaporated, the country it created disappeared from the map, and its economic legacy quickly became one of the world's most rapacious capitalist systems.

–PAUL DU QUENOY,
GEORGETOWN UNIVERSITY

References

Robert Conquest, *The Harvest of Sorrow: Soviet Collectivization and the Terror-Famine* (London: Hutchinson, 1986).

Alexander Dallin, *German Rule in Russia, 1941–1945: A Study of Occupation Policies* (New York: Octagon, 1980).

Loren R. Graham, *The Ghost of the Executed Engineer: Technology and the Fall of the Soviet Union* (Cambridge, Mass.: Harvard University Press, 1996).

Geoffrey Hosking, *The First Socialist Society: A History of the Soviet Union from Within* (Cambridge, Mass.: Harvard University Press, 1990).

Stephen Kotkin, *Magnetic Mountain: Stalinism as a Civilization* (Berkeley: University of California Press, 1995).

Alec Nove, *An Economic History of the USSR, 1917–1991* (London & New York: Penguin, 1992).

Lennart Samuelson, *Plans for Stalin's War Machine: Tukhachevskii and Military-Economic Planning, 1925–1941* (New York: Macmillan, 2000).

Robert Service, *A History of Twentieth-Century Russia* (London: Allen Lane, 1997).

David R. Stone, *Hammer and Rifle: The Militarization of the Soviet Union, 1926–1933* (Lawrence: University Press of Kansas, 2000).

Robert C. Tucker, *Stalin in Power: The Revolution from Above, 1928–1941* (New York: Norton, 1990).

Lynne Viola, *Peasant Rebels Under Stalin: Collectivization and the Culture of Peasant Resistance* (New York: Oxford University Press, 1996).

STALIN'S ECONOMIC POLICIES

THOUGHT AND CULTURE

Was the modernist revolt against rationalism in Europe bolstered by scientific discovery?

Viewpoint: Yes. New scientific and pseudoscientific inquiries that demonstrated the significance of random occurrence in nature and the role of the subconscious in human behavior propelled the movement against realism and rationality.

Viewpoint: No. Modernism was an expression of individuality in reaction to the stultifying standardization of life, government, and society.

Twentieth-century culture, often characterized by the terms *modernism* and *postmodernism,* was deeply influenced by irrational thought. Expressionist painting, fascist politics, psychological novels, and a host of other media revealed that earlier emphases on reason and rationality were on the wane as cultural values. Yet, science, a discipline identified quintessentially with reason and rationality, made unprecedented strides forward alongside this culture.

One argument suggests that science and an offshoot of it, pseudoscience, went a long way toward endorsing irrationality. The new discipline of psychology, pioneered in the nineteenth century but exploding in relevance and appeal after 1900, explicitly recognized that humans operate from instincts, desires, and other unconscious motivations that preclude rationality. New emphases on class, nation, and race, which often appealed to science (and more often pseudoscience) for justification, helped form the foundation of two of the distinct political philosophies of the century: communism and fascism.

One could also argue, however, that the explosion of cultural irrationality was a reaction to the growing primacy of rationality in daily life. Populations that were increasingly regimented, standardized, and controlled, processes that science facilitated to greater effect, urgently needed an outlet to express individuality. Creative irrationalism enabled them to satisfy that human need. New trends in culture allowed one to escape the pressures of the modern bureaucratic state, often without consequences.

Viewpoint:
Yes. New scientific and pseudoscientific inquiries that demonstrated the significance of random occurrence in nature and the role of the subconscious in human behavior propelled the movement against realism and rationality.

Much of twentieth-century European culture rejected rationalism as the basis of human thought and action. This development, which had deep roots in the Romantic Age of the nineteenth century, emerged in reaction to the Enlightenment's notions that the world and its creatures were part of a universal machine that could be organized and perfected according to rational principles. Nineteenth-century Romantics and their spiritual and intellectual heirs embraced myth, mysticism, emotion, dreams, and a host of other concepts and experiences that were at odds with a "rational" understanding of the world. Although the latter approach continued in philosophical positivism and literary realism, both were spent forces by 1900 and appeared wholly anachronistic after the carnage of World War I. Rather than supporting rationalism, by the turn of the twentieth century, new trends in scientific thought and its offspring, pseudoscience, came to complement and even endorse irrational values.

The Romantic emphasis on myth came to have a great deal of meaning in the twentieth century. Myths are thought to embody eternal truths and to offer timeless insights into the vagaries and contradictions of human nature. In the first half of the nineteenth century, the zenith of the Romantic Age, cultural figures throughout Europe took a renewed interest in folklore, fairy tales, legends, stories from antiquity, and other expressions of human experience that, despite having little traceable or provable basis in fact, captured the imagination and rang true to the spirit. The Brothers Grimm developed the first definitive compilation of German fairy tales at this time, just as the operas of Richard Wagner were drawn from the composer's study and amalgamation of medieval lore. The study of history as an academic discipline was another essentially Romantic development, one centered on narrative retellings of the past paired with higher moral messages. The Romantics pursued insights into the human experience which naturally defied reason or rationality. In their view of the world, humans were not merely creatures that operated from natural and rational instincts like survival and procreation, but beings

who also craved and needed such intangible and irrational values as spiritual fulfillment and the pursuit of destiny.

It was no accident that modern psychoanalysis has much of its basis in Romantic sensibilities. How else could one explain the idea of the human unconscious pioneered by the Austrian psychiatrist Sigmund Freud? Motivations hidden by the thin veil of civilization, a negotiated and largely artificial set of values, assumptions, and expectations that Freud thought to be the source of all modern human dysfunction, were quintessentially Romantic. Fears and desires that one could not articulate openly were expressed in dreams, a phenomenon that has captured the attention of humans since the dawn of time and that figures prominently in the primordial myths of most cultures. By attempting to interpret dreams scientifically, in terms of symbols and other common cultural referents, Freud integrated the ancient practice of dream interpretation into one of the most innovative fields of twentieth-century science.

Dreams and their interpretation were not the only mythological referents to come to light in modern psychoanalysis. As irrational behavior was explored, Freud and his growing number of colleagues came to realize that their scientific approach confirmed many truths that had been long explored in the human cultural experience, and which would continue to be explored in the modernist ethos that prevailed throughout the twentieth century. Freud was not merely being quaint when he theorized his Oedipus and Electra complexes, for their substance, socially taboo feelings of attraction that children have for parents of the opposite sex and the desire to strike down and replace parents of the same sex, had been realized by human societies for at least 2,500 years, back to the time when Sophocles wrote the first dramas featuring those characters and their incestuous relationships. The Swiss psychiatrist Carl Jung, a student and colleague of Freud, added to these concepts with his elaborate exploration of archetypes, characters, or phenomena that symbolize universal patterns of human behavior and personify aspects of the psyche.

It is not difficult to see the connection between the new discipline of psychiatry and European cultural developments, or to observe how they complemented each other. The Russian novelist Fedor Dostoevsky's *The Brothers Karamazov* (1879–1880), which explores the psychological bases of parricide among many other psychological phenomena, had a direct influence on Freud, just as Dostoevsky's earlier novel *Crime and Punishment* (1866) anticipated by about fifty years Freud's theorized relationship of guilt, paranoia, and the desire to confess.

THOUGHT AND CULTURE

Although it is not commonplace to identify Dostoevsky and other Russian Slavophiles, thinkers who saw the salvation of man in the traditional spirituality and communalism of the Slavic peoples, as European Romantics, their attachment to the spiritual, mistrust of Enlightenment models of reason, and profound insights into the psyche make them more similar than different. It should come as no surprise that Dostoevsky's values and judgments of human nature played an enormous role in shaping those of the twentieth- century West. The German novelist Thomas Mann, the quintessential modernist, kept his Russian predecessor's picture over his desk. Nor should it be any surprise that European communists, who extolled the Enlightenment, prized science over faith, promoted socialist realism over abstract creativity, and could, incidentally, never pretend to cultural and ideological hegemony without resorting to violence, hated Dostoevsky, despised modernism, and regarded Freudianism as a variety of "bourgeois decadence."

Yet, as much as twentieth-century political extremists claimed to reject irrationalism, their ostensibly scientific, or, more appropriately, pseudoscientific, worldview often led them to embrace it. Scientific models of politics and economics led Marxists to the conclusion that humanity was moving naturally toward a communist society free from exploitation and inequality. Since they attached so much value to that utopian future, they appealed to it to legitimize their goals and justify their actions. As long as one could argue that his actions furthered "the cause," he could claim that he was working in the name of forces no less irresistible than science, history, and justice. In time, commitment to this value came to be a faith unto itself, complete with its own prophecy, dogma, ritual, and saints. Recounting the contradictions and barbarities of communism falls outside the parameters of this essay, but it is worth noting that communists claiming a dedication to rationality could and did deliberately starve people to death, preside over slave-labor camps, tell as well as believe obvious lies, and consent to government by arbitrary dictatorship. If one could accept that these travesties of logic and rational thought would help in the long-term creation of paradise, suspending disbelief was the rational thing to do, no matter how many died or how much suffering was caused. As one Soviet secret police slogan put it, "With an iron fist, we will lead humanity to happiness!"

The world of Soviet science provided many stunning examples of such doublethink. Under Josef Stalin's dictatorship thousands of engineers were arrested after reporting that in their objective professional opinions, certain state-planned industrial projects were unfeasible. It did not matter that the engineers were applying their scientific and technical training in the most rational way. Rather the state, despite its professed commitment to scientific rationalism, quite irrationally interpreted their negative professional views as signs of disloyalty. "Why don't you want us to succeed?," the commissars would ask. The unfortunate takers of the Soviet Union's 1937 census (censuses themselves having been perfected by the rationalist nineteenth-century bureaucratic state) were eliminated after their all too scientific calculations indicated a major decline in the Soviet population following a period of devastating famine and intense political repression. Avoiding public admission, however tacit, of the state's failings thus became more valuable than the lives of its servants, to say nothing of the millions missing from the population at large. In the late 1940s the Soviet government ostracized scientists who presented hard objective evidence suggesting, before the discovery of DNA in 1953, that personal traits are inherited. Admitting the scientific truth that heredity has a powerful and (at least until recently) uncontrollable influence on human development was too much for ideologues devoted to the Enlightenment ideal that man and society can be shaped to perfection by the omnipotent state.

The role of heredity, despite its much more thoroughly understood nature today, was nevertheless another scientific complement to cultural irrationality. The Romantic idea of nation, which conceptualized an identity for otherwise vaguely defined cultural, linguistic, or historical communities, came to have endorsements that pretended to scientific validity. Yet, just as the division of Europe's peoples into nation-states defined the Continent's modern political structure, appeals to science also contributed to the development of a sinister side of nationalism. Adopting the British naturalist Charles Darwin's theory of evolution, which maintains that species compete for survival in an environment where the strongest and most adaptable prevail, many social and cultural figures argued that the "survival of the fittest" also applied to humanity. Although Darwin decried this perversion of his theory, the pseudoscientific attributes of social Darwinism lent imprimatur, however dubious and awful, to the arguments of those who maintained the superiority of one group, ethnicity, or nation over others.

Yet, the more these individuals appealed to science to back their claims, the less grounded in rationality their worldviews were. Indeed, in another Romantic exercise in mythology, nationalists who looked to the past to justify their pretensions to nationhood constructed communities

1937 CENSUS

Josef Stalin had high hopes for the Soviet census carried out in January 1937, as he wanted to show the world the prosperity of the U.S.S.R. However, the results stunned him. He had anticipated a total population of 177 million, but the figures (finally revealed in 1990) showed only 162 million. The deficit of 15 million revealed the extent of premature deaths resulting from imprisonment and famine. Stalin could not countenance such an embarrassment and had the data immediately destroyed and the Census Board members arrested. The following is the official explanation of what went wrong with the census:

To register all . . . changes in our country and build statistical accounts, a second all-union census was conducted in January 1937.

But it was disrupted by contemptible enemies of the people—Trotsky-Bukharinite spies and traitors to the motherland, having slipped at that time into the leadership of the Central Directory of People's Economic Accounting.

The census of 1937 was conducted with violations of government instructions, with the grossest violations of elementary principles of statistical science.

Enemies of the people set themselves the goal of distorting the real number of the population. Without the government's permission, they printed the wrecker's "Booklet for Censustakers," in which, against instructions, census-takers were ordered to strike out from their census forms all citizens (tabulated in preliminary filling of census lists), not spending the night of 5–6 January at home.

As a result, the census of 1937 dropped many such people (not spending the night of 5–6 January at home), who certainly could not have been counted anywhere else: railwaymen working night shifts, those carrying out official duties, those traveling to a market, or into the forest for wood, and many others. Deliberately, no provision was made for the census to count whole categories of the population, e.g.: all those traveling by cart, by automobile, or in freight trains; those out on the steppe; people waiting for trains at small stations and sidings, etc. Thus, the 1937 census was done without a full count of the population.

The plan for processing census data was also marked by wrecking. In order to distort the class structure of the population, enemies of the people treated family members of Collective farmers, working in household plots, as private farmers. Collective farmers, working in industrial trades at their collective farms (carpenters, cobblers, blacksmiths, etc.), were treated as "hired workers of the collective farms." There were cases when invalids and the aged were treated as non-working elements of the population. The wreckers tried to distort the distribution of population by occupation; according to their idea, the calculations should not include new occupations, characteristic of our socialist economy, for example chairmen of collective farms. Thus they "found" in the USSR such "professions" as servant and governess, which had long ceased to exist on Soviet territory.

The unmasking of the hostile work in the 1937 census obliges Soviet and Party organizations to take special political responsibility for the upcoming census.

Keep in mind, that a masked enemy can try by any "news" or provocateur's distortions to sow doubts about the census. The duty of every Soviet citizen is to watch vigilantly for all enemy machinations, unmask them in time, and cut them out at the root.

Source: *"The National Census—A Duty of the Whole People,"* Bolshevik: Theoretical and Political Journal of the Central Committee of the All-union Communist Party (of Bolsheviks), *nos. 23–24 (December 1938): 61–62.*

on mythological or semimythological foundations. From a rational perspective, this approach meant that emphasizing absolute differences between peoples would stretch objective fact to greater and more unreal degrees. It was difficult to say that Germans, for example, were immeasurably superior to Poles when both peoples had lived next to each other for at least a thousand years separated only by a porous, fluctuating border which enabled them to trade, intermarry, migrate, and live as neighbors, friends, and family. Making a scientific distinction between German Christians and German Jews was an even more arbitrary endeavor, for Germany's Jewish population was continental Europe's most integrated group before the rise of Nazism. As ruthless and methodical as the Nazis were, they faced huge bureaucratic dilemmas when they tried to decide who was to be considered Jewish and who was not (they eventually settled on people

THOUGHT AND CULTURE

Max Planck (l.) and Albert Einstein (r.) at the World Power Conference in Berlin, June 1930

(Bettmann/CORBIS)

repeating the common accusation that an international Jewish conspiracy was plotting to take control of the world—a conspiracy that, he paradoxically claimed, lay at the root of both international communism and international capitalism. Yet, if the Nazis believed Jews to be their inferiors, few appeared to wonder how such an inferior group could ever pose so dangerous a threat to the master race that it had to be exterminated.

Outside of the cultural and political realm, around 1900 new discoveries about the nature of energy, the atomic structure of matter, and the relative relationship of time and space—ushered in by the German physicists Max Planck and Albert Einstein—challenged long-held assumptions about reality and human powers of observation. If energy moves in imperceptible streams of units (quanta) rather than continuous beams, if matter is at the subatomic level more porous than solid, if the most powerful known form of energy derives from the smallest elements in nature, and if time is relative rather than constant, who could argue that the German philosopher Immanuel Kant, a progenitor of the Romantic ethos, was wrong to say that there are higher, unknowable truths operating in a noumenal realm inaccessible to human understanding. As ideologues and racists, perpetrators and victims, dreamers and psychiatrists, and everyone in between discovered, this irrationality was complemented by science or, more dangerously, pseudoscience in twentieth-century Europe.

—PAUL DU QUENOY,
GEORGETOWN UNIVERSITY

who had at least one Jewish grandparent, though there was a list of exceptions).

The centerpiece of Nazi and other racial ideologies, the idea of a master race, was itself rife with contradictions that forced their exponents to rely on an abstract Aryan identity—one that was fallacious in national or biological terms, subject to enormous variation even among the racists, and rarely spoken of by anyone before about 1870. Yet, these contradictions did not matter to cultural figures who relied on the science of observable phenomena (for example, height, hair color, and other superficial physical characteristics) to justify their irrationality. Like the communist ideologues who believed that their suspension of rational thought would ultimately help create paradise on earth, Nazis and other European racists found a malignant sense of purpose and identity in the "scientific" construction of "others" to persecute for the supposed benefit of mankind. In another notable exercise in irrational thought, racists usually portrayed their "inferiors" as a threat that had to be neutralized. Hitler never tired of saying that the Jews endangered Germany's racial purity or of

Viewpoint:
No. Modernism was an expression of individuality in reaction to the stultifying standardization of life, government, and society.

If the eighteenth century was the Age of Reason for European civilization, the twentieth could be called the Age of Irrationality. During the eighteenth century, intellectuals focused on the power of human reason to make the world understandable. Enlightened autocrats tried to develop rational law codes. Artists strove for geometric harmony in their works. Denis Diderot attempted to collect all of humanity's knowledge in his twenty-eight-volume *Encyclopedia* (1751–1772). Adam Smith explained how economies naturally tended toward rationality and justice, and Jeremy Bentham proposed that actions should be valued based on the relative amounts of pleasure and pain they produced. During the twentieth century, by contrast, intellectuals began to explore, even to embrace, the idea that irrationality played a significant and unavoidable role in human history. Political leaders proclaimed the value of struggle, not reason. The avant-garde rejected rational rules in art, to the point at which some (the Dadaists) deliberately created nonsense. Sigmund Freud proclaimed the power of instinct and the unconscious mind; Jean-Paul Sartre urged readers to accept the fact that life was absurd; and Max Planck developed a quantum theory suggesting, as Albert Einstein put it, that "God does not play dice with the universe." A world once perceived as a carefully designed clockwork mechanism had become a mass of colliding atoms ruled, at bottom, by chance.

One of the key characteristics of modernity is change. The idea that "everything flows, nothing remains" is as old as Heraclitus. In the nineteenth and twentieth centuries, though, the speed at which everything flowed became faster. Populations increased exponentially; laborsaving devices appeared one after the other; news crossed the ocean in hours, then minutes; computing machines became obsolete before they hit store shelves.

Modernity is also closely tied to rationality. In the eighteenth century, European intellectuals became committed to bringing about "the progress of mankind towards improvement," as Immanuel Kant put it. Following the Cartesian precept that "we should never allow ourselves to be persuaded except by the evidence of our reason," scholars defined *improvement* not in religious or moral terms but in rational terms. For them, the only true morality was a rational morality. Thus, by using reason—by calculating, analyzing, and connecting structures to functions—humanity was going to rid itself of useless beliefs and superstitions, gain control over its environment, and build a new, better world. This mind-set brought about the French Revolution and the Industrial Revolution, democratization, urbanization, standardization, consumerism, and mass production. It exalted the individual as possessor of reason, but it aimed to bring about improvements for all individuals, not just a select few. Beliefs in rationality and change lie at the bottom of what one late-nineteenth-century philosopher, Goldsworthy Lowes Dickinson, called "the prevailing characteristics of the modern spirit": "dissatisfaction with the world in which we live and determination to realize one that shall be better."

Nevertheless, modernity fostered irrationality. On a philosophical level, Kant and his intellectual heirs had no tangible goals for humanity. Everyone was simply supposed to become more knowledgeable and rational, more enlightened and free, until (presumably) the world was perfect. As the nineteenth and twentieth centuries wore on, though, two things happened as a result of Kantian "progress toward enlightenment": reasoning intellectuals reached areas where logic and reason no longer worked, and (not coincidentally) they began to analyze and attack the idea of rationality itself. Physics provides one of the best examples of the former development. Scientists looking deeper into the structure of matter arrived at subatomic space, where the ordinary rules of physics did not apply. Planck found that randomness, not rationality, governed particle decay. Werner Heisenberg discovered the seemingly illogical truth that the more one knew about the position of a particle in space, the less one could know about its velocity, and vice versa. As later researchers found their own tidy chains of logic dissolving into chaos, it seemed that modern science had reached those limits where, in the words of Friedrich Nietzsche, logic is like a snake that "curls about itself and bites its own tail."

Meanwhile, developments in other fields led people to question the idea that humanity ever would or could be free to behave rationally. In biology, evolutionary theory pointed to the "survival of the fittest," who were not necessarily the most rational; perhaps, people thought, states and civilizations would also prosper if they favored war over philosophy. In psychology, Freud and his followers argued that all humans were ruled not by reason but by sexual and sadistic instincts. Hans Blumenberg and other philosophers followed Nietzsche in arguing that irrational myths performed important functions for societies and individuals. Linguists such as Ludwig Wittgenstein analyzed and dissected language—the tool used to perform rational analyses—and found that the nonrational structure of language largely determined the outcome of the reasoning process. Even sociologists, many of whom argued that seemingly irrational beliefs (fascism, theories of comprehensive worldwide conspiracy, and so forth) and behaviors (using heroin, joining a cult, and so forth) were actually rational coping mechanisms, rejected logic when they talked about the unmet emotional requirements that necessitated the creation of such reactions. In other words, scholars made modern rational arguments in favor of the idea that irrationality should and/or did play an important role in human life. It is even possible that their arguments in turn made irrational behavior "respectable" among modern readers and increased its incidence.

At the same time, irrationality could and did represent a rejection of modernity. Some intellectuals and their followers embraced irrationality as an antidote to what they saw as the sterility, weakness, and falsity of modern life. This trend was already visible by the late eighteenth century, when Romanticists exalted emotion over reason. In 1863, Fedor Dostoevsky's "underground man" epitomized the rejection of modernity when he wrote that he

> wouldn't be surprised in the least, if, suddenly, for no reason at all, in the midst of this future, universal rationalism, some gentleman . . . [were to say]: "How about it, gentlemen, what if we knock over all this rationalism with one swift kick for the sole purpose of sending all these logarithms to hell, so that once again we can live according to our own stupid will!" But that wouldn't matter either; what's so annoying is that he would undoubtedly find some followers; such is the way man is made . . . man, always and everywhere, whoever he is, has preferred to act as he wished, and not at all as reason and advantage have dictated.

The underground man's prediction came true in the 1920s and 1930s, when millions embraced political doctrines—fascism and communism—that involved, according to sociologist Camillo Pellizzi, "opposition to reason and the abstract and empirical individuality of the men of the Enlightenment, the positivists, and the utilitarians." On the purely philosophical level, existentialists such as Jean-Paul Sartre and Albert Camus wrote that life had no rational goal and that existence itself was irrational. For them, "progress toward enlightenment" was a senseless, Sisyphean struggle with a rock that inevitably rolled back down the mountain each time it neared the summit.

Irrationality did not have free reign in the twentieth century, however. Just as the seventeenth-century Age of Reason coexisted with irrational great fears and budding romanticism, the twentieth century produced (along with computers and antibiotics) structuralists, empiricists, and pragmatists who continued to rely heavily on the ideas of reason and progress. Furthermore, the definitions of concepts such as *modernity* and *irrationality* can be seen as products of modern philosophy and social assumptions, so that, like Nietzsche's snake biting its tail, modernity defines itself and its relation to irrationality.

Given this situation, some twentieth-century thinkers tried to strike a balance between a wholesale acceptance of modernity and a wholesale rejection of it. Russian philosopher Sergei Bulgakov, for example, accepted modern science and rationalism as useful and necessary, but he added that "Sophia [eternal wisdom], which establishes the ultimate connection of all things, cannot be understood through science, which only observes nature's regularities and patterns . . . truth reveals itself in miraculous, intuitive ways independent of scientific cognition." Bulgakov wrote those lines in 1912. After World War I and World War II,

more people joined him in the conclusion that while rationality was useful to humanity, it was not enough to live by. They had seen the horrors of total war and the Holocaust, and they had realized that reason alone could not prevent those horrors; for, in the words of sociologist Zygmunt Bauman, "there is nothing in those rules [of 'instrumental rationality'] which disqualifies the Holocaust-style methods of 'social-engineering' as improper or, indeed, the actions they served as irrational." They knew from experience that morality could not be worked out by rational equations. As Arthur Koestler put it:

> In the social equation, the value of a single life is nil; in the cosmic equation it is infinite. Now every schoolboy knows that if you smuggle either a nought or the infinite into a finite calculation, the equation will be disrupted and you will be able to prove that three equals five, or five hundred. Not only Communism, but any political movement which implicitly relies on purely utilitarian ethics, must become a victim to the same fatal error. It is a fallacy as naïve as a mathematical teaser, and yet its consequences lead straight to Goya's Disasters, to the reign of the guillotine, the torture-chambers of the Inquisition, or the cellars of the Lubianka. Whether the road is paved with quotations from Rousseau, Marx, Christ or Mohammed, makes little difference.

The real question, such thinkers suggested, was not whether irrationality was a consequence of modernity, but rather whether modernity could gain an old-fashioned, "irrational" sense of the value of life in time to save itself.

—CATHERINE BLAIR, GEORGETOWN UNIVERSITY

References

Forrest E. Baird and Walter Kaufmann, eds., *Philosophic Classics: Nineteenth-Century Philosophy,* volume 4 (Upper Saddle River, N.J.: Prentice Hall, 1997).

Zygmunt Bauman, *Modernity and the Holocaust* (Ithaca, N.Y.: Cornell University Press, 1989).

Sergei Bulgakov, *Philosophy of Economy: The World as Household,* translated and edited by Catherine Evtuhov (New Haven: Yale University Press, 2000).

Robert Conquest, *Reflections on a Ravaged Century* (New York: Norton, 1999).

René Descartes, *Discourse on Method and Meditations on First Philosophy,* translated by Donald A. Cress (Indianapolis: Hackett, 1980).

THOUGHT AND CULTURE

Robert Donington, *Wagner's 'Ring' and Its Symbols: The Music and the Myth* (London: Faber & Faber, 1963).

Fedor Dostoevsky, *The Brothers Karamazov,* translated by David McDuff (London & New York: Penguin, 2003).

Dostoevsky, *Crime and Punishment,* translated by McDuff (London & New York: Penguin, 2003).

Dostoevsky, *Notes from Underground,* translated and edited by Michael R. Katz (New York & London: Norton, 1989).

Modris Eksteins, *Rites of Spring: The Great War and the Birth of the Modern Age* (New York: Anchor, 1990).

William R. Everdell, *The First Moderns: Profiles in the Origins of Twentieth-Century Thought* (Chicago: University of Chicago Press, 1997).

Leon Festinger and others, *When Prophecy Fails: A Social and Psychological Study of a Modern Group that Predicted the Destruction of the World* (New York: Harper & Row, 1964).

Sigmund Freud, *Civilization and Its Discontents* (New York: Cape & H. Smith, 1930).

François Furet, *The Passing of an Illusion: The Idea of Communism in the Twentieth Century,* translated by Deborah Furet (Chicago: University of Chicago Press, 1999).

Immanuel Kant, *On History,* edited by Lewis White Beck (New York: Macmillan, 1963).

Arthur Koestler, *The Invisible Writing: An Autobiography* (Boston: Beacon, 1956).

Harold D. Lasswell, review of "Our Age of Unreason: A Study of the Irrational Forces in Social Life," *Journal of Modern History,* 16 (June 1944): 137–138.

Ursula K. Le Guin, "The Ones Who Walk Away from Omelas (Variations on a Theme by William James)," in *The Norton Anthology of Short Fiction,* edited by R. V. Cassill, third edition (New York: Norton, 1986), pp. 870–875.

Hermann Lotze, *Microcosmus: An Essay Concerning Man and his Relation to the World,* translated by Elizabeth Hamilton and E. E. Constance Jones (Freeport, N.Y.: Books for Libraries Press, 1971).

L. Nathan Oaklander, ed., *Existentialist Philosophy: An Introduction,* second edition (Englewood Cliffs, N.J.: Prentice Hall, 1996).

Richard Rorty, *Truth and Progress: Philosophical Papers,* volume 3 (Cambridge: Cambridge University Press, 1998).

Max Weber, *The Protestant Ethic and the Spirit of Capitalism,* translated by Talcott Parsons (New York: Scribners, 1958).

UKRAINIAN FAMINE

Was the Ukrainian famine of 1932–1933 caused by genocidal government policies?

Viewpoint: Yes. Josef Stalin deliberately targeted the Ukrainian people for mass destruction and used starvation as his weapon.

Viewpoint: No. Although many Ukrainians died of starvation, there was no consistent plan to punish them collectively, and many members of other nationalities in the Soviet Union also died in the famine.

A terrible famine accompanied the government's collectivization of agriculture during the 1930s in Ukraine, a union republic of the Soviet Union. This policy, part of Soviet leader Josef Stalin's ambitious plan to socialize all aspects of his country's economic life, forced peasants to merge their small private farmsteads into huge collective farms organized and operated by state and Communist Party officials. The tensions and problems inherent in this process were enormous. Widespread resistance spread through the countryside, and the Soviet state used armed repression and wholesale confiscation of grain to enforce its policies. In Ukraine these conditions caused millions of deaths from starvation. Precise numbers of victims are unknown, but estimates range from four to ten million.

This chapter examines a serious accusation against Stalin's regime: that its policies in Ukraine were genocidal. Many witnesses and scholars believe that it was. Deliberate government policies, including some directly issued by Stalin, ensured the near total confiscation of food and prevented starving people from migrating to areas not affected by the famine. Officials spoke of collectivization in Ukraine as an important means of destroying Ukrainian nationalism. The Ukrainian people, in other words, were explicitly targeted for conditions in which many would die.

Others are reluctant to accept this interpretation. Many other nationalities, including Russians, suffered horrible losses during the Soviet Union's collectivization of agriculture, a fact that suggests Ukraine and its people were not targeted purposely or alone. Famine deaths appear to have been spread evenly among all regions that had offered meaningful resistance to the Soviet regime during the Russian Civil War (1918–1920). Though tragic, they say, it seems unlikely that genocide was the motivating factor.

Viewpoint:
Yes. Josef Stalin deliberately targeted the Ukrainian people for mass destruction and used starvation as his weapon.

There can be little doubt that the Soviet government's policies in and toward Ukraine and its people were genocidal, deliberately intended to cause the deaths of millions of people on the basis of who they were. Soviet leader Josef Stalin had consistently and violently opposed all signs of what he considered to be Ukrainian nationalism from the earliest days of the Russian Revolution. Before he initiated the economic policies that lead to the worst famine year, 1932–1933, Stalin purposely annihilated Ukraine's cultural intelligentsia—not so much its engineers, doctors, and technicians, but its linguists, historians, artists, folk singers, and others whose work and professional lives suggested a separate cultural or historical identity for Ukraine. This group included Ukrainian communists, many of whom advocated "nationalist" policies and were eliminated years before Stalin's general purge of Soviet Communist Party members in 1936–1938.

Stalin's next objective in attacking Ukrainian identity was diminishing the economic, demographic, and, thus, political relevance of the land's peasant farmers. Most Ukrainian farmers had historically owned and operated their own small farms, rather than having been serfs and communal farmers under the old regime, and they remained independent and relatively prosperous during the implementation of the New Economic Policy (NEP) in the 1920s. Although the collectivization of agriculture was a national policy that affected all of the Soviet Union's agricultural population, in Ukraine it was designed specifically to end individual proprietorship and the distinct, independent way of life it represented. "De-kulakization," a policy that targeted peasants who were believed to be economically better off and therefore a threat to state control in rural areas, naturally fell hardest on Ukraine's relatively more prosperous peasantry. Under its malignant implementation, hundreds of thousands of Ukraine's most talented farmers and rural community leaders were forcibly deported along with their families to distant parts of the Soviet Union where many died and from whence few returned. The collectivization of agriculture that followed was described in the official Soviet press as a "special task" that would "destroy the social basis of Ukrainian nationalism," clearly indicating a purposeful, anti-Ukrainian element in its application.

Once Ukraine's remaining peasants had been forced to enter state-managed collective farms, a process largely completed by 1932, several government measures actively and deliberately caused a large number of unnatural deaths among them. While all Soviet collective farms were assigned quotas of grain to deliver to central authorities for export or relocation to urban areas, Ukraine as a whole, which produced 27 percent of the country's crops, was ordered to deliver 38 percent of the Soviet Union's total grain quota—a requirement that proportionally exceeded production by more than 40 percent. A decree of August 1932 empowered local Communist Party and secret police officials, of whom almost all were non-Ukrainians at the time, to confiscate unlimited amounts of grain from peasant households. In practice this meant that every last ounce of wheat was seized from peasant families by armed agents who searched private homes, executed resisters, and received special psychological and ideological training to steel themselves against "saccharine humanitarianism" and feelings of remorse and guilt. Further state decrees made concealing grain, pilfering even small amounts of foodstuffs from communal fields and storage facilities, and criticizing the famine and policies that led to it serious crimes against the state, punishable by long and often lethal imprisonment in labor camps. Ukraine's internal borders were sealed, initially to prevent foreigners and unauthorized Soviet citizens from witnessing what was happening, and later—under direct orders issued in January 1933 by Stalin and titular Soviet head of state Vyacheslav Molotov—to prevent starving Ukrainians from escaping their fate by relocating to neighboring non-Ukrainian areas that were not suffering famine. Although the international community nevertheless heard news of what was happening, the Soviet government and its agents categorically denied reports of the famine and universally rejected offers of foreign assistance. Since the Soviet government had accepted American food relief a decade earlier—assistance that saved an estimated ten million lives—it is not unreasonable to suggest that its failure to do so again in the early 1930s was at least partly due to its desire to see certain elements of its population suffer and die.

Critics of interpreting the Ukrainian famine as genocide frequently argue that it was caused by a bad harvest and/or poor, yet nondeliberate, government mismanagement. While some scholars have found evidence of

THE GRAIN PROBLEM

Addendum to the minutes of Politburo [meeting] No. 93.

RESOLUTION OF THE COUNCIL OF PEOPLE'S COMMISSARS OF THE UKRAINIAN SOVIET SOCIALIST REPUBLIC AND OF THE CENTRAL COMMITTEE OF THE COMMUNIST PARTY (BOLSHEVIK) OF UKRAINE ON BLACKLISTING VILLAGES THAT MALICIOUSLY SABOTAGE THE COLLECTION OF GRAIN.

In view of the shameful collapse of grain collection in the more remote regions of Ukraine, the Council of People's Commissars and the Central Committee call upon the oblast executive committees and the oblast [party] committees as well as the raion executive committees and the raion [party] committees: to break up the sabotage of grain collection, which has been organized by kulak and counterrevolutionary elements; to liquidate the resistance of some of the rural communists, who in fact have become the leaders of the sabotage; to eliminate the passivity and complacency toward the saboteurs, incompatible with being a party member; and to ensure, with maximum speed, full and absolute compliance with the plan for grain collection.

The Council of People's Commissars and the Central Committee resolve:

To place the following villages on the black list for overt disruption of the grain collection plan and for malicious sabotage, organized by kulak and counterrevolutionary elements:

1.) village of Verbka in Pavlograd raion, Dnepropetrovsk oblast. . . .

5.) village of Sviatotroitskoe in Troitsk raion, Odessa oblast.

6.) village of Peski in Bashtan raion, Odessa oblast.

The following measures should be undertaken with respect to these villages:

1.) Immediate cessation of delivery of goods, complete suspension of cooperative and state trade in the villages, and removal of all available goods from cooperative and state stores.

2.) Full prohibition of collective farm trade for both collective farms and collective farmers, and for private farmers.

3.) Cessation of any sort of credit and demand for early repayment of credit and other financial obligations.

4.) Investigation and purge of all sorts of foreign and hostile elements from cooperative and state institutions, to be carried out by organs of the Workers and Peasants Inspectorate.

5.) Investigation and purge of collective farms in these villages, with removal of counterrevolutionary elements and organizers of grain collection disruption.

The Council of People's Commissars and the Central Committee call upon all collective and private farmers who are honest and dedicated to Soviet rule to organize all their efforts for a merciless struggle against kulaks and their accomplices in order to: defeat in their villages the kulak sabotage of grain collection; fulfill honestly and conscientiously their grain collection obligations to the Soviet authorities; and strengthen collective farms.

CHAIRMAN OF THE COUNCIL OF PEOPLE'S COMMISSARS OF THE UKRAINIAN SOVIET SOCIALIST REPUBLIC - V. CHUBAR'.

SECRETARY OF THE CENTRAL COMMITTEE OF THE COMMUNIST PARTY (BOLSHEVIK) OF UKRAINE - S. KOSIOR.

6 December 1932.

Source: *"Grain Problem," Revelations from the Russian Archives: Ukrainian Famine, Library of Congress Home Page <http://lcweb.loc.gov/exhibits/archives/k2grain.html>.*

UKRAINIAN FAMINE

confusion and dissension in state and Communist Party organs during the famine, eyewitness testimony and well-known economic facts disprove this conclusion. Virtually every firsthand account of Ukraine in the early 1930s—from victims of the famine as well as from its perpetrators—testifies to the opposite. In addition to the thorough searches, grain confiscations, and official state directives, most Ukrainian accounts include recollections of vast storehouses of wheat and other foodstuffs existing under guard in or near their villages. Many of these stores were emptied for export, but often they were simply left to rot while the peasants who had produced them continued to starve. The agents charged with confiscating grain almost uniformly remembered being told that no matter how unpleasant it was to condemn innocent people to death, their actions would guarantee a strong Soviet Union, destroy "separatist" Ukrainian nationalism, and help realize the fulfillment of the communist dream. This situation was not a case of overzealous officials requisitioning grain to fulfill their duties, or of an unfortunate land suffering from a bad harvest, but of a state that oppressed one of its most prosperous subject nationalities by willfully denying sustenance to its people. Those who argue the "mismanagement" thesis usually respond to these voluminous firsthand accounts with sweeping dismissal (claiming for example, all the witnesses lied), despite their inability to disprove them and even though scholars of other genocides, especially the Holocaust, identify such testimony as serious and crucially important primary evidence. As for the myth of Ukraine's bad harvest, even as the peasants starved, the Soviet government's crash industrialization policy dramatically increased the country's urban population, which consumed food rather than produced it (without mass starvation), while the country's foreign trade monopoly exported some 1.7 million tons of grain to foreign markets in 1932–1933. The latter figure alone was sufficient to provide between 1 and 2.5 pounds of food per day for a year to each Ukrainian who died in the famine, depending on the mortality number one uses—to say nothing of the domestic surpluses and the large wasted quantities that eyewitnesses later recalled.

Since most Ukrainians nevertheless survived, some have argued that these policies could not have been genocidal—in other words, because Stalin's actions did not appear to share or equal Adolf Hitler's determined attempt to annihilate entire peoples, it is inappropriate to call the Soviet regime genocidal. Under the prevailing legal definitions, however, the Soviet state's failure to cause the deaths of all or even most of its Ukrainian population does not absolve it of genocide. The United Nations' Convention on Genocide specifically states that the crime is characterized by the "intent to destroy, in whole or in part, a national, ethnical, racial, or religious group." This definition is thus not limited to perpetrators who kill all members or a majority of members of such a group. Any organized killing of people on the basis of their ethnicity fits the international legal definition, even if only a minority died as a result. With some 40 million Ukrainians living in the Soviet Union, there were limitations on what Stalin could do to them. When his successor, Nikita Khrushchev, who had been the secretary of the Ukrainian Soviet Socialist Republic in the late 1930s, partially revealed some of Stalin's crimes in a February 1956 speech to the Communist Party elite, he claimed that Stalin wanted to deport all of the Ukrainians to Siberia but realized he could not because of the sheer numbers involved. Since Stalin did deport Chechens, Crimean Tatars, Volga Germans, and other numerically smaller nationalities, however, there is no reason to doubt that the dictator could think in such terms or that he lacked the desire and intent to carry them out.

It is therefore perfectly reasonable to argue that Stalin's policies were genocidal: they were directed specifically at the Soviet Ukrainian population as a whole and caused enough deaths that its numbers dropped significantly, while the survivors remained cowed and intimidated thereafter. Creating conditions designed to cause death (as opposed to direct killing), it should be noted, is another definition of genocide elaborated in the UN's Convention, which refers specifically to "acts . . . deliberately inflicting on the group conditions of life calculated to bring about its physical destruction in whole or in part." Several consequences of the famine indicate that Stalin succeeded in meeting this definition. Millions of Ukrainians died in conditions created by a state that made great and deliberate efforts to leave them without even subsistence levels of food. The absolute number and relative proportion of Ukrainians living in the Soviet Union quickly and significantly declined, diminishing the influence that a larger, prosperous population would have had. The decline also helped facilitate large-scale ethnic Russian immigration into their homeland, a strategically important frontier region that shared its history and culture with freer Ukrainian populations living on the other side of the Soviet border with Eastern Europe. Ethnic Russians still make up more than 20 percent of independent Ukraine's population, a figure that was considerably higher

Ukrainian peasant girl
whose parents starved to
death, 1934

*(Hulton-Deutsch
Collection/CORBIS)*

UKRAINIAN FAMINE

in Soviet times. The statistical distribution of deaths among Ukrainian famine victims, moreover, fell disproportionately on children (an estimated one-third of whom perished) and added to the adverse long-term effects on Ukraine's demographic situation. Millions of the famine's survivors emerged from it malnourished, physically weakened, diseased, and knowing that their future survival depended on the good graces of a state that had just starved them and their millions of deceased countrymen. The postfamine Ukrainian population emerged measurably smaller, weaker, and less influential.

A final argument advanced by critics of the genocide interpretation is that Soviet terror and collectivization-related famine deaths were not confined to Ukraine. The Chechens and other nationalities deported from their homelands during World War II lost over one-half their number to starvation, exposure, and disease. Many other ethnic groups, including Russians, died from famine in the 1930s and at other times, and the cultural intelligentsias of many other minority nationalities were obliterated in a conscious effort to root out any sense or potential sense of ethnic separatism. The steppe nomads of Central Asia are believed to have suffered 40 percent mortality rates after they were forced to abandon their traditional way of life for permanent settlements under state control. Arguing that the Ukrainian famine was genocidal, however, does not at all deny or trivialize these atrocities. Soviet expert Robert Conquest, whose book *The Harvest of Sorrow: Soviet Collectivization and the Terror-Famine* (1986) directly endorses the genocide interpretation by comparing Ukraine in the 1930s to "a vast Belsen" (a Nazi concentration camp), also generously acknowledges other Soviet nationalities' suffering from famine and deportation, as do almost all other serious studies. Targeting multiple ethnicities, in other words, does not and cannot absolve a state of committing acts of genocide against individual ethnicities per se. Indeed, although Jews were the most prominent victims of the Holocaust, the Nazis also relentlessly persecuted and killed Gypsies, Poles, Russians, Jehovah's Witnesses, and a host of others, including Ukrainians, on the sole basis of their ethnic or religious identity. Yet, it would be ludicrous to claim that none of these groups was a victim of genocide because others were also victimized. The same logic should apply to the Ukrainians, whose deliberate murder through state-manufactured famine fits every current definition of genocide.

–PAUL DU QUENOY,
GEORGETOWN UNIVERSITY

**Viewpoint:
No. Although many Ukrainians died of starvation, there was no consistent plan to punish them collectively, and many members of other nationalities in the Soviet Union also died in the famine.**

The millions of Ukrainians who died during the famine of the early 1930s perished as the result of severe repression and deeply flawed state agricultural policies. Although the fact and scope of this tragedy are undeniable and stand as one of the twentieth century's greatest crimes against humanity, identifying Ukraine's suffering as genocidal is not necessarily accurate. Little direct evidence supports the conclusion that the Soviet government deliberately targeted the Ukrainian people alone for destruction, while substantial evidence indicates other causes of the famine. Focusing on famine-related deaths in Ukraine also excludes the catastrophes that befell other Soviet peoples, including the Soviet Union's dominant ethnic Russian population, many of whom also suffered from famine and political persecution.

The most important fact illustrating this essay's argument is that in more than a decade since the collapse of the Soviet Union, no documents have emerged to show that Soviet leader Josef Stalin or members of his ruling inner circle consciously conceived or ordered the implementation of genocidal policies in Ukraine. This fact does not deny that the Ukrainian people were subject to arbitrary rule, that they were terrorized by the Soviet secret police, or that they died unnaturally in large numbers because of the actions of their government. They shared that sad fate with all of the peoples of the Soviet Union. Its significance, however, is that there is no known Soviet record equivalent to Nazi Germany's Wannsee Protocol, the memorandum of a secret January 1942 meeting of high officials who adopted the extermination of Europe's Jews as an official policy. In the absence of such a document, scholars who argue that the Ukraine's famine was genocidal often base their case mostly on comments, actions, and other highly circumstantial evidence that support their conclusion.

Just as hard evidence of genocidal intent remains elusive, other evidence contradicts it. Even if one uses the highest estimated numbers of victims, an overwhelming majority—perhaps 75 or 80 percent—of Ukrainians living in the Soviet Union survived the famine years. More moderate numbers yield an even higher survival rate, exceeding 90 percent. Because the Soviet Ukrainians were under the state's complete control and entirely at its mercy, it is unlikely that so many would have lived if Stalin had been committed to their genocidal murder, especially since he remained in power for another twenty years after the famine. His ruthless treatment of the Chechens, Volga Germans, Crimean Tatars, Meshkhetian Turks, Balkars, and the Ingush people during World War II proved that when he wanted to, he could use the state's resources to carry out a people's wholesale deportation and cause huge proportions of them, often more than half, to die in the process. The fate of these peoples did not befall the Ukrainians in nearly as comprehensive a way or solely because of their ethnicity. Many did suffer and die, but this horror was shared by all of those unfortunate enough to live under Soviet rule.

Further, while Ukrainians did represent a substantial number of Soviet famine victims in the early 1930s, they were neither the phenomenon's only sufferers, nor, in a proportional sense, its greatest sufferers. "De-kulakization" (removing peasants who were considered a potential source of opposition), collectivization, and the other state agricultural policies that caused famine were not confined to Ukraine but were national measures that affected tens of millions of non-Ukrainians living in agricultural regions all over the Soviet Union. At least one million ethnic Russians living in the North Caucasus region and along the river Volga also died of starvation in the 1930s, as did many members of smaller ethnic groups. In Central Asia the region's nomadic peoples were forced to form permanent settlements, which prevented them from following their herds, and then to cultivate cotton and other nonedible crops that left them almost totally bereft of sustenance. Exact numbers remain unknown, but experts have estimated that 40 percent of the indigenous population of the Central Asian steppe died as a result of these policies. Nomadic tribes in Siberia and the Soviet Far East suffered deaths in similarly great proportions. Although the number of Ukrainian victims was larger in absolute terms, a greater percentage of these populations perished.

Was there any rhyme or reason to the geographic and ethnographic dispersal of famine deaths in the Soviet Union in the early 1930s? The first and most obvious factor shared by all of the affected regions was the predominance of agriculture as their main economic activity. The Soviet Union's cities, industrial regions, and forested rural areas did not suffer famine on nearly as great a scale as the farming regions did, if at all. This divergence implicates Stalin's economic policy of using the Soviet agricultural sector's produce to finance his program of rapid industrialization. In order to assure profitable exports and sufficient food supplies for the country's expanding urban areas and industrial workforce, the state imposed murderously strict control over the countryside. Eliminating kulaks and others who might have offered resistance, forcibly confiscating so much grain that farmers starved, and pushing peasants into collective farms accomplished this goal, but led to the famine and its millions of unnatural deaths. Since Ukraine had long been the breadbasket of Russia and the Soviet Union, and indeed of much of Europe, it was intrinsically one of the most likely places to suffer the consequences of Stalinist economics.

Second, as some analyses have suggested, the most vicious implementation of state policies that led to famine appears to have occurred in regions that offered the greatest resistance to Soviet power in the years after the Bolshevik coup d'état of November 1917. Once again, Ukraine represented a prime target. In January 1918 its autonomous government formally declared independence from Soviet Russia, and over the next two years a series of strongly anti-Soviet nationalist governments ruled the country. At various times during the Russian Civil War, Ukraine also hosted the anti-Bolshevik White Russian Armies of Generals Anton Denikin and Petr Wrangel, as well as the anti-Soviet partisan movement led by the anarchist Nestor Makhno. Only military conquest eventually assured Soviet control of Ukraine, and this experience was shared with most of the other regions that suffered in the famine in the 1930s. Of those regions the North Caucasus was both a major center of Cossack resistance and the main power base of Denikin's army throughout the Civil War; it, too, had to be conquered by the Red Army. Armed, organized peasant resistance inflamed the Volga provinces in 1919–1921 and was only suppressed by full-scale military operations. White armies based in the Far East continued to function until 1921–1922, often with the support of the indigenous peoples who opposed the Soviets and later suffered in the famine. In Central Asia, Soviet arms suppressed an autonomous anti-Soviet government in early 1918, and the Russian Empire's vassal states in the region, Khiva and Bukhara, resisted Soviet attempts to conquer them until 1920. Armed attacks by native rebels, the Basmachi, lasted well into the mid 1920s. While these rebellious peripheral regions all later suffered from the famine, the more passive and

UKRAINIAN FAMINE

urbanized areas of the Russian heartland did not or did to a much lesser degree. It is entirely reasonable to suggest that Stalin implemented famine-creating policies at least partly to punish and weaken past centers of resistance and unrest. Ukraine was not exceptional, and if it was singled out for punishment, it was as one part of a broad swath of Soviet territory that had posed sustained challenges to Moscow's rule.

–JOHN PAWL,
WASHINGTON, D.C.

References

Yaroslav Bilinsky, "Was the Ukrainian Famine of 1932–1933 Genocide?" *Journal of Genocide Research,* 1 (1999): 147–156.

Marco Carynnyk and others, eds., *The Foreign Office and the Famine: British Documents on Ukraine and the Great Famine of 1932–1933* (Kingston, Ontario: Limestone, 1988).

Robert Conquest, *The Harvest of Sorrow: Soviet Collectivization and the Terror-Famine* (London: Hutchinson, 1986).

Wasyl Hryshko, *The Ukrainian Holocaust of 1933*, edited and translated by Marco Carynnyk (Toronto: Bahriany Foundation, 1983).

Roman Serbyn and Bohdan Krawchenko, eds., *Famine in Ukraine, 1932–1933* (Edmonton: Canadian Institute of Ukrainian Studies, University of Alberta, 1986).

U.S. Commission on the Ukraine Famine, *Investigation of the Ukrainian Famine 1932–1933: Report to Congress* (Washington, D.C.: U.S. Government Printing Office, 1988).

UKRAINIAN FAMINE

WELFARE STATE

Has the welfare state been effective?

Viewpoint: Yes. Comprehensive state-sponsored social welfare programs and economic intervention have provided necessary remedies for the needs of European societies.

Viewpoint: No. The welfare state has long been an unwieldy and counter-productive burden that most European nations can no longer afford.

Responding to the pressures of industrialization and urbanization, many European governments took it upon themselves to play a larger and, it was hoped, more beneficial role in the lives of their citizens. Beginning in the 1880s, politicians of several ideological viewpoints advocated bureaucratized systems of social welfare to cover such needs as health insurance, old age pensions, and education. Some advocated redistributive financial programs to eliminate extremes of wealth and poverty and to address the economic bases of social problems. The trauma of World War I added an urgent and widespread need to care for veterans and the families of the dead. After facing the even greater social challenges of World War II, most Western European governments adopted "cradle to grave" care for their populations, providing material support for almost every conceivable need. The "welfare state," as it has come to be called, was perhaps the most prominent social institution of postwar Europe.

Recently, however, the welfare state has come under attack. As one essay in the chapter argues, it has engendered tremendous financial challenges that national economies and European workers may not be able to face much longer. As Europe's population ages demographically, serious questions about its citizens' ability and willingness to pay for comprehensive state support are asked with greater frequency. A culture of entitlement and benefits that may discourage productive work add to the dilemmas of the welfare state.

The counterargument presents a different perspective. Despite its great expense, the welfare state provides for Europeans on an unprecedented and unequaled scale. Even as more Europeans complain about high taxes and unfair policies, they are living longer, healthier, and safer lives than almost anyone else in the world. Their access to health care, child care, education, insurance, and employment opportunities are enormous and envied. Whatever flaws the welfare state may have, this argument maintains, the results prove its value in both theory and practice. As the question of the welfare state is raised not only across Europe but also all over the world in the twenty-first century, a consideration of its advantages and demerits is in order.

Viewpoint:
Yes. Comprehensive state-sponsored social welfare programs and economic intervention have provided necessary remedies for the needs of European societies.

At first glance, there seems no way to judge historically whether the European welfare state has been a success without wading into the waters of politics or political theory. Measures of success or failure rest upon many factors. Yet, it seems on balance that the European social welfare state has been a worthwhile endeavor, whatever its flaws.

Even in a country with the most comprehensive and generous welfare system, such as Sweden or Denmark, there is no shortage of critics. Some complain, for example, about unemployment benefits that pay 80 to 90 percent of lost wages. Where, the argument goes, is the incentive to work? More recently, there has also been some vigorous criticism of the extension of social welfare benefits to immigrants and refugees. Others criticize a system that allows students to remain subsidized at universities well into their thirties without any serious repercussions. Moreover, there are few who are enthusiastic about income taxes that can range from 40 to 80 percent.

One needs to balance these facts against the positive features of the welfare state in Europe, however. It would be impossible to give a complete list of social benefits provided to European citizens, but the benefits that can be found in the European Union today include the following: subsidized or free day care for children; free or subsidized nursing home or home health care for the elderly or for those who are unable to care for themselves; income supplements for families with lower incomes; rent support and comfortable, safe, public housing for the poor; shopping services for older people living on their own; income stipends for students; free education from kindergarten through postgraduate study; retirement pensions; and universal health insurance. Europe has sought to provide for the well-being of its citizens from the "cradle to the grave."

With such a scope of benefits, one can see why it is difficult to declare whether it has been successful. The effort has remained popular among the citizenry. When asked about the welfare state, many Europeans will express pride in their countries' effort to care for their fellow citizens. While Americans might see such an arrangement as an opportunity for freeloaders to take advantage of the situation, Europeans see the welfare state as a positive achievement. Americans, who normally see themselves as not being particularly dogmatic, are in this case actually clinging to their free-market view of the world: not only will the invisible hand provide for all needs but Americans also believe that anything else will morally corrupt the recipients of such aid. Compare this view to the one French prime minister Edouard Balladur expressed in a 1993 *Financial Times* interview: "What is the Market? It is the law of the jungle. And what is civilization? It is the struggle against nature." For Europeans, it is the duty of the state to protect its citizens against the vagaries of existence. While an American is willing to accept that the market creates winners and losers, the European wishes to use the power of the state to provide a better life for all members of a society, not just those at the top of the socio-economic ladder.

One way to measure the success of the welfare state is to determine whether the well-being of people is better for living in a welfare state. How to measure this is less clear, however. On a purely material level, it is hard to surpass the Americans, who consume more energy, electronic equipment, automobiles, and calories than just about anyone in the world. The country that most obviously can be compared to the United States, Canada, does not measure as high in terms of material consumption, but this situation might well be related to the fact that Canada has sought to build a welfare state much more akin to Europe's. Certainly, a social welfare state costs money that might be spent on private consumption. On a material level, then, perhaps, the welfare state has not been such a success.

If one examines the distinction between a fully developed country that chooses a welfare state (the countries of continental Europe) and one that does not (the United States), then perhaps some useful conclusions can be drawn. One might conclude that the welfare state has in fact been successful in producing a society that is happier and more peaceful than the alternative, in light of the stresses and strains that modern life can produce. If one looks for such indicators, perhaps then one could say that the European welfare society has been successful.

One of the arguments heard in America about proposals to adopt a state-directed health insurance program has been that such a system would inevitably be of a lower quality than a private system. This stance, of course, is a reflection of the American bias against its public sector. By many measures, however, it appears that Europeans are healthier than Americans. Life expectancy, for example, shows a gap between the Europeans and Americans. Figures from the *CIA World Factbook* for 2002 include the following life expectancy figures:

Country	Life Expectancy (combined male/female)
Sweden	79.84
France	79.05
Netherlands	78.58
Germany	77.78
Finland	77.75
United States	77.40

Source: *CIA World Factbook* <www.cia.gov/cia/publications/factbook/>.

The gap here is particularly great between the United States and the Netherlands, France, and Sweden. Germany's figures may be affected by the fact that a sizable portion of its population now includes people from former East Germany, where health care, diet, and environment are not up to normal German standards. Perhaps more useful figures for comparison are those for infant mortality, which depend greatly upon access to adequate medical care. Infant mortality is much higher in the United States than it is in Europe.

Country	Infant Mortality (deaths per 1,000 live births)
Sweden	3.44
Finland	3.76
Netherlands	4.31
France	4.41
Germany	4.65
United States	6.69

Source: *CIA World Factbook* <www.cia.gov/cia/publications/factbook/>.

One should also note that medical statistics in the United States can vary widely between urban and suburban populations. The *Detroit Free Press* recently reported that infant mortality rates in urban Detroit were three times those of the suburban areas. In Europe the difference between urban and nonurban populations is significantly less. Income is famously more evenly distributed in Europe than in the United States. The Gini Coefficient of income distribution is particularly illustrative in this regard.

Country	Gini Coefficient 0 = all families have equal incomes 100 = one family has all the income
Sweden	25.0
Finland	25.6
Germany	30.0
Netherlands	32.6
France	32.7
United States	40.8

Source: *CIA World Factbook* <www.cia.gov/cia/publications/factbook/>.

The Gini figures are quite surprising. A listing of countries with a Gini index more like that of the United States and less like that of Europe

yields the following countries: Cambodia (40.8), Guinea (40.3), Kyrgyzstan (40.5), Moldova (40.6), Turkmenistan (40.8), Morocco (39.5), Mozambique (39.6), Russia (39.9), and Ghana (39.6). Thailand, Tunisia, and Turkey all have figures in the 41 range. Europe's more even distribution of wealth is the result of deliberate government policy; similarly, the United States's figure is the result of a deliberate policy to promote individual liberty and consumption.

With an inequitable income distribution and a lack of social services, it might be expected that the disaffected in the United States have turned to crime in a system that they might see as stacked against them. Homicide rates certainly show a gap between Europe and the United States:

Country	Number of Homicides
Denmark	8
Norway	9
Switzerland	12
Sweden	21
Netherlands	21
Canada	121
United States	5,718

Source: *United Nations Demographic Yearbook, 1995*

Although to do so is speculative, it might be argued that the higher (272 times that of Sweden, for example) number of murders in the United States indicate unhappiness or desperation in American life. One needs to consider, however, whether there are extraneous factors at play here, given the great difference between the American case and the European one. For example, one ought to note the ready availability of guns in the United States, as compared to Europe. One also ought to take into account America's strong protection of the accused. Yet, if such liberties for the accused yield more criminals on the street and fewer behind bars, figures for incarceration do not indicate it:

Country	Incarceration Rate (inmates per 100,000 people)
Sweden	45.95
Netherlands	48.31
Germany	90.10
Canada	120*
United States	613.48

Source: *United Nations Crime and Justice Information Network, World Crime Surveys: Sixth Survey* <www.uncjin.org>; * *Statistics Canada* <www.statscan.ca>.

That America's crime rate is higher than Europe's derives from America's ethnic heterogeneity may have an element of truth to it, but one needs to compare Canada in this case, for the

BUILDING THE NEW EUROPE TOGETHER

Below is an excerpt from a speech by Romano Prodi, president of the European Commission, delivered at the Social Dialogue Summit in Brussels on 13 December 2001:

Ladies and Gentlemen:

This has been an important meeting, and I thank you for this opportunity to draw conclusions from it.

Clearly, Europe is facing several major challenges.

The challenge of enlargement.

The challenge of reforming European governance.

The challenge of modernizing the Welfare State.

The challenge of combining a healthy, competitive economy with a fair and caring society.

Most immediately, there is the challenge of the current economic slowdown, aggravated by the recent terrorist attacks.

The physical arrival of the Euro next month will certainly help. Handled successfully, it will give a real boost to consumer confidence.

But there is much else that needs to be done, and the European Commission is counting on both sides of industry to play their part.

Employers need to explore all the options for redeploying and retraining staff, improving the quality of work.

Employees, for their part, need to continue working with employers to improve labor relations and helping firms find innovative, socially responsible solutions to their problems.

These difficult times call for real solidarity and for even more constructive dialogue between the social partners.

The current crisis must not deflect us from our commitment to modernize our economy and society. Quite the opposite, in fact: it should spur us to greater efforts.

Those efforts must be directed at bringing our European social model up to date.

Some people deny that there is such a thing as a European social model. I disagree.

Certainly there are differences between, say, the Italian and Swedish versions of the Welfare State. But that is not the point. The point is that all European societies share the same fundamental social values.

It is unacceptable in any European country that a human being—whether an EU citizen or not—should die of cold and hunger on our streets. Every European country wants a fair society, and every European government recognizes that you can't have a fair society without fair pay.

The Welfare State, in its various national forms, is one of the greatest European achievements of the 20th century. Our task is to adapt it to our 21st century realities. Realities such as our aging population and our shrinking workforce.

Indeed, we have a moral duty to adapt our social model so as to preserve its benefits for future generations. . . .

The price of failure . . . is simply unaffordable. . . .

Let's build the new Europe together.

Source: *"Building the New Europe Together," EUROPA, EU internet web page <http:// europa.eu.int/futurum/documents/speech/ sp131201_en.pdf>.*

WELFARE STATE

ethnic mix there is as rich as it is in the United States, and Canada's incarceration rate seems more like Europe's. One has to wonder what the Canadians are doing to keep murder and incarceration rates so much lower than the United States. One obvious factor is that they are maintaining a welfare state.

The figures indicate that Europe, with its welfare state, seems to have produced a more peaceful society. It also appears that Europeans' health is better in the aggregate than in the nearest comparable countries. To provide comfort and security has certainly been the goal of the welfare state. By this measure, perhaps, it can be said to have succeeded. The greatest criticism leveled against the welfare state has been that its cost has weakened Europe's competitive position vis-à-vis America, but one has to wonder whether Europeans want to pay the price of high crime and incarceration rates and lower levels of health care than they currently enjoy. Such a tradeoff seems to be one that Europeans are hesitant to make. That situation perhaps is the best proof that the welfare state has been a success.

–PHIL GILTNER,
ALBANY ACADEMY

Viewpoint:
No. The welfare state has long been an unwieldy and counterproductive burden that most European nations can no longer afford.

When the Industrial Revolution emerged on the European continent, various countries began shifting resources from agrarian to industrial sectors. Cities became overcrowded as more people arrived looking for employment in the new factories that were springing up, practically overnight. Governments were faced with new domestic challenges to deal with multiple issues emerging from industrialization. One of the most significant results of this transition was the inception of the welfare state. For the first time in history, central governments took it upon themselves to insure a minimum level of health and financial welfare for their citizens.

The welfare state, as it exists in Europe today, while hailed as humane and egalitarian, has done little more than coddle its citizens in a state of perpetual dependence and effectively cripple state finances over the long run. By providing "cradle to grave" financial support for their citizens, many European states provide unemployment insurance, free medical care, and

generous public pensions, all derived from an enormous tax burden placed upon their citizens.

When Chancellor Otto von Bismarck instituted old-age insurance in Prussian-dominated Germany in the 1880s, he was hailed for the liberal move that would provide funds for elderly Germans rendered unable to work by the ravages of time. Of course, Bismarck was more concerned with undercutting the growing support of the liberal and socialist parties in the Reichstag, the German parliament. His plan was to tax laborers during their working lives and pay them a pension after they reached age sixty-five. Since most people never lived to reach age sixty-five in the nineteenth century, however, few people lived to collect their pensions. By the late twentieth century, when most Germans lived into their mid seventies, government financial support for the elderly consumed an enormous portion of the national budget. Liberal and other Left-wing governments throughout Western Europe subsequently adopted similar ideas and found themselves in the same dilemmas.

As for unemployment, after 1945 the welfare institutions of Western Europe were broadened in order to curb unemployment and combat growing communist sentiment. Many Word War II veterans were young men returning from violent circumstances and could be a force for political upheaval and revolution if left unemployed. Governments instituted mandatory retirement and extensive pension benefits in order to open up the job market for the returning veterans. The system of universal "cradle to grave" coverage, however, soon proved too expensive for Europe to maintain. Low birth rates and high longevity have revealed the cracks in the systems and created circumstances that will render the current state welfare systems unsustainable within the next few decades.

Contemporary Europe is going through an aging transition, along with many other countries around the world. The net result is that several European states have already begun to experience contracting labor forces. Meanwhile, the largest generation in Europe, born near the end of World War II, is moving into retirement. The departure of the "baby boomers" from the work force will create a vacuum that their younger cohorts cannot possibly fill and that the government will not be able to afford. The baby boomers of most European nations have paid payroll taxes ranging from 37 to 48 percent of their incomes for most or all of their working lives and expect their governments to honor their promises to pay their pensions. Unfortunately, their pensions will come from payroll deductions from the existing workforce, which will soon be too small to cover them.

A few statistical projections illustrate the demographic dilemma. According to United Nations figures, the German working-age population (ages twenty to sixty-four) is projected to decline by 31 percent by 2050. Over the same period of time, the number of Germans over age sixty-five will grow to more than 30 percent of the total population. Italy will be in even worse shape by 2050, with its working-age population declining by more than 41 percent and its elderly population increasing by 48 percent. Since 1950 the median age in Spain has grown from 27.7 years to 37.7 years, an increase of more than 26 percent. Low birth rates and low mortality will cause the median age in Spain to soar by a further 31 percent, to 55.2 years, in 2050. The aging of these countries will precipitate a fundamental shift in resources, as more government capital will need to be redirected towards the needs of the older population, which is poised to eclipse their younger cohorts and leave them to bear the burden of increased taxation.

In addition to the spiraling costs associated with the demographic problem, the structures of the welfare state are also problematic. In Germany, the national unemployment insurance program implemented in the 1950s and 1960s is so generous that the impetus and compulsion to seek work is effectively removed in many situations. The widely accepted concept that a person would rather earn their bread than be given it has been negated by an overly generous system that, among other things, does not compel jobless profession-

als to accept underemployment at work that is "beneath" them. In Germany one could literally retire at age sixty from a career of unemployment. The United Kingdom's national health coverage, administered by the National Health Service (NHS), is universal and includes all citizens. Conceived of in 1942 and implemented in 1945, it is today poorly managed, disorganized, and underfunded. It is not uncommon for patients to wait a year or more for surgery and other forms of treatment. Government hospitals and clinics frequently run out of widely prescribed drugs and frequently lose patient records. Many patients die from illnesses that private health care sectors, like that of the United States, treat in a far more timely and effective manner, while others suffer from scandalously negligent patient care. Many British patients seek health care abroad to avoid the sometimes fatal waiting periods, or purchase necessary treatment in Britain's limited private health care sector with their own resources. Despite its obvious problems, the NHS currently costs 7.1 percent of Britain's gross domestic product, a figure that is expected to climb despite a lack of improvement in medical care. In April 2002 the British government announced that the NHS could only be funded and improved in the future by substantial tax increases.

The circumstances in Italy are in some ways worse. Although Italy has no unemployment insurance, its labor laws prohibit layoffs, leading employers to develop an attitude that severely

French prime minister Alain Juppé (r.) with his predecessor, Edouard Balladur, at Matignon, 14 June 1996

(Jean Bernard Vernier/CORBIS SYGMA)

WELFARE STATE

inhibits hiring. In a competitive international economy, Italian employers are increasingly unwilling to hire workers whom they will never be able to let go in the event of a poor economy or serious business losses. Italy's powerful labor unions are staunchly against any efforts to liberalize labor policies, and in March 2002 members of one radical communist group murdered a government adviser who recommended such measures. With unemployment at more than 10 percent, many unemployed young men live with their families, sometimes until they are in their thirties or forties. The nickname *momoni*, or *mama's boys*, has developed as a result.

In France the structural problems of the welfare state are also acute. In 1995 Alain Juppé's Center-Right government attempted to raise the minimum number of years a civil servant had to work before he could receive his full pension benefits, from 37.5 to 40 years. The proposed reform incited such an enormous uproar that after weeks of continuous riots across the nation, the proposal was dropped and the government collapsed soon after. When a Left-wing coalition government came to power under the leadership of the socialist Lionel Jospin in 1997, the National Assembly passed a law that reduced the work week from forty hours to thirty-five and simultaneously prohibited employers from making corresponding reductions in pay. Productivity dropped while labor costs remained the same. Even though the measure was taken to reduce unemployment by creating more available work hours for the jobless, as of March 2002 unemployment in France still stood at more than 9 percent, nearly twice that of the United States's then recessing economy. Much of the "protest vote" that fueled the unexpectedly popular April–May 2002 presidential candidacies of the extreme Right-wing leader Jean-Marie Le Pen and various candidates of the extreme Left came from the disgruntled unemployed.

The nature of Western European political systems is rife with divisions over welfare state reforms. The impetus for drastic fiscal reform will remain absent so long as strong elements of these governments continue to play off the fears of the populace and refuse to act.

In certain respects the nations of Eastern Europe are far more amenable to sweeping reform of national welfare systems. Each of the former Soviet Bloc countries has had to enact economic reforms to separate their countries from their communist pasts and place themselves on the road to economic recovery. Eastern European nations have moved ahead of their Western neighbors in enacting and implementing reforms. Poland, for example, has taken tremendous strides in developing a pension system funded by a combination of direct payroll contributions and market funding to offset its dwindling labor supply. The Polish government developed a public relations campaign to promote the change. The campaign proved successful, and a subsequent referendum endorsed the government's will to act.

European populations are simultaneously outgrowing the resources of their national welfare institutions, and the net result of this process is that the same institutions that were designed to maintain their citizen's financial well-being will ultimately fail to deliver and continue to inflict financial harm. The riots and protests are likely to continue as the governments of Europe are forced to make unpopular changes to salvage already unsustainable systems. Across Europe, long-established welfare systems have stymied the Continent's tremendous natural potential for growth and economic expansion by maintaining exorbitant taxes to cover a flawed system that will soon collapse under its own weight. The governments of Europe are desperately seeking viable solutions to the dilemmas associated with the welfare state, but with tremendous political pressure being brought to bear by trade unions and older workers who fear for their futures, the outlook appears grim. These governments know that time is working against them as the first wave of the baby boom generation inches toward retirement. The loss of so many workers and their tax revenues will fundamentally change the nature of domestic policies for the foreseeable future. In order to fulfill their obligations to the financial well-being of Europe's citizenry throughout the twenty-first century, European governments must somehow reform or discard the institutions of yesterday.

–CRAIG ROMM,
CENTER FOR STRATEGIC AND
INTERNATIONAL STUDIES

References

Maurizio Ferrera and Martin Rhodes, eds., *Recasting European Welfare States* (London: Frank Cass, 2000).

Peter Flora, ed., *Growth to Limits: The Western European Welfare States Since World War II* (Berlin & New York: De Gruyter, 1986–).

Stein Kuhnle, ed., *Survival of the European Welfare State* (London & New York: Routledge, 2000).

Martin Rhodes, ed., *Southern European Welfare States: Between Crisis and Reform* (London: Frank Cass, 1997).

Robert Sykes, and others, eds., *Globalization and European Welfare States: Challenges and Change* (New York: Palgrave, 2001).

Has the emancipation of women in the twentieth century radically changed European social and political life?

Viewpoint: Yes. The inclusion of women into electorates, political parties, and professions has reordered social and political priorities.

Viewpoint: No. Most women who entered public life were moderates who advocated mainstream positions on political and social issues.

Tremendous advancement for women occurred in European society during the twentieth century. Over the century every European nation enfranchised the female half of its population. Women received suffrage, property ownership, equal treatment under the law, full admission to the worlds of education and labor, protection from discrimination, and many other rights that made them equal to men. Did the inclusion of women change, or even "feminize," the contours of Europe's debates, values, and institutions?

One argument suggests strongly that it has indeed affected European social and political priorities. Enjoying the freedom to express themselves and develop a public identity associated with their gender, women have added many new concerns to European society. Issues such as sexuality, abortion, birth control, marriage, divorce, and general concerns about gender equity have reached the forefront of debate and substantively reshaped the Continent's values on the subject. This development would have been impossible without the broader inclusion of women in social and political life.

Yet, an opposing argument maintains that Europe's mainstream feminists largely received what they wanted: legal equality with men. Except for a small number who saw gender liberation as part of a wider project of social and political change, most European women adopted moderate attitudes and embraced their new rights to shape society in much the same terms as men. Rather than "feminizing" European life, women simply contributed to it as the citizens that feminist leaders had always wanted them to become.

Viewpoint:
Yes. The inclusion of women into electorates, political parties, and professions has reordered social and political priorities.

By 1900 women had achieved only modest gains in European social and political life. Nowhere were they truly emancipated or treated equally under the law. They had neither gained the right to vote nor achieved parity with men in employment. It was assumed that men alone should occupy the public, political, and economic spheres. Society expected them to be fathers, husbands, and providers. Men exercised authority over those family members under their protection. Conversely, women were expected to occupy the private, moral, and domestic spheres. Society expected them to be mothers, wives, and nurturers. These restraints notwithstanding, women did exert considerable pressure in the male-dominated public arena through indirect means as moral reformers and political activists.

It would take several massive upheavals in Europe to cause enough disruption to allow women to increase their social equality, economic opportunities, and political rights. World War I, the Great Depression, World War II, and the Cold War each affected the nations of Europe and their female populations differently because of extreme pressures in the social and political environments. Neither evenness of gains nor consistency in ideology existed. Yet, overall, an examination of the broad sweep of the twentieth century indicates that women made great progress and thus changed European social and political life.

The four bloody years of World War I cost millions of lives and caused massive changes in European society and politics. When the conflict started, a clear division between women and men became visible as the men joined the military and assumed the role of warrior. Women stayed in their traditional roles of wife, nurturer, and mother. The lines between masculinity and femininity soon became blurred, however. In modern and total war a nation had to mobilize all its human, industrial, and natural resources. As the war effort required more industrial production and soldiers, nations desperately needed a larger labor force, one that increasingly included women. National needs gave women unparalleled opportunities to move beyond the limitations of the private sphere. They either entered the workforce for the first time or, more frequently, moved from their prewar domestic jobs to war-related industrial occupations. They enjoyed absolute increases in wages as they took these new jobs.

In France, women increased from 38 percent of the labor force in 1914 to approximately 50 percent by the end of the war. This development represented a significant gain because World War I helped France industrialize in a way that it had not done in the prewar era. Women, called *munitionettes,* made their most striking advances in the chemical, timber, transportation, and manufacturing industries. Their numbers in these vital areas increased from 5 percent of the workforce in 1914 to 25 percent in 1918. In Great Britain, women made similar progress. Female employment in commerce and industry rose from 3.2 million in 1914 to almost 5 million in 1918. The British government also established the Women's Army Auxiliary Corps, the Women's Royal Naval Service, and the Women's Royal Air Force to relieve the personnel shortages at the front.

Women in Germany and Russia followed different paths. Most German women stayed home throughout the conflict. They did piecework, and rather than making corsets or clocks as they had done in the prewar years, they manufactured tents, gas masks, or munitions. After the February Revolution of 1917, Russian women gained the highest level of equality with men, receiving the right to vote and even serving in organized combat units.

When World War I ended on 11 November 1918, European societies attempted to drive the wedge between feminine and masculine roles back into place, to return to gender normalcy. With the exception of some middle- and upper-class women who chose to remain in the public sphere, most European women were sent home to resume their peacetime activities. However, women gained voting rights in Russia under its Provisional Government in 1917, in Britain, Germany, Sweden, Poland, Austria, Hungary, and Czechoslovakia in 1918, and in the United States in 1920. Suffrage was and has been viewed as a reward for the service of women in the war effort. Many feminists in the 1920s heralded it as the culmination of decades of efforts for emancipation—as a watershed event for feminism. Suffrage gave women a legal forum and political representation. In France and Italy, however, women did not receive voting rights following World War I. These notable exceptions to the trend occurred because little solidarity existed between nonvoting women and the working-class men who had been voting for decades. Likewise, to truly return to normalcy, the French government reestablished the status quo in political and legal gender relations.

During the 1920s, women experienced many changes. They moved out of the domestic social sphere and increasingly began to transform their Victorian styles of dress emphasizing feminine curves into the more androgynous styles emphasizing freedom of movement and comfort. With the improvement and increased use of contraception and abortion, women also began to stretch the sexual limits placed on them by society and physiology.

With the Great Depression of the 1930s, women endured more challenges and restrictions in society and politics. Governments all over Europe fell from power as people struggled to handle extreme unemployment and economic stress. Women made few gains during this period. Instead, they frequently were objects of resentment and criticism because men viewed them as potential competition for the few jobs that existed. Thus, they were pushed further back into their separate domestic spheres even as they needed to work outside the home to help support their families. Indeed, the decade of the

Great Depression represented a period of stagnation for women. As the 1930s drew to a close, Europe plunged into yet another more destructive conflict—World War II. Once again, women increasingly took part in total war efforts, both as victims and participants. Millions of European women and children suffered and died because of genocide, starvation, rape, and bombings. The death toll among civilians when added to combat casualties exceeded all previous wars in human history.

Every European nation needed to harness all human, natural, and material resources to fight World War II. The ways in which the combatant nations utilized female resources illustrated much about the gender relations in those nations. Regardless of what they did or did not do, women fit into particular and calculated gender roles. Approximately 90 percent of British women worked in some war-related industry or served in some formal capacity with the military. Thousands joined the British military and served in both logistical and auxiliary combat roles. It should be noted that British women played supportive roles to free men for military or other essential service. In the Soviet Union, where a constant need for human resources existed, almost one million women saw combat in the

army and air force. Some of these women soldiers received decorations for valor. It should be noted that the Soviet Union had from its inception in 1920 accorded women a more public and equal status relative to men. Nazi Germany also made use of women as a resource, and after 1944 German women entered the industrial workforce en masse.

At the end of the conflict, Europe had been laid waste. Rationing of food and other consumer goods increased in the decade after 1945. This situation put a great strain on women as wives, mothers, and citizens. Still, some important gains can be counted. France and Italy finally offered women the vote partly as a reward for their activities in the Resistance movements.

As the reconstruction of Europe progressed, women themselves asserted their calls for more genuine equality in political, social, economic, and legal terms. They sought to further empower themselves. In her book *The Second Sex* (1949), French feminist Simone de Beauvoir called for women to break out of the paradigm in which they were relegated to inferiority. Any positive characteristics attributed to women were cast in masculine terms. Breaking of such a male-dominated paradigm meant breaking out of traditional roles as wives and mothers. The new

Angela Merkel, leader of the conservative German Christian Democratic Union, at the fourteenth general party meeting in Dresden, December 2001

(Reuters/CORBIS)

WOMEN

THE OTHER

For a long time I have hesitated to write a book on woman. The subject is irritating, especially to women; and it is not new. Enough ink has been spilled in quarreling over feminism, and perhaps we should say no more about it. It is still talked about, however, for the voluminous nonsense uttered during the last century seems to have done little to illuminate the problem. After all, is there a problem? And if so, what is it? Are there women, really? Most assuredly the theory of the eternal feminine still has its adherents who will whisper in your ear: 'Even in Russia women still are women'; and other erudite persons—sometimes the very same—say with a sigh: 'Woman is losing her way, woman is lost.' One wonders if women still exist, if they will always exist, whether or not it is desirable that they should, what place they occupy in this world, what their place should be. 'What has become of women?' was asked recently in an ephemeral magazine.

But first we must ask: what is a woman? 'Tota mulier in utero', says one, 'woman is a womb'. But in speaking of certain women, connoisseurs declare that they are not women, although they are equipped with a uterus like the rest. All agree in recognizing the fact that females exist in the human species; today as always they make up about one half of humanity. And yet we are told that femininity is in danger; we are exhorted to be women, remain women, become women. It would appear, then, that every female human being is not necessarily a woman; to be so considered she must share in that mysterious and threatened reality known as femininity. Is this attribute something secreted by the ovaries? Or is it a Platonic essence, a product of the philosophic imagination? Is a rustling petticoat enough to bring it down to earth? Although some women try zealously to incarnate this essence, it is hardly patentable. It is frequently described in vague and dazzling terms that seem to have been borrowed from the vocabulary of the seers, and indeed in the times of St. Thomas it was considered an essence as certainly defined as the somniferous virtue of the poppy.

But conceptualism has lost ground. The biological and social sciences no longer admit the existence of unchangeably fixed entities that determine given characteristics, such as those ascribed to woman, the Jew, or the Negro. Science regards any characteristic as a reaction dependent in part upon a *situation*.

If today femininity no longer exists, then it never existed. But does the word *woman*, then, have no specific content? This is stoutly affirmed by those who hold to the philosophy of the enlightenment, of rationalism, of nominalism; women, to them, are merely the human beings arbitrarily designated by the word *woman*. Many American women particularly are prepared to think that there is no longer any place for woman as such; if a backward individual still takes herself for a woman, her friends advise her to be psychoanalyzed and thus get rid of this obsession. In regard to a work, *Modern Woman: The Lost Sex*, which in other respects has its irritating features, Dorothy Parker has written: 'I cannot be just to books which treat of woman as woman. . . . My idea is that all of us, men as well as women, should be regarded as human beings.' But nominalism is a rather inadequate doctrine, and the antifeminists have had no trouble in showing that women simply *are* not men. Surely woman is, like man, a human being; but such a declaration is abstract. The fact is that every concrete human being is always a singular, separate individual. To decline to accept such notions as the eternal feminine, the black soul, the Jewish character, is not to deny that Jews, Negroes, women exist today—this denial does not represent a liberation for those concerned, but rather a flight from reality. Some years ago a well-known woman writer refused to permit her portrait to appear in a series of photographs especially devoted to women writers; she wished to be counted among the men. But in order to gain this privilege she made use of her husband's influence! Women who assert that they are men lay claim none the less to masculine consideration and respect. I recall also a young Trotskyite standing on a platform at a boisterous meeting and getting ready to use her fists, in spite of her evident fragility. She was denying her feminine weakness; but it was for love of a militant male whose equal she wished to be. The attitude of defiance of many American women proves that they are haunted by a sense of their femininity. In truth, to go for a walk with one's eyes open is enough to demonstrate that humanity is divided into two classes of individuals whose clothes, faces, bodies, smiles, gaits, interests, and occupations are manifestly different. Perhaps these differences are superficial, perhaps they are destined to disappear. What is certain is that they do most obviously exist.

If her functioning as a female is not enough to define woman, if we decline also to explain her through 'the eternal feminine', and if nevertheless we admit, provisionally, that women do exist, then we must face the question "what is a woman?"

To state the question is, to me, to suggest, at once, a preliminary answer. The fact that I ask it is in itself significant. A man would never set out to write a book on the peculiar situation of the human male. But if I wish to define myself, I must first of all say: 'I am a woman'; on this truth must be based all further discussion. A man never begins by presenting himself as an individual of a certain sex; it goes without saying that he is a man. The terms *masculine* and *feminine* are used symmetrically only as a matter of form, as on legal papers. In actuality the relation of the two sexes is not quite like that of two electrical poles, for man represents both the positive and the neutral, as is indicated by the common use of *man* to designate human beings in general; whereas woman represents only the negative, defined by limiting criteria, without reciprocity. In the midst of an abstract discussion it is vexing to hear a man say: 'To think thus and so because you are a woman'; but I know that my only defense is to reply: 'I think thus and so because it is true,' thereby removing my subjective self from the argument. It would be out of the question to reply: 'And you think the contrary because you are a man', for it is understood that the fact of being a man is no peculiarity. A man is in the right in being a man; it is the woman who is in the wrong. It amounts to this: just as for the ancients there was an absolute vertical with reference to which the oblique was defined, so there is an absolute human type, the masculine. Woman has ovaries, a uterus: these peculiarities imprison her in her subjectivity, circumscribe her within the limits of her own nature. It is often said that she thinks with her glands. Man superbly ignores the fact that his anatomy also includes glands, such as the testicles, and that they secrete hormones. He thinks of his body as a direct and normal connection with the world, which he believes he apprehends objectively, whereas he regards the body of woman as a hindrance, a prison, weighed down by everything peculiar to it. 'The female is a female by virtue of a certain lack of qualities,' said Aristotle; 'we should regard the female nature as afflicted with a natural defectiveness.' And St Thomas for his part pronounced woman to be an 'imperfect man', an 'incidental' being. This is symbolized in Genesis where Eve is depicted as made from what Bossuet called 'a supernumerary bone' of Adam.

Thus humanity is male and man defines woman not in herself but as relative to him; she is not regarded as an autonomous being. Michelet writes: 'Woman, the relative being. . . .' And Benda is most positive in his *Rapport d'Uriel:* 'The body of man makes sense in itself quite apart from that of woman, whereas the latter seems wanting in significance by itself. . . . Man can think of himself without woman. She cannot think of herself without man.' And she is simply what man decrees; thus she is called 'the sex', by which is meant that she appears essentially to the male as a sexual being. For him she is sex—absolute sex, no less. She is defined and differentiated with reference to man and not he with reference to her; she is the incidental, the inessential as opposed to the essential. He is the Subject, he is the Absolute—she is the Other.

Source: *Simone de Beauvoir, "Introduction, "The Second Sex, translated by H. M. Parshley (New York: Knopf, 1953), Marxists.org Internet Archive <http://www.marxists.org/reference/subject/philosophy/works/fr/debeauv.htm>.*

paradigm, according to de Beauvoir, would benefit women and men by liberating both from restrictive gender roles.

From the 1960s to the 1980s feminists asserted their rights in an international liberation movement that included mass demonstrations, advertising campaigns, political activities, and legal appeals. Gradually, women increased their autonomy and control over sexuality and reproduction. After much effort and incredible resistance, Britain legalized abortion in 1967, with other major European nations following suit soon thereafter. With medical advances as well as effective forms of birth control, European women lived longer lives and enjoyed more free time away from motherhood than ever before. Such freedom has undermined influential gender divisions. In terms of political, economic, and social status, women also made significant gains. In 1979 Margaret Thatcher became the first female prime minister in British history. Other women have served in many other high offices across Europe. No political party in the late twentieth century can ignore women's issues such as reproductive rights, social welfare, or divorce. In economics, women continue to break into more male-dominated professions and to increase their earnings relative to men. In the social sphere, lesbian rights activists also achieved more visibility and acceptance in recent decades.

The twentieth century has been one of the greatest periods of change in European society and politics. Few centuries have witnessed so many advances; yet, at the same time, so many setbacks. Women played important roles in these changes. While not completely equal or equitable, progress toward women's emancipation had been great by the year 2000.

–DAVID J. ULBRICH,
TEMPLE UNIVERSITY

Viewpoint:
No. Most women who entered public life were moderates who advocated mainstream positions on political and social issues.

The broader inclusion of women in European social and political life has not substantively changed its contours. Although the twentieth century saw an unprecedented inclusion of women into mainstream society, public life, electorates, and the working world, it would be difficult to argue that this situation resulted in a feminization of European life. In many respects

the concerns, actions, passions, and priorities of European societies remained consistent with what they had been before the inclusion of women.

The most basic feature that prevented women's liberation from changing Europe's social and political landscape lay in its original goals. Feminists of the late nineteenth and early twentieth century rarely demanded anything more than inclusion in public life on an equal footing with men. Generally coming from the upper classes and sharing the outlook of classical liberalism, few of the early feminists had any desire to upset the status quo apart from securing their own inclusion in mainstream society and using their new freedom to improve it. They supported the emerging liberal democratic order that European men advocated and were in the process of creating. Feminists wanted civic equality, the right to vote, legal independence, and all the other conventions that bourgeois democracy had already guaranteed to men. In other words, they saw the prevailing system for what it was and largely liked it. The only way in which they wanted to change it was to be a part of it.

For that reason feminism as it was became anathema to radical movements that advocated more sweeping social change. Most European socialists either opposed women's liberation outright or reacted to it with ambivalence because they saw it as unnecessary or counterproductive to their larger purposes. Marxists, who emphasized class struggle as the main engine of historical development, believed that feminism detracted time and energy from their main goal of revolutionary social and economic transformation. If, as they believed, a favorable resolution of class conflict would be the most efficient means of ending all types of inequality, then feminism was superfluous; the realization of its goals would be the natural product of a socialist society.

Revisionist socialists, who rejected revolution as the means of social transformation, remained hostile to feminism for tactical reasons. Realizing that mainstream women in, say, rural France or staid urban Germany were more likely to be culturally traditional, politically conservative, and devoutly religious, many European socialists argued that their inclusion in public life would merely reinforce the strength of their opponents. Even as early as the French Revolution of 1789, a male-dominated radical government looked with suspicion upon women who called for equal rights and sent their most prominent spokeswoman, Olympe de Gouges, to the guillotine. Modern Left-wing attitudes toward feminism notwithstanding, early-twentieth-century socialist and radical thought saw women's liberation as a threat. Almost every European socialist

WOMEN

party, and most liberal parties, expressly opposed women's suffrage until after World War I. France's strong socialist movement continued to oppose it in the interwar period, and when Charles de Gaulle's provisional government finally gave women the right to vote in 1945, it was because de Gaulle and his conservative allies realized what an important role traditional and conservative French women could play in checking the electoral strength of the Left.

Still another point of conflict between socialism and feminism was that the societies to which the early-twentieth-century Left aspired—whether they were utopian or simply better than what was—often had no place for the feminist ideal of the liberated woman. Particularly for revisionist socialists who wanted a peaceful transformation of social and economic relations, aspiring to the material comforts of the upper classes by definition ruled out much of the feminist program. One of the rank-and-file socialists' most important material goals was to increase wages and improve working and living conditions to the point where their wives and daughters did not have to work outside the home to support the family. It was well and good for upper-class feminists to moralize about lower-class women needing to enjoy the fruits of their labor, become productive citizens in their own right, and benefit from Virginia Woolf's ideal of "a room of one's own," but rarely did the prospect of giving women the right to work a hard factory day on par with men seem to be the most popular idea. Since World War I led to increased female participation in the workforce, moreover, working-class men and the socialist parties that represented their concerns feared that liberated women would keep the jobs they had taken and thus make it more difficult for men to support their families.

The European Left's doctrinaire attitudes toward women's liberation alienated many actualized women. All too often the Left seemed unconcerned with and even hostile to their immediate aim of taking part in the public sphere that was already there. Russian feminists, usually identifying with their country's liberal parties, fled for their lives and the preservation of their convictions after the Bolshevik Revolution of 1917. In Britain the first woman to be elected to Parliament (in 1919), Viscountess Astor, was a member of the Conservative Party. The British Conservatives were also among the first major European political parties to name a woman, Margaret Thatcher, as their leader in 1975 and then as the country's first female prime minister in 1979–1990. Germany's Right of center Christian Democratic Union became that country's first political party to name a female leader, Angela Merkel, in 2000. Like

mainstream male participation in politics, female participation in parliamentary government all over the Continent has tended to be moderate in political outlook and more concerned with tackling existing problems than with effecting radical social transformation.

Once equal civil rights were established for women, furthermore, issues of gender failed to rise to great prominence in European politics. Statistically, women make up just over one-half of Europe's population—a figure that was greater in the immediate aftermath of World War II—yet gender politics have played only a marginal role alongside traditional national debates about the economy, education, employment, foreign affairs, and social welfare. Women surely participate in the discussion of these topics—not just in government, but also in the media, universities, public interest groups, and other institutions of civil society—but they are by no means exclusively women's concerns. Even recently explored issues that feminists have tried to claim as their own or as issues predominantly concerning women are dubious indicators of sweeping social change. Debates and legislation involving health care, child rearing, marital rights, contraception, sexuality, and other so-called women's issues were already present in European social and political life long before women were included in the political process. Naturally, to say that such issues have been neither of interest nor of concern to men would be both unfair and untrue.

Finally, as women have come to play more active roles in European life and experience greater degrees of acceptance, tension between the sexes appears to be on the decline. This situation is especially true in the political realm, where individuals of all strands of political thought and both genders receive broad support from men as well as women. Feminists continue to argue that women remain underrepresented in parliaments with male majorities, and women in fact make up no more than 40 percent of any European legislature (and usually less). Yet, it is not unreasonable to suggest that since women do vote and make up slightly more than one-half of European electorates, many of them are perfectly comfortable having their political concerns expressed and represented by male legislators. Conversely, it would be difficult for female legislators to be elected at all without substantial male support. Thatcher's selection as her party's leader depended on her drawing support from a parliamentary caucus that was overwhelmingly male. It is much more the case that European women of leftist convictions have supported male candidates of the Left over female candidates of the Right, and vice versa.

In a society that teaches tolerance and acceptance as paramount virtues, that prizes demonstrated ability over ascribed background, and has found inclusion to be more productive and stable than exclusion, women have largely met the goals of early feminism. One major result of this success is that over the course of the twentieth century, socially and politically integrated women have contributed to and worked within the values, attitudes, debates, and concerns that shape European life rather than change them fundamentally. Many radicals objected to feminism's goals because they correctly saw liberated European women who did not agree with them as an additional hindrance to their programs, while many conservatives supported women's liberation for the same reason. Leaving these convolutions aside, it may be enough simply to state that modern European women, like modern European men, are overwhelmingly moderate in their political outlook and overwhelmingly settled in a modern society of tolerance and equality.

–JOHN PAWL,
WASHINGTON, D.C.

References

Bonnie S. Anderson and Judith P. Zinsser, *A History of the Their Own: Women in Europe from Prehistory to the Present,* 2 volumes, revised edition (New York & Oxford: Oxford University Press, 2000).

Gisela Bock, *Women in European History,* translated by Allison Brown (Oxford: Blackwell, 2002).

Renate Bridenthal and others, eds., *Becoming Visible: Women in European History* (Boston: Houghton Mifflin, 1998).

Simone de Beauvoir, *The Second Sex,* translated by H. M. Parshley (New York: Knopf, 1953).

Patrick Fridenson, ed., *The French Home Front, 1914-1918* (Providence, R.I.: Berg, 1992).

Margaret Randolph Higonnet and others, eds., *Behind the Lines: Gender and the Two World Wars* (New Haven: Yale University Press, 1987).

Gisela Kaplan, *Contemporary Western European Feminism* (New York: New York University Press, 1992).

Arthur Marwick, ed., *Total War and Social Change* (New York: St. Martin's Press, 1988).

Jill Stephenson, *Women in Nazi Germany* (New York: Longman, 2001).

Richard Stites, *The Women's Liberation Movement in Russia: Feminism, Nihilism, and Bolshevism, 1860-1930* (Princeton: Princeton University Press, 1978).

WOMEN

APPENDIX

European Union Charter of Fundamental Rights, 2000

CHAPTER I—DIGNITY

Article 1

Human dignity

Human dignity is inviolable. It must be respected and protected.

Article 2

Right to life

1. Everyone has the right to life.
2. No one shall be condemned to the death penalty, or executed.

Article 3

Right to the integrity of the person

1. Everyone has the right to respect for his or her physical and mental integrity.
2. In the fields of medicine and biology, the following must be respected in particular:
    —the free and informed consent of the person concerned, according to the procedures laid down by law;
    —the prohibition of eugenic practices, in particular those aiming at the selection of persons;
    —the prohibition on making the human body and its parts as such a source of financial gain;
    —the prohibition of the reproductive cloning of human beings.

Article 4

Prohibition of torture and inhuman or degrading treatment or punishment

No one shall be subjected to torture or to inhuman or degrading treatment or punishment.

Article 5

Prohibition of slavery and forced labor

1. No one shall be held in slavery or servitude.
2. No one shall be required to perform forced or compulsory labor.
3. Trafficking in human beings is prohibited.

CHAPTER II—FREEDOMS

Article 6

Right to liberty and security

Everyone has the right to liberty and security of person.

Article 7

Respect for private and family life

Everyone has the right to respect for his or her private and family life, home and communications.

Article 8

Protection of personal data

1. Everyone has the right to the protection of personal data concerning him or her.
2. Such data must be processed fairly for specified purposes and on the basis of the consent of the person concerned or some other legitimate basis laid down by law. Everyone has the right of access to data which has been collected concerning him or her, and the right to have it rectified.
3. Compliance with these rules shall be subject to control by an independent authority.

Article 9
Right to marry and right to found a family
The right to marry and the right to found a family shall be guaranteed in accordance with the national laws governing the exercise of these rights.

Article 10
Freedom of thought, conscience and religion
1. Everyone has the right to freedom of thought, conscience and religion. This right includes freedom to change religion or belief and freedom, either alone or in community with others and in public or in private, to manifest religion or belief, in worship, teaching, practice and observance.
2. The right to conscientious objection is recognized, in accordance with the national laws governing the exercise of this right.

Article 11
Freedom of expression and information
1. Everyone has the right to freedom of expression. This right shall include freedom to hold opinions and to receive and impart information and ideas without interference by public authority and regardless of frontiers.
2. The freedom and pluralism of the media shall be respected.

Article 12
Freedom of assembly and of association
1. Everyone has the right to freedom of peaceful assembly and to freedom of association at all levels, in particular in political, trade union and civic matters, which implies the right of everyone to form and to join trade unions for the protection of his or her interests.
2. Political parties at Union level contribute to expressing the political will of the citizens of the Union.

Article 13
Freedom of the arts and sciences
The arts and scientific research shall be free of constraint. Academic freedom shall be respected.

Article 14
Right to education
1. Everyone has the right to education and to have access to vocational and continuing training.
2. This right includes the possibility to receive free compulsory education.
3. The freedom to found educational establishments with due respect for democratic principles and the right of parents to ensure the education and teaching of their children in conformity with their religious, philosophical and pedagogical convictions shall be respected, in accordance with the national laws governing the exercise of such freedom and right.

Article 15
Freedom to choose an occupation and right to engage in work
1. Everyone has the right to engage in work and to pursue a freely chosen or accepted occupation.
2. Every citizen of the Union has the freedom to seek employment, to work, to exercise the right of establishment and to provide services in any Member State.
3. Nationals of third countries who are authorized to work in the territories of the Member States are entitled to working conditions equivalent to those of citizens of the Union.

Article 16
Freedom to conduct a business
The freedom to conduct a business in accordance with Community law and national laws and practices is recognized.

Article 17
Right to property
1. Everyone has the right to own, use, dispose of and bequeath his or her lawfully acquired possessions. No one may be deprived of his or her possessions, except in the public interest and in the cases and under the conditions provided for by law, subject to fair compensation being paid in good time for their loss. The use of property may be regulated by law insofar as is necessary for the general interest.
2. Intellectual property shall be protected.

Article 18
Right to asylum
The right to asylum shall be guaranteed with due respect for the rules of the Geneva Convention of 28 July 1951 and the Protocol of 31 January 1967 relating to the status of refugees and in accordance with the Treaty establishing the European Community.

Article 19
Protection in the event of removal, expulsion or extradition
1. Collective expulsions are prohibited.
2. No one may be removed, expelled or extradited to a State where there is a serious risk that he or she would be subjected to the death penalty, torture or other inhuman or degrading treatment or punishment.

CHAPTER III—EQUALITY
Article 20
Equality before the law
Everyone is equal before the law.

APPENDIX

Article 21
Non-discrimination
1. Any discrimination based on any ground such as sex, race, colour, ethnic or social origin, genetic features, language, religion or belief, political or any other opinion, membership of a national minority, property, birth, disability, age or sexual orientation shall be prohibited.
2. Within the scope of application of the Treaty establishing the European Community and of the Treaty on European Union, and without prejudice to the special provisions of those Treaties, any discrimination on grounds of nationality shall be prohibited.

Article 22
Cultural, religious and linguistic diversity
The Union shall respect cultural, religious and linguistic diversity.

Article 23
Equality between men and women
Equality between men and women must be ensured in all areas, including employment, work and pay. The principle of equality shall not prevent the maintenance or adoption of measures providing for specific advantages in favor of the under-represented sex.

Article 24
The rights of the child
1. Children shall have the right to such protection and care as is necessary for their well-being. They may express their views freely. Such views shall be taken into consideration on matters which concern them in accordance with their age and maturity.
2. In all actions relating to children, whether taken by public authorities or private institutions, the child's best interests must be a primary consideration.
3. Every child shall have the right to maintain on a regular basis a personal relationship and direct contact with both his or her parents, unless that is contrary to his or her interests.

Article 25
The rights of the elderly
The Union recognizes and respects the rights of the elderly to lead a life of dignity and independence and to participate in social and cultural life.

Article 26
Integration of persons with disabilities
The Union recognizes and respects the right of persons with disabilities to benefit from measures designed to ensure their independence, social and occupational integration and participation in the life of the community.

CHAPTER IV—SOLIDARITY
Article 27
Workers' right to information and consultation within the undertaking
Workers or their representatives must, at the appropriate levels, be guaranteed information and consultation in good time in the cases and under the conditions provided for by Community law and national laws and practices.

Article 28
Right of collective bargaining and action
Workers and employers, or their respective organizations, have, in accordance with Community law and national laws and practices, the right to negotiate and conclude collective agreements at the appropriate levels and, in cases of conflicts of interest, to take collective action to defend their interests, including strike action.

Article 29
Right of access to placement services
Everyone has the right of access to a free placement service.

Article 30
Protection in the event of unjustified dismissal
Every worker has the right to protection against unjustified dismissal, in accordance with Community law and national laws and practices.

Article 31
Fair and just working conditions
1. Every worker has the right to working conditions which respect his or her health, safety and dignity.
2. Every worker has the right to limitation of maximum working hours, to daily and weekly rest periods and to an annual period of paid leave.

Article 32
Prohibition of child labor and protection of young people at work
1. The employment of children is prohibited. The minimum age of admission to employment may not be lower than the minimum school-leaving age, without prejudice to such rules as may be more favorable to young people and except for limited derogations.
2. Young people admitted to work must have working conditions appropriate to their age and be protected against economic exploitation and any work likely to harm their safety, health or physical, mental, moral or social development or to interfere with their education.

APPENDIX

Article 33
Family and professional life
1. The family shall enjoy legal, economic and social protection.
2. To reconcile family and professional life, everyone shall have the right to protection from dismissal for a reason connected with maternity and the right to paid maternity leave and to parental leave following the birth or adoption of a child.

Article 34
Social security and social assistance
1. The Union recognizes and respects the entitlement to social security benefits and social services providing protection in cases such as maternity, illness, industrial accidents, dependency or old age, and in the case of loss of employment, in accordance with the procedures laid down by Community law and national laws and practices.
2. Everyone residing and moving legally within the European Union is entitled to social security benefits and social advantages in accordance with Community law and national laws and practices.
3. In order to combat social exclusion and poverty, the Union recognizes and respects the right to social and housing assistance so as to ensure a decent existence for all those who lack sufficient resources, in accordance with the procedures laid down by Community law and national laws and practices.

Article 35
Health care
Everyone has the right of access to preventive health care and the right to benefit from medical treatment under the conditions established by national laws and practices. A high level of human health protection shall be ensured in the definition and implementation of all Union policies and activities.

Article 36
Access to services of general economic interest
The Union recognizes and respects access to services of general economic interest as provided for in national laws and practices, in accordance with the Treaty establishing the European Community, in order to promote the social and territorial cohesion of the Union.

Article 37
Environmental protection
A high level of environmental protection and the improvement of the quality of the environment must be integrated into the policies of the Union and ensured in accordance with the principle of sustainable development.

Article 38
Consumer protection
Union policies shall ensure a high level of consumer protection.

CHAPTER V–CITIZENS' RIGHTS
Article 39
Right to vote and to stand as a candidate at elections to the European Parliament
1. Every citizen of the Union has the right to vote and to stand as a candidate at elections to the European Parliament in the Member State in which he or she resides, under the same conditions as nationals of that State.
2. Members of the European Parliament shall be elected by direct universal suffrage in a free and secret ballot.

Article 40
Right to vote and to stand as a candidate at municipal elections
Every citizen of the Union has the right to vote and to stand as a candidate at municipal elections in the Member State in which he or she resides under the same conditions as nationals of that State.

Article 41
Right to good administration
1. Every person has the right to have his or her affairs handled impartially, fairly and within a reasonable time by the institutions and bodies of the Union.
2. This right includes:
   —the right of every person to be heard, before any individual measure which would affect him or her adversely is taken;
   —the right of every person to have access to his or her file, while respecting the legitimate interests of confidentiality and of professional and business secrecy;
   —the obligation of the administration to give reasons for its decisions.
3. Every person has the right to have the Community make good any damage caused by its institutions or by its servants in the performance of their duties, in accordance with the general principles common to the laws of the Member States.
4. Every person may write to the institutions of the Union in one of the languages of the Treaties and must have an answer in the same language.

Article 42
Right of access to documents
Any citizen of the Union, and any natural or legal person residing or having its registered office in a Member State, has a right of access

APPENDIX

to European Parliament, Council and Commission documents.

Article 43
Ombudsman

Any citizen of the Union and any natural or legal person residing or having its registered office in a Member State has the right to refer to the Ombudsman of the Union cases of maladministration in the activities of the Community institutions or bodies, with the exception of the Court of Justice and the Court of First Instance acting in their judicial role.

Article 44
Right to petition

Any citizen of the Union and any natural or legal person residing or having its registered office in a Member State has the right to petition the European Parliament.

Article 45
Freedom of movement and of residence

1. Every citizen of the Union has the right to move and reside freely within the territory of the Member States.
2. Freedom of movement and residence may be granted, in accordance with the Treaty establishing the European Community, to nationals of third countries legally resident in the territory of a Member State.

Article 46
Diplomatic and consular protection

Every citizen of the Union shall, in the territory of a third country in which the Member State of which he or she is a national is not represented, be entitled to protection by the diplomatic or consular authorities of any Member State, on the same conditions as the nationals of that Member State.

CHAPTER VI—JUSTICE

Article 47
Right to an effective remedy and to a fair trial

1. Everyone whose rights and freedoms guaranteed by the law of the Union are violated has the right to an effective remedy before a tribunal in compliance with the conditions laid down in this Article.
2. Everyone is entitled to a fair and public hearing within a reasonable time by an independent and impartial tribunal previously established by law. Everyone shall have the possibility of being advised, defended and represented.
3. Legal aid shall be made available to those who lack sufficient resources insofar as such aid is necessary to ensure effective access to justice.

Article 48
Presumption of innocence and right of defense

1. Everyone who has been charged shall be presumed innocent until proved guilty according to law.
2. Respect for the rights of the defense of anyone who has been charged shall be guaranteed.

Article 49
Principles of legality and proportionality of criminal offences and penalties

1. No one shall be held guilty of any criminal offence on account of any act or omission which did not constitute a criminal offence under national law or international law at the time when it was committed. Nor shall a heavier penalty be imposed than that which was applicable at the time the criminal offence was committed. If, subsequent to the commission of a criminal offence, the law provides for a lighter penalty, that penalty shall be applicable.
2. This Article shall not prejudice the trial and punishment of any person for any act or omission which, at the time when it was committed, was criminal according to the general principles recognized by the community of nations.
3. The severity of penalties must not be disproportionate to the criminal offence.

Article 50
Right not to be tried or punished twice in criminal proceedings for the same criminal offence

No one shall be liable to be tried or punished again in criminal proceedings for an offence for which he or she has already been finally acquitted or convicted within the Union in accordance with the law.

CHAPTER VII—GENERAL PROVISIONS

Article 51
Scope

1. The provisions of this Charter are addressed to the institutions and bodies of the Union with due regard for the principle of subsidiarity and to the Member States only when they are implementing Union law. They shall therefore respect the rights, observe the principles and promote the application thereof in accordance with their respective powers.
2. This Charter does not establish any new power or task for the Community or the Union, or modify powers and tasks defined by the Treaties.

Article 52
Scope of guaranteed rights

1. Any limitation on the exercise of the rights and freedoms recognized by this Charter must be provided for by law and respect the essence of those rights and freedoms. Subject to the

APPENDIX

principle of proportionality, limitations may be made only if they are necessary and genuinely meet objectives of general interest recognized by the Union or the need to protect the rights and freedom of others.

2. Rights recognized by this Charter which are based on the Community Treaties or the Treaty on European Union shall be exercised under the conditions and within the limits defined by those Treaties.

3. In so far as this Charter contains rights which correspond to rights guaranteed by the Convention for the Protection of Human Rights and Fundamental Freedoms, the meaning and scope of those rights shall be the same as those laid down by the said Convention. This provision shall not prevent Union law providing more extensive protection.

Article 53
Level of protection

Nothing in this Charter shall be interpreted as restricting or adversely affecting human rights and fundamental freedoms as recognized, in their respective fields of application, by Union law and international law and by international agreements to which the Union, the Community or all the Member States are party, including the European Convention for the Protection of Human Rights and Fundamental Freedoms, and by the Member States' constitutions.

Article 54
Prohibition of abuse of rights

Nothing in this Charter shall be interpreted as implying any right to engage in any activity or to perform any act aimed at the destruction of any of the rights and freedoms recognized in this Charter or at their limitation to a greater extent than is provided for herein.

Source: *"European Union Charter of Fundamental Rights, 2000," Charter of Fundamental Rights: Home Page <http://www.europarl.eu.int/charter/pdf/ text_en.pdf>.*

APPENDIX

Europe at the beginning of the twentieth century

(©2003, Christos Nüssli)

APPENDIX

TERRITORIAL
CHANGES
FOLLOWING
WORLD WAR I

⬚ Territory lost by Germany
⬚ Territory lost by Russia
▦ Territory lost by Bulgaria
▥ Territory lost by Austria-Hungary

0   200   400
MILES

Courtesy Rand McNally & Company

EUROPE
in 1939

Atlantic
Ocean

NORWAY

SWEDEN

FIN.

Leningrad

Moscow

UNION of SOVIET
SOCIALIST REPUBLICS

Kharkov

Kiev

ESTONIA

LATVIA

LITHUANIA

Vilna Minsk

EAST
PRUSSIA

POLAND

Cracow

Warsaw

Danzig

DENMARK

Copenhagen

Hamburg

Bremen

Berlin

GERMANY

Weimar

Prague

CZECHOSLOVAKIA

RUTHENIA

SUDETENLAND

BESSARABIA

BUKO-
VINA

TRANSYLVANIA

ROUMANIA

Bucharest

BULGARIA

Sofia

SERBIA

Belgrade

CROATIA

YUGOSLAVIA

MACEDONIA

GREECE

Athens

ALBANIA

Budapest

HUNGARY

AUSTRIA

Vienna

Trieste

Munich

Zurich
SWITZ.

Annexed by
GERMANY
before 1939

SAAR

RHINE
LAND

Essen

LUX.

BELG.

Brussels

THE NETHERLANDS

Amsterdam

Lille

Paris

FRANCE

Geneva

Lyon

Milan

Venice

Genoa

ITALY

Rome

Naples

Nice

Marseille

CORSICA

SARDINIA

SICILY

Mediterranean Sea

Adriatic Sea

TUNIS

ALGERIA

MOROCCO

Gibraltar

SPAIN

Madrid

Burgos

Cordova

PORTUGAL

Lisbon

Barcelona

BALEARIC IS.

Bordeaux

Toulouse

Brest

GREAT
BRITAIN

Edinburgh

London

Dublin

IRISH
FREE
STATE

North
Sea

Baltic
Sea

Oslo

NORTH
SEA

TURKEY

Black Sea

CYPRUS

CRETE

APPENDIX

Europe at the end of the twentieth century

(Map by Mary Reilly)

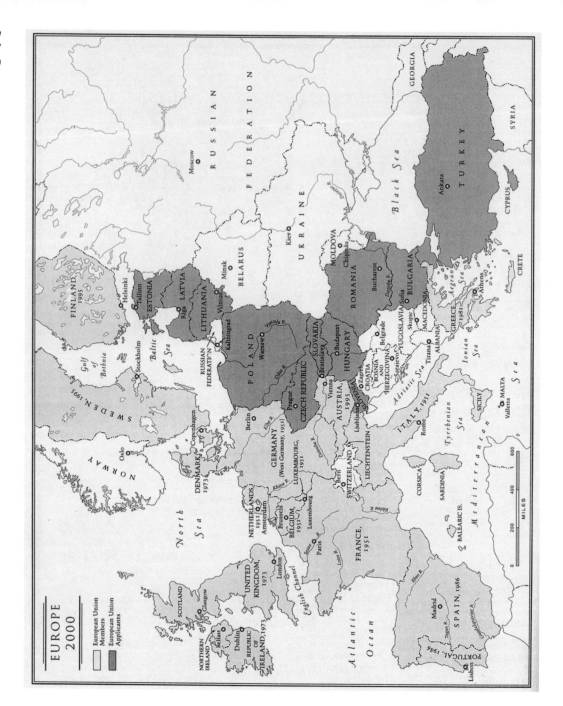

EUROPE 2000

European Union
Members

European Union
Applicants

REFERENCES

1. GENERAL

Angell, Norman. *The Great Illusion: A Study of the Relation of Military Power in Nations to their Economic and Social Advantage.* New York: Putnam, 1910.

Conquest, Robert. *Reflections on a Ravaged Century.* New York: Norton, 2000.

Ferguson, Niall. *The Cash Nexus: Money and Power in the Modern World, 1700–2000.* New York: Basic Books, 2001.

Fukuyama, Francis. *The End of History and the Last Man.* New York: Free Press, 1992.

Gilbert, Martin. *A History of the Twentieth Century.* New York: Perennial, 2000.

Gochberg, Donald S., ed. *The Twentieth Century.* Classics of Western Thought, Volume 4. New York: Harcourt Brace Jovanovich, 1980.

Goldstone, Jack A., ed. *Revolutions: Theoretical, Comparative, and Historical Studies.* San Diego: Harcourt Brace Jovanovich, 1986.

Hitchcock, William I. *The Struggle for Europe: The Turbulent History of a Divided Continent, 1945–2002.* New York: Doubleday, 2003.

Hobsbawm, Eric. *The Age of Extremes: A History of the World, 1914–1991.* New York: Pantheon, 1994.

Howard, Michael and Wm. Roger Louis. *The Oxford History of the Twentieth Century.* Oxford: Oxford University Press, 1998.

Knoebel, Edgar E. *Classics of Western Thought: The Modern World.* New York: Harcourt Brace Jovanovich, 1988.

Markoff, John. *Waves of Democracy: Social Movements and Political Change.* Thousand Oaks, Cal.: Pine Forge Press, 1996.

Muggeridge, Malcolm. *Chronicles of Wasted Time.* London: Collins, 1972.

Roberts, J. M. *Twentieth Century: The History of the World, 1901 to 2000.* New York: Penguin, 1999.

Sontag, Raymond J. *A Broken World, 1919–1939.* New York: Harper & Row, 1971.

Spielvogel, Jackson J. *Western Civilization.* Volume 2: *Since 1550.* Minneapolis/St. Paul: West, 1997.

Tuchman, Barbara. *The Proud Tower: A Portrait of the World Before the War, 1890–1914.* New York: Macmillan, 1966.

Wright, Gordon and Arthur Mejia Jr., eds. *An Age of Controversy: Discussion Problems in 20th Century European History.* New York: Harper & Row, 1973.

2. BIOGRAPHY

Cohen, Stephen F. *Bukharin and the Bolshevik Revolution: A Political Biography, 1888–1938.* New York: Knopf, 1973.

Kershaw, Ian. *Hitler, 1889–1936: Hubris.* London: Allen Lane, 1998.

Kershaw. *Hitler, 1936–1945: Nemesis.* London: Allen Lane, 2000.

Michie, Lindsay W. *Portrait of an Appeaser: Robert Hadow, First Secretary in the British Foreign Office, 1931–1939.* Westport, Conn.: Praeger, 1996.

Millington, Barry. *Wagner.* London: Dent, 1984.

Pipes, Richard, ed. *The Unknown Lenin: From the Secret Archive.* New Haven: Yale University Press, 1996.

Service, Robert. *Lenin: A Biography.* Cambridge, Mass.: Harvard University Press, 2000.

Taylor, S. J. *Stalin's Apologist: Walter Duranty, the New York Times's Man in Moscow.* New York: Oxford University Press, 1990.

3. COMMUNISM, FASCISM, SOCIALISM & TOTALITARIANISM

Allardyce, Gilbert, ed. *The Place of Fascism in European History.* Englewood Cliffs, N.J.: Prentice-Hall, 1971.

Anderson, Perry. *Lineages of the Absolutist State.* New York: Schocken, 1974.

Arendt, Hannah. *The Origins of Totalitarianism.* New York: Harcourt Brace Jovanovich, 1951.

Carsten, F. L. *The Rise of Fascism.* Berkeley: University of California Press, 1967.

Cohen, Carl, ed. *Communism, Fascism, and Democracy: The Theoretical Foundations.* Third edition. New York: McGraw-Hill, 1997.

Colorado University Department of Philosophy. *Readings on Fascism and National Socialism.* Chicago: Swallow Press, 1952.

Courtois, Stéphane and others. *The Black Book of Communism: Crimes, Terror, Repression.* Translated by Jonathan Murphy and Mark Kramer. London & Cambridge, Mass.: Harvard University Press, 1999.

Delzell, Charles F., ed. *Mediterranean Fascism, 1919–1945.* New York: Harper & Row, 1970.

Furet, François. *Fascism and Communism.* Lincoln: University of Nebraska Press, 2001.

Furet. *The Passing of an Illusion: The Idea of Communism in the Twentieth Century.* Translated by Deborah Furet. Chicago: University of Chicago Press, 1999.

Griffin, Roger, ed. *Fascism*. Oxford: Oxford University Press, 1995.

Hudson, Kate. *European Communism Since 1989: Towards a New European Left?* New York: St. Martin's Press, 2000.

Ingersoll, David E. and Richard K. Matthews. *The Philosophic Roots of Modern Ideology*. Englewood Cliffs, N.J.: Prentice Hall, 1991.

Kallis, Aristotle A., ed. *The Fascism Reader*. London & New York: Routledge, 2002.

Laqueur, Walter and George Mosse, eds. *International Fascism, 1920–1945*. New York: Harper & Row, 1966.

Larsen, Stein Ugelvik and others, eds. *Who Were the Fascists: Social Roots of European Fascism*. Bergen: Universitetsforlaget / Irvington-on-Hudson, N.Y.: Columbia University Press, 1980.

Ledeen, Michael Arthur. *Universal Fascism: The Theory and Practice of the Fascist International, 1928–1936*. New York: Fertig, 1972.

Lindemann, Albert S. *A History of European Socialism*. New Haven: Yale University Press, 1983.

Moschonas, Gerassimos. *In the Name of Social Democracy: The Great Transformation, 1945 to the Present*. London & New York: Verso, 2002.

Nagy-Talavera, Nicholas. *The Green Shirts and the Others: A History of Fascism in Hungary and Rumania*. Stanford, Cal.: Hoover Institution Press, 1970.

Nolte, Ernst. *Three Faces of Fascism: Action Française, Italian Fascism, National Socialism*. New York: Holt, Rinehart & Winston, 1966.

Payne, Stanley G. *Fascism: Comparison and Definition*. Madison: University of Wisconsin Press, 1980.

Payne. *A History of Fascism*. Madison: University of Wisconsin Press, 1995.

Rogger, Hans and Eugen Weber, eds. *The European Right: A Historical Profile*. Berkeley: University of California Press, 1965.

Skocpol, Theda. *States and Social Revolutions: A Comparative Analysis of France, Russia, and China*. Cambridge & New York: Cambridge University Press, 1979.

Soucy, Robert. *French Fascism: The First Wave, 1924–1933*. New Haven: Yale University Press, 1986.

Soucy. *French Fascism: The Second Wave, 1933–1939*. New Haven: Yale University Press, 1995.

Sternhell, Zeev and others. *The Birth of Fascist Ideology: From Cultural Rebellion to Political Revolution*. Translated by David Maisel. Princeton: Princeton University Press, 1994.

Talmon, J. L. *The Origins of Totalitarian Democracy*. London: Secker & Warburg, 1952.

Tucker, Robert C. *The Marxian Revolutionary Idea*. New York: Norton, 1969.

Vago, Bela. *The Shadow of the Swastika: The Rise of Fascism and Anti-Semitism in the Danube Basin, 1936–1939*. Farnborough, Hants, U.K.: Saxon House for the Institute of Jewish Affairs, 1975.

Walicki, Andrzej. *Marxism and the Leap to the Kingdom of Freedom: The Rise and Fall of the Communist Utopia*. Stanford, Cal.: Stanford University Press, 1995.

Weber, Eugen. *Varieties of Fascism: Doctrines of Revolution in the Twentieth Century*. Princeton, N.J.: D. Van Nostrand, 1964.

Wilde, Lawrence. *Modern European Socialism*. Aldershot, Hants, U.K. & Brookfield, Vt.: Dartmouth, 1994.

Wittfogel, Karl. *Oriental Despotism: A Comparative Study of Total Power*. New Haven: Yale University Press, 1957.

Woolf, S. J., ed. *The Nature of Fascism*. New York: Random House, 1969.

4. ECONOMICS

Clavin, Patricia. *The Great Depression in Europe, 1929–1939*. New York: St. Martin's Press, 2000.

Garraty, John A. *The Great Depression: An Inquiry into the Causes, Course, and Consequences of the Worldwide Depression of the Nineteen-thirties, as Seen by Contemporaries and in the Light of History*. San Diego: Harcourt Brace Jovanovich, 1986.

Hall, Thomas E. and J. David Ferguson. *The Great Depression: An International Disaster of Perverse Economic Policies*. Ann Arbor: University of Michigan Press, 1998.

5. ENVIRONMENTAL POLITICS

Carson, Rachel. *Silent Spring*. Boston: Houghton Mifflin, 1962.

Coleman, Daniel. *Ecopolitics: Building a Green Society*. New Brunswick, N.J.: Rutgers University Press, 1994.

Doherty, Brian and Marius de Geus, eds. *Democracy and Green Political Thought: Sustainability, Rights, and Citizenship*. London & New York: Routledge, 1996.

O'Neill, Michael. *Green Parties and Political Change in Contemporary Europe: New Politics, Old Predicaments*. Brookfield, Vt.: Ashgate, 1997.

Richardson, Dick and Chris Roots, eds. *The Green Challenge: The Development of Green Parties in Europe*. London & New York: Routledge, 1995.

Torgerson, Douglas. *The Promise of Green Politics: Environmentalism and the Public Sphere*. Durham, N.C.: Duke University Press, 1999.

6. EUROPEAN UNION

Dedman, Martin J. *Origins and Development of the European Union, 1945–95: A History of European Integration*. London & New York: Routledge, 1996.

Di Nolfo, Ennio, ed. *Power in Europe? II : Great Britain, France, Germany, and Italy, and the Origins of EEC, 1952–1957*. Berlin & New York: De Gruyter, 1992.

Giustino, David de. *A Reader in European Integration*. London & New York: Longman, 1996.

Gowan, Peter and Perry Anderson, eds. *The Question of Europe*. London & New York: Verso, 1997.

Koutrakou, Vassiliki N. and Lucie A. Emerson, eds. *The European Union and Britain: Debating the Challenges Ahead*. New York: St. Martin's Press, 2000.

Milward, Alan S. *The Reconstruction of Western Europe, 1945–51*. London: Methuen, 1984; Berkeley: University of California Press, 1984.

Rüb, Ulrike, ed. *European Governance: Views from the UK on Democracy, Participation and Policy-making in the EU*. London: The Federal Trust, 2002.

Urwin, Derek W. *The Community of Europe: A History of European Integration since 1945*. London & New York: Longman, 1991.

7. FRANCE

Allen, James Smith. *In the Public Eye: A History of Reading in Modern France, 1800–1940*. Princeton: Princeton University Press, 1991.

Bloch, Jean-Richard. *Destin du siècle*. Paris: Rieder, 1931.

Cox, Marvin R., ed. *The Place of the French Revolution in History*. Boston: Houghton Mifflin, 1998.

Doyle, William. *The French Revolution: A Very Short Introduction*. Oxford & New York: Oxford University Press, 2001.

Furet, François. *Interpreting the French Revolution*. Translated by Elborg Forster. Cambridge & New York:

REFERENCES

Cambridge University Press, 1981; Paris: Editions de la Maison des sciences de l'homme, 1981.

Larkin, Maurice. *France since the Popular Front: Government and People, 1936-1996.* Second edition. Oxford & New York: Clarendon Press, 1997.

Lefebvre, Georges. *The French Revolution.* Volume 2. *From 1793 to 1799.* Translated by John Hall Stewart and James Friguglietti. New York: Columbia University Press, 1964.

Marcus, Jonathan. *The National Front and French Politics: The Resistible Rise of Jean-Marie Le Pen.* Washington Square: New York University Press, 1995.

Mayer, Arno J. *The Furies: Violence and Terror in the French and Russian Revolutions.* Princeton: Princeton University Press, 2000.

Simmons, Harvey G. *The French National Front: The Extremist Challenge to Democracy.* Boulder, Colo.: Westview Press, 1996.

Sternhell, Zeev. *Neither Right Nor Left: Fascist Ideology in France.* Translated by David Maisel. Princeton: Princeton University Press, 1996.

Weber, Eugen. *Peasants into Frenchmen: The Modernization of Rural France, 1870-1914.* Stanford, Cal.: Stanford University Press, 1976.

8. GERMANY

Abraham, David. *The Collapse of the Weimar Republic: Political Economy and Crisis.* Princeton: Princeton University Press, 1981.

Balderston, Theo. *The Origins and Course of the German Economic Crisis: November 1923 to May 1932.* Berlin: Haude & Spener, 1993.

Bracher, Karl Dietrich. *The German Dictatorship: The Origins, Structure, and Effects of National Socialism.* Translated by Jean Steinberg. New York: Praeger, 1970.

Bramsted, Ernest K. *Germany.* Englewood Cliffs, N.J.: Prentice-Hall, 1972.

Bramsted. *Goebbels and National Socialist Propaganda, 1925-1945.* East Lansing: Michigan State University Press, 1965.

Childers, Thomas. *The Nazi Voter: The Social Foundations of Fascism in Germany, 1919-1933.* Chapel Hill: University of North Carolina, 1983.

Comfort, Richard A. *Revolutionary Hamburg: Labor Politics in the Early Weimar Republic.* Stanford, Cal.: Stanford University Press, 1966.

Davidson, Eugene. *The Trial of the Germans: An Account of the Twenty-two Defendants Before the International Military Tribunal at Nuremberg.* New York: Macmillan, 1966.

Donington, Robert. *Wagner's 'Ring' and Its Symbols: The Music and the Myth.* London: Faber & Faber, 1963.

Feldman, Gerald. *The Great Disorder: Politics, Economics, and Society in the German Inflation.* New York: Oxford University Press, 1993.

Gay, Peter. *Weimar Culture: The Outsider as Insider.* New York: Harper & Row, 1968.

Glass, James M. *Life Unworthy of Life: Racial Phobia and Mass Murder in Hitler's Germany.* New York: Basic Books, 1997.

Golomb, Jacob and Robert S. Wistrich, eds. *Nietzsche, Godfather of Fascism?: On the Uses and Abuses of a Philosophy.* Princeton: Princeton University Press, 2002.

Kershaw, Ian, ed. *Weimar: Why Did German Democracy Fail?* London: Weidenfeld & Nicolson, 1990.

Marshall, David E. "*Das Museum für Deutsche Geschichte:* A Study of the Presentation of History in the Former German Democratic Republic." Ph.D dissertation. University of California, Riverside, 2002.

Merson, Allan. *Communist Resistance in Nazi Germany.* London: Lawrence & Wishart, 1985.

Webb, Steven B. *Hyperinflation and Stabilization in Weimar Germany.* New York: Oxford University Press, 1989.

9. GLOBALIZATION

Baudrillard, Jean. *America.* Translated by Chris Turner. London & New York: Verso, 1988.

Falk, Richard. *Predatory Globalization: A Critique.* Cambridge: Polity Press, 1999.

Huntington, Samuel P. *The Clash of Civilizations and the Remaking of World Order.* New York: Simon & Schuster, 1996.

Judt, Tony. *Past Imperfect: French Intellectuals, 1944-1956.* Berkeley: University of California Press, 1992.

Kuisel, Richard F. *Seducing the French: The Dilemma of Americanization.* Berkeley: University of California Press, 1993.

Pells, Richard H. *Not Like Us: How Europeans Have Loved, Hated, and Transformed American Culture since World War II.* New York: Basic Books, 1997.

Strauss, David. *Menace in the West: The Rise of French Anti-Americanism in Modern Times.* Westport, Conn.: Greenwood Press, 1978.

10. GREAT BRITAIN

Black, Jeremy. *Convergence or Divergence?: Britain and the Continent.* New York: St. Martin's Press, 1994.

Carrick, Roger. *Britain and Europe: One Foot In and One Foot Out.* Milwaukee: Center for International Studies, University of Wisconsin-Milwaukee, 1999.

Greenwood, Sean. *Britain and European Cooperation since 1945.* Oxford & Cambridge, Mass.: Blackwell, 1992.

Greenwood, ed. *Britain and European Integration since the Second World War.* Manchester & New York: Manchester University Press, 1996.

Hitchens, Peter. *The Abolition of Britain: From Winston Churchill to Princess Diana.* San Francisco: Encounter, 2000.

Milfull, John, ed., *Britain in Europe: Prospects for Change.* Aldershot & Brookfield, Vt.: Ashgate, 1999.

Schmidt, Gustav. *The Politics and Economics of Appeasement: British Foreign Policy in the 1930s.* Translated by Jackie Bennett-Ruete. Leamington Spa, U.K. & New York: Berg, 1986.

11. HOLOCAUST & GENOCIDE

Bauman, Zygmunt. *Modernity and the Holocaust.* Ithaca, N.Y.: Cornell University Press, 1989.

Blet, Pierre. *Pius XII and the Second World War: According to the Archives of the Vatican.* Translated by Lawrence J. Johnson. New York: Paulist Press, 1999.

Chalk, Frank and Kurt Jonassohn. *The History and Sociology of Genocide: Analyses and Case Studies.* New Haven: Yale University Press, 1990.

Chartock, Roselle K. and Jack Spencer, eds. *Can It Happen Again?: Chronicles of the Holocaust.* New York: Black Dog & Leventhal, 1995.

Cornwell, John. *Hitler's Pope: The Secret History of Pius XII.* London & New York: Viking, 1999.

Friedlander, Saul. *Pius XII and the Third Reich.* New York: Knopf, 1966.

Gordon, Sarah. *Hitler, Germans and the "Jewish Question."* Princeton: Princeton University Press, 1984.

REFERENCES

Kertzer, David I. *The Kidnapping of Edgardo Mortara*. New York: Knopf, 1997.

Lang, Berel. *Act and Idea in the Nazi Genocide*. Chicago: University of Chicago Press, 1990.

Lapide, Pinchas E. *The Last Three Popes and the Jews*. London: Souvenir, 1967.

Laquer, Walter, ed. *The Holocaust Encyclopedia*. New Haven & London: Yale University Press, 2001.

Lewy, Guenter. *The Catholic Church and Nazi Germany*. New York: McGraw-Hill, 1964.

Marchione, Margherita. *Consensus and Controversy: Defending Pope Pius XII*. New York: Paulist Press, 2002.

Marchione. *Yours Is a Precious Witness: Memoirs of Jews and Catholics in Wartime Italy*. New York: Paulist Press, 1997.

Rychlak, Ronald J. *Hitler, the War, and the Pope*. Huntington, Ind.: Our Sunday Visitor Press, 2000.

Sanchez, Jose M. *Pius XII and the Holocaust: Understanding the Controversy*. Washington, D.C.: Catholic University of America Press, 2002.

Smith, Helmut Walser, ed. *The Holocaust and Other Genocides: History, Representation, Ethnics*. Nashville, Tenn.: Vanderbilt University Press, 2002.

12. INTERNATIONAL JUSTICE & WAR CRIMES

Borneman, John. *Settling Accounts: Violence, Justice, and Accountability in Postsocialist Europe*. Princeton: Princeton University Press, 1997.

Kritz, Neil J., ed. *Transitional Justice: How Emerging Democracies Reckon with Former Regimes*. Washington, D.C.: United States Institute of Peace Press, 1995.

Minow, Martha. *Between Vengeance and Forgiveness: Facing History after Genocide and Mass Violence*. Boston: Beacon, 1998.

Phillips, Raymond, ed. *Trial of Josef Kramer and Forty-Four Others: The Belsen Trial*. London: Hodge, 1949.

Rosenberg, Tina. *The Haunted Land: Facing Europe's Ghosts after Communism*. New York: Random House, 1995.

Scharf, Michael P. *Balkan Justice: The Story Behind the First International War Crimes Trial since Nuremberg*. Durham, N.C.: Carolina Academic Press, 1997.

13. MEMOIRS, AUTOBIOGRAPHIES & PRIMARY DOCUMENTS

Bliss, Howard, ed. *The Political Development of the European Community: A Documentary Collection*. Waltham, Mass.: Blaisdell, 1970.

Hitler, Adolf. *Hitler's Secret Conversations: 1941–1944*. Translated by Norman Cameron and R. H. Stevens. New York: Farrar, Straus & Young, 1953.

Koestler, Arthur. *The Invisible Writing: An Autobiography*. Boston: Beacon, 1956.

Nabokov, Vladimir. *Speak, Memory: A Memoir*. London: Gollancz, 1951.

Zolli, Eugenio. *Before the Dawn: Autobiographical Reflections*. New York: Sheed & Ward, 1954.

14. NATIONAL MINORITIES

Brown, Michael E. and others, eds. *Nationalism and Ethnic Conflict*. Cambridge, Mass.: MIT Press, 1997.

Frankel, Jonathan, ed. *Jews and Gender: The Challenge to Hierarchy*. Oxford & New York: Oxford University Press, 2000.

Heraclides, Alexis. *The Self-Determination of Minorities in International Politics*. London & Portland, Ore.: Cass, 1991.

Musgrave, Thomas D. *Self-Determination and National Minorities*. Oxford: Clarendon Press, 1997; New York: Oxford University Press, 1997.

Sellers, Mortimer. *The New World Order: Sovereignty, Human Rights, and the Self-Determination of Peoples*. Oxford & Washington, D.C.: Berg, 1996.

Thornberry, Patrick. *International Law and the Rights of Minorities*. Oxford: Clarendon Press, 1991; New York: Oxford University Press, 1991.

Wagner, Richard. *Judaism in Music and Other Essays*. Translated by William Ashton Ellis. Lincoln: University of Nebraska Press, 1995.

15. NATIONALISM

Anderson, Malcolm. *States and Nationalism in Europe since 1945*. London & New York: Routledge, 2000.

Gellner, Ernest. *Nations and Nationalism*. Oxford: Blackwell, 1983; Ithaca, N.Y.: Cornell University Press, 1983.

Höbelt, Lothar. *Defiant Populist: Jörg Haider and the Politics of Austria*. West Lafayette, Ind.: Purdue University Press, 2003.

Hobsbawm, Eric J. *Nations and Nationalism since 1780: Programme, Myth, Reality*. Second edition. Cambridge & New York: Cambridge University Press, 1992.

Jenkins, Brian and Spyros A. Sofos, eds. *Nation and Identity in Contemporary Europe*. London & New York: Routledge, 1996.

Milward, Alan S., with the assistance of George Brennan and Federico Romero. *The European Rescue of the Nation State*. Second edition. London & New York: Routledge, 2000.

Roessingh, Martijn A. *Ethnonationalism and Political Systems in Europe: A State of Tension*. Amsterdam: Amsterdam University Press, 1996.

Smith, Anthony D. *Nations and Nationalism in a Global Era*. Cambridge: Polity Press, 1995.

16. PHILOSOPHY

Baird, Forrest E. and Walter Kaufmann, eds. *Philosophic Classics: Nineteenth-Century Philosophy*. Volume 4. Upper Saddle River, N.J.: Prentice Hall, 1997.

Barrett, William. *Irrational Man: A Study in Existential Philosophy*. Garden City, N.Y.: Doubleday, 1958.

Bulgakov, Sergei. *Philosophy of Economy: The World as Household*. Translated and edited by Catherine Evtuhov. New Haven: Yale University Press, 2000.

Descartes, René. *Discourse on Method and Meditations on First Philosophy*. Translated by Donald A. Cress. Indianapolis: Hackett, 1980.

Everdell, William R. *The First Moderns: Profiles in the Origins of Twentieth-Century Thought*. Chicago: University of Chicago Press, 1997.

Festinger, Leon and others. *When Prophecy Fails: A Social and Psychological Study of a Modern Group that Predicted the Destruction of the World*. New York: Harper & Row, 1964.

Freud, Sigmund. *Civilization and Its Discontents*. New York: Cape & H. Smith, 1930.

Judt, Tony. *The Burden of Responsibility: Blum, Camus, Aron, and the French Twentieth Century*. Chicago: University of Chicago Press, 1998.

Judt. *Past Imperfect: French Intellectuals, 1944–1956*. Berkeley: University of California Press, 1992.

Kant, Immanuel. *On History*. Edited by Lewis White Beck. New York: Macmillan, 1963.

Lotze, Hermann. *Microcosmus: An Essay Concerning Man and His Relation to the World*. Translated by Elizabeth Hamilton and E. E. Constance Jones. Freeport, N.Y.: Books for Libraries Press, 1971.

Oaklander, L. Nathan, ed. *Existentialist Philosophy: An Introduction*. Second edition. Englewood Cliffs, N.J.: Prentice Hall, 1996.

Rorty, Richard. *Truth and Progress: Philosophical Papers*. Volume 3. Cambridge: Cambridge University Press, 1998.

Solomon, Robert C. *From Rationalism to Existentialism: The Existentialists and Their Nineteenth-Century Backgrounds*. Atlantic Highlands, N.J.: Humanities Press, 1978.

Weber, Max. *The Protestant Ethic and the Spirit of Capitalism*. Translated by Talcott Parsons. New York: Scribners, 1958.

Wicks, Robert. *Modern French Philosophy: From Existentialism and Postmodernism*. Oxford: Oneworld, 2003.

Wolin, Richard. *The Politics of Being: The Political Thought of Martin Heidegger*. New York: Columbia University Press, 1990.

17. PUBLIC INTELLECTUALS

Bauman, Zygmunt. *Legislators and Interpreters: On Modernity, Post-Modernity, and Intellectuals*. Cambridge: Polity Press, 1987; Ithaca, N.Y.: Cornell University Press, 1987.

Bourdieu, Pierre. *Acts of Resistance: Against the Tyranny of the Market*. Translated by Richard Nice. New York: New Press, 1998.

Datta, Venita. *Birth of a National Icon: The Literary Avant-Garde and the Origins of the Intellectual in France*. Albany: State University of New York Press, 1999.

Drake, David. *Intellectuals and Politics in Post-War France*. Houndmills, U.K. & New York: Palgrave Press, 2002.

Foucault, Michel. *Language, Counter-Memory, Practice: Selected Essays and Interviews*. Edited by Donald F. Bouchard. Translated by Bouchard and Sherry Simon. Ithaca, N.Y.: Cornell University Press, 1977.

Habermas, Jürgen. *The Structural Transformation of the Public Sphere: An Inquiry into a Category of Bourgeois Society*. Translated by Thomas Burger with the assistance of Frederick Lawrence. Cambridge, Mass.: MIT Press, 1989.

Jennings, Jeremy and Anthony Kemp-Welch, eds. *Intellectuals in Politics: From the Dreyfus Affair to Salman Rushdie*. London & New York: Routledge, 1997.

Joll, James. *Three Intellectuals in Politics*. New York: Pantheon, 1960.

Lasch, Christopher. *The Revolt of the Elites and the Betrayal of Democracy*. New York: Norton, 1995.

Lawrence, P. K., ed. *Knowledge and Power: The Changing Role of European Intellectuals*. Aldershot, U.K. & Brookfield, Vt.: Avebury, 1996.

Lyotard, Jean François. *Tombeau de l' intellectuel: et autre papiers*. Paris: Editions Galilée, 1984.

Negt, Oskar and Alexander Kluge. *Public Sphere and Experience: Toward an Analysis of the Bourgeois and Proletarian Public Sphere*. Translated by Peter Labanyi, Jamie Owen Daniel, and Assenka Oksiloff. Minneapolis: University of Minnesota Press, 1993.

Posner, Richard A. *Public Intellectuals: A Study in Decline*. Cambridge, Mass.: Harvard University Press, 2001.

Robbins, Bruce, ed. *Intellectuals: Aesthetics, Politics, Academics*. Minneapolis: University of Minnesota Press, 1990.

Said, Edward W. *Representations of the Intellectual: The 1993 Reith Lectures*. New York: Pantheon, 1994.

Walzer, Michael. *The Company of Critics: Social Criticism and Political Commitment in the Twentieth Century*. New York: Basic Books, 1988.

18. PUBLIC OPINION

Ebon, Martin. *The Soviet Propaganda Machine*. New York: McGraw-Hill, 1987.

Lippmann, Walter. *Public Opinion*. New York: Free Press, 1997.

Overy, Richard. *Why the Allies Won*. New York: Norton, 1996.

Remnick, David. *Lenin's Tomb: The Last Days of the Soviet Empire*. New York: Random House, 1993.

Welch, David. *The Third Reich: Politics and Propaganda*. London & New York: Routledge, 1993.

19. RUSSIA & THE SOVIET UNION

Applebaum, Anne. *Gulag: A History*. New York: Doubleday, 2003.

Cohen, Stephen F. *Rethinking the Soviet Experience: Politics and History since 1917*. New York: Oxford University Press, 1985.

Conquest, Robert. *The Great Terror: A Reassessment*. London: Hutchinson, 1990; New York: Oxford University Press, 1990.

Dallin, Alexander. *German Rule in Russia, 1941–1945: A Study of Occupation Policies*. New York: Octagon, 1980.

Dallin, David J. and Boris I. Nicolaevsky. *Forced Labor in Soviet Russia*. New Haven: Yale University Press, 1947.

Figes, Orlando. *A People's Tragedy: The Russian Revolution, 1891–1924*. New York: Viking, 1997.

Fitzpatrick, Sheila. *The Russian Revolution*. Oxford & New York: Oxford University Press, 1982.

Graham, Loren R. *The Ghost of the Executed Engineer: Technology and the Fall of the Soviet Union*. Cambridge, Mass.: Harvard University Press, 1996.

Handelman, Steven. *Comrade Criminal: Russia's New Mafiya*. New Haven: Yale University Press, 1995.

Hosking, Geoffrey. *The First Socialist Society: A History of the Soviet Union from Within*. Cambridge, Mass.: Harvard University Press, 1990.

Kotkin, Stephen. *Magnetic Mountain: Stalinism as a Civilization*. Berkeley: University of California Press, 1995.

Kotz, David M. and Fred Weir. *Revolution from Above: The Demise of the Soviet System*. London & New York: Routledge, 1997.

Lewin, Moshe. *The Making of the Soviet System: Essays in the Social History of Interwar Russia*. London: Methuen, 1985.

Marks, Steven G. *How Russia Shaped the Modern World: From Art to Anti-Semitism, Ballet to Bolshevism*. Princeton: Princeton University Press, 2003.

McReynolds, Louise. *The News Under Russia's Old Regime: The Development of a Mass-Circulation Press*. Princeton: Princeton University Press, 1991.

Neumann, Iver B. *Russia and the Idea of Europe: A Study in Identity and International Relations*. London & New York: Routledge, 1996.

Nove, Alec. *An Economic History of the USSR, 1917–1991*. London & New York: Penguin, 1992.

Pipes, Richard. *Russia Under the Bolshevik Regime*. New York: Knopf, 1994.

REFERENCES

Pipes. *Russia Under the Old Regime*. New York: Scribners, 1974.

Pipes. *The Russian Revolution*. New York: Knopf, 1990.

Remnick, David. *Lenin's Tomb: The Last Days of the Soviet Empire*. New York: Random House, 1993.

Sakwa, Richard. *The Rise and Fall of the Soviet Union, 1917–1991*. London & New York: Routledge, 1999.

Samuelson, Lennart. *Plans for Stalin's War Machine: Tukhachevskii and Military-Economic Planning, 1925–1941*. New York: Macmillan, 2000.

Service, Robert. *A History of Twentieth-Century Russia*. London: Allen Lane, 1997.

Shlapentokh, Dmitri. *The Counter-Revolution in Revolution: Images of Thermidor and Napoleon at the Time of the Russian Revolution and Civil War*. New York: St. Martin's Press, 1999.

Shlapentokh. *The French Revolution and the Russian Anti-democratic Tradition: A Case of False Consciousness*. New Brunswick: Transaction Publishers, 1997.

Shlapentokh. *The French Revolution in Russian Intellectual Life, 1865–1905*. Westport, Conn.: Praeger, 1996.

Stone, David R. *Hammer and Rifle: The Militarization of the Soviet Union, 1926–1933*. Lawrence: University Press of Kansas, 2000.

Suny, Ronald Grigor. *The Soviet Experiment: Russia, the USSR, and the Successor States*. New York: Oxford University Press, 1998.

Swift, E. Anthony. *Popular Theater and Society in Tsarist Russia*. Berkeley: University of California Press, 2002.

Thompson, John M. *A Vision Unfulfilled: Russia and the Soviet Union in the Twentieth Century*. Lexington, Mass.: Heath, 1996.

Treadgold, Donald. *The West in Russia and China: Religious and Secular Thought in Modern Times*. Volume 1. *Russia, 1472–1917*. Cambridge: Cambridge University Press, 1973.

Trotsky, Lev. *The Revolution Betrayed*. Garden City, N.Y.: Doubleday, Doran, 1937.

Tucker, Robert C. *Stalin in Power: The Revolution from Above, 1928–1941*. New York: Norton, 1990.

Viola, Lynne. *Peasant Rebels Under Stalin: Collectivization and the Culture of Peasant Resistance*. New York: Oxford University Press, 1996.

Webb, Sidney and Beatrice Webb. *Is Soviet Communism a New Civilisation?* London: Left Review, 1936.

Wren, Melvin C. *The Western Impact upon Tsarist Russia*. Huntington, N.Y.: Robert E. Krieger, 1971.

20. SOCIAL CLASSES

Glezerman, G. E. *Classes and Nations*. Translated by David Fidlon. Moscow: Progress Publishers, 1979.

Hill, Mike and Warren Montag, eds. *Masses, Classes and the Public Sphere*. London & New York: Verso, 2000.

Luebbert, Gregory M. *Liberalism, Fascism, or Social Democracy: Social Classes and the Political Origins of Regimes in Interwar Europe*. New York: Oxford University Press, 1991.

Vogler, Carolyn M. *The Nation State: The Neglected Dimension of Class*. Aldershot, U.K. & Brookfield, Vt.: Gower, 1985.

21. SPANISH CIVIL WAR

Bolloten, Burnett. *The Spanish Civil War: Revolution and Counterrevolution*. Chapel Hill: University of North Carolina Press, 1991.

Borkenau, Franz. *The Spanish Cockpit: An Eyewitness Account of the Political and Social Conflicts of the Spanish Civil War*. London: Faber & Faber, 1937.

Brenan, Gerald. *The Spanish Labyrinth: An Account of the Social and Political Background of the Civil War*. Cambridge: Cambridge University Press, 1943; New York: Macmillan, 1943.

Esenwein, George and Adrian Schubert. *Spain at War: The Spanish Civil War in Context, 1931–1939*. London & New York: Longman, 1995.

Fraser, Ronald. *Blood of Spain: An Oral History of the Spanish Civil War*. New York: Pantheon, 1979.

Jackson, Gabriel. *The Spanish Republic and the Civil War, 1931–1939*. Princeton: Princeton University Press, 1965.

Orwell, George. *Homage to Catalonia*. London: Secker & Warburg, 1938.

Preston, Paul. *A Concise History of the Spanish Civil War*. London: Fontana, 1996.

Preston, ed. *Revolution and War in Spain, 1931–1939*. London & New York: Methuen, 1984.

Radosh, Ronald, Mary R. Habeck, and Grigory Sevostianov, eds. *Spain Betrayed: The Soviet Union and the Spanish Civil War*. New Haven: Yale University Press, 2001.

Thomas, Hugh. *The Spanish Civil War*. Third edition. London: Harper & Row, 1986.

Tisa, John. *Recalling the Good Fight: An Autobiography of the Spanish Civil War*. South Hadley, Mass.: Bergin & Garvey, 1985.

22. UKRAINIAN FAMINE

Carynnyk, Marco and others, eds. *The Foreign Office and the Famine: British Documents on Ukraine and the Great Famine of 1932–1933*. Kingston, Ontario: Limestone, 1988.

Conquest, Robert. *The Harvest of Sorrow: Soviet Collectivization and the Terror-Famine*. London: Hutchinson, 1986.

Hryshko, Wasyl. *The Ukrainian Holocaust of 1933*. Edited and translated by Carynnyk. Toronto: Bahriany Foundation, 1983.

Serbyn, Roman and Bohdan Krawchenko, eds. *Famine in Ukraine, 1932–1933*. Edmonton: Canadian Institute of Ukrainian Studies, University of Alberta, 1986.

U.S. Commission on the Ukraine Famine. *Investigation of the Ukrainian Famine 1932–1933: Report to Congress*. Washington, D.C.: U.S. Government Printing Office, 1988.

23. WELFARE STATE

Ferrera, Maurizio and Martin Rhodes, eds. *Recasting European Welfare States*. London: Frank Cass, 2000.

Flora, Peter, ed. *Growth to Limits: The Western European Welfare States Since World War II*. Berlin & New York: W. de Gruyter, 1986– .

Kuhnle, Stein, ed. *Survival of the European Welfare State*. London & New York: Routledge, 2000.

Rhodes, Martin, ed. *Southern European Welfare States: Between Crisis and Reform*. London: Frank Cass, 1997.

Sykes, Robert and others, eds. *Globalization and European Welfare States: Challenges and Change*. New York: Palgrave, 2001.

24. WOMEN

Anderson, Bonnie S. and Judith P. Zinsser. *A History of Their Own: Women in Europe from Prehistory to the*

REFERENCES

Present. 2 volumes. Revised edition. New York & Oxford: Oxford University Press, 2000.

Beauvoir, Simone de. *The Second Sex*. Translated by H. M. Parshley. New York: Knopf, 1953.

Bock, Gisela. *Women in European History*. Translated by Allison Brown. Oxford: Blackwell, 2002.

Bridenthal, Renate and others, eds. *Becoming Visible: Women in European History*. Boston: Houghton Mifflin, 1998.

Higonnet, Margaret Randolph and others, eds. *Behind the Lines: Gender and the Two World Wars*. New Haven: Yale University Press, 1987.

Kaplan, Gisela. *Contemporary Western European Feminism*. New York: New York University Press, 1992.

Stephenson, Jill. *Women in Nazi Germany*. New York: Longman, 2001.

Stites, Richard. *The Women's Liberation Movement in Russia: Feminism, Nihilism, and Bolshevism, 1860–1930*. Princeton: Princeton University Press, 1978.

25. WORLD WARS I & II

Eksteins, Modris. *Rites of Spring: The Great War and the Birth of the Modern Age*. New York: Anchor, 1990.

Fridenson, Patrick, ed. *The French Home Front, 1914–1918*. Providence, R.I.: Berg, 1992.

Furnia, Arthur H. *The Diplomacy of Appeasement: Anglo-French Relations and the Prelude to World War 1931–1938*. Washington, D.C.: University Press, 1960.

Marwick, Arthur, ed. *Total War and Social Change*. New York: St. Martin's Press, 1988.

Overy, Richard. *Why the Allies Won*. New York: Norton, 1996.

Sharp, Alan. *The Versailles Settlement: Peacemaking in Paris, 1919*. New York: St. Martin's Press, 1991.

Winter, Jay, Geoffrey Parker, and Mary R. Habeck, eds. *The Great War and the Twentieth Century*. New Haven: Yale University Press, 2000.

26. YUGOSLAVIA

Denitch, Bogdan. *Ethnic Nationalism: The Tragic Death of Yugoslavia*. Minneapolis: University of Minnesota Press, 1994.

Judah, Tim. *The Serbs: History, Myth and the Destruction of Yugoslavia* (New Haven: Yale University Press, 2000).

Kumar, Radha. *Divide and Fall?: Bosnia in the Annals of Partition*. London & New York: Verso, 1997.

Rogel, Carole. *The Breakup of Yugoslavia and the War in Bosnia*. Westport, Conn.: Greenwood Press, 1998.

Woodward, Susan L. *Balkan Tragedy: Chaos and Dissolution after the Cold War*. Washington, D.C.: Brookings Institution, 1995.

CONTRIBUTORS

ABEND, Lisa: Oberlin College, Ohio.

BLAIR, Catherine: Doctoral student at Georgetown University; earned a B.A. in history and Russian from the University of North Carolina at Chapel Hill and an M.A. in history from Georgetown University; she is researching pretenders to the throne in seventeenth- and eighteenth-century Russia.

BUDJEVAC, Julijana: Independent scholar on Capitol Hill, Washington, D.C.; she has degrees in economics and international affairs from George Washington University; a former doctoral fellow at George Washington University and a past *History in Dispute* contributor.

DAVIS, Lawrence H.: Received a Ph.D. in European history from the University of Connecticut; visiting assistant professor of history at Salem State College in Salem, Massachusetts; presently writing a book on French historian Georges Lefebvre.

FEDYASHIN, Anton: Georgetown University.

FOLEY, Kerry: Earned an M.A. in Russian and Eastern European studies, with a certificate in refugees and humanitarian emergencies, from Georgetown University in 2002; worked for the Damascus office of the United Nations High Commissioner for Refugees (October 2002–December 2003); consulted for the Damascus office of the International Organization for Migration.

FRANK, Matthew: Visiting lecturer with the Civic Education Project at the history faculty of Omsk State University in western Siberia; doctoral candidate at St Antony's College, Oxford University; his thesis on Britain and the transfer of Germans from East Central Europe (1939–1947) will be submitted in 2004.

GILTNER, Philip: Earned his doctorate in modern European history from the University of Toronto; currently teaches at the Albany Academy; taught at the United States Military Academy at West Point, Pace University, and Mercy College; author of *"In the Friendliest Manner": German-Danish Economic Cooperation during the Nazi Occupation of 1940–1945* (1998); he lives in Kinderhook, New York.

GOLDFRANK, David: Georgetown University.

HANNA, Ray: Attorney at Law, Washington, D.C.

HELM, Lawrence A.: Strategic policy consultant for NASA; earned an M.A. in history from George Washington University; oversaw IT Research initiatives at NASA Headquarters for ten years and was involved in the earliest Internet deployments for the agency.

JUDAKEN, Jonathan: University of Memphis.

KALLIS, Aristotle: Lecturer in modern European history in the Department of Historical Studies at the University of Bristol; he is the author of *Fascist Ideology: Territory and Expansion in Italy and Germany, 1922–1945* (2000) and the editor of *The Fascism Reader* (2003).

MAIER, Wendy A.: Adjunct professor of history in Chicago; the author of several articles, book reviews, and essays; research interests include the Holocaust, Nazi Germany, and early modern European women's history.

MARSHALL, David E.: Earned his Ph.D. in modern European history from University of California, Riverside; holds an M.A. in history from University of California, Riverside and an M.A. in German literature from San Francisco State.

MAURIELLO, Christopher E.: Salem State College, Massachusetts.

NORMAN, York: Ph.D. candidate in history at Georgetown University; holds an M.A. in Eastern European history from Indiana University and an M.A. in Ottoman history from Bilkent University, Turkey; his fields of study are Ottoman history and early modern Europe.

PAWL, John: Independent scholar, Washington, D.C.

QUENOY, Paul du: Doctoral candidate in Russian history at Georgetown University; author of several articles on Russia, Ukraine, and the Soviet Union; co-editor of *History in Dispute, Volume 6: The Cold War, Second Series* (2000).

RAINOW, Peter: Author and co-author of six books and more than sixty chapters on international history published in the United States, United Kingdom, Italy, Russia, and Ukraine; visiting scholar at Stanford University (1996-1997); participated in the Consensus Project on the future of international relations at the John M. Olin Institute of Strategic Studies, Harvard University (1991-1992).

ROMM, Craig: Research associate at the Center for Strategic and International Studies; received an M.A. in contemporary Eastern European history from George Washington University; author of articles on the European Union and NATO; research interests include Central/Eastern Europe, international migration, and the relationship between demography and geopolitics.

SHOWALTER, Dennis: Professor of history at Colorado College; president of the Society for Military History; visiting professor at the U.S. Military Academy and U.S. Air Force Academy; author and editor of many books; joint editor of *War in History*.

SNYDER, Sarah: Georgetown University.

SOARES, John: Received a Ph.D. in history from George Washington University; he has taught courses on U.S. history and international relations at Montgomery College, George Washington University, and the University of Cincinnati; he is currently working on a book about the Cold War and international ice hockey.

TSYGANKOV, Andrei P.: Teaches international relations and political science at San Francisco State University; holds a candidate of sciences degree from Moscow State University and a Ph.D. from the University of Southern California; author of *Pathways after Empire: National Identity and Foreign Economic Policy in the Post-Soviet World* (2001) and *Whose World Order?* (2004); his current research explores Russian international relations theory and foreign policy; he is a native of Russia.

ULBRICH, David J.: Doctoral candidate in history at Temple University; awarded the 2003–2004 Lemuel C. Shepherd Dissertation Fellowship by the U.S. Marine Corps Heritage Foundation, which supports his research for "Managing Marine Mobilization: Thomas Holcomb and the U.S. Marine Corps, 1936–1943."

VARHO, Scott: Summa cum laude graduate of Amherst College in European studies; earned an M.A. with honors from the Politics and European Studies Department at Palacky University in Olomouc, Czech Republic; has done extensive research in European development; his undergraduate thesis was on the formation of Czechoslovakia during World War I; he focused on European integration issues throughout his graduate studies; co-author and presenter of a document outlining the state of Czech legislation in the areas of company law, audit, accounting, and intellectual property to the Senate of the Czech Republic Committee on European Integration (2002), which was unanimously adopted as the committee's official position regarding these legislative areas.

WHEATLEY, John: Independent scholar, Brooklyn Center, Minnesota.

302 HISTORY IN DISPUTE, VOLUME 17: TWENTIETH-CENTURY EUROPEAN SOCIAL AND POLITICAL MOVEMENTS, SECOND SERIES

INDEX

AIDS in VII 244
British colonization in XII 167, 171
casualties of WWI troops in Europe IX 115
colonization of freed blacks in XIII 2-3, 8, 19
communal work patterns XIII 204
complicity of Africans in slave trade XIII 35-40
corruption in XIV 48
dams in VII 1-9, 236-246, 287
deep-water sources in VII 62-68
drinking water in VII 2
economy of XIII 38
famine in XIII 40
genocide in VI 216
German interests in VIII 100
harm of slave trade upon XIII 39
hydroelectric power in VII 2, 5
independence of colonies in VI 13
influenza epidemic in VIII 89
kinship networks XIII 36
Muslims in XIII 193
oral tradition in XIII 141
slave trade XIII 130, 273
slavery in XIII 110
slaves from XIII 269, 270, 272, 273, 274
slaves from to Brazil XIII 65
Soviet activities in VI 2
U.S. policy in VI 87
water shortage in VII 280
World War I VIII 84-90
Africa, Southern VII 63-68
African Americans XI 72; XII 34, 259, 263, 293-300;
XIII 1-284
American Revolution XII 1-8, 89, 217
Confederate symbols XIII 270, 273, 275
development of culture during slavery XIII 138-
145
doctors banned by AMA XI 152
excluded from U.S. naturalization XII 7
exploitation of XIII 195
folktales XIII 139
impact of emancipation on XIII 50-57
impact of slavery upon XIII 197, 253-260, 261-
267
Loyalists XII 189
Muslims XIV 188
religion XIII 187, 189
retention of African culture XIII 11-15
socio-economic divisions III 118
white ancestry of XIII 222
World War I VIII 298, 301; IX 1-7
World War II III 213-219
African National Congress (ANC) VI 5; VII 239, 286
African Union XIV 284
Africans XIII 251
arrive in North America XIII 180
English views of XIII 250-251
enslavement of XIII 167
European views on XIII 179-180
racial discrimination XIII 181
Afrika Korps (Africa Corps) V 123, 181, 226, 232
Afrikaner Nationalist Party VII 239
Agadir, Morocco VIII 33
Agadir Crisis (1911) XVI 193
Age of Reason XII 109-110
Age of Sail VIII 136; IX 117
Agency for International Development XV 205
Agrarian Reform Law (1952) I 93, 123, 126
Agreement on German External Debts (1953) XI 215
Agreement on the Prevention of Nuclear War
(1972) XV 257
Agricultural Adjustment Act (1933) III 27, 30, 62, 66,
156-163
Supreme Court ruling III 25
Agricultural Adjustment Administration (AAA,
1933) III 154, 157; VI 124
agricultural revolution III 2
agricultural science II 83-85
agricultural technology III 1-8

Global Positioning Satellites (GPS) III 5
history III 2, 5
impact of tractors III 6
post–World War II mechanization III 3
time management III 4
Agua Caliente Reservation VII 170
Aid for Families with Dependent Children (AFDC) II
278
Airborne Warning and Control System (AWACS) VI
173
aircraft carrier
defeat of U-boats IV 4
role in World War II I 4; IV 1-7
AirLand Battle doctrine XVI 44
airplanes VIII 17
F-16 fighter (U.S.) VI 223
Illiushin (U.S.S.R.) XVI 163
Tiupolev (U.S.S.R.) XVI 163
WWI IX 9-14, 217-223
Ait Ahmed, Hocine XV 8-9
Akhmerov, Yitzhak VI 126
Akosombo Dam (Ghana) VII 4
Akron v. *Akron Center for Reproductive Health* (1983) II
222
Alabama
disfranchisement of blacks in XIII 56
grandfather clause XIII 56
meeting of Confederate Congress XIII 153
slavery in XIII 102, 195, 206, 221, 232, 282
use of Confederate symbols XIII 277
Alabama (Confederate ship) VIII 136-137
Albanians, enslavement of XIII 167
Al-Adil X 89, 256-258
Al-Afghani, Jamal al-Din X 61
Alamo Canal VII 152, 154-155, 157, 159
Al-Andalus X 8, 40-43, 60, 242
Al-Aqsa Martyrs Brigades XIV 102
Al-Aqsa *intifada* (uprising) XIV 19-27, 31, 33, 95, 97,
103, 105, 128, 155; XV 83, 90, 183, 185, 201,
261, 266-267
Al-Aqsa mosque X 198-199; XIV 19, 22, 159, 165-166;
XV 186
Al-Asad, Bashar XIV 61, 63, 64, 67, 174, 256
Al-Asad, Hafiz XIV 29, 64, 125, 128, 148, 174; XV 83,
150, 155, 214, 219-220, 222, 227, 238, 240-
241, 255, 260-261, 264, 266-267; XV 45,
153, 267
Al-Ashraf X 47, 49
Alaska VII 197
salmon range VII 196
Alawid dynasty XIV 206, 209
Albania I 294; VI 134, 175, 181, 261, 275, 280-281;
VIII 212; IX 205, 227, 270; XIV 176; XV
120; XVI 58, 60, 109, 124
lack of environmental control in VII 145
monarchy XVI 180
Soviet domination until 1968 I 107
Albanian Communist Party VI 280
Albert (England) XVI 181
Albert I IX 42, 44
Albert of Aix X 16, 97, 211, 215, 219, 237, 276
Albigensian (Cathar) heresy X 208
Albright, Madeline XIV 38; XV 265
Alcala, Pedro de X 8
Aleppo X 48, 51, 185; XV 275
Alessandri Rodríguez, Jorge I 124, 127
Alexander (Greek king) IX 208
Alexander (Serbian king) VIII 45
Alexander (Yugoslavia) XVI 180
Alexander I IX 268, 271; X 69; XII 308
Alexander II IX 155, 158, 190, 238; X 220, 224, 284;
XVI 16
Alexander III 234, 236; XVI 16, 53
Alexander, Harold IV 149, 181; V 73, 125
Italian campaign IV 144
Alexander, Leo T. XI 151-152
Alexandra IX 160, 237, 239-240, 243; XVI 17, 201

Alexandria, Egypt VII 147; X 76, 141, 152, 170, 185, 187
    construction of sewage plants in VII 148
    sack of (1365) X 67, 70
Alexandria Protocol (1944) XV 141, 146–147
Alexeyev, Mikhail IX 65
Alexius I Comnenus X 24, 26, 29, 74, 205, 209, 215, 220, 234, 238, 280, 285, 292
Alexius IV Angelus X 107, 110
Alfonso I X 242, 246
Alfonso II X 244
Alfonso III 242, 244
Alfonso VI 2, 41, 245, 289
Alfonso VIII X 133
Alfonso X X 160, 243
Alfonso, Pedro (Petrus Alfonsi) X 42, 44
Algeciras, Spain, conference in (1906) VIII 32; XVI 107
Algeria I 151, 281; VI 83, 103, 106–107, 188; VII 82; IX 111–112, 115–116; X 305; XIV 29, 31, 52, 55, 69–72, 74–75, 79, 81–82, 84–85, 88, 114, 134, 141, 177, 179, 183, 190, 201–203, 205, 209, 212, 215–216, 219, 230–231, 252–253, 255, 276, 283; XV 23, 37, 45, 49, 57, 136, 199, 216, 222, 244, 271; XVI 71, 79, 81, 84, 136, 139, 236, 238–240
    Algerian Communist Party (PCA) XV 14
    Algerian National Assembly XIV 203
    Armée de Libération Nationale (National Army of Liberation, ALN) XV 9
    arms from Russia XV 14
    Assemblée Populaire Comunale (APC) XV 8
    Assemblée Populaire de Wilaya (APW) XV 8
    colonial policy of French VI 80, 136; XIV 12
    Comite Revolutionnaire d'Unite et d'Action (CRUA) XV 11
    Committee of Public Safety XVI 136
    coup in (1958) VI 106
    economy XIV 51
    Egypt, aid from XIV 143
    environmental law in VII 145
    France in XVI 70
    Front de Libération Nationale (National Liberation Front, FLN) XV 11–12, 16; XVI 240
    Front National (National Front, FN) XV 9
    Haut Comité d'Etat (High Council of State, HCE) XV 2, 8
    independence from France I 278; XIV 121, 203
    Islamique Armé (Algerian Islamic Armed Movement) XV 6
    Majlis al-Shura XV 4
    National Charter (1976) XV 6
    National Liberation Front (FLN) XIV 69
    National Popular Assembly XV 2, 8
    1992 elections XV 1–10
    Organisation Armée Secrète (Secret Army Organization, OAS) XV 18
    Rassemblement pour la Culture et la Démocratie (Rally for Culture and Democracy, RCD) XV 9
    War of Liberation XV 6
    water XIV 269
    Western Sahara XIV 278, 280–282
    women 121, 123, 290
Algerian Revolution (1954–1962) XV 11–19
Algiers accord (1975) XV 100, 102
Algiers Charter (1964) XV 6
Algiers Conference (1973) VI 268
Al-Hakim X 101, 218, 273, 287
Al-Harawi X 249
Al-Husayni, Muhammed Amin VII 137
Ali 234–236
Al-Jazeera XIV 28–35, 61, 65, 91, 115, 217
Al-Kamil X 89–90, 92
All-American Canal VII 154–155
All Quiet on the Western Front (1929) VIII 55, 59, 188, 264; IX 212
All-Russian Fascist Party XVII 137, 139

Allegheny Mountains XII 199, 232, 236
Allen, Ethan XII 10, 11, 14, 44
Allen, Richard VI 229, 231
Allenby, Edmund VIII 37, 39, 41, 121, 213, 216; IX 69, 72; X 59, 171, 305
Allende Gossens, Salvador I 26, 68, 123–125, 127–140; VI 64, 86–87, 265; XI 88
Alliance for Progress I 17–26, 126, 132; II 115
Allied Expeditionary Force (AEF) V 20, 23, 25; XVI 312
Allied Mediterranean Expeditionary Force VIII 119
Allied Supreme Council IX 173
Allies IV 208–215; V 27–33
    relationship of IV 209; V 34–47
    strategy IV 143–150; V 19–26
Allison, Francis XII 296
All-Russian Council of Soviets VIII 171
Al-Mansuri, Baybars X 49
Al-Mirazi, Hafez XIV 29, 30
Almohads X 273–275; XIV 201, 206
Almoravids X 159, 163, 245, 274–275, 287; XIV 201, 206
al-Moualem, Walid XV 263–264, 266
Al-Mu'azzam X 89–90
Alp Arslan X 138
Alphonse of Potiers X 145
Alpine Regional Hydroelectric Group VII 98
Alps VII 229, 231; XI 175
Al-Qaida X 55, 61; XIV 1, 3, 7, 10–18, 28, 31, 38, 86–87, 91–93, 105, 175, 182, 184, 228–230, 237–239, 242, 250, 262; XV 54, 259; XVI 71, 245
    religious indoctrination XIV 92
Alsace-Lorraine VIII 71–72, 76, 151, 180, 226, 232, 234–237, 280–281; IX 46, 52, 102, 263; XVI 257, 292, 295, 302, 308
Al-Said, Nuri XV 31, 116, 121–122, 142, 146, 169
Al-Saiqa (Pioneers of the Popular War for Liberation) XV 90
Al-Sanusi, Idris XIV 192–193
Al-Shara, Farouk XV 265–267
Al-Thani, Hamad bin Khalifa XIV 28, 33
Altmühl River VII 204–207
Amalgamated Clothing Workers Union III 191
Amaury of Lautrec X 294
Amazon River VII 235
Ambrose, Stephen I 214; II 50
Ambrose X 97, 229
America First movement V 135–136
American and Foreign Anti-Slavery Society XIII 9
American Anti-Slavery Society XIII 4, 6–7, 9
American Civil Liberties Union (ACLU) II 283; III 39; V 224
    Scopes Trial III 33
    Scottsboro case III 185
American Coalition of Life Activists (ACLA) II 223
American colonies, Anglicization of XII 208–211
American Colonization Society XIII 19
American Communist Party III 221, 223–226
American Cotton Planters' Association XIII 51
American culture
    frontier and exploration as symbols of II 245
    hegemony II 213
    spread of II 213
American Eugenics Society III 21–22
American Expeditionary Forces (AEF) VIII 10–25, 182, 300; IX 21, 24, 30–31, 57, 105, 109–110, 146, 193
    African Americans in IX 1–7
    Catholics in VIII 205
    effect of gas on VIII 239
    homosexuals in IX 149
    women nurses in VIII 130
American Farm Bureau Federation III 159
American Federation of Labor (AFL) II 188; III 183
    attitudes toward opium III 134
    reasons for decline III 195

American Federation of Labor-Congress of Industrial Organizations (AFL-CIO) II 190; VI 237
American Federation of State, County, and Municipal Employees (AFSCME) II 190-191
American Federation of Teachers II 190
American Friends Service Committee IX 19
American Independent Party II 180
American Indian Defense Association (AIDA) III 141
American Institute of Public Opinion (AIPO) III 66
American Jewish Committee II 24
American Kurdish Information Network (AKIN) XIV 172
American Labor Party II 197
American Management Association III 68
American Medical Association (AMA) II 221
    bans African American doctors XI 152
American Party
    1968 presidential race II 281
American Revolution (1775-1783) I 88; XII 1-324; XIII 2, 7, 42, 45, 147, 156, 164, 175, 195, 233, 249, 272, 274, 280-281; XV 157; XVI 181
    African Americans in XII 1-8, 89, 217, 263; XIII 17-24
    British military strategy XII 267-275
    British Southern strategy XII 39
    British West Indies XII 310-316
    Canada XII 43-49, 86, 268
    causes XII 50-55
    Continental Army XII 85-91
    Conway Cabal XII 92-98
    culpability of George III XII 136-144
    Franco-American alliance XII 39, 41, 101, 103, 181-182, 186, 255, 306, 308
    French participation in XII 100-107
    guerilla warfare XII 27, 33
    Hessian deserters XII 89
    impact of Great Awakening upon XII 145-153
    impact on Great Britain XII 27-35, 164-172
    influence on French Revolution XII 127-134
    Loyalists XII 25, 30, 37, 39, 41, 82, 86, 139, 158, 160, 167, 169, 181-194, 218-219, 260, 268, 306, 316
    mercantilism as cause of XII 196-203
    mob action in XII 214-215
    nationalism in XII 204-212
    Native Americans XII 37, 44, 49, 173-180, 217, 268
    naval warfare XII 77-83
    Newburgh Conspiracy XII 221-229
    Parliamentary policies XII 230-237
    Parliamentary supremacy XII 239-245
    philisophical influences upon Founding Fathers XII 118-125
    popular support in Great Britain XII 248-256
    possibility of British victory in XII 36-41
    privateers XII 77-78, 81, 83, 106
    role of the elite XII 213-219
    slavery XII 37, 293-300; XIII 17-24
    women in XII 217, 317-324
American River VII 29
American-Syrian Crisis (1957) XV 270-271
American System XIII 283
American Telephone and Telegraph IX 21
American Type Culture Collection XV 78
American University of Beirut XV 205
Amery, Julian XV 15, 161
Amin, Hafizullah I 10-12, 15; VI 165-166
Amin, Idi VI 83; XI 71; XIV 197
Amnesty International I 146
Amphibians VII 216-217
Amphictionic Confederacy (circa sixteenth century B.C.E.) XII 19
Anabaptist Germans XII 235
Anarchism VIII 254; XVI 243-244
Anarcho-Syndicalism VIII 254
Anatolia VIII 189, 211-214; X 280, 282; XIV 168, 261
    Christians in VIII 211

    Greeks evacuated from IX 206
    Islamic rule in VIII 211
Anatolian Plain VII 10
Anderson, Sherwood III 177
André, John XII 11
Andre, Louis VIII 151
Andrew II X 89
Andrew of Strumi X 229
Andronicus II Palaeologus X 30
Andropov, Yuri I 13; II 60; VI 111, 116, 226, 239; XV 255
    domestic programs I 197
    foreign policy I 186
    views on Afghan war I 13
Angell, Norman IX 228
Angleton, James Jesus I 66
Anglican Church XVI 178
    American Revolution XII 148, 167, 314
    World War I VIII 202
Anglo-American Corporation VII 5
Anglo-American Financial Agreement (1945) VI 79
Anglo-American Mutual Aid Agreement (1942) VI 78
Anglo-Boer War (1899-1902) VIII 34, 73, 103, 200, 272
    opposition to VIII 77
Anglo-Egyptian accord (1954) XV 244, 255
Anglo-Egyptian Treaty (1936) XV 66
Anglo-French rivalry XII 252
Anglo-German naval rivalry VIII 29-36; XVI 193
Anglo-Iranian Oil Company (AIOC) I 69; VI 255; XV 108, 156, 160, 173, 176
Anglo-Iraqi Treaty (1930) XV 117
Anglo-Irish Treaty (1921) VIII 158, 160
Anglo-Irish War (1916-1921) IX 93
Anglo-Japanese Alliance (1902) IX 167
Anglo-Persian Oil Company XIV 211-212
Angola I 95, 105, 152; II 56; VI 7, 44, 50, 65-66, 83, 87, 165, 178, 188, 194, 221-222, 241, 256, 261, 265; VII 236, 239; XIII 11, 272
    Cuban troops in VI 41, 43
    female agricultural practices XIII 40
    Portuguese immigration to VII 237
    slave trade XIII 35, 130, 134
    Soviet support I 185
    withdrawal of Cuban troops VI 7
Annan, Kofi XIV 199, 280-282
Annapolis Convention (1786) XII 287, 289, 291
Anne (Queen) XII 141
Annie Hamilton Brown Wild Life Sanctuary VII 277
Anno of Cologne X 284
Anschluss (political union, 1938) IV 19-20, 126, 191, 224; V 293; XI 14, 149; XVI 10, 119, 220
    European reactions to IV 127
Anselm II of Lucca X 81, 85
Anthony, Susan B. II 74; III 199
Anti-Ballistic Missile (ABM) Treaty (1972) I 199, 200, 227, 231; II 61, 171; VI 18, 30, 35, 43; XIV 17; XVI 95
anti-ballistic missiles (ABMs) VI 17
anti-Catholicism XII 149
Anti-Comintern Pact (1936) V 115, 229; XVI 100
anticommunism V 114
    concensus builder II 211
    domestic II 211
    impact on labor movement II 189
    influence on foreign policy II 205
    legislation II 131
    propaganda II 130
Antifederalists XII 19, 21-22, 73-75, 121-122, 277-279, 281, 288, 291
Antigua XII 311-314
antinuclear weapons protests VI 15, 22
    impact on Soviet policy VI 17
Antioch X 25, 27, 35, 46-48, 52, 128, 138, 155, 187, 191, 201, 247-248, 251, 254, 256, 259, 282; XI 20
Antipodes XII 168
Anti-Saloon League III 262

Arnold, Henry Harley "Hap" V 5, 51, 88, 91, 98–99
Ar-Rashid, Harun X 287
Arrow Cross XI 177
Arrowrock Dam (United States) VII 26
Art, avant-garde IX 87
Articles of Confederation (1781) XII 17–26, 61, 68, 70,
        73, 65, 118, 120–122, 214, 222, 264, 279,
        282, 285, 286, 289, 290, 316
Articles of Faith XIII 32
artillery VIII 52, 56, 61, 68, 110, 112–115, 180, 220,
        272, 275; IX 14, 16, 64, 66, 122
    boring of VIII 199
    Prussian VIII 67
    United States VIII 16–17
Arun Dam (Nepal) VII 9
Aryan Paragraph XI 29, 31, 33, 35
Ascalon X 146, 170, 195, 254, 257–259, 261
Ashanti, slave trade XIII 40
Ashcroft, John XIV 14
Ashkenazi XIV 221, 257–258
Asia VI 77, 79, 189, 201, 264, 271; IX 112, 116, 162,
        167, 225–226; XII 200; XIV 88, 110, 112,
        176, 187; XV 203, 205; XVI 65–66, 85, 87–
        88, 107, 110–111, 193, 238, 254, 268
    British colonization in XII 171
    colonial trade from XII 197
    corruption in XIV 48
Asia Minor X 30, 221
Askaris VIII 84–85, 87, 90
Asmal, Kader VII 9
Aspinall, Wayne Norviel VII 114
Asquith, Herbert VIII 77–78, 81–82, 103–104, 106,
        155, 161–162; IX 55, 58, 100; XVI 28
Assad, Hafiz al- I 163, 314
Assassins X 184, 258; XIV 286
Association of Professional NGOs for Social Assistance
        in Baia Mare (ASSOC) VII 252
Association of South-East Asian Nations (ASEAN) VI
        271
Assyria XI 125, 169
Astoria, Oregon VII 53
Astrakhan, Russian conquest of XVI 70
Aswan Dam (Egypt) II 146, 148; VII 3; XV 21, 62, 70,
        244, 249–250
Aswan Declaration (1978) XV 223
Ataturk, Mustafa Kemal VIII 118, 211–214; XIV 134,
        168, 261; XV 108
Ataturk Dam (Turkey) VII 82
Atchafalaya River VII 161
Atlanta Exposition (1895) III 268, 271
Atlantic Charter (1941) I 301; II 99; V 45, 146–149;
        VI 9, 78–79; IX 250; XI 110; XVI 125, 224,
        315, 317–318
Atlantic Ocean IX 77, 79, 140, 142, 181, 245; XI 174;
        XII 78, 198, 202; XIII 42, 129, 133–134,
        164, 167; XIV 75, 192, 276; XV 275;XVI
        111, 213, 254
Atlantic slave trade XII 7
Atlas Mountains XIV 206, 209
atmospheric nuclear testing VI 16
atomic bomb II 228; III 10, 16; V 48–55; VI 20, 57,
        136, 154, 254–255; VIII 195
    American I 260, 262–263
    Anglo-American cooperation on VI 10
    data passed to Soviet Union II 231
    development V 44
    Hiroshima and Nagasaki III 10
    impact on World War II II 268; III 11
    introduction I 4
    Soviet development of II 229
    "Stockholm Appeal" II 47
Atomic Energy Act (1946) I 220–221
Atomic Energy Act (1954) VII 175
Atomic Energy Commission (AEC) I 27, 29–31, 214,
        220; II 82; VII 174–175, 178
Atoms for Peace I 216–217, 221; II 51
Atta, Muhammad XV 54
Attila the Hun XI 71

Attlee, Clement VI 11, 250
Attorney General's List I 76
Auchinleck, Sir Claude John Eyre V 76, 172
Auden, Wystan VIII 191
Audubon Society VII 31, 258
Aufmarschplan I (Deployment Plan I) VIII 247
Aufmarschplan II (Deployment Plan II) VIII 247–248
August Revolution (1945) V 146
Augustine of Hippo, Saint X 20, 80–81, 84–85, 103–
        104, 117, 135, 212, 229, 277; XI 19–20, 23,
        169; XIII 31; XIV 205
Aum Shinrikyo XIV 262
Aurul SA cyanide spill (Romania) VII 248–250, 252–
        255
Auschwitz (concentration camp) I 138; III 253–254,
        256; V 54, 56–57, 60, 158, 160–163, 219;
        VIII 94; XI 2, 4, 9, 11, 16, 45, 50, 69–70, 79,
        102–104, 111, 114, 131, 148, 180, 186, 188,
        206, 213–214, 217–221, 224, 227–228, 230–
        231, 235–237, 239–240, 250; XVI 138, 300
    theories of formation V 156
Ausgleich agreement (1867) IX 137
Aussaresses, Paul XV 13, 19
Australia VI 136; VIII 33, 133, 137, 160–161, 208; IX
        76, 173; XI 62, 93, 96; XII 165, 169; XIV
        166; XV 39; XVI 13, 80–81, 87
    Aborigines XI 57
    British convicts in XII 167
    British immigration to XII 168
    grain reserves VIII 290
    immigrants XI 57, 59, 62
    Japanese immigration to IX 162
    motivation of soldiers VIII
    represented at Evian Conference XI 55
    World War I VIII 54, 117–123, 220
Australia (Australian ship) VIII 137
Australia Light Horse IX 72
Australia Mounted Division IX 67
Australian and New Zealand Army Corps (ANZAC)
        VIII 121–122
Austria I 253, 293; VI 136; VIII 18, 82, 106, 251–252,
        266, 281; IX 49, 82, 93, 120, 158, 225–226;
        XI 14, 36, 56, 59, 88, 110, 123, 167, 175, 179,
        211; XII 105; XIV 171; XV 215; XVI 8, 10,
        13, 30, 34, 45, 102, 175, 192, 194, 206, 213,
        216, 272, 315
    alliance with Germany (1879) VIII 35
    annexation of XVII 195
    Central European Model I 108
    Concert of Europe XVI 72–78
    contribution of Jews in VIII 167
    customs union with Germany forbidden VIII 283
    dam agreement with Hungary VII 101
    dams in VII 101
    East German emigration through VI 118, 121
    Freedom Party XVII 83–84
    Jehovah's Witnesses in XI 129
    Jews in XI 55, 60, 93
    occupation of I 108
    pre–World War I alliances VIII 225–231
    Right-wing politics in XVII 80–86
    Socialists in VIII 260
    supports Slovak anti-nuclear activists VII 103
    union with Nazi Germany VIII 284
    World War I XVI 308
Austria-Hungary VIII 76, 95, 98, 104, 172, 178, 226,
        228, 230, 266–267, 280, 299; IX 30, 64–65,
        99, 102, 140, 154, 192–193, 204, 206, 225,
        227, 248, 266–272; XVI 51, 57, 99, 102, 175,
        192–196, 199, 204, 208, 214, 244; XVII 3,
        20, 48, 170, 231
    army VIII 69; IX 134, 158
    collapse of VIII 216–217; IX 81; XVI 29–37
    invades Poland VIII 72
    invades Serbia VIII 72
    monarchy XVI 177–178
    relations with Germany concerning Slavic lands
        VIII 94

Jews XVI 305
loss of African colonies VIII 280
monarchy XVI 178, 181
neutrality treaty (1839) IX 42, 44
occupies Ruhr VIII 285
postwar influence of Communist parties I 174
submarine bases in VIII 134
troops in Africa, World War I VII 84, 86
World War I IX 41–47; XVI 308
Belgrade VII 248
Belgrade Conference for Foreign Ministers (1978) VI 268
Belknap, Jeremy XII 206, 217
Bellevue, Washington VII 189, 191
Bellotti v. *Baird* (1979) II 222
Belorussia XVI 18, 189
U.N. membership I 300
Beloved (1987) XIII 145
Below, Fritz von IX 10
Belzec XI 220, 269
Ben Bella, Ahmed XV 6, 13
Benedict XV VII 206, 209; XVI 308
Benedictines X 116, 235
Benelux countries VI 275
Benes, Eduard XVI 11, 34, 125
Benezet, Anthony XIII 1
Ben-Gurion, David I 278, 281; XI 37–39, 42, 63, 123;
     XIV 143–144; XV 24, 31, 33, 35, 130, 135,
     226, 248; XVI 240
Benhadj, Ali XV 4–5, 7, 9
Benigni, Roberto XI 160
Benin XIV 198
slave trade XIII 35, 40
Benjamin of Tudela X 198
Benjedid, Chadli XV 2, 4, 6–7
Benso, Camillo IX 225
Berber Cultural Movement XIV 201–202
Berbers X 160, 163, 242, 274, 287; XIV 201–210, 231;
     XV 4, 6, 9; XVI 70
Berbice, slave rebellion XIII 231
Berchtold, Leopold VIII 46, 228; IX 99; XVI 32, 196
Berenguer, Ramon (the Elder) X 243
Berg, Alban IX 84
Bergen-Belsen XI 158, 220
Bergier Report (1998) XI 179
Bergson, Henri-Louis IX 224
Beria, Lavrenty I 38; VI 255; XVI 39, 124; XVII 173
nuclear spying I 184
Soviet nuclear weapons development I 238, 245
Berke X 187, 189
Berkeley, William XIII 23, 164, 249
Berlin I 33, 119–120; II 171; VI 73, 142, 169, 252
airlift (1948) II 42, 264; V 149; VI 9
blockade of (1948) II 36, 66; VI 49, 133, 141,
     173, 177, 252, 255; XV 160
bombing of V 5
German attack on (1945) VI 169
Soviet capture of VI 251
Berlin Crisis (1958–1959) I 33–39, 168 169; VI 104
Berlin Crisis (1961) I 171; XVI 158
Berlin Wall I 120; II 66; VI 51, 64, 104, 115, 118, 122,
     142, 235; XV 260; XVI 63, 85, 245, 289
erection I 34
fall of VI 51, 111
last E. German fugitive killed at VI 118
Berlin-to-Baghdad railroad XVI 23, 27
Berlin West Africa Conference (1885) VI 267
Bermuda XII 316
Bermuda Conference (1943) III 252
Bernard, Francis XII 53
Bernard of Clairvaux X 13, 33, 128, 133, 158, 161–162,
     165–166; XI 20, 23
Bernardone, Peter X 36
Bernstein, Eduard XVII 66, 204
Bessarabia XVI 99, 185
Bessmertnykh, Alexander A. VI 223
Bethlehem Steel IX 22

Bethmann Hollweg, Theobald VII 143, 164, 289; IX
     41, 44, 99, 253; XVI 27, 196, 308
Bettelheim, Bruno XI 224, 235–237
Betts v. *Brady* (1942) II 290
Beverly, Robert XII 296; XIII 150
Bevin, Ernest VI 101
Bhakhra Dam (India) VII 130
Bhopal, India (1984) II 86
Bible X 82, 212, 273; XIV 184, 188
slavery XIII 187
view of blacks XIII 182–183
Bidault, Georges I 175, 273; VI 101
Biddle, Francis V 187–188, 224; XI 258
Big Bend Dam (United States) VII 31
Big Brother and the Holding Company II 219
Bight of Benin XIII 35
slave trade XIII 39
Bill of Rights (1791) XII 61, 76, 108, 113, 120–122,
     131, 276–283, 290
Billboard II 217
charts II 214
classifications of music II 214
music categories II 218
Biltmore Conference (1942) II 145; XV 34
Binding, Karl XI 247
Bingham, William XII 79
bioengineering II 83–85
bipartisanship II 195
vs. concensus II 205
bipolarity VI 213
birds—
     bald eagle VII 215, 220, 234
     Black Capped Vireo VII 72
     brown-headed cowbird VII 216
     ducks VII 277
     European Starling VII 216
     Golden Cheeked Warbler VII 72
     in the Pacific flyway VII 151
     in the Atlantic flyway VII 277
     kingfisher VII 205
     southwestern willow flycatcher VII 211, 215–216
     spotted owl VII 226
     western yellow-billed cuckoo VII 215
     white-tailed sea eagle VII 252–253
     Yuma clapper rail VII 215
Birkenau (concentration camp) XI 70, 102, 240
birth control pill II 224–240
Birzeit University XV 94
Biscayne Bay VII 266
Bismarck, Otto von VI 9; VIII 35, 137, 207, 226, 249;
     IX 98–99, 101, 224, 226; XI 168; XIV 173;
     XV 101; XVI 74, 175, 192, 200, 257, 313;
     XVII 105, 272
Bizonia VI 101; XVI 267
Black, Hugo II 280, 284; III 105
Black and Tans IX 93
Black Codes XIII 5, 50, 53–55
Black Death (1347–1351) VIII 61, 189; XI 24; XIII
     161, 165, 181
Black Hand IX 102; XVI 196
Black Manhattan (1930) III 122
black nationalism II 89, 93; III 120
Black Panthers II 89, 165, 197
demonstration at the California State Assembly
     (1967) II 94
Party for Self-Defense II 94
Black Power II 24, 93–95, 162; III 120
Black Power conference (1966) II 93, 95
Black Sea VII 104, 148, 204–205, 210, 247; IX 181,
     205; X 53, 187; XIII 167; XVI 184, 206, 312
submarines in VIII 292
time needed to flush pollution from VII 142
Turkish control of IX 194
Black Sea Fleet VIII 33, 280
Black September XIV 198; XV 49, 149, 198–199; XVI
     245
Black Sharecroppers Union II 197
Black Student Union II 94

INDEX

INDEX

Congress of Vienna (1815) IX 45, 226; XVI 72, 75
Congressional Black Caucus XIII 198
Connally, John VI 257
Connecticut XII 10–12, 15, 66, 70, 205, 209, 215
    gradual emancipation in XIII 19
    impact of Shays's Rebellion in XII 287
    prohibits importation of slaves XIII 18
    religion in XII 148, 150, 263
    slave uprising in XIII 235
Connolly, Thomas T. II 208; III 31; VI 151
Conrad X 48, 286
Conrad III X 128, 294
Conrad of Montferrat X 256, 258
Conrad von Hotzendorf, Franz VIII 46–47, 49, 252;
    IX 64–65, 99, 135, 137; XVI 32–33, 196
Conradin X 142
Conscription Crisis (1917) VIII 158–159
Conservation in Action Series (1947) VII 278
Conservative Party (Great Britain) VI 13
Constantine (Greek king) IX 208
Constantine I (Roman emperor) X 80–82, 224, 228;
    XIV 159
Constantine IX X 284
Constantine Plan (1958) XV 18
Constantinople VIII 117–118, 122, 173, 212, 214–215,
    228; IX 208; X 27–30, 47, 58, 88, 108, 110,
    112–114, 121, 150, 152, 208–209, 220–221,
    239, 250, 262, 281, 284–286; XIV 261
    fall of (1204) X 24, 27, 36, 108
Constantinople Convention (1888) XV 247
Constitution of the United States (1787) II 98, 101; VI
    56, 283–284; XII 7, 18, 58, 60–62, 64, 66,
    108, 113, 118, 120–122, 127, 131, 134, 276–
    283, 288, 293, 297; XIII 7, 56, 272, 274;
    XVI 139
    economic interpretation of XII 68–76
    Eighteenth Amendment (1919) III 198–200,
        VIII 295
    Fifteenth Amendment (1870) III 270; XIII 5, 56
    Fifth Amendment II 132, 134, 281–282; III 107
    First Amendment II 166; XII 60, 61, 63
    Fourteenth Amendment II 20, 138, 224, 282,
        284; XIII 5, 57
        due process clause II 281
        equal protection clause II 138–139, 141, 221
    Fourth Amendment II 281
    fugitive slave clause XIII 173
    Nineteenth Amendment (1919) II 78; III 171–
        172, 206, VIII 295
    Ninth Amendment II 225, 281
    Second Amendment XII 276–283
    Seventeenth Amendment II 196
    Sixth Amendment II 281
    slavery XII 294; XIII 18, 195
    taking clause XII 274
    Tenth Amendment VI 57; XII 61
    Thirteenth Amendment (1865) XIII 5, 272
    Three-fifths Compromise XIII 7
    Twenty-first Amendment (1933) III 200
Constitutional Convention (1787) XII 18, 21, 25 62–
    64, 69, 75, 119, 214, 217, 281, 285, 288, 291,
    293, 297–299
Contadora peace process VI 194
containment I 142, 144, 154, 158, 160, 183–184, 187,
    262, 271–272, 274, 288, 293; II 30–31, 58,
    269; VI 59, 80, 83, 203
    Dulles criticism of I 273
    during Carter administration I 13
    strongpoint I 82–86
    universal I 82–90
Continental Army XII 9–10, 15, 33, 37–39, 78, 81, 92–
    93, 95–96, 106, 149, 155–156, 158, 182, 184,
    215–217, 222–223, 263, 272–273, 283, 301,
    305–307
    African Americans in XII 89
    billeted in Loyalist homes XII 191
    bounties for recruitment to XII 89

deserters XII 90
    Hessian deserters in XII 89
    punishments in XII 304
    soldiers in XII 85–91
Continental Association XII 189, 215
Continental Congress XII 1, 10, 12–13, 15, 22, 37, 41,
    44, 46, 52, 54–55, 61–62, 78–79, 86–87, 89,
    93, 95–96, 103, 106, 108–109, 113–114, 116,
    140–141, 156, 185, 189–191, 193, 215, 221–
    222, 224, 262, 278–279, 282, 286, 290, 294–
    295, 301–303, 306, 315–316
    Board of War XII 97
    naval policy of XII 77, 81
Continental Navy XII 77–83, 106
Continental System XVI 27
Contras VI 57, 61, 191–196, 237, 241
Conventional Forces in Europe (CFE) Treaty
    (1990) XVI 95
Convention on the Protection of the Mediterranean Sea
    against Pollution VII 143–144, 305–310
conventional warfare IV 46–52
convergence theory VI 241
Conway, Henry XII 57
Conway, Thomas XII 92–93, 97–98
Conyers, John XIII 197–198
Conyngham, Gustavus XII 79, 106
Cook, James XIII 133
Coolidge, Calvin III 22, 25, 47, 176, 178, 226; IX 92;
    XI 56
Coolidge administration IX 171
    authorizes Boulder Dam VII 28
Cooper v. *Aaron* (1958) II 286
Cooper, John Sherman VI 61
Cooper, Samuel XII 150
Cooper, Thomas XII 320; XIII 48
Cooper-Church amendment (1970) I 44; VI 60
Coordinating Committee for Mutual Export Controls
    (COCOM) XVI 45
Coordinating Unit for the Med Plan VII 145
Copenhagen Criteria (1993) XIV 173, 265
Coppola, Francis Ford VI 222
Cordier, Andrew VI 75
Corfu IX 207
Corfu Declaration XVI 103
Corn Laws XII 200
Corn Production Act (1917) IX 59
"Cornerstone Speech" (1861) XIII 277
Cornplanter XII 175, 177
Cornwallis, Charles XII 23, 39, 41, 164, 184, 187, 304,
    308
Cornwallis, George XII 103, 171
Corsica XVI 136, 249, 302
    terrorism XVI 249
Corsican Liberation Front XVI 248
Cortes, Hernan X 8
Costa Rica I 53
    invasion threats from Nicaragua (1949, 1955) I
        125
    U.S. intervention in mid 1950s I 15
cotton gin XIII 7, 43
Council for German Jewry XI 96
Council for Mutual Economic Assistance (CMEA) XVI
    282
Council of Clermont (1095) X 13–14, 17, 20, 32, 35, 72,
    81, 97–99, 102, 104–105, 116, 119, 122, 126–
    127, 130–131, 135, 149–150, 171, 205, 209,
    211, 213, 215, 218–219, 221, 227, 234, 238,
    245, 265, 269, 279, 281–283, 287, 289, 295
Council of Lyon (1245) X 141
Council of Nablus (1120) X 201
Council of Piacenza (1095) X 127, 216, 220, 286
Council of Pisa (1135) X 128, 225
Council of Sens (1140) X 166
Council of Ten VIII 282
Council of Troyes (1129) X 158
Council on Environmental Quality Rainfall VII 214,
    224
Council on Foreign Relations VI 199, 203

Czechoslovak (Sudeten) Crisis (1938) XVI 220–221, 225

Czechoslovak Legion XVI 6, 34

Czechoslovakia I 109–110, 112, 277, 293–294, 303; II 9; VI 103, 110, 119, 131, 133, 165–166, 178, 217, 227, 237, 246, 249, 251–252, 261, 274, 276; IX 93, 136, 272; XI 14–15, 56, 68, 86, 110, 167, 178–179, 207; XV 68, 70, 120; XVI 8, 11–14, 58, 76, 99–104, 114–115, 118–119, 123–124, 127, 157, 213, 220, 233, 238, 285, 289, 292, 294

    appeal of Marshall Plan I 178

    arms shipment to Guatemala (1954) I 49, 123, 126

    attempted alliance with France VI 255

    dams in VII 100

    fascism XVII 140

    frontiers recognized VIII 283

    Germany annexes border districts VIII 284

    human rights abuses I 146

    Munich Agreement (1938) I 300

    National Council XVI 34

    National Front XVI 124

    nationalism XVII 167

    occupation of VIII 284

    overthrow of communist regime XVI 282

    Police Coup XVI 271

    political changes in VII 101

    Soviet coup (1948) I 173, 182, 185

    Soviet invasion (1968) I 11–12, 218; VI 43, 116, 182, 249; XIV 2; XVI 288; XVII 231

    Ukrainian Ruthenians in XVI 101

Czerniakow, Adam XI 139–142

Czernin, Ottokar XVI 195

D

Dachau (concentration camp) XI 13, 45, 148, 151–152, 170, 213, 220, 222, 224, 232, 236, 255–256, 260

Dahomey XIII 11

    famine in XIII 38

    slave trade XIII 39, 40

Dakar, Vichy forces in XVI 300

Daladier, Edouard V 116; XVI 8, 11–12, 115, 117, 118

    appeasement policy IV 20

Dalmatia IX 136, 208; XVI 36

    enslavement of Dalmatians XIII 167

Damascus VIII 39, 41; IX 72; X 51, 77, 167, 172, 196, 305; XV 275

Damietta X 60, 87, 90, 92, 95, 139–140, 145–146, 262

Damodar Valley VII 130, 132

Damodar Valley Corporation VII 127, 132

Dams VII 1–9, 14, 25–32, 51–61, 100–107, 125–134, 196, 236–246

    benefits of VII 1, 28

    breaching of VII 31, 221, 224, 226

    fish VII 53, 196–203

    hydroelectric energy VII 226

    political economy of VII 129

Danbury Baptist Association XII 62

Dandalo, Enrico X 107, 149, 152

Danish West India Company XIII 274

Dante XI 129; XIII 262

Danube River VII 100, 101–104, 106, 204–207, 209–210, 247, 250, 253, 255; XVI 36

Danzig VIII 280–281; XI 179; XVI 294

Dardanelles VIII 38, 80, 117–123, 212, 214, 216; IX 114, 207; X 15; XVI 185

Darrow, Clarence III 32–34, 37–39

    relationship with NAACP III 186

    Scopes Trial III 33

Darwin, Charles III 32–33; VIII 93; XI 17–18; XVII 174, 254

Davenport, James XII 148

Davidic dynasty (tenth century B.C.E.) XIV 163

Davidiz, Sisnando X 2, 41

Davies, John Paton VI 158

Davis, Jefferson XIII 270, 274, 277

Davis Sr., Benjamin O. IX 7

Dawes, Charles VIII 285

Dawes Plan (1924) IV 270; V 119; VIII 298; IX 92, 171; XVI 148, 296; XVII 116, 121

Dawes Severalty Act (1887) III 140–143; VII 166, 167, 168, 171

Day, Nathaniel XII 48

Dayan, Moshe XV 23–24, 136, 221–222

Dayton Accords (1995) II 100, 154; XVI 57, 60; XVII 149

D-Day (6 June 1944) VI 168, 251

Deane, Silas XII 79, 100, 102–103, 105–106

Déat, Marcel XVI 142

De Bow, J. D. B. XIII 28, 101

De Bow's Review XIII 86

Debs, Eugene V. II 196; III 151, 175, 208, 222–223, 234

Decatur, Stephen XVI 70

Declaration of Independence (1776) VI 9; XII 18, 32, 34, 46, 54–55, 69, 71, 108–116, 118, 120, 129–131, 134, 136–137, 140, 143, 171, 191, 215, 235, 261–262, 265, 277, 282, 293, 314; XIII 18–19, 23, 147, 156, 272

Declaration of Paris (1856) VIII 136

Declaration of Punta del Este (1961) I 17

Declaration of St. James XI 261

Declaration of the Rights of Man and Citizen (1789) XII 130, 131, 265; XIII 156

Declaration on Liberated Europe (1945) XVI 122, 125, 127, 224

Declaratory Act (1720) XII 246

Declaratory Act (1766) XII 57, 141, 233, 237, 239–240

Decolonization VI 264; XVI 65

    effects of on Third World VI 83

Defense Intelligence Agency (DIA) XV 86

    NIE reports VI 257

    Soviet military strength VI 259

Defense of the Realm Act (1914) VIII 158; IX 58; XVI 173

Defense Policy Board XIV 97

Defense Readiness Condition (DEFCON) VI 163

Deism XII 151

Delaware XII 70, 78, 175–176, 306

    ratification of Constitution XII 74

Delaware River XII 271

Delbo, Charlotte XI 222–223

Demerara (Guyana) XIII 190

    slave revolts XIII 154, 159, 231

Democratic Front for the Liberation of Palestine (DFLP) XIV 195; XV 95

Democratic National Committee (DNC)
    headquarters broken into VI 24

Democratic National Convention
    (1964) II 28, 161–163
    (1968) II 162, 180; VI 25

Democratic Party II 49, 162–165, 180, 194–195, 198, 257; III 191–195; XIII 21, 56, 222, 276, 281–283

    association with labor movement II 187–192

    Mississippi Freedom Democratic Party II 28, 161, 197

    relationship with African Americans III 118

Democratic Republic of Vietnam. *See* North Vietnam

Denikin, Anton XVI 2, 5

Deng Xiaoping VI 4, 42, 44, 204

    visits United States VI 43

Denmark VIII 280, 283–284; IX 171, 225; XI 176; XIV 31; XVI 84, 114–115, 212–214, 272, 319

    homicides XVII 270

    Iceland's secession from XIV 171

    Jewish rescue in WWII XI 175

    Jews XVI 305

    monarchy XVI 178, 180–181

    slave trade XIII 270

    Social Democratic movement XVII 28

    social welfare XVII 269

Dennis v. *United States* I 78–79

East Germany I 107, 274; VI 110–111, 115–122, 141, 178, 182, 206–212, 217, 246, 249, 251, 261, 276; XI 214; XVI 77, 95, 124, 284–285, 289; XVII 2, 67, 70, 72, 81, 132, 200, 216, 221
   defectors VI 170
   dissidents in VI 117, 121, 211
   Dulles acceptance of Soviet influence I 273
   flight of citizens VI 141
   political parties in VI 121
   reforms I 154
   relations with Soviet Union I 253
   revolt against totalitarianism (1953) I 254
   shift in leadership VI 117
   Soviet suspicion of I 185
   strategic importance I 109
East India Company XII 197, 200, 234, 237; XIII 271; XVI 70
East Indies XVI 84
East Jerusalem XIV 19, 154, 157, 160, 162–163; XV 20–21, 42, 79, 134, 136, 183, 190–191, 194–195, 215, 219, 226
East Prussia VIII 249, 252, 280; IX 15, 158
East St. Louis, riot IX 7
East Timor, Indonesian invasion of VI 270
Easter Rising (1916) VIII 154–162, 209; IV 21; XVI 244
Eastern Europe VI 116, 120, 131, 148, 181, 201, 207–208, 221, 224, 226, 236, 251, 267, 281; VII 250; IV 81, 83; X 62, 67, 130, 178, 180–182, 206, 265, 301; XIV 2, 6, 82, 110, 112; XV 33, 253; XVI 41, 45, 92, 111, 121–122, 124–125, 157, 176, 226, 228–230, 233, 254, 264
   collapse of communist regimes in VII 101; XVI 281–289
   collapse of Soviet control in VI 216
   Crusades in X 66, 128, 270
   democracies in XV 82
   dissident movements in VI 229
   environmental crisis in VII 17–24
   fascism in XVI 141
   German occupation (World War I) VIII 91–101, 176
   German occupation (World War II) VIII 91–101
   NATO expansion in VI 54
   political repression in VII 18
   punishment of former communists XVII 213–221
   removal of Soviet forces VI 110
   Soviets block Marshall Plan to VI 255
   Soviets in VI 244–245, 250, 252
   state development after WWI XVI 99–105
   treatment of refuges VI 251
   U.S. support of dissidents in VI 3
   voter apathy on environmental issues VII 20
Eastern Orthodox Church VIII 207; X 25, 190, 208; XVI 30; XVI 60
Easton, James XII 11
Eban, Abba XV 135, 213, 217
Ebert, Friedrich VIII 257, 280; IX 32; XVI 151, 176
Ebro River VII 147
Echo Park Dam (United States) VII 27, 29, 30–31
Economic Commission for Latin America (ECLA) I 20–22
Economic Market of the Southern Cone (Mercosur) XIV 71
Economic Opportunity Act (1964) II 276
Economic Opportunity Act (1965) II 272
Ecuador XIII 104; XIV 212, 217
Eden, Anthony I 272, 280; V 41, 290, 312; VI 11; XV 160, 247; XVI 233, 237–238, 240
   "Mansion Speech" (1941) XV 146
Edessa X 48, 74, 92, 129–130, 167, 191, 270, 296–297
Edison, Thomas Alva VIII 197
Edmondson, W. T. VII 189, 192
Edward I X 189
Edward VII (England) X 57; XVI 193
Edward VIII (England) XVI 179, 181
Edwards, Jonathan XII 147–149

Edwards Aquifer VII 69–75
Egypt I 308–312, 273, 283; II 53; VI 11, 83, 137, 162–164, 172, 246, 271–27; VII 29, 82, 135, 149; VIII 31–32, 38, 168, 213; IX 96; X 24, 30, 46–51, 56, 60, 64, 66, 78, 89, 95, 107, 109, 139–142, 144–148, 155–156, 167, 170, 173–174, 182, 185, 187, 193, 239, 248, 251, 255–258, 273, 277, 282, 287, 292; XII 165, 168; XIV 7, 23, 31, 34, 52, 55–56, 61, 68, 79, 81–83, 85, 88, 105, 114, 116, 134, 141, 143, 146–149, 154, 176–183, 186, 190, 193–195, 197–201, 206, 217, 220, 225, 228, 235, 242, 252, 255, 282; XV 12, 14, 19–23, 27, 30–34, 40, 42, 45, 51–57, 58–59, 61–62, 73, 79, 81, 100–101, 116, 127, 134–137, 141–146, 150, 166, 168–169, 176, 184–185, 199, 204, 206–207, 213, 216, 219–220, 223, 226–227, 238–241, 254, 257, 261, 275; XVI 23, 80–81, 84, 88, 98, 136, 236, 269
   Arab-Israeli War (1967) II 150
   Arab Republic of Egypt XV 223
   Arab Socialist Union XV 70
   arms XV 68
   Aswan Dam II 146, 148; VII 3; XVI 238
   attack on Israel VI 10, 161, 163
   attacks on tourists XIV 191
   bankruptcy (1882) XVI 66
   boycotts XIV 50
   Central Security Forces XV 224
   conflict with Israel I 159
   Coptic Christians XV 276
   corruption in XIV 48
   cotton and textile exports XIV 45
   deportation of Jews VIII 166
   economy XIV 47, 51, 54
   education XIV 52
   environmental control in VII 145
   expels Soviet advisers XV 220, 223, 240
   Free Officers' regime II 148; XIV 193
   Free Officers Revolution (1952) XV 59, 63, 65–70, 101, 119, 220, 226, 244, 249
   Great Britain in VIII 35
   Hadeto (Democratic Movement for National Liberation) XV 69
   Jewish spying in XIV 129
   July Laws (1961) XV 70
   Kafara Dam VII 3
   labor XIV 52
   Marxists in XV 69
   National Assembly XV 56, 222
   National Union Party XV 273
   nuclear weapons development I 219
   relations with United States XIV 16
   Revolutionary Command Council (RCC) XV 66, 68, 70
   Soviet alliance I 161; II 146; VI 43, 81
   Soviet arms XV 40, 253
   Soviet-Egyptian Pact (1955) I 162
   Suez Canal I 308, 316
   Suez Crisis I 289; VI 135, 270; XVI 235–242
   Suez War I 277, 280; XV 244–251, 253
   Sunni Muslims XV 276
   United Arab Republic (UAR) XV 70, 147, 270–276
   U.S. resistance to return of Soviet troops VI 163
   U.S. support for authoritarian regime XIV 14
   Wafd Party XV 69
   water XIV 269–271
   weapons XIV 144
   Western Desert Project VII 2
   women XIV 116, 119, 121, 287, 291
   World War I VIII 37–42
   Young Egypt XV 70
Egyptian Center for Women Rights XIV 116
Egyptian Communist Party XV 69
Egyptian Space Channel (ESC) XIV 29
Egyptian-Israeli Armistice Agreement (1949) XV 247

Eshkol, Levi XV 23–24, 135–136

Esmeralda (mining company) VII 248, 250, 254

Espionage Act (1917) III 223, 229, 234

Estates-General XII 127, 129, 131, 133–134

Estonia VI 178; VIII 93–94, 96–97; IX 93; X 179; XI
260; XVI 18, 218
 annexed by Soviet Union VII 22
 environmental activism in VII 17–24
 first national park VII 22

Estonian Nature Conservation Society VII 22

Estonian Writers' Union VII 23

Ethiopia VI 4, 63, 68, 188, 261, 271; IX 96, 175; XIV
176–177, 198; XV 271; XVI 13, 110, 219
 claim to Ogaden VI 165
 Crisis (1935) IX 172
 Cuban troops in VI 41
 enslavement of Ethiopians XIII 167
 relations with Soviet Union VI 165
 Somalia attack on VI 165
 water XIV 269–270

Ethiopian-Somali crisis VI 166

ethnic cleansing VI 211

eugenics movement III 17–23

Eugenics Record Office (1910) III 18, 21

Eugenius III X 128–130, 225, 256, 265, 267, 270, 293,
295–297

Euphrates-Tigris Basin VII 76–84

Eurasia
 introduction of species from VII 217

Eureka, California VII 178

Euro-Mediterranean Partnership XIV 114

Europe VII 206, 229; XII 252; XIV 135, 178, 187, 190,
201, 211, 242, 261; XV 15, 78, 202, 205, 252;
XVI 44, 58, 87–88, 284
 anarchism XVI 244
 aristocracy in IX 81, 83
 backs Zionist settlements in Israel VII 136
 capitalism in VI 49
 colonialism XVI 64–71
 Crusades X 5, 32–33, 123, 135, 176, 190, 223–
229, 281, 295
 demographic changes XVI 107
 demographic impact of World War I VIII 189
 eclipse of XVI 106–112
 Jews in X 274; XI 93
 market for African beef VII 33
 monarchy XVI 177–183
 patriarchal society in VIII 129
 racism in XIII 246
 serfs XIII 117
 servitude in XIII 249
 slavery in XIII 162, 165, 167
 support for World War I in VIII 125
 terrorism XVI 243–250
 twentieth-century disarmament XVI 90–98
 U.S. influence in XVI 266–272
 U.S. troops in VI 251

European Advisory Commission XVI 315

European Bank for Construction and Development VI
120

European Coal and Steel Community (ECSC) XVI
268, 270–271; XVII 57, 59–60

European Community (EC) I 108, 209; XIV 69, 72,
265

European Court VII 250

European Court of Human Rights XIV 173

European Economic Community (EEC) VI 13, 106,
209; VII 33, 36; XVI 155, 268, 271; XVII
13, 20–21, 23, 57, 60, 232
 Spain XVI 180

European Free Trade Association (EFTA) I 108

European Recovery Plan. *See* Marshall Plan

European Union (EU) VI 51, 53, 216–217, 219; VII
34, 37, 83, 100, 106, 143, 146–148, 207, 248,
250; XIV 17, 69–70, 72, 76, 100, 106, 114,
170, 173, 247; XVI 60, 74, 77, 108, 129, 155,
245, 250, 266–268, 272; XVII 13, 18, 21, 29,

57, 60, 83–84, 86, 129, 132, 149, 166–167,
170–171, 216, 233
 Helsinki summit (1999) XIV 265
 Turkey XIV 261–267

eutrophication VII 90, 148, 265

Everglades VII 271

Everson v. Board of Education (1947) XII 64

Evert, Alexie IX 65, 243

Evian Accords (1962) XV 11, 18

Evian Conference (1938) XI 4, 55–64

Executive Committee of the National Security Council
(ExComm) VI 70, 73

Executive Order 9066 III 105; V 183, 188–189

Existentialism XVII 74–79

Expressionist School IX 84

Exxon (Standard Oil of New Jersey) XIV 211–212; XV
172–173, 176, 179

Exxon *Valdez* oil spill (1989) II 86

F

Fabian Society XVI 24

Fahd, King XIV 58, 62, 249

Faidherbe, Louis IX 114

Fair Employment Practices Committee (1941) IV 218

Fairfax, Ferdinando XII 295

Faisal I VIII 37–39, 214; XV 136, 220

Faisal II XV 116

Falconbridge, Alexander XIII 131–132

Falin, Valentin VI 117, 119

Falkenhayn, Erich VIII 114, 213, 252, 266; 65, 99, 207,
252–257, 263, 265

Falkland Islands VI 13; XVI 81

Falklands War (1983) VI 8; XVI 111

Fall, Albert III 127, 141, 178

Fanning, David XII 185

Farmer Labor Party II 197

Farabundo Marti movement XIV 198

Farmers' General XII 105

Farouk I XV 30, 66, 68, 70, 144

Fascism IV 77–84
 in France XVI 140–146
 international XVII 135–141
 origins XVII 180–187

Fashoda Incident (1898) VIII 33; XVI 23–24

Fatah XIV 102–103, 152; XV 41, 44, 48–49, 90, 95,
132, 135, 152, 193, 195, 198–199

Fatah Tanzeem XIV 24, 26
 Shabiba committee XIV 26

Fatamids X 51, 274, 277, 287; XIV 201

Faubus, Orval II 20, 137, 140

Faw Peninsula XV 98

FB 111 bomber VI 259

FBI. *See* Federal Bureau of Investigation

February Revolution (1917) VIII 171–173

fedayeen (guerrilla) XV 41–42, 44–47, 233

Federal Aid Highway Act (1956) II 109

Federal Aid Road Act (1916) II 106

Federal Bureau of Investigation (FBI) I 76, 292; II 5,
47; III 107; VI 24, 157, 257; XIV 14, 235
 communist spy investigations II 131
 NIE reports VI 25
 Rosenberg files II 228, 231
 terrorism XIV 126
 treatment of spies II 231
 wiretapping I 77

Federal Bureau of Public Roads II 109

Federal Communications Commission (FCC) II 123,
III 55

Federal Deposit Insurance Corporation (FDIC) III 62,
152

Federal Emergency Management Agency VII 214

Federal Emergency Relief Administration (FERA,
1933) III 149, 159

Federal Occupational Safety and Health Act (1970) II
192

Federal Oil Pollution Control Act (1924) VII 41

Federal Power Commission VII 53

Index

INDEX

Fourteen Points (1918) II 99, 101, 145; VI 77; VIII
    280–282, 298; IX 168, 225, 245, 250; XVI
    87, 237; XVII 7, 11, 166
Fourth Lateran Council X 88; XI 23
Fox, Charles James XII 30
Fox, George XIII 31
Fox, Vincente XIV 219
France I 34, 151, 278, 280, 283, 289, 293, 305; II 153,
    264; VI 11, 76, 97, 100–107, 137, 178, 183,
    189, 201, 209, 214, 234, 246–247, 264; VIII
    30, 44, 71, 76, 82, 104, 172, 176, 182, 212,
    245–246, 249, 251–252, 280; IX 26–27, 29–
    30, 48–49, 75, 91–92, 95, 99, 101, 103–105,
    140, 145, 158, 163, 173, 193, 207, 224–231,
    248, 252, 257, 263, 265; XI 2, 4, 15, 62, 79,
    96, 102, 108, 110, 117, 123, 126, 167, 175,
    178, 211, 253, 260, 266; XII 28, 33, 37, 92,
    98, 155, 167–169, 248–252, 256; XIII 236;
    XIV 143, 181, 239, 241, 277–278, 281; XV 9,
    15, 21, 24, 27, 30, 59, 62, 78, 135, 137, 146,
    168, 199, 275; XVI 17, 22–24, 32, 34, 60,
    93–94, 102, 104, 107, 111, 189, 192–194,
    198, 208–209, 212–213, 217–218, 220, 224,
    252, 255, 267, 269, 291–292, 296, 315, 318
    Action française (French Action) XVI 142–143
    aftermath of World War II I 173; VI 49
    Algeria XVI 70, 131
    Algerian Revolution XV 11–19
    alliance with Russia (1893) VIII 35, 212
    Allied invasion (1944) XVI 299
    American Revolution XII 15, 78, 100–107, 166,
        268
    anti-Catholic sentiment VIII 204
    anti-Semitism in VIII 168
    appeasement XVI 8–14
    army 17, 69, 179, 185, 232–238; IX 252
        African troops in IX 115
        cavalry IX 70, 72
        foreign troops in IX 116
        mutiny of VIII 67, 223, 269; IX 27
        offensive tactics of VIII 71
        rotation of units IX 234
        World War I VIII 218
    artillery VIII 199, 272
    as arm supplier VI 107
    as buyer of Chesapeake tobacco XII 202
    Assembly of Notables XII 131
    attack on Germany VIII 72
    attempted alliance with Czechoslovakia VI 255
    Bastille (1789) XVI 130
    Belgian neutrality IX 41–47
    Bourbon dynasty XVI 178
    Catholic movement XIV 256
    Catholicism of XII 211
    Catholics in World War I VIII 207
    Centre d'Instruction, Pacification et Contre-guérilla
        (Instruction Center for Pacification and
        Counter-Guerilla Tactics, CIPCG) XV 14
    Chamber of Deputies XVI 118
    colonial policy of VI 93; VII 81, 135; X 59, 199;
        XVI 67, 70; XVII 229
    Communist Party I 204, 208; XVI 135, 138, 141
    Concert of Europe XVI 72–78
    Constituent Assembly XVI 135
    Croix de feu (Cross of Fire) XVI 141–142, 146
    Croix de Guerre (War Cross) XVI 141
    Crusades X 10, 33, 35, 37, 62, 72–73, 88, 93–94,
        108, 116, 144, 151–152, 161, 167, 191, 198,
        206, 211, 216, 218–219, 226, 239, 257, 260,
        265, 285
    Cuban Missile Crisis VI 102
    decolonization policy VI 77–83; XVI 79–88
    disastrous harvests in XII 132
    Dunkirk Treaty I 208
    École Nationale d'Administration (National
        Administration School) XVI 137
    École Normale Supérieure XVI 142

ecological policy VII 92–99
Eleventh Shock commando unit XV 16
Elysée Palace XVI 134
Estates in XII 132
fall to Germany IV 70–76; V 35, 36; XI 14
fascism in XVI 140–146
Fifth Republic I 283; VI 106; XVI 129, 131, 134,
    136, 139
first nuclear test VI 106
foreign policy XVI 155–161
Fourth Republic I 283; VI 80; XVI 129, 131,
    135–136
German defeat of XVI 113–120
German invasion of VIII 110, 278
Grand Armee VIII 49, 233; XI 169
homosexuals, during Nazi occupation XI 246
impact of American Revolution upon XII 165
imperialism IX 111–112; X 300–306
in Algeria VI 80, 106, 136
in Indochina VI 106
in Middle East VI 161; VIII 37
in Morocco VIII 277
in Southeast Asia II 264
in Vietnam VI 102
in West Indies XII 314
inability to hold Vietnam II 266
Israel, military aid to XIV 143
Jacquiere in XIII 71
Jehovah's Witnesses in XI 129
Je suis partout (I am everywhere) XVI 142
Jeunesses partiotes (Patriotic Youths) XVI 142
Jews in VIII 164, 168; X 14, 16, 21–22, 209; XI
    93–94; XVI 299–300, 302
League of Nations IX 170
Lend Lease aid XVI 167
levée en masse (1793) XVI 255
literacy XII 132
Maison de la Presse (Press Office) XVI 173
Med Plan VII 145
Middle East XV 274
Ministry of the Interior VIII 255
monarchy XVI 177–178, 183
Multinational Force in Lebanon XV 148–155
Munich Agreement (1938) I 300
National Assembly XVI 137–138
National Front XVI 134, 138
NATO XVI 267
nuclear arsenal VI 103, 106, 187; XVI 108
Nuclear Non-Proliferation Treaty I 218
opposition to rearming Germany VI 9
Organisation Armée Secrète (Secret Army
    Organization, OAS) XV 14; XVI 137
Parti populaire français (French Popular
    Party) XVI 141
Parti social français (French Social Party) XVI 141
pays Germany indemnity VIII 278
Permanent Committee for National Defense XVI
    118
political democratization IX 81
Popular Front XVI 115, 117–118, 141, 220
Popular Party XVI 142
postwar decline I 285
post-World War II XVI 129–139
products from Saint Dominque XIII 210
Provisional Government XVI 135, 298
refuses to sign NPT VI 106
relations with Great Britain VIII 32; XII 211
relations with Native Americans XII 178
realtions with Russia XVI 200
relations with Soviet Union VI 145
relations with the United States VI 104; XII 53
religious strife in XIII 273
reluctance to declare war on Germany IV 117–
    120
Revolution of 1789 XVI 129; XVII 87–94
Revolution of 1848 XVI 130
Russia, intervention in (1918) XVI 1–7
Second Republic XVI 130

INDEX

INDEX

ethnic groups in XVI 30
Habsburgs XVI 104, 195, 211–213, 216, 294
Hachani, Abdelkader XV 4–5, 8
Hadid, Muhammad XV 122–123, 124
Hadrian XI 19
Hafiz El Assad II 146
Hafsids X 66, 146
Hague, The XVI 92
Hague Conference (1911–1912) III 137; VIII 240
Hague Conventions (1907) V 222, 264; VIII 244; XI
    258; XV 79
Haider, Jorg XVII 80, 82–84, 86, 167, 171
Haig, Alexander M. I 56; II 179; VI 44, 225, 229, 231;
    XIV 198
Haig, Douglas VIII 52, 56, 77, 79, 103–104, 106, 108,
    114, 218–221, 223, 26, 271–273; IX 34–39,
    107–108, 110, 120, 123, 211
Hainburg Dam Project (Austria) VII 105
Haiti I 51, 125; II 100; III 50; VI 58, 194, 213, 217,
    283; IX 96; XII 169; XIII 156, 209–216
Haitian Revolution XIII 209–216
Haldane Reforms (1906) IX 51
Haldeman, Harry R. VI 24
Halder, Franz V 126–127, 227
Ha-Levi, Yehuda ben Shemuel X 273, 275
Hallstein Doctrine VI 208, 210
Halsey Jr., William F. IV 173
Hamad XIV 61–63
Haman Act VII 47
Hamas XIV 24, 41, 93, 103, 105, 107, 127, 148, 184,
    230; XV 90, 182, 186, 194, 201, 264
Hamilton, Alexander XII 34, 58, 65, 68, 70, 73, 97,
    114, 119–122, 127, 162, 222–224, 228–229,
    258, 279, 289–291, 296; XIII 281; XVI 66
Hamilton, Ian VIII 118–119, 122
Hammarskjold, Dag XV 247
Hammond, James Henry XIII 27, 48, 81, 83, 87, 218–
    219, 240, 264–265
Hampton, Wade XIII 155, 233, 235
Hancock, John XII 110, 291; XIII 48
Handel, George XVI 23
Hankey, Maurice VIII 79
Hannibal VIII 179, 249
Hanoi I 41–47
Hanoverians XII 136
Haram al-Sharif 19, 22–23, 159–160, 165–167
Hardin, Garrett VII 47, 70, 72–73
Harding, Warren G. III 25, 69, 175–178; IX 92; XI 56
Harding administration IX 171
Harkin, Thomas R. VI 194
Harlan, John Marshall II 23, 282–283; XIII 57
Harlem Renaissance III 78–84, 118–120, 184; IX 1, 4
Harper, William XIII 70, 73–74, 165, 217, 267
Harper's Ferry (1859) XIII 4
Harriman, W. Averell I 306; II 264; V 312; XV 160;
    XVI 227, 315
Harrington, James XII 119, 122–123, 209
Harris, Sir Arthur "Bomber" V 87, 91
Harrison, Earl G. XI 122–124
Harrison Act (1914) III 133, 137
    narcotics legislation III 137
Hart, Sir Basil Henry Liddell V 23, 102
Harvard University VI 90, 129, 199, 203, 258; XIII
    198; XIV 14
Hashemite Arabs VIII 40–41; XIV 245
Hashemite Kingdom XIV 160, 166; XV 32, 34, 41–42,
    44–45, 116, 121, 142, 146, 273, 275
Hassan II XIV 74, 209, 278, 282–283; XV 44
Hat Act (1732) XII 198, 202, 243
Hatch Act (1939) III 11
Hauptmann, Bruno III 110–116
Hausner, Gideon XI 38–41
Havel, Vaclav XVII 200, 214–215
Hawaii IX 96
Hawatmah, Nayef XV 41, 90, 199
Hayden, Carl Trumbull VII 109, 112, 154–155
Hayes, James Allison VII 274
Hays, Mary Ludwig (Molly Pitcher) XII 263

Hazen, Moses XII 12
Heady, Earl O. VII 187
Hebrew University XIV 225
Hebron massacre (1994) XV 187
Hebron Protocol (1997) XV 185
Heeringen, Josias von VIII 180, 184
Hegel, Georg XIV 77, 84; XVII 77, 105, 174, 183
Heidegger, Martin XVII 75, 77–78
Heights of Abraham XII 160
Heine, Heinrich VI 121
Hells Canyon Dam (United States) VII 55
Helms, Richard M. VI 24
Helms-Burton Bill I 97–98
Helper, Hinton Rowan XIII 46, 69
Helsinki Accords VI 200
Helsinki Conference (1975) I 142
Hemingway, Ernest VIII 186, 188, 191; IX 4; XVII 41,
    44, 48, 238
Henderson, Loy XV 158–159, 161–162
Hendrix, Jimi II 219
Henry II X 260; XI 88
Henry III X 66, 143, 284
Henry IV X 15, 85, 115, 117–119, 121, 205, 216, 219–
    220, 224, 227–229, 284–285; XI 80
Henry VIII, founds Royal Navy VIII 30
Henry of Le Mans X 215–216
Henry, Patrick XII 76, 97, 110, 113–114, 139, 205, 241,
    263, 279, 281; XIII 18–19, 48
Hepburn Act (1906) III 243, III 245
Herder, Johann Gottfried XII 61
Herero/Nama Rebellion (1904) VIII 87
Herod the Great XIV 159
Herzl, Theodor XII 120, 126; XIV 163, 258; XV 33
Hess, Rudolf V 223–224; XI 103
Hessians XII 161
Heydrich, Reinhard XI 37, 87, 89, 91, 108, 211, 249,
    265
Hezb-i-Islami XIV 4, 6
Hideki Tojo V 112; VI 75
Highway Act (1987) II 112
Highway Revenue Act (1956) II 107
hijab (modest Islamic dress; also means head scarf) XIV
    118–124
Hildebrand X 119
Hillsborough, Lord XII 32, 141
Himmler, Heinrich I 305; IV 131; V 154, 162; XI 63,
    86, 89–90, 102–103, 116, 132, 151, 153, 178,
    186, 227–228, 244, 252, 265
Hindenburg, Paul von V 114–115, 120; VIII 54, 93,
    95–96, 140, 143, 252, 292; IX 15, 82, 120,
    122, 128, 257; XI 94; XVI 148–151, 154, 173
Hindenburg Line VIII 27, 53, 57
Hinton, Harold VI 41
Hippocrates XI 151
Hirabayashi, Gordon V 188–189
Hirabayashi v. *United States* (1943) III 103, 105–106; V
    188
Hirakud Dam (India) VII 130
Hirohito, Emperor V 49, 108–113; VIII 95
Hiroshima I 30, 230, 239, 242–246, 249; II 268; III
    12, 15, 216; V 1, 3, 8, 49, 50, 52, 55, 111,
    154, 192, 221; VI 31, 254; XI 159; XVI
    254–255
Hispaniola XIII 63, 210
    maroons in XIII 105
    slave revolt XIII 155
Hiss, Alger II 130–133, 229; III 34; VI 123–129, 154,
    156, 158
    conviction for perjury VI 124
    Pumpkin Papers VI 127, 129
    trip to Moscow VI 126
Hiss, Priscilla VI 124
Hitchcock, Alfred IX 257
Hitler, Adolf I 150, 235, 239, 256, 274, 288, 293, 300,
    305; II 156; III 38, 250–257; IV 17–19; V
    14, 35, 57–58, 61, 79, 81, 84, 93, 96, 98, 104,
    107–109, 122–125, 152–158, 173, 221, 226;
    VI 49, 61, 158, 176, 178, 251, 254, 275, 277,

281; VIII 30, 58, 92, 94–97, 99, 166, 186,
241, 263–264, 281, 284; IX 174, 264; X 20;
XI 2, 4–5, 8–11, 14, 17–20, 27–29, 32, 55,
59, 62, 67, 71, 74, 80–91, 93, 98, 102–104,
106, 110–112, 114, 131, 134–135, 156, 166,
168, 174–175, 177–178, 184–185, 187–192,
211, 227–228, 240, 243, 246, 249, 252, 259,
264–265, 271; XV 34–35; XVI 147–154;
XVI 8–14, 41, 76, 78, 81, 91, 94, 100, 102,
104, 113, 115, 117–119, 140–141, 162, 176,
209, 211–212, 215, 220–221, 225, 230, 238,
259–264, 291–294, 296, 299, 314, 317, 319
   annexation of Sudentenland IV 19; VIII 284
   appeasement of I 276
   cultural figure XVII 104–111
   declaration of war on U.S. V 131–136
   failure as war leader IV 108
   foreign policy IV 122–128
   German rearmament IV 116–117
   goals of foreign policy IV 123
   Hitler and Stalin I 134–139
   influence on the *Wehrmacht* V 137–144
   invasion of Rhineland IV 115
   invasion of Soviet Union IV 111
   Operation Barbarossa XVI 184–191
   remilitarizes the Rhineland VIII 284
   responsibility for World War II IV 114–120
   rise to power V 114–121; XVI 147–154
   vegetarianism XI 147
   war leader IV 104–112
Hizbollah (Party of God) VI 234; XIV 7, 41, 93, 103,
105, 125–132, 230; XV 98, 113, 131, 133,
142, 153, 201, 264, 266–267, 269
Ho Chi Minh I 46, 183, 290, 294, 296, 297, 298; II 97,
263–264, 266, 267; V 145–150, 174; VI 28,
80, 92–93, 98, 107, 203; IX 93; XII 33–34;
XIV 147
Ho Chi Minh Trail VI 142
Hoare-Laval Pact IX 175
Hobbes, Thomas XI 75; XII 109, 118–119, 121–122;
XVII 183, 186
Hoffmann, Max VIII 93, 252; IX 66
Hogan's Heroes (TV show, 1965–1971) XI 189
Hohenstaufen X 140, 142–143, 146, 204, 226
Hokkaido VI 147
Holbrooke, Richard XVI 269
Holland VIII 72, 245, 261, 280; X 10; XI 62, 108, 179,
193, 211; XII 251–252, 255; XV 14
   allies with Amerians in U.S. Revolution XII 39
   fights maroons XIII 107
   slave trade XIII 270
   visited by U.S. ships XII 79
   wars wih England XII 198
Holmes, Oliver Wendell II 280–281, 284; III 17–18;
VI 123; IX 4
Holocaust (1933–1945) III 251–257; IV 129–142; V
56–61, 151–166; VIII 166; X 20, 278; XI 1–
264; XIII 138, 198; XVI 9, 138, 254, 260,
298, 300, 302; XVII 97–98, 145–147
   advanced warning of XI 1–8
   air raids on concentration camps XI 8–16
   Catholic Church XI 191–201
   collaboration IV 129–135
   Communists in XI 66
   ethical representations of XI 45–53
   Final Solution, as irrational act XI 110–118
   Final Solution, genesis of XI 102–109
   Führer Order XI 81–91
   gendered experiences in XI 66–73, 93–100
   Gypsies in XI 66, 71, 73, 147, 149, 153, 171, 186,
190, 242–243, 247, 257
   homosexuals in XI 71, 186, 242–248
   humiliation of Jews XI 211
   Intentionalist/Structuralist debate XI 102–109
   Jehovah's Witnesses in XI 128–137, 186, 243, 246
   Jewish Councils in XI 138–145
   mentally ill in XI 242
   movie representations of XI 155–164

   Neutral states and the XI 174–181
   ordinary Germans and the XI 183–190, 264–271
   reparations XI 210–216
   resistence XI 240
   role in twentieth-century history V 163
   slave labor XI 210–216
   survival during XI 217–224
   survivor narratives XI 226–233
   theories IV 136–141
   use of medical data from Nazis XI 146–154
   victim psychology XI 235–240
   victims during XI 242–250
Holocaust (1978) XI 48
Holtzendorff, Henning von VIII 289, 292–293; IX 75
Holy Alliance IX 226; XVI 72
Holy Roman Empire X 93, 267, 285; XVI 211, 213, 216,
255
Holy Sepulcher X 94, 99, 101, 138, 215, 217, 287
Home Rule Bill (1885) XII 166
Home Rule Bill (1914) VIII 155, 158, 161
Home Rule Party VIII 158
Homer VIII 117
homosexuality
   in the Holocaust XI 242–248
   in World War I IX 146–153
   use of symbols XIII 270
Honduras VI 193–194
Honecker, Erich VI 117–118, 120–121, 211
Hong Kong XVI 64, 81, 109
Honorius II X 286
Honorius III X 89, 93–95
Hoover Dam (United States) VII 27, 29, 94, 109, 152
Hoover, Herbert I 285; II 49, 86; III 25–26, 50, 66,
VIII 285 ; IX 18; XI 56; XVI 296
   goodwill trip to South America (1928) III 46
   Prohibition III 174
   Reconstruction and Finance Corporation II 209
   signs the Colorado River Compact VII 152
Hoover administration IX 171
   Native American policies III 144
   Reconstruction Finance Corporation (RFC) III
154
Hoover Dam II 257
Hoover, J. Edgar I 76, 292; II 232; III 107, 233; VI
24, 158
Hopkins, Esek XII 77, 81
Hopkins, Harry L. I 306; V 196; VI 155; XVI 218
Hopkins, Joseph XII 287
Hopkins, Samuel XII 58
Hopkins, Stephen XII 152
Hopkinson, Francis XII 307
horizontal escalation VI 221
Horn of Africa VI 42, 164, 256; XIV 180
Hortobagy National Park VII 253
Hospitallers X 30, 49, 75, 90, 158, 174
Höss, Rudolf XI 131, 186
Hostiensis X 57, 178, 226, 236
House, Edward VIII 228; XVI 308
House of Burgesses XII 148, 241
House Un-American Activities Committee (HUAC) I
77, 79, 306; II 130–134, 207; VI 124, 127,
129, 178
Houston, Charles Hamilton II 19, 22, 137–138
Houston Accords (1997) XIV 279–280, 284
How the Other Half Lives (Riis) III 260
Howard University XIII 254
Howard v. *Howard* (1858) XIII 101
Howe, George Augustus XII 156, 159
Howe, Richard XII 37, 106, 155–158
Howe, William XII 30, 37, 39, 40, 44–45, 47–48, 94,
146, 155–158, 181–182, 267–268, 270–271,
273–274, 304–307
Hoxha, Enver VI 181
Hoyos Mission (1914) VIII 47
Huck, Christian XII 186
Hudson Bay XII 171
Hudson Bay Company XII 200
Hudson Motor Car Company IX 21

Index

INDEX

Anti-Normalization Committee XIV 65
Army abuses of Jewish gravestones XIV 165
British Army in XV 120
Civil War (1970, Black September) XV 40–50,
    127, 198
closes al-Jazeera office XIV 65
corruption XIV 48, 64
Crisis (1957) XV 58, 166
Crisis (1970) XV 149
Department of Forestry XV 209
dissolves parliament XIV 65
duty free investment XIV 64
economic reform XIV 54, 65
elections XIV 64
extra-parliamentary decrees XIV 65
Free Officers Movement XV 63, 169
free trade agreement with United States
    (2000) XIV 65
fundamentalist movements in I 163
labor XIV 52
mandate in VIII 168
Palestinians in XIV 67; XV 191
Pan-Arab campaign I 281
peace treaty with Israel (1994) XIV 65
relations with United States XIV 16
support of U.S. I 158; XIV 14
water XIV 269; XV 205
West Bank captured by Israel I 156
women XIV 116, 123–124, 287–288
Jordan River XIV 268–271; XV 20, 24, 34, 193, 205–
    206
Jordan River Basin VII 137–138
Jordan Valley Authority XV 205
Jordanian-Israeli treaty (1994) XIV 116
Jospin, Lionel XVI 137–138; XVII 81, 133, 274
Joyce, James VIII 191
Juan Carlos (Spain) XVI 180–182
Jud Süss (1940) XI 90, 185
Judaism XIV 19, 22, 81, 159, 183, 187, 191, 253
Judea XIV 151, 259
Judgment at Nuremberg (1961) XI 158
Jugurtha XIV 206
Jünger, Ernst VIII 59, 64, 263; IX 131, 149, 212
Jupiter missiles VI 71
Justin Martyr XI 20
Justinian I X 228

K

Kádár, János VI 130, 134
Kafara Dam (Egypt) VII 3
Kafue Dam (Zambia) VII 137, 240
Kafue River VII 2, 5, 137
Kahn, Agha Mohammad Yahya VI 88
Kalahari Desert VII 33–34, 36–37, 236
    lack of surface water in VII 38
Kalb, Johann de XII 101
Kamenev, Lev XVI 20
kamikaze VIII 60
Kampuchia VI 165
Kansas VII 10–11, 13, 181–182, 185, 187
    alfalfa production in VII 13
    sugar-beet production in VII 13
    violence in XIII 5
    water diverted from VII 13
    water policy in VII 185
    wheat sales XV 78
Kant, Immanuel XI 75; XVII 105, 256–257
Kapp Putsch (1920) IV 271
Karadzic, Radovan XVII 147, 149
Kardelj, Edvard VI 281
Karen Liberation Army XV 14
Kariba Dam VII 1, 4–5, 8, 239, 242–243
Kariba George VII 1, 237, 239, 245
Karine A (ship) XIV 101, 105
Karl I VIII 257; XVI 33, 308
Karmal, Babrak I 10–15; VI 238
Kashmir XIV 88, 93, 147; XVI 88

Katse Dam (Lesotho) VII 7, 237, 241, 244
Kattenburg, Paul VI 96
Katyn Forest massacre (1940) XI 169, 258, 260, 262;
    XVI 229
Kaufman, Irving R. II 131, 230, 232
Kazakhstan VI 109, 215; XIV 180, 228; XVI 98
Kazan, Russian conquest of XVI 70
Keating, Kenneth B. VI 73
Keitel, Wilhelm V 3, 127, 142–143, 223–224
Kelheim VII 204, 209
Kellogg, James L. VII 49
Kellogg-Briand Pact (1928) III 179; V 115; VIII 298;
    XI 258; XVI 218, 222, 224; XVII 11, 143,
    193
Kemble, Frances Anne XIII 83, 88, 189, 226
Keneally, Thomas XI 202, 205–206
Kennan, George F. I 22, 31, 75, 82, 138, 148, 150, 154,
    159, 284–285, 288; II 8, 60, 267; VI 188
    containment policy I 110, 274
    domino theory I 266
    later view of containment I 183
    "Long Telegram" I 261; II 34, 205, 264; VI 9
    Marshall Plan I 176
    Mr. X II 206
    rules for handling relations with the Soviet
        Union I 186
Kennedy, John F. I 23, 64, 68, 89, 92, 94, 119–121,
    130, 257, 291–292; II 8, 45, 52, 67–68, 93,
    114–120, 160; III 48; VI 64, 66, 70, 73, 93,
    96, 102–103, 138–145, 188; XI 129; XII 33;
    XV 19, 137, 168; XVI 12, 271
    Alliance for Progress I 17, 20, 23; II 115
    assasssination I 18; II 180; VI 138, 142
    Bay of Pigs I 71; II 115, 119
    Camelot mystique II 117
    Cold War policies II 117
    compared with Franklin D. Roosevelt II 115
    criticism of Eisenhower administration I 193; VI
        141
    critiques of performance in Cuban Missile
        Crisis VI 73
    Cuban Missile Crisis II 116, 120, 265
    decolonization policy VI 81
    Food for Peace II 116
    foreign policy II 117
    Inauguration Address I 23
    Jimmy Hoffa II 190
    Johnson as vice president running mate VI 142
    limited-nuclear-war doctrines I 169
    Nuclear Test Ban Treaty (1963) II 118
    Peace Corps II 116
    plot to overthrow Castro I 276
    presidential campaign I 17
    promotion of space program II 260
    Roman Catholicism of VI 142
    State of the Union address (1961) VI 140
    strategy in Southeast Asia VI 95
    support of British VI 11
    supports coup against Diem VI 98
    United Nations II 115
    Vietnam policy I 183
Kennedy, Robert F. II 9; VI 75, 96; XIII 277
    assassination of II 162, 180
    civil-rights issues II 22
    Cuban Missile Crisis VI 70–76
    nuclear disarmament in Turkey I 121
    U.S. Attorney General II 22
    War on Poverty involvement II 272
Kennedy administration VI 26, 56, 72, 92, 99, 138–
    145, 238
    Alliance for Progress I 17–26
    and civil rights II 26
    attempts to overthrow Fidel Castro I 24
    Berlin Wall Crisis I 119–120
    Cuban Missile Crisis I 120
    Cuban policy I 67
    "flexible response" I 115, 214
    Iran XV 158

Mein Kampf (1925-1927) IV 111, 123, 137, 186, 227; V 132; VIII 99; IX 264; XI 2, 5, 15, 19, 88, 91, 103-104, 135, 247; XVI 151

Meir, Golda VI 163; XV 135, 137, 186, 221, 223, 238, 241

Memminger, Christopher G. XIII 28

Mencken, H. L. III 32, 37, 78, 98, 128, 175
 flu epidemic III 101

Mengele, Josef XI 147-148

Mensheviks VIII 258; IX 198

mercantilism XII 171, 196-203

Merrill's Marauders V 198

Mesopotamia VIII 39-40, 121, 193, 212-213, 216; IX 67, 206
 mandate in VIII 168

Messersmith, George XI 60, 268

Methodists XII 148, 151, 235, 263
 slave religion XIII 186, 190

Metro Action Committee (MAC) VII 191

Metropolitan Problems Advisory Committee VII 190

Metternich, Clemens von XVI 73-74, 76

Meuse River IX 254, 257

Mexicali Valley VII 151-154, 157

Mexican American War (1846-1848) XIII 283

Mexican Revolution III 124-131

Mexican Water Treaty VII 151-159

Mexico III 124-131; VII 197; VIII 296, 298; IX 21, 168; X 8, 10; XIII 104; XIV 162; XVI 36
 cientificos (scientific ones) III 125
 criticism of Libertad Act I 98
 Cuban investment I 97
 departure of French army (1867) I 125
 escaped slaves to XIII 124
 land reform I 21
 mining industry III 125
 nationalization of U.S. businesses, 1930s I 130
 oil XIV 218
 relations with the United States VIII 16, 18, 22
 salmon range VII 196
 water policy in VII 151-159

Mfume, Kweisi XIII 277

Michael VI 252; XVI 180

Michael VII Ducas X 122, 285

Michel, Victor VIII 234-235

Michigan XII 22

Micronesia IX 163, 165

Middle Ages X 123-124, 130-131, 140, 152, 158, 166-168, 181, 208, 229, 236, 241-243, 250, 265; XI 23, 169; XII 242; XIII 117, 162; XIV 230

Middle Colonies
 ethnic diversity in XII 205
 religion in XII 208

Middle East I 157-158, 161, 277; VI 53, 79, 90, 135-136, 162, 171, 188, 266, 268, 271; VIII 109, 211, 228 ; IX 27, 34, 67, 72, 91; X 199; XIV (all); XV (all); 65, 73, 80-81, 85, 87, 110, 193, 236, 237, 239
 agricultural assistance to XIV 45
 al-Aqsa intifada XIV 19-27
 Alpha Plan XV 250
 Al-Jazeera, influence of XIV 28-35
 Arab leadership in XIV 60-68
 Arab Maghrib Union XIV 69-76
 Arab-Israeli conflict II 145
 business practices in XIV 44-47
 civil rights and political reforms XIV 61
 civil society XIV 77-85, 110
 control of Jerusalem XIV 159-167
 corruption in XIV 48-49
 democracy in XIV 110, 133-142
 demographic pressures XIV 52
 economic growth in XIV 51-59
 education XIV 52, 111
 fear of Westernization XIV 123
 foreign assistance for schools XIV 45
 foreign investment in XIV 44-47
 fundamentalist political parties XIV 252-260
 globalization XIV 109-116

hierarchal nature of society XIV 49
illiteracy XIV 111
image of the West in XIV 227-236
impact of technological advances XIV 90
income distribution XIV 56
influence of Saudi Arabia XIV 244-251
infrastructure I 158
Israeli-Palestinian conflict XIV 151-158
Kurdish independence XIV 168-174
maternal mortality rate XIV 56
natural resources XIV 45
North Africa XIV 201-210
nuclear weapons in XIV 143-150
oil XIV 47, 55, 62, 68, 111, 240
OPEC XIV 212-219
Palestinian refugees XIV 220-226
peace process I 289
political parties XIV 56
polygamy XIV 287
poverty XIV 56
purchase of arms XIV 89
relations with United States I 278
responses to modernization XIV 119-124
socio-economic structure XIV 79
Soviet influence VI 160-167, 261
Suez Canal Zone II 146
technology XIV 61
terrorism XIV 16, 125-132; XVI 248
U.S. foreign policy in XIV 16
U.S. interests I 162; VI 61
U.S. support for mujahideen in Afghanistan XIV 1-9
use of term *Middle East* XIV 175-181
water VII 76-84, 135-141, 280; XIV 268-275
women XIV 111, 115, 118-124, 286-292
women's clothing XIV 118-124
worker training XIV 45
World War I 37-42; XVI 312

Middle East Air Command XIV 176
Middle East Broadcasting Center (MBC) XIV 29
Middle East Command (MEC) XV 26, 30, 59
Middle East Defense Organization XV 26, 30, 59
Middle East Executive Training Program XIV 114
Middle East Nuclear Weapons Free Zone XIV 146
Middle East Radio Network XIV 233, 235
Middle East Research and Information Project (MERIP) XV 93

Middle Passage XIII 15
 mortality rates XIII 129-137

Middleton, George XV 160-162, 164

Midwest Holocaust Education Center, Overland Park, Kansas XI 238

Mifflin, Thomas XII 94, 97-98

Migratory Bird Conservation Act (1929) VII 277

Mihajlovic, Draza VI 275, 277-278

Mikolajczyk, Stanislaw XVI 230

Mikoyan, Anastas XVI 168

Mikva, Abner Joseph VII 121

military gap between U.S. and Soviet Union I 188-194

Military Intelligence Service (MIS) III 14-15

Military Service Act (1916) IX 58

Milites X 14, 16, 34

militias XII 277, 281-282

Millerand, Alexandre VIII 152, 255

Milliken v. *Bradley* (1974) II 293, 298

Milne, George VIII 214, 216; IX 206

Milosovic, Slobodan XI 71, 75; XIV 23; XVI 58-60, 63; XVII 99, 102, 146, 149, 216, 230

Milyukov, Pavel VIII 173-174

Mind of the South (1941) XIII 224

Minow, Newton II 121, 23

Miranda, Ernesto II 284

Miranda v. *Arizona* (1966) II 281, 284, 286

Missao do Fomento e Powoamento dio Zambeze (MFPZ) VII 240

missile gap I 182-194; II 260; VI 21, 141

Mission for the Referendum in Western Sahara (MINURSO) XIV 278

Israelis killed at XV 224; XVI 245
Municipality of Metropolitan Seattle (Metro) 188–195
Munitions of War Act (1915) IX 56
Murphy, Charles Francis III 262
Murphy, Justice Frank V 188
Murphy, Robert XV 62, 169
Murray, Wallace XI 57, 62
Musaddiq, Muhammad. *See* Mosaddeq
music
    "folk revival" II 214
    political force II 214
music industry
    impact of television II 218
    record companies at Monterey Music Festival II 219
    sheet music production II 217
    technological advances II 216
    youth market II 219
Muskie, Edmund Sixtus VII 176, 261, 263–264, 268
Muslim Brotherhood XIV 7, 127, 139, 190, 230, 255; XV 69, 271, 275
Muslims X 8, 10, 17, 19, 27, 29, 33–34, 37, 43–44, 47–48, 52, 54, 59–60, 65, 69, 78, 81, 88–90, 95, 101, 105, 108–109, 117, 128, 133, 140, 149–150, 153, 159, 169, 174, 176, 179–181, 195, 209, 212, 219–220, 223–224, 238, 248, 255, 265–266, 280–281, 284, 287, 289, 292, 297: XI 17; XVI 57, 60
    Christian treatment of X 177
    cultural interaction with Christians X 197–203
    enslavement of XIII 167, 192
    Latinization of X 43
    slavery among XIII 165
    slaves in Americas XIII 192
    Spain X 1–6, 40–45, 241–246
    suicide missions XIV 130
    treatment of in Crusader States X 190–196
    treatment of Jews X 272–278
Mussolini, Benito I 134; IV 14, 80; V 36, 108–109, 117, 135, 169, 175–177, 226, 233; VIII 95; IX 96, 175; X 305; XI 74, 167; XVI 11, 13, 105, 138, 140–141, 144, 182, 185–186, 260, 262, 264, 302, 319; XVII 80–81, 140–141, 179–181
    alliance with Hitler V 179
    downfall V 2
    invasion of Ethiopia V 118, 120
    March on Rome XVI 151
    proposal of the Four Power Pact V 120
    removal from power V 178, 179
    support of Franco IV 224, 226
Muste, A. J. II 7; III 184
Mutual Assured Destruction (MAD) I 154, 169–171, 191, 198, 202, 226–227, 230–232, 251–252; II 67; VI 31, 168, 174
Mutual Defense Assistance Act (1949) I 59
Mutual Security Act I 175; XV 202
Mutual Security Agency (MSA) XV 205, 206
Mutual Security Program (MSP) I 175
MX missile VI 17–18
Myalism XIII 190, 193
Mycenaean Greeks, as slave owners XIII 165
Myrdal, Gunnar XIII 257

N

Nader, Ralph VII 178, 265, 269
Nagasaki I 30, 230, 239, 242–245, 249, 268; III 12, 15; V 3, 8, 49, 52, 111, 154, 192; VI 31; VII 174; XI 159; XVI 254
Nagy, Imre VI 130–131, 134, 270
Nagymaros Dam (Hungary) VII 100–101, 104
Nahhas, Mustafa al- XV 146, 275
Naipaul, V. S. XV 232
Namibia VI 1 6; VII 7, 38, 236–237, 240–242
    U.N. Trust Territory VI 236
    withdrawal of South African troops VI 7
Nanking Massacre (1937) V 151
Napoleon I IX 116

Napoleon III IX 30, 116; XVI 130, 257
Napoleonic Wars (1803–1815) I 166, 259; VIII 233–234; XII 167–169
narcotics III 133–137
    Boxer Rebellion III 136
    Foster Bill (1910) III 137
    Harrison Act (1914) III 137
    history of legal regulation III 133
    progressive movement III 135
Narmada (Sardar Sarovar) Project (India) VII 127, 132
Narmada River VII 9, 134
Narodny Kommisariat Vnutrennikh Del (People's Commissariat for Internal Affairs, NKVD) IV 50; V 233; VI 275, 278; XVI 229
Nasrallah, Hasan XIV 127–128, 131
Nassau Agreement (1962) VI 11, 13
Nasser, Gamal Abdel I 110, 162, 273, 277–278, 283, 314; II 117, 146–147; VI 11, 80–81, 106, 161, 246, 268, 270; VII 3; X 56; XIV 82, 119, 143, 193–195, 197; 82, 193–195, 197, 253; XV 12, 19–22, 24–25, 31, 40, 42, 45–46, 48–49, 56, 58–59, 61–62, 65–68, 70, 100–101, 116, 119, 121, 135–137, 144, 147, 164–169, 193, 199, 218–220, 223, 225, 238, 244–246, 249, 254, 270–276; XVI 235–240, 242
    challenges Britain I 280
    Nasserism XIV 253; XV 166, 251
    pan-Arab campaign I 281
    "positive neutrality" II 148
Nation of Islam II 93–95
National Aeronautics and Space Administration (NASA) II 246, 258, 260; XI 152
    creation of II 242
    funding of II 261
National Association for the Advancement of Colored People (NAACP) II 19–20, 23, 25, 27, 44–45, 90, 94, 138, 140–141; III 80, 93, 118, 121, 182, 184–186, 217, 270–274; IX 2, 4; XIII 256, 277
    opposition to Model Cities housing projects II 277
    Scottsboro case III 185
National Association of Black Journalists II 96
National Association of Broadcasters II 123
National Association of Colored Women III 167
National Audubon Society VII 215
National Black Political Convention (1972) II 95, 198
National Committee of Negro Churchmen II 95
National Committee to Re-Open the Rosenberg Case II 228
National Conference of Christians and Jews XI 159
National Council of Negro Churchmen (NCNC) II 94
National Council of Mayors VII 258
National Council of Slovenes, Croats, and Serbs XVI 36, 100
National Defense and Interstate Highway Act (1956) II 107
National Defense Highway Act (1956) II 249
National Education Association II 190–191
National Environmental Policy Act (NEPA) II 183; VII 31, 176, 266, 269,
National Farmers Process Tax Recovery Association III 159
National Front for the Liberation of Angola (*Frente Nacional de Libertação de Angola* or FNLA) VI 1, 6, 87, 165
National Guard Act (1903) VIII 301
National Guidance Committee (NGC) XIV 25
National Industrial Recovery Act (NIRA, 1933) III 27–28, 62, 65, 149,154
    Supreme Court ruling III 25
National Intelligence Estimates (NIEs) VI 256–258, 260
National Iranian Oil Company (NIOC) XV 175
National Labor Relations Act (Wagner Act, 1935) III 149, 193

Index

INDEX

INDEX

Christian-Muslim relations X 40–45, 190
control of Mississippi River XII 25, 290
cost of Med plan to VII 146
free workers from XIII 168
Haitian Revolution XIII 209
impact of American Revolution upon XII 165
Jews in X 2, 4, 8, 22, 35, 40, 42, 274
Jews saved by XI 177
laws of slavery XIII 178
monarchy XVI 180–182
Muslims in X 1–6 ; XIV 201
pollution from industrial centers in VII 147
Popular Front IV 228; XVI 220
presence in Florida XII 295
racism XIII 179
Reconquista X 241–246
slave trade XIII 180, 270
slavery in XIII 167
socialism in VIII 254
Sociedad Estatal de Participaciones Industriales (State Industrial Holdings Company or SEPI) 280
support of Americans in Revolution XII 166
terrorism XVI 245, 248, 249
threat to western U.S. expansion XII 18
treatment of Native Americans X 7–12
views of blacks in XIII 181
views of Jews in XI 23
visited by U.S. ships XII 79
Western Sahara XIV 276–278, 280, 283
Spandau prison V 224
Spanish American War (1898) II 99; III 245; VIII 18, 22–23, 198, 296, 301; XVI 65
treatment of African American soldiers IV 217
Spanish Armada XII 28
Spanish Civil War (1936–1939) IV 167, 223–231; VI 154, 176; XVI 10, 13, 118, 220; XVII 234–242
Nationalists IV 228, 230
Spanish Influenza III 95; VIII 189; IX 31
Spartacus XIII 149
Spee, Maximilian von VIII 132–133, 135
Speer, Albert XI 205, 254, 258; XVI 302
Spiegelmann, Art XI 53, 233
Spielberg, Steven XI 45, 156–157, 159–161, 163–164, 202
Spingarn, Joel IX 2–3
Spirit of Laws, The (1748) XII 234
Spock, Dr. Benjamin III 169
Spokane, Portland, and Seattle Railroad VII 59
Sputnik I 182, 188–189, 192, 256; II 47, 64, 70, 257–258, 260
Staatsangehöriger (subjects of the state) IV 140
Staatsschutzkorps (State Protection Corps) V 214
Stalin, Joseph I 31, 35–36, 59, 66, 86, 102, 108–110, 112–113, 149, 151, 263, 288, 305; II 30–41, 49, 52, 68, 132, 156, 169, 193, 210; III 10, 12; IV 210; V 14, 25–26, 35, 41, 44, 46, 50, 54, 107, 109, 131, 136, 149, 151, 177, 194, 224, 226–227; VI 31, 36, 40, 109, 111, 131, 133, 137, 147, 150, 154–156, 158, 161, 175, 178–179, 207, 242, 244, 250–267; VII 22, 97, VIII 97; IX 9–10, 12, 15, 74–75, 79–80, 83, 167, 169, 261; XIV 181; XV 160, 253; XVI 4, 39, 76, 114, 118, 122, 124, 135, 168, 185, 186, 189–190, 217–218, 221, 224, 227–230, 232, 238, 244, 259–264, 314–315, 317–319
attempt to extract base rights from Turkey I 238
Balkans campaign V 71
compared to Lenin XVII 151–158
death VI 181
domestic atrocities I 260–261
economic policies XVII 243–251
"Election Speech" (1946) II 133
expansionist intentions I 262
foreign policy II 36
genocide practices V 166
German invasion of U.S.S.R. IV 233

lack of concern for Western European economies I 176
making trouble II 205
Marshall Plan I 208
Moscow winter offensive, 1941 IV 237
motivation II 36
postwar policy toward the United States I 258
postwar settlement I 110
Potsdam Conference I 263
propaganda IV 234, 236
purges VI 244; XVI 184
relationship with Allied leaders V 27
retribution for Nazi war crimes V 218
Soviet nuclear weapons development I 183, 245
Soviet recovery from Second World War I 182
speech of 9 February 1946 I 260–261
support of Operation Anvil/Dragoon V 241
Tito VI 273–281
view of postwar Germany I 252
war with Germany V 229; VI 274
World War II IV 232–237
Yalta Agreement (1945) I 300; V 309–315
Stalin-Hitler nonaggression pact (1939) II 193
Stamp Act (1765) XII 1, 51, 53, 56–57, 140–141, 143, 149, 152–153, 166, 192, 207, 214–215, 231, 233, 236, 241, 252, 254, 261, 314–315
Stamp Act Congress (1765) XII 54, 233, 236, 315
Standard Oil Company XIV 211–212
"Star Wars." *See* Strategic Defense Initiative
State v. *Boon* (1801) XIII 97
State v. *Caesar* (1849) XIII 98
State v. *Hale* (1823) XIII 97, 99
State v. *Hoover* (1839) XIII 98
State v. *Mann* (1829) XIII 97, 102
State v. *Tackett* (1820) XIII 97
State v. *Will* (1834) XIII 97
Statute of Westminster (1931) XVI 80
Stegner, Wallace VII 112
Steiger, Rod XI 159
Stephens, Alexander H. XIII 271, 277
Steuben, Frederick von XII 87, 304
Stevens, Isaac VII 56
Stevens, Thaddeus XIII 51
Stevenson, Adlai E. VI 75
Stevenson, Charles H. VII 46
Stewart, Walter XII 224, 228
Stiles, Ezra XII 146, 148
Stilwell, Joseph W. V 187, 191–199
Stimson, Henry L. I 28, 263; III 104, 109; V 53, 187; XI 257
Stolypin, Pyotr IX 156; XVI 17, 50–55, 200
Stone, Justice Harlan III 25
Stone, Livingston VII 197
Stono Rebellion (1739) XIII 124, 235
stormtroopers IX 126, 129–130
Stowe, Harriet Beecher XIII 4, 89
Strait of Tiran XV 20–21, 24, 135, 137, 225, 245, 247, 250, 254; XVI 239
Straits of Gibraltar XVI 65
Straits of Malacca XVI 65
Strategic Air Command (SAC) I 188; VI 263
Strategic Arms Limitation Treaty (SALT I) I 190, 199; II 171; VI 30, 35, 41, 43; XV 257; XVI 95
Strategic Arms Limitation Treaty (SALT II) I 10, 12, 143, 146, 191; VI 2, 35, 166
Soviet criticism of VI 43
Strategic Arms Reduction Treaty (START) I 199, 224; VI 44; XVI 95; XVI 98
Strategic bombing
postwar I 4, 6, 8
postwar role I 5
Strategic bombing in World War II I 3–4
Strategic Defense Initiative (SDI) I 186, 195–196, 199; II 58; VI 3, 22, 36, 109, 223, 226, 229, 234, 239; XVI 40, 45, 95
Strauss, Richard IX 84
Stravinsky, Igor IX 84
Streicher, Julius V 224; XI 185, 254, 258

INDEX

Index

Index

Windsor Castle XII 143; XVI 178, 180
Windward Coast XIII 272
Winter War (1939–1940) I 108; XVI 119, 125, 221, 224, 319; XVI 125, 221, 224, 319
Winters Doctrine VII 172–173
Winters v. United States (1908) VII 168, 172
Wisconsin VII 122, 264, 267; XII 22
    Native Americans XII 176
    pollution control in VII 264
Wisconsin State Committee on Water Pollution VII 122
Witte, Sergei XVI 16, 200
Wohlstetter, Albert J. I 213, II 65
Wolfowitz, Paul XV 84, 87
Wollstonecraft, Mary II 74
Wolman, Abel VII 47
Wool Act (1699) XII 198, 243
Women
    antebellum South XIII 224–230
    emancipation of in twentieth-century Europe XVII 275–282
    Middle East XIV 111, 115, 286–292
Women's Air Force Service Pilots (WASPs) V 303
Women's Army Corps (WAC) V 303
Women's movement II 162, 165
    Progressive Era III 165–173
    Prohibition III 198
    World War I VIII 124–130, 296, 298
Wood, Edward (Earl of Halifax) IX 83
Wood, Leonard IX 6
Woodhouse, Monty XV 160, 163
Woodstock II 257
Woodstock Dam (South Africa) VII 243
Woodwell, George M. VII 262
Woolf, Virginia VIII 130
Woolman, John XIII 1, 17, 149–150, 152
Workers World Party II 197
Works Progress Administration (WPA), 1935 III 150, 163
    ex-slave interviews XIII 226
World Bank I 20, 22, 124, 145; VI 120; VII 5, 7–8, 62, 83, 130, 132, 146, 241, 280, 287; XIV 58, 89, 111; XV 160; XVI 77, 87
    Resettlement Policy VII 244
    sets tone on water policy VII 286
World Bank Development Report XIV 58
World Bank Inspection Panel VII 8, 9
World Commission on Dams VII 9, 127, 130, 133, 242
    report of (2000) VII 317–332
World Commission on Water for the Twenty-First Century 286
World Court IX 171
World Economic Conference (London, 1933) XVI 218
World Health Organization (WHO) VII 143, 253
World Jewish Congress III 256; V 58; XI 181
World Trade Center attack (11 September 2001) XIV 10–11, 13, 27–28, 32, 37–38, 41, 43, 50, 61, 68, 77, 86–94, 95–96, 103, 108–109, 126, 129, 175, 182, 189–191, 216, 218, 227, 238–239, 243, 245, 247, 250, 256, 262, 264; XV 54, 83, 145, 259; XVI 71, 243, 245
World Trade Center bombing (1993) XIV 16, 191, 193
World Trade Organization (WTO) XIV 40, 54, 65, 109, 112, 114, 273
World War I (1914–1918) I 88, 112, 149, 284, 286; III 210, 223, 229, 244; VI 57, 176, 178, 267; VII 82; IX 22, 27; X 59, 62, 199, 304; XI 15, 28, 32, 82, 88, 97, 114, 126, 132, 174, 183, 215, 220, 266; XIV 65, 168, 171, 176, 178, 211, 220, 261; XV 11, 33–34, 65, 68–69, 73, 82, 98, 106, 116–117, 121, 141, 146, 152, 156, 172–173, 176, 274; XVI 1, 4, 8–9, 12–13, 15, 17, 20, 29–30, 32–33, 36, 49–50, 53, 55, 57, 61, 65, 72, 74, 80–81, 87, 91–95, 100, 102, 107, 111, 113–114, 117, 129–130, 140–141, 148, 151, 183, 189, 208, 211, 213–214, 216–218, 221, 228, 236, 245, 249, 267, 291, 294, 298, 307–313

African Americans III 268; IV 218; VIII 298, 301
African soldiers in IX 111–118
airplanes VIII 115, 193–197; IX 9–14, 38
Allied cooperation IX 104–110
Allied suplies to Russia IX 190
Anglo-German naval rivalry VIII 29–36
Armistice IX 72, 114
artillery IX 39
arts IX 84
Balkans IX 206, 266–272
balloons in IX 14
Belgian neutrality IX 41–47
British entry into XVI 22–24
British strategy IX 48–53
casualties IX 30
causes I 205; IX 224–229; XVI 192–198
chemical warfare VIII 239–244
combat tactics VIII 109–116
convoys IX 74–79
cultural watershed IX 80–90; XVII 40–50
East Africa VIII 84–90
Eastern Front VIII 49, 60, 79, 91, 94, 110, 114, 125, 182, 240, 242, 252 IX 27; 60–66, 71, 108, 120, 124, 127, 129, 135, 154, 159, 206, 238, 243, 252–253; XVI 2, 6, 308–309
European economics IX 83
European leadership IX 98–103
firepower and mobility VIII 109–116
gender roles VIII 124–130
German Jewish service in XI 94
homosexuality in IX 146–153
impact on American business in Mexico III 128
impact on European states XVI 171–176
impact on Jews VIII 163–169
impact on U.S. isolationism V 289; VIII 295–302
Japan in IX 162–169
Lost Generation VIII 186–192
mass mobilization III 19
Middle East VIII 37–42, 60
military innovations VIII 193–197
motivations of soldiers VIII 59–64, 263–269
naval war IX 139–142
New Women III 168, 172
Ottoman Empire VIII 117–123
prewar alliances VIII 225–231
prostitution in IX 146, 152
recreation for soldiers IX 234
religion VIII 202–210
Russia IX 237–243; XVI 199–207
shell shock IX 209–213
Socialists in Europe VIII 254–262
strategic bombing in IX 217–223
Supreme War Council IX 104
technology in IX 231
trench warfare IX 230–235
venereal disease IX 152
Western Front VIII 11–13, 16–19, 21, 24, 27–28, 39, 51, 56–57, 59, 61, 77–79, 90, 96, 102, 104, 106, 108–110, 112, 114, 117, 122, 177, 179–185, 187–188, 195, 197, 208, 221, 264, 272–273, 276, 282; IX 12–13, 15–16, 27, 29–31, 33–34, 38, 40, 48–49, 53, 61, 65–67, 71–73, 104–110, 114, 118, 120, 122, 124, 128, 131, 190, 193, 203, 225, 231–232, 234–235, 253–254; XVI 5–6, 34, 37, 201, 309, 312–313
women in VIII 296, 298
World War II (1939–1945) I 61, 91; III 11, 50, 250–257; VI 8, 27, 31, 36, 49, 77, 79, 126, 146, 179, 267; VII 27, 29, 53, 69, 90, 93, 109, 152, 168, 174, 188, 199, 202, 204, 236–237, 257, 263–264, 273, 278, 287; IX 22, 27; X 14, 272, 300, 305; XI 9–10, 14, 18, 36–37, 45, 56, 70, 81, 103, 106, 114, 117–118, 121, 126, 139–140, 148, 168, 171, 174, 181, 187, 191–192, 211, 214, 227, 243, 249, 252–253, 255–257, 260; XII 30, 33, 64, 171; XIII 198;

Index

XIV 2, 17, 37, 40, 71, 171, 174, 176, 181, 188,
192, 211, 230, 238, 245, 261; XV 12, 18, 29–
30, 34–35, 65, 70, 87, 106, 108, 116, 126,
141, 146, 156, 163, 172–173, 176–177, 202,
229, 252–253, 274; XVI 11, 36, 39, 41, 44,
61, 63, 65, 69, 76, 80–81, 84–85, 91, 94, 99,
100, 104–105, 111, 113, 118, 121–122, 125,
134, 137, 140, 158, 163, 171, 181, 208, 211,
213, 216, 218, 221, 226, 228–229, 233, 238,
240, 245, 254, 255, 262, 266, 267, 269, 281,
285, 298, 301
African American contributions IV 221; IX 115
Allied bombing XI 13
Allies V 27–33; VI 169
Anglo-American alliance IV 208; XVI 314–320
antisubmarine defense IX 79
Axis powers V 62–67
Balkans V 68–78
Catholic Church VIII 209
display of Confederate flag during XIII 277
Eastern Front IV 53–60; XI 169, 177; XVI 315
casualties IV 55
Soviet advantages IV 55
effect on Great Depression III 63
homefront segregation IV 218
impact on Civil Rights movement IV 220
impact on colonial powers VI 183
Japanese internment III 102–109
Kyushu invasion III 13
labor impressment IX 114
movies about XI 155
Okinawa III 15
Operation Olympic III 14
Operation Overlord II 39
Pacific theater III 13, 214; VI 254
Pearl Harbor III 214–215
relationship of Great Britain and U.S. II 31
resistance movements V 243–247
role of tanks IV 238–251
Soviet casualties II 38
strategy: IV 104–128; Allied V 19–26; Anglo-
American disputes V 34–40; Anglo-Americn
relations V 41–47; atomic bomb V 48–55;
Axis V 62–67; Balkans 68–78; bomber
offensive V 86–100; Eastern Front IV 53–
60; Italian campaign IV 143–150; Operation
Barbarossa V 226–234; Operation Dragoon
V 235–242; unconditional surrender V 270–
277; Yalta conference V 309–316
submarines V 255–261
Teheran Conference (1943) II 32
threat of Japanese invasion III 108
Tokyo trials (1945–1948) V 263–269
unconditional surrender policy V 270–276
U.S. combat effectiveness V 278–286
U.S. Marine Corps V 295–301
War Plan Orange III 108
women's roles V 302–308; VIII 130
Yalta Conference (1945) II 39
World's Fair, Chicago (1933) III 2
World's Fair, New York (1939) II 122
World's Fair, St. Louis (1904) III 242
World Water Commission VII 280, 281
World Water Forum (2000) VII 286
World Wildlife Fund (WWF) VII 107
World Zionist Organization XI 60, 124
Wyandot XII 175–176
Wye River Agreement (1998) 185, 264

X

Xangô XIII 192
Xhosa VII 67, 242

Y

Yad Vashem XI 161, 164, 202–203, 206
Yakama Reservation VII 60

Yakovlev, Aleksandr N. I 104, 152
Yale College XII 10
Yale University XIII 198
Yalta Conference (1945) I 73, 110, 252, 254, 256–257,
259, 273, 285, 288, 300–307; II 39, 205,
211; V 32, 75, 88, 252, 309–315; VI 126,
153, 158, 267; XI 261; XVI 74, 122, 127,
226–227, 230, 317
"betraying" east European countries I 59
criticism of I 302, 306
"Declaration of Liberated Europe" I 300
Far East I 303–304
German war reparations I 300
Poland V 310–311
Stalin's promise of elections I 151
United Nations V 310, 314
Yamagata Aritomo IX 164, 167
Yamamoto, Isoroku IV 2, 6
Yamani, Ahmed Zaki XIV 214, 218
Yamashita, Tomoyuki
trial of V 265
Yarmuk River VII 78, 81
Yasui, Minoru V 188–189
Yasui v. *U.S.* (1943) V 188
Yates v. *United States* (1957) I 81; II 281
Yatskov, Anatoli II 230
Year of Eating Bones VII 242
Yellow Sea VII 148
Yeltsin, Boris VI 113–114; XVI 77
Yemen VIII 39, 41, 212; XIV 52, 55, 68, 79, 146, 177,
179, 181, 248, 291; XV 57, 62, 81, 141, 144,
146, 166, 204
Arab Republic XV 276
assasination of Ahmad I 282
civil war (1962) II 150
Cole attack (2000) XIV 16
pan-Arab campaign I 281
People's Democratic Republic XV 276
revolution I 158
terrorism XIV 14
UAR XV 270, 271, 273, 276
water XIV 269
women XIV 291
Yom Kippur War. *See* Arab-Israeli War, 1973
Yosemite National Park VII 112
Young Lords II 94, 197
Young Plan (1929) IV 270; IX 92, 171; XVI 148, 296
Young Turks VIII 37, 45, 211; XI 172
Yugoslav Communist Party XVI 100
Yugoslav National Committee XVI 36
Yugoslav National Council (YNC) IX 267
Yugoslavia I 36, 108, 273, 277, 294; II 154, 156; VI
134, 136, 175, 181, 217, 219, 226–227, 243–
244, 265, 271, 273–275, 277; VII 248–249,
252–254; IX 93, 203, 208, 266–272; XI 10,
174; XV 68, 120, 167; XVI 36, 41, 76, 98–
100, 102–104, 115, 123–124, 213, 233, 248,
269, 272, 317
bombing of XVII 8
collapse of XVI 57–63
collectivization VI 274
Croats flying Confederate flags XIII 274
"ethnic cleansing" in XI 166; XIV 243
fascism XVII 137, 140
genocide XVII 95, 142, 147
monarchy XVI 180
NATO in VI 219
"non-aligned" movement I 283
Soviet domination until 1948 I 107; VI 54
U.S. aid I 86
Yuma County Water Users Association (YCWUA) VII
154
Yuma Valley VII 151, 155

Z

Zahedi, Fazlollah XV 158, 163
Zahniser, Howard VII 112

INDEX

ISBN 1-55862-480-5

90000